JIMMY CARTER

Jimmy Carter

FOREIGN POLICY AND POST-PRESIDENTIAL YEARS

EDITED BY
Herbert D. Rosenbaum
AND
Alexej Ugrinsky

Prepared under the auspices of
Hofstra University

Contributions in Political Science,
Number 328

GREENWOOD PRESS
Westport, Connecticut • London

Library of Congress Cataloging-in-Publication Data

Jimmy Carter : foreign policy and post-presidential years / edited by
Herbert D. Rosenbaum and Alexej Ugrinsky.
    p.   cm. — (Contributions in political science, ISSN 0147-1066
; no. 328)
    "Prepared under the auspices of Hofstra University."
    Includes bibliographical references and index.
    ISBN 0-313-28844-5 (alk. paper)
    1. Carter, Jimmy, 1924- . 2. United States — Foreign
relations — 1977-1981. I. Rosenbaum, Herbert D. II. Ugrinsky,
Alexej. III. Series.
E873.J56 1994
973.926 — dc20   93-9320

British Library Cataloguing in Publication Data is available.

Library of Congress Catalog Card Number: 93-9320
ISBN: 0-313-28844-5
ISSN: 0147-1066

First published in 1994

Greenwood Press, 88 Post Road West, Westport, CT 06881
An imprint of Greenwood Publishing Group, Inc.

Printed in the United States of America

The paper used in this book complies with the
Permanent Paper Standard issued by the National
Information Standards Organization (Z39.48-1984).

10 9 8 7 6 5 4 3 2 1

Contents

Contents

Preface: The Carter Foreign Policy
and the Post-Presidential Years

This volume of proceedings of Hofstra University's Conference on the Carter presidency brings together the work of ten of the conference panels. Eight of these deal with foreign policy, testimony to the prominence of those concerns in the Carter years, and to the hazards and opportunities the Carter administration faced.

The panels have been organized under six topical part headings. A suitable introduction characterizing the contents has been provided for each part.

It has long been asserted that the American presidency is a divided one: that in the foreign policy arena many of the restraints of domestic policy-making are absent, that opportunities for acting in that sphere abound, in comparison with the constitutionally and politically much more limited scope of domestic affairs. This distinction is in need of revision. President Jimmy Carter, like all of his predecessors since World War II, experienced the blurring of lines between foreign and domestic politics even while, paradoxically, the contrasts between them became more pronounced. In nearly every arena of domestic and foreign policy he had to deal with the intrusion of the politics of each sphere into the other. The freedom to act in foreign affairs is a tempting target for the enlargement of one's cope, but the cost in domestic politics for such expansion is often quite high. On the other hand, the greater constraints on the president's scope in domestic affairs do not lessen their impact on foreign policy.

These observations seem particularly apt in characterizing President Carter's foreign policies. Each instance of foreign policy examined at this conference can be said to have such characteristics: staffing the foreign policy apparatus, elevating human rights to the forefront of basic policy considerations, creating peaceful conditions in the Middle East, contributing to the emergence of underdeveloped countries, lessening Cold War tensions, ending the drawn-out negotiations about the Panama Canal, not to speak of freeing the hostages taken in Iran. All of them made clear the interlocking nature of domestic and international policy-making.

This volume's last two parts concern President Carter's career since his return to private life. He continues to pursue and enlarge his post-presidential role in a unique way. The Carter Presidential Center in Atlanta, designed to study, discuss, and act on a large number of significant domestic and international social, economic, and political issues, reflects that intent. Carter's role as an observer in overseas elections, his new involvement in the city of Atlanta, in inviting political leaders and experts from around the world to discuss their vital concerns--indeed, in his willingness to attend Hofstra's presidential conferences--all point to a distinctive public career.

The possibility of devising a formal, institutionalized role in the American political system for former presidents has been discussed from time to time. Carter's post-presidential career thus far seems to indicate that an ex-president's determination to shape a career of public-spirited service can find fulfillment without adopting either constitutional or legislative measures. So active and multifaceted an example of that has been the Carters' life since January 1981 that the long-standing discussion may well come to an end because of it.

Herbert D. Rosenbaum
Conference Director

Part I

Major Principles and Guidelines
of the Carter Foreign Policy

The first part of this volume brings together the papers and commentaries of two panels. The first, titled "Overviews," appraises the general impact of Jimmy Carter's values on the conduct of American foreign policy. The evidence for that impact is drawn from four distinct perspectives One deals with the values reflected in the appointments of the secretary of state and the national security adviser; another, with the management of the Western alliance's response to the Soviet invasion of Afghanistan. Attempts to create a post-Cold War foreign policy is the focus of the third paper, and the fourth considers Carter's overall view of conflict and war in the international arena.

Together with the commentary of a leading scholar of American foreign policy and a long-established practitioner and writer, these perspectives provide a sharply etched portrait of the attitudes the president broguht to his task as international leader.

In this part's second portion the focus is narrowed in order to examine the character and impact of Carter's human rights initiatives. Although there are two papers dealing with that subject in the panel on Africa and Asia, the primacy accorded to human rights in the Carter foreign policy called for a more detailed examination. We were fortunate to have three papers discussing the policy at very close range. Two of these focus on particular applications, and one deals with an assessment of the conflict between the ideal of human rights as a premise of policy-making and the "realities" of international relations. Commentary was supplied by a former assistant secretary of state for human rights in the Carter administration and by a leading attorney in the field.

Taken together, the work in this portion of the conference and the volume supplies us with the framework by which to assess nearly the entire scope of the Carter foreign policy.

OVERVIEWS

1

An Examination of the Carter Administration's Selection of Secretary of State and National Security Adviser

LAWRENCE X. CLIFFORD

Approaching two years in office . . . as a foreign policy decision maker . . . Jimmy Carter, it would appear that "le style c'est l'homme même." So far, both in substance and in manner, it has seemed more Carter's policy than Vance's or Brzezinski's.[1]

British political scientist Coral Bell's observation about the Carter administration's foreign policy performance, valid when made at its midway point and still valid more than a decade later, underlines the importance of understanding the way in which this neophyte in global politics chose his principal foreign policy advisers.[2, 3] For if the man in the Oval Office, a man--unlike most of his predecessors in the twentieth century--without any substantive prior experience in international affairs, was indeed running the show, then any effort to evaluate the Carter presidency's record in foreign affairs must rest, in part, on an appreciation of how he came to select his secretary of state and national security advisor.[4, 5] It is the contention of this paper that the appointment of Cyrus Vance and Zbigniew Brzezinski was the product both of Jimmy Carter's long-held attitudes about the proper exercise of government power and his short association, in the years immediately preceding and during his race for the White House, with a new organization called the Trilateral Commission.[6, 7] This paper will also analyze how these attitudes, associations, and appointments shaped the Carter foreign policy.

Although Jimmy Carter as a candidate for the nation's highest office presented himself as a hardworking peanut farmer, the man from Plains, Georgia, hardly fit the stereotype of the dirt poor Southerner.[8, 9, 10] In addition to cultivating his own land, Carter's father ran the gin and the grain and feed store that served all of Sumter County. The elder Carter was a highly respected leader of his community who possessed sufficient political influence to secure an appointment for his oldest son to the U.S. Naval Academy. When his father died several years later and the family's businesses demanded his attention, Jimmy Carter was able to enlist the assistance of Georgia's senior senator in gaining a release from his Navy commitment.[11]

Returning home, Carter not only revived and expanded the peanut operations but also plunged into community service. In addition to joining the local school board, he became a member of the Southwest Georgia Regional Planning Board, which in turn led to his appointment to the Georgia Planning Board.[12] In these positions, the Navy-trained engineer was able to advance the ideas of conceptualization, coordination, and cooperation as essential to efficient management in the public sector.

Carter's successful run for the Georgia governorship in 1970, achieved largely by tireless campaigning and superb organization, made him something of a minor national figure.[13, 14, 15] Replacing the diehard segregationist Lester Maddox, Carter, along with several others, was seen as leading the South into a new era of race relations. But if the national press focused on the racial issue, Carter's own priority as governor was building up the Georgia economy. Proud of his own achievements as a businessman aside from the political dividends they bestowed, Carter embarked upon a spirited crusade to make Georgia a more conspicuous player in both American and overseas markets. It was this activity that brought Jimmy Carter to the attention of the founders of the Trilateral Commission in 1973.[16, 17]

Primarily the handiwork of David Rockefeller, head of the Chase Manhattan Bank, the Trilateral Commission sought to promote global economic stability. Bringing together established leaders from the governmental, business, and academic sectors of the United States (and Canada), Western Europe, and Japan, the commission advocated coordination and cooperation among the capitalist economic superpowers as the means to this end.[18] As director, Rockefeller chose Zbigniew Brzezinski, a professor of international relations at Columbia University. It was part of Brzezinski's duties to invite prominent individuals to join the commission.[19]

In selecting governmental leaders from the United States, the commission steered clear of officeholders in the federal executive branch, with the result that as the Trilateral Commission took shape in 1973, it had a distinctly Democratic cast to it.[20] With the members coming from Congress and from the corporate world fairly evenly split between the parties, it was among the former government officials that the Democrats predominated. Prominent in this latter group were former Under Secretary of State George Ball and former Vietnam peace talks negotiator Cyrus Vance.[21]

As he put the commission's membership list together, Brzezinski decided that he wanted two state governors--one from each party--on it. As he looked over the names of the Democratic incumbents--a generally undistiguished lot--his attention focused on two Southerners: Carter and Reuben Askew of Florida. According to Brzezinski's memoirs, his initial reaction was to go with Askew, who, coming from a larger and more glamorous state, had a higher national profile than Carter.[22] But when some of Brzezinski's associates pointed out that Carter was making a name for himself on economic issues, the decision was made to invite the Georgian, an invitation he quickly accepted.

The Carter selection was little noticed at the time--after all, he was just a governor from a relatively small state and the commission, itself not widely known, had three hundred members--but it would have significant consequences. Jimmy Carter received his initial and only significant pre-White House exposure to international issues in the context of the Trilateral Commission's concern for safeguarding the interests of multinational corporations in an uncertain environment made even more volatile by the Yom Kippur War and Arab oil embargo. Although lacking the wealth and power possessed by most of his fellow commission members, the businessman's outlook and engineering background that Carter brought to the commission's deliberations made him sympathetic to the its search for stability.[23, 24]   Carter's deep religious faith and love of country provided him with the broad outlines of the foreign policy he would pursue in the White House, but the priorities and details of that diplomacy would largely result from his contact with the Trilateral Commission.[25, 26]

The most crucial contribution the Trilateral Commission made to the Carter presidency was personnel. Moving in circles closed to him previously, the Georgian came to know most of the Democratic Party's foreign policy elite. More than twenty-five members of the commission were given important posts in his administration, including his secretaries of the Treasury (Michael Blumenthal) and defense (Harold Brown), as well as his national security adviser and his secretary of state.

The development of the Carter-Vance relationship had its roots in the Trilateral Commission, but it flowered with substance from several difference sources. Several years older than Carter, Vance appeared on the surface--with his Yale education, extensive service in the federal govenrment, and international law practice--to be cut from a completely different cloth.[27, 28] But on closer acquaintance the two men found a lot in common.[29] Vance's family came from West Virginia, and although he moved to New York as a child after the death of his father, Vance remained an enthusiastic fisherman and hiker, pleasures he and Carter had occasion to share in the two years before the primary campaign took up all of Carter's time. Their mothers were remarkably similar: Mrs. Vance, like Miss Lillian, was known among friends for her outspoken and independent views. And both Jimmy Carter and Cyrus Vance had been commissioned officers aboard Navy destroyers, a bond made especially strong because their experiences had occurred "in harm's way."[30]

In addition to these personal considerations, Carter was drawn to Vance by the lawyer's extraordinary skills at laying out points at issue and the ways in which they could be settled. Vance was a problem solver, and the engineer in Carter found Vance's attention to detail and his ability to find the precise word to suit a given situation a tremendous asset. When the Democrats started gearing up for the presidential primaries in 1975, Vance initially cast his lot with Sargent Shriver, an old friend from the Kennedy and Johnson days, but when the Shriver campaign failed to survive the early primaries, Vance was warmly welcomed into the Carter camp.[31, 32]

It is interesting to note that one person whom the candidate Carter appeared to want to link to the campaign, at least publicly, but did not was George Ball. In the spring of 1976, when Carter's candidacy was beginning to be taken more seriously but questions were being raised about his foreign policy credentials, the Carter staff indicated that Ball was one of the people--along with Vance--with whom the Georgian was in touch on international issues. When reporters contacted Ball, however, they found that this was not the case, and Carter suffered some embarrassment from the episode.[33, 34] In many ways Vance's twin in regard to education and experience, the thoroughly urbane Ball never hit it off personally with Carter. Aside from this difficulty, Carter's hestitation about Ball may have stemmed from Ball's much heralded dissent from the policies of the Johnson administration, of which he had been a member. Vance, by contrast, had alway been the good soldier during those tumultuous years, and Carter may have felt more comfortable with him at his side than the more independent Ball.[35, 36]

If the precise Vance appealed to one side of Carter's character, the philosophical Brzezinski found a receptive listener in the planning side of Carter. Like most well-educated Americans, Carter had a working familiarity with global politics, but until he struck up his relationship with the Columbia professor, he had not attempted to put international affairs into any schematic framework. With Brzezinski easily assuming the role of teacher and Carter willingly accepting the role of student, Brzezinski provided the engineer in Carter with a conceptual outlook that fit the various pieces of the world scene into a unified system. The generalities of Brzezinski's approach also fit in with the politician Carter's need to appear different from his rivals without having to be specific about how this difference would work out in practice.[37]

Jimmy Carter enjoyed the unusual luxury of being able to get through the Democratic primaries and the fall election campaign without having his lack of foreign policy experience seriously questioned or his views on global questions drawn out for public discussion. With the shadow of Watergate hanging over the political landscape, the traditional issues did not carry much weight, and Carter was undeniably the major beneficiary of this peculiar state of affairs. Even when one of the debates between candidates Ford and Carter was specifically labeled as being on foreign policy, the public's attention was focused on Ford's mistake in identifying Poland as free of Soviet control rather than on anything Carter may or may not have said. Carter was permitted to get away with criticizing Ford for having abdicated responsibility for foreign affairs to Henry Kissinger without being pressured on what presidential control of foreign policy would mean in practice. The closeness of the balloting may have reflected some uneasiness among the electorate about Carter--about either his personality or his qualifications--but foreign policy was just one of a bundle of ill-defined concerns.[38, 39, 40, 41]

Equally remarkable was the absence of uncertainty about who would hold the top foreign policy positions in the Carter administration. Of the three prior presidential transitions since the start of the Cold War, only John Foster Dulles had been the obvious selection for secretary of state from the start of the process to the end. Kennedy's choice of Dean Rusk and Richard Nixon's appointment of William Rogers were both surprises and were designed in each instance to affirm the chief executive's command of diplomacy.[42] (Reagan's choice of Alexander Haig was also unexpected, but the message there was unclear.) Vance's appointment, by contrast, was a foregone conclusion, despite Hamilton Jordan's comment earlier in the year that if Vance became secretary of state, it would represent a repudiation of the Carter promise to sweep a new broom into Washington and that he, Jordan, would not be a party to such a breach of faith. (He changed his mind, of course.) There was no alternative to Vance--no one Carter knew well enough to trust with this delicate assignment. Not only was Vance's position the first appointment announced, but it was paired with the selection of Carter's old friend Bert Lance to the top domestic job of director of the Office of Management and Budget.[43]

Brzezinski's reward also was never in doubt. The fountain of wisdom on whom Carter relied in preparing for his debate with Ford, Brzezinski possessed the academic credentials that McGeorge Bundy and Walt Rostow had first brought to the job of national security adviser, and that Henry Kissinger had all but made sine qua non for the position. The official announcement of his appointment came three weeks after the

Vance appointment, but the groundwork for his taking the post had been laid immediately following the election. In retrospect, the most interesting facet of the selection process was not the choices themselves but the failure of Carter, Vance, and Brzezinski to come to any understanding about their respective roles. After the Nixon-Ford-Kissinger experience, this was not an abstract issue, but in the euphoria of electoral triumph and the launching of a new administration, no one wanted to bring it up. This is particularly surprising in the case of Vance, whose knowledge of bureaucratic wars and legal mind should have set off alarms about the problem and made him eager to pin down the details. His failure to do so led not only to his eventual departure from the administration but also to the overall failure of the Carter presidency.[44, 45, 46]

Four episodes representative of the Carter administration's performance in foreign affairs have been chosen as a means of judging the consequences of the Vance and Brzezinski appointments: (1) the Panama Canal treaties; (2) the Camp David accords; (3) the SALT II negotiations; and (4) the Iranian crisis.

The first three reflected the priorities of the Trilateral Commission in its quest for global economic stability.[47] The improvement in U.S.-Latin American relations resulting from the settlement with Panama, the lessening of tension between Egypt and Israel flowing from the Camp David accords, and the prospect of a slowed arms race offered by the SALT II agreements were all important objectives of the Trilateral Commission. To be sure, these achievements were long-standing goals of American foreign policy, but that the Carter administration chose to focus its energies in these areas was undoubtedly the product of Carter's association with the Trilateral Commission and his having Vance and Brzezinski as his top aides. That in each case the groundwork for successful resolution of these issues had been laid by Henry Kissinger is also to be noted, since Kissinger joined the Trilateral Commission immediately after leaving the post of secretary of state.[48, 49, 50]

The Panama Canal treaties were primarily the product of Carter's appreciation of Latin America's historic grievances against the colossus to the north and Vance's skills as a negotiator and manager. If it was clear to anyone with a rudimentary understanding of hemispheric diplomacy that the maintenance of U.S. control of the Panama Canal in its present form was not sustainable, then Carter's decision to push for the treaties was not so much visionary as it was eminently practicable. But given the history of chauvinism on the issue, it was almost heroic. Even with the foreign policy establishment behind him,[51] the narrowness of the Senate vote for ratification (66-32) reveals how difficult the struggle was.[52]

Carter's success here owed much not only to his own willingness to take a stand but also to Vance's ability to fashion an agreement that would satisfy both the Panamanians and two-thirds of the Senate. The secretary of state assembled a topflight negotiating team composed of foreign service professionals and able lawyers. Keeping in constant touch with his surrogates, Vance hammered out a settlement that either delayed important shifts of power for long periods of time or put off resolution of other delicate subjects until a later date. It was diplomacy at its artful, evasive best, but it worked and U.S.-Latin American relations became noticeably warmer in the treaties' glow.[53, 54]

Panama was a Carter-Vance operation; Camp David demonstrated what Carter, Vance, and Brzezinski were capable of when they operated in harmony. The president approached the task with the single-mindedness of a man on a mission. Indicative of his obsession with bringing peace to the land of the Bible was his admission that, quite out of character, he took some satisfaction in being able to succeed where the twentieth-century "Cardinal Richelieu" (Henry Kissinger) had failed. If Carter supplied the passion, Brzezinski provided the overall framework for the talks. Besides continually reminding each participant in the three-cornered discussions of the advantages that could be expected from an agreement, Brzezinski suggested that the resulting accord would add up to more than the sum of its parts. His abstractions were complemented by the ability of Vance and his State Department aides to devise countless new proposals that could be arranged and rearranged to suit everyone's needs.[55, 56]

Critics of the Camp David accords have rightly pointed out that the agreements served the interests of Egypt and Israel without promoting the American goal of a general Middle East peace settlement; but against the almost totally bleak record of American involvement in that tragically divided region's affairs since the 1940s, the Carter administration's performance at Camp David certainly shines. Carter, Vance, Brzezinski, and the Trilateralists could justly believe that they had begun to relieve the threat posed to the industrialized world's petroleum supplies by Middle Eastern instability.[57]

But Trilateralism provided no usable umbrella for conducting U.S.-Soviet relations. A reduction in American-Soviet tensions was the common goal of the foreign policy establishment, but the means for achieving it lacked a similar unanimity of opinion, and here the Carter administration began to fly apart. Strategic arms limitation had been established in the Nixon-Ford years as the focus for U.S.-Soviet diplomacy, and the Carter administration followed this precedent. But if divisions within the executive branch during the Nixon-Ford period had followed the expected State Department vs. Defense Department lines, with the president and his national security adviser generally supporting accommodation with the Soviets, the Carter administration developed a maze of fractures, with the chief executive contributing to the disarray by his own vacillation.[58, 59, 60, 61]

The SALT II negotiations revealed the problems in Carter's organization of his foreign policy apparatus, for it was here that Brzezinski's conception of the big picture came into direct collision with Vance's building blocks approach. Whereas Vance thought U.S.-Soviet understanding and trust could be built up block by block, by stressing the aspects of their relationship where their interests were in common--for instance, reducing spending on strategic weapons and the danger of all-out nuclear war--Brzezinki insisted that no agreement with the Soviets on these issues could take place before Moscow ceased being a global troublemaker. At the midpoint of the Carter presidency, the national security adviser identified no fewer than twenty-eight low-intensity wars and conflicts in the Third World that were directly sponsored and supported by the Soviet Union or one of its satellites in Eastern Europe. Viewing any progress in strategic arms limitation as being more beneficial to the Russians than to the United States, Brzezinski demanded a "quid pro quo" from the Soviets in the form of cutting off aid to these destabilizing movements.[62, 63, 64, 65]

With his secretary of state and national security adviser at loggerheads, and with his secretary of defense and the joint chiefs of staff also at odds, President Carter proved indecisive. Confronted with conflicting advice and lacking the experience and assurance that come from an extended exposure to complex foreign policy issues, the chief executive moved first one way and then another. As Hamilton Jordan observed in dismay: "Who the hell knows whether the president will not veer in some direction tomorrow or the day after tomorrow?" Carter's signing of the SALT II Treaty in Vienna in June 1979, although a victory for Secretary Vance, was not the end of the story. The subsequent Senate ratification hearings revealed an administration in almost total disarray, and even if Brzezinski did not testify, his unhappiness with the treaty was obvious to all. The Soviet occupation of Afghanistan in December provided Carter with another opportunity to reverse himself, and he took it. Even before the Iranian crisis, the Carter foreign policy was in tatters.[66]

The mess in Iran supplied the coup de grace. To be sure, the Carter administration cannot be held responsible for the decades of diplomatic folly that preceded the shah's fall in the winter of 1979, but it does bear responsibility, as any administration in power must, for the failures committed on its own watch. In a nutshell, Iran fell through the cracks of the structure of foreign policy-making put together by Jimmy Carter. Vance, the tactician, did not have his attention pulled to Iran until the shah was already on the ropes. Brzezinski, the strategist, counted the shah among the pillars of American power in that part of the world, totally oblivious to the depth of hatred the people of Iran felt for their leader and to the strength of Islamic fundamentalism. Carter, the moralist, had no independent familiarity with the dynamics of this country and its people, and played the opportunistic game pursued by all of his predecessors. Whether there was anything that Jimmy Carter might have done before January 1979 to protect American long-term interests in Iran is problematic, but one thing is certain: his acceptance of the status quo was disastrous.

Trilateralism had never come to grips with the needs and yearnings of the Third World, and thus, as in regard to U.S.-Soviet relations, it had no ready design for Carter to follow in Iran. But the Trilateral connection would figure heavily in the deepening Iranian tragedy that followed. However humanitarian a gesture it might have seemed at the time, the decision to allow the shah into the United States in the fall of 1979--a step initiated by David Rockfeller and Henry Kissinger--played into the hands of Muslim militants and set off the hostage crisis. While Vance and Brzezinski were in accord on receiving the shah, the deterioration of their relationship because of Cold War issues hindered development of an effective response to this unprecedented breach of diplomatic protocol. When decisive action was finally taken in the spring of 1980, it came at the cost of the secretary of state's resignation.

The Constitution of the United States lodges prime responsibility for the conduct of this nation's foreign policy with the president. In 1976, the American people elected as their chief executive a man with no experience in global affairs who was also a virtual stranger to the ins and outs of Washington. Jimmy Carter captured the hearts of the American electorate at a peculiar time in this country's two-hundred-year experiment with democracy and rode that passion to victory. After four years, Carter stood repudiated by that same electorate, largely because of his failures in foreign policy.

Carter's failures derived largely from that inexperience. Aside from some very general views about the world and America's place in it, Carter's approach to foreign policy was largely set from his contacts with the Trilateral Commission. The engineer, planner, and businessman in Carter found the commission's search for political and economic stability appealing and, to a remarkable degree, his administration actively pursued these objectives and achieved them where they were clearly recognizable. But when Trilateralism offered few or no guidelines, as in the case of U.S.-Soviet relations or the Iranian situation, Carter was at a loss.

Jimmy Carter's growth and development were shaped by a number of powerful experiences. In the early years the family vicariously modeled and reinforced the values of hard work, fairness in relations with others, and a deep religious/church commitment. Strengthened and forged by these values, Jimmy Carter developed a personality characterized by strong commitment, confident leadership attitudes, and a sense that with hard work one could accomplish any task or meet any goal. Certainly his successes as farmer, businessman, and politician continued to reinforce his belief that he was in charge of his own destiny. Social psychologists refer to this kind of personality as one with an internalized locus of control.

Jimmy Carter was clearly deficient in his understanding of world affairs. The Trilateral endeavor provided powerful knowledge and complementary experience. However, the experience did not correct the deficiency, a fact that was never understood by President Carter. Success and power make it extremely difficult to step back in the heat of mental battle in order to take stock. Even if Carter had been able to step back and reflect on his own abilities, his internal locus of control prevented him from being introspective.

As a result, Jimmy Carter continued to maintain full responsibility for foreign policy decision making. His deficiency and lack of experience with world affairs did not allow his wealth of management experience to come to his aid in directing the affairs of his secretary of state and national security adviser. But more important, Carter was not able to manage the relationship between Vance, Brzezinski, and himself--particularly in a crisis situation.

His choice of top advisers only exaggerated his weakness. By appointing two men with two very different approaches--both operationally and ideologically--Carter found himself confronted with contradictory advice that in the end produced only vacillation and paralysis. If Carter prided himself on his managerial skills and for being a decision maker, the poverty of his background in foreign policy prevented him from acting with consistency and purpose. In the end it was the *Carter* foreign policy that was generated, but it was a foreign policy little understood by our friends, our adversaries, or our own people.

NOTES

1. Coral Bell, "Virtue Unrewarded: Carter's Foreign Policy at Mid-Term," *International Affairs*, 54, no. 4 (October 1978):149-170.

2. Carl M. Brauer, *Presidential Transitions, Eisenhower Through Reagan* (New York: Oxford University Press, 1986), pp. 173-176.

3. Erwin C. Hargrove, *Jimmy Carter as President* (Baton Rouge: Louisiana State University Press, 1988), p. 3.

4. Brauer, op. cit., p. xv.

5. Vincent Davis, "Carter Tries on the World for Size," *Society*, 16, no. 1 (November/December 1978):36-42.

6. Jimmy Carter, *Keeping Faith: Memoirs of a President* (New York: Bantam Books, 1982), pp. 17-21.

7. Holly Sklar, ed., *Trilateralism: The Trilateral Commission and Elite Planning for World Management* (Boston: South End Press, 1980), p. 32.

8. Gary M. Fink, *Prelude to the Presidency* (Westport, CT: Greenwood Press, 1980), pp. 49-55.

9. Haynes Johnson, *In the Absence of Power: Governing America* (New York: Viking Press, 1980), pp. 58-61.

10. Robert Strauss, "Reflections on the Presidency," in *Twelve Virginia Papers Presented at the Miller Center Forums, 1985* (Lanham, MD: University Press of America, 1985), p. 4.

11. John Dennis, "Jimmy Carter's Fierce Campaign," *The Nation*, May 17, 1975, p. 593.

12. Fink, op. cit., p. 68.

13. Linda Charlton, "Carter Watches the Convention and Confers on Energy Policy," *New York Times*, August 18, 1976, p. 20.

14. Brauer, op. cit., p. 39.

15. Johnson, op. cit., p. 65.

16. Zbigniew Brzezinski, *Power and Principle: Memoirs of the National Security Advisor* (New York: Farrar, Straus and Giroux, 1983), p. 5.

17. Gloria Duffy, "Shaping Carter's World View," *Washington Post*, August 15, 1976, p. C-5.

18. Sklar, op. cit., p. 4.

19. Brzezinski, op. cit., p. 5.

20. *Who's Who*, 1972, p. 684; 1973, p. 617; 1974, p. 693.

21. Sklar, op. cit., p. 14.

22. Brzezinski, op. cit., p. 7.

23. Carter, op. cit., p. 49.

24. Linda Charlton, "Policy Briefings Begun by Carter," *New York Times*, July 27, 1976, p. 1.

25. Carter, op. cit., p. 53.

26. Brzezinski, op. cit., p. 9.

27. Carter, op. cit., p. 70.

28. William E. Farrell, "Reagan Defeats Ford in Indiana and Also Wins Georgia Primary: Carter Is Victor in Both States," *New York Times*, May 5, 1976, p. 1.

29. David McLellan, *Cyrus Vance* (Totowa, NJ: Rowman and Allanheld, 1985), pp. 20-24.

30. Ibid.

31. Brzezinski, op. cit., pp. 10-15.

32. Leslie H. Gelb, "The Secretary of State Sweepstakes," *New York Times Magazine*, May 23, 1976, pp. 13ff.

33. Hargrove, op. cit., p. 121.

34. Dennis, op. cit., pp. 594-595.

35. Carter, op. cit., p. 70.

36. Joseph G. Bock, "The White House Staff and the National Security Assistant: Friendship and Friction at the Water's Edge," in *Contributions in Political Science*, no. 170 (Westport, CT: Greenwood Press, 1987), p. 133.

37. Leslie Gelb, "Carter Is Expected to Appoint Vance as Secretary of State," *New York Times*, December 3, 1976, p. 1.

38. Gelb, op. cit., pp. 13ff.

39. "The Government in Waiting," *The New Republic*, 175, no. 25, iss. 3232 (December 18, 1976):5-6.

40. Wayne King, "Carter Redux," *New York Times Magazine*, December 10, 1989, pp. 17ff.

41. Stephen Klaidman, "The New Foreign Policy Crowd," *Washington Post*, June 27, 1976, p. C-1.

42. Carl M. Brauer, "Organizing Policy-Making: Presidential Transitions and Foreign Policy," in *Seven Virginia Papers Presented at the Miller Center Forums and Conversations, 1986-87, Part I* (Lanham, MD: University Press of America, 1987), pp. 165-172.

43. "Picking the New Team," *Newsweek*, December 13, 1976, pp. 20-21.

44. Anthony Lake, "Third World Radical Regimes, U.S. Policy Under Carter and Reagan," *Foreign Policy Association Headline Series*, no. 272 (January/February 1985):110-112.

45. Murray Marder, "Brzezinski: A Voluble Critic of His Predecessor, Kissinger," *Washington Post*, December 19, 1976, p. A-18.

46. "Vance and Lance: The Selection Begins," *Time*, December 13, 1976, pp. 12-13.

47. Bruce Mazlish and Edwin Diamond, *Jimmy Carter, A Character Portrait* (New York: Simon and Schuster, 1979), p. 79.

48. Philip Ogden, "The President and National Security," in *Five Virginia Papers Presented at the Miller Center Forums, 1984, Part II* (Lanham, MD: University Press of America, 1984), p. 2.

49. Craig Allen Smith, "Leadership, Orientation, and Rhetorical Vision: Jimmy Carter, the New Right, and the Panama Canal," *Presidential Studies Quarterly*, 16, no. 2 (September 1986).

50. Sklar, op. cit., p. 12.

51. McLellan, op. cit., pp. 79-80.

52. Brzezinski, op. cit., pp. 14-24.

53. McLellan, op. cit., p. 79.

54. William Clinton Olson, "The World from Both Ends of Pennsylvania Avenue," *The Round Table*, no. 272 (October 1978):333-340.

55. McLellan, op. cit., p. 110.

56. Brzezinski, op. cit.

57. Alan Wolfe, "Reflections on Trilateralism and the Carter Administration: Changed World Realities vs. Vested Interests," in Sklar, ed., *The Trilateral Commission* (Boston: South End Press, 1980), p. 90.

58. Ibid., p. 92.

59. Brzezinski, op. cit., p. 17.

60. Sander Vanocur, "The President, the Secretary of State, and the National Security Advisor," in *Four Virginia Papers Presented at the Miller Center Forums, 1983, Part III* (Lanham, MD: University Press of America, 1983), p. 41.

61. Ogden, op. cit., p. 23.

62. Brzezinski, op. cit., p. 257.

63. McLellan, op. cit., p. 138.

64. Griffin Bell, "Cabinet Government: An Alternative for Organizing Policymaking," in *Five Virginia Papers Presented at the Miller Center Forums, 1984, Part III* (Lanham, MD: University Press of America, 1984), p. 62.

65. Hargrove, op. cit., p. 134.

66. Bell, op. cit., p. 65.

REFERENCES

Periodical Articles and Books

Beck's Business Almanac. Chicago: Rand McNally, 1974.

Bell, Coral. "Virtue Unrewarded: Carter's Foreign Policy at Mid-Term." *International Affairs* 54, no. 4 (October 1978).

---. "From Carter to Reagan." *Foreign Affairs* 65, no. 3, 1985.

Bell, Griffin. "Cabinet Government: An Alternative for Organizing Policymaking." In *Five Virginia Papers Presented at the Miller Center Forums, 1984, Part III*. Lanham, MD: University Press of America, 1984.

Benze, James G., Jr. *Presidential Power and Management Techniques*. Westport, CT: Greenwood Press, 1987.

Bercovitch, Jacob. "A Case Study of Mediation as a Method of International Conflict Resolution: The Camp David Experience." *Review of International Studies* 12 (1986).

Bock, Joseph G. "The White House Staff and the National Security Assistant: Friendship and Friction at the Water's Edge." *Contributions in Political Science*, no. 170. Westport, CT: Greenwood Press, 1987.

Brauer, Carl M. "Organizing Policy-Making: Presidential Transitions and Foreign Policy." In *Seven Virginia Papers Presented at the Miller Center Forums and Conversations, 1986-87, Part I*. Lanham, MD: University Press of America, 1987.

Brzezinski, Zbigniew. *Power and Principle: Memoirs of the National Security Advisor*. New York: Farrar, Straus and Giroux, 1983.

Burns, William F. "Arms Control Administration: The Reagan Administration Legacy." *Presidential Studies Quarterly* 19, no. 2 (Winter 1988).

Carter, Jimmy. *Keeping Faith: Memoirs of a President*. New York: Bantam Books, 1988.

Cronin, Thomas E., ed. *The Presidential Advisory System*. New York: Harper and Row , 1969.

Davis, Vincent. "Carter Tries on the World for Size." *Society* 16, no. 1 (November/December 1978).

deMause, Lloyd, and Henry Ebel, eds. *Jimmy Carter and American Fantasy: Psychohistorical Explorations*. New York: Two Continents/Psychohistory Press, 1977.

Dennis, John. "Jimmy Carter's Fierce Campaign." *The Nation*, May 17, 1975.

Fink, Gary M. *Prelude to the Presidency*. Westport, CT: Greenwood Press, 1980.

"The Government in Waiting." *The New Republic,* December 18, 1976.

Graber, Doris A., ed. *The President and the Public*. Philadelphia: ISHI Publications, 1980.

Hamilton, Andrew. "Redressing the Conventional Balance: NATO's Reserve Military Manpower." *International Security* 10, no. 1 (Summer 1985):111-136.

Hargrove, Edwin C. *Jimmy Carter as President*. Baton Rouge: Louisiana State University Press, 1988.

Helms, Richard. "The Presidency and the Intelligence System." In *Six Virginia Papers Presented at the Miller Center Forums, 1983, Part IV*. Lanham, MD: University Press of America, 1984.

Johnson, Donald Bruce, comp. *National Party Platforms, vol. II, 1960-1976*. Urbana: University of Illinois Press, 1978.

Johnson, Haynes. *In the Absence of Power: Governing America*. New York: Viking Press, 1980.

Jones, Charles O. "Carter and Congress: From the Outside In." *British Journal of Political Science* 15, pt. 3 (July 1985):269-298.

Komer, Robert W. "What 'Decade of Neglect?'" *International Security*, Summer 1985.

Lake, Anthony. "Third World Radical Regimes, U.S. Policy Under Carter and Reagan." *Foreign Policy Association Headline Series*, no. 272 (January/February 1985).

Lebovic, James H. "National Interests and U.S. Foreign Aid: The Carter and Reagan Years." *Journal of Peace Research* 25, no. 2 (June 1988):115-136.

McLellan, David S. *Cyrus Vance*. Totowa, NJ: Rowman and Allanheld, 1985.

Mazlish, Bruce, and Edwin Diamond. *Jimmy Carter, a Character Portrait*. New York: Simon and Schuster, 1979.

Mulcahy, Kevin V. "The Secretary of State and the National Security Advisor: Foreign Policy Making in the Carter and Reagan Administration." *Presidential Studies Quarterly* 16, no. 2 (Spring 1986).

Ogden, Philip. "The President and National Security." In *Five Virginia Papers Presented at the Miller Center Forums, 1984, Part II*. Lanham, MD: University Press of America, 1984.

Olson, William Clinton. "The World from Both Ends of Pennsylvania Avenue." *The Round Table*, no. 272 (October 1978).

Rovere, Richard H. "Letter from Washington." *The New Yorker*, December 20, 1976.

Shafer, D. Michael. *Deadly Paradigms: The Failure of U.S. Counterinsurgency Policy*. Princeton: Princeton University Press, 1988.

Sklar, Holly, ed. *Trilateralism: The Trilateral Commission and Elite Planning for World Management*. Boston: South End Press, 1980.

Smith, Craig Allen. "Leadership, Orientation, and Rhetorical Vision: Jimmy Carter, the New Right, and the Panama Canal." *Presidential Studies Quarterly* 16, no. 2 (September 1986).

Starbuck, Kathy. "Mr. Sincere Runs for President." *The New Leader*, March 17, 1975.

Strauss, Robert. "Reflections on the Presidency." In *Twelve Virginia Papers Presented at the Miller Center Forums, 1985*. Lanham, MD: University Press of America, 1985.

Suetonius. "Cyrus Robert Vance, Everybody's Man." *The New Republic*, December 18, 1976.

Szulc, Tad. "Carter's Foreign Policy Team: Who's in Charge Here?" *The New Republic*, January 1 and 8, 1977.

Vanocur, Sander. "The President, the Secretary of State, and the National Security Advisor." In *Four Virginia Papers Presented at the Miller Center Forums, 1983, Part III*. Lanham, MD: University Press of America, 1983.

Whitehead, John C. "The Department of State: Requirements for an Effective Foreign Policy in the 1990's." *Presidential Studies Quarterly* 19, no. 1 (Winter 1989).

Wolfe, Alan. Reflections on Trilateralism and the Carter Administration: Changed World Realities vs. Vested Interests." In Holly Sklar, ed., *The Trilateral Commission*. Boston: South End Press, 1980, pp. 533-534.

Zwick, Charles. "The Future of Public Diplomacy." *Presidential Studies Quarterly* 19, no. 2 (1988).

Newspaper and Newsmagazine Articles

"Arts of Cabinet-Making." *Newsweek*, December 20, 1976.

Braden, Tom. "The Next Secretary of State." *Washington Post*, August 21, 1976.

Burns, John F. "Vorster Assails U.S. Africa Policy as a Payoff by Carter for Blacks." *New York Times*, October 7, 1977.

"Carter: Seeking Clear Goals." *Time*, May 10, 1976.

"Carter! Election '76." *Time*, November 15, 1976.

"Carter's Brain Trusts." *Time*, December 20, 1976.

Carter, Jimmy. "Excerpts from Carter Speech on Nuclear Policy as prepared for delivery at the United Nations." *New York Times*, May 14, 1976.

Charlton, Linda. "Carter Watches the Convention and Confers on Energy Policy." *New York Times*, August 18, 1976.

---. "Policy Briefings Begun by Carter." *New York Times*, July 27, 1976.

Clymer, Adam. "Senators Reject Public Financing of Their Races." *New York Times*, August 3, 1977.

"The Crisis Manager." *Newsweek*, December 13, 1976.

Duffy, Gloria. "Shaping Carter's World View." *Washington Post*, August 15, 1976.

Farrell, William E. "Reagan Defeats Ford in Indiana and Also Wins Georgia Primary; Carter Is Victor in Both States." *New York Times*, May 5, 1976.

Fritchey, Clayton. "Kissinger in 'Opposition.'" *Washington Post*, December 11, 1976.

Gelb, Leslie H. "Top Experts Helping Guide Candidates' Foreign Views." *New York Times*, March 27, 1976.

---. "Aides Say Carter Is Courted by Russians." *New York Times*, May 13, 1976.

---. "The Secretary of State Sweepstakes." *New York Times Magazine*, May 23, 1976.

---. "Brzezinski Is Viewed as Key Advisor to Carter." *New York Times*, October 6, 1976.

---. "Carter Is Expected to Appoint Vance Secretary of State." *New York Times*, December 3, 1976.

Gwertzman, Bernard. "U.S. Reports Accord with Israel Raises Hope of Peace Talks." *New York Times*, October 6, 1977.

Halloran, Richard. "U.S.-Japanese-European Body off to a Shaky Start in Tokyo." *New York Times*, October 6, 1973.

Johnston, Laurie. "Jimmy Carter's Foreign Policy." *New York Times*, May 29, 1975.

King, Wayne. "Carter Redux." *New York Times Magazine*, December 10, 1989.

Klaidman, Stephen. "The New Foreign Policy Crowd." *Washington Post*, June 27, 1976.

Marder, Murray. "Brzezinski: A Voluble Critic of His Predecessor, Kissinger." *Washington Post*, December 14, 1976.

Mohr, Charles. "Vance Is Selected by Carter to Run State Department." *New York Times*, December 4, 1976.

"Picking the New Team." *Newsweek*, December 13, 1976.

Smith, Hendrick. "The Love-in." *New York Times*, July 23, 1976.

---. "An American Accord." *New York Times*, August 14, 1977.

---. "Problems of a Problem Solver." *New York Times Magazine*, January 8, 1978.

"U.S. Reviews Commitment to the Indochina Refugees, Issue and Debate." *New York Times*, August 3, 1977.

"Vance and Lance: The Selection Begins." *Time*, December 13, 1976.

Weaver, Warren, Jr. "Democrats' Big Worry is Not Enough Worrying." *New York Times*, July 17, 1976.

Weinraub, Bernard. "Defense Chief Backs Start on a System of Mobile Missiles." *New York Times*, October 6, 1977.

2

President Carter, Western Europe, and Afghanistan in 1980: Inter-Allied Differences over Policy toward the Soviet Invasion

MINTON F. GOLDMAN

In the early months of 1980 the Carter administration's policy toward the Soviet invasion of Afghanistan had three major objectives: to prod the Soviets to withdraw their military forces from Afghanistan; to punish them for an aggressive act President Carter considered illegal; and to prevent them from using Afghanistan as a springboard for further expansion southward toward the Persian Gulf. To achieve these objectives, President Carter announced an extensive curtailment of American trade with the Soviet Union involving the sale of grain and high technology, threatened American withdrawal from the Olympic Games to be held in Moscow, and pledged protection of the Persian Gulf, by force if necessary.

For these objectives to succeed, President Carter believed he needed a strong, unified response to the Soviet invasion from the Western European Allies. In the early months of 1980 he exerted intense pressure on Britain, Germany, France, and Norway, along with other members of the European Community (EC), to cooperate with American efforts to punish the Soviets and force a reversal of their policy in Afghanistan.

Initially, they were responsive. For example, on January 17, 1980, EC foreign ministers reaffirmed their "grave concern" over the Soviet invasion, which, they said, represented "a serious violation of the principles of the United Nations . . . a flagrant interference in the internal affairs of a non-aligned country, and a threat to peace, security and stability." They also agreed to review all economic, credit, and financial relations between the EC and the Soviet Union; to cancel the 1978 EC food and aid program for Afghanistan, and to assure that European agricultural supplies should not substitute for those denied by the U.S. embargo; and to call upon the International Olympic Committee as well as national Olympic committees of member states to reconsider whether the Summer Olympic Games should be held in Moscow if the occupation of Afghanistan continued.[1]

Despite this and similar gestures of opposition to the Soviet invasion, however, the Western European Allies were unwilling to press the Afghan issue in the same way as the United States. Indeed, they had serious misgivings about the Carter administration's policies toward the Kremlin in the Afghan crisis. Before long it was apparent to Washington that the Allies would not back the U.S. sanctions policy, would not increase military deployments in the greater Persian Gulf region, and would not participate in the arming of Pakistan.

ALLIED SKEPTICISM

Several considerations inspired Allied skepticism of American policy toward the Soviet invasion of Afghanistan. They were less willing than the United States to confront the Soviets on the Afghan issue because of the risk to détente, which had brought them so many political, economic, and strategic advantages throughout the 1970s. Indeed, by the early 1980s, détente with the East bloc had become important and valuable to the Western European countries if only because of their geographic proximity and, therefore, vulnerability to the Warsaw Pact members.

Other differences with the United States involved strategic questions. The Allies tended to see Soviet policy in Afghanistan primarily in regional terms rather than as another dimension of the Cold War. Regional problems, in their view, were best left to local resolution.

Moreover, they never really accepted President Carter's view, embodied in the so-called Carter Doctrine, that Soviet action in Afghanistan was a prelude to further expansion southward into the Persian Gulf, and therefore a threat to the security of Western oil sources in the Arabian Peninsula. Therefore, they did not share the president's sense of urgency in responding to the Afghan invasion.

At the same time, most of the Allies ultimately disagreed with President Carter's insistence in the "Carter Doctrine" speech to Congress on January 23, 1980, on the obligation of the West to counter the Soviet invasion. They did not acknowledge NATO's substantive responsibilities outside of continental Europe and did not approve of an expansion of NATO military power in the Persian Gulf.

In addition, the Allied governments in the early months of 1980 did not believe that the Soviet invasion of Afghanistan was as much of a threat to Western economic and strategic interests as the Carter administration said it was. Rather, they saw some merit in the Kremlin's argument, dismissed out of hand by many Carter administration officials, of having had to move into Kabul for reasons of defense and security. To deal with these concerns, the West Europeans preferred diplomacy that would take into account the Soviets' legitimate security concerns and provide the Kremlin with a face-saving way out of a sitaution that had provoked such international opposition.[2]

The Allies also questioned the efficacy of American policy. They doubted that the trade embargo and the Olympic boycott could have much influence on the Kremlin, especially in light of the Soviets' repeated assertions that they would never negotiate under pressure. Moreover, rather than isolate and ostracize the insecure and defensive Soviet leadership, and thereby encourage its stubbornness and belligerence, the Allies preferred to keep lines of communication open with the Kremlin to give diplomacy a chance to induce a reversal of policy in Afghanistan.

Finally, the Allies were sensitive to strong pressures from the Carter administration almost immediately after the Soviet invasion, inasmuch as their interests in the crisis were far from identical to those of the United States. While affirming to American diplomats their deep and abiding commitment to the traditionally strong friendship they had always had and would continue to have with the United States, they sought a margin of discretion in dealing with the Soviet Union in accordance with their national interests, which required the continuation of détente.

Beyond these considerations were others of national interest peculiar to each of the major European Allies. Britain, West Germany, France, and Norway, which were the objects of the strongest appeals from the Carter administration, had their own strategic, economic and other reasons for proceeding with caution and restraint.

Britain

Consistent with its past closeness to the United States on East-West issues and with its long experience countering tsarist Russian expansionism in Central Asia during the nineteenth century, Britain condemned the Soviet invasion and was the strongest supporter of the Carter administration. The British government thought, as did the United States, that the Soviet invasion of Afghanistan signaled a Soviet effort to obtain control of a country outside the Warsaw Pact; that the Kremlin could continue to seek opportunities to expand Soviet influence in the Third World; that strong actions were necessary to induce a reversal of Soviet policy; and that NATO must expand its military operations outside of continental Europe.[3]

The government of Prime Minister Margaret Thatcher seemed to be as good as its word in backing the Carter administration on the Afghan issue. On January 22, the prime minister endorsed the American idea of a punitive gesture toward the Soviets in the form of a boycott of the Summer Olympic Games, and asked British Olympic athletes not to participate in the upcoming games unless they were relocated outside the Soviet Union. On January 24, the British government announced a broad program of diplomatic reprisals against the Soviet Union that included the suspension of ministerial and other high-level contacts, an increase in foreign-language broadcasts to the Soviet Union and Afghanistan, a tightening of credit restrictions, a review of the rules governing the transfer of sensitive technology to the Soviet Union, and a proposal to remove the Summer Olympic Games from Soviet cities.[4]

The British also shared an American concern with the security of the Indian subcontinent and were willing to help mobilize Pakistan and India against Soviet policy in Afghanistan. Foreign Secretary Lord Carrington went to Islamabad in January to re-assure Pakistan of Western Europe's concern over its defense in the aftermath of the Afghan invasion and to offer President Zia ul-Haq's government economic assistance.[5]

Lord Carrington also discussed Afghanistan with the Indian leadership to persuade Prime Minister Indira Gandhi that India faced a greater threat from Soviet forces in Afghanistan than from the American attempt to strengthen Pakistan's defense. Though there were differences over how to respond to the Soviet invasion--the Indians refused to condemn Soviet policy, urged restraint, and told Carrington they were more worried about an American arming of Pakistan than about Soviet troops in Kabul-- both sides agreed that the Soviet invasion represented a threat to peace in the region.[6]

The British also sought to mobilize the rest of Europe behind American opposition to Soviet policy in Afghanistan. In a speech to Parliament on January 28, a week before the EC was scheduled to discuss joint policies toward the American trade embargo and the proposed Olympic boycott, Thatcher called on the EC countries to put aside their differences of emphasis and unite behind President Carter's "clear leadership."[7] In February, Foreign Secretary Lord Carrington proposed to a meeting of EC foreign ministers in Rome that the Soviets be offered a European-guaranteed neutralization of Afghanistan that implied--but did not explicitly provide for--an end of Western military assistance to the anticommunist resistance that had battled the Marxist regime in Kabul since its establishment in April 1978.[8]

When the Soviets rejected the EC proposal on February 23, the Allies followed the British lead and toughened their position. On April 29, the EC Council meeting in Luxembourg expressed deep concern that Soviet military forces had not been withdrawn from Afghanistan; emphasized the need more than ever before for European unity on the Afghan issue; and reiterated the European commitment to Afghan self-determination and to ending all outside interference in Afghan affairs. At a NATO meeting in May, the British and West Europeans again spoke strongly against the Soviet invasion. They seemed to affirm the American view of the broad geographic area to which détente applied and stipulated, as the Carter administration had done earlier, that Soviet military control of Afghanistan negatively affected the overall strategic situation; that the stability of regions outside NATO boundaries was of crucial importance to all members; and that the invasion had done serious damage to détente. At the Venice summit in June, the Western Europeans, along with the United States, Canada, and Japan, stated firmly that "the Soviet military occupation of Afghanistan is unacceptable now"; that "we are determined not to accept it in the future"; and that "it undermines the foundation of peace both in the region and in the world."[9]

The British also agreed to increase spending on defense, as the Carter administration had been urging all the NATO Allies to do in the aftermath of the Soviet invasion. The Ministry of Defense in April announced an increase in the military budget of 3.5 percent for 1980-1981 while overall public expenditures were to decrease. The ministry also indicated willingness to increase the British share of NATO's military operations outside the North Atlantic area.[10]

While these British actions were substantial--and considerably more than other Western European countries were willing to take in response to the Soviet invasion-- they were far less than the Carter administration wanted, and they marked the end rather than the beginning of what London was willing to do to pressure the Soviets to reverse course in Afghanistan. Indeed, despite their inclination to support the Carter administration, British leaders had some serious reservations about U.S. policy in the Afghan crisis.

They did not want to go so far as to close lines of communication with the Kremlin or to curtail their trade with the Soviet Union in imitation of the American embargo. Indeed, Lord Carrington said in January that Britain would continue "to search for arms control agreements, commercially justified trade, and other arrangements of mutual benefit." Nor were the British ready to expand in a substantial way their deployment of military power east of Suez and help the United States enforce the Carter Doctrine to defend the Persian Gulf against an expected Soviet attack, or to participate in a full-scale rearming of Pakistan.[11]

More evidence of British differences with the United States over Afghanistan was apparent when Prime Minister Thatcher refused to go beyond her January 22 request for the boycott of the Olympic Games. On February 14, she announced that the British government would only "advise" British athletes not to attend the games in the Soviet Union. When the British Olympic Committee on March 25, acting partly in response to strong public sentiment in favor of British participation in the games, recommended sending British athletes to the Summer Games, Thatcher accepted this decision.[12]

Behind this British restraint were several considerations, among them the fact that Britain, with its North Sea oil, was not dependent on Persian Gulf oil and therefore was less anxious over Soviet policy in Afghanistan than the United States. Also, the British were aware of their limited military capability, summed up rather bluntly by the *London Times* when it said in early January that "it is not suggested that partly toothless Britannia could or should charge off on any leadership crusade."[13]

Former Prime Minister Sir Alec Douglas Home offered another reason for British unwillingness to follow the American lead in the Afghan crisis. He was quoted as saying that "no military operation of the kind envisaged by President Carter in his pledge to defend the Persian Gulf could possibly make sense for NATO because the Soviets did not go into Afghanistan to seize control of the Persian Gulf."[14]

Moreover, holding the British back from arming Pakistan and other Third World countries against the Soviets, a policy the Carter administration was pursuing, was not only the cost to their economy, which already was burdened by a high social budget, but also the risk of provoking anti-Western sentiment. The British were especially concerned about alienating India and driving her closer to the Soviet Union in the Afghan crisis.

The British also believed that eventually the Russians would be hoist by their own petard in Afghanistan. They thought the Kremlin would end up paying a very high diplomatic price for aggression in Afghanistan, with diminished credit in the Muslim world and dissatisfaction among some of the Warsaw Pact members, already uncomfortable over the deterioration of détente, and with diminished opportunities to obtain concessions from the United States in the areas of trade and arms control.[15]

West Germany

Like the British, the West German government sympathized with the Carter administration's strong reaction to the Soviet invasion of Afghanistan and to a degree was willing to speak strongly to the Kremlin. Because of the need for Persian Gulf oil, the Germans were sympathetic to the American view that the presence of Soviet troops in Afghanistan posed a threat to secure oil supplies. Also, they feared the precedent that would be set should the Soviets be allowed to get away with their invasion of Afghanistan. Germany is vulnerable to an "Afghanlike" Soviet military thrust arising out of its contiguity to the Warsaw Pact nations: a quarter of German industry and 30 percent of the German population are within one hundred kilometers of the West German border with what was then socialist East Germany and Czechoslovakia. Bonn also was sensitive to the lessons of the past. According to Rolf

Pauls, the West German ambassador to NATO, at an emergency meeting of NATO ministers on January 1, 1980, if the West had challenged Nazi policies, say by a boycott of the 1936 Olympic Games held in Berlin, they might have undermined Hitler and discouraged further Nazi development.[16]

The Germans were also somewhat sympathetic to U.S. policy in the Afghan crisis because of their special relationship with the United States. As Chancellor Helmut Schmidt put it to President Carter in March, during his visit to Washington, Germany was linked to the United States for its security and as "an ally who owes so much, we stand side by side . . . in the aftermath of Afghanistan."[17] The Social Democratic Party also affirmed West Germany's loyalty to American leadership of the Western alliance at its 1980 congress, which adopted a resolution linking the peace and security of Europe to the political and strategic unity of NATO under U.S leadership.[18]

Thus, in the early months of 1980, West Germany was prepared to show some solidarity with the Carter administration's tough responses to the Kremlin. For example, German leaders repeatedly condemned the invasion and called for withdrawal of Soviet troops from Afghanistan. In January, Bonn agreed not to sell substitutes to the Soviet Union for goods embargoed by the Americans; to discuss a reassessment by NATO countries and Japan of exports of high-tech goods to the Soviet Union; and to give financial aid to Turkey and Pakistan to strengthen their defense capabilities. The Germans also expressed willingness--albeit with much reluctance--to increase their own defense expenditures.[19]

In February, Foreign Minister Hans Dietrich Genscher spoke supportively of the U.S. proposal to boycott the Olympic Games if the Soviets did not withdraw their military forces from Afghanistan. He observed that it was up to the Kremlin to re-create the conditions that ought to exist for holding the games and for West German participation in them, namely, a military withdrawal from Afghanistan. He thus overruled Interior Minister Gerhard Baum, who earlier had suggested West Germany would not go along with an Olympic boycott, declaring that "sports cannot be used for political ends," a view of many German citizens.[20]

During his conversations with President Carter in March, Chancellor Schmidt offered additional German cooperation with U.S. policy in the Afghan crisis. He reiterated German willingness to limit the export of strategic goods to the Soviet Union provided other NATO Allies would do the same. He also raised the possibility of his government's willingness to review its policies concerning guarantees of private loans to firms exporting to the Soviet Union.[21]

As in the case of Great Britain, however, German support of the Carter administration in fact was very limited. Bonn was determined to keep the lines of communication open with the Kremlin at a time when the Carter administration was working hard to close them. The only concrete German action in protest against Soviet policy in Afghanistan was the decision not to participate in the Summer Olympic Games. The Germans did not restrict their trade with the Soviets, which seemed to continue in a normal way throughout 1980.[22]

Furthermore, Chancellor Schmidt did not support the Carter administration's policy to expand Western military capabilities in the Middle East and Central Asia. He believed that such a move would encourage popular domestic opposition in those volatile areas and thereby weaken conservative regimes oriented toward the West.

Rather, Schmidt advocated large scale economic aid similar to the Marshall Plan of the late 1940s to Third World countries--in particular, Turkey and Pakistan--to counter Soviet influence. The Germans also were reluctant to increase defense spending or to agree in any other way to a formal extension of NATO's military responsibilities outside Europe.[23]

Behind German caution in the Afghan crisis were several considerations, not least of which was the *Ostpolitik*, a policy of maintaining good relations with Germany's eastern neighbors, notably socialist East Germany and the Soviet Union. Although the *Ostpolitik*, which German statesmen had practiced since the time of Otto von Bismarck in the late nineteenth century, had lapsed in the Cold War atmosphere of the 1950s and 1960s, Vice Chancellor and Foreign Minister Willy Brandt had revived it in the late 1960s.

By the end of the 1970s, *Ostpolitik* had brought West Germany substantial advantages: it had led to a surge in West German trade with the East bloc at a time of economic difficulty in Europe caused by the Arab oil embargo and the consequent energy crunch; had contributed to the psychological feeling of a diminished risk of East-West conflict in Central Europe; and had led to tangible rewards, such as freer access to Berlin and East Germany and the emigration of over two hundred thousand ethnic Germans from the Soviet Union and Eastern Europe to the West. West German ministers emphasized in the weeks and months following the Soviet invasion the need to keep trade flowing, to keep a dialogue going, and to avoid doing anything that could bring back the Cold War.[24]

Bonn also was critical of the Carter administration's leadership of NATO, especially its relations with the Soviet Union. Chancellor Schmidt believed that President Carter's belligerent attitude toward the Soviet government in 1980 was based less on principle than on domestic political expediency. In Schmidt's view, the president wanted to appear tough toward the Soviets to increase his popularity in the 1980 presidential campaign. Moreover, Schmidt was critical of Carter's failure to consult the Allies before the formulation of policy toward the Soviet Union for which he sought their support.[25]

Furthermore, Schmidt preferred to view the invasion not in the context of the Soviet-American global rivalry but as a regional problem best left to regional powers, such as Pakistan, to solve. In addition, Schmidt had to take into account the views of other influential Social Democratic Party leaders like Egon Bahr, Herbert Wehner, and Willy Brandt. They accepted the prospect of the further growth of Soviet influence in Europe as well as a further reduction of American influence and therefore favored a modus vivendi with the Russians on Afghanistan that would help assure preservation of good West German-Soviet relations, even if it must be at the expense of the United States.[26]

As a principal architect of *Ostpolitik* in the 1970s, Wehner in particular was opposed to West Germany's alignment with the Carter administration in the Afghan crisis. Arguing a far less confrontational line than the Americans in March 1980, Wehner said that "the Soviet intervention in Afghanistan was essentially a 'preventive' strike and the world would have to be patient about a Soviet withdrawal just as it had been patient in waiting for an American pull-out from Vietnam."[27]

The Germans also were sensitive to Soviet efforts to encourage their independence of the United States on the Afghan issue. The Kremlin had warned the West Europeans in early January that détente, which had brought so many advantages to Europe in recent years, would certainly be threatened by their support of a trade embargo and a boycott of the Summer Olympic Games.

The Soviets called into question American reliability, an issue on which they knew the West German government was sensitive. In an article that appeared in the March 3, 1980, issue of *Pravda*, Georgy Arbatov, head of the USSR Academy of Sciences' Institute of the USA and Canada and a leading analyst of American policy, wrote about abrupt swings in U.S. foreign policy and of the "contrived" American view about a growing Soviet military threat. He implied that Carter was influenced by presidential electoral politics in his harsh response to Soviet policy in Afghanistan.[28]

In early 1980, the Soviets also tried threats and intimidation to influence West German policy. They spoke about the irreparable damage to Soviet-German trade if sanctions were imposed, and suggested a possible curtailment in the supply of Soviet natural gas.[29] In early February, the Soviets withheld consummation of an earlier $11.6 billion deal to deliver Siberian natural gas to West Germany.[30] And in response to Schmidt's meeting with French President Valery Giscard d'Estaing at the beginning of February 1980, to condemn the invasion of Afghanistan, the Soviets accused West Germany of using the Afghan crisis to dominate Western Europe. Appealing to latent German nationalism, they emphasized German dependence on, and subservience to, the United States in the Afghan crisis, and said that Bonn was pursuing an American inspired anti-Soviet campaign.[31]

Some of the Soviet Union's allies in Eastern Europe, undoubtedly on signal from the Kremlin, also helped to exert pressure on Bonn to proceed carefully in the Afghan crisis. For example, in the early months of 1980, as if to reinforce Soviet predictions of what might happen on a long-term basis if West Germany cooperated with the United States against the Soviet Union in the Afghan crisis, the Czechs asked for delay of a projected visit of West German Foreign Minister Genscher to Prague; the Hungarians called off a visit to West Germany by their foreign minister; and East German Communist Party leader Erich Honecker deferred a planned summit meeting with Chancellor Schmidt.[32]

In the spring, the Soviets undertook another kind of tactic in their campaign to influence the West German government and stressed West Germany's independence of American influence. They spoke of West Germany's successful resistance to the dangerous bullying by the Americans. In various public pronouncements in early 1980, the Soviets presented Bonn's caution in the Afghan crisis as a wise course of independence and as evidence of West Germany's not being in the "American pocket," so to speak. And in May, the Soviets observed that despite unrelenting American presure, the West German government still refused to restrict trade with the Soviet Union because of an appreciation of the risk of losing important markets and needed sources of raw materials.[33]

The Soviets also gave a lot of publicity to Chancellor Schmidt's plans to visit Moscow at the end of June. They said this demonstrated that whatever criticism of Soviet policy in Afghanistan he had endorsed at the Venice summit, in deference to his American ally, he was still concerned to maintain Germany's friendship with the Soviet

Union and to protect détente. In this spirit, the Soviets also tried to suggest that the Americans were "worried" about Schmidt's independence and his readiness to give priority to Germany's national interests in East-West relations.[34]

When Schmidt did visit Moscow, starting on June 20, the Soviets tried hard to show that he was indeed proceeding independently of the Americans, calling attention to the chancellor's stated reservations about the aggressiveness of U.S. reactions to Soviet policy in Afghanistan. Commenting on the Soviet-German summit, Communist party foreign policy spokesman Leonid Zamyatin said in *Literaturnaya Gazeta* that both sides had opposed confrontation and had pledged efforts to restore détente.[35]

The Kremlin also undertook a conciliatory approach with the West Germans, trying to convince them of future gains if they resisted American pressures to pursue anti-Soviet policies in the Afghan crisis. In early February, Soviet Ambassador to East Germany Pyotr A. Abrasimov said Moscow would cut back of Soviet military forces in East Germany by twenty thousand troops and one thousand tanks, as pledged by Leonid Brezhnev in October 1979.[36] And at the end of June, during Chancellor Schmidt's visit to Moscow, the Soviets hinted of a willingness to negotiate the balance of medium-range nuclear missiles in Europe.[37]

Thus, in the first half of 1980, the Soviets shrewdly increased the costs to West Germany of engagement in the kind of forceful resistance to their policy in Afghanistan sought by the Americans. The Kremlin successfully supported Chancellor Schmidt's inclination to proceed cautiously in responding to the Carter administration's pressure to back its anti-Afghan policies and encouraged his determination to avoid a confrontation between West Germany and the Soviet Union over the Afghan crisis.

France

While it is true that at the beginning of February 1980, President Giscard d'Estaing joined West German Chancellor Schmidt in a statement calling the Soviet invasion "unacceptable" and "dangerous to the stability of the region," and demanding an immediate Soviet withdrawal to save a weakened détente,[38] the French were determined not to participate in American efforts to pressure the Soviets, never mind punish them for the invasion, and not to use coercion to induce a military withdrawal from Afghanistan. In January, French Foreign Minister Jean François-Poncet had said that France had no intention of doing anything that might revive the Cold War in East-West relations.[39]

Furthermore, François-Poncet made it clear to U.S. Secretary of State Cyrus Vance, during his visit to Paris at the end of February to enlist French support, that French criticism of Soviet behavior in Afghanistan was independent of American policy. To demonstrate this independence, the French government refused to attend a meeting of Western foreign ministers to discuss a common response to the Soviet invasion of Afghanistan proposed by the United States. It also linked its endorsement of the proposed Olympic boycott--which, incidentally, it originally had opposed--to the Soviet exile of Andrei Sakharov and to a perceived Soviet failure in other ways to live up to the human rights provisions of the Helsinki agreements.[40]

Further evidence of French determination to proceed with caution and independently of the United States in responding to the Afghan crisis was unwillingness to protest or interfere with a decision of the French Olympic Committee to send French athletes to the Soviet Union in the summer, despite a French government endorsement of the boycott. The French also provided little substantive support for the U.S. trade embargo. Although Foreign Minister François-Poncet said that France would not take advantage of the restrictions on U.S. sales to increase its exports to the Soviet Union, the French government did not prevent French firms from selling goods to the Soviets similar to those embargoed by the United States. It raised no objection to the conclusion by the French firm Rhône-Poulenc of a ten-year contract with the Soviet Union worth $6.5 to $6.8 billion to exchange for Soviet crude oil and other materials a variety of French agricultural products, including the kind of animal feed embargoed by the Carter administration. Indeed, by the end of 1980, the French were asking Washington to terminate the U.S. embargo.[41]

At the same time, a bland joint statement issued by President Giscard and Indian Prime Minister Indira Gandhi following their talks on Afghanistan at the end of January in New Dehli made no mention of the Soviet invasion. It merely stipulated that the use of force in international relations was inadmissible and it called for the diffusion of tensions on the subcontinent and the avoidance of actions that would intensify great power rivalry.[42]

French leaders also made clear their intention to maintain full and friendly diplomatic relations with the Soviets in the aftermath of their invasion. In April, the French gave a hospitable reception to Soviet Foreign Minister Andrei Gromyko, who had come to Paris expressly to discuss the Afghan issue. Gromyko's dialogue with the French marked the first direct and open Soviet contacts with a Western government since the invasion.[43] Then, in May, without prior consultation with the Allies--indeed, he had insisted on secrecy to the last minute--President Giscard met Soviet President and Communist Party leader Brezhnev for five hours in Warsaw for talks on a wide range of international issues, including Afghanistan.[44]

From the vantage point of Washington, France was undermining the Carter administration's efforts to promote a unified Western opposition to the Soviet invasion. While in Washington's view nothing positive was accomplished toward a settlement of the Afghan crisis in these Franco-Soviet exchanges beyond an affirmation of the French preference for diplomacy in dealing with the Soviets on Afghanistan, the Americans were convinced that the Giscard-Brezhnev meeting helped the Kremlin lessen its isolation in the international community and especially in the West. Furthermore, the Americans believed that French policy encouraged the Soviet strategy of playing on the evident differences among the Allies over how to respond to events in Afghanistan.[45]

The French pursued an independent policy, despite the perceived irritation of the Americans, because of the high value Paris always had placed on good relations with the Soviet Union. By maintaining friendly diplomatic links with the Kremlin involving periodic summit meetings between the two powers, past and present French leaders had been able to strengthen French relations with the Soviet Union and to offer Western Europe an alternative to close alignment with the United States in the development of East-West détente, thereby enhancing their efforts to exert French leadership in Europe. In turn, friendship with the Soviets strengthened France's independence of American policies.

Furthermore, Franco-Soviet trade had expanded substantially in the 1970s as a result of détente. In the first nine months of 1980, the value of French exports had increased by one-third in comparison with the corresponding period in 1979. And, as was true in the case of West Germany, this East-West trade had developed at a difficult time for the French economy, which had experienced growing domestic unemployment and balance-of-payments deficits because of the effects of the Arab oil embargo and the consequent energy crunch.[46]

The French also believed that a confrontation with the Soviets over Afghanistan would adversely affect French relations with the Eastern European countries. President Giscard spoke of a recent transformation of French ties with Poland, Hungary, and Romania that would be compromised by a deterioration of French relations with the Soviet Union. A disruption of détente, by contributing to their isolation from the West, would increase their dependence on, and subordination to, the Soviet Union and restrict the limited independence of Moscow the East Europeans had thus far achieved in domestic and foreign policies.[47]

Finally, the French believed that some of the Carter administration's responses to the Soviet invasion of Afghanistan were ineffective and counterproductive. Writing in the *New York Times* at the end of January 1980 to explain French policy in the Afghan crisis, *Le Monde*'s editor André Fontaine said that the Carter administration's military threats in the Persian Gulf would provoke an explosive situation in the region and vindicate the Soviet argument of having had to go into Afghanistan with massive military force for reasons of Soviet security and national defense. He said also that nobody in Europe believed that the threat of an Olympic boycott would persuade the Russians to evacuate Afghanistan. He argued that American economic sanctions against the Soviet Union would hurt consumers in Eastern Europe more than they would influence the Kremlin. Indeed, sanctions, he correctly predicted, would probably encourage the Soviets to dig their heels more deeply into Afghanistan.[48]

Norway

Norway and its neighbors, Sweden and Finland, were alarmed by the Afghan invasion. It was the first time the Soviet Union had attacked a neutral, nonaligned neighbor that had been trying to act as a buffer between East and West in Central Asia. In this respect, they saw parallels between themselves and Afghanistan, and were concerned about Soviet actions that had threatened their security and heightened their sense of vulnerability. Soviet submarines repeatedly had violated Swedish territorial waters, presumably to warn the Swedes against changing their policy of neutrality, say by tilting toward NATO.[49] In 1979, the Soviets also had increased pressure momentarily on the Finns, as in the instance when Soviet Defense Minister Dmitrii Federovich Ustinov, during a visit to Helsinki, tried to persuade the Finnish government to agree to hold joint military maneuvers with the Soviet Union.[50]

Soviet political-military pressure had been most intense on Norway, probably as a result of Norway's proximity to Soviet territory, its membership in NATO, and

Norwegian accommodation of Carter administration requests to position NATO military equipment on Norwegian soil near the Soviet frontier to strengthen the Western capability to defend Norway in case of a Soviet attack. The Soviets complained that while the post-World War II period in Northern Europe had been peaceful and stable, despite crises in East-West relations, by the late 1970s American and NATO policies involving a military buildup in Norway had brought tension to the whole region.[51]

On the eve of the Soviet invasion of Afghanistan, there had been repeated violations of Norwegian territorial waters by Soviet intelligence-gathering naval vessels and an ominous increase in Soviet military activity not only at the Soviet helicopter base on Spitsbergen, near Murmansk, but also on the Kola Peninsula, which houses the Soviet northern fleet. In the event of Soviet military action in Scandinavia, Soviet forces could quickly occupy Norwegian territory, dominate the Baltic, and interdict Western aid to Sweden and Finland.[52]

To respond to this expansion of Soviet naval capabilities in Scandinavia, as well as to increase Soviet isolation and vulnerability in the Afghan crisis, the Carter administration throughout 1980 tried to persuade the Norwegian leadership to allow the stockpiling of weapons and equipment to arm an amphibious brigade of ten thousand U.S. Marines. On March 27, 1980, it obtained from Oslo a "lines of communication" agreement under which the Norwegians would provide certain facilities and services in the event U.S. forces were deployed in Norway.[53]

But the Norwegian government had mixed feelings about accommodating Carter administration's demands for an expansion of NATO facilities on Norwegian territory. Though there was some sympathy in Oslo for strengthening NATO's defense capabilities in Northern Europe because of the Soviet invasion of Afghanistan and because of the steady Soviet military buildup in the Kola Peninsula, ut was feared that deployment of NATO military equipment and American military forces, however modest in scope, would surely provoke the Soviets, who viewed the stockpiling of NATO weapons and equipment as the equivalent of a foreign base on Norwegian soil and an aggressive Norwegian posture linked to American policy in the Afghan crisis.[54] Indeed, there was a sense among Norwegian politicans that agreeing to the Carter administration's request to stockpile would lead to the very actions dangerous to Norwegian security that the whole prepositioning strategy was intended to deter.[55]

To encourage the Norwegian government's resistance to the stockpiling agreement, the Soviets throughout 1980 tried to play on Oslo's faer of retaliation. For example, commenting on Norwegian-American discussion of stockpiling in early January, a TASS commentator accused Norway of consolidating its forces along the Soviet border "in connection with events in Afghanistan."[56] At the same time, the Soviet Ambassador in Oslo told G. Harlem Bruntland, then deputy chairman of the Norwegian Labor Party, that if prepositioning was approved, "we [the Soviets] would know how to react, how to make trouble for you."[57] Finally, on February 19, 1980, *Pravda* warned, in connection with a perceived willingness of Oslo to cooperate with NATO efforts to expand deployment of military power on Norwegian territory, that "an anti-Soviet 'arch of crisis' is being created in the North."[58]

While the Soviets also tried conciliatory tactics to encourage Norwegian neutrality in the Afghan crisis by agreeing to reopen talks on the disputed border in the Barents

Sea, an issue on which there had been no negotiation for three years, and invited Norwegian Foreign Minister Knut Freydenland to visit the Soviet Union to discuss issues in Norwegian-Soviet relations, they continued to keep the Norwegian government on edge for the remainder of 1980.[59] For example, they demanded a border in the Barents Sea giving them some 155,000 square kilometers of resource-rich continental shelf; they continued testing of the Norwegian air defense system; their sumbarines continued to violate Norwegian territorial waters; and they deployed more missiles on the Kola Peninsula.[60]

Thus, while Norway justified to Moscow its willingness to allow a limited warehousing of NATO military equipment on the ground that increased Soviet capacity to interdict seaborne transportation across the Atlantic required equivalent reinforcement measures by the West, Norway was unwilling to further complicate its relations with the Kremlin by close cooperation with the Carter administration's Afghan policies.[61] Moreover, Norwegian leaders worried about being dragged into a Soviet-American confrontation that would compromise Scandinavia's effort to serve as a "bridge builder" between East and West, a role perceived as essential to the peace and security of all of Europe and one the Scandinavian countries wanted their Soviet neighbor to acknowledge. The Norwegians also made clear their determination to avoid involvement in areas far from Europe, where their national interests were nowhere near as great as those of the United States.

Furthermore, while the Norwegians criticized Soviet policy in Afghanistan, they carefully abstained from the kind of punitive actions that could provoke the Kremlin. Although they participated in the Olympic boycott in an expression of solidarity with the United States, they did not restrict trade with the Soviets. They also conveyed to Moscow their sensitivity to Soviet security concerns in Northern Europe and their willingess to be responsive to them.[62] Indeed, in 1980, Norwegian Defense Minister Thorvald Stoltenberg slowed down discussion with Carter administration officials of stockpiling matériel for U.S. Marines.[63] The Norwegian government also continued its policy of military restraint with regard to membership in NATO and prohibited NATO maneuvers near the Norwegian frontier with the Soviet Union and the positioning of Allied aircraft and naval forces beyond 24° east longitude.[64] In 1981, after agreeing to allow NATO to stockpile military equipment, Norwegian Prime Minister Odvar Nordli insisted that it be confined to the central part of the country, far from any area that could arouse Soviet anxiety.

CONCLUSIONS

In the early months of 1980, while the Allies paid only lip service to American policy toward the Soviet invasion of Afghanistan, they did give some backing to it. But increasingly they pursued their separate and independent approaches. They were unwilling to punish the Soviets and use coercion to force their withdrawal from Afghanistan. Allied behavior ultimately compromised American initiatives and prevented the formation of a cohesive Western opposition to the Soviets.

President Carter could not prevail on the Allies to solidly support his sanctions against the Soviets in the Afghan crisis, perhaps because he did not fully understand,

and therefore could not respond to, their divergent interests. The president was convinced that the Soviet invasion was wrong and his efforts to reverse it were right. And once he had made up his mind on this issue, the Allies could not persuade him to consider a negotiated resolution of the U.S.-Soviet confrontation over Afghanistan.

As a result of Allied differences with the United States, the Carter administration could not present the Soviets with the unified Western resistance it considered necessary to force a prompt Soviet military withdrawal from Afghanistan. Furthermore, the Soviets could proceed in Afghanistan without fear of seriously disrupting détente with the Western European countries or of forfeiting the enormous advantages they, as well as the West Europeans, had obtained from improved relations in the 1970s.

Allied behavior also encouraged the Americans to employ other problem-ridden means of reversing Soviet policy in Afghanistan. For example, the Carter administration armed Pakistan, which strained American relations with India and reinforced New Dehli's pro-Soviet orientation, and strengthened ties with China that involved controversial concessions to Beijing, such as curtailment of military aid to Taiwan. Eventually, under President Ronald Reagan, the United States gave substantial military assistance to the Afghan anticommunist guerrillas (Mujahideen) that led the Soviets to dig their heels still more deeply into Afghanistan.

Finally, Allied independence of the United States in the Afghan crisis accentuated development of a rather serious rift within the Western community regarding American leadership. The United States could no longer assume automatic Western European support of its foreign policy initiatives. Moreover, it now was clear that the interests of Western Europe and the United States, especially in the Third World, were far from identical, and that the Allies were far less willing than the Americans to challenge Soviet initiatives outside continental Europe.

NOTES

1. "Resolution of the European Parliament, January 17, 1980," Carter Library, Box FG 29, Brzezinski-Executive File (November 1, 1979-January 31, 1980). See also *Economist*, January 19, 1980, p. 44.

2. *London Times*, January 13, 1980. Hereafter cited as *LT*.

3. *New York Times*, April 20, 1980. Hereafter cited as *NYT*.

4. *An Assessment of the Afghanistan Sanctions: Implications for Trade and Diplomacy in the 1980s*, a report prepared for the Subcommittee on Europe and the Middle East of the Committee on Foreign Affairs, U.S. House of Representatives (Washington D. C.: U.S. Government Printing Office, 1981), pp. 85-86, hereafter cited as *Assessment*; *LT*, January 18, 1980; *NYT*, January 18, 25, 1980.

5. *NYT*, January 17, 1980.

6. *LT*, January 16, 18, 1980; *NYT*, January 17, 18, 1980.

7. *Assessment*, p. 103.

8. *Economist*, February 23, 1980, p. 59; March 8, 1980, pp. 13-14; *NYT*, February 20, 1980.

9. *NATO After Afghanistan*, a report prepared for the Subcommittee on Europe and the Middle East of the Committee on Foreign Affairs, U.S. House of Representatives (Washington, D. C.: U.S.Government Printing Office, 1980), pp. 52, 55, 56, hereafter cited as *NAA*. See also Zbigniew

Brzezinski, *Power and Principle: Memoirs of a National Security Advisor, 1977-1981* (New York: Farrar, Straus and Giroux, 1981), p. 461; *NYT*, May 15, 1980.

10. *NYT*, April 20, 1980.
11. *NYT*, January 25, 1980.
12. *Assessment*, p. 86; *LT*, January 18, 19, 1980.
13. *LT*, January 5, 1980.
14. *LT*, June 19, 1980.
15. *LT*, January 13, 1980, January 17, 1980, and June 15, 1980.
16. *Assessment*, p. 85; F. Bolkestein, "The Alliance in Disarray: A Dutch View," *The Atlantic Community Quarterly*, 19, no. 2 (Summer 1981):146.
17. *NYT*, March 6, 1980.
18. *NAA*, p. 11.
19. *NYT*, January 25, 1980.
20. *NYT*, January 6, 1980.
21. *NYT*, March 5, 1980 and March 6, 1980. See also Office of the White House, "Joint Press Statement, March 5, 1980," Carter Library, Box CO 54-2 (January 1, 1980-January 21, 1981).
22. *Assessment*, p. 105; *LT*, May 31, 1980.
23. *Assessment*, p. 99; *NYT*, June 22, 1980.
24. *Assessment*, p. 87; *International Herald Tribune*, July 17, 1980 (hereafter cited as *IHT*); *LT*, January 14, 1980; see also Gunther Gillessen, "German-American Relations: A German View," Carter Library, Box FG-Organizations, Brzezinski-General File, F6-1-1 (January 1, 1980-February 29, 1980), pp. 2-4.
25. *NYT*, February 15, 1980.
26. Gillessen, "Germany-American Relations," pp. 2-3.
27. *NYT*, March 29, 1980.
28. *Pravda*, March 3, 1980, p. 6, in *Current Digest of the Soviet Press*, 32, no. 9, (1980):1-4.
29. *Assessment*, p. 101.
30. *NYT*, February 8, 1980.
31. *LT*, March 6, 1980; *Le Monde*, February 8, 1980.
32. *Soviet World Outlook*, 5, no. 2 (February 15, 1980): hereafter cited as *SWO*. See also *Le Monde*, February 1, 1980.
33. *SWO*, 5, no. 6 (June 1980).
34. Ibid.
35. *Yearbook on International Communist Affairs, 1981* (Stanford, California: Hoover Institution Press, 1982), p. 319.
36. *NYT*, February 2, 1980.
37. *IHT*, July 17, 1980.
38. *Le Monde*, February 6, 1980.
39. *Le Monde*, January 8, 1980, January 12, 1980, February 10, 1980; *Assessment*, pp. 104-105.
40. Ibid., February 9, 1980; *NYT*, February 6, 1980; *Assessment*, p. 87.
41. *NYT*, February 6, 1980; *Assessment*, pp. 87, 104-105.
42. *NYT*, January 30, 1980.
43. *NYT*, April 25, 1980; *LT*, April 24, 1980 and April 26, 1980.
44. *Le Monde*, April 20, 1980 and April 21, 1980; *NYT*, May 19, 1980.
45. Michael J. Sodaro, "Moscow and Mitterand," *Problems of Communism*, 29 (July/August 1980):23-35; *NYT*, May 20, 1980.
46. *Assessment*, p. 104.
47. *NAA*, p. 8.
48. *NYT*, January 30, 1980.

49. Trond Gilberg, George K. Osborn, William J. Taylor, Jr., and John R. Fairlane, "The Soviet Union and Northern Europe," *Problems of Communism*, 30 (March/April 1981):15.

50. *NYT*, April 1, 1979.

51. Organ Berner, *Soviet Policies Toward the Nordic Countries* (Cambridge, Mass: Center for International Affairs, Harvard University, 1986), p. 161.

52. Ibid., p. 163; *NYT*, April 1, August 14, 1980; Gilbert et al., "The Soviet Union and Northern Europe," p. 15.

53. *NYT*, May 10, 1980.

54. Berner, *Soviet Policies*, p. 172.

55. *NYT*, August 14, 1980.

56. Bruce D. Porter, "The USSR and Norway Since the Invasion of Afghanistan," *Radio Liberty Research*, 489/80 (December 22, 1980)3.

57. Ibid.

58. Berner, *Soviet Policies,* p. 161.

59. Porter, "The USSR and Norway," p. 3.

60. Ibid.

61. Berner, *Soviet Policy*, p. 172.

62. Ibid., p. 161.

63. *NYT*, May 10, 1980.

64. Berner, *Soviet Policies*, p. 169.

3

The Rise and Fall of America's First Post-Cold War Foreign Policy

JEREL A. ROSATI

Public evaluations of President Jimmy Carter have fluctuated dramatically over time. Upon winning the presidency in 1976, Carter symbolized in the minds of many Americans the effort to restore a sense of honesty, morality, and optimism in the White House and the country following the Vietnam War and Watergate. By the end of his administration in 1980, Carter was overwhelmingly seen as a failed president--a leader whose weakness was evidenced by double-digit unemployment and inflation, the Iran hostage crisis, and the Soviet invasion of Afghanistan. Yet by the late 1980s public perceptions of Carter began to change for the better as he won a new sense of respect and admiration for his post-presidential activities.

Assessments of the Carter administration's foreign policy reveal that they, too, have evolved with time. During the late 1970s and early 1980s there were conflicting interpretations of the Carter administration's worldview and its foreign policy. Some individuals, such as John Lewis Gaddis, James Fallows, and Arthur Schlesinger, Jr., argued that its foreign policy was confusing and inconsistent, for high-level policymakers never developed a coherent worldview. Instead, different officials, especially Brzezinski and Vance, represented and promoted different worldviews, with the president gravitating from one set of foreign policy beliefs to another. Other individuals, such as Robert Tucker, Leslie Gelb and Simon Sefarty, argued that Carter administration policymakers did share a common optimistic and complex view of the world from the beginning. They believed that this worldview changed with time, although there has been little agreement among them concerning how it changed, when this happened, and why.[1]

By the end of the 1980s, a consensus position increasingly formed among students of U.S. foreign policy that the Carter administration entered office with a foreign policy based on an idealistic view of the world. This optimistic image began to crack due to growing splits among policymakers: first in 1978 with Brzezinski emphasizing the need to contain Soviet expansionism; then intensifying in 1979, with Carter wavering between the optimistic policy views of Vance and the hard-line policy views of Brzezinski. By the last year in office the Carter administration's foreign policy change was complete: its worldview became decidedly pessimistic, symbolized by

Vance's resignation; the containment of Soviet expansionism was restored to the forefront of U.S. foreign policy. This interpretation has been documented in two book-length studies of the Carter administration's foreign policy published in the late 1980s: first by historian Gaddis Smith in *Morality, Reason and Power: American Diplomacy in the Carter Years*; subsequently by political scientist Jerel Rosati in *The Carter Administration's Quest for Global Community*.[2]

Although there now appears to be a consensus concerning the evolution of the Carter administration's worldview and its foreign policy, there remains disagreement over to what extent Carter's early foreign policy represented a change from the Cold War past. Some argue that the Carter administration's foreign policy represented "containment by other means"--that it operated within the tradition of detente initiated under the stewardship of Henry Kissinger during the Nixon and Ford administrations. Others argue that the Carter administration's foreign policy was based on the "rejection of containment" that has dominated U.S. foreign policy since World War II and, thus, represented a major foreign policy change. Overall, however, there has been little effort to fully explore the level of continuity and change represented by the Carter administration's foreign policy and its ultimate implications for understanding the postwar history of U.S. foreign policy.

The purpose of this paper is to determine the significance and meaning of President Carter's national security policy when his administration first came into office and to place the Carter years in historical perspective. As Gaddis Smith argues, "The four years of the Carter Administration were among the most significant in the history of American foreign policy in the twentieth century," both for the uniqueness of its foreign policy and for the light it sheds for better understanding the broad sweep of U.S. foreign policy over time.[3] Three questions are addressed: To what extent did Carter administration policymakers, especially in the first two years, see the world differently than their predecessors? To what extent did the theory and practice of the Carter administration's foreign policy represent change from the Cold War patterns that had dominated U.S. foreign policy since World War II? What explains why the Carter administration's initial foreign policy met with failure and reversal by its fourth year in office?

I take the position that the Carter administration entered office with a world order approach that ultimately supplanted the strategy of containment. That approach was intended to replace the Cold War and détente policies of its post-World War II predecessors, which were based on strategies of containment: global containment of Soviet communism during the Cold War years from Truman to Johnson, followed by selective containment of the Soviet Union under Nixon and Ford. Therefore, not only did the Carter administration reject the strategy of containment as the basis of its foreign policy when it entered office; it can be argued that it represented the first "post-Cold War foreign policy" since World War II.

Thinking of the Carter administration's approach toward the world as the first post-Cold War foreign policy should be easier to understand in light of the rise of Mikhail Gorbachev, the collapse of communism in the Soviet Union and Eastern Europe, the reunification of Germany, and proclamations about "the end of the Cold War." In this respect, Jimmy Carter was the first, and only, postwar American leader to take the initiative and promote a post-Cold War foreign policy--almost a decade before Gorbachev's initiatives.   The rest of the paper examines to what extent the Carter administration's post-Cold War foreign policy differed from the Cold War policies of the past, why Carter's foreign policy collapsed over time, and what the implications are for a post-Cold War U.S. foreign policy in the future.

CARTER'S POST-COLD WAR FOREIGN POLICY

As most observers of U.S. foreign policy have concluded, a considerable amount of continuity existed in U.S. foreign policy from President Truman to President Johnson.[4]   Continuity in American Cold War policies was based on three major underlying intellectual roots:

1. A strategy of containment
2. A realpolitik approach to international relations, and
3. An ideology of anticommunism.

These three elements operated in tandem and were mutually reinforcing, thus providing the basis of American Cold War policies throughout the 1950s and 1960s. Ultimately, this led to shorthand concepts such as the "domino theory" and the continuing escalation of American intervention in the Vietnam War.

The Vietnam War shattered the Cold War consensus throughout society and the foreign policy establishment that supported American Cold War policies. The lesson of Vietnam for many foreign policy elites was to reject Cold War global policies based on containment, realpolitik, and anticommunism.   U.S. Cold War policies, in fact, began to change during the presidencies of Richard Nixon and Gerald Ford, under the direction of Henry Kissinger. The major break in U.S. Cold War policies, however, came with President Carter, who was the first American leader to pursue a post-Cold War foreign policy.

Carter staffed his administration with personnel who believed "Vietnam had changed the world and America's role in it so drastically that early [Cold War] 'lessons' had become largely irrelevant."[5]   Its members identified more with a world order approach based on three underlying intellectual roots very different from previous Cold War policies:

1. A strategy of adjustment and preventive diplomacy
2. A complex interdependence approach to international relations
3. The pursuit of human rights and global community.

In order to better understand the significant foreign policy changes that occurred under President Carter, each of the three elements that laid the foundation of American Cold War policies is examined separately so as to demonstrate how they were superseded by another approach during the early Carter years in order to pursue a post-Cold War foreign policy.

From Containment to Preventive Diplomacy

American foreign policy during the postwar years came to be based on the strategy of containment, in which Soviet communist expansion was to be deterred and contained through the threat of force, first in Europe, then in Asia, and eventually throughout the world. The development of the American strategy of containment following World War II was heavily influenced by George Kennan, a diplomat in the State Department at the time, and embodied in NSC-68 (National Security Council document 68) approved in 1950.[6] Bruce Jentleson has summed up the assumptions of the global strategy of containment, or what he called "global commitments theory."[7] The U.S. strategy of containment was based on three key postulates:

1. Commitments must be made on a global scale because threats are interdependent.
2. Commitments, once made, must be maintained as inviolable.
3. Commitments must be reinforced, as necessary, by political uses of military force.

The U.S. strategy was to surround the Soviet Union, and its allies in Eastern Europe and mainland Asia, with American allies, alliances, and military forces, thereby forming global commitments intended to deter the Soviet Union from initiating a military strike for fear of triggering World War III. Containment of the Soviet Union and the People's Republic of China in Eurasia was to be accomplished principally through the threat and use of conventional and, especially, nuclear military force. In the Third World, where the U.S.-Soviet confrontation tended to be fought more indirectly over the "hearts and minds" of local elites and peoples, the United States relied on assistance, counterinsurgency, and the use of covert paramilitary action. Diplomacy, and other non-coercive instruments of policy, were pushed to the side in East-West relations and superseded by the threat and use of force. Hence, the United States used overt military force in Korea, Lebanon, the Dominican Republic, and Vietnam, and relied heavily on covert operations in responding to what American leaders saw as major challenges to American commitments.

Differences in emphasis and policy instruments did occur with each new administration as Cold War policies evolved, but they were variations on the same containment theme. Under the Truman administration the initial focus was on the economic rebuilding of Western Europe through the Marshall Plan while the containment policy was in the process of being globalized in the Korean War. During the Eisenhower administration, containment was based on the threat of nuclear "massive retaliation" and the use of the CIA to maintain friendly Third World regimes. The Kennedy and Johnson administrations emphasized counterinsurgency and nation-building in fighting the Cold War throughout the Third World. All these variations were part and parcel of the global strategy of containment, ultimately leading to the Americanization of the war in Vietnam.

Although the Nixon and Ford administrations, with Henry Kissinger as secretary of state, replaced a strategy of global containment with selective containment of the Soviet Union in their détente policies, the Carter administration supplanted the strategy of containment as the basis of its foreign policy when it took office in 1977. This position was made clear in President Jimmy Carter's first and most famous public address at Notre Dame University, on June 13, when he declared that American Cold War policies "during this period [were] guided by two principles--a belief that Soviet expansion was almost inevitable, but it must be contained, and the corresponding belief in the importance of an almost exclusive alliance among non-Communist nations on both sides of the Atlantic. That system could not last forever unchanged."[8] Vietnam demonstrated the bankruptcy of that kind of strategic thinking. Since that time, "We've learned that this world, no matter how technology has shrunk distances, is nevertheless too large and too varied to come under the sway of either one of two superpowers."[9]

A belief in the end of the Cold War and the need to move beyond containment was not mere window dressing nor limited solely to President Carter. This was a perception that was widely shared among major officials early in the Carter administration. In an address before the American Foreign Service Association in Washington, D.C., on December 9, 1977, National Security Adviser Zbigniew Brzezinski reiterated the same themes: "We have witnessed perhaps the end of a phase in our own foreign policy, shaped largely since 1945, in which preoccupation particularly with the Cold War as a dominant [concern] of U.S. foreign policy no longer seems warranted by the complex realities within which we operate."[10]

Whereas Cold War administrations feared global change as a threat to international stability and the status quo, Carter officials were optimistic about the potential of change and the ability to take a leadership position. They emphasized the importance of a *strategy of adjustment* to the inevitability of global change. Brzezinski communicated this sense of optimism about the future of global change and U.S. foreign policy in an address before the Trilateral Commission on October 25, 1977:

We have sensed that, for far too long, the United States had been seen--often correctly--as opposed to change, committed primarily to stability for the sake of stability, preoccupied with the balance of power for the sake of the preservation of privilege. We deliberately set out to identify the United States with the notion that change is a positive phenomenon; that we believe that change can be channeled in constructive directions; and that internationally change can be made compatible with our own underlying spiritual values.[11]

A strategy of adjustment meant that U.S. foreign policy no longer could revolve around the Soviet Union and the maintenance of the international status quo. Instead, the Carter administration emphasized the need to address a variety of national security issues and to take a *preventive diplomacy* approach. In this respect, the key was to address problems by working closely with the parties directly involved to resolve conflict and promote constructive change before they led to heightened conflict and war. Soviet-American conflict, for example, was best addressed through the pursuit of arms control. More important was the perceived need to tackle regional conflicts by addressing their fundamental causes rather than seeing them in East-West terms and treating the symptoms by relying on containment and force.

Secretary of State Cyrus Vance was particularly active in addressing regional conflict. He explained the preventive diplomacy approach with respect to Africa thus: "The history of the past 15 years suggests that efforts by outside powers to dominate African nations will fail. Our challenge is to find ways of being supportive without becoming interventionist or intrusive." This meant that the United States needed to "work with African nations, and with our European allies, in positive efforts to resolve such disputes. . . . *The most effective policies toward Africa are affirmative policies.* They should not be reactive to what other powers do, nor to crises as they arise."[12] Hence, major preventive diplomacy initiatives were taken, for example, to bring to fruition the Panama Canal treaties, to address the Arab-Israeli conflict through the Camp David accords, and to resolve the racial conflict in Rhodesia by promoting black majority rule in the new country of Zimbabwe.

In the minds of Carter officials, the policy of containment was anachronistic and counterproductive in a new world of great change and global complexity. Yet, members of the Carter administration understood that a strategy of adjustment and preventive diplomacy would be a difficult undertaking. As President Carter stated before the United Nations, "We can only improve this world if we are realistic about its complexities. The disagreements that we face are deeply rooted, and they often raise difficult philosophical as well as territorial issues. They will not be solved easily. They will not be solved quickly."[13] This was why the Carter administration felt it was imperative to work with others in resolving problems and adjusting to the global change. It was this worldview of global complexity held by Carter policymakers that compelled them to downplay realpolitik, the second element behind the Cold War policies.

From Realpolitik to Complex Interdependence

The U.S. strategy of containment was heavily a function of a realpolitik, or power politics, view of the world. Political realists believe that states act to promote their "national interests" through an international struggle for power. Therefore, international peace and stability can be maintained only through a precarious "balance of power." The major threat to international peace and stability comes from the rise of unsatisfied and "revolutionary" states that challenge the status quo and attempt to change the system.[14] In accordance with this realpolitik vision of the world, American Cold War policies following World War II attempted to maintain a favorable balance of power to contain the threat to international peace and stability posed by Soviet expansionism.

Three assumptions provided the basis for the intellectual tradition of realpolitik and, likewise, for U.S. national security policy during the Cold War. First, states, especially great ones, are the dominant actors in international politics. Other actors exist, but they are peripheral players. Second, the threat and use of force is the most effective instrument of statecraft. Other instruments are available, but none as important and effective as military force. Finally, realists assume a hierarchy of issues in world politics in which the "high politics" of national security issues dominates the "low politics" of economics and other issues. The high politics of national security "constitutes a single issue occurring in a single system and entails a ceaseless and repetitive competition for the single stake of power."[15] From Truman to Ford, the practice of U.S. foreign policy revolved around the struggle for power between the two great powers--the United States (and its allies) and the Soviet Union (and its allies)--where American interests, international peace, and global stability were pursued principally through the threat and use of force embodied in the containment strategy.[16]

Carter administration officials saw a world of much greater global complexity than their predecessors. U.S. foreign policy at the beginning of the Carter years did not operate on the assumptions of realpolitik. Instead, it was much more consistent with an approach to international relations referred to as *complex interdependence*. A complex interdependence approach to world politics is based on three assumptions very different from the realpolitik tradition as outlined in Stanley Hoffman's *Primacy or World Order* or Robert Keohane and Joseph Nye's *Power and Interdependence*.[17] First, a multitude of different actors comprise the international system. Such a world is extremely pluralistic, consisting of a large number of states, as well as nonstate actors. Second, the utility of military force has declined and, correspondingly, there has been a rise in the importance of other instruments of foreign policy. Third, the agenda of world politics consists of multiple issues that are not arranged in a clear or consistent hierarchy. "Foreign affairs agendas--that is, sets of issues relevant to foreign policy with which governments are concerned--have become larger and more diverse. No longer can all issues be subordinated to military security."[18]

In accordance with the assumptions of complex interdependence, the Carter administration's vision of global complexity downplayed the role of great powers such as the Soviet Union, the utility of force, and a preoccupation with traditional security issues. Instead, Carter officials saw a world of great complexity where pluralism and interdependence reigned supreme. In this new world neither the United States nor the Soviet Union could control the destiny of the planet. Where national security issues previously revolved around American leaders' preoccupation with the U.S.-Soviet relationship, a variety of actors had become globally important. In the words of President Carter, "Europe and Japan rose from the rubble of war to become great economic powers. Communist parties and governments have become more widespread and more varied, and I might say more independent from one another. Newly independent nations emerged into what has now become known as the 'Third World.' Their role in world affairs is becoming increasingly significant."[19] In fact, for Brzezinski these changes had led to the conclusion of a "long chapter in the history of the West, namely the West's predominance over the globe as a whole."[20]

Therefore, the United States could lead, but it could no longer command or control. "However wealthy and powerful the United States may be--however capable the leadership," stated President Carter, "this power is increasingly only relative, the leadership increasingly is in need of being shared. No nation has a monopoly of vision, of creativity, or of ideas. Bringing these together from many nations is our common responsibility and our common challenge."[21] Given this vision of global complexity, Carter administration officials felt they had no choice but to address a variety of international issues that involved numerous actors. As Brzezinski explained, "We do not have a realistic choice between an approach centered on the Soviet Union, or cooperation with our trilateral friends, or on North-South relations. Indeed, each set of issues must be approached on its own terms. . . . We did not wish the world to be this complex; but we must deal with it in all of its complexity."[22]

Hence, the traditional focus on the Soviet Union and the high politics of East-West security issues was deemed anachronistic by members of the Carter administration. Not only were the Soviets no longer the dominant priority, they were not seen in a particularly threatening light. Indeed, they were portrayed rather optimistically-- having a limited capability to affect the environment, constrained by the complexity of the international system, and, although occasionally opportunistic, generally cooperative in their intentions. Secretary of State Vance and, in particular, President Carter were the most optimistic in this regard.

This image of complex interdependence accounts for Vance's position that "When our Administration came into office, we decided that we were not merely going to react to situations, but that we were going to shape an agenda of items which we considered to be of the highest priority and would proceed to deal with those issues."[23] In fact, the Carter team attempted to tackle numerous issues: the promotion of human rights and democracy, the normalization of relations with former adversaries (such as the People's Republic of China), the pursuit of arms control, the resolution of Third World conflicts, a concern with Third World development, and the maintenance of a healthy global economy. The taking of such a full foreign policy agenda can best be understood in light of a vision of complex interdependence.

From Anticommunism to Human Rights and Global Community

The post-Cold War policies of the Carter administration differed from their Cold War predecessors in a third way by no longer being ideologically driven by the fear of communism. It was the combination of realpolitik and anticommunism that provided the basis for a strategy of global containment that dominated U.S. foreign policy throughout the Cold War. As explained by Bruce Jentleson, "For all their criticism of isolationism and idealism, traditional realists have definite limits to the commitments they were prepared to support." Yet, "global commitments theorists dropped all such limits on the scope of American commitments."[24] It was the ideology of anticommunism fused with a realpolitik approach that made Americans so fearful of the Soviet Union and so willing to treat world politics in tight, bipolar, zero-sum terms.

Anticommunism became a prominent issue in U.S. foreign policy following World War II, with the collapse of Europe and the rise of the United States and the Soviet Union as two competing great powers. Problems over a divided Germany, the communist coup d'état in Czechoslovakia, the "fall" of China, and the North Korean attack on South Korea convinced most Americans, in and out of government, that the Soviet Union was indeed a revolutionary, communist state bent on achieving world domination. The paramount lesson of World War II that was conveyed--that the "appeasement" of Adolf Hitler and fascism by England and France at Munich only produced more aggression--was transferred to the postwar international environment: The United States must not appease Stalin and communist aggression. Instead, the American response was that the United States must build up its military and contain communist aggression wherever it occurred.[25]

Anticommunism has been a dominant strain in American politics throughout the twentieth century. And during the postwar years, especially with the fall of China to communism and the outbreak of the Korean War, McCarthyism rose as a political force throughout American society, made anticommunism the most prominent issue on the foreign policy agenda, and attacked the U.S. government--especially under President Truman--for being "soft on communism." The political challenge represented by McCarthyism helped to generate an anticommunist consensus at home and conformity behind a U.S. global policy of containment of Soviet communism reliant on the threat and use of force.[26]

This Cold War and bipolar vision of the world divided into two opposing forces was reinforced by the political culture, in which Americans saw themselves not as self-interested or imperialistic (more in accordance with realpolitik) but as an innocent society, a benevolent and exceptional people who symbolized progress and a hopeful future. This strong sense of American nationalism was shared by most Americans, including American political leaders, thus infusing the U.S.-Soviet struggle for power with an ideological struggle between good and evil, democracy and totalitarianism, capitalism and communism, and Christianity and atheism.[27] In short, the U.S.-Soviet confrontation represented more than great power politics; it symbolized the struggle between the "free world" led by the United States and "communism" under the control of the Soviet Union.

The Nixon and Ford administrations, under the tutelage of Henry Kissinger, were the first to shed the anticommunist ideological baggage that had influenced American Cold War policies of containment. However, Kissinger's realpolitik orientation did not alter a preoccupation with containing the Soviet Union in modified form during the détente years. Therefore, not until President Carter entered office was the effort made to move beyond anticommunism, realpolitik, and containment in initiating a post-Cold War foreign policy.

The people who staffed the Carter administration did not see a bipolar world that pitted communism against the free world in a global Cold War. As stated by President Carter in the most memorable part of his address at Notre Dame University:

Being confident of our future, we are now free of that inordinate fear of communism which once led us to embrace any dictator who joined us in that fear. . . . For too many years, we have been willing to adopt the flawed and erroneous principles and tactics of our adversaries, sometimes abandoning our own values for theirs. We have fought fire with fire, never thinking that fire is better quenched with water. This approach failed, with Vietnam the best example of its intellectual and moral poverty. But through failure, we have found our way back to our own principles and values and we have regained our lost confidence.[28]

What was to replace anticommunism? The promotion of human rights and the quest for global community. For President Carter, *human rights and democracy* were the essence of what America represented. This was "testimony of a neo-Wilsonian populist who saw American diplomacy not primariy in terms of geopolitical interests but as the external reflection of popular 'ideals and goals and hopes.'"[29] These principles allowed the United States to respond to and take the lead alongside global change, as well as to act as a beacon to attract support from people throughout the world. As Carter stated with typical optimism, America's commitment to the goals of human rights, freedom, and justice "are [*sic*] the wave of the future. We should not fight this wave. We should ride it, be part of it, encourage it, let it nurture a better life for those who yearn and for those of us who already enjoy."[30] This view was widely shared within the administration. As Brzezinski suggested, "If we do not stand for something more than anticommunism, then indeed we may confront the decline of the West."[31]

The larger goal of the Carter administration was to promote a new system of world order--a *quest for global community*. The principal architect of this quest was Zbigniew Brzezinski, as shown by his 1970 book *Between Two Ages: America's Role in the Technetronic Era*, and his directorship of the Trilateral Commission.[32] Brzezinski described his vision of what he meant by a global community before the Trilateral Commission on October 30, 1977:

A secure and economically cooperative community of the advanced industrial democracies is the necessary source of stability for a broad system of international cooperation. We are aware of the pitfalls of constructing a geometric world--whether bilateral or trilateral or pentagonal--that leaves out the majority of mankind who live in the developing countries. . . . At the same time, a wider and more cooperative world system has to include also that part of the world which is ruled by communist governments. . . . We are therefore seeking to create a new political and international order that is truly more participatory and genuinely more responsive to the global desire for greater social justice, equity, and more opportunity for individual self-fulfillment.[33]

In sum, the Carter administration attempted to implement the first post-Cold War foreign policy. Like its predecessors, it continued to exercise a global leadership role. However, instead of developing a foreign policy revolving around a strategy of containment, a realpolitik vision, and an ideology of anticommunism, Carter administration officials shared a post-Cold War foreign policy approach based on a strategy of adjustment and preventive diplomacy, an image of complex interdependence, and the promotion of human rights and global community. According to Richard Melanson, "As a result of this redirection the Carter Administration defined 'world order' in less hegemonic terms than any of its post-war predecessors."[34]

THE COLLAPSE OF THE POST-COLD WAR APPROACH

Despite some notable foreign policy achievements, such as the Panama Canal treaties, the peaceful transition to majority rule in Zimbabwe, the Camp David accords, the normalizaton of relations with the People's Republic of China, and the SALT II Treaty with the Soviet Union, Carter's post-Cold War foreign policy collapsed over time. By its last year in office, in fact, the Carter administration reinstated the strategy of containment based on a realpolitik orientation and a growing concern with anticommunism--best symbolized by the Carter Doctrine--thus repudiating its initial post-Cold War orientation. It justified the Carter Doctrine by no longer emphasizing change, but continuity with America's Cold War past. Brzezinski specifically argued that the Persian Gulf represented the "third central strategic zone"--first being Western

Europe and the second the Far East--vital to the United States and the West after World War II that was under challenge by Soviet expansionism.[35]

Thus, the policy innovation initiated under President Carter at the beginning of his administration failed. Why did Carter's post-Cold War foreign policy collapse? According to Gaddis Smith,

Carter failed because he asked the American people to think as citizens of the world with an obligation toward future generations. He offered a morally responsible and farsighted vision. But the clamor of political critics, the behavior of the Soviet Union, the discordant voices of his advisers, and the impossibility of seeing clearly what needed to be done--all combined to make Carter's vision appear naive. In 1980, he fell back on the appeal to the combative, nationalistic instincts of the American people.[36]

More specifically, there were five mutually reinforcing reasons that explained the collapse of Carter's post-Cold War foreign policy: resistance to a post-Cold War approach throughout much of the national security bureaucracy; policymaker infighting due to Brzezinski's early change in image; Carter's naïveté (and bad luck) concerning the international environment and, in particular, the Soviet Union; Carter's lack of strong leadership to promote and maintain domestic support for his policies; and the rise of conservatism as a powerful political force in the domestic arena. Each contributed to a growing perception among the American public of Jimmy Carter as a failed president, resulting in his inability to be reelected in 1980.

President Carter's effort to promote a post-Cold War foreign policy met considerable resistance throughout much of the national security bureaucracy. This is a problem that all presidents face when they enter office, especially if they want to promote policies different from those the bureaucracy has been implementing for some time. In President Carter's case, he presided over a huge national security bureaucracy born out of World War II and the Cold War that for thirty years had been in the business of implementing Cold War policies based on containment, realpolitik, and anticommunism. Not surprisingly, for example, the national security bureaucracy resisted Carter's proposal to reduce the number of American troops in South Korea.

The bureaucratic resistance to many of Carter's post-Cold War policy initiatives also existed among his senior advisors, who tended to be much more pragmatic as to what was achievable. According to Leslie Gelb, director of the Bureau of Political-Military Affairs in the State Department under Vance, "What fascinated me was the subtle struggle between the President on the one hand and almost all of his senior foreign policy advisors, including Vance, on the other."[37] They "were, to varying degrees, to the right of Mr. Carter on most matters."[38] Unlike the bureaucratic resistance, however, most of this early resistance by senior officials represented efforts to moderate some of President Carter's more optimistic inclinations.

Second, by 1978, National Security Adviser Zbigniew Brzezinski began to argue in favor of a realpolitik approach and containment strategy to prevent threats to global instability posed by growing Soviet expansionism, thus undercutting Carter's post-Cold War foreign policy. Brzezinski from the beginning was not as deeply committed to a post-Cold War foreign policy based on preventive diplomacy, complex interdependence, and human rights as were Carter and Vance. In fact, he had a long history as a Cold Warrior that quickly resurfaced in response to events in the Horn of Africa in 1978. Therefore, when the Soviet Union and Cuban-backed Ethiopia appeared to be threatening Somalia's territorial integrity in 1978, Brzezinski reverted to his earlier, pessimistic orientation emphasizing power politics and the need to contain Soviet expansionism.[39] From that time on, he highlighted the importance of the "arc of crisis" from the Persian Gulf down to South Africa as an area of great instabiilty and vulnerability to Soviet expansionism. Brzezinski thus came to represent a critical perspective that dominated the National Security Council staff and permeated other parts of the national security bureaucracy, resulting in considerable governmental infighting that reached its peak in 1979.

One point of clarification needs to be made about Brzezinski's role in the Carter administration's foreign policy process. Conventional wisdom has portrayed Brzezinski as a "hawk" who focused on Soviet expansionism and global instability from the very beginning, in opposition to Vance and Carter--a view promoted by Brzezinski in parts of his memoirs. There is no doubt that during the first year he was less optimistic about Soviet intentions and behavior than Vance and, in particular, Carter. Brzezinski was of two minds, "hopeful yet skeptical" that the Soviet Union would act in a "more cooperative, less imperially assertive fashion and begin participating in what is gradually, truly emerging: namely, a global community."[40] This subtle difference in image of the Soviet Union did contribute to some disagreements between Brzezinski and Vance, reinforced by two very different personal styles of interaction. This being said, Carter, Vance, and Brzezinski nevertheless shared an optimistic image of the world and were in agreement in promoting a post-Cold War foreign policy. As stated above, Brzezinski was very much the architect and, in fact, acted as Carter's major foreign policy tutor before he entered office. A close reading of his memoirs supports this interpretation, for instance, when he states that "the first phase of Carter's foreign policy, which lasted till early 1978, was thus dominated by high expectations and ambitious goals." Substantive policy differences, especially between him and Vance, arose "first, over the issue of the Soviet-Cuban role in the African Horn, and the likely impact of that on SALT."[41]

Third, many of Carter's foreign policy beliefs were quite naive. Carter lacked the pragmatism of Vance, who had considerable governmental experience and involvement in diplomacy, and of Brzezinski, given his tenure as a professor and Sovietologist. Carter's experience level and personality were such that his positive view of human nature and the future pro vided the guideposts by which he evaluated much of the world around him. Quite naturally, this led him to harbor optimistic impressions and to set high standards of behavior for many of the world's actors, most notably the Soviet Union. It is in this respect that he was naive: to assume a cooperative and forthcoming Soviet Union under General Secretary Leonid Brezhnev; to think that he could lecture Soviet leaders on human rights; and to believe that he could downplay and ignore the role of the Soviet Union after thirty years of American and Soviet preoccupation with each other. As Stanley Hoffman, a sympathetic observer warned, it would be a mistake for an American president to pursue a new world order policy while, at the same time, downplaying the very real conflict in Soviet-American relations, for this would damage the need for sufficient order in a fragmented and complex world. This is why Hoffman advocated a world order policy of "moderation plus," and why Keohane and Nye argued in terms of "power and interdependence."[42]

In fact, whenever the Soviets acted opportunistically abroad and violated Carter's high expectations, he experienced periods of dissonance. Two events beyond Carter's control in particular overwhelmed his thinking: the taking of American hostages in revolutionary Iran and the Soviet military intervention in Afghanistan. They compelled Carter to reassess his optimistic notions of the Soviet Union and the world. His naïveté was clearly revealed when he confessed on national television that the Soviet invasion of Afghanistan profoundly affected his thinking: "My opinion of the Russians has changed most drastically in the last week than even the previous two and a half years before that. . . . to repeat myself, this action of the Soviets has made a more dramatic change in my own opinion of what the Soviets' ultimate goals are than anything they've done in the previous time I've been in office."[43] This new realization about the Soviet Union made President Carter much more receptive to the containment policies that were being pushed by Brzezinski.

Fourth, President Carter was unable to provide the political leadership necessary to promote and maintain domestic support for his post-Cold War foreign policy. In the post-Vietnam years the foreign policy consensus had collapsed. Hence it was difficult for any president to gain sufficient support for his policies over a prolonged period of time.[44] But there was an extra burden on President Carter because he was attempting to initiate a post-Cold War foreign policy that went against the political grain of thirty years of Cold War conditioning. As Keohane and Nye warned those attempting to pursue a foreign policy based on complex interdependence, "Foreign policy leaders dealing with these new issues will have to pay even more attention than usual to domestic politics."[45]

It was an innovative and complex foreign policy that he had to sell to Americans throughout the government and society. In this he clearly failed. President Carter never developed the leadership skills that might have allowed the American public to understand and support his policies.[46] But he also failed, as Stanley Hoffman has repeatedly pointed out, to develop priorities and agree on a coherent strategy in pursuing a post-Cold War foreign policy.[47] Instead, after entering office the Carter administration went on an activist foreign policy binge, addressing numerous issues that gave observers little appearance of any rhyme or reason.

Finally, Carter's foreign policy was attacked, and he was placed on the political defensive, as the power of conservatism grew in the late 1970s. With the onset of the Iran hostage crisis and the Soviet invasion of Afghanistan, double-digit inflation and unemployment, and a growing perception of him as a weak leader, Carter was unable to counteract the rise of the political right throughout American society. This increasingly conservative domestic environment and the approaching 1980 presidential election helped to spur the reinstatement of containment to the forefront of U.S. foreign policy. Although Carter's new Cold War foreign policy was consistent with the mood of the country, the public was disenchanted with Carter and his administration. That led to the election of Ronald Reagan as president of the United States in 1980.[48]

DEFEAT, ISOLATION, AND RENEWAL?

Under the Reagan administration a Cold War foreign policy based on containment, realpolitik, and anticommunism, reminiscent of that during the Cold War years, was instituted. Thus, the effort by President Carter to engage in a post-Cold War foreign policy resulted completely collapsed. As Stanley Hoffman wrote at the time, "The tragedy of the Carter failure is that, far from furthering an intelligent discussion of the issues, it has thrown us back to the simplicities of Cold War containment and bipolarity. The absence of a strategy has paved the way for those who seem to have one, however inadequate or antiquated it may be."[49]

Certainly the Carter years have not helped to legitimize a post-Cold War foreign policy in the minds of many Americans. If anything, the perception of a failed Carter presidency has made it that much more difficult to circumvent the Cold War legacy that continues to permeate beliefs and institutions throughout the government and the society. Yet the rise of Mikhail Gorbachev as general secretary of the Communist Party of the Soviet Union opened up new opportunities for a post-Cold War U.S. foreign policy. Communism has collapsed in the Soviet Union and Eastern Europe; Germany has been reunified; and greater integration of the European Community is rapidly taking place. Clearly, the East-West conflict that had been the justification for a Cold War foreign policy based on containment, realpolitik, and anticommunism no longer seems to exist.

More and more Americans appear to have acknowledged the existence of a post-Cold War global era. In such a climate a post-Cold War foreign policy has a greater chance of being successful and gaining political support. Such a post-Cold War environment helps to account for the renewed public interest and admiration that Jimmy Carter has received for his post-presidential activities, such as his involvement in the promotion of human rights, the overseeing of foreign elections, the negotiation of regional conflicts, and his assistance in promoting Third World development. Therefore, Jimmy Carter may have been, at least in the area of foreign and national security policy, a man ahead of his time.

The 1988 election of George Bush, however, brought a president whose foreign policy remained heavily conditioned by the Cold War past. Therefore, even though America's Cold War with communism and the Soviet Union is at an end, the U.S. response to Iraq's invasion of Kuwait was heavily conditioned by the legacy of the Cold War. Although President Bush promoted a multilateral response through the use of the United Nations, at the same time he took the lead in relying on the threat and use of force by placing over two hundred thousand American troops in the Persian Gulf in order to contain and roll back the threat that Saddam Hussein of Iraq was seen to pose to regional and global stability. Such a policy, although free of anticommunism, represents a global containment strategy based on a realpolitik view of the world.

President Bush's foreign policy in a post-Cold War era demonstrated the continued power of Cold War thinking. In this respect, the major obstacle to an American post-Cold War foreign policy is the Cold War legacy that continues to permeate the government and society: the beliefs of political leaders, the institutions that make up the national security bureaucracy, and the beliefs of a public conditioned for over forty years to respond to international conflict predominantly through intervention and the use of force. Therefore, a post-Cold War approach in U.S. foreign policy remains at best a future possibility. More important, the institutionalization of a U.S. post-Cold War foreign policy will require a president of vision and strong leadership to overcome the powerful legacies of America's Cold War past.

NOTES

I would like to thank John Creed, Ray Goldstein, Paul Kattenburg, Ken Menkhaus, Raymond Moore, Donald Puchala, Steven Twing, Art VandenHouten, Steven Walker, and Brian Whitmore for their very helpful comments and suggestions.

1. See Jerel A. Rosati, *The Carter Administration's Quest for Global Community: Beliefs and Their Impact on Behavior* (Columbia: University of South Carolina Press, 1987), ch.1.

2. Gaddis Smith, *Morality, Reason and Power: American Diplomacy in the Carter Years* (New York: Hill and Wang, 1986); Rosati, *Carter Administration's Quest*.

3. Smith, *Morality, Reason and Power*, p. 4.

4. See Seyom Brown, *The Faces of Power: Constancy and Change in United States Foreign Policy from Truman to Reagan* (New York: Columbia University Press, 1983); Charles W. Kegley, Jr., and Eugene Wittkopf, *American Foreign Policy: Pattern and Process* (New York: St. Martin's Press, 1987); John Spanier, *American Foreign Policy Since World War II* (Washington, D.C.: Congressional Quarterly Press, 1988).

5. Richard A. Melanson, *Writing History and Making Policy: The Cold War, Vietnam, and Revisionism* (Lanham, MD: University Press of America, 1983), p. 178.

6. See George F. Kennan, "Long Telegram" (February 22, 1946), in Thomas G. Paterson, ed., *Major Problems in American Foreign Policy, Documents and Essays*, vol. II: *Since 1914* (Lexington, MA: D.C. Heath, 1984); George F. Kennan, "The Sources of Soviet Conduct," *Foreign Affairs, 26* (July 1947); U.S. Department of State, "A Report to the President Pursuant to the President's Directive of January 31, 1950" (NSC-68, April 7, 1950), *Foreign Relations of the United States, 1950*, vol. I, pp. 235-292.

7. Bruce Jentleson, "American Commitments in the Third World," *International Organization*, 41 (1987):667-704. See also Alexander L. George and Richard Smoke, *Deterrence in American Foreign Policy: Theory and Practice* (New York: Columbia University Press, 1974); John Lewis Gaddis, *Strategies of Containment: A Critical Appraisal of Postwar American National Security Policy* (New York: Oxford University Press, 1982).

8. President Jimmy Carter, "A Foreign Policy Based on America's Essential Character," address at Notre Dame University, May 22, 1977, *Department of State Bulletin*, June 13, 1977, p. 622.

9. Jimmy Carter, "The U.S.-Soviet Relationship," remarks made before the Southern Legislative Conference at Charleston, SC, July 21, 1977, *Department of State Bulletin*, August 15, 1977, p. 194.

10. Zbigniew Brzezinski, address to the American Foreign Service Association, Washington, DC, December 9, 1977, *Department of Defense Selected Statements*, March 1, 1978, p. 19.

11. Zbigniew Brzezinski, "American Policy and Global Change," address to the Trilateral Commission, Bonn, Germany, October 25, 1977, *Congressional Record*, November 1, 1977, p. H-11999.

12. Cyrus Vance, "The United States and Africa: Building Positive Relationships," address to the annual convention of the National Association for the Advancement of Colored People, St. Louis, July 1, 1977, *Department of State Bulletin*, August 8, 1977, pp. 166, 169. Emphasis in the original.

13. Jimmy Carter, "Peace, Arms Control, World Economic Progress, Human Rights: Basic Priorities of U.S. Foreign Policy," address to the U.N. General Assembly, March 17, 1977, *Department of State Bulletin*, April 11, 1977, p. 329.

14. See E. H. Carr, *The Twenty Years Crisis, 1919-1939* (New York: Harper and Row, 1964); Hans J. Morgenthau, *Politics Among Nations: The Struggle for Power and Peace* (New York: Alfred A. Knopf, 1978); A. F. K. Organski, *World Politics* (New York: Alfred A. Knopf, 1958).

15. Richard W. Mansback and John A. Vasquez, *In Search of Theory: A New Paradigm for Global Politics* (New York: Columbia University Press, 1981), p. 8. See also Robert Gilpin, *War and Change in World Politics* (Cambridge: Cambridge University Press, 1981); John A. Vasquez, *The Power of Power Politics* (New Brunswick, NJ: Rutgers University Press, 1983).

16. See Richard Barnet, *Roots of War: The Men and Institutions Behind U.S. Foreign Policy* (Baltimore: Penguin, 1971); Leslie H. Gelb and Richard K. Betts, *The Irony of Vietnam: The System Worked* (Washington, DC: Brookings Institution, 1979); David Halberstam, *The Best and the Brightest* (New York: Random House, 1971); Walter Isaacson and Evan Thomas, *The Wise Men: Six Friends and the World They Made* (New York: Touchstone, 1986).

17. Stanley Hoffman, *Primacy or World Order: American Foreign Policy Since the Cold War* (New York: McGraw-Hill, 1978), Robert O. Keohane and Joseph S. Nye, *Power and Interdependence* (Boston: Scott, Foresman, 1989). See also Seyom Brown, *New Forces in World Politics* (Washington, DC: Brookings Institution, 1974); Edward L. Morse, *Foreign Policy and Interdependence in Gaulist France* (Princeton: Princeton University Press, 1973).

18. Keohane and Nye, *Power and Interdependence*, p. 26.

19. Carter, "The U.S.-Soviet Relationship," p. 194.

20. Brzezinski, address to the American Foreign Service Association, p. 19.

21. Jimmy Carter, "U.S. Role in a Peaceful Global Community," address to the U.N. General Assembly, October 4, 1977, *Department of State Bulletin*, October 24, 1977, p. 552.

22. Brzezinski, "American Policy and Global Change," p. H-11999.

23. Cyrus Vance, interview on "Issues and Answers," June 19, 1977, *Department of State Bulletin*, July 18, 1977, p. 81.

24. Jentleson, "American Commitments in the Third World," p. 671.

25. See Gabriel Almond, *The American People and Foreign Policy* (New York: Praeger, 1960); R. B. Levering, *The Public and American Foreign Policy, 1918-1978* (New York: William Morrow, 1978); M. J. Rosenberg, "Images in Relation to the Policy Process: American Public Opinion on Cold War Issues," in Herbert C. Kelman, ed., *International Behavior: A Social-Psychological Analysis*, (New York: Holt, Rinehart and Winston, 1965), pp. 277-334.

26. See Eric F. Goldman, *The Crucial Decade--and After. America, 1945-1960* (New York: Vantage, 1961); Robert Griffith, *The Politics of Fear: Joseph R. McCarthy and the Senate* (Hasbrouk Heights, NJ: Hayden, 1970); Godfrey Hodgson, *America in Our Time: From World War II to Nixon. What Happened and Why* (New York: Vintage, 1976); Daniel Yergin, *Shattered Peace: The Origins of the Cold War and the National Security State* (Boston: Houghton Mifflin, 1978).

27. See Loren Baritz, *Backfire: A History of How American Culture Led Us into Vietnam and Made Us Fight the Way We Did* (New York: William Morrow, 1985); Tamil R. Davis and Sean M. Lynn-Jones, "City upon a Hill," *Foreign Policy*, 66 (1987):20-38; Hodgson, *America in Our Time*; Stanley Hoffman, *Gulliver's Troubles or the Setting of American Foreign Policy* (New York: McGraw-Hill, 1968); Michael H. Hunt, *Ideology and U.S. Foreign Policy* (New Haven: Yale University Press, 1987).

28. Carter, "Foreign Policy Based," pp. 621-622.

29. Melanson, *Writing History and Making Policy*, p. 143.

30. Jimmy Carter, "The United States and Its Economic Responsibilities," remarks made at the opening session of the 26th World Conference of the International Chamber of Commerce, Orlando, FL, October 1, 1978, *Department of State Bulletin*, 78 (December 1978):13.

31. Brzezinski, address to the American Foreign Service Association, p. 25.

32. Zbigniew Brzezinski, *Between Two Ages: America's Role in the Technetronic Age* (New York: Penguin, 1973).

33. Brzezinski, "American Policy and Global Change," p. H-12000.

34. Melanson, *Writing History and Making Policy*, p. 191.

35. Zbigniew Brzezinski, "Remarks Before the Women's National Democratic Club," Washington, DC, February 21, 1980, White House press release, February 21, 1980; Zbigniew Brzezinski, "The Quest for Global Security: The Third Phase," remarks before the Council on Foreign Relations, Denver, October 25, 1980, White House press release, October 25, 1980.

36. Smith, *Morality, Reason and Power*, p. 247.

37. Leslie H. Gelb, "Beyond the Carter Doctrine," *New York Times Magazine*, February 10, 1980, p. 26.

38. Leslie H. Gelb, "The Struggle over Foreign Policy: Muskie and Brzezinski," *New York Times Magazine*, July 20, 1980, p. 39.

39. See Simon Sefarty, "Brzezinski: Play it Again, Zbig," *Foreign Policy*, 32 (1978):3-21.

40. Zbigniew Brzezinski, interview with *Washington Post*, October 9, 1977, *Department of Defense Selected Statements*, November 1, 1977, p. 29.

41. Zbigniew Brzezinski, *Power and Principle: Memoirs of a National Security Advisor, 1977-1981* (New York: Farrar, Straus and Giroux, 1983), pp. 81, 193. See also Rosati, *Carter Administration's Quest*, pp. 107-111. It is interesting to note that Richard Melanson's study of U.S. foreign policy during the Carter years arrived at the same conclusion, although based on a different method--interviews of NSC and State Department Policy Planning staff officials. Melanson, *Writing History and Making Policy*, chs. 6 and 7.

42. Hoffman, *Primacy or World Order*; Keohane and Nye, *Power and Interdependence*.

43. Jimmy Carter, interview with Frank Reynolds on ABC-TV's "World News Tonight," January 19, 1980, *New York Times*, January 20, 1980, p. 4.

44. See I. M. Destler, Leslie H. Gelb, and Anthony Lake, *Our Own Worst Enemy: The Unmaking of American Foreign Policy* (New York: Simon and Schuster, 1984); Oli R. Holsti and James N. Rosenau, *American Leadership in World Affairs: Vietnam and the Breakdown of Consensus* (Boston: Allan and Unwin, 1984); Jerel A. Rosati, "The Domestic Environment," in Peter J. Schraeder, ed., *Intervention in the 1980s: U.S. Foreign Policy in the Third World* (Boulder, CO: Lynne Rienner, 1989), pp. 147-160.

45. Keohane and Nye, *Power and Interdependence*, p. 237.

46. See Erwin Hargrove, *Jimmy Carter as President: Leadership and the Politics of the Public Good* (Baton Rouge: Louisiana State University Press, 1988); Charles O. Jones, *The Trusteeship Presidency: Jimmy Carter and the United States Congress* (Baton Rouge: Louisiana State University Press, 1988).

47. See, for example, Stanley Hoffman, "The Hell of Good Intentions," *Foreign Policy*, 29 (Winter 1977-1978):3-26.

48. It is important to point out that Carter's commitment to a Cold War approach at the end of his administration did not outlast his losing bid for reelection. His farewell address in January 1981 focused on three major themes that reflected his earlier post-Cold War foreign policy: the threat of nuclear destruction, the stewardship of the physical resources of the planet, and the preeminence of the basic rights of human beings. His post-Cold War approach has continued to inform his activities

since he left office. Jimmy Carter, "Farewell Address," January 14, 1981, *New York Times*, January 15, 1981, p. B-10.

49.   Stanley Hoffman, "Requiem," *Foreign Policy*, 42 (Spring 1981):17.

4

Negotiations at Home and Abroad:
Carter's Alternatives to Conflict and War

KENNETH W. THOMPSON

Jimmy Carter has been variously described as a new kind of president, a bridge president between the old and the new, and the first president to be elected from the Deep South since the Civil War. He was the first outsider to become president since Woodrow Wilson. My colleague James Sterling Young, who directed an extensive oral history of the Carter White House at the University of Virginia's Miller Center of Public Affairs, has described him as "the first president to open his presidency to intense, sober and objective examination by scholars before his library was opened up." The inquiry has resulted in twenty-two volumes of some three thousand pages that will be available to historians and scholars.

In foreign policy, Jimmy Carter was both a new and an old kind of president. He was committed to goals that, clustered together, offered a vision of a new world. It would be no exaggeration to say that he carried the banner of Woodrow Wilson and Franklin D. Roosevelt in a changing world. Some of his views on human rights and the responsibility of the executive echo Wilson's Fourteen Points and Roosevelt's Four Freedoms. As was sometimes said of these two liberal predecessors, historians may judge that Carter was ahead of his time on the great fundamental issues of his time, including the environment, human rights, and defense and arms control. More difficult to assess are two other reformist views Carter advanced once he left office. First, he proposed that presidents be elected for a single six-year term. Second, he wished to change the two-thirds vote required for Senate ratification of treaties either to a simple majority vote or a two-thirds vote to override an agreement a president has negotiated with a foreign nation. It remains to be seen whether either reform will be approved in the coming decades. Anthony Lake, who was director of the Policy Planning Staff in the State Department during the Carter administration, considers that the true impact of Carter's vision of the future will not be fully recognized for ten or twenty years.

Evidence that President Carter saw himself as speaking for a new age in world affairs comes out in a second Miller Center oral history, this one based on interviews with a group of cabinet and department officials. Without exception, they called attention to the aim of the administration to look ahead. In October 1976, Secretary of State designate Cyrus Vance and a few of his colleagues prepared a white paper at

Carter's request, laying out what they saw as the major foreign policy issues of the next four years. Discussing uses of the paper, Vance explained: "One of the things I recommended was that each year we ought to update our priorities and see whether they still stood, and if not to change those priorities and to have the assistant secretaries who had responsibility in those functional and geographical areas to do this at the beginning of each year."[1]   Establishing priorities and reconsidering their importance each year were examples of the Carter administration's attempt to look ahead and to anticipate the future. For most Americans, Carter as a man of vision in foreign policy was the hallmark of his administration. If there is a Carter who is known to a wide public, it is the Carter of human rights, the global environment, and worldwide arms limitation. Yet important as these areas of foreign policy were for him, another sphere of his interest has become increasingly visible, especially in his life as a former president. It is in the area of negotiations, reflected in the title of his Mercer Lectures, *Negotiation: An Alternative to Hostility*. The unknown Carter is the Carter of negotiations and accommodation; the discussion that follows seeks to analyze his contributions here.

In the Carl Vinson Inaugural Memorial Lecture, delivered on April 28, 1983, in Macon, Georgia, former President Carter sought to lay down some general principles and procedures that he found helpful in resolving disputes. He explained that as president he had sometimes been the principal negotiator. At other times he monitored "each step" in the negotiations of his chosen representatives, and at still other times he drew up a general formula or framework within which negotiators enjoyed considerable freedom of action. He stressed that negotiations are especially complicated for Americans because of the unique relationships between the executive and Congress, the media, public and special interest groups, and leaders in other world capitals.

Negotiators confront a series of important decisions at the outset of any negotiation: when to act, whether to make the first initiative public or private, the diplomatic level at which to establish contact, what forum to use, what incentives to offer the other side--whether carrots or sticks--how to assess the prevailing support for and opposition to negotiations in one's own country, and at what point the president should become personally involved. The list of decisions is reminiscent of a pilot's checklist that must be completed at the end of the runway before requesting clearance to take off.

It is especially important to recognize the nature of the international system within which negotiations are conducted. President Carter understood well that no single judge or jury presided over the system, and therefore the decisions of negotiators had to be *voluntary* and *unanimous*. In a particularly graphic descripton, he wrote:

Often I would sit by a large globe, imagine myself to be Brezhnev, Sadat, Begin, Den Xiaoping or Torrijos, and try to understand the issues in question from their points of view. At the same time, for me as president, the interests of the United States . . . would always be paramount.[2]

Perhaps without knowing it, Carter was enacting what Sir Herbert Butterfield once described as the essence of diplomacy. For Carter as for Butterfield, diplomacy is the art of putting oneself in another leader's or people's shoes or looking over the shoulder of a policymaker as a decision is made.

The most difficult step in any negotiation, according to Carter, was getting the parties to agree to commence negotiation and deciding what should be included on the agenda. Sometimes the parties are unwilling to meet for fear of granting the other side diplomatic recognition, one of the reasons the Palestinians and the Israelis have thus far not come together at a negotiating table. I remember Ralph Bunche telling the story of his becoming so frustrated when Arabs and Jews could not reach an agreement, even when he carried messages back and forth between them, that he finally blurted out, "Why can't you act like Christians?" Carter acknowledges that the Soviets postponed SALT II negotiations for months "partially to retaliate against our strong human rights stand,"[3] an admission that no Carter official made at the time and that some deny to the present day.

Carter rightly emphasizes patience and persistence in negotiations, and reminds his readers that the SALT II negotiations went on for more than six years, on and off, under three presidents. Law of the Sea discussions lasted for a decade, and the Panama Canal treaty negotiations were begun by Lyndon Johnson and concluded fourteen years later by Carter. He might have mentioned other examples such as the Austrian Peace Treaty of 1955, requiring nearly five hundred negotiating sessions. It is admirable that Carter praises those who can find "five new ways to measure the height of a tall building by using a barometer," an appeal for new paradigms of negotiating techniques. However, history more than science is the school of the statesman who seeks political settlements and arms agreements. Hugh Sidey has argued that John Kennedy was the last president with a sense of history.

One of the most creative aspects of Carter's approach is his call for a general framework to guide negotiators. He wisely proposed that such a framework permit the negotiators maneuvering room and flexibility, and enable them to withdraw from untenable positions taken in anger or war. It can help them rationalize their positions without losing face. The framework for Camp David provided that Israel, in exchange for peace and normalized relations with Egypt, would withdraw from Sinai. Following an interim period, a final agreement would assure autonomy for the Palestinians and Israeli withdrawal from Gaza and the West Bank. The framework for release of the American hostages in Iran provided for their freedom in return for recovery of part of Iran's frozen assets. In the absence of an overall framework, Carter recommends that negotiators seek agreement on one or two relatively simple preliminary accords from which a general formula might later emerge.

Even though his rhetoric and his concept of openness against secrecy pushed him in another diection, President Carter came to understand with Winston Churchill that effective negotiations must be conducted in private. He wrote: "Had we not isolated the negotiators within the confines of Camp David and totally excluded the reporters, I am convinced that we could never have reached agreement." Nonetheless, even private diplomacy can be threatened by premature press releases and provocative unilateral statements, as by Prime Minister Menachem Begin after Camp David, that are intended primarily for domestic political constituencies.

Carter's view of deadlines in negotiations runs counter to those of most students of traditional diplomacy, including Sir Harold Nicolson and Hugh Gibson. They argue that negotiators who have run out of time cannot face the prospect of returning empty-handed to their constituents. Therefore, they agree to empty and meaningless formulas that obscure and conceal the fact that their differences remain largely unresolved.

By contrast, Carter argues that deadlines can promote successful negotiations. "Without a deadline of some sort, talks tend to drag on interminably."[4] (He gives as an example the Mutual and Balanced Force Reduction talks between NATO and Warsaw Pact countries.) He cites three examples in which substantial concessions were made at the eleventh hour: Panama, in which August 10, 1977, was known to be the last day that Ambassador Sol Linowitz could serve as the American negotiator; Camp David, where Carter announced the Americans would leave with or without an agreement on September 17, 1978; and January 20, 1981, when the Ayatollah Khomeini, knowing that Carter was leaving office, recognized that without an agreement the Iranians would face new talks with the Reagan administration, the results of which were impossible to predict.

Mr. Carter believes that negotiators must constantly be reminded of the benefits of success and the risks of failure. Every time deadlock appears likely, they must be ready to try new approaches. "If they are well prepared, each side will have many options ready to put forward--sometimes just a change in language--both to reach their own goals and to react successfully to the proposals of others."[5] "Understanding the enemy" is crucial. While Carter is not particulary forthcoming on diplomatic tactics and stratagems, he does say:

Often it is possible to convince at least some key members of the opposing [negotiating] team and then let them use their influence to encourage movement toward agreement by the entire delegation. A real or implied threat that proposals will be made public sometimes helps to prevent the rejection of patently attractive or fair offers. We used this device in dealing with Prime Minister Begin, who was almost always the most recalcitrant member of the Israeli delegation. Sadat . . . was always the most constructive and generous among the Egyptians.[6]

For those who see him only as a starry-eyed idealist with little grasp of the need for hardheaded realism, such reflections reveal the unknown Carter, who thought seriously about diplomacy and has continued to construct his own concepts of and approach to negotiations and peaceful settlement.

The foremost American exponent of political realism, Hans J. Morgenthau, often said of Carter that he could not remember an American president whose goals and values he respected more but who appeared more inept in pursuing them. Yet the Carter record in foreign policy is one of the most impressive of any postwar presidency measured by the weight of substantive accomplishments. What accounts for the gulf between the public image of Jimmy Carter and the reality?

Three explanations are offered by participants in the Carter oral history, and their interconnections and mutual reinforcement may provide answers to our question. First, the shadow of internecine conflict between the White House and the State Department was present from the earliest days of the administration, and President Carter did nothing to diminish or control the struggle. Second, Carter never gained the personal loyalty of the bureaucracy, in part because he was seen as anti-

Washington, in part because of his style of governing, and in part because of the bureaucracy's feeling that he seldom treated it with the respect it deserved. Third, foreign policy crises, such as the Iran hostage problem, had domestic political consequences. This may have been the most important factor because, in Anthony Lake's words:

Foreign policy issues are politically important in two indirect ways. First, they provide a test of the character of the candidates. People seem less interested in the details of what candidates say they will do than in whether the candidate seems capable of taking care of business in a dangerous world. And secondly, a foreign policy problem can become symbolic of other things that are bothering Americans.[7]

Lake concludes: "I think that to some degree a public sense of helplessness over Iran reflected a sense of helplessness over the economy."[8]

The first explanation--that of conflict within the administration, and especially between Secretary of State Vance and National Security Council Adviser Zbigniew Brzezinski--is raised by virtually every participant in the oral history. Secretary Vance explained:

I do not feel the President adequately enforced what . . . is essential in dealing with foreign affairs and national security issues--namely, to tell the principal players in the White House and in the departments that he expected them to work together in a collegial fashion to advance the best interests of the country and those of the President. He did not tell them that he did not want them going out and building empires for themselves, because if they were going to do that, they had better get themselves a job elsewhere. He did not say that if he caught any of the people doing it that he was going to fire either one or both of them, as, for example, if there was such an incident involving the Secretary of State and National Security Advisor.[9]

This lack of a tough policy by the president toward senior advisers fed back a harmful virus into the stream of public perception. If Carter's sense of diplomacy was not fully appreciated, it was in part because the administration's principal executors represented and spoke for divergent viewpoints. In Lake's view, "Brzezinski was more concerned with the Soviet Union as a global threat, Vance more with resolving regional issues and negotiating SALT II."[10] The public grew increasingly confused concerning who spoke for American foreign policy? The famous Carter Annapolis speech, in which paragraphs representing opposing State Department and National Security Council views were pasted together, was only the most egregious example of an administration speaking with two voices. The more Brzezinski seized opportunities to appear on Sunday talk shows, according to Lake, "the more an impression was created of more than one voice speaking for the administration."[11] Explaining his relationship with the Brzezinski, Vance's successor, Edmund Muskie, remembered that "the first thing I wanted to know was whether I would be his [Carter's] foreign policy spokeman or whether I would be sharing that responsibility with someone else."[12] It is surprisng that President Carter, who promptly reassured Muskie on this score, would not have recognized the depth of the problem in the public's mind, the question having come from his newly designated secretary of state.

The second factor that may have contributed to the failure of the public to give full credit to Carter was his administrative style. Speaking of the Namibian and Rhodesian nego-tiations, Ambassador Donald McHenry observed: "There were times when he knew more about the subject . . . than I did."[13] On the hostage crisis, which McHenry described as literally consuming the president, he found Carter approaching "it in the same manner that he approached other problems," involving himself "in the slightest of details."[14] McHenry believed that attention to details stood in the way of Carter's success as a communicator: "His attention to detail tended to carry over to the way he discussed policy matters with the public. The public doesn't want . . . to hear a recitation of the detailed complications of foreign policy. . . . The public wants to know how you, as president, are going to act."[15] In Carter's efforts to project leadership, as in the "malaise" speech or the Notre Dame speech, "one doesn't get the impression of this man as leader"[16] because of his tendency to introduce too many details. Paradoxically, Carter's grasp of details, which was sometimes a strength, could also be a weakness in diverting him from the need to frame a general strategy.

A further question concerns President Carter's authority and the respect he commanded in the bureaucracy and the Congress. Lake suggests that Carter failed in reaching out to members of these two important governmental bodies. The bureaucracy in particular cannot be led by fear but only "by treating it like any other political constituency--by capturing its loyalty and imagination." Having failed to gain the bureaucracy's allegiance, Carter lost a potential means for communicating his ideas. Not proving his leadership with those closest to him, he was bound to lose out with those more remote. Perhaps this failure was linked to the fact that President Carter was a very "private, public man." Lake sums up this weakness thus: "He did not convey his personal qualities with the kind of warmth that can inspire a bureaucracy or the Congress."[17] Not inspiring the two bodies with whom he maintained an ongoing relationship, he could scarcely hope to motivate and educate the vast, amorphous public. Lake suggests "that what the historians will say is that his foreign policy was a tremendous substantive success even while it failed politically at home."[18] This theme runs through the testimony of many Carter staffers and may explain why he remained to the end an unknown leader despite his considerable foreign policy skills.

The revisionists are only now begining to influence the public perception of President Carter. His stature is being elevated significantly by his dedication to the quest for global peace and the well-being of mankind around the world. No living president has given himself more fully to the cause of peace and justice, whatever the personal sacrifice required. It is still premature to expect a definitive judgment of his place in American history. Among the questions worth asking as historians seek to judge the Carter foreign policy are the reasons for the curious and thus far unexplained gulf between perception and reality. How could so many who were otherwise sympathetic not recognize his grasp of the art of diplomatic negotiations and his tireless pursuit of the peaceful settlement of international disputes? How can we explain the strange fact that these qualities remained largely unknown in the public at large throughout most of his administration? Accounting for the known and the unknown Jimmy Carter in foreign policy may be the primary task of historians for generations to come. Two important texts for pursuing the question may prove to be, first, the historical record of the Carter approach to diplomacy and, second, a series of his fugitive and litte known writings, such as *Negotiation: The Alternative to Hostility*.

We ask of our leaders that "they stand for something again" in world affairs, but their public pronouncements on current questions may divert attention from their more fundamental political and diplomatic principles. We know that methods and procedures hold less appeal in public discourse than do clarion calls for an end to the arms race or a crusade for human rights or the war against environmental deterioration. It is tempting to measure a president solely by public statements and lose sight of the broad directions and guiding principles he is following. If this should prove true of President Carter, future studies of the Carter approach to foreign policy may help us to bring the known and the unknown Carter on-line. I would hope at least some Carter scholars might recognize such inquiries as worthy of investigation in the future.

NOTES

1. Kenneth W. Thompson, ed., *The Carter Presidency: Fourteen Intimate Perspectives of Jimmy Carter* (Lanham, MD: University Press of America, 1990), pp. 136-137.

2. Jimmy Carter, *Negotiation: The Alternative to Hostility, The Carl Vinson Memorial Lecture Series* (Macon, GA: Mercer University Press, 1984), p. 13.

3. Ibid., p. 14.

4. Ibid., p. 19.

5. Ibid., p. 18.

6. Ibid., pp. 18-19.

7. Thompson, *The Carter Presidency*, p. 155.

8. Ibid.

9. Ibid., p. 141.

10. Ibid., p. 150.

11. Ibid., p. 151.

12. Ibid., p. 179.

13. Ibid., p. 163.

14. Ibid., p. 165.

15. Ibid., p. 171.

16. Ibid.

17. Ibid., p. 147.

18. Ibid., p. 153.

Discussant: William B. Quandt

I should probably confess to my most obvious bias at the beginning. I participated in the Camp David negotiations. I probably saw President Carter at his best, and that probably does color the kinds of comments that I'm going to make, although I don't want to try to draw exclusively from that personal experience in reacting to the papers, which were all very interesting.

Just based on what we've heard today, I think it's hard to get a clear picture of Jimmy Carter, and that's also true when you've worked with him. But two images seem to come across from the papers, and I want to see if I can do a little bit to sharpen the image. One image is Jimmy Carter the skilled negotiator; the man ahead of his time, with a vision that encompasses considerable complexity and tries to break loose of the Cold War shibboleths with which we had lived for so long. The other image is of a rather naive, ill-informed man who came to the presidency and fouled up time after time, including on such matters as managing the alliance against the Soviet invasion of Afghanistan. Now, is this really the same person we're talking about, or is it, like the *Rashomon* story, everybody seeing a different part of the picture? I'm not quite sure. I have certain preferences for some of those interpretations over others, but let me, for the moment, give you my image of what Carter seemed like from the standpoint I had of working on the National Security Council staff, and then I'll have a few comments about the papers.

It seems to me that Carter did bring some impressive strengths to the presidency, strengths that we can appreciate after some of the weaknesses of his successor. He was a man of considerable intelligence; he was very serious about foreign policy issues; he was a very diligent student. He would read everything that was sent to him, and ask for more. He worked long hours, and I think one can hardly doubt his commitment to peace and a vision of a world in which nuclear weapons were no longer a threat to mankind. So in terms of his dedication, intelligence, hard work, and values, I would say there is very little that I would hold against him. I think all of those served him well in the presidency. He had a moral compass, which is often useful, and he had a mind that worked well. His background as an engineer did predispose him to think of things in rather discrete packages. Problems had solutions, and you could attack them one by one. This leads me to the less impressive side of what he brought to the presidency, and we've heard some of that today.

Obviously, he was a man who had not been deeply involved in foreign policy prior to his coming to office, and this inexperience--plus, perhaps, the predisposition as an engineer to see problems in very discrete, solvable packages--made it difficult for him to set priorities. If he saw a problem, he wanted to solve it, and that was all there was to it. At various times while I worked at the White House, we were told to try to come up with lists of priorities in the foreign policy arena, and we would send lists to the president and say, "Here are twenty issues or so that are of concern, that need attention. You can devote attention to only two or three of them and really hope to do very much. Which two or three are most important to you?" And the checklist would come back with a note to do all twenty of them. None of them were unimportant. That was a failing. A president cannot be the desk officer for everything. He maybe should not even try to be the desk officer for a single problem. But President Carter certainly did not have the inclination or capacity to make the grand strategic trade-offs.

For example, at the time of the SALT negotiations, Cyrus Vance very much wanted to push forward, get the negotiations concluded quickly, and move for quick ratification. He was worried about the problems of dragging out the negotiations endlessly. Brzezinski said, "No, there's no need to rush; we can get a better deal if we get a little bit more leverage over the Soviets. We should normalize relations with the Chinese first, and then we will have a stronger bargaining position vis-à-vis the Soviets." And Carter's response was, "I want to do both of those things. I want to normalize relations with China, because it's a desirable objective, and I want to get the SALT negotiations concluded quickly." Now, those both sound like perfectly reasonable things to want, but in the real world, it was impossible to get both simultaneously. If we were going to go down the track of quick normalization of relations with China, it would be at the expense of SALT II. If we wanted to do SALT II quickly, we needed to slow down on the normalization with China. Carter could not make the choice; he said, "Do both of them." That was, in fact, a problem, and a persistent problem.

Carter also had a surprising failure as a politician. You would think that a man who managed to get himself elected president would be particularly adept at reading the public mood, mobilizing support through speeches, dealing with Congress--doing all the things that politicians presumably should be able to do. He certainly had been a politician; he'd served as governor, he'd gotten himself elected. And yet, it was really in this arena that I saw the greatest failures in the man.

I don't buy the argument that his lack of experience was his main liability as foreign policymaker. I think he was a very quick study, and he soon knew enough to make reasonably informed judgments. His real failure seems to me to have been his almost total belief that if he made the right decision--through diligent study, hard work, sincere application, looking at that globe, putting himself in the shoes of the other person--people would support it because it was right. And of course, that goes back to a kind of moralistic streak: You do the right thing, people will recognize it as right, and they will therefore support you. You don't need to pick up the phone and call the majority leader of the Senate and say, "Why don't you drop by and have a drink, and we'll schmooze a little bit?" That kind of politics was almost beneath him.

Politics, for President Carter, was a moral crusade where you take the right position and people will fall in line. That is not American politics. In American politics, you have to talk and you have to persuade. You have to say it over and over and over again, and you have to spend a lot of time with people in Congress, because they have very big egos and they think they ought to be involved in everything. Carter was incapable of doing that. So where I, at least, see his great failures--his inability to get, for example, ratification of the SALT II treaty--comes down more to his failures as a politician, not so much as a conceptualizer of foreign policy.

Now, a word or two on the papers. I don't want to ignore them; they were all interesting in their own ways. For the paper by Professor Goldman, the question I would have after both reading it and listening to his presentation is how much better Jimmy Carter could have done in mobilizing support from the Allies, given that they did have divergent interests. All we have heard is that he should have consulted with them more. Well, no doubt that would have been good, but I'm not sure it would have solved the problem. Goldman also suggested that we should have looked more into Soviet motivations for going into Afghanistan. I'm not sure what that would have led us to. It's like saying that if we understood Saddam Hussein's motivations today, we would know better what we ought to do about him. I think I have a pretty good idea of why Saddam Hussein went into Kuwait; but that doesn't exactly help me solve the problem of what to do about it. And I'm not sure it would have helped had we concluded that the Soviet intervention in Afghanistan was defensive as opposed to offensive. We still probably would have wanted to impose some cost on the Soviet Union for pursuing such a policy.

Let me say just a brief word about Professor Thompson's paper. In passing, there was one reference in the paper to the fact that the Camp David accords provided for the withdrawal of Israeli forces from the West Bank and Gaza after an interim period. That isn't true. I wish it had done so; it would have probably set the stage for a much more productive negotiation. But the fact of the matter is that that was one of the things we could not and did not get in the Camp David accords, and of course it has been a problem ever since.

Professor Rosati's paper was extremely interesting, and by and large, I would agree with a great deal of what he said--perhaps almost all of it. It does seem to me that there's a little bit of an exaggeration in terms of how much of a break with the past there really was. Some of the seeds of the early Carter policy were, after all, planted and quite visible in part of the Nixon-Kissinger foreign policy. The real opening toward China, of course, came then, and that was really the break with anticommunism as a dominant theme; after all, China was the largest communist power. And in terms of the crumbling of the ideological overlay of the Cold War, I think you can begin to see it there, and in a sense, there's a sort of continuity from then on in American foreign policy. The difference was that Nixon and Kissinger were still obsessed with the power of the Soviet Union and, at least at the outset, Carter and Brzezinski and Vance were more persuaded that that was no longer such a great problem, and it could be dealt with through negotiations and through building a structure around the Soviet Union that would eventually bring about a moderating of Soviet foreign policy.

I also think it would be interesting, if you have any occasion to add to the paper or revise it, to note that one of the first examples of this post-Cold War approach--that is, to undertake foreign policy initiatives with the Soviet Union--took the form of the U.S.-Soviet joint communiqué on the Middle East on October 1, 1977. I happened to be involved in that a bit. It was an interesting initiative. It also lasted all of three days, which makes one wonder how deeply committed to the post-Cold War era we were when the domestic costs of pursuing that kind of an approach became very evident very quickly.

Finally, on Clifford's paper, I think the basic thesis is wrong. I'm sorry to be so blunt about it, but I have only a couple of minutes to conclude. The assumption in the paper is that if Carter had had more experience, and had been better informed, we would have had better foreign policy. That sounds perfectly plausible, and perhaps, in some very broad sense, it is much to be desired that you have presidents experienced in foreign policy. His successor wasn't terribly experienced, however, and we managed to survive those eight years. I think, however, that on-the-job learning is always a necessity, no matter how well prepared a president may be in some general sense. He knows a little bit about the world, and he's been exposed to foreign policy issues; there is no perfect preparation for being president. The combination of pressures from domestic politics and the real issues that you have to face in foreign policy--it's very, very hard to be fully prepared for them. Therefore, I would much rather have--if I had to take my choice--someone who could learn very quickly the special requirements of this job for which there is no preparation, and who had an open enough mind to learn the facts as they came to his attention, rather than someone who lived a lot of experience in foreign policy, and all of a sudden faced issues thinking he knew all the answers, but in fact the experience was from ten or fifteen years earlier and had very little to do with the kinds of issues that he was going to have to deal with in the real world.

I also thought that the paper by Clifford was too harsh on the Carter record. It's true that Iran was a terrible blunder, and it deserves considerable attention in any serious study of the Carter foreign policy. But it also requires an answer--how would you have done better? Iran was a revolution; we're not terribly good at riding the tides of revolution, and I'm not sure that any president--even a better-prepared one, even one who spoke Persian and knew everything that you could possibly know about Iran --would have been able to come up with a great policy to deal with a totally unprecedented revolutionary situation in Iran. So unless you can tell me how we would have done better in Iran, I'm not sure I can draw the conclusion that Carter contributed to the foul-up any more than anybody else would have.

Finally, I think the Carter presidency deserves a bit more credit than was given in this paper. Camp David, with all of its flaws--I've written a whole book about Camp David, including its shortcomings--does still stand, more than ten years later, as a solid achievement, and I don't know too many people who would rather have seen that not be achieved. Likewise, the Panama Canal treaty negotiations--again, with all of their shortcomings--have stood the test of time pretty well, and I think we're better off for their being in place. SALT II, although it was never ratified, was nonetheless observed, and that helped to cap the arms race in some sense. The Carter Doctrine, even though it reflects the latter stage of the Carter presidency--which Professor Rosati correctly sees as a rather different phase of the Carter administration, although I don't think it was primarily an anticommunist statement; I think it was more an anti-Soviet statement, a statement against Soviet power, not against Soviet ideology--nonetheless set in motion the building of a kind of force that could be used in the Gulf region and has served us extremely well in this current crisis with Iraq. The Reagan administration basically built on that and elaborated a bit more what was implied by the Carter Doctrine. Of course, some people may not like the fact that we're in this position, but I think it was desirable to have the capabilities to confront the kind of aggression carried out by Saddam Hussein. I'm still uneasy about where that is taking us, but having the capabilities is directly related to the Carter Doctrine, and I think that also was a positive achievement.

So with those few comments, let me step down and pass it back to the chairman.

Discussant: Gaddis Smith

In my comments, I'd like to focus on the papers, and some of the things that I will say are very similar to what Bill Quandt has just said.

The papers in this panel enable us to contemplate the foreign policy of the Carter presidency in four dimensions. There's the dimension of time in Professor Rosati's paper, relating the foreign policy of the administration to the long transformation of the Cold War. There's the dimension of personality in Dr. Clifford's discussion of the appointment and roles of Vance and Brzezinski. There's the dimension of method in Professor Thompson's essay on Jimmy Carter and negotiation. And there's the dimension of place--or more precisely, foreign place, foreign perspective--in Professor Goldman's analysis of the Western European response to American policy in the Afghanistan crisis.

Professor Rosati asks us if Jimmy Carter was a man ahead of his time, and gives an affirmative answer. I agree. One can recall by contrast the attitudes of the high Cold War--or the low Cold War, whatever adjective you prefer. The first secretary of defense, James Forrestal, once said, "We must always remember that the principal export of the Soviet Union is chaos." And the corollary was that wherever you find any chaos, it's a Soviet export directed against us. Ronald Reagan said much the same thing with his remark that the Soviets were behind all of the hot spots in the world. By contrast, as we know, Jimmy Carter and most of his advisers understood mankind's inherent capacity to create chaos, without the help of the Soviet Union (or the United States, for that matter), and the necessity of dealing with that chaos without constantly referring it to possible Soviet manipulation.

I agree with Bill Quandt that the contrast between Carter and previous administrations may be a bit overdone. Advocates of previous presidencies could argue that Carter was not the first to think beyond the Cold War. Harry Truman had Point Four; Dwight Eisenhower had Atoms for Peace, and indeed had severe doubts about the utility of military force; Kennedy had his call to "make the world safe for diversity"; Nixon and Kissinger had détente and the opening to China. None of these gestures were as conceptually broad as the ideas that came forward in the Carter years, but their existence argues for a bit more continuity, and slightly less originality, than Professor Rosati suggests.

Also, those who contend that Carter pursued the Cold War by other means should not be dismissed too quickly. The Soviet Union, at all times in the Carter presidency, was the principal adversary, and he called it an adversary throughout. The focus on such issues as peace in the Middle East, or normalization of relations with the People's Republic of China, was not entirely separate from perceptions of Soviet-American relations. Carter said that fire is better fought with water than with fire, but he still talked about fighting fire, and fire meant the Soviet Union and its expansionist tendencies.

Let me stress that I'm in agreement with much of what Professor Rosati said, and I certainly applaud the Carter administration, and have done so, for trying more than any predecessor to get beyond the Cold War. Perhaps what I'm doing is indulging in the propensity of historians to say that nothing is ever quite as clear-cut as you think. Or that Carter and his advisers tried to think for the long term. The advocacy of racial equality in Africa was based both on general conceptions of human rights and on an estimate of how events would unfold over generations on that continent. The Panama Canal treaties looked to the twenty-first century. Camp David was to lay foundations that would be built on for decades. The administration's concern for international environmental problems--a concern that was, unfortunately, swamped by more pressing political issues and never given the attention President Carter hoped it would be given--dealt with the ultimate sustainability of life on earth. And how hard it is, and how rare it is, for a government to attempt to look that far ahead, when the political bottom line for a president comes every four years, and the approval polls come out every few days. And how do we, in foreign policy, get governments and people to think and act beyond tomorrow, beyond their own lifetimes--beyond even the lifetimes of their children? No one has that answer. But Carter, I think, tried harder than most.

Dr. Clifford's paper on Vance and Brzezinski adds some details to a fairly well-known story. Hundreds of writers--and I'm among them--have taken advantage of the dramatic contrast between those two principal advisers; they give us a plot line. The students love it when we lecture on them, and on their differences. But I think a lot of us--and I'm among them--are guilty of overplaying the role of personality in the foreign policy of the administration.

Professor Thompson's essay stressing Jimmy Carter's deep commitment to negotiation, in preference to coercion, as an instrument for dealing with disputes draws heavily on Carter's statements and work in his post-presidential years. But there's a real congruence between those statements and what he did at the time. This isn't always true of public figures who reminisce about what they have done. They often create a situation that didn't exist. I think President Carter has been very, very sound, and has not distorted his past record. A skillful, realistic commitment to negotiation is admirable but, alas, it does not guarantee broad political support. Professor Thompson wondered why there wasn't much support. I think it's very, very hard for a president to sell negotiating skill as a political asset. Too many of our leaders have acted as if negotiation equaled appeasement, and that's part of the rhetoric of our culture. Dean Acheson used to say that we must have negotiation from strength, which meant in practice that you never negotiate unless you know you're stronger. And if you know you're stronger, you don't need to negotiate. President Kennedy kept secret the negotiations that brought the Cuban missile crisis to a peaceful resolution, and it's only been in the last year or two that the secret aspect of those negotiations has come out. President Carter, I think, understood the sterility of the "negotiation from strength" position, but he suffered politically from those who said that negotiation with Panama was surrender of sovereign American rights, or that maneuvering Begin into the Camp David accords was a betrayal of Israel, or that the drawn-out negotiations for the release of the hostages in Iran were unworthy of American honor and power. Oh, how it simplifies life to have an enemy of unmitigated evil, preferably one you can compare with Adolf Hitler! No need to negotiate; no ambiguity; no uncertainty.

Now to the dimension of place: Professor Goldman's paper is valuable for reminding us that a full understanding of foreign policy demands that we take note of the behavior of other governments and peoples. I think too often we academics who write about American foreign policy write about one hand clapping, as if all of the explanatory data can be found within the United States, within the bureaucracy, within the personalities, within the special interest groups--Congress and so on. I'm guilty of this. We build on what we know, on the languages we can read, on the sources that are most accessible, and on the people we know or can interview. It's simpler to carry out such research, uncluttered by too much inconvenient and hard-to-find detail. As scholars, we may in fact be mimicking, in part, the foreign policy process itself, where the higher up you go, the more the details about the perspectives of specific countries get filtered out. But the data are available, especially from countries that enjoy an open society. Our embassies report information in real time, and as scholars, we can retrieve much of it even before the archives are open, as Professor Goldman's paper shows. We have to ask more questions and work harder than is sometimes our wont.

But what of those places that don't have open societies--specifically, of course, the Soviet Union, the Soviet Union of the Brezhnev years? It's intriguing, by the way, to speculate on what might have happened had Mikhail Gorbachev become the Soviet leader during Carter's presidency. Would he have had a more positive attitude toward Carter than did Brezhnev and his cohorts? We don't know. We know what Brezhnev said in public about Carter, and what the propaganda machine of the Soviet Union said. Is that what they believed in private? It would be very, very interesting to know. I was extremely surprised, almost shocked, during the Carter administration to talk to Soviet academics. I was full of admiration for Jimmy Carter at the time, and believed that he really was offering a new relationship with the Soviet Union. My Soviet counterparts abhorred him! They thought he was totally untrustworthy, and they said there were only two American presidents who were worth respect from the Soviet point of view: Franklin Roosevelt and Richard Nixon. That was a very common line. They believed that Richard Nixon was a martyr, had been made a martyr to the cause of peace, had been undone by the enemies of détente. It was a very common cliché in the Soviet Union, at least in the late 1970s and early 1980s.

Professor Rosati has shown that Carter's initial impulse for post-Cold War policy was defeated for a variety of reasons. I think the most important reason was Soviet behavior--the Soviet invasion of Afghanistan. It's interesting that the Soviets today-- or many of them, including Foreign Minister Eduard Schevardnadze--look back on that as an immoral blunder. Schevardnadze has given speeches that sound like Jimmy Carter, saying, "We have sinned in the past, and we must reform ourselves. We must be born again in our foreign policy." Very, very remarkable. Perhaps with *glasnost*, and if the Soviet Union does not collapse entirely--and we don't know whether that will be the case or not--we might be able to answer some of those questions before too long. It would be very interesting to have a Russian counterpart of Hofstra--Hofstra on the Moscow River--mount a conference such as this one on the Brezhnev years, bringing the people who took part in the Soviet foreign policy together to tell what they remember. If we had such a conference, I think we'd have a better perspective, and could speak a bit more confidently, on whether Carter really was a post-Cold War president, or whether he was truly blocked from any possibility of reaching that status by Soviet attitudes.

Questions and Answers

Q: My question goes to Professor Rosati. As I look at Carter, and I see his Presidential Directive number 59, and the whole big Russophobic rhetoric of Brzezinski, I find it hard, in terms of the sincerity of these men, to see them as guides into the post-Cold War era. I wonder what to make of Directive 59. I'd like your response to that, and also if Mr. Quandt and Mr. Smith could comment.

Rosati: I think one of the unanswered questions--it will be very interesting to see how it plays out in time--is Brzezinski's role in the whole thing. I think Bill Quandt can maybe shed some light on this. There was a debate about Brzezinski, whether or not he was--and I'll oversimplify it--a closet hawk when he came into office, or whether he sincerely shared the--I'll just use my term for now--post-Cold War values of Vance and of Carter. I believe he shared the views. If he was a hawk, he was a hawk in the shower. He wasn't a hawk in the NSC meetings or in the White House. I think the triggering factor for Brzezinski was the Somalia-Ethiopia War, where you had a lot of Cuban troops with Soviet support that were threatening Somalia. That really was, I think, the straw that broke the camel's back, and from that moment on, the old Brzezinski, if you will, came to the forefront and the new, complex, interdependent Brzezinski that rose up during the early 1970s tended to be in decline.

In terms of the PD 59, one of the things--and I think it goes back to the point that Gaddis Smith made--is, anytime you look at an administration, a foreign policy is composed of an aggregate of individual policies. Even though the leaders may have a common or a particular direction, it doesn't mean that all the policies are going to be consistent with that. You're going to have contradictory policies, for a variety of different reasons. In a nutshell, one would have to delve more into the bureaucracy when it comes to something like PD 59. But that's a very short response, and probably an inadequate response, on the PD 59 part of your question.

Goldman: I would like to jump in and add that I tend to agree with the thrust of Professor Rosati's argument. And with regard to Brzezinski, he, in point of fact, seemed to disagree with President Carter in the weeks immediately following the Soviet invasion on the issue of what to do about, and to, the Soviets. Brzezinski made the point that however bad the Soviet action was, however offensive and repulsive it was, it should not result in a complete collapse of the Soviet-American relationship. Carter was so angry, he was ready to do anything, and Brzezinski, for all of his reputation of being hostile to the Soviet Union, and being a Russophobe, in fact counseled caution and said we should keep some political channels open; we should not completely cut ourselves off from the Soviets. I think he was looking down the long hall, down the pike, in terms of the future of the Soviet-American relationship. So this tends to throw a different kind of light on Brzezinski--different from what seems to be the light when you read about his rhetoric at first blush.

Clifford: I think that Professor Goldman's example is a very excellent instance of a student having not learned his lessons very well. He was put into a situation where the time and experience necessary, the caution that Brzezinski offered at the time--as pointed out by Professor Goldman--is something that you don't learn easily, and sometimes you need time and background to learn that.

Q: I wonder to what extent the two different aspects of what we have come to call the Cold War--the propaganda aspect and the real or perceived threat by the Soviet Union--have contributed very importantly to the many, many foreign policy problems, and not only of the Carter administration. And I would like to say something here which can be said now: The Soviet Union, after the war, has never gone beyond expanding into any country beyond its empire.

Smith: Sort of like the Texan who had no ambition except for the next ranch, and the territory continguous to whatever he had.

Q: Considering the longer range of American policy, we seem to have done pretty well with promoting--and this dates back to Wilson, perhaps--the self-determination of nations, as long as the British empire and the French empire and other empires were concerned. But no sooner did those imperial nations abdicate their empires, than we somehow got involved in those very colonial countries, and we are still involved. We are victims of our own refusal to see that the Soviets have provided more of a power vacuum than we think they really have.

Rosati: If I understand you correctly, I'm partially or very sympathetic to what you're saying. One of the points that I was trying to make in the paper--and I wasn't really explicit about it, because the focus was on Carter--is that the Cold War years not only had a heavy anticommunist dimension but there was also a heavy underlying realpolitik dimension that preceded World War II, as you point out quite correctly; it goes way back in time, and certainly throughout Latin America since the United States has been actively involved in Latin America. A lot of people who study foreign policy make an argument--and I'll just give it very, very briefly--that American foreign policy has changed over time from idealism, whatever that means, to realism, whatever that means. But I think that's a very artificial and simplistic argument, because what you find is, for almost any administration--Kissinger maybe being the major exception to the rule, and obviously it's not his administration; we're talking Nixon-Ford here, so with the Nixon and Ford administration as being the major exception to the rule--you often see a fusion of realpolitik and some kind of moral element. It happened to be predominantly in the form of anticommunism during the 1950s and 1960s, and both of those elements were very, very powerful. In fact, the Persian Gulf situation has made me rethink the role of realpolitik throughout the history of U.S. foreign policy, because I have a very difficult time making sense of the Bush administration's response other than in terms of realpolitik, power politics, although obviously the administration is having a very difficult time selling that at a moral level. Jim Baker is now trying to sell it in terms of jobs. But I really think if you want to understand the Bush administration's policy, you almost have to see it through Kissinger's eyes.

Q: I find the idea of Carter being the first post-Cold War president intriguing. However, by the end of his administration, with the Soviets going into Afghanistan, we had the Cold War back again. Leonid Brezhnev obviously was acting in terms of Cold War years.

Rosati: Which goes back to Gaddis Smith's point: It would be interesting to see Gorbachev and Carter at the same point in time, early Carter.

Q: Brezhnev completely fouled up the situation by going into Afghanistan.   In retrospect, Afghanistan is probably the end of the Soviet empire.

Q: I have a problem with the early Carter years, particularly the NATO agreement that we pushed to increase military spending by 3 percent per year, in real terms, until 1985. Was that left over from the Ford years, or was that initiated in the Carter years?

Smith: I would tend to take more of your former position on that. Let me give you one example. There's a debate on the defense budget. Carter promised a cut in the defense budget in his 1976 campaign. Some people say he cut it; some people say he didn't. Well, it all depends on what one's definition is, because the way it operates, a president doesn't come into office in 1977 and operate on his own defense budget in 1977. He's operating on President Ford's defense project, which was submitted to Congress two years previously. And what happened was that Carter a resolution before Congress that cut Ford's initial request. So if you look at it from what Ford proposed, it was a cut. If you look at what it was from the year before, it was an increase. Is that a cut, or is that an increase? I have a feeling that your question reflects a similar kind of puzzlement.

Goldman: I was just thinking about realpolitik. It seems to me that Brzezinski and other administration officials acknowledged publicly, to make the point, that the turn toward China was meant as a message to the Soviet Union, which Carter may not have intended. Carter, to his credit, I think, saw the obvious liabilities and flaws of the United States not having gone beyond the reconciliation that was initiated by Nixon. But I think Brzezinski turned it around and made it a little bit more sinister than perhaps Carter wanted. So again, we're back to the problem of who's making policy, and is realpolitik really dead, or is it simply the point of view of some but not all members of the administration?

In that connection, I would like to give my own view of the Brzezinski-Vance conflict; I think that justice has not been done to President Carter with regard to their differences. Obviously, Carter knew them and lived with them, and obviously he didn't do anything about them. And maybe he didn't do anything about them because he didn't want to. I've always felt that what distinguished President Carter from other presidents was that he was a very intellectual person, and if given a multiple-choice examination, he would almost always say, "None of the above," because "None of the above" was absolutely correct. I think that intellectually, it probably was very stimulating and helpful to him, in terms of policy-making, to have these two advisers combating one another and coming up with different points of view--whatever impression that might have given to others. And I think maybe he lived with that situation not because he was unable to resolve the conflict, or bang heads together, but because he wanted it that way.

One more point: Bill Quandt wanted to know what else President Carter could have done with regard to mobilizing the Allies. Well, he could have done what I think Mr. Bush is not doing--and that is negotiate. He brushed aside the idea of a neutralized Afghanistan that had been put forward by the Europeans. I think that the negotiation tactic was not given fair attention in the early months of the Afghanistan crisis because the President was--understandably, and perhaps justifiably--absolutely furious with Brezhnev and wouldn't sit down with him, or his representative, to negotiate what was at stake in Afghanistan. And that bothers me about President Bush in the present crisis. And maybe, if President Bush and President Carter could sit down and decide what America could have done better in the Afghan crisis, our policy in the present Iraq crisis might be a little better. But I think the whole negotiation tack--which was what the Europeans wanted then and what they want now--was not given a fair assessment by the administration. And that was a mistake.

Quandt: Do we have time for just one more word on Brzezinski and Vance? I saw them work quite closely on the Middle East, which is a very controversial area, and in that particular area, they saw the issues more or less in the same way, as did the President. Whatever their personalities may have been, they didn't have any trouble getting along, and there was a pretty good division of labor. I think Carter valued the advice from both of them; he never screened one out at the expense of the other. So it wasn't the case that they were at loggerheads on all issues. There were two areas where they fundamentally disagreed. Brzezinski was more of a hard-liner on the Soviets than Vance, no doubt about it. And on that issue, Carter had a hard time deciding. His heart, I think, was with Vance; he wanted an accommodation with the Soviet Union, he wanted to try to develop this post-Cold War relationship, if we can talk about it at that time; he was a bit suspicious of Brzezinski's hard-line views. But there were also certain realities. Brezhnev was building up military capabilities; Carter had to take certain developments seriously. And then Afghanistan really did tip the balance. Carter was always a little bit caught between the two advisers. His hardheaded side saw some merit in what Brzezinski said; his sympathies were certainly with Vance. And I don't think he knew how to choose.

Where I think the rivalry between the two became absolutely debilitating was the Iran crisis--not the hostage part of it, but what to do about the shah's collapse and the beginnings of the revolution, before the shah had left. There, Vance and Brzezinski presented Carter with fundamentally different recommendations. Brzezinski wanted an American-supported coup d'état, led by the Iranian army, that would put down the revolution, and he didn't care much whether we kept the shah around or not. He simply wanted to crush the revolution--with force, if necessary. And he had a slew of historical analogies to peddle, to show how this might work. Vance was appalled by that notion; he thought that there was no way of saving the shah, that the shah had brought a lot of this on himself--he was indecisive, he was out of touch with his own people--and that we would simply have to ride this wave of history and hope for the best. Carter listened to them both; he didn't know what to do. He didn't know whether it was the wave of the future that couldn't be stopped, or whether giving the order to the Iranian army to shed blood would prevent this wave from cresting and might turn it back. And so he did the worst thing possible: a bit of both. It seems to me that that is the tragic moment in the Carter presidency, where the different advice he was getting paralyzed him, and he did a little bit of this and a little bit of that, and in the end he became a great hawk on Iran. In the very last few weeks, at a point when it was far too late, Carter was all in favor of the Heiser Mission telling the Iranian army to put this thing down by force.

So I think that if there was a moment when this rivalry really cost Carter, it was on Iran, and that's the part of the Iran policy that I was asking for advice on--not on how to handle the hostages. Of course, he screwed up the hostage thing by letting the shah into the United States and the whole way he handled it. But how do you stop a revolution in the making? How do you ride the wave of history? That debate was posed for him by the advisers. If I were president, I would think I would want advisers around me arguing both of those cases. The problem was, he couldn't make up his mind. Can you?

Q: Could I ask Mr. Quandt to comment on the degree to which perhaps the differences between Brzezinski and Vance--on that particular point, but also on many other points -- may have been more institutional than personal? That is, clearly Brzezinski was reflecting the attitudes of the national security complex, including the intelligence community, and Vance was clearly reflecting the point of view of the Department of State. Many of us had the feeling that Brzezinski was the conduit of the intelligence community to the president, which Vance frequently opposed.

Quandt: I think it's true that Vance represented a view that was fairly widespread in the State Department. Brzezinski, however, I don't think was anybody's puppet on this one. He was on his own, and I certainly don't think that the CIA was pushing any particular line, as far as I can recall. The CIA thought the shah was finished; there wasn't much you could do about it. Brzezinski was more, I think, influenced by his own reading of history--not Middle Eastern history but European history--and he thought that if a tough stand was taken, the revolution might be stopped. And he had any number of examples, which I can't remember now. My colleague on the National Security Council staff, Gary Sick, certainly wasn't pushing him in this direction. If anything, he agreed more with the Vance line, that this probably was nothing we could stop, and we ought to start planning for the post-shah era. Brzezinski was really on his own, and making his own recommendations to the president; this was his personal crusade. It wasn't institutionalized, as far as I could see.

Smith: May I add a footnote to that comment--a bookish footnote? The individual that Brzezinski admired was Crane Brinton. Crane Brinton's book, *Anatomy of Revolution*, contains a marvelously circular argument that no regime in history threatened by revolution has been overthrown by that revolution if it was tough enough to suppress it. It doesn't tell you anything, but it appears as great wisdom.

Clifford: I'd like to make one comment about Quandt's remarks, with respect to "he couldn't make up his mind. Can you?" Being president requires that you do make up your mind. It's not a question of you can't; you *must* make up your mind. You're the leader. You need to have people around you who can argue for you, that's true; it's good to have the arguments set forth and placed in front of you. But when you're the leader, you must make up your mind.

HUMAN RIGHTS

5

Free Elections Based on Human Rights Protection: The Carter Contribution

HENRY F. CAREY

Jimmy Carter's human rights initiatives are generally remembered favorably around the world. Other presidents--Wilson, Franklin Roosevelt, and Kennedy--also promoted freedom in terms of the language of basic rights, but without achieving realization in significant measure. While Carter's success during his four years in office was also circumscribed, scholars should note the continuing impact of the human rights movement generally. One dimension of the movement--the emergence of freely elected governments--is an accomplished fact, an international norm, and an important component of U.S. foreign policy. Free elections are a human right promoted by President Carter, the first world leader to do so.

In accepting the Democratic presidential nomination in July 1976, Carter declared:

Ours was the first nation to dedicate itself clearly to basic moral and philosophical principles . . . a revolutionary development that captured the imagination of mankind.

At the 1977 Notre Dame Commencement, President Carter made his most explicit assertions on human rights:

Because we know that democracy works, we can reject the arguments of those rulers who deny human rights to their people. . . . We are confident that democracy's example will be compelling, and so we seek to bring that example closer to those from whom in the past few years we have been separated and who are not yet convinced about the advantages of our kind of life. We are confident that democratic methods are the most effective.

In his farewell address, President Carter sought an impact that Washington and Eisenhower had achieved on similar occasions, regarding "foreign entanglements" and the "military-industrial complex," respectively. Carter exhorted the incoming Reagan administration to continue emphasizing human rights. Even though he himself had occasionally found it necessary to deemphasize rights, such as when advocating SALT II's ratification, Carter left office sounding the same note as he had on his arrival:

America must always stand for these basic human rights. America did not invent human rights. Human rights invented America. Ours was the first nation in the history of the world to be founded explicitly on such an idea.

By the 1990s, the United States had developed a practice of exerting pressure for reasonably fair elections as a response to regime polarization. This has acted to the detriment of authoritarian allies like the Philippines' Ferdinand Marcos and to the benefit of self-avowed anti-imperialist socialists like Haiti's Jean-Bertrand Aristide. The fairness of the October 24, 1990, election in Pakistan became a condition for the continuation of some $500 million in U.S. assistance, of which Pakistan is the third largest recipient.[1] Normalization of U.S. relations with the Sandinista government and reduced support for the Contras appeared to have stemmed from the improved political rights of the Nicaraguan opposition and the credible February 25, 1990, elections, conditioned on an end to support for the Salvadoran rebels. Whereas past U.S. support for authoritarian regimes had often harmed civil and political rights, U.S. promotion of free elections under Reagan's foreign policy usually, if unpredictably, had the opposite effect.

Although international law and human rights will continue to ebb and flow in importance, human rights generally and one right in particular--to free and periodic elections--have come to enjoy a seemingly permanent significance in international politics and world public opinion. While many have contributed to this historic development, few can claim a more lasting impact than President Carter. Monitors of human rights and of the election process are only Carter's most obvious legacies. He initiated a liberalization policy applying to friendly authoritarian regimes whose gross human rights abuses were both destabilizing and delegitimizing, as well as to more rigid totalitarian regimes.

President Carter's efforts admittedly were not specifically focused on electoral promotion. The veritable industry of election monitoring was not an offshoot but an inevitable consequence of the international human rights movement generally and of nongovernmental human rights organizations inspired by the possibility that U.S. foreign policy would take rights seriously for the first time.

Ironically, Jeane Kirkpatrick's doctrine, which criticized the Carter liberalization policy toward authoritarian allies, was responsible for the very continuation of Carter's policy under Reagan.[2] In passing, she made a crucial qualification of her overall assertion that the United States should not undermine authoritarian allies with human rights pressure when their political survival is threatened by apparently totalitarian movements seeking power through force. Kirkpatrick added *except when there are alternatives to the authoritarian rule.* U.S. policy may encourage "a process of liberalization and democratization, provided that the effort is not made at a time when the incumbent government is fighting for its life against violent adversaries, and that proposed reforms are aimed at producing gradual change rather than perfect democracy overnight." Human rights pressure generally promoted human rights protection for a noncommunist political opposition as well as demands for the right to free elections, giving an opposition a chance to win power in a nonviolent fashion. Perhaps unwittingly, Kirkpatrick provided the intellectual justification for the Reagan administration to abandon its long-standing policy, which Franklin Roosevelt encapsulated in his dictum about the Somoza dynasty. "He's an SOB, but he's our SOB."

At first blush, most could consider Reagan administration methods--like Contra funding, mining harbors and embargoes--to be the antithesis of human rights promotion.[3] Indeed, it is doubtful that President Carter would have used all these techniques to promote liberalization. Reagan and Bush have clearly been more prepared to use force to promote human rights, a seeming contradiction that is beyond the scope of this paper. A significant change is the bipartisan consensus in U.S. foreign policy over the past three administrations in support of the goal of free elections. Despite the nearly barbarous methods of Reagan and Bush in Central America, for example, it is free elections, not dictatorship, that is the object of U.S. support.

Many have belittled this change in policy.[4] Yet the promotion of free elections to create a quasi-democratic alternative to authoritarian allies has had liberalizing impacts on both U.S. foreign policy and authoritarian regimes. Despite his rhetoric of realpolitik and his militarization policies, Reagan also continued and expanded Carter's human rights policy, in such a way that his own policies helped to inaugurate democracy in authoritarian regimes in Latin America and Asia, and to enhance the transition from totalitarianism to authoritarianism in Eastern Europe and Nicaragua.

By the time of the Bush administration, the normal U.S. policy was no longer automatic support for a friendly authoritarian dictator, the prevailing U.S. policy since World War II and particulary since President Johnson supported the 1964 coup in Brazil. The current U.S. policy, which President Carter can be credited with initiating, is to sponsor democratization by holding free elections under conditions of imperfect but improving human rights protection.

Carter's contributions were indispensable to the initiation of the trend to world democratization that has occurred since the Andean transitions of the late 1970s. This is so even though he was not necessarily aware of what he was starting or that the human rights consequences would be even greater under his successor. Carter's approach was not just to promote human rights in the abstract, hoping that military or revolutionary governments would provide more space to opposition groups. He insisted that none of the authoritarian regimes prevalent during his presidency could be ultimately expected to protect human rights and that these regimes were implicitly illegal under international law. Democratically elected governments do not necessarily gain control over military and security forces that are so often agents of violent human rights violations.[5] The republican norm, and a probability under electoral democracies (except under conditions of insurgency, succession, or civil war), is civilian supremacy and military accountability. When human rights are not well protected, civil society can, and is likely to try to, elect a government that can protect them.

Obviously, elections and human rights have not been the only factors in inspiring the decline of authoritarianism and the rise of worldwide electoral legitimacy.[6] In all the recent commotion about changes in the communist world since 1989, it should be acknowledged that these are only part of an overall democratization trend that began during Carter's presidency and has continued, from the Eastern bloc to Africa. Many authoritarian regimes in Southern Europe, East Asia, and Latin America initiated transitions toward democracy after Carter left office in January 1981. He has received little credit for influencing the international environment that encouraged these transitions.

The human right to representative government based on a secret and universal ballot is found in most basic human rights treaties except the African Charter. Article 21(3) of the 1948 Universal Declaration of Human Rights enacted by the U.N. General Assembly states:

The will of the people shall be the basis of the authority of government; this will shall be expressed in periodic and genuine elections which shall be by universal and equal suffrage and shall be held by secret vote or by equivalent free voting procedures.

President Carter signed two international human rights covenants in 1977 but failed to convince the Senate to ratify them, making the United States prominent among the countries that still have not done so. Nevertheless, Carter was solidly behind them, including the International Covenant on Civil and Political Rights, whose Article 25 states:

Every citizen shall have the right and opportunity . . . without unreasonable restrictions:
  a) to take part in the conduct of public affairs, directly or through freely chosen representatives;
  b) to vote and to be elected at genuine periodic elections which shall be held by secret ballot, guaranteeing the free expression of the will of the electors.

Other presidents had discussed human rights. Franklin D. Roosevelt and John F. Kennedy mentioned them, Roosevelt in the Atlantic Charter and both in their inaugural addresses. But they never touted human rights as a basis for U.S. foreign policy. They emphasized military solutions to protecting freedom, while Carter was as likely to employ the carrot as the stick. They were also more likely to give precedence to U.S. national interests where they seemed to conflict with the rights of foreigners.

Nor was Carter the first politician to emphasize democratization as a human right. Congress in the mid-1970s enacted human rights legislation that required termination of U.S. military assistance to gross and systematic human rights violators. Daniel Patrick Moynihan, as president Ford's ambassador to the United Nations, undertook an exuberant campaign in the 1975 General Assembly session against members that were actually dictatorships. He asserted that they lacked the moral credibility to speak on behalf of the citizens they represented.

In the context of these antecedents, Carter, as a newly elected president, became the first to assert unabashedly that human rights were a main goal of his foreign policy. On January 21, 1977, he proclaimed, "Our commitment to human rights must be absolute."

In order to promote these aims, Carter insisted that it was the business of the United States, as well as of international organizations and nongovernmental organizations, to monitor violations. This view directly confronted the traditional notion that human rights were strictly a matter of internal policy. At the same time, the United Nations began criticizing countries other than South Africa and Israel for human rights violations, beginning with Chile in 1977.

The promotion of human rights by these different groups necessarily required intrusive monitoring of the domestic affairs of other countries. External vigilance of the treatment of opposition groups meant that the concept that they enjoyed rights became more understood and acceptable.

In dealing with states seeking to hold power by suppressing oppositions, Carter's was the first U.S. administration to nudge regimes to accept oppositions by recognizing their rights, or risk losing U.S. military assistance. President Carter's horizons encompassed all human rights, including foreign monitoring of elections. He thus helped strengthen opposition to the point that the possibility of a free election became conceivable for the first time in decades in those countries where the United States had leverage. Longtime Carter Latin American affairs adviser Robert Pastor wrote:

With President Carter's personal leadership, the United States became identified with a hemisphere-wide movement for freedom and democracy. This movement gained strength, and within ten years military government would be swept from power in all but two nations in South America.[7]

Carter understood that promoting democracy and promoting human rights were not processes independent of each other. It would have been illogical to condemn human rights violations without considering the political system in which they occurred. Democracy was not a panacea, but it did offer the possibility of greater protection for opposition movements. Human rights violations were inevitable in authoritarian regimes whose existence was threatened by legitimate oppositions.

The notion of interrelationship between human rights and democracy was subsequently adopted by others. The Inter-American Institute of Human Rights in San José, Costa Rica, for example, was founded in 1980, with the slogan "Human rights are impossible without democracy, and democracy is impossible without human rights." This principle does not assure that democracy will guarantee human rights protection, but democracy is certainly a necessary, if not a sufficient, condition, to use academic parlance. Elections are a necessary, but not a sufficient, condition for establishing democracy. Then it follows that fair elections are a necessary, but not a sufficient, condition for promoting human rights (a basic mathematical principle of transitivity). Stated more pragmatically, free elections in developing countries were not possible without legalizing political parties, trade unions, opposition newspapers, radio and televison stations, or counting votes honestly--in short, by promoting democracy.

This notion was more controversially advocated by Reagan administration officials like Elliott Abrams. His emphasis on electoral democracy was criticized for hypocritical overlooking of human rights violations, for example, by the Salvadoran military in its counterinsurgengy or by "democratic" guerrillas like the former Nicaraguan Contras or the UNITA forces in Angola.[8] Yet in these controversial elections, there were tremendous democratic counterpressures to authoritarian institutions and practices. To hold fair elections, domestic human rights organizations, the news media, and political parties all insisted that their rights be respected, and gradually they were enhanced, albeit still incompletely. However imperfect the electoral conditions, political organizations acquired the capacity to seek to win elections through more balanced competition, not only in the technical honesty of registration and balloting but also in the freeness of expression, association, and information. By the end of 1988, even Abrams was stressing that the nascent democracies supported by the United States still had a long way to go before becoming democratic.[9]

Carter's idealism was neither ephemeral nor unrealistic. His was not, despite the rhetoric, an absolute human rights standard, which would have been destructive of certain other U.S. interests linked to the predominant authoritarian regimes, some of whom were key allies. He nonetheless did give more weight to human rights than any other president.

Some allies lost their military assistance because of their violations. The only alternative for military governments like Argentina and Guatemala was to hold fair elections and leave power, which they refused to do at the time. Anastazio Somoza declined to hold elections in 1978, and the loss of U.S. assistance was crucial. Then the Sandinistas promised to hold fair elections before taking power in July 1979, and were therefore initially recognized by the Carter government. When it became clear by April of the following year that they were only consolidating the power of the Sandinista Front and limiting the human rights of other civilian groups that had been participating in the junta, Carter ended the U.S. assistance that had initially been so generous. The Sandinistas showed no signs of holding fair elections soon.

Likewise, the new ruling Salvadoran military faction promised to hold fair elections when it took power on October 15, 1979. It was replaced by a more hard-line military faction three months later, and Carter cut off assistance. It was restored only in his final month in office, after a further communist threat to overthrow the government, which had renewed a pledge to hold elections, albeit in wartime conditions. Thus, a pattern emerged that U.S. assistance would not be continued in the face of human rights violations, unless there were signs that a democratic transition would be initiated, with some assurance that the opposition would be legitimated and the need to suppress its rights reduced.

Where there was the possibility of an election, as in Zimbabwe, Peru, and Ecuador, Carter supported fair elections. Where the degree of regime polarization had not yet reached crisis proportions, as in Argentina, Haiti, and South Korea, he offered moral support to the struggling opposition movements, enhancing their legitimacy.

Because democracy was cast as a universal, not an American, ideal, many countries antagonistic to the United States came to accept democratic movements as part of their human rights obligations. Most countries in the world claimed to allow a legal opposition, often asserted to be only a minority. In the new human rights environment, the only way to prove this was through an open electoral contest. Some states eventually became enmeshed in their own spiders' webs, as the oppositions developed more support.

Of course, the democratization that ensued proved that human rights are not always improved, especially if elections fail to end a civil war. The legitimation of new regimes that continue to oppress civilian oppositions beclouds elections, but that subject is beyond the scope of this paper. Whether elections solve regime crises or not, they do enhance some of the rights and influence of oppositions.

Carter identified U.S. interests with helping governments promote human rights and democracy and trying to replace governments that refused to do so. Because he saw human rights as a binding commitment of all governments, such replacement coincided with U.S. interests. In his *Memoirs*, he noted, "It was time for us to capture the imagination of the world again."[10] Carter's contribution was to couch such a campaign that benefited the United States in terms that were comprehensible to the rest of the world. Many heard, understood, and embraced the more general Carter human rights policy of predicating U.S. support on the human rights practices of a regime, not just on its ideology and alliances. A U.S. administration that would really sacrifice its national interests to respect universal standards was unprecedented to the extent practiced by Carter.

Some viewed Carter as being too principled and others as not enough so. Pastor commented on these contrary reactions:

Without a slogan, the [Carter] Administration's approach became known not by its principles but by its salient features--human rights and democracy by those who were sympathetic to the administration and the revolutions in Nicaragua and Grenada and the problem of Cuban refugees by those who were not.[11]

Those who regarded his foreign policy as unacceptably weak emphasized geopolitical setbacks from the Persian Gulf across Africa to Central America. Human rights standards were only part of the criticism of his policy that is best epitomized in Kirkpatrick's influential article.[12]

Contempt for Carter's politics, including the human rights emphasis that was only partly responsible for these setbacks, should be kept in perspective. More important was the belief by citizens in countries like Nicaragua and Iran that their new leaders were telling the truth when they promised to establish liberal, democratic republics. Furthermore, events in Afghanistan, Angola, and Ethiopia were largely unrelated to human rights. Finally, the solution to these and other conflicts in Cambodia and Palestine have been pursued along paths reminiscent of Carter's criteria of human rights and free elections.

President Carter's visible monitoring and evaluation of recent elections represent the fulfillment of his presidential efforts to include freedom and reconciliation by promoting democratic practices.[13] Like Richard Nixon, who has written a number of impressive books, the Democratic ex-president continues to haunt those who taunted him as president. The reputations of both have improved, partly because their recent activities cast light on similar themes and efforts of their presidencies, under-appreciated at the time.

The omnipresent president, once accused of "losing Nicaragua and Iran," has been charged by the U.S. right wing with enhancing Soviet interests. Jack Fowler of *The National Review*, in referring to the 1990 UNO victory in Nicaragua, commented:

Carter has also left observer staff chief Robert Pastor, the Carter White House's Latin American expert who set the disastrous policy that helped the Sandinistas gain power in 1979, to advise Mrs. Chamorro during the transition period.[14]

Carter's advice, in those circumstances, could only be controversial in such a divided country.

As the surprising vote returns showed the defeat of the Sandinistas, Nicaraguan President Daniel Ortega requested a meeting with Carter. The latter then successfully urged the Sandinistas to recognize the will of the people and to hand over the government. Ortega had asserted several times during the previous year that the Sandinistas could "lose an election but never lose power." Carter helped convince Ortega to announce two days later that he would hand over formal power despite the opposition in his government. Along with the United Nations and Organization of American States representatives, Carter helped to facilitate the Toncontín transition accords between the outgoing Sandinista government and the new Chamorro administration, which helped achieve a negotiated end to the nine-year civil war.

Even though Reagan's admirers would find the notion comical, Jimmy Carter deserves to bask in some of the glory that Richard Viguerie's new right and Norman Podhoretz's neoconservatives have claimed. They mistakenly assert that the Reagan policy was the first to emphasize democratization as the engine of human rights improvements. Joshua Murchavik argues that the Carter government promoted human rights without considering a country's potential for a democratic regime change or threats from communists. Short-term violations were less important than the type of regime that was evolving:

President Carter erred in not recognizing, or pretending not to recognize, that the cause of human rights rested above all on the cause of democracy. But people around the world readily enough recognized the relationship.[15]

Similarly, then Secretary of State George Shultz pointed to a contrast:

The Reagan Administration approaches the human rights question on a deeper level. . . . We have a duty not only to react to specific cases but also to understand and to seek to shape the basic structural conditions in which human rights are more likely to flourish. This is why President Reagan has placed so much emphasis on democracy.[16]

Both Carter and Reagan emphasized democratization by allies such as the Philippines to excuse violations of human rights while more readily criticizing violations by enemies like the Soviet Union. Critics have overlooked how Carter in fact made electoral democracy acceptable to the developing world because human rights standards were more equally applicable to all types of regimes. Carter was more apt to ignore national interests than Reagan, as in South Korea, where U.S. remarks were considered unusually blunt and unwelcome by the Park government.[17]

President Carter foreshadowed the democratization trends that followed his government when he wrote that he

hoped and believed that the expansion of human rights might be the wave of the future of the rest of the world, and I wanted the United States to be on the crest of that movement.[18]

Pastor emphasized that Carter was particularly interested in democratization even if the U.S. interests in the country involved were marginal:

Carter's vision was a tolerant one, that aimed to align the United States with changes that had occurred in the world, most notably the demand for respect in the Third World.[19]

The main difference between Carter and the Republicans who followed him concerned timing. Carter appeared to promote regime liberalization first, instead of elections first, because rulers were not yet ready to compromise with civil society and offer to hold elections. Yet it is questionable whether so many countries would have moved toward electoral democracy if the pressure of human rights movements had not been initiated. Carter stimulated this evolution by promoting the new international infrastructure of human rights principles, which civil society leaders learned they could demand.

Human rights provided the legal and ethical foundation for oppositions to do battle. The human rights movement has engendered greater popular attempts to minimize authoritarian control rather than submitting or deferring to its authority. Following Carter's efforts, a state lacking an electoral sanction lost legitimacy. Rulers who renounced competitive elections had to convince their citizens that hereditary, religious, or revolutionary reasons excused their absence. Leaders in Iran, Indonesia, Mexico, and the Soviet Union have had to explain, ultimately without success, why elections have been only partly competitive. Their day of reckoning is probably not far off. What is impressive is the large number of countries that have already decided that the only resolution to the crisis of illegitimacy and human rights violations is the compromise of holding elections.

In his 1990 New Year's Day inauguration, New York City Mayor David Dinkins called human rights "the most important idea of this generation." The first black mayor of the largest U.S. city knew that his election was possible only because a human rights movement, then known as the civil rights movement, had laid the foundations for electoral changes for disenfranchised and oppressed black citizens. The human rights movement internationally played the same role for the new generation of elected leaders in the 1980s and beyond.

Before Carter, the international human rights movement was in its infancy. As president, Carter stood for a policy that governments that became less repressive were not only more trustworthy at home and abroad, but also were more likely to hold democratic elections in due course. Otherwise, all the talk about human rights improvements by regimes was untested. Without Carter, ours would have been a different world, with particularistic views of rights and legitimacy. Now, elections have become the sine qua non for resolving disputes within and among nations.

Promoting elections was a partly intended outcome of Carter's path-breaking human rights policy. While the policy was not specifically focused on free and periodic elections, they were its ineluctable consequence. Carter's more recent monitoring of elections in Panama, Nicaragua, the Dominican Republic, and Haiti was a logical sequel to his earlier efforts. He may not have realized what he set in motion when he announced the importance of human rights in his inaugural address, but he helped to make countries better off and U.S. foreign policy less unenlightened by insisting that elections help promote human rights, and human rights improve elections.

NOTES

1. The Mikulski Amendment was not actually responsible for the October 1990 moratorium in U.S. funding, which resulted from the Pressler Amendment, relating to Pakistan's effort to develop nuclear weaponry.

2. Jeane Kirkpatrick, "Dictatorships and Double Standards," *Commentary,* November 1979, p. 34ff, asserts that totalitarian regimes could not become authoritarian. The collapse of East European communism would fail to overturn her thesis only if external pressure was primarily responsible for the transition in totalitarian regimes. Kirkpatrick may have based her dichotomy on Juan Linz's typology differentiating these two types of regime. He shared her view that totalitarian regimes did not change because of largely internal forces. See Juan Linz, "Totalitarian and Authoritarian Regimes," in Fred I. Greenstein and Nelson Polsby, eds., *Handbook of Political Science* (Reading: Addison-Wesley, 1975), vol. 3, pp. 175-411. It could be argued that the suddenness of 1989's events shows how unlikely totalitarian liberalization can be. What Kirkpatrick really feared, it seems, was not totalitarianism per se but the threat of a Soviet-allied rival force. To this extent, her explanation is flawed because it is based on differences in regime type, not forces of international politics, or at least the relationship between these two.

3. The Sandinista regime argued, and the World Court concurred, that these methods violated international law. Even the embargo, which proved successful in South Africa, was considered a violation of economic and social rights.

4. See, for example, Frank Broadhead and Edward S. Herman, *Demonstration Elections* (Boston: South End Press, 1984).

5. See, for example, Alfred Stepan, *Rethinking Military Politics: Brazil and the Southern Cone* (Princeton: Princeton University Press, 1988), especially the chapter on military prerogatives.

6. The decline of leftist dictatorships has been attributed by some to President Reagan's firm resolve to confront Soviet imperialism, U.S. rearmament, and internal economic decline (as predicted by George Kennan in his famous 1949 "X" article in *Foreign Affairs*). Others, like Arno J. Mayer, cite declining foreign dangers and internal pressures. See his "Europe After the Great Thaw," *The Nation,* April 9, 1990, p. 490. Analysts of earlier transitions in Latin American and southern Europe emphasize internal decisions and factors, not U.S. foreign policy. See Guillermo O'Donnell, Philippa C. Schmitter, and Laurence Whitehead, eds., *Transitions from Authoritarian Rule* (Baltimore: Johns Hopkins University Press, 1986). Jorge Dominguez has noted the importance of "demonstration impacts in democratization." See his article "Latin American Politics" in Samuel P. Huntington and Myron Weiner, eds., *What is Political Development?* (Boston: Little, Brown, 1987).

7. Robert A. Pastor, "The Carter Administration and Latin America: A Test of Principle," in John D. Martz, ed., *United States Policy in Latin America: A Quarter Century of Crisis and Challenge* (Lincoln: University of Nebraska Press, 1988), p. 91.

8. The human rights practices of these Reagan-supported groups may in fact have been not much worse than those of the groups they were fighting. For example, a November 1989 report by Americas Watch documented seventy-four murders and fourteen disappearances by the Sandinistas in northern Nicaragua from 1987 to early 1989. The point should have been that the violations were unacceptably high on both sides.

9. Interview, C-SPAN, December 26, 1988.

10. Jimmy Carter, *Keeping Faith: Memoirs of a President* (New York: Bantam Books, 1982), p. 144.

11. Pastor, op. cit., p. 91.

12. Kirkpatrick, op. cit.

13. He condemned Panama's electoral fraud of May 7, 1979; brokered improvements in Nicaragua's campaign that ended on February 25, 1990; and controversially certified the Balaguer victory in the Dominican Republic on May 22, 1990.

14. Jack Fowler, *The National Review*, April 1, 1990, p. 38.

15. Joshua Murchavik, "Dictatorships and Single Standards," *Crisis,* February 1990, p. 21.

16. George Shultz, address at the Washington Day banquet of the Creve Coeur Club of Illinois, February 22, 1984. Published as U.S. Department of State, *Current Policy*, no. 551 (1984).

17. See, for example, William H. Gleysteen, Jr., "Korea: A Special Target of American Concern," in David D. Newsom, ed., *The Diplomacy of Human Rights* (Lanham, MD: University Press of America, 1986), pp. 85-100.

18. Carter, op. cit., p. 144.

19. Robert A. Pastor, "The Canal Treaties: The Other Debate on Central America," *Caribbean Review*, 15, no. 4 (Spring 1987):38.

6

American-Romanian Relations, 1977-1981:
A Case Study in Carter's Human Rights Policy

JOSEPH F. HARRINGTON

The 1974 Trade Act, initially designed to facilitate trade with the Soviet Union, was passed with language requiring all nonmarket economy countries to implement a freedom-of-emigration policy if they wanted their products to receive most-favored-nation (MFN) treatment from the United States. While the administration decried this provision, known as Section 402 (more commohly called the Jackson-Vanik Amendment), the White House did manage to get one concession. Jackson agreed that if a communist country could annually give the president of the United States oral assurance that its policies would lead to freer emigration, the president could convey this assurance to Congress and request the waiver of Section 402. Congressional approval would mean that the products of the country in question could receive, or continue to receive, MFN treatment. Section 402 required that this waiver request process be annual, permit hearings in both houses of Congress, and enable either house to deny MFN by passing a resolution of disapproval. If neither house took any action to disapprove the waiver request, MFN would automatically be extended for another year. If a communist country could annually assure the president that its policies would lead to emigration, the president could convey this assurance to Congress and request waiver of Section 402 of the Trade Act, which was the Jackson-Vanik amendment. If neither house approved a resolution of disapproval, MFN would be automatically renewed for another year.[1]

Moscow refused to accept the Jackson-Vanik language, viewing it as a deliberate attempt to intervene in its internal affairs. This refusal opened the door for Romania. Bucharest had tried since 1964 to secure MFN treatment, and nearly succeeded in 1971. Wilbur Mills, the controversial and powerful chairman of the House Ways and Means Committee, indicated that all he needed was a call from the president, and he would ensure that Romania received MFN.[2] In spite of his warm feelings toward Romania, Nixon would not make the call and incur an IOU with Mills.

However, Bucharest quickly seized the moment and signed a trade agreement with Washington in 1975 that included provisions for MFN treatment of Romanian exports to the United States. President Nicolae Ceausescu quickly assured President Ford that Bucharest's policies would lead to freer emigration. Ford relayed the assurances to

Congress and requested a waiver of Section 402 of the Trade Act of 1974. Congress approved the waiver in 1975, and an annual process that continued through 1988.

This waiver process serves as a wonderful vehicle to measure President Carter's approach to human rights during his four years in office. Each year he had to request a waiver, justify the request, and have administration witnesses explain the White House position at hearings before the relevant House and Senate subcommittees.

Jimmy Carter's arrival in the White House certainly appeared to be a victory for human rights supporters. When he announced his presidential candidacy in December 1974, he said "that this country set a standard within the community of nations of courage, compassion, integrity, and dedication to basic human rights and freedoms."[3] Throughout his campaign he repeated his interest in human rights. On January 20, 1977, the new president used his inaugural address to tell the American people that his government was committed to human rights. He also had broadcast a global message stating that while the United States "alone cannot guarantee the basic rights of every human being to be free of poverty and hunger and disease and political repression . . . the United States can and will take the lead in such effort."[4]

Carter's new secretary of state, Cyrus Vance, shared the president's commitment to improving human rights.[5] He had indicated his views in a memo to Carter in October 1976. Following the inauguration, he told a press conference that rather than being "strident or polemical," he preferred to use "quiet diplomacy" to improve an individual nation's human rights practices.[6] While critics would argue that Carter was inconsistent in his human rights policy, and was "too quiet" in his diplomacy,[7] the new president did make some significant changes. He upgraded the Office of Human Affairs to the Bureau of Human Rights and Humanitarian Affairs, headed by an assistant secretary of state, Patricia Derian.[8] He also appointed Deputy Secretary of State Warren Christopher to lead a committee to actively coordinate foreign aid programs with a country's human rights practices. Within a short time, the "Christopher Committee" forced many administration officials to become more aware of the relationship between human rights violations and America's foreign policy.[9]

Congress, too, had a human rights watchdog. Don Fraser of Minnesota chaired the House Subcommittee on International Organizations and Movements, and between 1973 and 1977, he held over 150 hearings with testimony from more than 500 witnesses. While the emphasis was on countries that were involved in "gross violations" of human rights, the fact of the hearings and the amount of testimony, much of it from government witnesses, educated many people on the need for America to take a more active role to improve human rights practices worldwide.[10] These hearings, coupled with the Carter admnistration's commitment to human rights, provided a new climate for Romanian-American relations.

Within the first few months of the Carter presidency, stories emanated from Romania detailing a number of human rights abuses. The Romanian dissident Paul Goma sent an open letter to the Helsinki Conference on Security and Cooperation in Europe (CSCE) in Belgrade, criticizing Ceausescu's indifference to human rights. This caused a stir among some American congressmen, most notably Representative Edward Koch of New York.[11] However, Koch's efforts went for naught. On March 4, a devastating earthquake struck Romania and quickly diverted congressional attention from human rights violations to humanitarian assistance. By mid-April, Carter had signed legislation providing $20 million worth of aid to Bucharest.[12]

In May, the Senate Judiciary Committee sent a staff team to visit Romania and make a firsthand report on the earthquake devastation. The team, led by Dale deHaan, counsel to the committee, and Jerry Tinker, staff consultant, arrived in Bucharest on May 1 and departed May 4. The two traveled extensively throughout the affected area. They talked with American Ambassador Harry Barnes, and discussed the earthquake and other elements of American-Romanian relations with President Ceausescu and Minister of Foreign Affairs George Macovescu.[13] Without question, they told Ceausescu of Congress's growing concern about Romania's human rights practices. They particularly stressed the present importance of the issue since Congress would soon consider the president's request to extend MFN for another year.

Ceausescu understood deHaan and Tinker's warning. Within a week of their departure, he issued an amnesty providing full pardons for individuals serving less than five years in prison and partial pardons for those interned from five to ten years. The amnesty affected about twenty-eight thousand persons, including political prisoners and dissidents, such as Paul Goma.[14]

Meanwhile, the State Department and the Treasury gathered data and recommended that the president ask Congress to extend the waiver of Section 402 of the Trade Act of 1974. On June 2, Carter submitted his first waiver recommendation. In his request to Congress, the president noted the increased trade between the two countries, and emphasized Bucharest's relative independence from Moscow. Further, the waiver extension would provide Washington with continued access to government officials in Romania who could facilitate family reunification and improved emigration practices. Carter did indicate that his administration would monitor Romanian emigration, and if Bucharest's performance did not comply with the intent of the waiver, "I would want to reconsider my recommendation." Further, the president promised that he would bring to the attention of the Romanian government "any actions or emigration trends" that did not conform to the assurances they had made in the past to "treat emigration in a humanitarian manner."[15] These latter statements were the first time a president had shown a willingness to reconsider the waiver request in the event of Romanian noncompliance.

The presidential waiver request meant that either house of Congress had until September 3 to disapprove the recommendation, otherwise, the waiver would continue for another twelve months and, with it, Romanian MFN. Ceausescu totally understood this legislative timetable, and over the years there developed an annual summer ritual between Washington and Bucharest. The high point of the ritual normally was a significant increase in the number of people permitted to emigrate from Romania to the United States, Israel, and elsewhere. For several years, the May through October figures were higher than those of other months.

In anticipation of the House hearings, the administration sent members of the Subcommittee on Trade several documents. A memo dated June 29 explained Romania's emigration practices and noted that in spite of a developing cyclical pattern, there was an overall moderate upward trend in the number of emigration visas granted since January 1975.[16] The second document was a synopsis of Romania's emigration procedures prepared by the American Embassy in Bucharest. At the outset, an applicant was aware that Bucharest officially discouraged emigration. Therefore, the applicant was viewed as either a deserter, an ingrate, or possibly a traitor. As for family reunification, Bucharest believed that family members living outside Romania should return home. With these standards as starting points, the government's emigration process was, as could be anticipated, burdensome and time-consuming.[17]

The July 18 hearing was lengthy. The administration sent five representatives to support the president, and of the more than twenty witnesses who followed, the vast majority favored the waiver. Representatives from Control Data Corporation, Island Creek Coal Company, Moody International, and Promethean Corporation joined with Congressmen John Breaux of Louisiana, Edward Derwinski and Paul Findley of Illinois, and Christopher Dodd of Connecticut in support of MFN renewal. While Jacob Birnbaum of the Center for Russian and East European Jewry used the hearings to encourage emigration, and remained neutral on the issue of the presidential request, Rabbi Israel Miller, representing the Conference of Presidents of Major American Jewish Organizations, urged approval of the request for one more year as a means to increase Romanian emigration. However, he added a caveat. If Jewish emigration did not improve during the next year, his organization would not support another presidential waiver.[18]

The Senate Finance Committee's Subcommittee on International Trade also held hearings on the waiver request, and while fewer witnesses testified, their statements corroborated the evidence presented at the House hearing. Since there were few reasons given to deny Romania continued MFN, neither house took any negative action, thereby automatically extending Romanian MFN through July 1978.

Congressional approval of the president's first waiver request was due to a number of factors. First, the earthquake had produced a humanitarian response to Romania, one of sympathy rather than of punishment. Second, Carter's identification with human rights gave greater credibility to his assurances to Congress that the waiver would lead to freer emigration practices. Third, the president's pledge to monitor Romania's behavior and his willingness to reconsider his position if Bucharest failed to keep its assurances won support for his recommendation. Fourth, American-Romanian trade continued to expand. Fifth, Romania's foreign policy appeared to challenge Soviet efforts to control Eastern Europe's behavior, and Congress wanted to reward Bucharest for her autonomy.[19] And sixth, the need for an annual renewal of the emigration waiver, and therefore continued MFN, appeared to many to give Washington leverage to negotiate improved emigration and human rights practices in Romania.

In continuing to set its own mark on government, the Carter administration reviewed its foreign service postings and decided to appoint a new ambassador to Romania. On September 27, Carter nominated O. Rudolph Aggrey to replace Harry Barnes as ambassador.[20] Aggrey's appointment made a statement that, if a defector's story is to be believed, did not please Ceausescu. According to Ion Pacepa, who fled Romania in 1978, the fact that Aggrey was black infuriated Ceausescu.[21] The Romanian president ignored the fact that he was a career diplomat who had already served as envoy to Senegal and Gambia.[22] Undoubtedly, one reason Carter chose Aggrey was to remind Ceausescu that the White House believed in human rights and human equality. Congress approved Aggrey's appointment unanimously.

In January 1978, Karoly Kiraly, an ethnic Hungarian and former member of the Romanian Communist Party hierarchy, wrote a memo in which he claimed the Communist Party discriminated against Hungarians and other minorities. A copy of the memo reached the West and appeared in the *Manchester Guardian*, the *London Times*, and the *Washington Post*. Kiraly accused the government of fraudulent behavior. It preached noble principles but pursued discriminatory practices that limited educational, cultural, and employment opportunities of non-Romanians.[23]

To counter the Kiraly memo and other stories circulating in the West about Romanian discrimination, Ceausescu invited Amnesty International to visit the country in February 1978. The government cooperated with the human rights monitoring organization, and the subsequent report did not indicate any particularly abnormal discriminatory practices.[24] In March, Ceausescu told a Joint Plenum of the Councils of Working People of Magyar and German Nationality that "a number of shortcomings still exist in our activity, that mistakes are still made," but he assured the delegates that the Communist Party would "eliminate" those errors."[25] He also alluded to Kiraly and other dissidents, describing them as people who had to "cover up their helplessness . . . by . . . speaking ill in every way" of those who were able and willing to sacrifice to continue the struggle toward communism.[26]

Meanwhile, human rights continued to be a major topic of discussion in Washington. The Carter administration had struggled for over a year to develop a human rights policy, as distinct from human rights statements. Finally, on February 17, 1978, Carter signed Presidential Directive 30, which defined America's policy. The elements were not new, but for the first time they were combined into a single statement. The United States set priorities in its human rights objectives, foremost being no support to governments guilty of gross violations of human rights, unless there were "exceptional circumstances." Further, Washington would work on a global scale to reduce government violations of people's civil, political, economic, and social rights. Finally, America would reward those countries which improved their human rights practices with generous aid programs.[27]

In practice, Carter viewed human rights violations differently when they occurred in a country governed by a rightist dictatorship and in a state under communist control. He believed that American condemnation of human rights violations in conservative regimes could be more effective "than in Communist countries, where repression was so complete that it could not easily be observed or rooted out."[28] And therein lay the basis for Carter's annual renewal of Romania's emigration waiver. He saw the waiver and MFN as one of the few means America had to effect human rights changes in Romania. Whether the mechanism worked was not the issue. The fact that the waiver and MFN kept alive a means for change was the purpose of annual renewal.

Meanwhile, the administration prepared for a White House visit by President Ceausescu. Carter's invitation stemmed from President Ford's visit to Romania in 1975. At 10:30 A.M. on April 12, Carter officially welcomed President and Mrs. Ceausescu in the Oval Office. The opening remarks of both presidents mentioned human rights, which was one of the recurrent themes throughout Ceausescu's six-day visit. In the afternoon, Barbara Walters, an ABC Television commentator, interviewed the Romanian president. In response to a question concerning human rights, Ceausescu praised his country's efforts and reiterated his view that he saw human rights in a broad context that included disarmament, the right to work, and the right to an education.[29] Within days after returning from his Washington visit, Ceausescu took action to show Carter that his promises were not set on sand. On April 18, he granted forty-seven Romanians passports and exit visas.[30] Considering that this number was nearly equal to a winter month's emigration, the gesture carried weight.

On June 2, President Carter sent Congress his second annual request for an emigration waiver for Romania, which began the summer ritual of MFN hearings. In his recommendation to Congress, the president noted the overall increase of emigration from Romania, especially to West Germany. He was still concerned about the decline in Jewish emigration, but noted that a number of high-level talks had "led to the favorable resolution of many emigration and humanitarian problems."[31]

Congress showed little opposition to renewing the emigration waiver. Ceausescu's April visit, coupled with Carter's 1977 pledge to monitor Romania's emigration practices, silenced most critics. In fact, no member of Congress introduced any resolution of disapproval before or during the hearings. Legislative opposition was also curtailed by the strength of the administration's presentation made at the outset of the hearings. From the opening testimony before the House Ways and Means Subcommittee on Trade, administration officials addressed the issue of emigration, and especially Jewish emigration to Israel. On June 15, William Luers, deputy assistant secretary of state for European affairs, reviewed the State Department's role in increasing Jewish emigration to Israel. In effect, the department played no direct role. Washington did not give Romania lists of Jews who wished to emigrate to Israel. The department, however, did provide such lists to the Israeli Embassy in Bucharest, thereby making the issue one between Israel and Romania. President Ceausescu and Premier Menachem Begin had discussed the matter of Jewish emigration, and they were trying to work out a solution. One of the problems was that Israeli authorities did not want all of the Romanian Jews who wished to go to Israel. Furthermore, Washington did not want to support only those Jews who wanted to emigrate to Israel. What about those who chose Canada, or France, or elsewhere?[32]

In response to queries concerning numbers, Luers noted that the official American Embassy emigration figures were less than the actual number of emigrants. There were two reasons for this. First, many Romanians who actually wished to emigrate to another country applied for permission to emigrate to the United States, since they believed that this increased their chances of approval. Once the Romanian government approved their emigration, they were free to go to any country that would accept them. Second, a number of Romanians applied for entry into the United States from third countries as refugees, and were not included in Washington's emigration figures. Unless a person received a visa at the American Embassy in Bucharest, the emigrant would not be recorded in the embassy statistics.[33] Since the hearings did not produce any resolutions to disapprove the emigraton waiver, the waiver and Romanian MFN were extended until July 1979.

During the last two years of the Carter administration, the relative importance of American-Romanian relations declined. Washington's attention in 1979 focused on recognition of the People's Republic of China, Ayatollah Khomeini's Islamic revolution, the SALT II agreement, the seizure of the American Embassy in Tehran and the ensuing 444-day hostage crisis, and the Soviet invasion of Afghanistan.

The administration's support of Romania carried over into Congress at the beginning of 1979. In January, Senator George McGovern of South Dakota reported to the Committee on Foreign Relations on his summer visit to Romania.[34] The ten-page summary gave a historical overview of Romania, emphasizing her nationalism and desire for economic and political independence. McGovern credited Romania with "pioneering détente" since Nixon's 1969 visit, and noted Ceausescu's continued willingness to take foreign policy initiatives quite independent of Moscow, most notably in the Middle East. While the report noted that emigration procedures were lengthy and burdensome, the fact was that "there has been a dramatic improvement" in the number of people permitted to leave Romania during the past several years. McGovern met Ceausescu, whom he described as "among the world's leading proponents of arms control," and without question was impressed by the Romanian president. In sum, the report gave evidence that America's East European policy, designed to encourage political independence among the Warsaw Pact countries, had made measurable gains in Romania. Washington should continue to expand relations with Bucharest.[35]

The growing importance placed on human rights in Washington was seen in the number of special congressional hearings devoted to the topic. On May 2, the House Subcommittee on International Organizations began hearings on human rights and American foreign policy. The principal administration spokesman was Warren Christopher, deputy secretary of state. He told the subcommittee that "human rights are a central facet" of American foreign policy.[36] He described the administration's approach to human rights as a "dramatic" change from the past. Human rights issues, such as the fate of political prisoners, were now discussed "face-to-face" between diplomats, forcing governments to confront the issue rather than letting it be "conveniently ignored" (as had been done by previous administrations).[37]

On June 1, Carter sent his annual recommendation to waive the freedom-of-emigration requirements in Section 402 of the Trade Act of 1974. In his letter to Congress, the president based his decision on the successful resolution of "many emigration and other humanitarian problems" as a result of high-level bilateral talks.[38] While there would be some opposition to the president's request, Congress was ready to extend the emigration waiver and Romanian MFN for another year. The primary reason for this attitude was the status of the American economy. In the last year of the Ford administration, America had a trade deficit of nearly $9 billion. In 1977, the deficit leaped to $29 billion, and in 1978 to $31 billion. The Consumer Price Index indicated a 6.5 percent annual rate of inflation in 1977 and a 7.7 percent rate in 1978, and experts predicted a double-digit inflation rate for 1979, which proved correct at 11.3 percent.[39]

On June 14, Richard Schulze of Pennsylvania, Larry McDonald of Georgia, and Robert Dornan of California introduced a resolution in the House, H. R. 317, disapproving the waiver extension for Romania.[40] They argued that Romania had consistently violated human rights, institutionalized emigration obstacles, persecuted Hungarians, and operated forced labor camps to construct the Black Sea-Danube River Canal. The resolution went to the House Ways and Means Committee for consideration.[41]

Eight days later the House Subcommittee on Trade began two days of hearings on the president's request for emigration waivers for both Romania and Hungary, which had just received MFN status. On June 22, administration witnesses appeared before the subcommittee. Charles Vanik chaired the meeting, and in his introductory remarks supported the waiver for Romania. Emigration figures showed that the former cyclical pattern had ended. Monthly numbers no longer showed an increase during the months immediately preceding and during the waiver hearings. Romanian emigration to America showed a consistent pattern.[42] Vanik noted that emigration to Israel had again declined, but justified this on the basis that the remaining Jews in Romania, approximately thirty-five thousand, were mostly elderly people who did not want to leave their homeland. Further, Romanian authorities had assured Washington that "all Jewish applications in 1979 have been resolved."[43]

By day's end, there were still a number of people who wanted to testify on the Romanian and Hungarian emigration waivers. Vanik announced that the hearings would continue on July 9. The delay was due to the traditional July 4 celebrations and ongoing emigration negotiations in Bucharest.

The negotiations stemmed from the continued decline in Jewish emigration from Romania to Israel. In 1974, 3,700 Romanians emigrated to Israel; in 1977, 1,500 emigrated; in 1978, 1,200 emigrated; and during the first five months of 1979, only 254 Romanians had left for Israel.[44] This dramatic decline greatly concerned the American Jewish community. In an effort to resolve the problem, representatives from the Conference of Presidents of Major American Jewish Organizations went to Bucharest in June to talk directly with the Romanian authorities. Aided by Ambassador Ionescu of Romania and Corneliu Bogdan, Romania's former ambassador to the United States, the American delegation negotiated an arrangement with Romania's chief rabbi, Moses Rosen, and the Romanian government. Bucharest agreed to permit any Romanian Jew to emigrate to Israel and assured the Conference of Presidents that Jewish applications would be processed expeditiously. As Bogdan described the solution, "anyone who wanted to go to Israel could go."[45]

On July 6, the Conference of Presidents sent an aide-mémoire to Congress indicating the settlement. Three days later, Vanik resumed the House Subcommittee on Trade's hearings on the emigration waiver. Without question, the success of the Bucharest negotiations undermined much of the opposition's position. Nonetheless, Congressman Richard Schulze, author of H. R. 217 to disapprove the president's waiver request for Romania, maintained his position and focused on Bucharest's continued persecution of Hungarians.[46] On July 25, the House voted down Schulze's resolution of disapproval by 271-126.[47] Since there was no resolution of disapproval in the Senate and neither house took any further action on Romanian emigration, the waiver authority automatically extended through July 2, 1980.

However, on August 3, seventy-six members of the House signed a letter and sent it to President Carter with a copy to President Ceausescu. The congressmen urged the president to ensure that Romania kept its promises to the Conference of Presidents of Major American Jewish Organizations. This was the primary reason that the House had supported the president's waiver. The letter indicated that if Bucharest did not implement its assurances, MFN renewal would be jeopardized. Further, the letter indicated that Congress was also concerned about Romania's human rights practices.[48]

This was the first time Congress had indicated in writing that it viewed emigration as part of the larger issue of human rights. This theme was repeated and made more specific by the Senate Finance Committee on August 23. Russell Long, chairman of the committee, sent President Carter a statement that the committee had adopted. While urging the administration to be more aggressive in its monitoring of Romanian emigration, the statement's last paragraph made a leap from the Jackson-Vanik emigration requirement to human rights concerns. The committee noted that

within the human rights framework, though not always directly related to emigration, the Committee had continued to receive allegations of cultural represssion and violations of individual human rights against ethnic minorities. . . . The Committee is deeply concerned about these charges and wishes to indicate its intent to carefully monitor this situation, reviewing the record in detail next year.[49]

Carter did not want to expand the Jackson-Vanik criteria to include all of Romania's human rights. He knew that Bucharest could not meet the standards Congress wanted to impose. He further knew that demanding these new criteria would end Romania's MFN and, in the process, end Washington's primary source of leverage to affect Romania's human rights practices. Consequently, the administration response was bland and noncommittal.[50]

In May 1980, Carter submitted what proved to be his last waiver request to Congress. He based his May 28 recommendation on Bucharest's improved emigration record. He also cited the success of high-level bilateral consultations that he believed would continue to ensure favorable resolution of emigration and humanitarian problems.[51]

The waiver request began the review process. The House Subcommittee on Trade held its hearings on June 10, and the Senate Subcommittee on International Trade held theirs on July 21. Most witnesses at both hearings supported the president's recommendation. The opposition rarely mentioned Romanian emigration because Carter's policy had worked. Through "quiet diplomacy" the White House had convinced Romania to increase its emigration so that by 1980, it was no longer an issue. Romania complied with the Jackson-Vanik waiver requirement. In 1979, 2,886 Romanians came to the United States and nearly 13,000 went to West Germany.[52] The Jewish emigration issue, too, played a much smaller role in the hearings, in part because of the arrangements made in the summer of 1979 between the Romanian government and the Conference of Presidents of Major American Jewish Organizations. In 1980, 1,061 Romanian Jews emigrated to Israel.[53]

Opposition to MFN renewal now focused on Romania's discrimination against religious and national minorities. However, since neither of these issues was an MFN criterion under the Jackson-Vanik Amendment, no member of either house took any action on the president's recommendation until August 27, when Richard Schulze introduced H. R. 775 to disapprove the waiver extension. The resolution never left the House Ways and Means Committee, and the president's authority automatically extended the waiver through July 2, 1981.[54]

On November 4, Americans elected Ronald Wilson Reagan as their fortieth president. Jimmy Carter received only 41 percent of the popular vote. The fact that on the previous day, Washington and Bucharest had signed a four-year agreement on trade in wool and man-made fiber textiles did not produce many Election Day votes.[55] Neither did the fact that during his four years in office, Carter had doubled the number of Romanians coming to America. In 1977, the American Embassy in Bucharest issued 1,228 visas, and in 1980, it issued 2,882. As evidence that this was not a normal increase, in Reagan's first year as president, the number dipped to 2,347.[56] Furthermore, through high-level dialogues with Bucharest, including the June 1979 meeting between Rabbi Rosen and the representatives of the American Jewish community, Carter established a mechanism to easily resolve special cases, especially those involving family reunification. Finally, as for trade, which ostensibly was the purpose of MFN, the Carter years saw two-way trade grow from $492 million in 1977 to over $1.6 billion in 1980. Even more important than the increase was the fact that the United States enjoyed a $400 million trade advantage with Romania in 1980, a figure that has not been equaled since.[57] Indeed, while "quiet diplomacy" won few votes on Election Day, it was certainly an effective approach to dealing with Romania. Through Carter's efforts, tens of thousands of people were able to emigrate to lands where they could freely exercise their human rights.

NOTES

1. I. M. Destler, *Making Foreign Economic Policy* (Washington, D.C.: Brookings Institution, 1980), p. 173.

2. Author interview with Corneliu Bogdan, Romanian ambassador to the United States (1967-1976), Washington, D.C., January 11, 1989.

3. Jimmy Carter, *Keeping Faith: Memoirs of a President* (New York: Bantam Books, 1982), p. 143.

4. *Facts on File, 1977*, pp. 25-26.

5. See Carter, *Keeping Faith: Memoirs of a President*, p. 50.

6. Cyrus Vance, *Hard Choices: Critical Years in America's Foreign Policy* (New York: Simon and Schuster, 1983), pp. 46, 441.

7. Carter, *Keeping Faith*, p. 145.

8. Derian was the founder of the Mississippi Civil Liberties Union and organizer of the biracial Loyalist Mississippi Democratic Party that unsuccessfully challenged the all-white delegation to the 1968 Democratic Party convention (David McLellen, *Cyrus Vance* [New York: Rowman Publishers, 1985], pp. 73-74), Derian credits Don Fraser with upgrading the status of her job from that of coordinator, as determined by Henry Kissinger, to that of assistant secretary of state, as intended in the authorizing legislation. She noted that the upgrade gave her a "bathroom and an American flag" (Patricia Derian, "Jimmy Carter: Keeping the Faith," Hofstra University's Eighth Presidential Conference, November 17, 1990).

9. David P. Forsythe, *Human Rights and U.S. Foreign Policy: Congress Reconsidered* (Gainesville: University Presses of Florida, 1988), p. 57.

10. John Salzberg, "A View from the Hill: U.S. Legislation and Human Rights," *The Diplomacy of Human Rights*, David D. Newsom, ed., (New York: University Press of America, 1986), p. 16.

11. Vojtech Mastny, *Helsinki, Human Rights and European Security* (Durham: Duke University Press, 1986), p. 195; *Congressional Record*, 95th Cong., 1st sess., vol. 123 (1977):8735-8736.

12. "Humanitarian Assistance to Earthquake Victims in Romania," staff report prepared for the Committee on the Judiciary, U.S. Senate, May 28, 1977, p. 4; *Washington Post*, April 20, 1977, p. 6.

13. "Humanitarian Assistance to Earthquake Victims in Romania," p. 5.

14. Letter from Frank Moore to Jerome A. Ambro, June 23, 1977, 2 pgs., Folder CO-130, 1/20/77-12/31/77, Box CO-51, WHCF, Jimmy Carter Presidential Library; letter from Zbigniew Brzezinski to Stuart Eizenstat, May 16, 1977, 2 pgs., Folder Foreign Affairs-Human Rights, Box 208, Eizenstat Domestic Policy Staff, Jimmy Carter Presidential Library.

15. *Public Papers of the Presidents, Jimmy Carter, 1977* (Washington, D.C.: U.S. Government Printing Office, 1978), vol. I, pp. 1055-1077.

16. U.S. Congress, House Committee on Ways and Means, *Most-Favored-Nation Treatment with Respect to the Products of the Socialist Republic of Romania*, hearing before the Subcommittee on Trade, 95th Cong., 1st sess., 1977, p. 5. Hereafter cited as House, Subcommittee on Trade, *MFN*, 1977.

17. Ibid., pp. 19-21.

18. Ibid., p. 58.

19. At the 1990 Hofstra Presidential Conference, Patricia Derian admitted her embarrassment at the administration's willingness to reward Romania for its maverick behavior. She noted that "America's policy was absolutely pegged on the demented notion that Ceausescu was some sort of tough individualist, a tiny little potentate facing down a giant Soviet bear. And that by supporting him, we were going to drive a wedge into the devotion of the Eastern European nations. When you look back at it, it is quite embarrassing" ("Jimmy Carter: Keeping the Faith").

20. *Public Papers of the Presidents, Jimmy Carter, 1977*, vol. II, pp. 1673-1674.

21. Ion Pacepa, *Red Horizons: Chronicles of a Communist Spy Chief* (Washington, D.C.: Regnery Gateway, 1987), p. 11. Pacepa was the former chief of the Romanian equivalent of the CIA.

22. Author interview with O. Rudolph Aggrey, Washington, D.C., October 1989.

23. "The Hungarian View: An Interview with Karoly Kiraly," *East European Reporter*, 2, no. 3 (1987):48; Richard F. Staar, ed., *Yearbook on International Communist Affairs, 1979* (Stanford, Calif.: Hoover Institution Press, 1979), p. 65.

24. U.S. Congress, *Country Reports on Human Rights Practices for 1979*, report submitted to the House Committee on Foreign Affairs and the Senate Committee on Foreign Relations by the Department of State, 96th Cong., 2nd sess., 1980, p. 656.

25. Nicolae Ceausescu, *Romania on the Way* (Bucharest: Meridiane Publishing House, 1979), vol. XV, p. 501.

26. Ibid., p. 514.

27. Zbigniew Brzezinski, *Power and Principle: Memoirs of the National Security Advisor, 1977-1981* (New York: Farrar, Straus and Giroux, 1983), p. 126.

28. Carter, *Keeping Faith*, p. 143.

29. *President Nicolae Ceausescu's State Visit to the USA: April 12-17, 1978* (Bucharest: Meridiane Publishing House, 1978), pp. 87ff.

30. *Christian Science Monitor*, April 18, 1978, p. 10.

31. *Public Papers of the Presidents, Jimmy Carter, 1978* (Washington, D.C.: U.S. Government Printing Office, 1979), vol. I, pp. 1031-1033. The president did not tell Congress that this increase was due to an arrangement between Bonn and Bucharest. Romania promised to allow approximately eleven thousand ethnic Germans to emigrate annually to West Germany in return for credits and payments of up to DM 8,000 per person. Vlad Georgescu, "Romania in the 1980s: The Legacy of Dynastic Socialism," *Eastern European Politics and Society*, 2, no. 1 (1988):90, n. 57.

32. U.S. Congress, House, Subcommittee on Trade, *Nondiscriminatory Treatment of Romanian Products, 1978*, pp. 106-107.

33. Ibid., pp. 68-71.

34. *Romanian Bulletin* (New York), September 1978, p. 2; U.S. Congress, Senate Committee on Foreign Relations, *Perspectives on Détente: Austria, Romania and Czechoslovakia*, a report by Senator George McGovern, 96th Cong., 1st sess., 1979.

35. Ibid.

36. Zbigniew Brzezinksi, *In Quest of National Security*, Marín Strmecki, ed. (Boulder, CO: Westview Press, 1988), p. 105. Christopher repeated Brzezinski's remarks of December 6, 1978.

37. U.S. Congress, House Committee on Foreign Affairs, *Human Rights and U.S. Foreign Policy*, hearings before the Subcommittee on International Organizations, 96th Cong., 1st sess., 1979, p. 16.

38. *Public Papers of the Presidents, Jimmy Carter, 1979* (Washington, D.C.: U.S. Government Printing Office, 1980), vol. I, p. 979.

39. U.S. Bureau of the Census, *Statistical Abstract of the United States, 1984* (Washington, D.C.: U.S. Government Printing Office, 1983), pp. 494-831.

40. U.S. Congress, House Committee on Ways and Means, *Waiver of Freedom of Emigration Requirement to the Socialist Republic of Romania and the Hungarian People's Republic*, hearings before the Subcommittee on Trade, 96th Cong., 1st sess., 1979, pp. 10. Hereafter cited as House, *Waiver, 1979*.

41. U.S. Congress, Senate Committee on Finance, *Continuing the President's Authority to Waive the Trade Act Freedom of Emigration Provisions*, hearing before the Subcommittee on International Trade, 96th Cong., 1st sess., 1979, p. 53.

42. U.S. Congress, House Committee on Ways and Means, *Trade Waiver Authority Extension*, hearing before the Subcommittee on Trade, 96th Cong., 2nd sess., 1980, pp. 46-47.

43. House, *Waiver, 1979*, pp. 1-2.

44. Ibid.

45. U.S. Congress, Senate Committee on Finance, *Extension of the President's Authority to Waive Section 402 (Freedom of Emigration Requirements) of the Trade Act of 1974*, hearing before the Subcommittee on International Trade, 96th Cong., 2nd sess., 1980, pp. 119, 298. Author interview with Corneliu Bogdan, Washington, D.C., January 11, 1989.

46. House, *Waiver, 1979*, pp. 266-269.

47. *Congressional Record*, 96th Cong., 1st sess., 1979, p. 20660.

48. Letter from Representative Ted Weiss et al. to President Jimmy Carter, August 3, 1979, 6 pgs., Folder CO-130, 1/1/79-12/31/79, Box CO-52, CO, WHCF, Jimmy Carter Presidential Library.

49. Letter from Russell B. Long to President Jimmy Carter, August 23, 1979, attachment, p. 2, Folder CO-130, 1/1/79-12/31/79, Box CO-52, CO, WHCF, Jimmy Carter Presidential Library.

50. See letter from Nelson C. Ledsky to Ted Weiss, August 31, 1979, 2 pgs., Folder CO-130, 1/1/79-12/31/79, Box CO-52, CO, WHCF, Jimmy Carter Presidential Library.

51. *Public Papers of the Presidents, Jimmy Carter, 1980-1981* (Washington, D.C.: U.S. Government Printing Office, 1981), vol. II, pp. 980-982.

52. U.S. Congress, House, *Disapproval of Extension of Presidential Authority to Waive Freedom of Emigration Requirements Under Section 402 of the Trade Act of 1974 with Respect to Romania*, Report No. 97-743, 97th Cong., 2nd sess., 1982, p. 4.

53. Ibid.

54. Vladimir Pregelj, "Most Favored Nation Treatment of Foreign Trading Partners by the United States: A Summary, January 28, 1986," prepared for Congressional Research Service, Library of Congress, 1986, p. 18.

55. Vladimir Pregelj, "U.S. Commercial Relations with Communist Countries," prepared for Congressional Research Service, Library of Congress, 1984, p. 13.

56. U.S. Congress, House Ways and Means Committee, *Presidential Recommendation to Continue Waivers Applicable to Romania, Hungary and the People's Republic of China, and to*

Extend the Trade Act Waiver Authority, hearing before the Subcommittee on Trade, 98th Cong., 1st sess., 1983, p. 17.

57. U.S. Congress, Joint Economic Committee of the Congress, *East-West Trade: The Prospect to 1985*, 97th Cong., 2nd sess., 1982, p. 265.

7

The Carter Human Rights Policy: Political Idealism and Realpolitik

VERNON J. VAVRINA

Recent events in Leipzig, Soweto, Medellín, Panama City, and Beijing demonstrate clearly that the struggle for human rights is always present. As the Bush administration fashions U.S. foreign policy to deal with these problems, a study of previous American efforts to promote human rights is extremely relevant.

The beginning of the 1990s will mark a decade since the end of the Jimmy Carter era. This is an appropriate time to reevaluate his human rights policy. Even proponents of this policy have been critical of it. Former U.S. Ambassador to the United Nations Donald McHenry has stated that it took too long for the policy to be enunciated.[1] Deputy Assistant Secretary of State Stephen Cohen, who worked during the Carter administration in the Human Rights Bureau, has described the policy as "oversold and sanctimonious." He believes the Carter administration did not adequately explain to the American people the connection between the cause of human rights and the self-interest of the United States.[2]

More strident critics of Carter, such as Jeane Kirkpatrick and Joshua Murvachik, have blasted his policy for being grossly inconsistent; they believe it was far too easy on hostile totalitarian regimes and too hard on America's authoritarian allies. Carter's approch, it is alleged, failed to give enough attention to building in other countries the institutions that are vitally necessary to support human rights. Too much time was spent on bureaucratic infighting over mainly symbolic issues.[3]

There is a great deal of empirical evidence to support many of these criticisms. Some will be presented in this paper. However, as will be explained, the Carter approach to human rights also left in its wake substantial contributions that should not be forgotten. Many of the problems confronting the Carter human rights policy were inherent in the attempt of any world power to reconcile its ideals and its self-interests. It is also imperative to understand that the U.S. Congress had begun to champion the cause of human rights years before Carter occupied the Oval Office. An evaluation of U.S. human rights policy between 1977 an 1980 must take into account the role of the Congress as well as that of the Executive. In addition, Carter's policy should be compared and contrasted with the human rights initiatives of other presidents.

The most serious charge against Carter's human rights policy is that it was extremely inconsistent. Some critics of the president complain that his policy utilized the Soviet Union as a whipping boy.[4] Kirkpatrick and Muravchik argue the reverse: Carter was too easy on communist regimes at the expense of allies such as Iran, Nicaragua, and Chile. Indeed, there was virtually no consistent American human rights policy founded upon commensurate response during the Carter era. Inconsistent policy was a result of the choice by U.S. decision makers to take each case on its merits. Inconsistency resulted as well when the United States chose to subordinate human rights concerns to those of national security. American foreign policy under Carter, as well as under Nixon and Ford, did in fact differ for similar human rights offenses according to various characteristics of the perpetrator, the relationship of the perpetrator with the United States, and the context in which the offense took place.[5] This paper will document some of the more glaring shifts.

INCONSISTENCIES

Shifts are particulary noticeable during the Carter administration because of its high-visibility human rights program, which emphasized a case-by-case approach. "The painful point is that to have a consistent human rights policy, we must be indifferent to some outcomes, particularly strategic outcomes."[6] The Carter administration, like its predecessors, was not indifferent to strategic outcomes.

Iran and Chile

Iran, for example, did receive special treatment because of its strategic importance. Despite many examples of violations of the integrity of the person[7]--credible reports of torture, large numbers of state security prisoners, brutal treatment of demonstrators, and SAVAK terrorism[8]--Iranian human rights abuses were not mentioned by presidents Nixon and Ford. President Carter chose to include human rights only in his private conversations with the shah. U.S. leaders could not cut economic assistance to Iran because rising oil prices made Iran fabulously wealthy and rendered such assistance moot. The shah continued to be the largest buyer of American arms, and no major arms systems were denied him by the United States. There were congressional hearings on human rights in Iran, but no legislation specifically punishing Iran for its abuses under the shah was enacted.

It is instructive to contrast the treatment of Iran with that of Chile. Chilean human rights conditions, including violations of the integrity of the person, were deplorable. There was reliable evidence of torture, execution without trial, political disappearances, and mistreatment of detainees.[9] Unlike Iran, Chile was small; had no valuable, difficult-to-obtain minerals; and was not an important trading partner of the United States. Although the cutting of military assistance to Chile because of human rights violations was judged counterproductive by the Nixon administration, Congress eventually forced the issue. By the Foreign Assistance Act of 1974, military assistance to Chile was prohibited and economic assistance was limited. Several other laws affecting U.S. policy were enacted. Congressional hearings on human rights abuses in Chile were perhaps the most extensive of those for any country. Numerous witnesses were called and significant amounts of material documenting abuses were inserted into the records. The special congressional scrutiny to which Chile was subjected may be partly ascribed to the alleged involvement of President Nixon, Henry Kissinger, other administration officials, and leaders of American firms operating in Chile in the attempt to prevent Salvador Allende Gossens from acceding to power. Members of Congress, infuriated by what they considered unwarranted interference in the domestic affairs of a democratically elected government, closely watched the activities of the new Pinochet regime. Whoever succeeded Allende was destined to be scrutinized, and Pinochet gave detractors much ammunition with which to attack him on human rights grounds.

Because of human rights abuses the Ford and Carter administrations failed to support multilateral development loans for Chile on six occasions. Under President Carter, Export-Import Bank loans for Chile were refused consideration, as were Overseas Private Investment Corporation insurance applications. U.S. human rights policy toward Chile, unlike its policy toward Iran, was aggressive. One can speculate whether it would have been so if Chile had enjoyed a more prominent position on the international scene. What is not so open to speculation is the contention that American approaches to human rights violations in Iran and Chile differed to an extent that confused some and alienated others. It is likely that Chile's democratic history was a key factor in subjecting her to so many sanctions. American foreign policymakers, especially during the Carter era, believed they could rightfully expect better human rights performance from Chile than from a country such as Iran, which did not have a history of liberal democracy.

South Korea and North Korea

U.S. human rights policy toward South Korea (Republic of Korea) was for the most part dominated by congressional initiatives, and lengthy hearings were held on the subject.[10] Legislation specifically citing South Korea was passed, and measures were taken that denied or limited some economic and military assistance until substantial progress in human rights could be reported. The effect was mitigated by an increase in World Bank loans and the fact that South Korea nevertheless continued to receive large amounts of military and economic aid from the United States. Active trade between the two nations continued, and much American money was invested in South Korea.

Like other presidents, Carter tended not to discuss publicly specific human rights violations in South Korea although a general dissatisfaction with the situation was made apparent. Secretary of State Vance announced that because of overriding security concerns, the United States opposed linking human rights in South Korea to security assistance--the same basic position in practice espoused by Nixon and Ford. The Carter White House registered its disapproval of the South Korean human rights situation by failing to approve Asian Development Bank loans destined for that country. During the 1979 official visit to South Korea by President Carter, a privately compiled list of more than one hundred alleged political prisoners was presented to the Korean foreign minister.

U.S. human rights policy toward North Korea was characterized by a lack of action during the Nixon, Ford, and Carter presidencies. This was partly due to the absence of diplomatic and economic ties with the Democratic People's Republic of Korea, but primarily because of the dearth of information about that isolated country.

Congress did hold limited hearings on the human rights situation in North Korea, but much of the discussion time was addressed to South Korea. Witnesses testified that although not a great deal was understood about North Korea, it was known that North Koreans did not enjoy even a modicum of human rights and that the authoritarian government of South Korea was a personification of perfect democracy compared with North Korea. Another witness characterized totalitarian North Korea as still in a Stalinist phase regarding human rights, but maintained that torture was not employed as extensively as in South Korea.

Presidential references in the 1970s to North Korea were almost nonexistent. President Carter did note on one occasion that North Korea was suppressing human rights. Nevertheless, he lifted American travel restrictions to that nation.

A weighing of American responses to human rights violations in North and South Korea shows that South Korea received the major share of attention. That was due both to the abundance of information about human rights abuses there and the sense of responsibility toward South Korea shared by many American policymakers. The United States and South Korea have enjoyed a special relationship since the Korean War. The "Koreagate" scandal forced Congress to study South Korea closely. Unlike North Korea, South Korea was the recipient of large amounts of U.S. economic and security assistance. The American executive and legislative branches therefore could use the leverage such monies afforded by threatening cuts.

South Korea no doubt merited much of the criticism it received for human rights abuses, but North Korea, a country that consistently earned the lowest possible ratings from Freedom House for both "political rights" and "civil liberties," and "where no private or public rights appear to be inviolable," escaped censure. Despite the conclusion by Freedom House that there were political prisoners in North Korea and that "torture may be assumed to be common," human rights abuses in North Korea were largely ignored. This was true despite reports that more than one hundred thousand North Koreans were in prison camps for ideological offenses.[11]

Soviet Union

Examples of the inconsistency of application of Carter's human rights policy abound. Even with respect to the same country over time the policy zigged and zagged. The case of the Soviet Union illustrates this point. The human rights policy of the U.S. executive branch toward the Soviet Union differed markedly in the Nixon/Ford and Carter eras. The Nixon/Ford years were characterized by quiet diplomacy; the Carter years displayed a vacillation between quiet diplomacy and a more vociferous approach. President Nixon, noting the dramatic increase in the number of Soviet Jews allowed to emigrate from the Soviet Union during a period of détente, credited the calm diplomacy of his administration with advancing the cause of Soviet Jewry. President Carter, early in his term, decided to forgo the quiet approach when he personally responded to a letter from Soviet prisoner of conscience Andrei Sakharov and then condemned the imprisonment of Aleksandr Ginzburg. Carter met briefly with released dissident Vladimir Bukovsky in the White House, although no pictures were allowed of the meeting. Soviet criticism of these actions was quick and sharp. Stung by the accusations flung against him, Carter was reminded even from friendly quarters that the Soviet Union was not the only violator of human rights. Accordingly, in subsequent weeks, the Carter administration toned down its anti-Soviet rhetoric.

Secretary of State Vance privately instructed the U.S. representative to the U.N. Human Rights Commission that he was under no circumstances to mention the name Yuri Orlov, another famous dissident arrested by the Soviets. However, during the Belgrade Review Conference on Security and Cooperation in Europe which began in October 1977, U.S. Ambassador to the United Nations Arthur Goldberg cited the Soviet treatment of specific dissenters. Carter himself spoke of the Soviet abuse of basic human rights[12] during the June 1978 U.S. Naval Academy graduation exercises.

Carter did not want his human rights policy to be linked with other issues, such as strategic arms limitations or mutual and balanced force reductions. He did not believe his policy would undermine détente, which was based on mutual advantage. Despite the trials of human rights activists Anatoly Shcharansky and Aleksandr Ginzburg, Secretary of State Vance continued with scheduled plans to meet with the Soviet foreign minister, although visits to the Soviet Union by relatively minor American delegations were canceled. A major computer sale to the Soviet Union was halted in retaliation for the trials of Soviet dissidents and two Moscow-based American reporters. The Soviet invasion of Afghanistan soured U.S.-Soviet relations during the last portion of the Carter administration. Carter decried the banishment into internal exile of Andrei Sakharov and said the Soviets dishonored the principles of Helsinki.

Other Cases

One additional frequently voiced criticism of Carter's human rights policy is that it continually lambasted authorities in El Salvador while scarcely mentioning a far graver situation in Pol Pot's Kampuchea. Kid glove treatment was likewise given to Yugoslavia and Romania at the same time the full hand of the administration came down upon weak and relatively friendly Latin American regimes. The People's Republic of China was let off the hook altogether. South Africa was soundly criticized while human rights transgressions in black African states went unnoticed.[13]

CONTRIBUTIONS

Given that the Carter human rights policy had such obvious flaws, what can be said in its behalf? One may argue that Carter's policy, albeit inconsistent, was an improvement over the policy of his predecessors. In the Nixon and Ford administrations, the norm was "quiet diplomacy." In practice this often became "no diplomacy" on the part of the United States to enhance international human rights. The scales had tipped too far in the direction of self-interest and too far from that of our American ideals. Clearly, a precarious balance must exist between the two poles; Carter acted to keep things from getting further out of kilter. Any human rights policy is an amalgam of often conflicting, competing interests. To insist that it be completely non-capricious and nonselective in application means in the end to abandon the policy altogether.[14]

Avoiding U.S. Identification with Repressors

David D. Newsom, Carter's under secretary of state, has expressed dismay that little is said or written about the problem of identification with repressive regimes despite the fact that the problem is considered crucial by those who work in the human rights field. He believes the totalitarian/authoritarian controversy misses the point. No one, for example, claims that Soviet dissidents identify and associate the United States with human rights violations perpetrated by the totalitarian Soviet government. On the other hand, dissidents in authoritarian countries such as El Salvador do feel that if the United States is silent about abuses committed there, American policy is to support repressive governments. If the United States totally abandons sending signals of support for human rights in these cases, it in practice gives an opposite signal.[15] Disassociating the United States from repressive regimes of all types is in the best long-term interest of the country.

Stressing Integrity of Person

Violations of the integrity of the person include torture; cruel, inhuman, or degrading treatment or punishment; and abitrary arrest or imprisonment. Muravchik has argued that the Carter administration's tendency to emphasize, in fact if not in rhetoric, the human rights category "integrity of the person" encouraged it to single out for criticism countries that may not have had the most repressive governments when measured by other standards--for example, civil and political rights. He writes of the irony that

an older, better established, more thorough tyranny whose population has all but given up hope for effective dissent may have less "need" to engage in eye-catching domestic violence than a newer, less repressive government struggling to impose and preserve its authority.[16]

While there is truth in this, it still seems harsh to criticize the Carter administration for emphasizing violations of the integrity of the person. The harsh reality is that during the Carter era, the worldwide situation with respect to human rights had gotten completely out of hand. International nongovernmental organizations such as Amnesty International documented that scores of countries were involved in torturing or inhumanely treating their citizens.[17] Millions of people were deprived of civil and political rights, and millions more lived without economic, social, and cultural rights. The same grim reality is with us today. To build the institutions necessary to protect some or all of the aforementioned kinds of rights is truly a worthy goal, but will in all likelihood take many generations at best. In a multicultural world, experience has shown it to be very difficult even to achieve agreement on the priority given to these various types of rights. Thus there was a need for two international human rights covenants rather than one. In 1977, the best way to promote human rights was to concentrate on a category about which people throughout the world could readily agree. Most human beings find the notion of torture repugnant. By concentrating on violations of the integrity of the person, the Carter administration quite properly was seeking to use this minimal consensus as a foundation upon which to support other human rights.

Building on Work of Congress

A great contribution of Carter was to build on the work already done by Congress in the early 1970s and to fortify the institutionalization of human rights concerns in American foreign policy. It was Congress that first moved to institutionalize the human rights component in the American foreign policy-making process. A 1974 report of the Fraser Subcommittee of the House Committee on International Relations noted that there was only one official in the entire Department of State who dealt solely with human rights, and recommended that a human rights officer be placed in each regional bureau. This recommendation was subsequently enacted, an officer having human rights responsibilities was placed in the International Organization Affairs section, and an Office of Assistant Legal Adviser on Human Rights was created. Personnel in policy planning were given human rights responsibilities. In addition, human rights elements were included in training for foreign service and military officers. In 1975, the Office of the Deputy Secretary of State was reorganized to embrace the new position of coordinator for humanitarian affairs. In 1976, Congress, in PL 94-329, inaugurated the Office of Coordinator for Human Rights and Humanitarian Affairs, and gave it specific responsibilities, such as the preparation of detailed information on human rights observance in countries receiving U.S. aid. In PL 95-105, Congress, with President Carter's approval, elevated the coordinator to assistant secretary of state rank. In an important bureaucratic move, the Coordinator's office was upgraded to bureau status. During the Carter era, the Bureau of Human Rights and Humanitarian Affairs (HA) was composed of three divisions: the Office of Human Rights (thirteen officers who worked along both functional and geographical lines); the Office of Refugee and Migration Affairs; and a section devoted to POWs and MIAs. HA was represented on the Inter-Agency Group on Human Rights and Foreign Assistance and on the Arms Export Control Board.

Congressional interest in human rights was at its peak during the Nixon/Ford years, when it was felt that those administrations paid scant attention to the subject. Individual congressmen and Congress as a whole prodded both administrations, especially with respect to the situations in Chile and South Korea. Liberals in

Congress were concerned that PL 480 Title I loans were being used to indirectly assist the repressive Pinochet regime in its arms purchases.

When President Carter assumed office, human rights advocates within Congress were relieved, but neverthleess continued to press for restrictive human rights legislation. Some wanted to pass laws that the president felt would needlessly tie his hands. Carter, the most noted advocate of international human rights since Eleanor Roosevelt, was placed in the anomalous position of lobbying to thwart congressional human rights initiatives. Finally, Congress, convinced of Carter's sincerity about human rights concerns, acceded to the president's wishes.

Advocating International Human Rights

In 1977, Carter signed the International Covenants on Civil and Political Rights and on Economic, Social and Cultural Rights. These had been opened for signature in 1966. During his tenure, Carter also signed the American Convention on Human Rights. He was not able, however, to persuade the U.S. Senate to ratify these treaties, nor was he any more successful with regard to securing ratification of the Genocide Convention and the Convention on the Elimination of All Forms of Racial Discrimination. The mere signing of the major human rights conventions by President Carter removed a public relations albatross from the necks of American foreign policymakers. In the past, it had been all too easy for unfriendly governments to chide the United States. After all, how could that nation be so aggressive in its approach to human rights at the very same time it had failed to sign the most important international agreements on the subject? True, the latter are imperfect and raise questions in American constitutional law. They may, for example, conflict with First Amendment protections. Over a dozen reservations, understandings, statements, and declarations were provided by the Carter administration to deal with these legal problems. Cuba, Chile, and the Soviet Union, among other countries, have followed a similar approach when signing or ratifying major human rights instruments. In a multicultural world composed of independent sovereign states, perhaps the only feasible way to build international human rights treaty law incrementally is through liberal use of reservations. In any event, the net effect of Carter's stance with respect to the treaties was to mute outside criticism of the United States for failing to move on the documents. American constitutional safeguards were protected simultaneously through the various undertandings and reservations.

The impact of the Carter human rights policy on improving the situations of people around the world is difficult to measure. Like presidents before him, Carter was careful not to take much public credit for apparent human rights successes. Seldom is it abundantly clear what motivates the torturer to stop torturing or the incarcerator to release a political prisoner from jail.

What is clear is that the Carter presidency changed the way many Americans thought about human rights. The number of references to the concept of human rights skyrocketed during the Carter era. Jimmy Carter was responsible for an explosion of interest in human rights. A casual persual of holdings in a public library will document this point. Today, "human rights" is a separate subject heading in card catalogs and bibliographical indexes. No one deserves more credit for this than President Carter.

Perhaps the biggest success of the Carter human rights policy was its unique concern to draw upon the work and interest of people in Congress, academia, intergovernmental organizations, and nongovernmental organizations. By urging people to probe, think, speak, and write about human rights, Carter gave strength and audience to the view that states are under a legal obligation to respect human rights.

The negligible role vis-à-vis the promotion of international human rights played by the United States under presidents Nixon and Ford has been asserted by writers such as Thomas Farer, Henry Shue and Lars Schoultz.[18] In those administrations, there was rarely someone in the decision-making process who would or could ask, "Is it right?" without being dismissed as a "bleeding heart."[19] In this context, the advent of the Carter presidency brought a much needed boost in morale to many human rights groups, both in the United States and around the world.

While the Carter administration did deemphasize human rights abuses occurring in Iran and often dealt quietly with infringements in other noncommunist states, it cannot seriously be concluded that transgressions in right-wing regimes were totally ignored. The Christopher Committee, for example, invested much time and effort determining whether the United States should support El Salvador, the Philippines, and South Korea in the international financial institutions. On the other end of the political spectrum, Carter, in the first months of office, lashed out at the Soviet Union and Cuba in a way never done by his two predecessors. However, the president did not maintain steady pressure on those countries. Suppression of human rights by North Korea, Kampuchea, and the PRC was scarcely mentioned.

President Carter's human rights policy, although based on substantial doses of political idealism, had aspects of realpolitik.[20] It was argued that a forceful human rights policy was in the best interests of the United States because it would disassociate this country from repressive regimes that were bound to fail. When the repressive regimes were overthrown, the position of the United States with the new governments would be much stronger, since there would be no history of U.S. support for repression. Carter's human rights policy was in much closer alignment with the wishes of Congress than that of his predecessors. Carter called much-needed attention to a viable issue, but by so doing risked raising public expectations too high. Realpolitik dictates that the United States depends on other nations to varying degrees and, conversely, that other nations depend on the United States to varying extents. It is, then, impossible to have a human rights policy based completely on commensurate response. The problem of a human rights policy is that to act is often to be inconsistent, and an inconsistent policy is difficult to sell and hard for the public to understand.

Because human rights policy is a classic example of the never-ending conflict between ideals and self-interest, it will always place the decision maker in a dilemma. To be sure, Jimmy Carter's human rights campaign suffered painful moments of sitting on horns. Yet a retrospective look at his unique crusade reveals substantial contributions as well as serious flaws. As George Bush shapes U.S. human rights policy in the 1990s, he will profit from a detailed understanding of both.

NOTES

1. Interview with Ambassador Donald F. McHenry, Washington, D.C., October 7, 1981.

2. Interview with Stephen Cohen, Washington, D.C., February 23, 1983.

3. Jeane Kirkpatrick, "Dictatorships and Double Standards," *Commentary*, 68 no. 5 (November 1979):34-35. See also Joshua Muravchik, *The Uncertain Crusade: Jimmy Carter and the Dilemmas of Human Rights Policy* (Lanham, MD: Hamilton Press, 1986); Tamar Jacoby, "The Reagan Turnabout on Human Rights," *Foreign Affairs*, 64 (Summer 1986):1068. The so-called Christopher Committee (Interagency Group on Human Rights and Foreign Assistance), chaired by Deputy Secretary of State Warren Christopher forced many top-level officials into long hours of debate on whether the United States should vote to disapprove international financial institution funding to certain violator countries even though there were never enough total votes to kill a measure.

4. For example, Jonathan Dimbleby of the BBC pressed Carter on why he concentrated so much on Russia at the expense of other countries. See Muravchik, *Uncertain Crusades*, p. 113.

5. Vernon J. Vavrina, "Human Rights and American Foreign Policy: Violations of the Integrity of the Person, Selected Cases, 1969-1980" (Ph.D. diss., Georgetown University, 1984). See also U.S. Congress, Senate, Committee on Foreign Relations, *Human Rights and U.S. Foreign Assistance: Experiences and Issues in Policy Implementation, 1977-1978*, report prepared for the Committee on Foreign Relations by the Foreign Affairs and National Defense Division, Congressional Research Service, Library of Congress, 96th Cong., 1st sess., November 1979, pp. 47-48, 63.

6. Earl Ravenal, "The Crisis of Liberal Internationalism: Human Rights Hypocrisies," *Inquiry*, January 23, 1978.

7. According to Secretary of State Cyrus Vance, in his Law Day address at the University of Georgia Law School, April 30, 1977, such violations include torture; cruel, inhuman, or degrading treatment or punishment; and abitrary arrest or imprisonment. They also include denial of fair public trial and invasion of the home.

8. U.S. Congress, House, Committee on International Relations, *Human Rights in Iran*, hearings before the Subcommittee on International Relations, House, 94th Cong., 2nd sess., August 2 and September 8, 1976.

9. U.S. Congress, House, Committee on International Relations, *Chile: The Status of Human Rights and Its Relationship to U.S. Economic Assistance Programs*, hearing before the Subcommittee on International Organizations of the Committee on International Relations, House, 94th Cong., 2nd sess., April 29 and May 5, 1976.

10. U.S. Congress, House, Committee on International Relations, *Human Rights in South Korea and the Philippines: Implications for U.S. Policy*, hearings before the Subcommittee on International Organization, 94th Cong., 1st sess., May 20, 22, June 3, 5, 10, 12, 17, 24, 1975.

11. Dr. Tai Sung An, professor of political science at Washington College, Chestertown, MD, and specialist in Asian affairs, in a telephone interview with the author, April 18, 1984, expressed the view that human rights abuses in North Korea were much more severe than those in the South. See. Tai Sung An, *North Korea: A Political Handbook* (Wilmington, DE: Scholarly Resources, 1983), pp. 82-83; *North Korea in Transition* (Westport, CT: Greenwood Press, 1983). See also *New York Times*, April 11, 1982, p. 3; and Raymond D. Gastil, *Freedom in the World: Political Rights and Civil Liberties* (Boston: G. K. Hall, 1978).

12. U.S. Congress, House, Committee on International Relations, *Psychiatric Abuse of Political Prisoners in the Soviet Union*, hearing before the Subcommittee on International Organizations, 94th Cong., 2nd sess., March 30, 1976.

13. Muravchik, *Uncertain Crusade*, pp. 145-149.

14. Interview with Ambassador David D. Newsom, Washington, D.C., September 9, 1981. See David D. Newsom, ed., *The Diplomacy of Human Rights* (Lanham, MD: University Press of

America, 1986); Cyrus R. Vance, "The Human Rights Imperative," *Foreign Policy*, 63 (Summer 1986):3-19; Larry Minear, "The Forgotten Human Agenda," *Foreign Policy*, 73 (Winter 1988-1989):76-93.

15. Ibid.

16. Muravchik, *Uncertain Crusades*, p. 131.

17. Amnesty International, *Report on Torture* (New York: Farrar, Straus and Giroux, 1975).

18. Thomas J. Farer, *Toward a Humanitarian Diplomacy: A Primer for Policy* (New York: New York University Press, 1980); Henry Shue, *Basic Rights: Subsistence, Affluence, and U.S. Foreign Policy* (Princeton: Princeton University Press, 1980); Lars Schoultz, *Human Rights and United States Policy Toward Latin America* (Princeton: Princeton University Press, 1981); David P. Forsythe, *Human Rights and World Politics* (Lincoln: University of Nebraska Press, 1983).

19. Interview with Ambassador Donald F. McHenry, Washington, D.C., October 7, 1981.

20. See, for example, the statement of Warren Christopher: "We realize that there are compelling reasons why we must season our idealism with realism. There is no blinking the fact that our ability to change human rights practices in other societies is limited, even where we use all the mechanisms and approaches at our disposal. We must not proceed as if we had unlimited power. . . . In addition, we must recognize that our actions may provoke retaliation against our short-term interests or even sometimes agaist the victims of repression we seek to assist." *Department of State Bulletin*, 77 (November 17, 1977):270-271.

Discussant: Eric Lane

I'm also someone who, in the words of Professor Vavrina, was inspired by the Carter administration's work on human rights, and ended up, partially, at least, receiving my tenure at Hofstra through the ideas and the excitement of the Carter administration.

In 1976, when Carter was elected, he said in his inaugural speech, "The world itself is dominated by a new spirit, and . . . people more numerous and more politically aware are craving and now demanding their place in the sun, not just for the benefit of their own physical conditions, but for basic human rights." And within a year from that date, Mark Schneider, who I think was Mr. Derian's deputy, was reporting to a congressional committee that had asked him what the Carter successes had been in human rights, that they were "the recognition of foreign states and their citizens; of the United States concern for human rights; consideration of foreign states of the cost of represssion; a change in worldwide perception of the United States; the release of some political prisoners; the admission of several foreign states to international organization for purposes of investigation; and at that time, . . . the signing of the American Convention on Human Rights," which was probably the most radical of the documents that President Carter signed.

Also, at the same time that was going on, Mr. Brzezinski, also a representative of the president, was announcing that "we have tried to make human rights an issue." I think the point is worth bearing in mind--and I'm quoting Brzezinski--"to confirm the American commitment to the notion that this is an idea whose time has come, that the strength of the idea, in its specific political expression within individual countries, really is, but when we get to specific bilateral discussions of important bilateral issues," he says, "we will not make it a precondition or central issue of bilateral relations." And in that same year, as we watched the destruction and death of millions of people in Cambodia and Uganda, James Reston--then the resident guru of the *New York Times*--said, "Can nothing be done by the so-called great nations, at least to investigate the report of such human suffering? Do the sovereign rights of national states include the power to treat or dispose of their people in any way their temporary rulers decide?"

As I listened to the comments of all of the presenters, while I agree with many of the comments, particularly with Vernon Vavrina, it struck me that what was missing from an analysis of the Carter adminstration's record on human rights is a context for understanding human rights as they apply in international relations. I mean that what I would I would call it is not a battle between the ideal and the real, although frequently we see it that way and often it is true. I would call it, basically, a battle between the ideal and the ideal. And by that I mean that the primary obstacle to the recognition of human rights in this world is, partially at least, a structural obstacle: the state system. Now, the state system, as you know--I don't mean the states of the United States; we in the international world call nation-states "states"--is not an eternal arrangement by which authority is distributed in the world. In fact, it's a somewhat recent invention.

Many people identify the beginnings of the seventeenth century as the time at which the centralized powers of the emperor and the pope were destroyed by the Thirty Yeras War, and the Enlightenment, Renaissance, and Reformation became accommodated in a legal, governmental structure known as the state system. Indeed, I think it was Pope Innocent X who, at the signing of the Treaty of Westphalia, which ended the war, criticized the treaty becuase it permitted "each state to allow for religious freedom, notwithstanding the church's position that there should be only one church"--the Catholic Church; the rest of these fellows were heretics.

Now, when you start to think about a state system, and the context of its creation, in conflict with a centrally dominated order, you can readily see that the notion of a state taking care of its domestic affairs and not allowing intervention from any other force carries with it a currency that I think is hard. It misses the point to characterize it simply as parochial or small or narrow-minded. In effect, the system under which we presently exist contemplates--and it was part of the politics and history of the moment--that the international order would be established among all of these states, all with equal votes and all belonging to friendly or not-so-friendly alliances; and that the domestic order--and to a large extent, constitutional democracies were starting to be created--would be left to the individual states. Everything about the international world legal order, and about international law, is directed toward that goal, including one of the msot significant provisions of the United Nations Charter: Article II, Section 7, which prohibits a nation--any nation--from intruding into the internal workings of another nation. And those prerogatives have been very, very jealously guarded.

Now, as a result of that, the way that human rights have been treated has been under the table and not on the table. I'm reminded of a story that Professor John G. Stoessinger once told me, that his "buddy" Henry Kissinger told him. Kissinger went hunting with Brezhnev--boar hunting--and Brezhnev shot a boar. He was so elated that he jumped into Kissinger's arms and said, "Anything you want, Henry!" Henry said, "Let some more Jews free," and within the next several months, several thousand Jews emigrated from Russia. Now whether that's apocryphal or not, it certainly represents the concept of human rights in international relations prior to the Carter administration.

I think that the difficulty we see now, what the Carter human rights movement saw in its implementation of a human rights policy, is noticeable in other areas of international concern even more vividly, and is also a product of the state system. Take, for example, the rain forest. It's in Brazil. Brazil is cutting it down. We don't like its being cut down. What can we do about it? Can we send our troops in to protect the rain forest? Doesn't Brazil have the right to control its domestic affairs? The same might be said about our food supplies in the face of starving nations. I only give you these examples to suggest that the obstacles to overcome when you try to implement a human rights policy in the world are very, very immense. The external forces, the institutional forces, against its implementation are very powerful. We know--as a result of the First World War and of the Second World War, of the interdependent economic relationships we see through oil, and of the Holocaust and subsequent human rights violations--that the old notions of a totally independent nation-state world may not work in the way we once thought they might work, and that there are other methods that we may be moving toward trying. I think that the Carter administration's efforts in this area reflect this. But in undertaking them, the power of the idea of the state, it seems to me, has to remain very central to your thinking so you can try to understand the extraordinary difficulties in implementing any human rights policy, particularly when you really want to make it your policy, as the Carter administration did.

I end this by giving you one last illustration of this point. It comes from Gabriel Marquez's book *The Autumn of the Patriarch*. It's a scene in the book where the patriarch, fat as he is, is lying in his hammock, licking his brutal lips and talking with his mother. "A nation was the best thing ever invented, Mother," he sighs.

Part II

Middle East Problems and Policies

Among the places in the world where American foreign policy has been called upon to exert extraordinary efforts, the Middle East must surely rank near the top, if it is not actually at the apex. This second part reflects the prominent place given to that policy area at the Hofstra Conference. The detailed descriptions and analyses were fitted into three distinct panels. The first of these was devoted to the Middle East peace process, the second to the Camp David accords, and the third to the Iranian hostage crisis.

In considering the Middle East as a policy arena upon which President Carter left his most distinctive marks, one cannot escape a sense of deep irony. It was there that he both achieved his most marked success and experienced the torture of his most serious debacle. The Hofstra Conference's ability to do justice to such grave matters depended upon the generous contributions of people deeply familiar with both sets of events at close range.

The first panel reflects the importance of two major points of tension in the design and execution of U.S. policy: the arms-length "relations" with the Palestine Liberation Organization, one of Israel's major antagonists, and the U.S. role in the relationship between Israel and Jordan. Both topics are dealt with in great detail, and the commentary is provided by two former U.N. officials and close observers of Middle East politics.

The forum on the Camp David accords was unusual and noteworthy because it featured four former diplomats directly involved as participants in the crafting and negotiation of that agreement, and a State Department official who is at present involved in the U.S. policy effort in the area. The panel was organized by one of the notable American scholars of the Middle East, and President Carter's major post-presidential aide in his continuing efforts in the Middle East. This account of the Carter-Sadat-Begin summit at this forum was the first time these participants had come together to discuss that fruitful diplomatic moment since then, though one of them, Dr. William Quandt, has written a highly regarded analysis of that period.

The Iran hostage crisis stands in sharp contrast to the success at Camp David. Entrapped by unyielding forces, and operating under the brilliant glare of continuous public scrutiny by the mass media, the president, having successfully managed the secret negotiations for the release of the hostages, was denied the political fruits of his unrelenting effort. Two papers concentrate on the diplomatic implications of the crisis and on Mr. Carter's relations with Congress during that period. A third focuses on the U.S. government's deportation of Iranian students. Several active participants in the crisis served as discussants, including two former hostages, one now-retired diplomat, one of the Carter administration's leading negotiators, and one scholarly student of the affair.

THE MIDDLE EAST PEACE PROCESS

8

National and International Consequences of Ambassador Andrew Young's Meeting with PLO Observer Terzi

BARTLETT C. JONES

The Carter administration was torn internally in the summer of 1979. Alarmed by national unrest and a "crisis of confidence," the president dismissed five cabinet officers, centralized the White House staff, and demanded more discipline in his official family. In mid-August, the news leaked that Ambassador Andrew Young had violated U.S. policy by meeting with a PLO representative. Young had not reported the meeting to the State Department, and then he told less than the whole truth--giving him a charitable evaluation. Carter's approval rating was only 25 percent; the secretary of state had been placed in an untenable position. Young had repeatedly embarrassed the administration by his gaffes. Despite his extraordinary achievements, particularly relating to negotiations in southern Africa and improved relations with the Third World, Young was compelled to resign.

AFTERMATH AT THE UNITED NATIONS

During Young's last days at the United Nations, the Palestine Liberation Organization (PLO) exploited the publicity surrounding his resignation. PLO Observer Zehdi Labib Terzi was present on August 23 when the Security Council began debate on the Palestinians' "rights of self-determination, national independence, and sovereignty." The following day Kuwait's representative Abdulla Yaccoub Bishara said that the Arab states, as a tribute to Young, would postpone a vote to save the United States the embarrassment of a veto.[1] Young was generously applauded that day for his personal farewell statement to the Security Council.

Young expressed pride in the record of the Carter administration in foreign affairs. He noted the U.S. role in the Namibia negotiations, in which he had played so large a part, and the improvement in our Latin American relations following the Panama Canal Treaty. He cited improved relations with Russia, China, and the Arabs while keeping Israel's friendship. Continuing to deny that he was the "victim," Young said that he had jeopardized his job with his eyes open. He defended his actions by analyzing the risks of broken communications between nations. The wars in Korea and Vietnam might have been averted if we had been willing to negotiate with the Chinese communists after their 1949 victory. (Based upon a private conservation after the resignation, a former U.N. official told me that Young was upset because he liked his job and was proud to be president of the Security Council; but he found the restrictions on whom he could talk with intolerable. The U.N. official, who had dwelt upon the bad consequence of our not recognizing China, suggested that echoes of the conversation appeared in Young's farewell remarks. Certainly he and Young had probed the issues posed by a great power moralistically refusing to recognize or talk to governments and groups of which it disapproved.) Young's most memorable remarks dealt with the PLO and Israel.

Assigning blame for the Middle East impasse to all parties, Young said:

I've said that it's ridiculous policy not to talk to the PLO, and I think it is a ridiculous policy. But if it is ridiculous not to talk to the PLO on the part of the United States and the Nation of Israel, it's also ridiculous for many of you around this table not to have good relations with the Nation of Israel.[2]

Both Israel and the Arabs had to renounce violence. The moral basis of the Palestinian people had been eroded by the attempts to destroy Israel; Israel was currently spending its moral capital in attacks on Lebanon and the building of illegal settlements. Violence had failed; efforts to isolate the opponent had failed. Talking together was the best hope for resolving differences. Although there was no change in Washington's PLO stance during the Carter era, both PLO and Israeli officials noted a new receptivity in Washington to dealing with the PLO. On August 31, Young's successor, Donald F. McHenry, found merit in Young's views. Although he avoided calling American policy "ridiculous" and referring to the PLO by name, McHenry generally applauded communication between rivals and including the Palestinians in the Middle East peace process.[3]

Certain reactions to Young's resignation provide perspective. Israel's Ambassador, Yehuda Z. Blum, told the Security Council that he was sorry to see Young leave the United Nations. Israeli officials in Jerusalem reportedly said that their protest over Young's meeting with Terzi was aimed at a suspected shift in U.S. policy toward the PLO rather than at Young personally. Singapore's U.N. ambassador, T. T. B. Koh, said that Young helped "turn Africans away from the anti-Israeli position they were locked into." For example, African states had refused to expel Egypt from the Organization of African Unity despite the Arab suggestions to do so following the Egyptian-Israeli peace treaty.

YOUNG AND THE STATE DEPARTMENT

Young had not told State about his meeting with Terzi "because the less they know, the less they would be responsible." He had probably caused State to issue a misleading explanation on August 13 by not disclosing that the meeting was substantive. On August 14, Young admitted misleading Vance and State on this point. "That was not a lie; it was just not the whole truth." Young suggested on the next day that State should have been wary about his answer because he had said that he was giving an "official version."[4] This scenario was consistent with administration press leaks asserting that Young's grave offense was not the meeting but his failure to inform State about it, and then further to embarrass the administration by his deceptive explanation. Administrative necessity, not Jewish pressure, was thus the administration's rationale for Young's departure.

On August 18, however, Young made assertions that made State a villain in his ouster. By July 30, he said, State had a virtually verbatim account of his conservation with Terzi: "I read it and it was very accurate." Young contended that this report and an August 11 conversation with William Maynes gave State all pertinent information before the issue became public. In conflict with his August 14 and 15 statements, Young now said that he had told Maynes that the Terzi conversation was substantive rather than merely social amenities. (He admitted withholding from Maynes the fact that he had arranged the Terzi meeting.) Maynes reportedly said that Young had not reported his dis cussion of the postponement with Terzi. Consistent with his claims that he had not been driven from office, Young said that the only pressure for his resignation came from a State Department group that had long criticized his methods and policies. Furthermore, Young said that he had filed a report of a chance meeting with a Palestinian official in 1977, and had been told by a high State Department official (not Vance) to keep it out of official channels. State had then denied that the meeting took place. In sum, Young suggested that he should not be blamed for failure to report the meeting because State had proved that it did not wish to know about such encounters. He had not misled State because State *already knew* that the meeting with Terzi was substantive. Finally, a group within State, the agency that pretended not to know the pertinent details of the Terzi meeting, had pressured him to leave.

The conflict between Young and Maynes respecting reported substance in the Terzi meeting would be relatively unimportant if State already had a transcript of that meeting. On August 20, the *New York Times* reported that senior intelligence officials had confirmed that State knew the substance of Young's talk with Terzi *before* it asked Young for an account. State responded that Vance did not know of the meeting until August 11, that on July 30 it had only a report that a meeting between Young and Terzi had been suggested, and that it had no account of the meeting prior to August 11. The next day, State reiterated its position with support from the CIA and the Justice Department. Young's supporters claimed that State had used the meeting to embarrass Young, but State denied that it had undercut him. Denouncing reports from anonymous intelligence sources, State refused further comment on the Young meeting with Terzi. Its credibility had been damaged by the disclosure that our ambassador to Austria, Milton A. Wolf, had met three times with a PLO representative and had only been reminded by State that he had violated policy. But State had the last word.

On October 28, Les Aspin (chairman of a House intelligence subcommittee), who had investigated the Young resignation for two months, reported no evidence of an intelligence report about Young's meeting with Terzi the evening of July 26. (State did have a report of a luncheon that day at which Arab representatives suggested such a meeting.) Young told the press that he would not argue with Aspin's conclusions, but offered an unsupported claim that State had a "pretty good idea of what was going on" within days of his meeting with Terzi. One matter has been clarified. Aspin thought Young might have seen a report of the lunch meeting and falsely concluded that it was a report of the evening meeting. After denying such confusion, Young told Aspin that "to his knowledge there is no and was no intelligence report of the evening meeting." Recall that Young had claimed he had read that report.

BLACK-JEWISH DISSENSION

Although both blacks and Jews were considered elements in the liberal coalition, there was much bitterness between them before 1979 over affirmative action and Israel's ties to South Africa, and there was strident conflict in New York State's 1988 Democratic primary and New York City's 1989 mayoral race. During 1979, however, there was two months of black-Jewish dissension that most participants and analysts linked directly to the Young resignation. Israel and American Jews were outraged by what Young had said and done; angry blacks blamed them for Young's ouster. The *New York Times* aired the controversy in articles, editorials, opinion pieces, and letters.

Jewish spokespersons expressed fear that the Young meeting presaged changing American policy toward the PLO, and denied that Jewish pressure had forced Young's ouster. Both Jesse Jackson and Vernon Jordan, head of the National Urban League, pointed out that Ambassador Wolf had meetings with PLO representatives without penalty. Jackson said that the Carter administration had capitulated to Jewish pressure, that Young was the "fall guy" for the administration's effort to change policy. Young said that he had warned the Israeli ambassador not to break the story because the backlash would create a pro-Palestinian constituency in the United States. After resigning, Young repeatedly voiced his passionate identification with the displaced Palestinians and blamed Israeli intelligence for bugging the Terzi meeting. He balanced these inflammatory comments with conciliatory statements to mitigate the black-Jewish clash, once phoning black mayors and opinion makers until the wee hours. Several militant black leaders announced that they would meet with Jewish leaders to promote reconciliation, and with Palestinian leaders to continue Young's efforts to bring the Palestinians into the peace process.

Congressman Walter E. Fauntroy, chair of the Southern Christian Leadership Conference's (SCLC) national board, said that Young's resignation compelled black leaders to become informed and active respecting Middle East problems. Mayor Richard G. Hatcher of Gary, Indiana, called the Young resignation "a benchmark." Blacks could no longer acquiesce passively to U.S. Middle East policy. Joseph E. Lowery, SCLC president, met with PLO observer Terzi on August 20. (Jewish critics lamented the meeting between representatives of an American civil rights organization and a terrorist group.) Although Lowery urged the PLO to recognize Israel, Terzi was pleased with the meeting because "the black community in the United States identifies with struggles for liberation and human rights." Terzi thought that it "would have taken much longer without the Andrew Young affair for the SCLC and the PLO to come together."

On August 22, the National Association for the Advancement of Colored People (NAACP) convened a meeting of more than two hundred black leaders in New York City that included representatives of the National Urban League, SCLC, People United to Serve Humanity (PUSH), Congressional Black Caucus, A. Philip Randolph Institute, clergymen's groups, and state caucuses. Their discussion of the Young resignation produced the following grievances against Jews:

1. Jews had been insensitive to black needs and had, without consultation, taken public positions that adversely affected blacks.
2. Jews had opposed the interest of the black community through stands against affirmative action (e.g., the DeFunis and Bakke cases).
3. Israel had important economic and military ties to South Africa and Rhodesia.
4. Jews purportedly had desired Young's resignation. (The president of the American Zionist Federation had called for Young's ouster, but other Jewish groups denied taking that position.)

The group resolutions supported Young, condemned an alleged "double standard" in judging him, asserted black rights to express opinions on foreign policy, approved the SCLC initiative to meet with the PLO, and called for black-Jewish meetings to reappraise their relationship. The participants were ecstatic. One called the conference a "watershed"; the noted psychologist Kenneth Clark said it was the black "Declaration of Independence" on the Middle East problem. To underscore the determination of blacks not to be confined to "ghetto politics," TransAfrica (a ten thousand-member black American lobby for foreign affairs) criticized Israel on August 27 and supported a Palestinian state.

In late August, both Patricia Roberts Harris, the new secretary of health, education and welfare, and President Carter, in a speech at Emory University in Atlanta, tried to promote black-Jewish reconciliation. News analysis in September suggested, however, that the Carter administration had lost both black and Jewish support. Blacks thought that accepting Young's resignation suggested that Young had violated American foreign policy, that black perspectives on foreign policy were rejected. Jews said that the administration needed to say it had dismissed Young for insubordination. (This explanation would exonerate Israel and American Jews.) At the swearing in of Young's successor, Donald F. McHenry, President Carter said that no American Jewish leader or anyone else had asked him to seek Young's resignation. Four days later, however, William Safire's *New York Times* article blasted Carter, and especially Vance, for covering up the real reason for Young's dismissal--a betrayed secretary of state could never have credibility if Young remained in the administration. By refusing to rule out Israeli influence on the decision, Vance had contributed to an orgy of anti-Semitism.

For three weeks beginning in mid-September, SCLC and PUSH leaders toured the Middle East and met with Yasir Arafat and other Arab leaders. (Just prior to the visit, Arafat expressed regret for the dismissal of his "good friend" Andrew Young.) Ten SCLC representatives, led by Fauntroy and Lowery, made a five-day tour of Lebanon. Jesse Jackson and a PUSH delegation visited Israel and Lebanon. Both groups engaged in some cross-cultural exchanges with the Palestinians: hugging and kissing Arafat, singing "We Shall Overcome," and exchanging "soul brother" handshakes, plus chanting Jackson's consciousness-raising slogans along with combined cheers for Jackson and Arafat. Although both groups urged recognition of Israel and an end to terror, Israel's Prime Minister, Menachem Begin, refused to receive them--despite the pleas of some American Jews and members of his government who thereby hoped to reduce black-Jewish conflict in America. The visits also divided the civil rights movement. Vernon E. Jordan, president of the National Urban League, Benjamin L. Hooks of the NAACP, and Bayard Rustin called the black meetings with the PLO divisive, morally inappropriate, and unwise because they bypassed the State Department. Days after Jackson's return, Bayard Rustin and a delegation of black labor leaders were received by Israeli labor officials and by Begin himself. There was unanimous agreement that these black tours of the Middle East were triggered by the Young resignation.

If Young had kept silent concerning the frequent press reports that *Newsweek* magazine's Israel correspondent had been tipped about the Terzi meeting, and that Israeli agents had bugged that meeting, the black-Jewish clash might have been less severe. But Young reportedly supported the theory of Israeli bugging. (An *Atlanta Constitution* story said that the Israeli ambassador had knowledge of the substance of the Young-Terzi meeting before Young discussed it with him.) On September 24--his first full day after leaving the United Nations--Young said that Israel's foreign minister, Moshe Dayan, had broken the Terzi story. Young's aides said privately that *Newsweek* sources had named Dayan as the tipster. Two days later, Young met with Dayan in a New York hotel. Young accepted Dayan's denial and their rift was healed. Young also kept the controversy between blacks and Jews hot by urging the Congressional Black Caucus to be more active in such foreign policy areas as the Middle East. On October 16, moreover, Young told a House subcommittee that the White House had discussed with Israel the possibility of an Israeli statement opposing the Young resignation. Young suggested that Israel had been receptive, that only Begin's illness had prevented a timely statement. Administration sources said that Israel had quashed the proposal at the outset. Regardless, it was an irritant to black-Jewish relations to learn that Israel had not accepted an opportunity to support Young.

Young's accusation against Isreal, like those he leveled against the State Department, was divisive; but even he later appeared to accept denials and refutations. All the evidence suggests that he was quite distraught over leaving the United Nations which makes his conduct more understandable. (At the swearing in of Donald McHenry, Young said, "I ran my part of the race and while I wasn't getting tired, my time was probably over.") His prophecy that an Israeli protest woud produce a pro-Palestinian backlash in the United States proved true. In early September, a PLO spokesman credited Young for a deluge of supportive letters, lecture invitations, and interview requests. According to the *New York Times*, "Western diplomats here say the PLO has gained tremendous political mileage from Mr. Young's actions."[5]

INTERNATIONAL REACTION

The U.S. State Department monitored international reaction to Young's resignation. Black African nations said that their relations with the United States were jeopardized. Black Africa and the Arabs blamed Israeli influence, as did press comment in Ireland and Poland. Secretary Vance denied such Israeli influence. State made a concerted effort to convince black Africa that U.S. policy remained unchanged, and issued confirming statements to the American press. Isreal reported some preresignation statements by Young to the Israeli ambassador that cast doubt on America's unqualified economic support, and insisted that tensions with Washington were not eased by Young's resignation. America's ability to influence the Middle East peace process was altered.

SUMMATION

The Young affair was devastating to the Carter administration's credibility, both internationally and domestically. Support from both blacks and Jews was eroded. But it marked a new era for black Americans. Martin Luther King, Jr., had led them to the promised land of full citizenship; Young had led them across the Jordan to committed involvement in foreign affairs.

NOTES

1. *Inter Dependent*, vol. 5, October 1979.

2. *Congressional Record*, September 11, 1979, p. 24901.

3. Ibid.

4. Encyclopedia Americana/CBS News Audio Resource Library, *Vital History Cassettes* (August 1979).

5. *New York Times*, September 8, 1979.

9

Did President Carter Miss an Opportunity for Peace Between Israel and Jordan-- Or Is the "Jordanian Option" Still a Viable Solution?

SAMUEL SEGEV

Ever since the signing of the Camp David accords in September 1978, and especially since the signing of the Egyptian-Israeli peace treaty in Washington on March 26, 1979, questions have repeatedly arisen as to whether President Carter had missed an opportunity to bring both Jordan and the Palestinians into the peace process. Some politicians, scholars, and commentators in the United States (William Quandt, in particular), Israel, and the Arab world are of the opinion that had the Camp David framework given the idea of self-rule for the Palestinians more of substantive value, such as full control over land and water resources; or had President Carter forced Israeli Prime Minister Menachem Begin to commit himself to the cessation of all settlement activities in the West Bank and the Gaza Strip during the autonomy negotiations; or if a way could have been found to include East Jerusalem Palestinians in the electoral process, then there would have been a chance to change the course of history in the Middle East.

I am not among those who share this point of view. In my judgment, President Carter did not miss any opportunity, because in 1978 there was not a chance for the inclusion of Jordan and the Palestinians within the framework of the Camp David accords. The wealth of information gathered both before and after the signing of the Egyptian-Israeli peace treaty, and based upon personal background discussions with the late Israeli Foreign Minister Moshe Dayan and President Anwar Sadat, as well as on unpublished protocols of private consultations within the Labor Party in Israel in 1968 (i.e., ten years earlier), led to the conclusion that both Egypt and Israel, for totally differnt reasons, did not wish to have Jordan participate in the Camp David process. Despite public statements to the contrary, both Begin and Sadat were determined to reach a separate peace between their nations--yes, a separate peace--and hence, the agreement reached at Camp David was the maximum that President Carter could achieve at that time. The Camp David accords were a kind of Israeli-Egyptian "collusion" behind King Hussein's back, without President Carter's knowledge, and this explains why King Hussein was waiting in London for a telephone call from President Sadat to join him at Camp David--but the phone did not ring. Sadat proposed to meet with the Jordanian monarch in Morocco on his way back from the

United States. King Hussein declined the invitation, and instead joined the "rejectionist front" that included Iraq, Syria, Jordan, Libya, and the Palestine Liberation Organization (PLO).

It is nearly impossible to explain Begin's and Dayan's opposition to Jordan's participation in the Camp David process without discussing at length the positions of Israel and Jordan expressed during high-level, secret meetings in London between King Hussein and Israeli leaders in May and September of 1968. Since September 1963, King Hussein had been meeting regularly with Israeli emissaries to discuss problems of interest to both countries. (An effort to meet with Prime Minister David Ben-Gurion in Tehran in 1961 had failed.) Hussein met with Jacob Herzog--then political adviser to Prime Minister Levi Eshkol--at the medical clinic of Dr. Emmanuel Herbert (Hertzberg) at 21 Devonshire Street, in London, on September 23, 1963, and in the fall of 1965 with Foreign Minister Golda Meir in Paris. While the first meeting dealt with the problems of sharing water resources, the meeting with Meir dealt with Nasser's subversion in the Middle East. Three weeks after the Six-Day War (on July 2, 1967), Prime Minister Eshkol sent Jacob Herzog to London again to meet with the Jordanian monarch and to explore the possibilities for peace between the two countries. King Hussein explained that it was too soon to discuss this matter, but agreed to continue his secret dialogue with Israel. In May 1968, the first high-level meeting between King Hussein and Foreign Minister Abba Eban took place at the private residence of Dr. Herbert, at 1 Longford Place, in London. This meeting set the tone for future encounters. Neither Hussein nor Eban committed himself to any possible compromise, and both talked about peace in very general terms. However, Hussein insisted that a future meeting should deal with substance and not just with principles.

For that purpose, on May 29, 1968, Prime Minister Eshkol convened a meeting with Eban, Defense Minister Moshe Dayan, and Deputy Prime Minister Yigal Allon. At the meeting, Eban said that King Hussein wanted a clear Israeli answer as to the parameters of a possible settlement. He therefore proposed that Prime Minister Eshkol should meet with Hussein in London and convey to him the Israeli position. But both Dayan and Allon opposed the idea and insisted that before a decision was taken, the entire political committee of the Labor Party should discuss the matter and decide on the issues. Dayan and Allon argued that at that stage, it was still unclear what was the best option for Israel--a settlement with Jordan or a settlement with the Palestinians, independent of Jordan. Prime Minister Eshkol argued that in his consultations with Palestinan leaders in the West Bank, he reached the conclusion that the Palestinians would not participate in any autonomy talks without Jordan's permission, and that all of his interlocutors suggested that Israel should reach an agreement only with King Hussein. Dayan replied that in such a case, Israel should continue to be responsible for the security, water resources, and land in the West Bank, whereas Hussein would be responsible for the remaining fields and the Palestinians would once again become his subjects. Because of conflicting views, no agreement was reached in that meeting.

On July 3, 1968, Eshkol convened twelve members of his party's political committee, including Dayan, Eban, Allon, and Eliahou Sasson, a veteran orientalist with rich experience in secret meetings with Arab leaders, to discuss the parameters for peace with Jordan. Jacob Herzog reported that Zeid Rifai, a confidante of Hussein, conveyed to him the message that Jordan would oppose any territorial compromise with Israel, whether it was based on the Allon plan or any other Israeli plan. As a result, Eshkol concluded: "In that case, I do not think I should meet with King Hussein. Just to satisfy my ego, it is not that important." However, all the participants agreed that a high-level meeting with King Hussein should take place as soon as possible.

On September 20, 1968, Eshkol convened the full political committee of the Labor Party to discuss this matter. This forum was selected in order to avoid a premature debate within the cabinet, of which Menachem Begin was a member as part of the national unity government that was formed on the eve of the Six-Day War. Eshkol suggested that Eban and Dayan should meet with King Hussein. But Dayan rejected the idea: "I am the last man who is suited for such a meeting . . . small talk is not one of my strengths. After two minutes, I would want to talk business with him and would tell him exactly what are my ideas for a solution, and it all would have gone up in smoke." Following Dayan's rejection, it was decided that Abba Eban and Yigal Allon, together with Jacob Herzog, would meet with King Hussein in London at the end of September. The meeting was held at Dr. Herbert's clinic, and for the first time since he began his encounters with Israeli leaders, King Hussein came to London accompanied by Zeid Rifai.

Eban opened the discussion by stating that it was a historical moment and that it was the intention of Israel to verify whether Hussein indeed wanted a peaceful settlement. Eban had a veiled threat: should the negotiations fail, Israel would have to settle with the Palestinians, with no connection at all with Jordan.

King Hussein replied that his dream was to achieve peace. However, for peace to be achieved, it should be honorable. "If peace will be based on Israel's armed power, then there is no chance for a settlement and the entire region will be in constant danger of continued war. You can win many wars but you cannot afford to lose one single battle. So Israel too is vulnerable, and needs peace no less than the Arabs need it," the king argued.

Eban then presented Israel's demands for a settlement with Jordan:

a. Contractual peace
b. Considerable border modifications, and no return to pre-war lines
c. Demilitarization of the West Bank
d. United Jerusalem, under Israeli sovereignty, with a religious status for Jordan in the Muslim holy places and on the Temple Mount.

Eban went on to explain that Israel would consider a corridor to serve as a territorial link between East Jerusalem and the autonomous West Bank, under Jordanian sovereignty.

King Hussein replied that he understood Israeli security concerns very well. But Israel should ask itself what security is--is it a few kilometers, or the sense of security of the population? "If there is . . . trust and confidence between our two nations, then there is security for both. But if there is no confidence, then a few kilometers won't give you the security you need," the king said.

Zeid Rifai played the role of the "bad guy." He told Eban that the fact that King Hussein did not address himself specifically to the problem of East Jerusalem should not be interpreted as an acceptance of the Israeli position. On the contrary, Rifai said, Jordan insisted on total Israeli withdrawal from East Jerusalem. "For the peace to hold, it should be honorable, and therefore, Jordan rejects the Allon plan and considers it to be totally unacceptable," Rifai concluded.

One week later, Rifai submitted to Herzog a written memorandum containing Jordan's answers to Eban's proposals. The memorandum stated:

a. Jordan proposed that settlement should be based on resolution 242, under U.N. auspices.
b. Regarding border modifications, Jordan accepted the preamble of resolution 242, which spoke about the inadmissibility of the acquisition of territory by force. This principle should apply to East Jerusalem as well. However, if security concerns required border modifications, these should be made on a reciprocal basis.
c. In Jerusalem, Jordan was prepared to accept Israel's sovereignty over the Jewish holy places only. The Muslim and Christian holy places in East Jeusalem should return to Jordan's sovereignty. Jordan also accepted that the city of Jerusalem should have a new status that would guarantee free access to all religions.
d. As for security, without going into the question of who started the Six-Day War, Jordan felt that its own security, and not Israel's, was at stake. Therefore, Jordan needed to be able to defend the Palestinians on the West Bank. Jordan also rejected Israeli demands for permanent military presence and for unrestricted permission for Jews to settle on the West Bank.

Rifai's memorandum reiterated Jordan's position that the Allon plan was "totally unacceptable," and that any peaceful agreement with Israel should be arranged under U.N. auspices. He concluded by saying: "His Majesty's ability to contribute to a peaceful settlement depends to a very large extent on his ability to show the Arab world that peace is honorable, and that the settlement was not imposed. Therefore, before any date for a new meeting with Israeli leadesr could be fixed, the Israeli government has to respond if it would accept these guidelines."

From 1968 on, King Hussein consistently held the position outlined in the above memorandum. The Jordanian position aroused many doubts in Israel as to Hussein's ability to reach an agreement with Israel. During a discussion in the Labor Party's political committee about King Hussein's reply, Moshe Dayan observed that he did not believe in King Hussein's ability to reach a peaceful agreement with Israel by himself, with no backing from other Arab countries.

Eban admitted that during the meeting in London, King Hussein remarked that he was too weak to conclude a separate peace with Israel. Hussein recalled that he was in East Jerusalem when his grandfather, King Abdullah, was murdered by Palestinians, and he did not want history to repeat itself with him. Therefore, Hussein suggested that any peace process should begin in negotiations between Israel and Egypt.

That was the point that interested Dayan most, and he shared the details of the secret negotiations with King Hussein with Menachem Begin, who was then a minister without portfolio in Levi Eshkol's government. He and Begin agreed that there was no chance for a "Jordanian option," and they shared the view that the main Israeli effort should be directed toward Egypt. Nevertheless, the official Israeli position remained based on the Jordanian option and the meetings with Hussein continued, including two secret visits the Jordanian monarch made to Tel Aviv long before Sadat came to Jerusalem. That was the situation when Moshe Dayan became the foreign minister in Begin's cabinet, after the right-wing Likud Party had defeated the Labor Party in the May 1977 Knesset elections.

But before analyzing the Israeli and Egyptian positions on the eve of Camp David, one should focus on how President Carter's Middle East policy was perceived by Cairo and Jerusalem. During the 1976 election campaign, little was known about Carter's view of the Arab-Israeli conflict. In the only major address on the Middle East, delivered by Carter on June 6, 1976, the presidential candidate asserted that the precondition for peace was a change in the Arab attitude toward Israel:

Now this change of attitude on the part of the Arab states must be reflected in tangible and concrete actions, including, first of all, the recognition of Israel, which they have not yet done; secondly, diplomatic relations with Israel; third, a peace treaty with Israel; fourth, open frontiers with Israel's neighbors; lastly, an end to the embargo and official hostile propaganda against the state of Israel.

In the same address, Carter was also quite explicit on the Palestinian problem: "There ought to be territories ceded for the use of the Palestinians. I think they should be part of Jordan, and be administered by Jordan. I think that half the people in Jordan are Palestinians themselves, and that would be my own preference."

However, once Carter became president, the Middle East policy that was emerging in his administration was in sharp contrast to what he had said in the past, and was generally perceived by Israel as being openly hostile. I will cite here just two examples. One, Carter canceled the sale of concussion bombs to Israel, at the same time approving the sale of sophisticated Maverick air-to-ground missiles to Saudi Arabia, thus providing the Arabs with new technology they previously lacked. Two, despite promises made by the Ford administration, Carter vetoed the sale of $150 million worth of Israeli-built Kfir jets to Ecuador. Israeli suspicions about Carter's Middle East policies grew even stronger after the president had met in Washington with Isreali Prime Minister Yitzhak Rabin on March 7, 1977, and especially after his speech in Clinton, Massachusetts, on March 16, where the president spoke for the first time of a "homeland for the Palestinians." After meetings with President Sadat and King Hussein in Washington, Carter also met with Syrian President Hafez Assad in Geneva. After the meeting, Carter described Assad as "a strong supporter in the search for peace in the Middle East." If those meetings meant anything for Israel, they meant that President Carter was courting the most radical elements in the Arab world --Syria and the PLO.

Carter's meeting with Assad came just a week before crucial Knesset elections were to be held in Israel. Despite the weakness of the Israeli Labor Party--due mainly to corruption and scandal among its top leaders, the resignation of Rabin, runaway inflation, and frequent strikes--Israeli leaders were frequently reminded that the United States would soon be offering ideas of its own concerning an Arab-Israeli settlement. And when Labor, as expected, lost the elections and Begin formed the new Israeli cabinet, the United States was quick to remind Israel that Carter stood firm on his insistence that Israel should give up most of the West Bank and that he intended to bring pressure to bear on the new Begin government to compromise on that issue.

That was, then, the situation when Begin and Dayan resumed their personal cooperation in the new Israeli government. Begin was determined not to surrender the West Bank to Arab sovereignty, and Dayan, while amenable to a territorial compromise in the West Bank, did not think highly of King Hussein, believing he was "too weak to deliver." Therefore, Begin and Dayan disconnected themselves from the "Jordanian option" and turned toward Egypt. Thus, when Cyrus Vance toured the Middle East in the summer of 1977, and when Begin later went to Washington, on both occasions the Israeli prime minister asked for U.S. assistance in arranging a meeting between him and President Sadat.

However, Israeli efforts were not limited to Washington. Much has been said about the role that Romania had played in Sadat's decision to go to Jerusalem in November 1977. Much less was said about Morocco's role. Except for Jordan, Israel has had the longest relationship with Morocco, which continues to this date on different levels. Israeli leaders, including Dayan, Rabin, and Shimon Peres, had visited Rabat on several occasions, and according to numerous international press accounts, the two countries had cooperated in the field of intelligence. Using the Mossad channel, Dayan asked King Hassan's assistance in arranging a meeting between Begin and Sadat.

But before the Moroccan reply was received, Dayan wanted to be absolutely certain that the "Jordanian option" was dead. Therefore, again through private channels, he arranged a personal meeting with King Hussein at Dr. Herbert's clinic in London in August 1977. Dayan spoke briefly about this encounter in his memoirs. But in a personal discussion with me following Camp David, Dayan said that he returned from London definitely convinced that King Hussein was not yet ripe for a peaceful agreement with Israel. He quoted Hussein as saying that he could not suggest even to one village in the West Bank that it come under Israeli rule, and that no agreement could be reached in which East Jerusalem would be returned to Jordan.

That is exactly what Begin and Dayan wanted to hear from Hussein, and henceforth they devoted all of their energies to the Egyptian option. A few days after the Dayan-Hussein meeting, a positive response came from Cairo and, under Moroccan auspices, Dayan met with Egyptian envoy Mohammed Hassan Tuhamy in advance of Sadat's historic visit to Jerusalem.

One has to raise a question here: Why was President Sadat responsive to Israeli overtures, and why would he act in an opposite direction to the policy that was being shaped by President Carter? Here again, based upon private discussions with both Dayan and Sadat, it is now clear that Egypt, too, was not enthusiastic about Carter's intentions. Sadat did not like Carter's courting Syria's President Assad, and he was opposed in particular to Carter's intention to reconvene the Geneva peace conference, thereby giving Moscow a role in the peace process. Although less vocal than Israel, and certainly not hostile at all to Carter (on the contrary, in private communication with Carter and in public statements, he expressed a cordial preference for the U.S. president), President Sadat was deterred at that stage to reach a separate agreement with Israel. The association of Syria or Jordan in the process would have interfered with this intention.

This is not to suggest that Sadat betrayed Jordan or the Palestinians. On the contrary, on every occasion the Egyptian president insisted on the need to solve the

Palestinian problem, and to grant the Palestinians in the West Bank and the Gaza Strip the right to self-determination. Sadat also insisted on total Israeli withdrawal from the occupied territories, according to his own interpretation of UN resolutions 242 and 338, but he had a set of priorities different from President Carter's. He was desperate to have the Sinai returned to Egypt, and he sincerely believed that once Egypt had achieved its objectives, he (Sadat) would be able to bring the Jordanians and the Palestinans into the peace process.

Did Sadat overestimate Egypt's leadership capability, or did he exaggerate his own role in the process? It is difficult to answer these questions now, although history shows that was the case. Nevertheless, in the meetings between Israel and Egypt that preceded Sadat's visit to Jerusalem, there was a subtle, unofficial "understanding" between the two countries that when a final agreement was reached, Jordan should remain outside the process. Sadat told both Begin and Dayan that King Hussein "is hesitant, and lacks leadership." Begin, too, had contempt for King Hussein. He was ready to give Sadat all of Sinai, but in a way that could not be interpreted as a separate peace. Hence, the framework of the Camp David accords gave both leaders what they wanted, although both continued to pay lip service to the need to move toward an overall settlement.

However, it soon became clear that President Carter's success at Camp David could not be repeated. The dramatic developments in Iran in the summer of 1978, which resulted in the overthrow of the shah in January 1979, forced President Carter to divert all his attention to the defense of the Persian Gulf. For Sadat and Begin, it became clear that Carter would not be able to invest the time required to arrange a settlement with Jordan and the Palestinians. This became even more evident after Iranian radicals had taken the American Embassy in Tehran, and kept fifty-two American diplomats as hostages until the very last day of Carter's presidency. The Khomeini revolution not only humiliated the United States but also weakened President Carter's authority. Prime Minister Begin was the first to draw the correct conclusion from the American weakness.

Despite the stalemate in the peace process, the Jordanian option remained the only viable option for a Palestinian solution. Despite his anger at Sadat, King Hussein's meetings with Israeli leaders continued as usual, the last one being held at an undisclosed place with Prime Minister Yitzhak Shamir in the winter of 1978. In this, as in all previous meetings, Hussein reiterated that he could not settle with Israel without a prior commitment by Israel to withdraw from all territories, including East Jerusalem.

The latest exchange of messages between King Hussein and Israeli leaders took place in July 1988, three days before the Jordanian monarch announced his intention to disengage from the West Bank. The language of the messages, as well as their form, are a case study in itself. The letters are never on an official letterhead, and the name of the addressee is always missing. In a letter from Jerusalem, dated July 26, 1988, hand-delivered by a special emissary who crossed the Jordan River, and addressed only to "Your Majesty," Foreign Minister Shimon Peres urged King Hussein not to kill the Jordanian option. King Hussein replied the next day--via the same messenger--his reply addressed to "My dear friend."

Jerusalem, July 26, 1988

Your Majesty,

When we launched our effort to alter the tragic course of events in our region and to offer prospects of security and prosperity in peace to our peoples, we were under no illusions. We knew the undertaking was demanding. We knew the obstacles were many. Yet we were able to visualize the consequences of failure as well as of success.

Reflecting on these four years, we can recall both gratifying as well as agonizing occasions. Moreover, in this process we have experienced moments when we misjudged each other's intention or misunderstood a move, along [with] moments of instant understanding. I am prompted to send you this message out of concern that we may be in the midst of yet another move which may affect the future of peace.

We have heard that your Majesty is contemplating policy changes regarding the West Bank. These published speculations have reinforced public perception in Israel that our policy, commonly dubbed "the Jordanian-Palestinian option," is no longer viable. Hence, the internal context and timetable make it imperative that we proclaim the availability of other options that are not necessarily in contradiction to this. Palestinians, for example, are not excluded from the Jordanian-Palestinian option. It is precisely for this reason that I am writing to reiterate my commitment to the London document approach. Indeed, I am no less convinced today that it holds the most promising prospects for progress. May I add that the time of decisions at home should not be the time for hurried decision and possibly irreversible steps abroad. Clearly, our respective ability to signal to each other, as well as to each other's audiences, our commitment to the desired course of action gave credibility to, and hence solidified, support for this option. The reverse may prove equally true.

When we are approached by Palestinians we indicate to them that the road to negotiations is open, provided the vehicle on which they travel is the one already agreed upon: UNSC resolutions 242 and 338, the renunciation of violence and terror, and a joint Jordanian-Palestinian delegation. Concurrently, we notice intriguing signs that the PLO is being forced to undergo a process of re-evaluation of the need to renew its link to Jordan. Your Majesty has on many occasions introduced a voice, both sober and moving, in favour of peace. Your voice and policies in the days to come will be listened to with great care by everyone concerned.

With best wishes,

Sincerely yours,
Shimon Peres

TOP SECRET--PERSONAL

My Dear Friend,

Thank you for your message and all the sentiments it contained. I wish to assure you that my total commitment to a negotiated peaceful settlement of the Arab-Israeli conflict remains unshakable. Any action which we might take is directed at breaking the impasse in the peace process which has prevailed for too long. We might disengage from the West Bank, but we will never disengage from the peace process. We might disengage from the administration of the people under occupation, but we can never disengage from the Palestinian people and the Palestinian problem. I still share with you the vision of peace and agree that the vehicle for peace is the international conference on the basis we arrived at in London: 242, 338, renunciation of violence and terror, and a Jordanian-Palestinian delegation to the conference will remain valid, even after our proposed actions. Indeed, we hope that our actions will cause the Palestinians to see the light and come to terms with the reality of what is required of them if peace is to reign in our region.

With best wishes for your continued good health, happiness and every future success. May you continue your efforts to achieve our common objectives of peace and good neighbourliness. You can always count on my friendship and support in this noble endeavour.

Hussein

27.7.88

As we can see from this exchange of messages, although Shimon Peres was out of power, King Hussein did not close the door to future involvement in the peace process. In my opinion, such an involvement cannot and will not take place as long as the Likud government remains in power in Israel.

However, once the crisis in the Persian Gulf is solved, one should expect a revival of the peace process between Israel and its neighbors. King Hussein's personal involvement is vital to the success of this effort.

Discussant: Seymour Maxwell Finger

I'll discuss the two papers in order, and separately. First, on the national consequences of Ambassador Young's meeting with PLO observer Terzi: both the meeting itself and the way Young handled it, to my mind, were a disaster for the black community, the Jewish community, and the Carter administration.

With the first paragraph, I would certainly agree. Carter, in July, had just fired five cabinet officers in order to enforce discipline within the government, and to make it clear that the president was running policy. The disclosure of Young's indiscretion and disobedience of established policy came one month later. It would have been very difficult for Carter not to dismiss Young under those circumstances. And, as this paper points out, Secretary of State Cyrus Vance had been placed in an untenable position: news of the meeting leaked, became public, and was brought to his attention through public media and other governments. I had lunch with Vance shortly after he resigned over the botched rescue attempt in Iran, and asked him about this particular incident with Young. He said, "If he had picked up the phone and told me that he had the meeting--that night, the next day--there would have been no problem at all. Unfortunately, that phone call did not come." And Vance, as anyone who knows him would attest, is a man of integrity and great decency. So there was the problem.

In my book *American Ambassadors at the United Nations*, I covered the Young period and gave him, in general, good marks, because I think, overall, his performance up to that point was excellent. He certainly restored our relations with Third World countries. I think he was substantially responsible for the achievement of independence in Zimbabwe through peaceful procedures, because he was trusted by both the Africans and the Western governments. I think the work that he and Don McHenry did to bring about a settlement in Namibia basically paved the way for Namibia's peaceful achievement of independence. So these were substantial achievements. But Young had a problem; one part of my chapter on Young, I labeled "Open Mouth Diplomacy." It is a very good thing for a columnist, or a professor, to have independent views in conflict with government policy, and often the government is wrong. I could give you many examples of when the government was wrong. However, when you're working for the government, when you're working for the president, you can argue internally. I've had many, many disputes with people in Washington as to what the policy should be. Sometimes you win; sometimes you lose. That's the nature of government. But once the policy has been decided, once the president has laid down a policy, you cannot publicly disagree with that policy if there's going to be any sort of believability and credibility in the government. Therefore, the resignation was inevitable.

Further, I agree completely with Young that communication is enormously important, and particularly communication with adversaries. With your friends, it's easy. I am convinced that the war in Vietnam would never have involved the United States if we had correctly understood China's position and objectives, the Soviet Union's position and objectives, and Ho Chi Minh's objectives. The line then was that we had to stop Moscow in Vietnam; that China was a subsidiary of the Soviet Union; and Ho Chi Minh was simply a puppet of China and Moscow. Well, of course, that was completely wrong. Ho Chi Minh was nobody's puppet; China and the Soviet Union were then at loggerheads on many aspects of policy; and we could very profitably have stayed out of that war, had we had good communication with Moscow and Beijing. When I was at the U.S. Mission to the United Nations, I tried to have lunch once a month with my Soviet counterpart--good times, bad times--just to find out what the Soviets were doing, and of course always reporting, as I'm sure he did to his government, what was said. So communication, I think, is essential, but discipline within the government is equally essential. And that turned out to be the problem.

It was not Jewish pressure that caused Andrew Young's dismissal, and I think that both the Carter administration and Young himself should have made that much clearer. The charge by Jesse Jackson that the Carter administration had capitulated to Jewish pressure was both unfounded and reckless, and very damaging--as were, for example, the meetings of certain black American leaders with the PLO. Of course, Arafat was delighted to meet with them. Since they opposed the U.S. government policy, and the United States did not recognize the PLO, he was glad to have the support of any group in the United States. The problem is that this showed an insentivity to Jewish concerns. Young, in one statement, said that the PLO leaders that he met in the United Nations were polite, civil, nice guys, and I suppose they were nice to him. I could have said the same about the people who represented the government of South Africa. But I doubt whether I would have told that to the NAACP under those circumstances, and I think that was not good judgment.

The visits to the PLO really divided the civil rights movement. After Young's resignation, I arranged a meeting with him at the U.S. Mission to the United Nations of some Jewish and some black leaders, to try to see whether we could minimize the damage to relations between the black and Jewish communities. After all, as minorities in the United States, they had shared many hardships; they had shared both difficulties and losses of lives in the civil rights movement; and in fact, many of the people who were at the meeting with Young had been with him during the civil rights struggles of the 1960s. The whole point was to try to minimize the damage. Unfortunately, as Professor Jones's paper points out, Young kept the controversy hot. He made the irresponsible charge that Moshe Dayan had leaked the story to *Newsweek*. Subsequently he accepted Dayan's denial, but the damage had been done.

I found particular difficulty with the final paragraph, stating that as a result of these incidents, the black community had crossed the Jordan to commitment in foreign affairs. The author seems to forget which people crossed the Jordan in the Bible. I think that these incidents did not help the position of black people in the area of foreign policy. Don McHenry, Young's successor, did, because he acted quite responsibly. And I think the real future for the black community, in terms of effect on foreign policy, is developing more trained people to share in the government. I'm involved now in a program of Ralph Bunche fellowships for minority students to study, take doctorates, in international affairs, and hopefully become important opinion leaders. The percentage now is pitifully low; probably about 1 percent of those with a Ph.D. in international affairs are black, when the part of our population that is black is about 11 or 12 percent. So I think that has to be rectified.

Now, turning to Professor Segev's paper--and I'll try to be quite brief and keep to the time limitations--I certainly agree that there was no possibility for Carter to achieve an agreement with Jordan, or to achieve any more than he did. The positions were so far apart. The Israeli government was not willing to give up any significant part of the West Bank, and certainly no part of Jerusalem. And Hussein was unwilling to do business unless he got back practically all of the West Bank. So the positions clearly could not be reconciled. Even had Hussein wanted to accept that kind of deal, his position was too weak for him to do so. I think that, as much of a tyrant as Assad is, the prospects for negotiation with Syria offer somewhat more hope, because you don't have that irreconcilable difference over territory and Assad has power to negotiate.

I conclude by saying to Professor Segev that there was a wealth of material that was new to me. Being an academic, I wished for some footnotes to give authority. Of course, a journalist doesn't have to do that, but I hope that before too long, he'll be able to provide them.

Discussant: Murray Silberman

I, too, will comment on the papers in order. I share Ambassador Finger's feelings about the Young meeting with the PLO representative to the United Nations. Young was an ambassador who not only was responsible for implementing policy but, like others before him, also wanted to shape policy. So his meeting with Terzi responded to that part of his political and psychological makeup that made him try to be a prime mover in events rather than to carry out policy shaped by others.

I think that at the time Young's meeting with Terzi was extremely important in terms of coverage in the newspapers, but it was blown out of proportion in terms of Carter's ability to act as a peacemaker. I think it had, perhaps, more implications for American domestic policy than for American foreign policy, particularly its impact on black-Jewish relations in the United States. If it had any effect, it was there; and, unfortunately, it did much to harm relations between blacks and Jews, particularly the statements made by Young toward the very end, which served to keep the issue alive. Certainly, the real reason for his resignation was the fact that he did not follow instructions; he was not to meet with PLO representatives. That was standing policy for all American officials at the time, and he violated that. The way Vance learned about this certainly did not help things, and Young's resignation was inevitable.

I, too, disagree with the conclusion that Young led blacks across the Jordan to become committed in foreign affairs. I don't think this incident has led to the involvement of American blacks in foreign affairs to the extent suggested in the paper. There was then, and there is today, a sort of episodic involvement of American blacks in foreign policy matters. To think that this incident had a permanent impact on the American black community, in terms of wanting to become involved in foreign policy matters, is, as far as I'm concerned, overstated. Certainly, in areas where the blacks might have a natural involvement, or an area where they would want to be involved-- namely, in Africa--one sees very little involvement. Take events in Ethiopia; take the great famines that are currently devastating the southern part of Sudan and parts of Ethiopia; the issue of Mozambique and Angola. There is very little involvement of black leadership in these areas, except for occasional statements. There is not a continuous involvement by the black community, which is to be deplored. So I think the concluding remarks of this otherwise very fine paper are overstated.

Now, about the paper of Professor Segev, I do agree that there was not much hope for an agreement with Jordan, and Begin and Sadat had agendas of their own. I think both of them should, in their own way, be thankful to President Carter for making the Camp David agreement possible. The October 1, 1977, statement--which is not mentioned in Professor Segev's paper--of the Soviet Union and the United States calling for a reconvening of the Geneva conference, if it did anything, pushed Sadat to meet with Begin. And one point should not be overlooked about the political makeup of Sadat: unlike his predecessor, Gamal Abdel Nasser, he was not a Pan-Arab leader. He had very little interest in Pan-Arab issues. He was more a leader of the Egyptian state, which is also an Arab state but at the same time is a state in the Middle

East that has interests of its own, independent of Arab interests. And one area where it had a clear interest that was independent, say, of Palestinian interests, or Jordanian interests, was the need to recover the Sinai. Had there been another leader in power who was more concerned with Pan-Arab sentiments, Sadat might have been prepared --at least at that moment--to sacrifice the Sinai and permit the Israelis to continue occupying this land. But he was more concerned with the needs of Egypt.

I have a number of points, but I know the hour is getting late, and I'm sure everyone has questions. One point that I'm not certain I agree with in this paper is to what extent the Jordanian option is still alive. Certainly it would be very difficult for Israel now to negotiate with the PLO; it would be very difficult for almost anyone to negotiate with the PLO, given the fact that it has sided almost totally with Saddam Hussein. But King Hussein has also thrown his lot in with Saddam Hussein, although he's been a little more deft in this. He sends signals to both sides. But nonetheless, the message is clear, at least to the Saudis, who've broken off all meaningful ties with him. They've stopped sending him money and oil; they're not going to have anything to do with him. And if the Saudis are not going to have much to do with him, I doubt that the Israelis would. I also feel that the Israelis are partly responsible for weakening the Jordanian option. On the one hand, they have always wanted Jordan to be--as the French would say, *interlocuteur palabre*--a person they could deal with--but they've always imposed very difficult conditions upon him, based on the fact that they won militarily; and they clearly are not going to give back at the diplomatic table what they won on the battlefield. But if the Jordanian option is to be a realistic option, it would seem that the Israelis would have to be a little more forthcoming, to make Hussein's acceptance of a deal with Israel more palatable to other Arabs. There has always been a resistance to that.

So there is something of a contradiction between the Israeli position, on the one hand--especially the Labor government--wanting to keep the Jordanian option alive; and on the other hand the very tough condition they've insisted upon, which to some extent, has weakened if not killed that option. So I think there has to be a rethinking of the terms and conditions under which that option could be acceptable to both sides, although I fundamentally believe that, given the lack of interest in Israel of returning much of this territory, this option is not a realistic one anymore. And I believe, as Ambassador Finger has said, that the next step is likely to be negotiations with Assad of Syria. Not too long ago, we must remember, no less a person than Prime Minister Shamir invited Assad to come to Jerusalem. I think the lines of communication should be kept open, not only to Assad but also to the PLO. There's nothing wrong in talking to people; it doesn't you mean you validate or accept their principles, but at least you can understand what they think, so there are no possibilities of miscalculation.

I think the Israeli position of talking to states, rather than to the Palestinians, is likely to be the next step. However, I believe that the core of this dispute is still the Arab-Palestinian dispute, not the Israeli-Arab dispute; and until the Israelis deal with the Palestinians--not necessarily with Arafat or the PLO--there won't be a meaningful solution. But as a next step in defusing this explosive situation, if Israel could strike a deal with Assad and return a good part of the Golan to Syria, which a number of Israelis have said is a realistic option, I think Israel could take out of the conflict the second most threatening country in the coalition against it--the first having been Egypt and the second, Syria.

There is one new participant in this equation: Iraq. The fact that Iraq has a tremendous military force, the fact that Iraq has managed to mobilize the more radical elements in the Arab world, makes Saddam Hussein a serious person in future negotiations or discussions about the Arab-Israel conflict.

THE CAMP DAVID ACCORDS

Moderator: Kenneth W. Stein

I grew up no more than two miles from here: it's quite gratifying to be back in Hempstead. It's also very gratifying to be here in the company of these five gentlemen, individuals who have an enormous amount of public policy experience dealing with the Middle East; individuals whose reputations far outweigh my own, and probably will for the rest of my life; individuals who have given enormous time to the pursuit of peace in the Middle East, and continue to do so, even though some of them are no longer involved in official public service.

No one who studies the Middle East or observes the conduct of American foreign policy can overestimate the extraordinary political achievement of President Jimmy Carter in negotiating the 1978 Camp David accords. Given the depth of historical animosity between Arabs and Israelis, it was remarkable that an agreement--however imperfect--was reached between Israel and Egypt in 1978. Since the September 1978 signing, the countries and people of the region have reacted to this historical benchmark. The accords proved that negotiation and not belligerency can begin to characterize Israeli-Arab relations. The legacy of the accords is their durability in the face of severe criticism and enormous political change in the Middle East.

When Anwar Sadat stated to the Egyptian People's Assembly on November 9, 1977, "I'm ready to go to their . . . Knesset to talk to them," most hardened cynics dismissed his statement as rhetoric. After his visit to Jerusalem, official Washington remained somewhat skeptical of this bold initiative. The Carter administration had spent almost all of the first year in office concentrating on seeking to reconvene a Geneva Middle East peace conference. Public endorsement of Sadat's venture was slow in coming from either the White House or the State Department.

During and after the October 1973 war, Secretary of State Kissinger had successfully established a working rapport with Sadat. The United States had become an interlocutor and intermediary. We had negotiated two successful disengagement agreements with Egypt, and one with Syria. In addition, Anwar Sadat began to trust Americans. He began to trust Kissinger; ultimately, he trusted Jimmy Carter.

In March 1977, at Clinton, Massachusetts, Jimmy Carter gave his historic speech in which he spoke about the necessity to establish a Palestinian homeland--the first president to make a positive statement about the Palestinian future. Subsequently President Carter met with virtually every major Middle Eastern leader, and he met with Menachem Begin after he was elected prime minister in May 1977. From April to August 1977, Carter and his foreign policy aides sought to overcome procedural problems involved in reconvening a Geneva conference. The sticking point then, as now, was the PLO, or Palestinian, representation. Israel opposed separate Palestinian representation at Geneva, and it adamantly opposed the establishment of a Palestinian political infrastructure, which would endanger Israel's survival. Ultimately, by the end of September 1977, Israel accepted the concept of Palestinian representation in a unified delegation at Geneva. After the opening session at Geneva, bilateral talks between Israel and Egypt were to take place. How the Palestinian question was to be resolved remained an outstanding issue.

But Anwar Sadat grew impatient because the Syrians perhaps were going to be involved. He may have grown impatient because the United States, on October 1, 1977, had offered the opportunity for a renewed Soviet involvement in Middle East diplomacy with the joint statement issued by the Soviet Union and the United States. So in November 1977, Anwar Sadat traveled to Jerusalem. During the first nine days of November, he kept the idea of going to the Knesset to himself; finally he went. He met the Israeli leaders; he met people with whom he had been enemies for many years. He had said, in 1972, that peace would come in the next generation, and five years later he was in Jerusalem. But it was much easeir during those first forty-eight hours in Jerusalem, with euphoria and expectations high, than it would be in the subsequent eight or nine months leading up to Camp David, to achieve anything substantial between the sides.

Subsequent to Sadat's trip to Jerusalem, talks took place in Ismailia, Egypt, Jerusalem, and Leeds Castle in England. It all led up to the decision by President Carter in mid-1978 to invite Menachem Begin and Anwar Sadat to Camp David. The letters of invitation, which were signed by President Carter and were hand-delivered by Secretary Vance, are now in the Jimmy Carter Presidential Library in Atlanta. If you want to see an example of the economy of word usage by the thirty-ninth president of the United States, I recommend that you read those letters. They are also found in the back of Bill Quandt's book on Camp David.

In September 1978, President Carter invited Menachem Begin and Anwar Sadat and their delegations to Camp David. Tonight, these five gentlemen will speak to us about their recollections surrounding events of Camp David. We have asked each of the principals this evening to speak for fifteen minutes. We will then have questions and answers. We want to give our principals an opportunity to query each other, to probe into the memories of one another.

Discussant: Hermann F. Eilts

Stein: Our first speaker this evening is Hermann Frederick Eilts, a distinguished university professor of international relations at Boston University. Ambassador Eilts was born in Germany, and received his B.A. from Ursinus College and his M.A. from the School of Advanced International Studies at Johns Hopkins University. He is a graduate of the National War College and the Army War College. After serving in the U.S. Army in North Africa and Europe as an officer in World War II, Hermann Eilts joined the U.S. foreign service in 1947. He's seen diplomatic service in Tehran, Jidda, Baghdad, Aden, Yemen, London, and Tripoli. He served as U.S. ambassador to Saudi Arabia from 1965 to 1970; was deputy commandant of the Army War College at Carlisle Barracks, Pennsylvania, from 1970 to 1973; and was U.S. ambassador to Egypt from 1973 to 1979, participating in the Sinai I and Sinai II disengagement talks and the Camp David negotiations. He retired from the foreign service in 1979, and that year joined Boston University. It is with great pleasure that I present to you Ambassador Hermann Frederick Eilts.

Eilts: Fifteen minutes is not a great deal of time to talk about events that were so momentous as those of Camp David. What I would like to do in the time that I have is speak on the subject of President Carter and the Egyptian leadership at Camp David.

Dr. Stein spoke a few moments ago of some of the events leading up to Camp David. There's one event that I think deserves particular mention, because it has tended to be forgotten. It happened in the first meeting in Washington that President Carter had with President Sadat, shortly after the Carter administration took office. President Sadat, at the time, had a certain sense of uneasiness about Carter. He felt that during the election campaign, Carter had shown very pro-Israeli tendencies in some of his remarks, and he was worried, initially, about the promise President Ford had made that if he was reelected, the Ford administration would seek to work out a comprehensive settlement rather than continue the Nixon-Kissinger step-by-step approach. Sadat had pretty much concluded after Sinai II that the step-by-step approach was no longer viable. He was delighted when President Carter, very quickly after assuming office, accepted the concept of working toward a comprehensive settlement. It was in that context that the effort of the Carter administration in its first year in office was to get to a Geneva conference.

At that first meeting in February 1977, President Sadat said to President Carter that if we could work out a cessation of hostilities and peace, that should be enough. President Carter responded, "You must understand, Mr. President, I cannot possibly urge the Israelis to take the necessary action to withdraw from Sinai if there is not also a willingness of the part of the Egyptian government to formally recognize and establish diplomatic relations with Israel as part of any such package." Of course, diplomatic relations between the two states have existed for a long time, but I want to emphasize that in 1977, this was an extraordinarily candid statement. No one in previous administrations had gone so far as to say openly to the Egyptian president-- nor, for that matter, to other Arab leaders with whom negotiations were taking place--

that what was critical, if one was going to try to get Israeli withdrawal from occupied territory, was a willingness on the Arab side to recognize Israel formally and to have diplomatic relations with that state.

President Sadat showed a bit of surprise that this had been put to him. He said something like "Well, maybe we can think about that in five years' time." To his credit, President Carter said, "Five years, no. We can't wait that long. The two things must happen at the same time." In a sense, of course, that was a very normal thing, but it was unusual for the Egyptian leadership to hear that proposition stated so unequivocally. In due course, as the Camp David agreements were worked out, and then the peace treaty between Egypt and Israel, the diplomatic relations became part of it.

Now, a word about Camp David. When the Camp David meetings took place, one of the immediate problems President Carter had to face was that Sadat--and I'm sure we'll hear about the views of Mr. Begin from my colleague, Ambassador Lewis--was primed for bear. Whatever positive spirit had come out of his trip to Jerusalem, and out of the talks that were subsequently held by the two leaders in Ismailia, had disappeared for a variety of reasons. Sadat had become convinced that the Israeli leadership failed, as he put it, to recognize the psychological breakthrough that he had attempted to make in visiting Jerusalem. So he made it very clear that he, Sadat, was looking for a confrontation with Mr. Begin at Camp David, and that he hoped President Carter would support him in this. Thus, Carter's first problem was to cool down, calm down, Sadat so that he did not come to the meeting, as he was ready to do, looking for a confrontation, and sour the conference at the outset.

A second problem that President Carter faced very, very quickly was a growing split between President Sadat and the members of the Egyptian delegation. The Egyptian delegation, very soon after Camp David had begun, concluded that President Carter was having too much influence on President Sadat; that Sadat was making concessions to President Carter. President Carter certainly worked very, very hard on Sadat; Sadat had the greatest admiration for President Carter. And some of the concessions Sadat seemed to be giving Carter went beyond what the Egyptian government had assured its Arab friends it was willing to make at Camp David. Thus, there was pressure on Sadat from his delegation, which included the deputy prime minister (who had met with Moshe Dayan on two separate occasions in Morocco as a result of the efforts of the king of Morocco), the minister of state for foreign affairs, the minister of foreign affairs, and a number of very able and influential officials in the Foreign Ministry.

The issue developed in this sense: What the Egyptians had wanted for some time-- even before Camp David--was a U.S. proposal that would take into account the views of Israel and the views of Egypt, and could be used as a negotiating document. Now that was indeed done, but Mr. Begin made it very clear that a single document that included both Sinai matters--that is, Egyptian-Israeli matters--and West Bank/Gaza matters was unacceptable. It was therefore up to President Carter to persuade Sadat to agree not only to split the single document into two separate drafts but also to insist that these two documents not be linked. In other words, each document would stand independently, and each would have to be implemented independently, so that if something happened on one and nothing happened on the other, this would not bring the implementation process to a halt.

The fact that Sadat was persuaded by President Carter to accept that split, and the legal separation of the two documents, was a source of enormous concern to the rest of the Egyptian delegation, which constantly sought to persuade President Sadat to stop making the kinds of concessions that President Carter sought. The Egyptian delegation tried hard to bring those two now separate documents together again, so there would be at least some kind of formal relationship between them. Generally speaking, the Egyptian delegation was unsuccessful.

The point I'm making is that the spirit of the Egyptian delegation at Camp David, their morale, was very tense--partly because of the concern that the relationship between President Carter and President Sadat had become so close that Sadat was willing to make the kinds of concessions that President Carter wanted, and that the members of the delegation felt were deleterious to Egyptian interests and to the Arab world as a whole. It was a very difficult situation. President Carter deserves great credit for handling Sadat so that the Egyptian president had developed a degree of confidence in Carter, in Carter's willingness to be evenhanded, to work out something that was fair to both sides. Sadat frequently said to Carter, "I will not let you down." That was clearly a statement welcome to President Carter, and obviously very helpful to him. At the same time, from the point of view of the rest of the Egyptian delegation, it was a source of trouble.

The eventual outcome of this tense situation was that the Egyptian foreign minister resigned at the very end of the Camp David conference, on the Friday before the meeting ended. And when the Camp David agreements were signed at the White House on Sunday evening, the minister could not be prevailed upon to attend the signing ceremony, he was so bitter about the whole matter. It was President Carter, through his efforts and the great confidence that Sadat had in him, who made it possible to move forward against the wishes of the members of the Egyptian delegation.

I would add a final point or two. Some of you may have seen the film that appeared a year or two ago on Camp David, which had a scene in which Begin and Sadat met in the woods of Camp David, and talked to each other, saying, "We two old terrorists, we know what it's about. Let's forget it all and work it out." No such thing happened; it was pure fiction.

Indeed, another of the problems that President Carter had was to try to get Sadat and Begin together. My colleague, Ambassador Lewis, and I had urged President Carter, just before the Camp David meeting, that given the state of tension between Sadat and Begin, he should not try to get them together at the beginning; we had warned that this would not work. President Carter nevertheless tried to do so. The first day went all right, but the second day did not go well at all. From that point on, Sadat and Begin rarely talked to each other. Certainly they did not talk in any negotiating fashion. It was necessary for the American delegation to go back and forth between the Israelis and the Egyptians in order to get anything done. The two principal leaders, whatever had come out of the earlier Jerusalem talks and the Ismailia talks, had become very bitter toward each other. I must say in fairness that Begin was less bitter and President Sadat more so, for he had concluded that the "spirit" of his Jerusalem visit should have been appreciated more by the Israeli prime minister.

As I recall the Camp David meeting, the elements affecting the Egyptian side were the principal problems that quickly emerged. President Carter had to be the mediator not only between the Israeli delegation and the Egyptian delegation, but also, in a sense, between Sadat and the objecting members of the Egyptian delegation. It was not an easy task, and it wasn't made any easier by the close confines of Camp David.

I've always recalled with a great deal of nostalgia that this was the only time in my diplomatic experience--which goes back to the end of World War II--and my involvement in the Arab-Israeli problem, which dates from the inception of the state of Israel, that it was possible to get senior Israeli officials (the prime minister), Egyptian officials including the president, and Americans together, even though their dialogue was limited to nonsubstantive matters. And despite the enormous difficulties of bringing them together and of finally getting a few on each side to talk to each other, it turned out be possible to draft and sign the two Camp David agreements. They may have been modest in substance, but they were nevertheless the greatest success in this very difficult Arab-Israeli issue that we had had until that time--and, for that matter, that we have had since.

Discussant: Samuel W. Lewis

Stein: Just as Ambassador Eilts has given you a sense of Egypt's view, or a view, perhaps, through Sadat's prism, we are fortunate this evening to have Ambassador Samuel W. Lewis, who is president of the United States Institute of Peace, and during the Camp David process was U.S. ambassador to Israel.

Mr. Lewis was born in Houston, Texas. He's a cum laude graduate of Yale University with a master's degree in international relations from Johns Hopkins University. He was in the foreign service for thirty-one years. In his last post, he served for eight years as ambassador to Israel. He was a prominent actor in the Arab-Israeli negotiations, including participation in the Camp David accords. Ambassador Lewis also served as assistant secretary of state for international organization affairs; as deputy director of the Policy Planning Staff; as a senior staff member of the National Security Council; as a member of the United States Agency for International Development Mission to Brazil; and had lengthy assignments in Italy and Afghanistan. He retired from the State Department in 1985, and he has served on numerous occasions as Bill Quandt's tennis partner.

Before assuming the presidency of the U.S. Institute of Peace on November 1, 1987, he was diplomat-in-residence at the Johns Hopkins Foreign Policy Institute, and guest scholar at the Brookings Institution. It is with great pleasure that I present to you Ambassador Samuel W. Lewis.

Lewis: Ken Stein has set out quite a task for this disparate group of old diplomatic colleagues, and we each come at it, I suppose, with slightly different prejudices. Bill Quandt, who's going to speak very shortly, has written the definitive book, *Camp David*, about the negotiations themselves, all the events that led up to the Camp David conference, and some of those after it. It's hard to do better than Bill in describing the diplomacy or the details of the negotiating dilemmas; or, indeed, to describe better than he has President Carter's unique contribution and role.

What I want to do is what Hermann Eilts has just done, from the other side of the mirror: talk about the role personality played in this outcome, especially the personalities of Menacham Begin and of Jimmy Carter. To do so, it's important to go back a bit before Camp David.

Begin, you will recall, was elected prime minister of Israel in May 1977, just four months after Carter took office, well after Carter had launched his effort to reconvene the Geneva conference to achieve a comprehensive peace settlement in the region. And Begin, who had a reputation as an underground fighter, a radical right-wing politician, and a warmonger, was the last Israeli prime minister anyone would have predicted to be the first to achieve peace with an Arab neighbor.

I arrived in Israel the day after Begin's election. I spent several hours with him informally over lunch three days after I arrived, well before he had taken office. And I came, in that informal exposure to him, to understand some things about him that ran through the next three years as an important leitmotif in his relationship to President Carter. I found that Menacham Begin was an enormous admirer of the United States, and in particular of the American presidency and of American presidents. As an outcast in Israeli politics all of his career, he yearned for acceptance as a legitimate political leader and as Israel's proper prime minister. Those two elements--his admiration for American presidents, whoever they were, and the United States; and his yearning for acceptance and legitimacy as Israel's leader--were interwoven in the way he reacted to Carter's diplomacy. Carter came to understand those characteristics of Prime Minister Begin, and I think his understanding enabled him to work through a very difficult series of policy conflicts with Begin over the next eighteen months in a constructive and ultimately successful way.

There was a big debate in Washington, prior to Begin's first visit as prime minister in July 1977, as to whether he should be treated with honey or with vinegar. His views on the West Bank and its permanent role in Israeli life, and its historical connection to the Jewish state, were well known. There were many in Washington at the time who felt that President Carter should lay the law down to Prime Minister Begin at the beginning, and make clear what was acceptable to the United States and what wasn't. Having some role in recommending to President Carter how to deal with Begin, I argued that in the long run, President Carter would achieve more success in bringing Begin to accept the necessary compromises for peace if he gave him honor and legitimacy at their first encounter.

For that first session, Carter accepted that strategy, and until March of the following year attempted to follow it rather consistently. It was a tough time for President Carter. Menacham Begin was a very difficult prime minister to deal with: proud; very concerned with legalities and the details of every negotiation and every document; immersed in Israel's tragic history and in the much longer tragic history of the Jewish people; highly defensive about any impugning of Israel's legitimacy or of its equality with other nations; very sensitive to personal slights.

But there developed between Carter and Begin a unique and interesting positive connection over months of meetings and negotiations and messages, and disagreements. That bond was grounded, I think, in Carter's religious convictions, in his upbringing as a Christian who understood the centrality of the Holy Land for American culture and for his own religion, and in an understanding of the history of the Jewish people in its biblical context. This provided an avenue for Begin and Carter to communicate, often when they could not carry on useful discussions about current issues. They could talk about the Bible, and they could talk about events of Jewish history that revealed something about Israeli behavior that Carter could understand.

Carter studied Begin very carefully, as I assume he studied Sadat. And as with every aspect of his Middle East diplomacy, he immersed himself in the details of Begin's history: he read his autobiography; he learned as much as he could about Begin's personal experiences during World War II. President Carter also came to realize that the tiresome, lengthy, legal dissertations about history and about the interpretation of language in documents that Begin so often subjected him to had to be endured, for they were an important part of Begin's psyche. This need to explain his actions in legal and in historical terms was central to his personality. Carter came to understand that, and as a man with an extraordinary degree of self-control and self-discipline, he sat through some very, very wearying sessions over those eighteen months before Camp David, without ever--except on rare occasions--letting his anger show.

I referred a moment ago to Begin's admiration for American presidents. Begin, throughout their relationship, desperately wanted Jimmy Carter's approval and friendship. He wanted them because Carter was president of the United States; he wanted them on personal terms, because he admired Carter, and Carter's enormous attention to detail, capacity for work, and wish to help bring peace to the region. At the same time, Begin was anxious for Sadat's friendship, and one of his great disappointments during the eighteen months before Camp David was the gradual realization that Sadat disliked him. After the initial visit--that almost miraculous visit to Jerusalem by an Egyptian president after decades of warfare and bloodshed-- relations between Sadat and Begin steadily soured. During Sadat's visit, Begin believed that he and Sadat had struck up a special friendship. And he continued to hope that their friendship was going to endure and be a bridge for the building of peace between the two nations. It was only in the spring of 1978 that Begin began to realize that Sadat found him quite disagreeable, and really didn't care to be in his presence. Begin was a very proud person; he hated to admit this, even to himself. It gnawed at him, for it then became more and more clear that President Carter, whom Begin admired and wanted as a friend, greatly preferred Sadat.

There was a fascinating triangular relationship here. Begin was the one most eager for acceptance, yet he was the odd man out. That, Carter understood; Sadat, I suppose, also understood it. Begin came to understand it later than the other two, and he tried to suppress, throughout the rest of his relationship with President Carter, his disappointment, his envy, about Sadat's preferred position among Carter's diplomatic friends. But it was difficult for him, and it often came out in small ways. It led me to encourage President Carter to try to find opportunities to send notes to Prime Minister Begin, to speak to him on personal matters, for Begin was a man not only of great pride, but also of considerable emotion about human relationships. So even when a policy dispute was unbridgeable, if you could communicate with Begin about something that had to do with his family or his personal concerns, it helped to get you over that immediate crisis in the policy arena. President Carter came to use personal correspondence with Begin to this end very effectively.

Now, as regards Camp David itself, I want to make one remark about Hermann Eilts's comment that after the second day, Sadat and Begin didn't spend much time together. Bill Quandt, in his book, makes it quite clear that this was Carter's decision. Begin was still anxious to meet with Sadat; Sadat was, I think, worn out from meetings with Begin. It was Carter's decision that if he continued his approach of the first two days, bringing the two men together with him as a triumvirate, letting them talk frankly to each other in his presence, the conference would blow up. Carter had planned on gradually getting a lot of the misunderstandings out of the way, and moving on to policy issues, but the chemistry was so unworkable that each meeting became less and less promising, and more and more explosive. Carter concluded by the end of the second day that he had to keep the other two principals apart; otherwise, the conference would fail prematurely. I think he was probably correct about that. So until the deal was finally struck, they didn't meet again. All the communication was done through their subordinates or through Carter.

I want to say just one quick word about the Israeli delegation at Camp David. It was, as usual in Israel, very disputatious, very noisy, very talented, and very important. Whereas Sadat was apparently struggling alone against the combined views of his delegation, who were trying to hold him back from making concessions, the Israeli delegation was the other way around. It was Begin who was standing fast against his delegation, who, in different ways, were pushing him to be more accommodating and more accepting of compromise formulas--proposed, usually, by the United States. Moshe Dayan, Ezer Weizman, and Attorney General Aharon Barak, now a Supreme Court justice, were the three key members of the Israeli delegation. In different ways, they all played crucial roles in helping Begin find ways to accept formulations of language that, in the first instance, his legal mind found totally unacceptable.

At Camp David, President Carter came up with one of the most unusual devices any negotiator has ever introduced in an international conference. Early in the second week, the effort to work out the overall framework for the Palestinian part of the problem was foundering. The issues had been divided into two separate frameworks: one for Israeli-Egyptian relations and the withdrawal from Sinai, which, by and large, was going fairly well; and one much more complex framework dealing with the West Bank and Gaza, which was still a long way from any agreement. Carter realized that the techniques being used--the United States producing a paper, getting comments separately from the Egyptians and from the Israelis, rewriting the paper, then giving it to each side for new comments, all the while controlling the drafts--although excellent, were not cracking the fundamental difference, which was that Begin was totally convinced Israel should never leave those territories. Sadat had to have some kind of commitment in principle to withdrawal if he was to take care of what he conceived to be his Arab and Palestinian audience.

So Carter persuaded Begin and Sadat each to name one senior member of his delegation to a drafting committee, and Carter selected Cyrus Vance as his member. Carter then chaired--as president--this working group: Barak for the Israelis, Osama el-Baz for the Egyptians, and Vance for the Americans. They worked with Carter for fifteen, twenty, or thirty hours--drafting and redrafting the language. Carter, as president, was of course not dealing with equals but with subordinates. Once he had Barak and el-Baz committed to a new draft, he would charge Barak with the job of selling Begin on what the committee had produced. El-Baz had the same task with the Egyptians. It turned out that Begin had great confidence in Barak as a jurist; he was persuaded by him to accept language that he would never have accepted directly from Carter, or directly from Sadat. Dayan, Weizman, and others in Begin's delegtion pushed Begin in the same direction; and Barak proved to be particularly ingenious at formulating arguments to show Begin in legal terms why he could accept something that seemed to him, at first blush, to be impossible.

This was only one of a number of ingenious innovations that Carter brought to Camp David, like keeping the press away and forcing all the delegations to speak only through one press spokesperson--the U.S.spokesperson, Jody Powell. This minimized the impact of domestic political pressures on Begin from Israel and on Sadat from Egypt or elsewhere in the Arab would, which would have resulted from free press access to leaks from within the Camp David walls.

Unfortunately, by the time the conference was over, all of Carter's efforts to keep his self-control had almost worn away before the very difficult negotiating tactics Begin employed. Late on the night before the conference ended, there developed a misunderstanding about Carter's insistence that Begin commit himself to freeze all new settlements in the West Bank and Gaza for the entire period of negotiation of the autonomy agreement that was to be the follow-on stage to Camp David. Begin never afterward admitted that he had committed himself to such a prolonged freeze; Carter was convinced--and is convinced today--that Begin did, and that he changed his mind overnight. This issue, although it did not hold up the signing of the agreement, came to poison the relationship between Begin and Carter in the months ahead, and was one of the most important reasons why the follow-on negotiations to Camp David over autonomy for the West Bank and Gaza were ultimately unsuccessful. What was at stake here was the tenuous mutual trust that Carter had established with Begin, which survived with difficulty through Camp David, though somehwat frayed, and was then practically destroyed by the disagreement about what had occurred right at the end of the conference. Had Carter and Begin had a stronger relationship before Camp David, I suppose it would not have suffered so much from that misunderstanding. Indeed, the two men managed with considerable difficulty to work together to complete the formal peace treaty over the next nine months. But the fundamentals of their personal relationship were established, and then soured, by the way Camp David ended. This episode again suggests that, with these three unique leaders, personality interaction played an enormous role in the outcome of President Carter's greatest diplomatic triumph.

Discussant: William B. Quandt

Stein: Our next speaker is William B. Quandt, senior fellow in foreign policy studies at the Brookings Institution. Dr. Quandt is an expert on the Middle East and American policy toward the Arab-Israel conflict.

Dr. Quandt was born in Los Angeles in 1941, the second year that Anwar Sadat was at the Military College; their paths would cross thirty years later. From Stanford University in 1963, Dr. Quandt received his B.A. degree, and his Ph.D. in political science from MIT in 1968. Before coming to Brookings in 1979, Dr. Quandt served as a staff member of the National Security Council. He was also an associate professor of political science at the University of Pennsylvania, and worked at the Rand Corporation in the Department of Social Science from 1968 to 1972. During 1987-1988, he was president of the Middle East Studies Association, and he's a member of the Middle East Institute Council on Foreign Relations.

This evening, at the Axinn Library, I typed in Bill Quandt's name and came up with nine books. I won't read them all to you. Among his better-known ones are *The United States and Egypt*; *Camp David: Peacemaking and Politics*; *Decades of Decision: American Foreign Policy Toward the Arab-Israeli Conflict*; and *The Politics of Palestinian Nationalism*. I might say that his book on Camp David, *Peacemaking and Politics*, is a treasure, and I commend it to you all. Bill tells me it's in paperback and still available.

During the Camp David process, Dr. Quandt was a staff member of the National Security Council, a position he held from 1972 to 1974, and again from 1977 through 1979. It's with great pleasure that I present to you Dr. William B. Quandt.

Quandt: The perspective that I want to try to develop is derived from the position that I had during this period. I worked on the National Security Council staff; I basically had two bosses--Zbigniew Brzezinski and Jimmy Carter. And in order to keep them satisfied--and they had a very big appetite for information about the Middle East--I depended very heavily on the kinds of reports that these two excellent ambassadors filed from Cairo and Tel Aviv, and on the advice and judgment of my colleague Hal Saunders, who was the assistant secretary at the State Department. We worked about as much as a team as one could imagine.

I want to try to give you my perception of how the president approached Camp David, and I want to reflect a bit on something of a paradox about the particular individual who is the focus of this conference, Jimmy Carter. On the one hand, you could say that he had a streak of optimism about human relations and about the way the world works--perhaps even a streak of naïveté; he often talked about resolving disputes through understanding and reaching harmony--"harmony" was a word that came up over and over again; and I think he deeply believed that most conflicts were based on misunderstandings that could be resolved through evenhanded mediation. Therefore, when he looked at the Arab-Israeli conflict, he was not particularly overwhelmed by the magnitude of the task. He thought it could be resolved. That went against the grain of many of the experts, who thought that it would be extraordinarily difficult to resolve such a deep-rooted conflict.

And that's the Jimmy Carter with deep roots in his religious beliefs, who came out of the civil rights struggle, and saw in one generation the change in black-white relations in the South. And it is the Jimmy Carter who was, in fact, a bit optimistic and a bit naive about the world. But another Jimmy Carter came through in the Camp David accords who was a rather tough-minded character about how you get people to agree, and was not above making some pretty strong threats and exercising some pretty heavy-handed influence. And I think anybody who tries to describe the man as having only one set of these characteristics is missing the complexity of the human being we're talking about.

Let me give you two anecdotes that show the different sides of the president. In the preparations for Camp David, as always happens, the bureaucracy was asked to generate briefing books, which turned out to be enormous volumes--often rather unreadable in their bulk. In this case, Secretary of State Cyrus Vance decided to get a few of us together to develop the key memo in this briefing book for President Carter. We spent several days on a very nice retreat in Virginia--Hal Saunders was there, Roy Atherton, and myself--and we tried to develop what we thought was the key memorandum that was going to clarify for the president exactly what he had to achieve at Camp David. We tried to focus on the issue of linkage, which, simply stated, was how the U.S. government would come down on the issue of whether the Egyptian-Israeli agreement should be a stand-alone agreement that had no relationship to the Palestinian issue, or whether, in some way, it should be linked to the resolution of the Palestinian issue. The Egyptian preference was for linkage; the Israeli preference was strongly against linkage; and we thought that, one way or another, Carter's major task was going to be to straddle this divide and find some way to get accommodation between these two starkly different views.

As I recall, Carter took this bulky book with him on a fishing vacation before going to Camp David, thereby clearing his mind before the onslaught. Shortly before meeting at Camp David, he called a number of us up and said, "I've read this book, and it hasn't helped me very much. First of all, I don't get the big point about this linkage issue. You're trying to make something very big out of something relatively simple. Of course, we want an Egyptian-Isreali agreement, and of course we want to do the best we can on the Palestinian issue . . . I don't see what you're talking about with this linkage issue." As I recall, we sort of went down the line. The secretary of state tried to explain it, and Brzezinski tried to explain it, and perhaps Hermann did and Sam did and Hal did. I was at the end of the line because I was the most junior, and I finally tried. He said:

You've got it all wrong, all of you. Let me tell you what's going to happen at Camp David. I've invited Sadat and Begin here to help overcome the real problem, and that is the fact that they don't trust one another, and they don't see the good points in each other's position. And by getting them to Camp David, away from the press and out of the glare of publicity, and away from their own political constituencies, I think I can bring them to understand each other's positions better. My intention is to meet with them for a couple of days, try to work through the misunderstandings, and within a very few days--two or three days at the most--we will reach agreement on broad principles. Then we can give instructions to the foreign ministers, and they can go off and negotiate an agreement. That's what we're going to do at Camp David.

I don't know how the rest of you felt. My reaction was, "Oh, my goodness, we're here for group therapy. What are we doing?" My impression was, from everything I had read, that Begin and Sadat could not stand one another, and that this was going to turn out to be a disaster. Nonetheless, the president convened Begin and Sadat the first day; the first round was not an easy one, because Sadat came, as Hermann Eilts mentioned, "loaded for bear." He had a document with him that he insisted on reading aloud that was very tough, and Prime Minister Begin had a very hard time controlling himself. The president kept saying, "Calm down, calm down, you'll have your chance." The next day, Prime Minister Begin had his chance, and the whole thing fell apart. And as you have heard, they didn't really meet again for any substantive purpose.

So this was a side of Jimmy Carter that was overly optimistic; that was a bit naive; that thought reasonable human beings could sit around the table and, in due course, reach an understanding. But that's not the only side of Jimmy Carter. Had that been the only dimension of the man, Camp David would have ended on that third day, and we all would have gone home.

The other side of Jimmy Carter was a man who understood that politics was the art of making the deal that was available. And very early on, he sensed--certainly before I sensed it, and before many of the others did--that the most readily attainable deal was one between Egypt and Israel; whatever else we could get was fine, but we shouldn't miss the opportunity to get that. The great advantage of working at the White House is that you get to participate in the briefing book that's done at the State Department--that is, if you have good relations with the assistant secretary; you also get to put your own memo on top of it before it goes to the president. So the memo that went on top of this briefing book was a scenario for how Camp David should unfold. We advised him to try to reach agreement with Begin and Sadat on broad principles that would address a comprehensive settlement in the Middle East, and not detailed agreements. And we had several scenarios for how he might try to do this.

Carter's reaction after reading this--and he was a reader; he read virtually everything that went to him--was to say, "You're not aiming high enough. We can do better than just get broad principles. At a minimum, we can get the framework for an Egyptian-Israeli peace treaty." Most us were surprised that that was what he had in mind. We had been working on the assumption that we were trying to get something more general, within which we could develop the framework for an Egyptian-Israeli treaty. He said, "I think we can get it, and I think Sadat's ready for it."

Looking back on what Carter had in mind, he was, on the one hand, more ambitious; he wanted full treaties, everything except the signatures, at Camp David. But it also had a narrower focus, and ultimately, it was more realistic than what we had in mind. I've tried to figure out where Carter got the notion that this was what was attainable. I trace it back to meetings that he had with President Sadat at Camp David in February 1978. None of us were present after the first meeting, which was a rather gloomy one. Sadat was very discouraged, very depressed. We left, and they spent the weekend together at Camp David. I've never known for sure what happened there, but I do know that when President Carter came away from those meetings, he asked us to try to think through what the implications of a separate Egyptian-Israeli agreement would be. I think we sent a cable to our embassies in Cairo and in Israel and elsewhere, asking precisely that question. Carter already had started thinking about what we could really get, and he was on to that much earlier than we. And he was right. Sadat ultimately was prepared to go for a separate agreement.

At Camp David, President Carter played many different roles, but the role he played that I think was most impressive was taking the issue of the bilateral agreement between Egypt and Israel, and becoming the desk officer for it. Hal Saunders did most of the drafting of the initial agreement, the overall comprehensive settlement. But Jimmy Carter wrote the first draft of the Egyptian-Israeli agreement. It went through several variations, as did Hal's draft, and I think that some twenty versions later, we finally got agreement on a much different version. But Jimmy Carter, in his own handwriting, drew up the first version of the Egyptian-Israeli agreement. This suggests to me that here was a man who, despite his naïveté and optimism, was also a fairly crafty politician who knew that there were certain things you could get and certain things you could not.

So I think we need to understand that the man had two dimensions, not just one: not just the naive optimist, not just the shrewd politician or negotiator. The two came in a package, and at various times each served him very well, and at other times each tended to exasperate us. But in the end, it was the combination of Carter's optimism-- his belief that peace was possible, despite the advice of some of the pundits--and the realization that there was a particular angle to this conflict that was susceptible to resolution now, that made it possible to reach the agreement we reached in 1978. And in that sense, Camp David really is Jimmy Carter's finest achievement.

Discussant: Harold H. Saunders

Stein: The next speaker is Dr. Harold Saunders. For twenty years, Hal Saunders worked continuously on the National Security Council (NSC) staff in the White House, or in the State Department. He has been at the center of Washington policy-making on the Middle East. After leaving government in 1981, he focused more broadly on the conduct of international relationshps in our changing world. From 1981 to 1986, he was a resident fellow at the American Enterprise Institute for Public Policy Research; he is now a visiting fellow at the Brookings Institution in Washington, D.C.

A Philadelphian, Dr. Saunders received an A.B. in English and American civilization from Princeton University in 1952, and a Ph.D. in American studies from Yale in 1956. As a U.S. Air Force lieutenant from 1956 to 1959, he served in the Central Intelligence Agency, and stayed as intelligence analyst until he moved to the NSC staff in 1961. In the State Department, he served last as assistant secretary for Near Eastern and South Asian affairs from 1978 to 1981. He was a key member of the small U.S. team that mediated five Arab-Israeli agreements from 1974 to 1979, including the Kissinger shuttle agreements, the Camp David accords, and the Egyptian-Israeli peace treaty. He also helped negotiate the release of American hostages from Tehran in 1981.

His most important book, *The Other Wall: The Politics of the Arab-Israel Peace Process*, published in 1985, builds on earlier writing about negotiation and describes the Arab-Israel peace process as negotiation embedded in larger political processes. His current project is a book extending that approach to the politics of international relationships globally. A longer-term project is a study of presidential policy-making in regard to the Arab-Israeli conflict. I'm sure any of these gentlemen at this table would attest that Hal Saunders is a gentleman's gentleman, the quintessential diplomat. He has given advice and counsel to all of us. It is with great pleasure that I present to you Dr. Harold H. Saunders.

Saunders: I have to say two words of introduction. First of all, I did, and do, respect Jimmy Carter enormously, and the remarks this evening are reflections in no way intended to be critical. The other thing I want to say is that I have often thought about our shared experience at Camp David as one of the finest human experiences of my career. I think it was one of the finest professional experiences as well, but more important was the human experience. I say that for two reasons. First of all, I worked with these gentlemen and our absent colleague, Roy Atherton, throughout the peace process, from the end of the 1973 war, when Bill Quandt and I were colleagues in the NSC, through the Camp David accords and the Egyptian-Israeli peace treaty. I have never known a finer group of human beings or a more capable group of professionals. We liked working together, and I think it showed in what we did.

But to follow up Bill Quandt's insights into Jimmy Carter, my primary point in speaking of this as a human experience was that in my book--I worked for five presidents--it was a model of how a president can use the professionals around him.

At Camp David, Carter learned that if he was about to see Begin, he could call Sam over and try out a few ideas on him, and Hermann when he was going to see Sadat; when he really wanted something thought through privately with his staff--with Zbig and Ham Jordan and Jody Powell--he got Bill to do the drafting; and if it was a larger issue, he'd get me over there on the drafting. He really learned how to work with us as individuals, and I think all of us are deeply proud not only to have been part of the achievement, but also to have worked with Jimmy Carter in that way. I cannot pass up the opportunity at this conference on the presidency of Jimmy Carter to say that.

When I talk about Camp David, in many cases I'm asked to talk about the negotiations. I usually spend three-quarters of the time talking about the Arab-Israeli peace process before Camp David, and about a quarter talking about negotiations at Camp David itself. As Ken said in his introduction, I came away from the 1970s seeing the Arab-Israeli peace process as a series of negotiations embedded in a larger political process. Now, in this case, we are focusing on the person of Jimmy Carter. Therefore, I need to go back and think a little about how Jimmy Carter got that way; why did that person, with the attributes described by my colleagues, come to Camp David to deal with this particular problem?

This point has broader applicability in the series of conferences that Hofstra has run on the postwar presidents. It would be my thesis about any president that the picture of a problem that a president brings to the Oval Office shapes his approach to that problem throughout his presidency. He certainly learns from experience; he may refine that picture from experience; but it is likely to color his approach through much of his administration. So an important question to ask is what was the President's early exposure to the problem? This question points to a more specific body of evidence than, for instance, the notion of some scholars that a president's worldview shapes his approach to policy problems. Of course it does, but what we're interested in here is what his particular exposure was, and how he interpreted that exposure in the context of his larger worldview.

Looking at the postwar presidents in relation to this particular problem is interesting. I always knew when I worked for Lyndon Johnson that he had a soft spot in his heart for Israel, and I wondered why. And then I realized, years later, that during the 1930s, when he was a young congressman, he came to know leaders of the American Jewish community, and he worked to help escapees from the impending Nazi holocaust come through Cuba and find haven here in the United States. He had a formative human experience helping people deal with that horrible situation, so of course he had a soft spot in his heart for the Jewish experience at that time. Each of the presidents has his own story. Jack Kennedy, as a second-term junior at Harvard, spent part of the summer in 1939 in Palestine. There's a wonderful four-and-a-half page letter he wrote to his father--then the ambassador to Britain--about that experience: a nice description of the future job of a future president of the United States.

Well, in a nutshell now, turning to Carter and his exposure to this problem, I would say that he saw the Arab-Israeli conflict more as a human rights problem than as a human or political problem. Let me elaborate. What was his exposure to this problem? The first two elements come together. There was, of course, his education in the Bible, which, as we all know, has been a serious part of the life of Jimmy Carter since his early days. Then there was his 1973 trip to Israel, a trip arranged for him--as for many other American public figures--by the government of Israel. I think it's fair to say that Carter's predominant experience on that trip was more one of placing the biblical experience in its geographical setting than it was one of deep thought about the policies of the government of Israel. Although these two elements account for a greater exposure to the Israeli side of the problem than to the Arab side, the interesting point is that Jimmy Carter came to the presidency, almost uniquely among postwar American presidents, knowing that there were two sides to this conflict.

By March 1977, at a Town Meeting in Clinton, Massachusetts, he spoke of a homeland for the Palestinians and shook a lot of people up by doing so. I asked him, "Why, Mr. President, did you, of all people, come to office putting the Palestinian dimension of this conflict as far forward in your perception of the problem as you did?" His answer was one sentence: "I saw it as a human rights problem." And that answer led to a discussion of how he came out on the liberal end of the spectrum in his Georgia community and in his Southern Baptist Conference. The detailed answer to that is appropriate to other panels in this conference, but I simply wanted to record for purposes here tonight his response to the question "Why, Mr. President, did you wind up at the liberal end of the spectrum?" His answer was, "My mother was a nurse who treated people who were sick, regardless of color."

In some way, though, Carter saw the plight of the Palestinians through lenses shaped by his experience with segregation and desegregation in Georgia. But, at the same time, to use his words, "Before I became president, I never met an Arab." And then he corrected himself. "Oh, yes, I did. A friend of mine took me to a racetrack in Florida, and there were a couple of young Arab gentlemen there, . . . they were friends of my friend, and he introduced me to them. But I never met an Arab." Carter speaks of learning about this and other problems from reading. He is an avid reader and scholar. To use his own words again, "I took delight--it wasn't a chore; I took delight --in learning as much as I could. I read all of Henry Kissinger's transcripts of his talks with Chou En-lai, and Nixon's with Mao Tse-tung. I read all about the U.S.-Soviet negotiations." He was a learner, but he did it from reading.

When I talked with him about what he had read, Carter couldn't come up quickly with titles of books, but for a presidential candidate, it's not so much that he read books; it's that he reads. People were always sending him memos and one thing and another; no wonder he couldn't remember everything he saw! But he did read. One of the documents that we know he read--and it might be interesting to hear Bill talk a little bit about this later--came to be called the Brookings Report. It was one of those things that prominent think tanks do in election years to take a look at a pressing problem that the new president would face, and to put it in perspective. The team that wrote the first Brookings Report was a collection of American scholars, former practitioners in government, Jewish Americans, Arab Americans; they tried to get a really good cross-section. But the interesting thing to me was not that it said, "Well, there should be a Palestinian entity of some kind. We should go back to Geneva." Rather, in the context here tonight, it was that from the perspective of somebody like myself in the government, this was a document that recorded what we all thought. This was the prevailing mode of thinking among those who had been in the peace process. I even think I remember that the president of the foundation that funded the exercise had permission from Henry Kissinger to produce a public study that would say what we in the government could not yet say. Therefore, it was part of the wisdom of all of those who had been close to the process, in government and out.

I make the point because Carter absorbed that, and he wasn't so far, therefore, from the community of people who cared about this problem. And the remarkable thing to me was that Cy Vance came in as secretary of state; it was Carter and Zbig Brzezinski and Bill Quandt over in the White House, and myself and Roy Atherton and colleagues. We got together on our strategy of trying to move the peace process back to Geneva without writing more than two or three memos. We knew where we were going because it was in the air that that's where we should go. If Henry Kissinger had been returned to the secretary of state's office and Gerald Ford to the Oval Office, we would have done about the same thing as the Carter administration did at the beginning, I think. Carter put his own particular spin on this because, as I said, he had a particular readiness to recognize that there were two sides to the conflict.

My point in all this was that he came to his views by reading, not by dealing with human beings. And it's interesting what this can do to someone. Again, after he left the presidency, after he traveled to the Middle East for the first time out of office, he said to me--he'd had a wonderful meeting with people, with Palestinians in the West Bank and Gaza--"You know, you and Bill Quandt told me a great deal about the Palestinians and their needs and their interests . . . Crown Prince Hassan of Jordan is a wonderful student of this problem, and he talked to me about it . . . I discounted most of what you said, because I thought that you were pressing an expert's point of view. But now I've met them, and I understand."

But Carter didn't meet them before he became president. So he didn't have the formative experience that Johnson had of helping Jewish refugees escape the Nazi holocaust; he didn't learn from people the way Johnson and Kennedy and others did. Even in the campaign, his relationship with the Jewish community wasn't particularly close; the Jewish vote, in the end, was critical, but it was, as he thought, grudging and very late in the campaign. So he came to office with an analytical view of the problem. He had a biblically inspired sympathy for the Jewish experience, historically, over four millennia; but he also had an unusually balancing human rights perspective on the Palestinian experience, and an analytical recognition that you couldn't bring about peace unless you dealt with both sides of the problem.

Now, returning for a moment to some of my larger thoughts about the presidency, it's my feeling that a president doesn't have his own policy toward a problem until he's a half a dozen months or more into the administration and has had a chance to grapple with this problem as president. And of course, during that time, Carter had his meetings with Sadat and with first Prime Minister Rabin of Israel and then Menacham Begin. I think his exposure to Sadat was certainly more gratifying than his initial meeting with Rabin, and probably than his initial meeting with Begin, so his tendency to see the Arab side of the problem as worthy of attention was analytically reinforced by his personal rapport with Sadat.

This leads me to a much shorter series of comments about Camp David itself, since my colleagues have dealt with it in some detail. Camp David was a triumph of mediation and negotiation, not just a triumph of politics. I would say that just as Carter's picture of the problem was drawn analytically rather than from human and political exposure, so was his approach to a solution. In brief, he relied heavily on negotiation. His dramatic political intervention--the Camp David accords themselves, the process--and his trip to the Middle East afterward to wrap up the details of the Egyptian-Israeli peace treaty were directed at bringing about a successful negotiation. Sam and Bill described the work of Carter--his ingenious work with his drafting group and his writing the first draft of the Egyptian-Israeli peace treaty. That was his ability; he was, indeed, the engineer putting the pieces together to form a structure.

I believe that the Camp David accords and the peace treaty that followed were a dramatic and historic achievement; I believe there was a genius in them; I'm proud, as I said, to have been part of them. But all of us here at this table understand where they fell short. I personally had the job, about a month after Camp David, of going to the Middle East and trying to persuade King Hussein of Jordan and Crown Prince Fahd of Saudi Arabia and the West Bank Palestinians that there was something in Camp David for them. I think there's no point in mincing words: I failed. I didn't convince them, because there were too many shortcomings in the approach as they saw it. The accords fell short because they did not transform the Arabs' political environment, or the Israeli-Palestinian relationship, enough to permit full implementation. My conclusion about the peace process is the one that Ken stated: the peace process was a series of negotiations embedded in a larger political process. Only when the politicians had changed the political environment did we, as mediators, have a prayer. Change isn't initiated in the negotiating room; it's initiated in the political arena, and the mediators and negotiators only capture it on paper.

We did not succeed in generating between Israelis and Palestinians a political process for transforming their relationship comparable with that between Egypt and Israel. Part of the reason for that, to come back to my original point, is that President Carter saw this more as a problem in negotiating human rights than as a political and human problem of transforming a relationship. Having made that statement, I will now answer it, in part, by saying that the Camp David accords were one of those instruments in history that are essential to staking out a framework for the evolution of a subsequent negotiating and political process. I believe that if we had been able to implement the Camp David accords in the years after 1979--1980 through 1983--the political process would have emerged from that. So I am not denigrating the achievement at Camp David. I'm simply saying it wasn't allowed to be realized in a political process.

My final judgment is not one of criticism but an analytical suggestion. It comes from the way King Hussein of Jordan described his concerns to me during that trip in October 1978. And I would paraphrase him in these words: "The Camp David framework is certainly sincere; it might even be a reasonable approach at getting something started between the Israelis and Palestinians. But I just don't think you are politically able to deliver its full implementation as you describe your purpose." And we haven't.

Discussant: Daniel C. Kurtzer

Stein: Hal has set a very formidable stage for our last speaker, Dan Kurtzer. Since the accords signing ultimately resulted in the March 1979 peace treaty between Egypt and Israel, many political leaders have blamed the accords for removing Egypt from physical confrontation with Israel, for making it easier for Israel to go into Lebanon in 1982, for allowing the Israelis to impose a policy on the Arab world in the 1980s of "Do unto others before they do unto you." What is quite clear is that since the Camp David accords were negotiated, there have been many other ideas, many other plans, many other declarations, by various groups, by organizations--the Arab League--by the European Community, by our government, that have sought to build on, emend, or tear down the Camp David accords--the framework, if you will. In essence, the accords have become a benchmark; they have become a basis from which many other ideas and plans have emerged.

We are going to leave it to our colleague from the State Department, Dan Kurtzer, to speak about what has happened to the intent, the tone, and the substance of those accords in the ten years since. Dr. Dan Kurtzer, a foreign service officer, was appointed deputy assistant secretary of state for Near Eastern and South Asian affairs in June 1989. His reponsibilities include the Middle East peace process, U.S. bilateral relations with Israel and Egypt, and Palestinian affairs; he is not responsible for Saddam Hussein's invasion of Kuwait.

Dr. Kurtzer was born in Elizabeth, New Jersey, and received his B.A. from Yeshiva University, and his M.A., his M.Phil. Middle East certificate, and his Ph.D. from Columbia University. Dr. Kurtzer and Jimmy Carter joined the federal government the same year, 1976. Dan Kurtzer was assigned to the Bureau of International Organization Affairs; Jimmy Carter went to the White House. In 1977, Dr. Kurtzer took a leave of absence from the State Department to accept an appointment as dean of Yeshiva College; he returned to the Department of State in 1979, and was assigned as first secretary for political affairs at the U.S. Embassy in Cairo. In 1982, he was appointed first secretary for political affairs in Tel Aviv. He returned to Washington in 1986 to become deputy director of the Office of Egyptian Affairs; in 1987, he was appointed a member of the secretary of state's policy planning staff, where he was a speech writer for the secretary of the state; and he was an adviser to the secretary and assistant secretary for Near Eastern affairs on issues relating to the Middle East peace process. He has twice received the State Department's Superior Honor Award, and in 1985, the award of the director general of the foreign service for political reporting. Every academic, every scholar in the United States who teaches Middle Eastern history, would like to write like Dan Kurtzer.

During the Camp David process, Dan was at Yeshiva College. It's with pleasure that I present to you a dear personal friend, Dr. Daniel Kurtzer.

Kurtzer: It is a tough act to follow four of the greatest practitioners of the art of diplomacy who have told us their experiences and shared with us their wisdom about what contributed to the success of Camp David. I feel very much like the character at the end of the "Rocky and Bullwinkle" show, who is left to sweep up the leftover pieces--described, quite graphically, by both Hal Saunders and Sam Lewis as the unfinished business of the Camp David accords.

Let me start with three reflections on the unfinished business of Camp David, which will answer, in a rather complicated way, the simple question of what has gone wrong since, and why successive American administrations have been unable to build on Camp David and to fulfill its promise.

First, immediately upon the completion of Camp David, as Ambassador Lewis noted, there were problems concerning the accords themselves--problems that not only would bedevil the treaty negotiations but also were to prove particularly troublesome in the negotiations that related to the resolution of the Palestinian problem, Israeli-Palestinian relations, and the future of the West Bank and Gaza. Inherent in those difficulties was the added dimension that for both Egypt and Israel, for different reasons, as well as for the United States, the Egyptian-Israeli component of the Camp David process became paramount. And so, although a great deal of time was spent by Israeli, Egyptian, and American delegations moving back and forth between Cairo and Tel Aviv to try to negotiate a self-governing authority, to try to negotiate Palestinian autonomy, to see whether the promise of the second half of Camp David could be fulfilled, in fact, the leadership of the three countries had their eyes very much on April 1982--the date by which Israel's withdrawal from Sinai was to be completed, and the real promise of the peace treaty was to be seen: full normalization of relations, full diplomatic relations, and full peace.

In a sense, the negotiations to implement the second half of Camp David became a bit of a sideshow. There was, in fact, as Ambassador Lewis indicated, a challenge from the outset in the efforts by both Egypt and Israel to revise Camp David, to reinterpret Camp David, and to lend to Camp David interpretations that were really inconsistent with the spirit, if not the letter, of the accords. This is manifest in the dispute that erupted immediately after Camp David, and which continues today, over whether the United States and Israel could reach an understanding about the Israeli policy of building new settlements in the process of trying to bring about a peaceful settlement of the Arab-Israeli dispute.

The environment after Camp David immediately was beset by other very pressing regional concerns, as well as global concerns. The Soviet invasion of Afghanistan; the Iranian revolution; and Israel's 1982 invasion of Lebanon became primary moving factors in the politics of the three key parties of Camp David, and they became excuses for all to focus less much attention on the Israeli-Palestinian dimension.

A second way to look at Camp David and its aftermath is to look at politics. Several speakers have talked about domestic politics and regional politics, that is, the influence of the political process within states on the ability of states to negotiate, and how they define their interests. The politics after Camp David--particularly in the Untied States but also in Israel and Egypt--changed considerably. If there was one lesson that successive administrations would learn about President Carter's effort at Camp David, it is that it did not pay off politically. Jimmy Carter became vilified in the communities that should have supported him the most: the Jewish and Arab. In fact, the only place where Jimmy Carter ended up the hero in the aftermath of Camp David was in Egypt, where President Sadat and the leadership--even those who opposed Sadat's policies--saw Carter's efforts as the harbinger of an American attempt to try to bring about a comprehensive settlement.

But Egypt does not vote in this country, and so the presidents who followed Jimmy Carter had to wonder whether it paid politically to invest the kind of time and attention that Carter did in trying to bring about a Middle East accord. This did not necessarily lead to a decision to ignore the Middle East, but it had to raise doubts in the minds of advisers as to whether Carter's kind of involvement in the Middle East was worth the price that he ultimately paid.

What followed Carter's efforts was a prolonged period of stagnation in American policy with regard to the peace process, in which the United States said that it could not want peace more than the parties themselves. This is a truism that happens to be true. But the one thing that Jimmy Carter demonstrated beyond a doubt is that the parties may want peace, but they cannot achieve it without outside help. They cannot do themselves what the United States helps them to do. This attitude gave way to the view that the parties needed to demonstrate an interest before the United States would try to move the peace process forward.

In the Middle East, everyone is a politician. The same kinds of considerations that motivate American presidents to shy away from the Middle East motivate the parties themselves to shy away from the Middle East peace process. In Israel, after Camp David, great disappointment set in almost immediately over the terms of the peace process, and particularly over the relationship that developed between Israel and Egypt. The promise of normalization, trade, open borders, and a new dimension in Israel's relations with its neighbors never materialized. In Egypt, opposition to the treaty among a significant political elite continues. Although there is a basic acceptance of the principle of peace on both sides, and the basic institutional framework of peace remains intact, the relationship that was envisaged by all parties before Camp David never came about. This led the political leadership in both Israel and Egypt to raise the same kinds of questions about the costs of a peace process that American presidents would raise in the United States.

Let me suggest a third factor. In addition to the environment that was changing, in addition to the politics that militated against the fulfillment of Camp David, there was the element of leadership. A colleague of mine at the State Department has a thesis that the age of heroic politics in the Middle East has ended. In fact, if we look around, there are no David Ben-Gurions or Menachem Begins on the scene; and there are no Gamal Abdel Nassers or Anwar Sadats on the scene. In Israel since Camp David, there has been a prolonged period of political succession, starting with Begin's resignation and not yet finished. In Egypt, only until recently, the same problem existed; many questioned whether the leadership existed to move Egypt beyond a kind of status quo policy. An unlikely source, the late Kamal Jumblatt, once said that the Middle East has room for everyone to live in, but it does not have room for everyone's ambitions. And that probably characterizes the way leadership today looks at the Middle East. What drives many leaders today--not only in the Middle East core countries but also at the periphery--is the concept that ideology is more important than the practical movement toward a peaceful settlement.

In some respects, Arabs and Israelis have reversed roles over these years. In the past, Israelis said, "We'll sit down anywhere, any time, with anyone to talk about peace"; today, one hears conditions attached to finding an Arab partner. Similarly, one could always count, in the past, on Arab partners rejecting the idea of sitting down with Israel. And yet, now there are indications in some quarters that perhaps there are changes under way in the Arab world. Questions do remain as to whether the Palestinian movement has come to grips with the reality and significance of the state of Israel in the Middle East.

All is not lost, however, and those of us who work on this issue are neither crazy nor blind optimists. Part of the reason that we do continue is that the beauty and the genius of Camp David still persists, and they provide us with tools, ideas, and ways to approach the problem of resolving the Arab-Israeli conflict.

One story illustrates this point. In 1983, when Secretary of State George Shultz began to move around the Middle East in the aftermath of the Lebanon invasion, a cable came in from one of our posts in Middle East country that, at that time, was characterized as rejecting the peace process. The ambassador reported a question that was posed to him by the foreign minister: What is the U.S. attitude toward Palestinian self-determination?

With everyone otherwise occupied, a junior officer was assigned to answer the question, and sent back a response drawn from the Camp David accords: that Palestinians should participate in the determination of their own future. Through the process of self-government and the process of voting on the agreement that was to be negotiated, they would have participated in the determination of their own future. The reaction to this was quite instructive. The host country thought that the United States had changed its policy, and was amazed at how far forward, how far-reaching, U.S. policy was. In fact, all that had been done was to quote from the Camp David accords.

There is still enough in Camp David to be worked on, and to be implemented, that we do not necessarily need a new framework to start a negotiating process. The idea of a transition period; the idea of self-governance for Palestinians as a means of establishing a new relationship between them and Israel; the idea of providing Palestinians with political and economic decision-making power over their future-- these ideas have not changed over the years, but they continue to take on increased and important salience in the resolution of this conflict.

So we leave this Camp David discussion with a kind of bittersweet attitude. We are left a bit disappointed by the failure of all of us--the United States and the parties in the region--to understand that a breakthrough achieved in 1978, and not fulfilled in 1990, is an unfulfilled breakthrough. As we pursue this peace process, we look back to the Camp David accords for inspiration, because they still provide us with a pathway to pursue. We still look for the kind of leadership qualities, the kind of political qualities, that were demonstrated by all sides at that particular moment in time, when the leadership of the three countries joined together in an effort that proved so successful in resolving an element of the Arab-Israeli conflict.

NOTE

The views expressed in this article are those solely of the author, and do not necessarily represent the views or policy of the United States government.

Questions and Answers

Stein: You can tell why it was easy to bring this panel together. These gentlemen know more, and can express it much better, than any of us possibly could. And rather than lose the poignancy of Dan's conclusion, I would like to turn immediately to the panelists and ask them if they have any questions of one another, and then to the audience for questions that I hope they will pose directly to the individual panelists.

Gentlemen, if there's anything that you'd like to clarify, please go ahead. This will be a free exchange, and we'll just pretend the audience is listening to a conversation.

Lewis: Can I ask a question of Hermann? Dan talked about the failure of leadership in the recent seven or eight years, and it does strike me that none of us have actually accented the loss of all three of the Camp David leaders from the process. Begin retired, unexpectedly, inexplicably, in midcareer; Sadat was assassinated; Carter was defeated. Do you think, Hermann, if Sadat had not been assassinated, and Carter had not been defeated--leave Begin aside; leave him out of the equation--would we have succeeded in completing the promise of Camp David?

Eilts: I think we would have had a very good chance of doing so. Sadat realized, by the end of Camp David, that it was the concessions that he had made--at least from his point of view--that had made Camp David a success. Now, granted, there was an egocentric aspect about that, but he had to take that position since, as I've indicated, his own people were criticizing him. He counted very heavily on the second Camp David agreement--that is, the West Bank-Gaza autonomy agreement--working out, and he counted on President Carter to make it work. He realized that in the year 1979-1980, President Carter was involved in the election campaign, and that the president had to deal with a very serious hostage crisis with Iran. Sadat was hoping very much, somehow, to be able to defer substantive discussions, which, as had been pointed out, were not working well on autonomy, until what he hoped would be Carter's reelection. And he was confident that Carter would then reinvolve himself in a major way in the negotiations, as he had at Camp David, and that something would come out of it.

There was, though, an essential difference--which I'm not sure that even Carter could have overcome--between Sadat and Begin on the issue of autonomy. As fas as Begin was concerned, West Bank-Gaza-Palestinian autonomy meant narrow powers and responsibilities for the Palestinian self-governing body; it meant no participation in the electoral process on the part of the hundred thousand or so Arabs of Jerusalem; and it certainly meant that whatever might come out of the five-year transition period of autonomy would be such, in terms of the narrow powers and responsibilities of the self-governing body, that there was not going to be any chance of self-determination. Moreover, Begin's point was that autonomy would apply to people and not to land. The Sadat view was totally different. The Sadat view was that autonomy powers and responsibilities of the self-governing body should be broad; second, that not only should the autonomy apply, the self-governing body should have control over both people and land--a very, very significant issue; and third, that the Palestinians of East Jerusalem should participate.

Incidentally, it ought to be borne in mind that Sadat was not a particular lover of Palestinians. In fact, he was very much an Egyptian nationalist. He wasn't even a great lover of other Arabs. Nevertheless, by the end of Camp David, because of the negative reaction that Camp David received even in friendly Arab countries--Saudi Arabia, Jordan, Morocco--Sadat had come to realize that something more had to be done for the Palestinians than had been done at Camp David. Hence, the importance that he attached to having those autonomy talks work, and while he understood that in 1979 President Carter could not involve himself, he desperately hoped that once the election was over and Carter was reelected, something could be worked out. There was still hope for compromise, but not a great deal.

I think if those leaders had remained in power, something would have resulted, because there would have been a greater willingness to focus on the issue, and focusing on the issue would have meant compromise by both sides. In my view, what really went wrong after Carter was out was that there was no longer as much focus on the issue as there had been.

Quandt: I think there's a lot to that argument, but I do think also that there was a fatal flaw in the autonomy negotiating process, and it would have continued even if Carter and Sadat had been in office; it was the flaw Hal Saunders alluded to. After Camp David, we failed to persuade either Palestinians in the territories or the Jordanians to enter the negotiations, as Camp David had planned for them to do. We failed, in part, because Sadat mishandled this issue and didn't help us very much in the persuading process. We failed, also, because Begin was preoccupied with his internal opposition, and said things publicly that interpreted Camp David in ways that drove Palestinians away rather than attracted them to it. And we failed for other reasons as well. And then Sadat said, "Okay, Egypt will represent the Palestinian position." I think, in retrospect, that was a fatal flaw that could not be overcome, for it was clear throughout the autonomy negotiations that Egypt could not make concessions on behalf of the Palestinians without running unacceptable political risks. If the Israelis were to be brought to a more realistic interpretation of autonomy, it had to be face to face with the people who were going to be living the autonomy; the deals had to be made directly with them. The failure to get them into the act, I think, was the worm that would have rotted the apple, even if the two leaders had survived.

Saunders: I'd like to pick up on a number of things that were said. I'll make one comment very quickly and then leave it aside. And I say this having worked for two Republican presidents in the White House, as I worked for two Democrats before that, and then for Jimmy Carter. Just picture what might have happened--to supplement Sam's original question--if Ronald Reagan, with his overwhelming electoral mandate, had picked up rather than dropped the autonomy talks. That would have injected a politically supported American involvement; it wouldn't have been the same as Carter's, but nevertheless it would have been there. But instead it was put on the back burner. So I think we bear some responsibility there.

But the conversation that I wanted to get into was the question of linkage. I guess I speak here, for a moment, in October 1978, as the emissary to the absent parties--

Jordan and the Palestinians, particularly. I remember a night at Camp David when probably all four of us were in a little room in the recreation building around the table, and found ourselves all of a sudden writing that Jordan would do this or that. And then we stopped and said, "You know, we can't say this." Even in a bureaucracy, it's a simple practice that if you're going to speak for somebody else, you'd better clear what you're saying with them, and Jordan wasn't there for us to clear these words. It was then we adopted the conditional: Jordan would be invited, too, if Jordan did this, etc. After Camp David, Carter called King Hussein and said, "Please don't say anything about the Camp David accords until we have a chance to sit down with you and tell you about them and their contents." An exhuasted Cy Vance was put on a plane and sent to talk to Hussein, and I was sent out later to continue the dialogue more broadly.

One thing we see in that situation was that we were left to sell the Camp David accords to the Saudis and to the Jordanians and to the Palestinians. For all my admiration for Sadat, I really do have to fault him for acting out of his negative feeling about Palestinians and other Arabs, which Hermann just described. What would have happened had Sadat been able to go to Hussein and Assad and the Saudi leadership and the Palestinians and say, "I didn't get everything I hoped to get at Camp David, but there's really more linkage here betwen the Sinai agreement and the West Bank agreement than is in that document because I have certain assurances from the U.S. leadership"? What if Sadat had made the appropriate gesture, and visited them, and said, "I didn't do what I promised you I would do, but here's why. We did the best we could, and we think we can keep this process going." So, in that sense, there was a failure in the politics of Sadat at that moment.

The question of linkage is a fascinating one. We could go on here all evening among ourselves about this, because in the very first draft of the Camp David accords that Bill referred to, we had a sentence that explicitly linked the withdrawal from the Sinai to the implementation, or the inauguration, of the first self-governing authority in the West Bank and Gaza. I remember on that Saturday when we first showed this to Vance and Brzezinski in the morning, and revised it and then showed it to President Carter around one in the afternoon. This was *shabbat*, so there was a kind of downtime in the dealings with the Israelis and the Egyptians, and we worked among ourselves. I still had that sentence in there about linkage. I think if you went back and looked at the draft, you'd find various annotations in the second and third drafts that say, in effect, "This doesn't make any sense; drop this; get rid of it; we don't need it"-- and it dropped out. And yet, linkage remained an issue throughout the negotiation of the peace treaty, six and seven months later. The refrain from the Americans to the Egyptians was "However we handle this in a legal document, and there probably will be no formal linkage"--and in retrospect, it's probably well that there wasn't--"the fact is that the quality of normalization of relations between Eypgt and Israel will depend on the quality of the continuing peace process and the involvement of the Palestinians and, later, the Jordanians and Saudis."

So we had the same problem with the word "linkage" that we had with the Soviets. There is a question of quid pro quo legal linkage, which we rejected; and then there is the problem of the real-world fact that the issues are intertwined, they are linked. It was that second form of linkage, in a way, that did us in. When I had to try to explain the Camp David accords to people in the West Bank and Gaza, I think it's fair to say that if I could have had one more thing, it might have been possible to get them to come along with us. The "one more thing" would have been the ability to deliver on what we thought was the Israeli commitment to stop settlement. That, more than any other thing, undid the Camp David accords because it convinced the Palestinians and the Jordanians that we wouldn't be able to deliver. But we had been able to deliver and say, "Look, this is a serious effort that we're going to make on the West Bank-Gaza. There's a political process that will unfold here; you Palestinians will be governing--however minimally--the land defined by the 1967 line, except for the area around Jerusalem. Take it, whatever it is, and work with it, and build yourselves here as responsible governors in this area; then you will have a different relationship with Israel. But we couldn't sell that; we couldn't establish that kind of real-world linkage.

Lewis: We also had going on simultaneously, Hal, a very vehement campaign by the PLO in the territories, trying to stop your persuasive abilities from having an effect on the population, and I think that was an important factor. Had the PLO seen the Camp David accords for what they really portended as a possibility for Palestinians and behaved differently, they today would have a far different situation, I think, in the Middle East in general. Dan did not refer to the fact that during the last four years, as we've gone through a series of iterations of American peace plans and peace initiatives, all based essentially on the Camp David idea, more and more plaintively, the Palestinians--including PLO members--have said, "We didn't see Camp David at the time for what was in it. If we only had, we'd be almost there by this time." It's another example of how repeatedly, since the 1950s, good ideas have been accepted by either Israelis or Palestinians several years after they were offered, too late to be effective.

Saunders: I agree with your point, Sam. In those conversations of October 1978, I met with a lot of people in the West Bank, but principally with two different groups. One was a group of people that you might describe as technocrats from the West Bank and Gaza, at a dinner in an American's home; these were the people running the hospitals and the services under occupation. They really thought the Camp David accords had something for them. They were asking really pratical questions; Will we get to control our own budgets? Can we import medical supplies on our own authority? Things like that. They saw real potential. The other meeting was with the "notables"--the political figures on the West Bank--and they were all scared. They said, "We were elected to govern a municipality; we weren't elected to negotiate for the Palestinians." And this went on and on.

I said, "Well, look: If you were really ingenious, why couldn't you get yourselves deputized by the PLO? Why didn't you have the dialogue? If you think this has possibilities, persuade the PLO. Get yourselves deputized by them to negotiate in this and consult with them; have your own constituent assembly--do whatever you want, but come on in." Finally, one of them just threw up his hands and he said, "Ach! We are all sheep. We can only follow; we can't lead." And that was a castigation of his fellows, not of me. I agree that the failure of the Palestinians--and I would have to say the other Arabs--to come in strong on this was partly because I couldn't persuade them, and partly because they had Baghdad breathing down their necks. Part of my mission was to persuade the Saudis and the Jordanians to defer an Arab summit that the Iraqis were trying to put together; indeed, they did have a summit, and they condemned the Camp David accords. The Saudis tried to resist it. There was a recess in the talks, and they went back to Saudi Arabia, and we had intelligence reports that the Iraqis had threatened to assassinate the Saudi leaders if they didn't go along with the condemnation of the accords. So that's what Hussein and the Saudis were up against--then, as they are again today.

Eilts: May I suggest another thought? I share Hal Saunders's view that the major reason the Camp David agreements were not more widely accepted in the Arab world was the unresolved issue of a protracted settlement freeze in the West Bank and Gaza. But apart from that, the question was Saudi Arabia. Sadat counted very much on getting Saudi endorsement; if he got it, he felt, given the influence of the Saudis with the PLO and other elements--influence brought about largely through the use of what you might call financial diplomacy--they would at least be accepted widely enough to be viable. And here, I think, we--specifically President Carter--made a mistake. Carter believed that the Saudis would go along with whatever came out of this effort. Just where the president got that idea, I don't know; I can only assume from our ambassador in Saudi Arabia, but he denied indicating that the Saudis would support anything, and I know we had discussions at Camp David as to whether what was evolving was likely to be acceptable to the Saudis. Sadat counted on Carter's assurance that the Saudis would support him. But as it turned out, the signing took place on Sunday night; by Monday morning, the Saudis had already denounced the accords. So all the other efforts then to get the Saudis to act a little more positively toward the accords at the Baghdad summit that the Iraqis were calling were too late. But it was a question of the protracted settlement, in my judgment, and the fact that we could not get the Saudis to accept it.

Stein: Let me, at this juncture, turn the microphone over to those in the audience who want to pose questions--not statements--to our assembled guests. If you would please approach the microphone on either the left or the right side, we'll take the first question. Please address it to a particular panel member.

Q: I'd like to address my question to Dan Kurtzer. Given the optimism you raised that the framework for Camp David is still basically alive, at the same time there is pessimism because you say the three primary participants aren't there and we don't have that kind of leadership in Israel, in Egypt, and in the United States, how do you see this ever shaping up again? How do you see the process picking up some steam in the future?

Kurtzer: As Sam Lewis suggested, very often ideas that don't find support when they're first proposed over time will gain support. One of the most interesting vignettes from our diplomacy of the last year and a half came after the Israeli elections proposal--of May 14--was published. At that time, we were engaged in a dialogue with the PLO in Tunis. One of the most significant questions that came back to us was phrased somewhat as follows: We understand what the Israeli plan is intending to do. What we don't understand is why it's not as good as Camp David. The PLO had undertaken its own study of Camp David; had not yet come to grips with Camp David fully enough to be prepared to endorse it; but clearly understood what the strengths of

Camp David held out as a possibility for Palestinians in a negotiating process. So, with that understanding, as it grows over time, the challenge for the diplomats, as the leaders assess whether their own environment is correct and ready for decision making, is to try to build little bridges between the parties and find out whether some of these changed attitudes can be translated into changed positions and changed policies, and see where things can work.

This is one of the things that we have tried to do over this last year and a half: taking an Israeli election proposal that had a lot of weaknesses in it but had one inherent strength: that it provided a potential pathway to a process that would lead, through a series of steps, to a comprehensive settlement. And it was for the promise of starting out rather modestly in an Israeli-Palestinian dialogue--through an election, through negotiations, in multiple stages--that we tried to attract some support, and have not yet been able to do so. You don't find a ready-made formula, but over time, as the different parties assimilate the importance of different aspects of this process, you try to find those bridges that can be built and see if the political environment can sustain them.

Q: It seemed from the discussion we just heard that the prime thing we learned from the statements that were made here--and I want to thank you gentlemen for giving us these little bits of the inside workings of the diplomatic process--is that the only success we've had so far in the Middle East was when there were direct negotiations between the heads of the states in dispute. Why does our government, and individuals in our government--particularly in the Bush administration--keep bringing up the concept of an international conference, which we know is unacceptable? In my experience and the little knowledge of history that I have, I don't know of any major dispute between nations that was solved in an international conference--only by direct negotiations of the parties in dispute. I'd like to hear from those who follow this particular idea of an international conference.

Lewis: I think you ought to ask Dr. Stein this question. I'll tell you why. The U.S. Institute of Peace--for which I have the honor to be the president--has made a grant to Dr. Stein--not to bribe him to bring me here tonight, I assure you, but for a project directly related to your question. His study is of all the peace conferences that have taken place on Middle East issues and what can be learned from their successes and failures. And there have been some successes; they haven't all been failures. But before he answers, let me say this: It is clear that even at Camp David, when you had the three principals together, locked up in a diplomatic prison, direct negotiations weren't the answer. It was, in fact, an indirect negotiation, with the United States moving back and forth between the two delegations. There was social contact, but the negotiating was all indirect. And I suspect that will be the pattern for success in the future.

Kurtzer: Let me add two comments, if I may. Number one, I think there has been a misunderstanding of American policy since 1980. The Reagan and the Bush administrations have both indicated their quite severe reservations about the viability of an international conference, and have adopted positions that indicate support for a properly structured conference to be convened at an appropriate time--two important caveats to the convening of a conference. That said, there is nothing inherently wrong with a conference as a vehicle to launch, or to help facilitate, or to help support, a negotiating process. A key element in the Shultz plan in 1988 was use of an international conference. None of the parties really expect negotiations per se to take place in a conference format, but many of the parties need the conference as a kind of umbrella or cover or facilitator for the process itself. So one of the arguments that we've had with both those who favor a conference and those who oppose it is not to inflate the importance of a conference, but also not to denigrate the kind of use that a conference can be in helping to bring about, or to support, a negotiating process once launched.

Stein: Let me very briefly give you some information about an international conference format. Each side believes in self-determination, but each would like to determine by itself what the other side will bring to the talks. In other words, each wants to be there alone, but each wants to determine the procedure or the conditions that will allow the other to come to the talks. No side wants the other side to determine the outcome alone. Each side fears the unknown, and as soon as they feel that they're getting close to some sort of negotiating dynamic, they get very cold feet, because they're afraid that they're going to get into a dark tunnel; they don't know whether it's really light at the end of the tunnel, or it's an oncoming train.

Q: But this is the nature of any negotiation.

Stein: I'm just telling you what I know from what the respective sides have said. And most important, some elements of each side are willing to say, "Let's go to an international conference," and each side demands active, vigorous U.S. participation.

Q: No, that's not the position of Israel, as I understand it. The position of Israel is that we are ready to sit down with any one or all of the Arab states and resolve this dispute face to face.

Stein: An international conference is one mechanism; it's not an exclusive means, as Dan pointed out.

Q: But what is wrong with face-to-face negotiations?

Stein: Nothing. If they want to go face to face, that's their business. I'm just telling you what the research has told me so far. Let's get on to the next question. This is a discussion about Camp David, not about convening an international conference.

Q: Since it's impossible to assemble so many American Middle East experts who've actually had successful dealings with the Middle East, I'd like to ask the gentlemen on the panel to comment on the Iraq situation, and in particular to comment on its likely impact on the Arab-Israeli dispute.

Quandt: Let me take a crack at the end of that. However the Iraq crisis comes out, the Middle East is not going to be the same. There may be a series of regime changes; certainly, if war is the outcome, that's likely. And if Saddam Hussein gains a diplomatic victory, I think our friends in the coalition are in serious internal trouble as well. Therefore, it's very hard to predict what the Palestinian-Israeli problem is going to look like until you know which outcome of the Gulf crisis you're dealing with. But one thing is clear: The crisis already has produced a deadly blow to the peace camp in

Israel, and to those people who had been moving in the direction of accepting the necessity for eventually negotiating with the PLO and the Palestinians. That's been set back dramatically. The suspicion between the two communities has been heightened enormously, and therefore, I would say that while there will undoubtedly be international pressure, in the wake of the Iraq crisis, to move on to an international conference or some other format for dealing with this long-standing major issue between Palestinians and Israelis, the prospects for doing it very quickly in the aftermath of this crisis are, I'm afraid, very poor.

Q: My question is for Dr. Eilts. Mr. Ambassador, during the remarks you mentioned the objections raised by the Egyptian staff during the early negotiations at Camp David. Were those objections reasonable or legitimate representations of Muslim, Pan-Arab objections or concerns? And if so, why were they not taken into consideration, given that they may have been legitimate?

Eilts: I would not characterize them as consistent, necessarily, with overall Muslim concerns, because the Islamic world goes beyond the Arab world. But as far as the members of the Egyptian delegation who were critical of Sadat--everyone other than the president himself--they felt that what Sadat was doing, in terms of conceding various points at Carter's request, was going to cause precisely the kind of problems that arose after Camp David; that Sadat, as I pointed out, had made concessions that went beyond what he had told the Arab leaders he would do--that is, limit the concessions he would make. With every passing concession--especially the separation of the Egyptian-Israeli effort in Sinai and the West Bank-Gaza autonomy--they argued that whatever came out of it probably was not going to be accepted in Egypt itself, and they did not want to be part of it. That was why the foreign minister resigned at Camp David. And in terms of Arab reaction, they were right. The overall Arab reaction was exactly what they had predicted.

Why wasn't that realized by Sadat? Well, Sadat was mesmerized, in many ways, by President Carter; the personal relationship between them was one I'd never seen between two leaders before. Sadat had enormous confidence that Camp David, even though it was a small and in many ways imperfect step, was the first step toward a more comprehensive peace process. And he counted on President Carter's personal involvement in the future to make it work. The other members of his delegation were dubious that it would work.

Q: I'd like to ask Dr. Saunders a question. What prompted President Carter to join with the Soviet Union in October 1977 to go to Geneva, and was that decision a factor that prompted President Sadat to go to Jerusalem?

Saunders: Bill may want to add something to my response, because he was part of those negotiations in New York. My picture of what happened there is as follows: As we all know, most of the diplomatic effort of 1977 was directed at trying to reconvene the Middle East peace conference in Geneva. Most of that effort in the first half of the year was an American effort; we went to the Middle East twice with Vance, and Carter saw the principal leaders himself. Then we realized, in midsummer, that there was another chairman to the Geneva Middle East peace conference that had met before Christmas in 1973: the Soviet Union. The calendar of diplomacy includes the fact that in September-October, many of the foreign ministers of the world come to the U.N. General Assembly, and that conclave provides a moment for many bilateral discussions; very often, if the Soviet foreign minister comes, he includes on his itinerary a visit to Washington to see the president, especially if he and the secretary of state get together in New York.

So, after a trip to the Middle East to try to move the process further toward Geneva, and having a deadline of trying to get there by the end of 1977, it was natural that we would think of using New York talks between Secretary Vance and Foreign Minister Andrei Gromyko to bring the Soviets up to date on the thinking and the work that we had done to pave the way for a resumption of the conference through writing terms of reference. When you're going to have a meeting of that kind, you also, as staff members, recognize that after the principals meet--especially if the press knows they have been talking about resuming the Middle East peace conference--the spokesmen for the two ministers will need something to say. If one is judicious, one wants to have that something pretty well prepared. So I think it was worked out that maybe this time, given the importance of the issue, we should consult with the Soviets before the foreign ministers even met. I can't remember--maybe Bill will--whether we sent a draft to the Soviets for them to comment on, or they provided the draft; it usually goes from the Americans to the Soviets.

In any case, when the Soviets came to New York, there were intense discussions between the staffs of the foreign ministers about that communiqué. I think the Americans felt pretty much that the language in it was quite satisfactory to us; we had not given anything away. We'd made a few advances, but it was essentially something we could be comfortable with. And a document was released after the Vance-Gromyko meeting. If there was a failure in the process, it was not a failure of diplomacy but a failure to anticipate the reaction of Israel, and some elements of the American Jewish community working through the Congress. Part of the surprise, I think, was the fact that during these talks with the Soviets, the American team had checked out the current draft with both the Egyptian foreign minister and with Foreign Minister Dayan, who were in New York. I think perhaps Dayan was as surprised as anybody at the rocket that he got back from the Israeli government, objecting to this coming together of the United States and the Soviet Union.

I see it much more--as you can tell--as the product of normal, high-level diplomatic dialogue, and not as a major shock in diplomatic language itself. Now, your second question is did that trigger Sadat's visit to Jerusalem? I know there's been that theory around; I personally haven't subscribed to it, but others from the panel may disagree with me.

Quandt: It was the Soviet team who prepared the first draft when they came to New York, and by any standards, it was a better draft than we had any reason to expect. Most of the slogans and jargon were missing, and therefore there was an inclination to work on it. It was not given tremendously high priority, insofar as there were a lot of other things going on. Insofar as there was a strategic rationale for going ahead with this, there was the feeling that Syria was going to be a problem as we tried to move forward, however we moved foward, because it seemed to be the most reluctant of the Arab states around Israel. And the Soviets had a better relationship by far with Syria than we, and we thought they might be prepared to use some of their influence as the entry to getting this honorary role of cochairman, which they had had in 1973. Insofar as there was some political reason for it, it was to try to get some leverage over the Syrians through the Soviets--and that's exactly what the Syrians read into it. My recollection--and I think Ambassador Eilts will confirm this--is that the initial Egyptian reaction was very positive, because they thought we had gotten a handle on the Syrians. The initial Syrian reaction was very negative; they thought they were cornered, with both the Americans and the Soviets pressuring them. My recollection is that Sadat's words to Ambassador Eilts were something like "master stroke" or "brilliant stroke."

Eilts: It was "brilliant."

Quandt: Sadat thought it was going to solve his main problem in going to Geneva, which was to get the Syrians to stop being so obstructive. My feeling is that when he realized that wasn't in the cards, and hadn't been worked out, and that Carter himself, after the domestic reaction to the October 1, 1977, statement, was, in a sense, retreating from it, Sadat knew that he didn't have anything to corner the Syrians. That made him start to worry about the Geneva conference, particularly as he saw Carter's own domestic stock fading during October. So it's only in an extraordinarily convoluted way that the October 1, 1977, communiqué is related to Sadat's decision to go to Jerusalem. His initial reaction was a very positive one, not a negative one.

Eilts: May I add a brief point? I think it's very important to try to explain why Sadat went to Jerusalem. Contrary to some revisionist history, he was not at all upset about that U.S.-Soviet statement. He called it "brilliant," for the reasons that Bill Quandt has given, and also because he felt that it was possible to have the Soviets present at such a conference and yet limit their potential mischief-making capabilities by, for example, the chairman--not the cochairmen, the Soviets and ourselves--not participating in committee sessions. The expectation was that the committee sessions, which would involve Arabs and Israelis, Egyptians and Israelis, would not work, and very quickly, the parties would rush out to seek the assistance of the cochairmen.

The Soviets had no relations with Israel, so they were hardly in a mediator's role; the United States did. So Sadat was not worried that that Soviet mischief-making capabilities were dangerous. He decided to go to Jerusalem when in October a series of working papers developed. The working papers were, in effect, the agenda for the Geneva conference. Moshe Dayan came to Washington; President Carter suggested that Dayan write what he thought should be the agenda. He did so. Several days later Ismail Fahmi, the Egyptian minister, came; President Carter asked him to look at the agenda, and Fahmi said, "My God, this is an Israeli draft; it's no good." So the president said, "Rewrite it," and Fahmi rewrote it. In due course, Moshe Dayan came again and said, "My God, this is an Egyptian draft; it's not acceptable." And so on. This working paper was finally sent to Egypt after the last Dayan revision, but we couldn't get the Egyptians to accept it. They would not accept the fact that this was what we called an American draft; they said, "This is nonsense; this is an Israeli draft." So one was stuck.

At that point--because we were reaching the end of the year; and the end of the year, or early January, had been the target time frame, the objective--President Carter proposed that we all go to Geneva without terms of reference; that we make the writing of terms of reference the first item at Geneva, no matter how long it took. At least we would be in Geneva, and that had a symbolic importance. The various parties--some with greater reluctance than others--agreed to that, with the exception of the Syrians. The Syrians never answered. And so days passed, and Sadat saw, as he put it, "Peace is slipping through my fingers for procedural reasons." The United States did not have enough influence on Assad to get him to change.

So President Carter sent Sadat a hand-written letter. He said, "I need your help. I need some bold action." And when you said "bold action" to Sadat, this was the kind of thing that he loved. So he came up with various ideas, one of which was going to Jerusalem, not to shift the peace process away from Geneva but as a step to getting it toward Geneva. The idea of going to Jerusalem was a product of two things. First, over the years, Sadat had been meeting regularly on his trips to Europe with very prominent Jewish financiers in Austria, Paris, and London. They had all urged him-- they were all anti-Begin--that the way to handle Begin was to go to Jerusalem and have direct talks. Second was King Hassan of Morocco. He had, several months before, sent Sadat a message from a very prominent Jewish leader saying the same kinds of things: Why don't you go to Jerusalem or have direct talks? It was direct talks; it wasn't Jerusalem.

And Sadat, in that dramatic fashion characteristic of him--Sadat was a showman, first and foremost--put together these suggestions and the message he had received from Hassan, and added to that his own flair for the dramatic. He would go to Jerusalem during the Muslim holiday, and use that venue to present the Arab case--to break, as he put it, the psychological barrier. That would be the way to break this impasse that had developed because the Syrians were not answering on the issue of terms of reference. Sadat seriously believed that was the way it was going to work. When he came back from Jerusalem, he called me and said, "We're going to be in Geneva in two weeks. And next week, we're going to have a preparatory conference here. You'll see. I've done it." The preparatory conference was held, but hardly anybody attended. As a result, the peace process shifted away from Geneva. It was that issue of not being able to have terms of reference that would allow the parties to go, that caused the trip to Jerusalem.

Q: First, I want to thank all of you gentlemen for a most enlightening and interesting and educational evening. The question I have is, Egypt had its Sadat, Israel had its Begin, but the Palestinians were really fragmented. Arafat spoke for only a very small portion of them. Who, therfore, could negotiate for the Palestinians and make any successful meeting of the minds in this kind of an environment? I'll address it to Mr. Kurtzer, and whoever else would like to enter into.

Kurtzer: It's a short question, and it's a question that has not had an answer yet. As Ken indicated in his introductory remarks tonight, perhaps the most bedeviling question in the peace process has been that of Palestinian representation. And it's been that way because the conditions under which the two key parties are prepared to meet with each other have not yet been close enough to bridge. Over the course of the past couple of years, we've tried a variety of formulas to get around the obstacles of, on the one hand, conditions set by the government of Israel with regard to PLO participation, and on the other, the conditions set by the Palestinian community with regard to PLO participation. We have come very close to finding formulas over the years that would allow a Palestinian partner to join the process, that partner being legitimized through a variety of ways by the PLO, but not in a way that would be so overt as to drive Israel from the table.

But having come close doesn't get you a cigar. We haven't yet found a formula that both sides can live with. It is far more, I would suggest, than a procedural question, because both sides, the Israeli and the Palestinian, have invested in the question of Palestinian representation rather far-reaching implications for the peace process. For Israel--and I speak in generalizations here--the question of PLO involvement in some ways is seen as a question of almost delegitimizing the state of Israel, because the PLO is seen, in the minds of many Israelis, as antithetical in its very nature--by its charter, by its meaning--to Israel's secure existence. And there are those in the Palestinian community who hold a vision of a political settlement that in fact would negate Israel's security and perhaps Israel's existence.

So it's not simply a question of representation, but the representation question is a way of getting at the issue that I suggested is at the heart of this conflict, and that is, Is there room--physical, psychological, and political--in Palestinian-Arab Israel for both Jewish nationalism and Palestinian nationalism? And if you can psychologically, politically, get to the answer of that question, then the issue of how you represent both sides in the negotiating process would, I think, be easier to address.

Stein: I'm tempted to end it here, but I asked each of my panelists when I wrote to them several months, if not a year, ago to bring an anecdote about the Camp David process, and share it with the audience. If you will permit me, I'd like to give them each an opportunity to tell an interesting story.

Eilts: When the Egyptian delegation came to Camp David, they looked around and said, "My God, what are we doing here? Why do we have to be up here in the mountains of Maryland"--which they didn't care about--"surrounded by barbed wire, by Marines, far from any city? Why do we have to stay here?" The senior members, especially the deputy prime minister, who most desperately wanted to go to Washington, kept trying to get over the fence, and of course were not allowed to do so. The only person in the Egyptian delegation who accepted it was President Sadat. I asked him, "How is it, Mr. President, that you are so calm about this?" He, too, liked the city life. He thought about it a bit, then said, "Well, it's better than Cell 20." That was the cell in which he had been imprisoned for four years many years earlier in Egypt, for participation in a terrorist action against a very unpopular leader at the time; that's where he learned English.

Saunders: I have to tell two quick ones. Sam Lewis commented that a way to Begin's heart was to get to the personal side of life. Carter tells the story that on the last day of Camp David, when the negotiations really almost fell apart, things were very tense. He had to go to Begin's cabin and try to resolve an issue related to Jerusalem--the toughest issue of them all. As he walked out of his study, he saw a pile of photographs of himself. Begin had asked Susan Clough, Carter's secretary, for autographed photographs for each of his grandchildren, and Susan gave the president the name of each grandchild. Carter had inscribed each of these photos to the name, and signed them "Jimmy Carter." So he picked up the photographs, found Begin on the porch of his cabin, and they headed for a very tense meeting. In the cabin, Carter casually and tentatively put the photographs on the table, and Begin saw that they were inscribed to his grandchildren. He started turning them over and talking about his grandchildren. At the end, according to Carter, he said, "Mr. President, this is what we're all about, isn't it? Our grandchildren."

My personal story is that later that afternoon, I was called over to Carter's lodge. Brzezinski and Vance were in the living room when I walked in the front door. As I entered, Carter and Sadat had obviously just finished their meeting in Carter's study. I stepped aside because Carter obviously was going to say good-bye and Sadat was going to go out the door and back to his cabin. After they shook hands, Sadat went out. Carter turned around, and because I'd stepped aside, I happened to be face to face with him. As nearly as I can remember the words, he looked at me and said, "I think we have an agreement, but I was afraid to ask him."

Ken asked us, when he wrote, to say a little bit about what we felt at the end of the Camp David accords. When we went down to the White House and were in the East Room in front of the television cameras, watching the signing and all the smiles, I looked at Sadat and thought, This is not the jubilant celebration that most of the world is going to think it is. This is a very sober moment.

Quandt: Picking up on Hal's anecdote, about half an hour after that, as we had all been briefed and an agreement had been reached--we thought--the planning madly began for the PR coup at the end of all this: Could we have a White House signing ceremony that night? At that point, they called in all the media people and started asking how quickly they could do this and that; could they get people from Congress, and so forth. They finally said, "It'll take us four hours to do it." It was about 6:30 or so at that point, and Carter said, "No, it's got to be 10 o'clock. You've got to do it faster." So everybody started rushing to get things ready. My recollection is that just as we were all getting ready to go, an enormous thunderstorm began. We all paused and thought that somebody up there took notice.

Just one other brief anecdote, because that was the tail-end of Hal's: Before going to Camp David, the issue arose--as it inevitably does from the intelligence types-- should we bug the cabins so we will know what they're saying to one another? Presumably, people do this on a fairly routine basis. But this created a bit of a division within the American camp. Brzezinski thought, of course, we should; the more we knew, the better. And Vance, the gentleman that he was, thought we shouldn't. Carter decided that we shouldn't, and so, as far as I know, during the entire proceedings, we did not have access to that kind of information. But I can tell you that the Egyptians and the Israelis thought we were doing it, and they had all of their private conversations outdoors.

Lewis: Well, I guess I have to tell two quickies also, one humorous and one not so humorous. In between meetings, there was a lot of tension released in various kinds of athletic enterprises. Brzezinski played chess with Begin, and Jody Powell--as I think Bill recounts in his book--and Hamilton Jordan pleaded with Begin to please beat Brzezinski, because if he allowed him to win, he would be insufferable for the rest of the conference. Begin did, in fact, come out (I think) in a draw. But one of the kinds of athletic endeavors that was most interesting to me was tennis. There were two very nice tennis courts at Camp David, and there was a lot of tennis in between meetings. One time, Bill Quandt and I were playing against the Israeli ambassador, Simcha Dinitz, and Dr. Lewis, who was the doctor to the Israeli delegation. Carter was playing on the court next to us, with Begin looking on, against somebody else. Bill and I were having a hard time at that moment. Carter turned and yelled to us, "You guys better win, because you're playing for the West Bank."

And now a more sober anecdote. It was one night, midway through the conference, when Carter had finished an extremely unpleasant, difficult, querulous, long, and wearing meeting with Prime Minister Begin, then briefed our delegation about it. I walked out after him; he was heading back to his cabin. He said, "Come walk with me." We walked through the woods, just the two of us, back toward our cabins. He said, "Damn, I don't think Begin wants peace!" And I said, "There's no Israeli who doesn't want peace, Mr. President, least of all Menachem Begin. What we're talking about here is how much would you pay and how much can you risk for a formal agreement." He grumbled a little bit. "Well, I don't know. I'm not sure." And then, at the very end of the conference, after the deal was made, the agreement was reached, we were walking, and Carter turned to me and said, "You know, I think you were right about Begin. It was the price."

Stein: Let me thank my colleagues. I think tonight some of us remember Walter Cronkite: "You are there."

THE IRAN HOSTAGE CRISIS

10

The Iranian Hostages Case:
Its Implications for the Future of the
International Law of Diplomacy

MICHAEL M. GUNTER

Iran's seizure of the American Embassy in Tehran on November 4, 1979, and the holding of its diplomatic staff as hostages, followed on the next day by a similar seizure of the consulates in Tabriz and Shiraz, violated two of the supposedly cardinal principles of the international law of diplomacy as codified by the 1961 Vienna Convention on Diplomatic Relations: (1) the immunity of diplomatic personnel from local arrest, detention, or trial, and (2) the inviolability of embassy premises.[1] In committing these acts, moreover, the Iranian officials proudly proclaimed their inherent right to violate the inviolable in the name of some vague, higher law.

International law and conventions, as well as all man-made laws, have been enacted to serve mankind. Men and their quests for principles take precedence over every man-made rule, at the highest value level. Seeking justice, truth and solid relationships is at question in the current Iranian situation--not whether certain laws are being upheld.[2]

Asked whether Iran was prepared to violate international law to achieve its objectives, Mohammed Javad Bahonar, a leading figure on Iran's fifteen-man Revolutionary Council, replied:

Your insistence on the legalistic aspects of the embassy siege is specious. . . . You think you can get away with murder by hiding behind the law. The Islamic canon recognizes the right of an oppressed people, faced by a government that cites the law in order to betray justice, to rebellion. The Iranian people's occupation of the U.S. embassy falls squarely within this principle.[3]

The student militants holding the hostages responded in a similar vein:

For 2,500 years, Iran has been oppressed by monarchy. Where in the world do oppressed people have the right to talk, even today? Everywhere you have the domination of the superpowers. Everywhere the superpowers make the law for themselves, and when someone breaks this law they call him a terrorist, violator of international law. What law? Law which approved the crimes of America in Vietnam, in Chile, in Africa, in Iran? Is this international law? Sixty thousand people were killed in Iran, yet no one came here to say that international law was being broken. What kind of laws are these? Are these laws for the superpowers, for capitalism, or for humanity? If they are for humanity, why did they not come here and say anthing last year or before that, during the 25 years of torture in Iran?[4]

The unwillingness of some around the world to back the U.S. position more energetically might be interpreted as giving a certain amount of sanction to the Iranian violation of the inviolable. While conceding Iran's action was not in keeping with international law, for example, an official commentary in *Pravda* nevertheless made it clear that the Soviets had sympathy for the Iranians: "This act [the seizure of the U.S. Embassy] cannot be taken out of the overall context of American-Iranian relations. . . . Does the stand of those in Washington who reject the demand of the Iranian people for the extradition of the Shah and the return to Iran of his plundered wealth have much in common with international law?"[5]

In Japan the daily *Mainichi* assessed the blame equally between the United Staes and Iran: "America's refusal to comply with its [Iran's] demands for the deposed Shah's extradition cannot be accepted. It is natural that the Iranians' hatred of the Shah is now directed at the United States which protects and harbors him."[6] Pakistani students were quoted as saying: "The Americans have weapons, the Russians have weapons, but Iran has no weapons and must use such tactics."[7] When one adds to this the rash of attacks throughout the world that have occurred on other supposedly inviolable embassies,[8] it becomes clear that the international law of diplomacy is being called into question.

As is true of most human institutions, diplomacy is a dynamic process that, if it is to survive, must change with the times. In the twentieth century, especially following the end of each world war and again in the 1950s and 1960s with the birth of the new Afro-Asian states, substantial changes did occur in diplomatic practices. These alterations helped result in the creation of what has often been called the "new" diplomacy.[9] Might not the events in Iran be still another step in what Harold Nicolson has called "the evolution of the diplomatic method"?[10]

The purpose of this paper is to analyze the implications for the future of the international law of diplomacy in light of the precedents set by the Iranian hostages case. Are the traditional laws becoming obsolescent, and, if so, what role has and will the Iranian case play? First, however, we must survey the unique historical background of Iran, which provided the setting, and indeed part of the impetus, for what happened.

THE MULTICULTURAL DIVERSITY OF THE WORLD

At a time when most ritualistically proclaim the essential unity of Spaceship Earth, some wisely question the future of international law in a multicultural world.[11] Analyzing the diverse cultural realms in the Islamic Middle East, Africa south of the Sahara, Indianized Asia, China, and the West, Adda Bruemmer Bozeman concluded: "Anyone attempting a comparative study of Western and Near Eastern approaches to law and organization . . . must face the fact that he is confronted here with totally different conceptions of the roles of law and government in society."[12] And these "locally and regionally prevalent theories . . . are likely to remain dominant in the future . . . [T]he world will continue to be multicultural under the surface of unifying technological and rhetorical arrangements."[13]

R. P. Anand, a prominent Indian scholar, seconded these conclusions when he pointed out "that traditional international law, the more or less accepted body of international rules of conduct inherited by the worldwide community of states, as developed among the Western European countries or countries of European origin, . . . is naturally coloured by their unmistakable influence."[14] On the other hand, he continued: "Most of the new states of Asia and Africa . . . have a different cultural and social background. . . . The[ir] political and legal ideas are different, and philosophically, they are quite apart from the Christian West."[15]

Iran is a case in point, for beneath its thin and superficial veneer of Westernized modernity, there lay still vibrant the rich heritage of its unique past.[16] Given the proper stimulus, this latent past burst suddenly into the present to influence the future when the Ayatollah Ruhollah Khomeini overthrew the shah early in 1979.[17] Thus, to begin fathoming the impetus to this event and the taking of the American hostages that followed, one must analyze Iran's unique cultural foundations.[18]

Shiism in Iran

Iran is the birthplace of several major world religions. Zoroastrianism, her ancient, pre-Islamic faith, still numbers a few faithful adherents in the land of its origin. In the early years of the present era, Iran produced Mithraism and Manichaeism, two religions that competed mightily with, and certainly influenced, early Christianity before finally succumbing. Illustrating that this religious heritage was still extant, Iran fathered still another world faith a little more than a century ago in Bahaism.

While these earlier religions, as well as other ancient events, no doubt have a lingering influence on contemporary Iran,[19] it is to Islam that we now must turn. For it is in the name of this latter faith that the Arabs swept out of the desert to overthrow the mighty Sassanian (Persian) empire in A.D. 642 and Islamize Persia.

Upon the death of the Prophet Muhammad, Islam divided into two main sects, the Sunnite and the Shiite. The former, in the majority, derives its name from the claim that its followers are orthodox adherents to the Sunna, traditions of the Prophet. The latter take their name from the term *shia*, which means "faction" or "partisan" (of Ali, the fourth caliph).[20]

When Muhammad died, he left no clear guidance concerning who should succeed him. The Sunnites believed that whoever was the outstanding member of the community could be elected as its imam, or leader. Thus Abu Bekr, Omar, and Othman were chosen as the first three caliphs, successors to the Prophet.

The Shiites, however, maintained what might be called the legitimist position; the caliph or imam ought to be a man with close family connections to the Prophet. Since Muhammad left no son, the Shiite candidate for imam was Ali, the Prophet's first cousin and son-in-law. Thus, the Shiites rejected the first three caliphs as usurpers and in Iran celebrated, until recently, the anniversary of Omar's death by burning in effigy the Arab caliph who conquered Sassanian Persia.[21]

Ali finally did become (the fourth) caliph, but during his tenure the Shiites failed to establish their legitimist position. Ali's assassination and the ensuing civil war, which the Shiites lost, led to the creation of the particular sect of Shiism practiced in Iran today, *Imamiyah shia*, the "twelver" variety. According to this belief, the imamate, following Ali, passed in succession to his eleven heirs of the flesh, the first two of whom were his sons, Hasan and Husain. Iranians believe that Husain married the daughter of their last Sassanian king, Yazdgerd III, and that, therefore, the subsequent imams descended from this union were Aryanized.[22]

Shortly after he assumed the leadership of the Shiites, Husain and his small band were massacred on the tenth of Muharram (Ashura, the day of repentance; October 10, 680) by the rival (according to the Shiites, the false or illegitimate) caliph, Yazid I, on the site of Kerbela in what is now Iraq. For the Shiites, this event has come to symbolize heroic martyrdom against illegitimate tyranny. Until the shah prohibited it, the occasion was annually observed in Iran by intense emotionalism that included processions of flagellants drawing blood from their own bodies.[23]

The commemoration of Husain's martyrdom fueled the final riots against the shah late in 1978 and galvanized the anti-American demonstrations in 1979 after the hostages were seized. As one Iranian commentator explained: "Because such men [Ali and Husain] and such stories are in the Iranian culture, the people during the crisis of the [1978-1979] revolution resorted to these emotional-concept-images and gained a connection with external values."[24]

Further illustrating the Shiite heritage's influence was the claim that "the Shah has come to personify Yazid--the Muslim world's most hated symbol of political and social evil."[25] From here it was easy to identify America as "the mother of corruption itself,"[26] to characterize Iran's struggle against that country as one "between Islam and blasphemy,"[27] and to proclaim an almost eager willingness to emulate Husain's martyrdom.[28]

The Islamic tradition of *taqiya*, which permits a Muslim to dissimulate if threatened with death, is relevant here. As a minority sect in an often hostile environment, Shiites obviously had occasion to employ dissimulation to gain their ends or to survive. In time the Shiites expanded this notion to permit dissimulation for a righteous cause. Thus, Khomeini's calling the diplomats in the U.S. Embassy in Tehran a "bunch of spies,"[29] and otherwise exaggerating his charges against the United States,[30] became justified by the higher cause he sought.

The Iranian Shiites believe that the twelfth imam descended from Ali miraculously disappeared (the great occultation) in A.D. 873. At some unknown time in the future, when the world is in dire trouble, this twelfth or hidden imam will reappear as the Mahdi, or Messiah.

Although he has never claimed to be this twelfth imam returned, Ayatollah Khomeini repeatedly allowed himself to be addressed as "imam," terminology that, under the unique circumstances described above, had obvious messianic implications for Iranians.[31] As one ecstatic account put it: "Victories, like the entry of the blessed Muhammad into Mecca, are very rare . . . in human history. Muhammad's victory showed that good can defeat evil and that Justice can triumph. For me Khomeini's return to Iran was another Mecca."[32] The description continues: "When Khomeini enters the room there is no sound. He seems to be walking on air. . . . There is a glow in his face, a combination of physical vitality and spiritual power, with an indefinable humility and gentleness which seems to be based on tremendous wisdom and understanding."[33]

The fact that Khomeini returned on the eve of the new Muslim century (1400 on the lunar calendar)[34] to overthrow unjust rule adds further overtones to the situation. His role as *faghi* (the all-powerful trustee or delegate of the hidden imam) under the new Iranian Constitution--which empowers him to declare war, dismiss an elected president, appoint military commanders and also jurists who may veto the laws of the Majlis (Parliament), and grant amnesties--formally institutionalizes his religious powers as imam.

The political consequences of Islam entail still more significant aspects. For one thing, the Christian concept of the separation of church and state, symbolized by the biblical injunction to render unto Caesar what is Caesar's and unto God what is God's, is foreign to Muslims.[35] Thus, any secular government in a Muslim country can be, and often is, impugned as illegitimate. Assassinations, coups d'état, and civil wars are the logical consequence. Seen in this cultural light, the overthrow of the shah does not appear so unusual, particularly given the Shiite belief in the hidden imam. Only the imam's rule can be just and legitimate; all other are illegitimate by definition.

This inherent Shiite tendency to contest the authority of Iran's secular government is intensified whenever that government appears to be letting foreign influences corrupt Islamic culture and tradition. Thus, as long ago as the nineteenth century, Shiism acted as the functional equivalent of an anti-imperialist or nationalist movement.[36]

The Muslim clerics, for example, were instrumental in launching Iran into a disastrous war against Russia in 1826. Three years later they incited the mob that attacked the Russian Embassy in Tehran and brutally murdered that country's ambassador. In 1872, the Shiite clergy played a leading role in canceling the fabulous monopoly granted Baron Paul Julius von Reuter for mines, forests, railroads, banks, customs, and telegraphic communications. The tobacco concession granted to a British company in 1890 was withdrawn a year later for similar reasons. The nationalism that emerged during 1906 over the granting of a constitution, and again in the early 1950s under Mohammed Mossadegh, also saw important Shiite roles.

In all these examples, the close association between religion and nationalism manifested an obvious difference from the West's secular brand of nationalism. Nevertheless, it would be a mistake to explain the hostage taking solely in terms of Shiism or even Shiite nationalism.

The Iranians clearly saw their action as the venting of justified nationalist wrath against "the imperialist"[37] Americans and, in general, a further development of the Third World's struggle against the West. As the Iranian foreign minister, Sadegh Ghotbzadeh, put it: "The moral responsibility for disgracing international imperialism rests upon the shoulders of the young Islamic revolution."[38] The seizure of the American Embassy, declared an Iranian Foreign Ministry statement, "expressed not only the emotions and feelings of our people but those of all the *mostazafs* [oppressed peoples] of the world."[39] Still another Iranian source stated that the "uprising in Iran is of interest to all . . . neo-colonized peoples."[40]

DIPLOMATIC IMMUNITIES AND INVIOLABILITY

From time immemorial, antedating perhaps all other rules of international law, the diplomatic agents sent by one state to another have been accorded special protections and immunities. As one authority noted, "Everywhere in antiquity ambassadors were considered inviolable."[41]

In ancient Greece, the Spartans recognized they had flagrantly violated a fundamental principle of law by killing the envoys of the Persian king Darius. But when two Spartan nobles later offered their own lives in retribution, the new Persian king, "Xerxes answered with true greatness of soul that he would not act like the Lacedaemonians, who, by killing the heralds, had broken the laws which all men hold in common."[42]

Cicero expressed the Roman attitude when he wrote: "The inviolability of ambassadors is protected both by divine and human law; they are sacred and respected so as to be inviolable not only when in an allied country but also whenever they happen to be in forces of the enemy."[43] The so-called father of international law, Hugo Grotius, wrote in 1625 that there were "two points with regard to ambassadors which are everywhere recognized as prescribed by the law of nations, first that they be admitted, and then that they be not violated."[44]

It is also important to note that the Prophet Muhammad himself recognized the inviolability of ambassadors. When faced with the emissaries of "the liar prophet," Musaylima, Muhammad remarked: "If I were in the habit of executing emissaries, I would have ordered you killed."[45] In an analysis of Islamic authority, M. Cherif Bassiouni concluded: "The seizure and continued detention of the detainees [the American hostages] are in violation of Islamic law . . . [and] Islamic international law."[46]

Although the law of diplomatic inviolability is general and ancient, exceptions and outright violations are more numerous than many believe. According to Arthur Nussbaum, the ancient Egyptians considered envoys "as a kind of hostage,"[47] and in early India, "the inviolability of envoys was not definitely recognized except for the sparing of their lives."[48]

Of related interest, if not exactly a precedent, is the fate of the Roman Emperor Valerian. When the Sassanian King Shapur I defeated and captured him in A.D. 260, Valerian was kept prisoner and treated as a slave for the rest of his life. "Few if any events in history have produced a greater moral effect. . . . The impression at the time must have been overwhelming, and the news must have resounded like a thunder-clap throughout Europe and Asia."[49]

In his study of Renaissance diplomacy, Garrett Mattingly wrote that "[d]own to the end of the seventeenth century" some still claimed that "delinquent diplomats escaped the penalties of the [host state's] law rather by clemency than by right."[50] It is also interesting to note that E. R. Adair, one of the best authorities on the matter, felt that diplomatic immunities were "more as a result of political pressure than any very strong respect for international law."[51]

The modern institution of permanent embassies developed during the Renaissance within the Italian city-states and soon spread to the rest of Europe.[52] In the following centuries, the history of diplomacy was full of conflicts between states over precedence in rank, as well as questions about diplo matic immunities. The Congress of Vienna in 1815 and that of Aix-la-Chapelle in 1818 were landmarks in the development of formal diplomatic practices.[53] It was not until the Vienna Convention on Diplomatic Relations[54] was signed in 1961 and entered into force in 1964, however, that a comprehensive treaty on all phases of diplomacy existed. As of January 1, 1978, 128 states, including the United States and Iran, were parties to it. It is to this convention, with its usage and interpretation, that we must now turn.

THE INTERNATIONAL LAW OF DIPLOMACY UPHELD

When the Iranians seized and occupied the American Embassy in Tehran and held as hostages the members of its diplomatic staff, the United States made a number of responses. Two that were germane for the purposes of the present analysis were the appeals to the International Court of Justice and to the U.N. Security Council. To the former we may turn for evidence of the legal implications for the international law of diplomacy, while in the latter we may find indications of the political consequences.

International Court of Justice

The International Court of Justice is identified by the Charter of the United Nations as its "principal judicial organ"[55] and is generally considered to be the highest organ for interpreting international law. Thus, a decision by the Court is a definitive statement of what the relevant international law is.

On November 29, 1979, the United States filed in the Registry of the International Court of Justice a request for interim measures of protection[56] relating to the takeover of its embassy in Tehran and the holding as hostages of some fifty of its diplomatic personnel. Acting with unaccustomed alacrity, the Court unanimously delivered its opinion without any obscuring concurring statements on December 15, 1979, just sixteen days later. Thus, the presumption is reinforced that the Order of the Court was indisputably a statement of the relevant international law of diplomacy.

In reaching its opinion, the Court's first problem was to establish its jurisdiction, since under international law no state can be sued without its consent, and in a letter of December 9, 1979, Iran urged the Court that it

should not take cognizance of the case . . . .

2. For this question only represents a marginal and secondary aspect of an overall problem, one such that it cannot be studied separately, and which involves, *inter alia*, more than 25 years of continual interference by the United States in the internal affairs of Iran, the shameless exploitation of our country, and numerous crimes perpetrated against the Iranian people, contrary to and in conflict with all international and humanitarian norms.

3. The problem involved in the conflict between Iran and the United States is thus not one of the interpretation and the application of the treaties upon which the American Application is based, but results from an overall situation containing much more fundamental and more complex elements. Consequently, the Court cannot examine the American Application divorced from its proper context,

namely the whole political dossier of the relations between Iran and the United States over the last 25 years. This dossier includes, *inter alia*, all the crimes perpetrated in Iran by the American Government, in particular the *coup d'état* of 1953 stirred up and carried out by the CIA, the overthrow of the lawful national government of Dr. Mossadegh, the restoration of the Shah and of his regime which was under the control of American interests, and all the social, economic, cultural and political consequences of the direct interventions in our international affairs, as well as grave, flagrant and continuous violations of all international norms committed by the United States in Iran. . . . In conclusion, the Government of the Islamic Republic of Iran respectfully draws the attention of the Court to the deep-rootedness and the essential character of the Islamic revolution of Iran, a revolution of a whole oppressed nation against its oppressors and their masters; any examination of the numerous repercussions thereof is a matter essentially and directly within the national sovereignty of Iran.[57]

The Court, however, emphatically rejected the Iranian position, declaring: "A dispute which concerns diplomatic and consular premises and the detention of internationally protected persons, and involves the interpretation or application of multilateral conventions codifying the international law governing diplomatic and consular relations, is one which by its very nature falls within international jurisdiction."[58]

The events that, in the opinion of the United States, required the Court to issue interim measures of relief were listed as follows:

(i) On 4 November 1979, in the course of a demonstration outside the United States Embassy compound in Tehran, demonstrators attacked the Embassy premises; no Iranian security forces intervened or were sent to relieve the situation, despite repeated calls for help from the Embassy to the Iranian authorities. Ultimately the whole of the Embassy premises was invaded. The Embassy personnel, including consular and non-American staff, and visitors who were present in the Embassy at the time, were seized . . . ;

(ii) Since that time, the premises of the United States Embassy in Tehran . . . have remained in the hands of the persons who seized them. These persons have ransacked the archives and documents both of the diplomatic mission and of its consular section. The Embassy personnel and other persons seized at the time of the attack have been held hostage with the exception of 13 persons released on 18 and 20 November 1979. Those holding the hostages have refused to release them, save on condition of the fulfillment by the United States of various demands regarded by it as unacceptable. The hostages are stated to have frequently been bound, blindfolded, and subject to severe discomfort, complete isolation and threats that they would be put on trial or even put to death . . . ;

(iii) The Government of the United States considers that not merely has the Iranian Government failed to prevent the events described above, but also that there is clear evidence of its complicity in, and approval of, those events;

(iv) The persons held hostage in the premises of the United States Embassy in Tehran include, according to the information furnished to the Court by the Agent of the United States, at least 28 persons having the status duly recognized by the Government of Iran of "members of the diplomatic staff" within the meaning of the Vienna Convention on Diplomatic Relations of 1961, and at least 20 persons having the status, similarly recognized, of "members of the administrative and technical staff" within the meaning of that Convention . . . ;

(v) In addition to the persons held hostage in the premises of the Tehran Embassy, the United States Chargé d'Affaires in Iran and two other United States diplomatic agents are detained in the premises of the Iranian Ministry for Foreign Affairs, in circumstances which the Government of the United States has not been able to make entirely clear, but which apparently involve restriction of their freedom of movement, and a threat to their inviolability as diplomats.[59]

The United States argued that these Iranian actions "violated . . . Articles 22, 24, 25, 27, 29, 31, 37 and 47 of the Vienna Convention on Diplomatic Relations."[60] The most significant parts of these articles are as follows:

Article 22

1. The premises of the mission shall be inviolable. The agents of the receiving state may not enter them, except with the consent of the head of the mission.

2. The receiving state is under a special duty to take all appropriate steps to protect the premises of the mission against any intrusion or damage and to prevent any disturbance of the peace of the mission or impairment of its dignity.

Article 24

The archives and documents of the mission shall be inviolable at any time and wherever they may be.

Article 25

The receiving state shall accord full facilities for the performance of the functions of the mission.

Article 27

The receiving state shall permit and protect free communication on the part of the mission for all official purposes . . . .

Article 29

The person of a diplomatic agent shall be inviolable. He shall not be liable to any form of arrest or detention. The receiving state shall treat him with due respect and shall take all appropriate steps to prevent any attack on his person, freedom or dignity.

Article 31

A diplomatic agent shall enjoy immunity from the criminal jurisdiction of the receiving state. He shall also enjoy immunity from its civil and administrative jurisdiction . . . .

Article 47

In the application of the provisions of the present Convention, the receiving state shall not discriminate as between states . . . .[61]

The Court unanimously and unequivocally upheld the international law of diplomatic immunity and inviolability, as codified by the Vienna Convention, arguing that:

there is no more fundamental prerequisite for the conduct of relations between States than the inviolability of diplomatic envoys and embassies. . . . [T]hroughout history nations of all creeds and cultures have observed reciprocal obligations for that purpose. . . . [T]he obligations thus assumed, notably those for assuring the personal safety of diplomats and their freedom from prosecution, are essential, unqualified, and inherent in their representative character and their diplomatic function. . . . .[62]

Accordingly, the Court unanimously stated that "Iran should immediately ensure that the premises of the United States Embassy . . . be restored to . . . the United States . . . and should ensure their inviolability,"[63] as well as ensuring "the immediate release, without any exception, of all . . . hostages."[64] On May 24, 1980, the Court delivered its final judgment in the matter, ordering Iran to release the hostages, return the embassy, and pay reparations. The United States was reprimanded for its aborted military attempt to free the hostages in April 1980.[65]

Security Council

The Charter of the United Nations confers upon "the Security Council primary responsibility for the maintenance of international peace and security,[66] and declares that the "members of the United Nations agree to accept and carry out the decisions of the Security Council in accordance with the present Charter."[67] Thus, in bringing its case to the Security Council, the United States was turning to a political organ of the world body, as well as to its judicial organ. What is more, the Security Council not only was mandated to recommend methods of peaceful settlement of disputes but also was the only U.N. organ empowered to order enforcement actions.

Ironically, however, when the hostage crisis first arose in November 1979, the United States initially opposed its consideration by the Security Council, as proposed by Iran, on the grounds that it would divert attention from the hostages to Iran's grievances about the deposed shah and his reputed American support.[68] In doing so, it is possible that the United States squandered an opportunity to arrange an early settlement of the crisis around a face-saving denunciation of the shah in the Security Council.

Iran's interim foreign minister (and later President), the relatively moderate Abolhassan Bani Sadr, was prepared to come to the United Nations, and had been quoted as saying that if the United States denounced the shah, "we could quickly solve the crisis."[69] But even as Bani Sadr was further stating that he was "already of the opinion that they [the hostages] must be released,"[70] the United States continued to demand the unconditional release of the hostages before a Security Council meeting could be held.

Although the United States publicly was supported in its stand by the Security Council's Western members--Britain, France, Norway, and Portugal--it privately was argued by one of them, whose delegate asked not to be identified, that "the Americans were being unnecessarily provocative by insisting that release of the hostages was a precondition for a hearing on a complaint against the United States."[71] By the time the United States was ready to turn to the Security Council, Bani Sadr had been removed from his position. Ayatollah Khomeini, who only a few days earlier was prepared to bring his case to it, now denounced the Security Council in no uncertain terms:

Carter, after political and military maneuvers, is willing that the Security Council should sit solely to study this case [of the hostages]. . . . [O]ur nation knows that the verdict of any council or court that sits under the direct influence of the United States has been dictated by the United States from the start. . . . Our nation does not agree with the made-to-order Security Council meeting, whose course has been predetermined.[72]

The Iranians were convinced that the Security Council was "a tool of the superpowers."[73]

Be that as it may, the Security Council finally did have ample occasion to consider the matter in escalating steps of concern. Shortly after the crisis erupted, it held consultations, as distinguished from a formal meeting, and unanimously agreed upon a brief statement that it issued through its president.[74] Although "not wishing to interfere in the internal affairs of any country," the statement "emphasize[d] that the principle of the inviolability of diplomatic personnel and establishments be respected in all cases in accordance with internationally accepted norms."[75] Accordingly, the Security Council urged "in the strongest terms" that the hostages "be released without delay."[76]

At the end of November, the secretary-general employed his significant but seldom-used power to "bring to the attention of the Security Council any matter which in his opinion may threaten the maintenance of international peace and security."[77] The Security Council proceeded to hold five meetings in which Iran's actions were almost universally condemned by the Western, communist, and Third World states. B. Akporode Clark of Nigeria, for example, stated that "one of the most indestructible pillars of international relations was the inviolability of diplomatic personnel and establishments."[78] The Soviet representative, Oleg Troyanovsky, said that "the USSR was in favour of strict compliance with the 1961 Vienna Convention."[79] The Norwegian ambassador, Ole Algard, declared that Iran's actions "amounted to flagrant violations of some of the basic rules of international law enshrined in the 1961 Vienna Convention on Diplomatic Relations."[80] Seldom had an American-backed position received such broad support in recent years.

The result of these considerations was the unanimous adoption of a resolution reaffirming "the solemn obligation of all States to . . . the Vienna Convention on Diplomatic Relations . . . to respect the inviolability of diplomatic personnel and the premises of their missions."[81] Iran was called upon "*urgently* . . . to release immediately the personnel of the Embassy of the United States . . . being held in Teheran."[82]

When Iran failed to react positively, the Security Council reaffirmed "its Resolution 457 . . . in all respects," deplored "the continued retention of the hostages," and called "once again on . . . Iran to relase immediately all . . . hostages."[83] In the final provision of its new resolution, the Council decided "to meet on 7 January 1980 in order to review the situation and, in the event of non-compliance . . . to adopt effective measures under Articles 39 and 41 of the Charter."[84] This overt threat to adopt mandatory economic sanctions under Chapter VII of the U.N. Charter was approved by a vote of eleven in favor, with four abstentions (Bangladesh, Czechoslovakia, Kuwait, and the Soviet Union). The action of the Soviets boded ill for the imposition of such measures.

While the Security Council was considering the hostages' case, the secretary-general did not remain inactive. From the start of the crisis, he had been involved; moreover, Security Council resolutions 457 and 461 had requested him "to lend his good offices" to resolving the situation. The latter resolution also had taken "note of his readiness to go personally to Iran." In light of this proposed trip, and to grant further time for reflection, the Security Council postponed the deadline (January 7, 1980) for considering sanctions against Iran set in Resolution 461.

The secretary-general visited Iran January 1-4, 1980, holding discussions with Foreign Minister Sadegh Ghotbzadeh and members of the Revolutionary Council.[85] He was not permitted, however, to meet with Ayatollah Khomeini, see the hostages, or confer with the militants holding them. Thus, although the trip gave him "a clearer insight into the position of the Iranian leaders," it "in no way contained a solution to the most delicate and complex problem of the hostages."[86]

The secretary-general emphasized "the grave violation of international conventions and international law"[87] committed by Iran. Ghotbzadeh, however, told the secretary-general that his country's present actions should be looked at in light of the history of the relationship between it and the United States over the past twenty-five years. He also broached the idea of establishing a committee of international inquiry, which had been discussed in earlier contacts, to investigate Iran's complaints against the United States. The report of the committee would be submitted to the appropriate U.N. organs for action. While the secretary-general said that the hostages must be released before or simultaneously with the creation of such a committee, the foreign minister maintained that the release could come only as a result of the entire procedure.

On January 10, 1980, the United States submitted a draft resolution to the Security Council calling for mandatory economic sanctions against Iran under Chapter VII of the U.N. Charter.[88] The proposal called for the release of the hostages and declared that until this was effected, all members of the United Nations should "prevent the sale or supply and shipment of all items, commodities, or products, except food, medicine and medical supplies" to Iran.[89] In addition, no UN member should "make available to the Iranian authorities or to any person in Iran or to any enterprise controlled by any Iranian governmental entity any new credits or loans."[90]

Although only two of the fifteen members of the Security Council (the German Democratic Republic and the Soviet Union) voted against the U.S. draft proposal, the measure failed because the Soviet opposition constituted a veto. Ten members approved the proposal, two abstained (Bangladesh and Mexico), and China did not vote. The statements made in the Security Council at this time help to illustrate why that organ was unwilling to enforce its call for the release of the hostages.[91]

The representative of the German Democratic Republic perhaps came closest to the mark when he declared, "Sanctions would only further worsen a complex situation and would make more difficult a peaceful solution."[92] The representative of Bangladesh argued similarly: "The imposition of economic sanctions . . . would not be effective in achieving its objective, but might aggravate the situation and unleash a chain of events with far-reaching implications."[93]

The two previous attempts by the Security Council to impose mandatory economic sanctions (Rhodesia and South Africa) were largely failures. "Ten years of sanctions didn't bring Rhodesia to its knees,"[94] said a European diplomat. "There are always

ways of getting around them,"[95] declared another. The mandatory arms boycott against South Africa not only had been ineffective but had stimulated a major domestic arms industry. Apart from the self-interest of many states in buying Iranian oil, sanctions against Iran could also bring unwanted side effects. Enforcement action, argued some diplomats, "might serve Ayatollah Ruhollah Khomeini, helping him to heal internal splits and strengthening his call for martyrs."[96]

The bottom line, of coure, was the Soviet desire to pose as a friend of Iran while punishing its superpower adversary. In explaining his country's action, the Soviet representative declared: "the Soviet Union had undermined the [U.S.] attempt to use the United Nations for covert plans to intervene flagrantly in Iran."[97] The Chinese delegate, however, characterized the Soviet behavior as an attempt "to make cheap political capital."[98] His American counterpart declared that "the USSR's vote was a cynical and irresponsible exercise of its veto power."[99]

Thus, the attempt to impose mandatory economic sanctions against Iran foundered on the twin rocks of doubt as to their ultimate effectiveness and renewed Cold War animosities between the two superpowers. Nevertheless, the United Nations, speaking through two of its principal organs--the International Court of Justice and the Security Council--had spoken out unmistakably in defense of the existing international law of diplomacy and its rules concerning diplomatic inviolability.[100] Despite the failure to adopt sanctions in the Security Council, the various members of the United Nations seldom had shown so much unity of purpose in recent years. Both legally and politically, Iran stood censured by the international community. The Iranians could take little comfort in what had transpired in the world organization.

CONCLUSIONS

There have been numerous, profound challenges in the twentieth century in what is historically Western-derived international law. The Russians, Chinese, and numerous Third World states from time to time have expressed reluctance to be bound by a law they not only had no role in developing but that often, by definition, has worked against their interests. As a result, contemporary international law has had to accommodate itself to some important alterations in recent decades. Changing norms concerning colonialism, the use of force, the expropriation of property, and the continuity of states are noteworthy examples.

What is more, even Western states have sanctioned important changes--as witness the obsolescence today of the international law of war and neutrality as it stood early in the twentieth century. Indeed, when it has suited its political purpose, the United States has proved just as ready as the Soviet Union to ignore strict international legal mandates, as illustrated by American actions during the Cuban missile crisis in 1962 and in the Dominican Republic three years later.

Might not the same fate befall the international law of diplomacy? After all, law would seem to exist because it serves perceived needs. Eliminate these exigencies and the rationale for the law disappears.

The present international law of diplomacy arose because it served the interests of the parties involved. In its work, which was used as a model for the 1961 Vienna

Convention on Diplomatic Relations, the International Law Commission stated that diplomatic privileges and immunities had been justified earlier on the basis of "extraterritoriality" and "representative character." According to the first, the premises of a diplomatic mission represent an extension of the territory of the sending state, and according to the second, privileges and immunities are predicated on the assumption that the diplomatic mission and its staff personify the sending state. In recent years, however, observed the commission, a "functional necessity" theory has been gaining adherents. This new rationale "justifies privileges and immunities as being necessary to enable the mission to perform its functions."[101] In other words, the international law of diplomacy is law because it serves the reciprocal needs and interests of the members of the international system.

Today, however, the traditional role of the diplomat as an international decision maker, negotiator, representative or information gatherer is being rendered obsolete by instant communications and travel. Diplomacy through conferences in bodies such as the United Nations and its numerous ancillary organs, summitry between heads of states such as the Carter-Brezhnev meeting in Vienna during 1979, and shuttle diplomacy à la Henry Kissinger or Robert Strauss in the Mideast are all playing a major role. At the same time, terrorists of one stripe or another are increasingly looking upon embassies as highly visible targets of opportunity that enable them easily to make their various points. Given these facts, so highly publicized by the Iran hostages' case, one might legitimately question the future of the international law of diplomacy.

Unlike so many other aspects of international law, however, the norms regarding diplomacy are not simply a Western invention for the good of the West. On the contrary, as was made clear above, they constitute possibly the oldest area of international law. In a world divided along national, ideological, and religious lines, there are few questions on which most members of the United Nations agree. Speaking through both its judicial and its political organs, however, the world organization did strongly agree that the international law of diplomacy should be supported and preserved. Otherwise, every embassy and every diplomat everywhere would be at the mercy of terrorists.

Thus, the Iranians were not challenging merely a partisan, Western international law but one sanctioned down through the ages by virtually every known civilization, including, as noted above, the Islmaic world. Violations of this law, when they have occurred, usually have been labeled "aberrations" at best and "barbarous" on the whole. Although it is possible to sympathize with the Iranian complaint about an international law that is so manifestly supportive of the United States in the hostages case, while at the same time permitting that state to subvert the constitutional government of Iran in 1953[102] and allowed U.S. Embassy personnel to help establish SAVAK,[103] it is not likely that time-honored international legal norms, which still serve the needs of the world community, will be overthrown so lightly.

It is conceivable, however, that certain aspects of the institution of modern diplomacy may be altered to conform to the new situation. Permanent embassies, for example, increasingly might be deemphasized in favor of either special roving envoys[104] or conference diplomacy through international organizations. Even then, however, diplomatic inviolability will have to be honored for any semblance of orderly international relations to prevail.

NOTES

1. See specifically Articles 22, 29, and 31 of the Vienna Convention on Diplomatic Relations, 500 *United Nations Treaty Series* 95.

2. *IranVoice* (published by the Embassy of the Islamic Republic of Iran in the United States), December 24, 1979, p. 8. The Quran, sura Taubah, is then quoted: "take them and confine them, and lie in wait for them in every place of ambush." Another observer sympathetic to the Iranian position wrote scathingly about the "lifestyle of the West with its social conventions such as the 'immunity' of diplomats living in embassies where I have seen cocktail parties given before sunset during the month of Ramadan." He added, "[M]ore than any other country, the United States . . . symbolized those features of Western civilization that Islamic revivalists consider to be base and objectionable." Irving, "The Looming Crescent: Carter's Canossa," *Islamic Revolution* (published under the auspices of the Islamic Republic of Iran), August 1980, p. 3.

3. *Time*, November 26, 1977, p. 31.

4. Christos P. Ioannides, "The Hostages of Iran: A Discussion with the Militants," *Washington Quarterly* 23 (Summer 1980). For the western observer, whose legal background is based on the English common law or the Continental system, the response to this Iranian position is immediate: if the Iranians feel they have a case, they should present it in a jurisprudential hearing, prior to any act of vigilantism or revenge.

5. *New York Times*, December 6, 1979, p. A-18. A Soviet diplomat in Canada compared the events in Iran with the detention of a Soviet airliner at Kennedy Airport in New York in the summer of 1978. See *New York Times*, December 5, 1979, p. A-19. See *New York Times*, December 17, 1979, p. 13, for statements from East European states critical of the United States. For further such examples from around the world, see *New York Times*, November 23, 1979, p. A-20, and November 24, 1979, p. A-8. A statement issued by a "group of concerned scholars" active in the World Order Models Project condemned the United States for its militarism in Iran, which created the conditions for the seizure of the embassy. "The Iranian Crisis: A World Order Statement," *Macroscope*, no. 8 (Fall 1980):12.

6. *New York Times*, November 16, 1979, p. A-17.

7. *New York Times*, November 26, 1979, p. A-14. Nevertheless, as will be shown below, the vast majority of the world gave at least its vocal support to the United States.

8. There have been forty-two terrorist assaults on diplomatic missions in twenty-five states since 1971. Almost half of these attacks occurred in the past two years. See *Time*, March 17, 1980, p. 28.

9. For an analysis of the transition from the "old" to the "new" diplomacy, see two studies by Harold Nicolson, *Diplomacy*, 3d ed. (London, New York: Oxford University Press, 1964); and *Curzon: The Last Phase* (London: Constable and Co., Ltd., 1934). Other observers have discerned a plethora of further changes in the art of diplomacy. A partial listing includes such varieties as "quiet," "summit," "crisis," "total," "conference," "parliamentary," "personal," "preventive," and "corridor" diplomacy.

10. See Harold Nicolson, *The Evolution of the Diplomatic Method* (London,   Melbourne: Macmillan, 1954).

11. See Adda Bruemmer Bozeman, *The Future of Law in a Multicultural World* (Princeton, NJ: Princeton University Press, 1971).

12. Ibid., p. 78.

13. Ibid., p. 61. Also see Bozeman's *Politics and Culture in International History* (Princeton, NJ: Princeton University Press, 1960).

14. Ram Prakash Anand, *New States and International Law*, (New Delhi: Vikas, 1972), p. 6.

15. Ibid., p. 7. Also see H. S. Bhatia, ed., *International Law and Practice in Ancient India* (New Delhi: Deep and Deep, 1977), pp. 139-161.

16. Unlike their Semitic coreligionists, the Arabs, the Iranians are ethnically Aryan, from which the name of their country, Iran, derives. The Iranian languge, however, is called Farsi or Persian, after the country's southern province, Fars. It was from Fars that the Achaemenids, the builders of the original Persian empire of Cyrus, Darius, and Xerxes, sprang. Thus, the entire land was referred to by foreigners as "Persia," a term that today has an old-fashioned ring.

17. For a general discussion of the fall of the Pahlavi regime, see Fereydoun Hoveyda, *The Fall of the Shah* (London: Weidenfeld and Nicolson, 1979); Amin Saikal, *The Rise and Fall of the Shah* (Princeton, NJ: Princeton University Press, 1980); Sepehr Zabih, *Iran's Revolutionary Upheaval: An Interpretative Essay* (San Francisco: Alchemy Books, 1979); and William H. Forbis, *Fall of the Peacock Throne: The Story of Iran* (New York: Harper and Row, 1980). For an analysis of events after the shah's fall, see Eric Rouleau, "Khomeini's Iran," *Foreign Affairs* 1 (1980):59. And for an examination of the Islamic revival in general, see Richard Pipes, "'This World Is Political!' The Islamic Revival of the Seventies," *Orbis* 9 (1980):24; and William E. Griffith, "The Revival of Islamic Fundamentalism: The Case of Iran," *International Security* 4, no. 1 (1979):132-138.

18. See, in general, Percy M. Sykes, *A History of Persia*, 2 vol. (London: Macmillan, 1951); and Richard N. Frye, *The Heritage of Persia* (Cleveland: World, 1963). For a survey of the more recent past, see Richard Cottam, *Nationalism in Iran*, 2nd rev. ed. (Pittsburgh: University of Pittsburgh Press, 1979). Finally, for a view that places the present events in their cultural context, see Adda Bruemmer Bozeman, "Iran: U.S. Foreign Policy and the Tradition of Persian Statecraft," *Orbis*, 387 (1979):8.

19. The similarity of the idea of a savior in Zoroastrianism and Shiite Islam is striking. For further parallels, see Henry Corbin, *Les motifs zoroastriens dans la philosophies de sohrawardi* (1946), and *Corps spirituel et terre céleste: Corps de résurrection de l'Iran mazdéen à l'Iran shiite* (Paris: Buchet/Chastel, 1961). Iran's mythical, pre-Islamic past finds voice in its great national epic poem, *The Shahnama* (Book of Kings), a work of some sixty thousand lines by the poet Firdawsi in the tenth century. Although it deals only with the pre-Islamic past and contains but a modicum of true history, *The Shahnama* is known to, fully believed in, and respected by contemporary Iranians. For summaries of this great national epic, see Clement Imbault Huart, *Ancient Persia and Iranian Civilization* (New York: Knopf, 1927), p. 205; and Sykes, *History of Persia*, vol. I, p. 133.

20. Iran is the only Muslim country in which the Shiites constitute a clear majority; overall they number less than 10 percent of the Islamic faith.

21. On this point, see Sykes, *History of Persia*, vol. I, p. 530.

22. The Shiite belief in the Sassanian (Persian) origin of their new religious rulers in Iran is strikingly similar to the claim in *The Shahnama* that Alexander the Great was of Achaemenid (Persian) descent. Whether Zoroastrian or Muslim, the Iranians used an identical means to help mitigate their humiliation at being conquered by an alien race. For an excellent discussion of Shiite Islam and its heritage and practice in Iran, see Mahmood Shehabi, "Shi'a," in Kenneth William Morgan, ed., *Islam--The Straight Path: Islam Interpreted by Muslims* (New York: Ronald Press, 1958), p. 180.

23. See the accounts in *New York Times*, November 29, 1979, p. A-18, and December 1, 1979, p. A-5, of the revival of these practices under Khomeini's new Islamic government.

24. *Islamic Revolution*, November 1979, p. 24.

25. *IranVoice*, January 14, 1980, p. 14.

26. See *New York Times*, November 21, 1979, p. A-13.

27. *New York Times*, November 23, 1979, p. A-1.

28. See, for example, Khomeini's statement that "we are not afraid [of America], because we believe there is another world, a better world" (*IranVoice*, December 24, 1979, p. 2) and the injunction to his followers "to put on white robes so the blood from their wounds would show better." *New York Times*, November 14, 1979, p. A-14. "Why should we be afraid?" asked Khomeini. "We consider martyrdom a great honor." *New York Times*, November 23, 1979, p. A-1.

29. *New York Times*, November 19, 1979, p. A-12.

30. Khomeini's accusation that the United States was "attempting to occupy" the Grand Mosque in Mecca comes readily to mind. See *New York Times*, November 25, 1979, p. A-1. For further comments on dissimulation in the Shiite tradition, see William S. Haas, *Iran* (New York: Columbia University Press, 1946), p. 19.

31. Khomeini holds the degree of *ijtihad* (the authority to render views on the sacred law) and the title of *marja'i taqlid* (one who is to be emulated by the Shiite faithful). For a brief but comprehensive biographical sketch of the ayatollah, see *Current Biography* 22 (November 1979):40.

32. *Islamic Revolution*, November 1979, p. 14.

33. Ibid., p. 15. A popular political poster in Iran depicts the shah as "the devil fleeing before the angel [Khomeini]." For a reproduction, see *IranVoice*, January 21, 1980, p. 5.

34. Shiites believe that 1400, being an "even year," would be a particularly likely time for the Mahdi to appear.

35. The modern Turkey created by Komal Ataturk after World War I is the only Islamic state that is officially secular.

36. For scholarly analyses of this general topic, see Shahrough Akhavi, *Religion and Politics in Contemporary Iran: Clergy-State Relations in the Pahlavi Period* (1980); and Farhad Kazemi, "The Shi'i Clergy and the State in Iran: From the Safavids to the Pahlavis," *Journal of the American Institute for the Study of Middle Eastern Civilization* 34 (Summer 1980):1.

37. *IranVoice*, January 21, 1980, p. 7. Perceived foreign intervention is nothing novel. For many decades before 1945, Russia and Britain exercised a tremendous influence over Iran, a control that at times bordered on a condominium or protectorate. The only reason Iran was not completely colonized was that neither Russia nor Britain wished to risk a major war with the other. See Richard Cottam, *Nationalism in Iran* (Pittsburgh: University of Pittsburgh Press, 1964), p. 158.

38. *IranVoice*, December 24, 1979, p. 7. The occasion was the call for an "international tribunal to investigate the crimes of U.S. imperialism." Even here, however, Ghotbzadeh manages to color nationalism with religious overtones by referring to the "Islamic revolution." "Our movement is Islamic before being Iranian," declared Khomeini. *New York Times*, November 25, 1979, p. A-1.

39. *New York Times*, December 9, 1979, p. 12.

40. *Islamic Revolution*, April 1979, p. 3.

41. Coleman Phillipson, *The International Law and Custom of Ancient Greece and Rome*, vol. I (London: Macmillan, 1911), p. 328.

42. Herodotus, *History* (New York: Modern Library, 1942), bk. 7, para. 136. Persian behavior has not necessarily become more honorable over the millennia.

43. Cicero, in *Verrem III*, as quoted in Graham H. Stuart, *American Diplomatic and Consular Practice* (New York, London: D. Appleton-Century, 1936), p. 6.

44. *De jure belli ac pacis*, bk. II, ch. 18, para. iii, as quoted in Charles G. Fenwick, *International Law*, 4th ed. (New York: D. Appleton-Century, 1965), p. 562. For a thorough analysis of the traditional immunities of diplomatic agents and a lengthy list of relevant precedents, see Ernest M. Satow, *A Guide to Diplomatic Practice*, 4th ed. (London, New York: Longman, 1958), p. 174.

45. A *hadith* (tradition of the Prophet), quoted in Majid Khadduri, *War and Peace in the Law of Islam* (Baltimore: Johns Hopkins Press, 1955), p. 239. See also Muhammad Talaat al-Ghunaimi, *The Muslim Conception of International Law and the Western Approach* (The Hague: Martinus

Nijhoff, 1968), pp. 31-32; and Afzal Iqbal, *Diplomacy in Islam* (Lahore: Institute of Islamic Culture, 1977), pp. 61-92.

46. M. Cherif Bassiouni, "Protection of Diplomats Under Islamic Law," *American Journal of International Law* 74 (1980):631.

47. Arthur Nussbaum, *A Concise History of the Law of Nations* (New York: Macmillan, 1947), p. 11.

48. Ibid.

49. Sykes, *History of Persia* vol. I, p. 401. An enormous bas relief at Nakh-i-Rustam commemorates the event. The fetters on Valerian's arms are clearly visible.

50. Garrett Mattingly, *Renaissance Diplomacy* (London: Cape, 1955), p. 278. For specific examples of exceptions to or violations of the rule of diplomatic inviolability, see Mattingly, *Renaissance Diplomacy*, pp. 47, 48, 49, 270, 274, 275, 278-279. Nevertheless, Mattingly concluded: "Although the fifteenth century was a violent and anarchic time . . . [w]ith remarkably few exceptions, ambassadors, and even minor diplomatic agents, did enjoy the privileges and immunities." (p. 46). Similarly, despite the listing of numerous violations of diplomatic immunities (pp. 10ff., 298ff.), Graham Henry Stuart declared: "The inviolability of the person of the diplomatic agent is the fundamental principle from whence flow all other immunities. . . . [T]he state must not only abstain from any act which infringes upon the rights of the diplomatic agent, but it must prevent the commission of such act, and punish any individuals who may have committed such an offense." *American Diplomatic and Consular Practice*, (New York: Appleton-Century-Crofts, 1952), p. 298.

51. Edward Robert Adair, *The Extraterritoriality of Ambassadors in the Sixteenth and Seventeenth Centuries* (London, New York: Longmans Green, 1929), p. 251. Adair continued, however, by asking, "But what of that? The fact that they [diplomatic immunities] were established is enough, for precedents made the law." Ibid.

52. On this point, see Mattingly, *Renaissance Diplomacy*, p. 155.

53. For a useful discussion, see Harold Nicolson, *The Congress of Vienna* (New York: Harcourt Brace, 1946). Also see Charles Wheeler Thayer, *Diplomat* (New York: Harper, 1959), for a good analysis of the traditional role of the diplomat. Elmer Plischke, ed., *Modern Diplomacy: The Art and the Artisans* (Washington, D.C.: American Enterprise Institute for Public Policy Research, 1979), p. 435, contains a helpful essay on the literature on diplomacy and a selected bibliography.

54. 500 *United Nations Treaty Series* 95, reprinted in *American Journal of International Law 55* (1962):1062-1082. Also see Ernest L. Kerley, "Some Aspects of the Vienna Convention on Diplomatic Intercourse and Immunities," *American Journal of International Law 56* (1962):88; and Philippe Cahier, "Vienna Convention on Diplomatic Relations," *International Conciliation 571* (1969).

55. U.N. Charter, Art. 92.

56. *International Court of Justice 7* (1979), reprinted in *American Journal of International Law* 74 (1980):266-283; and hereafter referred to as "Interim Order." For a discussion of this decision, see Leo Gross, *American Journal of International Law 74* (1980):395-410.

57. Interim Order, paras. 1-4.

58. Ibid., para. 25

59. Ibid., para. 34.

60. Ibid., para. 1. The United States also maintainted that the Iranians had violated various articles of (1) the Vienna Convention on Consular Relations, (2) the Convention on the Prevention and Punishment of Crimes Against Internationally Protected Persons, Including Diplomatic Agents, (3) the Treaty of Amity, Economic Relations, and Consular Rights between the United States and Iran, and (4) U.N. Charter (Ibid.). Since the present analysis is concerned specifically with the international law of diplomacy as codified by the 1961 Vienna Convention, however, it is not necessary to pursue the details of the other conventions alleged to have been violated.

61. 500 *UNTS* 95. These articles would seem to constitute the heart of the international law of diplomatic immunity and inviolability.

62. Interim Order, para. 38.

63. Ibid., para. 47.

64. Ibid.

65. See [1980] *I.C.J.* 3. Also see "World Court Calls on Iran to Free United States Nationals, Make Reparations," *U.N. Monthly Chronicle* 14 (July 1980):17.

66. U.N. Charter, Art. 24 (1).

67. Ibid., Art. 25.

68. See *New York Times*, November 14, 1979, p. A-1, and November 26, 1979, p. A-1.

69. *New York Times*, November 29, 1979, p. A-18.

70. Ibid.

71. *New York Times*, November 15, 1979, p. A-17.

72. *New York Times*, November 28, 1979, p. A-10. Several days later Khomeini explained that he had not allowed his foreign minister to attend the meetings of the Security Council because its permanent members "have the right to veto but we have no right except to bear our miseries and never utter a word." *New York Times*, December 18, 1979, p. A-1.

73. *IranVoice*, January 21, 1980, p. 3.

74. U.N. Doc. S/13616, November 9, 1979.

75. Ibid.

76. Ibid. The secretary-general was asked "to continue to use his good offices to assist toward this objective." Ibid. The president of the Security Council reiterated the appeal a few weeks later. See U.N. Doc. S/13652, November 27, 1979.

77. U.N. Charter, Art. 99. The secretary-general's request is in U.N. Doc. S/13646, November 25, 1979. The Security Council also had before it three letters from Iran. U.N. Doc. S/13650, November 27, 1979, requested that the Council's deliberations be postponed out of respect for the holy days of Tassua and Ashura, and to allow Bani Sadr to arrive at the United Nations to participate in the Council's debate. U.N. Docs. S/13626, November 13, 1979, and S/13671, December 1, 1979, listed Iranian grievances against the United States.

78. "Council Calls on Iran to Release Detained U.S. Embassy Personnel," *U.N. Monthly Chronicle*, January 1980, p. 9.

79. Ibid., p. 8.

80. Ibid.

81. U.N. Security Council Resolution 457, December 4, 1979.

82. Ibid.

83. Security Council Resolution 461, December 31, 1979. There were several documents before the Council during its con sideration of this resolution. A letter from the registrar of the International Court of Justice informed the Security Council of the Court's provisional order to Iran to free the hostages. See U.N. Doc. S/13697, December 15, 1979. A report from the secretary-general covered his attempts at good offices since Security Council Resolution 457 had been passed, but concluded that "the expectation which had previously arisen for early progress toward a settlement of the crisis could, for the time being, not be fulfilled." See U.N. Doc. S/13704, December 22, 1979. Finally, a letter from the United States said that Iran had not responded to any U.N. appeals and that, therefore, the Security Council should consider further measures. See U.N. Doc. S/13705, December 22, 1979.

84. U.N. Doc. S/13704, December 22, 1979.

85. For his report to the Security Council on this trip, see U.N. Doc. S/13730, January 6, 1980. The following discussion is based on this document.

86. Ibid. The Iranians continued to link the release of the hostages to the extradition of the shah and the return of the assets allegedly taken out illegally by him.

87. Ibid.

88. See U.N. Doc. S/13735, January 10, 1980.

89. Ibid.

90. Ibid.

91. See "Council Fails to Agree on Sanctions Against Iran," *U.N. Monthly Chronicle,* March 1980, p. 23.

92. Ibid., p. 24.

93. Ibid.

94. *New York Times*, December 13, 1979, p. A-14.

95. Ibid.

96. Ibid.

97. *U.N. Monthly Chronicle,* March 1980, p. 25.

98. Ibid.

99. Ibid.

100. The secretary-general himself concluded: "The United Nations Security Council and the International Court of Justice have pronounced themselves firmly on the principles involved." *U.N. Monthly Chronicle,* June 1980, p. 62.

101. [1958] 2 *Ybk. I.L.C.*, p. 95.

102. Richard Cottam, a former State Department officer and an Iran specialist, flatly asserts that the shah was put back into power in 1953 "as a result of a CIA-backed and in large part CIA-directed coup." Richard Cottam, *Nationalism in Iran,* 2nd rev. ed. (Pittsburgh: University of Pittsburgh Press, 1979), p. 332. Also see Kermit Roosevelt, *Countercoup: The Struggle for the Control of Iran* (New York: McGraw-Hill, 1979).

103. As one Iranian source put it: "No one brought up the question when you help a tyrant, overtly and covertly, to terrorize his nation, do you violate international laws of humanity, or is international law merely the name of certain procedures of protocol?" *Islamic Revolution,* November 1979, p. 2. The American attempt to cover up its role in Iran has been termed "Irangate." Ibid., p. 6. Also see the articles entitled "U.S. Embassies Abroad: CIA 'Safe Houses'" and "CIA Intervention in Islamic Movements," *IranVoice*, December 24, 1979, p. 6.

104. Norway has considered abolishing all its permanent embassies in favor of teams of experts who fly to other countries when necessity demands. See David W. Ziegler, *War, Peace and International Politics* (Boston: Little Brown, 1977), p. 266. See also Tom Boudreau, *A New International Diplomatic Order* (Muscatine, Iowa: Stanley Foundation, 1980).

11

The Deportation of Iranian Students During the Iranian Hostage Crisis

CHRISTINE REILLY

Iran has long been torn between its deeply revered religious culture and the vast new-found wealth from a growing oil industry. This conflict created divisions between those who wanted to modernize and those who wanted to keep its age-old customs intact. Eventually, revolution erupted and, in turn, created a strain on U.S.-Iranian relations. Conflicting U.S. interests between humanitarian concerns on the one hand and economic concerns on the other, made the situation more complex. When the Carter administration decided to offer the Shah asylum in the United States in 1979, militant Iranian students seized sixty-three Americans in the U.S. Embassy in Tehran. This political maneuver by the students quickly escalated into a "crisis situation" that resulted in retaliatory action by the Carter administration.

On November 10, 1979, six days after the hostages were taken in Iran, President Carter ordered Attorney General Benjamin Civiletti to promulgate regulation 8 CRF, Section 214.5, which required all Iranian students in the United States, and no others, to submit to investigation by the Immigration and Naturalization Service (INS) to verify their student status, or suffer deportation. The attorney general directed the INS to carry out a two-phase investigation on the seventy-five thousand Iranian students believed to be in the country.

Phase one took place from mid-November through December 31, 1979, when INS interviewed about fifty-seven thousand students at schools and campuses across the country. Roughly fifty thousand were found to be in full compliance with their visas. During this time, INS also set up special entry and departure controls on Iranian students and required them to submit to second inspections to ensure that their documents were valid. During the second phase, which began on January 1, 1980, INS sought to identify and to schedule deportation hearings for those students who had not reported for investigation. After hearings, 3,000 students were ordered to leave the country, although ultimately only 445 actually did so.

A class action lawsuit was brought by the Iranian students to have the order declared unconstitutional, which resulted in a judgment for an injunction against the order. The government appealed, and a stay was obtained. The Ninth Circuit later ruled that the regulation was constitutional. But while 445 Iranian students were expelled under this policy, another 1,200 Iranian students were admitted to the United States without question. Thus, the directive appears to have largely been an attempt by the president to create a highly visible illusion that forceful administrative action was being taken in response to the hostage crisis. For this political aim the result was that seventy-five thousand students were denied the rights to equal protection, free speech and due process. All Iranian students in the United States, regardless of their political affiliation or innocence of any involvement in the hostage situation, were used as pawns in a foreign policy crisis that occurred during an election year.

The plenary power of Congress with regard to immigration has long been recognized. Congress may exclude persons deemed, for one reason or another or for no reason at all, undesirable.[1] Along with this broad power developed the unfortunate and distasteful policy of racial exclusion that dominated immigration law for some seventy years.[2] Moreover, once legally admitted into this country, an alien has historically been far from secure, since Congress also holds plenary power to deport even legally admitted aliens.

The American government first asserted this right in 1798, when the Federalists determined that the country was filled with alien spies who were sympathetic to France and were being protected by Thomas Jefferson and the Democratic Republicans. In response to this fear, the Alien and Sedition Acts were passed; they provided that the president could seize or remove all resident aliens who were citizens of enemy nations, were considered dangerous, or were believed to be plotting against the country. Fortunately, the acts expired in 1800 without having ever been used, and having been criticized as unconstitutional. Finally, in 1893, the Supreme Court settled the constitutional questions raised in the Alien and Sedition Acts and decided that Congress's right to deport aliens was indeed "absolute" and "unqualified."[3]

Thus, despite legal entry, admission of an alien creates no legal obligation on the part of the government. The right to expel all aliens or any class of aliens in war or peace is exclusively vested in the Congress and is binding on the courts. Due process of law ensures access to the judiciary only when a person is charged with a crime. An alien subject to deportation for a statuatory violation therefore is not entitled to the right to trial or other provisions of the Constitution. The justification is that since deportation is not punishment for a crime, access to the courts and protection from unreasonable searches and seizures and cruel and unusual punishment is not required. The Supreme Court has upheld this proposition in several cases and has held that as long as reasonable notice, a fair hearing, and an order supported by some evidence is provided for, the administrative decision will not, and cannot, be reviewed by the court.[4]

Therefore, it is Congress alone, to the exclusion of the executive and judicial branches, that establishes when and how aliens may be admitted, permitted to stay, or be deported. When Congress acts on immigration matters, it has the extraordinary power to override constitutional rights of aliens or citizens as long as the regulation is not wholly irrational. In absence of such legislation, constitutional rights prevail. Section 8 of the United States Code specifically eliminates national origin as a criterion for the administration and enforcement of immigration laws. By now we have come a long way since our immigration laws deliberately discriminated on the basis of national origin, but along the way there have been many unfortunate examples of outrageous behavior sanctioned by Congress's plenary power.

After World War I, aliens were deported during the "Red Scare" of 1917-1921, when "red" and "foreigner" were associated with opposition to World War I and secret agents. A frenzy overtook the nation, and thousands of aliens were illegally arrested in their homes, searched without warrants, deprived of counsel, jailed without trial, and deported. Private mail was opened, property was seized, and civil rights all but abandoned. A similar climate existed after World War II when McCarthyism was supported by "crisis" legislation such as the Smith Act, the McCarran Act, the Alien Registration Act, and the Internal Security Act, which in one way or another were means to control and deport "subversive" elements.

Perhaps the most shocking abuse was perpetrated by President Roosevelt during World War II. The president authorized Executive Order 9066, which called for the imprisonment of over one hundred thousand Japanese aliens and citizens solely because of their race. Congress ratified the president's actions, and the Supreme Court upheld the relocation project as authorized by the foreign affairs power.[5] While Congress is authorized to take these and other constitutionally offensive actions, in retrospect such legislation has tainted the history of the country. But what is even more offensive than Congress asserting its power to initiate such disturbing legislation is the executive branch, acting outside of any legal authority, issuing directives that violate basic civil rights. President Carter's directive calling for the deportation of Iranian students during the 1979 hostage crisis exemplifies how in time of perceived crisis, when public officials must deal with international ramifications of their actions and pressure from their constituents, we revert to unconstitutional practices we thought were long abandoned.

Arguably, even the broadly defined foreign affairs power cannot be the basis for such action. History and judicial precedent establish limits on the Executive's foreign affairs power, and only those actions expressly or implicitly derived from the Constitution are exempt from judicial review. Where Congress has specifically prohibited the use of national origin as a criterion for administering and enforcing immigration laws, the president may not undermine the law by imposing conditions on aliens legally in the country. "The Executive itself cannot extend a delegation of Congressional authority, even in the foreign affairs area, into an open-ended power to create legislative ends not encompassed within Congressional authorization or not otherwise lawful."[6] Encroachment into congressional power in the name of foreign affairs is dangerous because very few problems arise that are not in some way connected with foreign matters. In fact, the Department of State has said "that there is no longer any real distinction between domestic and foreign affairs."[7] If this were true, then the foreign affairs power could be expanded and applied to virtually all areas of politics and the president could effectively preempt the function of Congress entirely. One INS official said about the directive, "there is absolutely no precedent for this kind of action during . . . peacetime . . . ."[8] Toleration of such action offends the basic doctrine of separation of powers.

Besides being illegally issued, the regulation had a procedural flaw in that it did not comply with the notice re quirements of the Administration and Procedure Act (9 U.S.C. 553[b][B]), which requires publication of a proposed regulation and an opportunity for public comment before it can be put into effect. Waiver is permitted if notice would be impracticable, unnecessary, or contrary to the public interest. Since the regulation affected the status of over seventy-five thousand foreign students who were legally in this country, notice and opportunity for public comment would seem particularly appropriate.

Perhaps more important than being illegally issued or procedurally flawed, the directive wrongfully deprives the students of basic constitutional rights that apply to all people within U.S. borders, even those here illegally. In this instance, students legally admitted were deprived of their rights to equal protection of the law under the Fifth Amendment due process clause, the First Amendment right to free speech and association, and the Fourth Amendment right to be free from seizure without probable cause or even reasonable suspicion.

Equal protection applies to aliens as well as citizens, and classifications based on nationality are suspect and presumed to be unconstitutional since they are almost never justified by legitimate government interests.[9] Although Congress may override this standard in areas of immigration because of its plenary power, it may not do so if the measure is wholly irrational. The president, since he does not have plenary power, is held to a stricter standard and must demonstrate an overriding national interest before he can issue unconstitutional directives based on the Foreign Powers Act. But all legislation, whether from Congress or the president, that distinguishes on the basis of nationality is presumed to be unconstitutional because a governmental interest of any degree is almost never legitimately served. Under this hard-won view of equal protection, it is shocking to think that over fifty thousand students could have been rounded up for interrogation merely because they were Iranian. These students were questioned by INS investigators and threatened with the possibility that they would be found "out of status" and deported without being able to finish the education in which they had invested both time and money.

One prominent immigration attorney wrote:

I have been deluged with phone calls from Iranian students seeking representation at deportation hearings. Almost all of the students I have encountered had only very minor technicalities that rendered them out of status. They may have transferred schools without permission yet remained bona fide full time students; they may have requested permission to transfer or to renew their visas, yet filed the forms a few days late; or they may have filed the proper papers in a timely fashion yet, due to the great time it takes the INS to process the paperwork (often several months in these types of cases), the students had not received an answer from INS by the time they needed to begin classes. It has been my experience in the past that students with these sorts of technical violations are NEVER set up for deportation hearings. Rather, their applications are uniformly approved. It is clear to me that the Iranian students are being treated in a completely different manner than any other students have been treated in the past. If action is not taken by the courts, over 100 students will be unjustly deported from this country in the San Francisco area alone.[10]

This statement describes how the presidential directive drastically changed the way the law was applied and demonstrates that it was only the Iranian students who were affected. Such disparate treatment is reminiscent of less enlightened days of the Chinese exclusion, the deportation rush of the 1920s, or the Japanese internment. It is therefore shocking and frightening to think that, forty years after the Japanese, similar offenses to yet another target ethnic group could be justified by a lesser crisis. It is difficult to see how deportation is any less an injustice than internment when both actions are taken simply because of ethnic origin and deprive persons of basic freedoms.

Although the directive, first and foremost, was a blatant violation of equal protection, First Amendment rights to free speech were also undermined. In fact, White House officials said the "Presidential Order came one day after Iranian students around the United States demonstrated in support of demands for extradition of the deposed Shah because it was designed to lower the possibility of additional demonstrations."[11] And an INS official stated, "We would like to be out at the demonstrations rounding them up."[12] The "roundup," which was supposed to check student credentials, ended up being an inquisition regarding their political beliefs and their participation in political discussions and demonstrations. A government memorandum instructing investigators on how to conduct the interviews required that the officers determine whether "the student had demonstrated before, and if so, when, where, how and why," and also directed them to inquire "whether they were members of any organizations pro or con the present Government of Iran or of the USA."[13] The chilling effect of such questioning prevented many Iranian students from participating in political demonstrations. "Many Iranian students expressed great fear of arrest and deportation by Immigration and Naturalization officials if they demonstrated. Many expressed that the new regula tion indicated official hostility directed toward Iranian students, which made them fearful for their physical safety as well as their immigration status. At the demonstration only 15, far fewer than expected, appeared, I believe, because of the regulation directed solely at Iranian students."[14] These remarks indicate that the government objective to curb student speech was effective, even if unjustified by the laws of the United States.

The third major constitutional violation imposed by the directive is that of the Fourth Amendment's guarantee of freedom from illegal seizure. It has been a long-standing proposition that an illegal seizure need not be an arrest, but is any restraint or forcible detention for the purpose of interrogation when probable cause or reasonable suspicion is lacking.[15] In this instance, the Iranian students were not free to refuse the detention because failure to report resulted in deportation. All of this was carried out without the slightest reason to believe that Iranian students were more likely or even as likely as other foreign students to be out of status. In fact, according to the General Accounting Office, 45 percent of *all* foreign students had technically violated their status.[16]

In the class action suit brought by the Iranian students, the district court recognized blatant procedural and substantive constitutional violations, and enjoined enforcement of the regulation on December 11, 1979. Judge Harold H. Green's well-reasoned opinion held that the regulation was not authorized by Congress, that the attorney general could not discriminate on the basis of nationality, that the president had no inherent authority under the foreign affairs power to promulgate regulations that denied fundamental liberties for no legitimate government interest, and that the Fifth Amendment due process clause was violated because discrimination based on nationality is unconstitutional by any standard of equal protection.[17] A decision on the First and Fourth Amendment violations was not reached. Judge Green specifically commented on the invalid psychological purpose of the regulation and found that assuaging the anger of the American people by demonstrating that something was being done in the face of crisis was not a legitimate national interest. Therefore, the regulation in no way could justify an abridgment of fundamental rights. This decision reflects a more enlightened view of equal protection and is more in keeping with the Carter administration's commitment to human rights, to which this directive was a glaring exception.

On appeal to the U.S. District Court of Appeals for the District of Columbia, Judge Green's opinion was reversed in a two-page decision that cited little or no precedent in support of the reasoning. Judge Roger Robb concluded that "for reasons long recognized as valid" (no precedent cited), it was not the business of this court to pass judgment on the decisions of the president relating to foreign policy. He refused to view this regulation as anything but a purely political question. In a concurring opinion, Judge George E. MacKinnon's view is particularly curious in that, also without citing any precedent, he rationalized the disparate treatment of the Iranian students by claiming that "the treatment afforded the students is justified by the fact that the Government of their home country has committed a number of violent and lawless acts aginst the United States and that these actions place the Iranian students in a distinctly separate class."[18] He added that when a foreign nation becomes our enemy, the alien also becomes an enemy, and as such is susceptible to explusion, internment, and property seizure and confiscation. Furthermore, the judge stated that "war is not required to bring the power of deportation into existence or to authorize its exercise." It is disturbing to find a contemporary jurist resting on the same principles that justified the Japanese internment that, in retrospect, attracted universal criticism.

This decision, which is little more than a reversal without opinion, raises questions about the independence of the judiciary, as does the fact that the Supreme Court denied certiorari without dissent. The courts should not defer to the executive in a crisis where tension and public opinion are running high, because it is precisely during these times that independent review by the judiciary is most important. The Constitution is most apt to be distorted in a crisis by public officials who have momentous decisions to make quickly. By refusing to hear the case on the merits, the courts allowed the directive, which was made under stressful conditions, to stand as law.

After the Court of Appeals lifted the injunction on the directive, the investigations continued, but the mismanagement and disorganization of the INS resulted in even more civil rights violations. At the outset of the investigations, the INS sent letters to universities demanding that the registrars turn over student information regarding grades, financial status, affiliations, and course load. When the universities protested because the information was privileged and protected under the Buckley Amendment to the Privacy Act, INS responded by threatening to revoke government certifications that permit the enrollment of foreign students.[19] After a letter of apology was sent to the universities regarding the "oversight," the policy was changed to allow the students to bring their own documentation to the hearings. This change still effectively revealed protected information to INS officials, but did not directly require schools to violate federal law. A second "oversight" occurred when INS agents began questioning the students about their political affiliations and participation in demonstrations in a manner reminiscent of the infamous McCarthy hearings question "Are you now or have you ever been a member of the Communist Party?" This questioning eventually was halted because it was apparently offensive to Carter's promise that "the procedure would go forward in accordance with American law and with American fairness, in accordance with the full principles of the U.S. Constitution."[20] Thus, on the eve of being deported from the country simply because they were Iranian, the students could be comforted by the fact that the president was concerned that the questions they were being asked were offensive to the principles of democracy.

Perhaps the most outrageous oversight was that in the first months of the hostage crisis, the INS *admitted* 7,592 Iranians, including 1,212 students, during a period when INS officials were looking for Iranian students who could be deported.[21] These figures were provided by Vern Jervis, a spokesman for the INS, who said he saw no inconsistency in admitting Iranian students to the country at this time. This contradiction in policy seems even more ridiculous in light of the fact that while 1,212 students were admitted into the country in the first two months of the student roundup, the entire investigation resulted in the deportation of only 445 Iranian students. Furthermore, the INS told Congress "that they could not give assurances that the deported students actually left the country because they were relying on airline forms which didn't guarantee that the person named on the form actually left."[22]

These administrative problems led to a special investigation of the INS by Elizabeth Holtzman, chairman of a House Immigration subcommittee. The findings indicated that the "attempted crackdown on Iranian students hurt INS more than it hurt Iran."[23] A special management review by a team of experts from the President's Management Improvement Council confirmed that the INS "is a bureaucratic nightmare."[24] In one year, the agency spent more than three million dollars and could not confirm the number of students who had actually been deported and had left the country. The records were illegible, unorganized, and unreliable, and were not computerized. INS paperwork indicated that deportation proceedings were begun against individuals for "no reason," because "I could not find the form," because "I could not read the form," or because "he was inadvertently set up for deportation."[25] These remarks, taken from documents sent to the main office from the field, indicate the inability of the INS to efficiently interview over fifty thousand students across the country within a matter of weeks without utter chaos and infringements of constitutional rights, which raises the question of whether the president was justified in mandating such an order. This order was issued in the face of mounting emotions among the American people, and was one of several presidential orders issued as a result of the hostage situation. President Carter emphasized in statements and messages the gravity of the crisis and referred to the situation as a national emergency. But an "emergency" cannot justify a president's overstepping his authority and effectively legislating away the basic constitutional rights of legally admitted foreign students. Such action sets a dangerous precedent for chief executives to promulgate sweeping measures based solely on the suspect classification of national origin.

The pretense for this directive was to ensure the safety of the hostages. But if the roundup was aimed, as the attorney general claimed, at removing Iranian students in order to reduce the potential for domestic violence that would adversely affect delicate international negotiations and threaten the lives of the hostages,[26] it was clearly undermined by the fact that twelve hundred additional students entered the country. Furthermore, many students married American citizens in order to remain in the United States and thereby avoided deportation. If the target of the directive was to curb the violent actions that *some* students engaged in, the government could have proceeded either with criminal charges against those individuals or acted to monitor the demonstrations. If deportation was to be used as a diplomatic tool and bargaining chip, it was ineffective and aimed at the wrong targets. The students who were being deported did not necessarily have any ties to the new regime, nor were they necessarily the ones violently protesting.

What is even more peculiar is that President Carter was a strong advocate of civil and human rights, and this directive was not in keeping with his reputation. The actions of the INS were in direct conflict with what he was continually espousing. He stated that "it would be a mistake for the people of our country to have hatred toward anyone; not against the people of Iran, and certainly not against the Iranians who may be in our country as guests. We certainly do not want to be guilty of the same violations of human decency and basic human principles that have proven so embarrassing to many of the Iranian citizens themselves."[27] This statement and others seem to conflict with the directive. One particular example can be found in a presidential proclamation on "Bill of Rights Day," in which Carter stated--in the midst of the deportation process--that "fundamental human liberties are continually threatened by the silencing of our dissenters, by discrimination based on race, sex, religion, *ethnic origin*, and by the violation of freedom of assembly, expression, and movement. Bill of Rights Day and Human Rights Week should be marked by redoubled support for international efforts on behalf of the full range of international rights."[28] These statements seem to diametrically oppose and condemn the practices that were being carried out against the students at this time. But the fact of the matter was that this statement was made in the midst of the court battle over the legality of the directive.

Perhaps the only explanation can be found in the fact that the Executive was under pressure to take some action on the hostage situation, and quickly responded with this highly visible regulation directed against the Iranian students. It is also pertinent that "by the end of November, President Carter's political standing had risen dramatically. The public and Congress strongly approved of his restraint in dealing with the crisis, as well as his firmness in refusing to capitulate to Iran's demands for extradition of the Shah and for an apology."[29] This becomes especially important because, prior to the taking of the hostages, many believed that "Carter's presidency would not receive an opportunity for a second term because of his difficulty in working with Congress,"[30] and because "senators and representatives in overwhelming numbers were giving Jimmy Carter flunking grades as president."[31] While Carter may have been genuinely concerned about the safety of the hostages, his mind was also on the upcoming primaries and presidential election. Since the president was receiving positive feedback from the press and his popularity was growing with every action he took with regard to the hostages, there was no reason to second-guess the measures he had taken. Finally, it is curious to note that none of the major works on the Iranian hostage crisis mention the directive even in the footnotes.[32] It may well be that, unfortunately for the Iranian students, the mandate was so widely supported that it went unchallenged by the American people, and the press was far more concerned with the hostages themselves and the economic sanctions that the administration was pursuing.

The ultimate evil is that bona fide, well-meaning students were deported because of violations of immigration regulations that would not have occurred if the foreign student program had been administered with common sense. The evil is all the more ugly because it made Iranian students the scapegoats for a show of leadership strength by the president. The courts abandoned their duty to guard the Constitution and thereby allowed the Exective to establish the precedent that only showing that the action is "wholly irrational" will permit judicial review of presidential actions taken under the foreign affairs power. Judging individuals solely on their nationality, regardless of their respective guilt or innocence, is dangerous precedent. Although the immigration laws and standards of equal protection may look enlightened on the books, as long as they are applied to reach ends like this, the country has not come very far from the Alien and Sedition Acts.

NOTES

1. *Chae Chan Pin* v. *United States*, 130 U.S. 581 (1889). In this Chinese exclusion case, the court unanimously held that Congress had the power, unrestricted by constitutional limitations, to suspend or prohibit immigration of all foreigners or members of a particular race, nation, or group. It is still good law.

2. In 1879 Congress passed a bill to exclude Chinese laborers that was vetoed by President Hayes. In 1882, Congress passed another act calling for the suspension of Chinese immigration for twenty years, which was vetoed by President Arthur. Then Congress passed this act, calling for a ten-year suspension of Chinese immigration, which was extended for another ten years, and subsequently lasted until 1943. 27 Stat. 25 (1892). In 1907, President Theodore Roosevelt negotiated the Gentlemen's Agreement with Japan that ended Japanese immigration; this agreement was codified into the Immigration Act of 1924.

3. *Fong Yue Ting* v. *United States*, 149 U.S. 698 (1983).

4. *United States* v. *Curtiss Wrught Export Corp.*, 299 U.S. 304 (1936). However, from the beginning there were strong dissenters on the Supreme Court who criticized the propositions that Congress has the plenary power to deport aliens and that aliens are not entitled to constitutional protections of due process by judicial review. In his *Fung Yue Ting* dissent, Justice David Brewer called the doctrine "indefinite and dangerous, and . . . the expulsion of a race of persons because of their race may be within the inherent powers of deportism, but no such power was delegated to Congress." Justice David Field agreed, and added, "Other nations have asserted sovereign power to expel: Spain expelled the Moors; England, under Edward I, expelled 14,000 Jews; France in 1685 drove out the Huguenots, but all these instances have been condemned for their barbarity and cruelty, and no power to perpetuate such barbarity is to be implied from the nature of our government, and certainly is not found in any delegated powers of the Constitution."

5. See *Hirabayashi* v. *United States*, 320 U.S. 81 (1973); *Koramatsu* v. *United States*, 323 U.S. 214 (1944). Fortunately, after years of legal battles and condemnation, the litigation surrounding the Japanese internment was finally overturned in 1983.

6. Appellees' brief, p. 19.

7. *Briehl* v. *Dulles*, 248 F. 2d, 561, 591 (D.C. Circuit, 1957).

8. "50,000 Iranian Students Face Quiz," *New York Post*, November 13, 1979.

9. *Vick Wo* v. *Hopkins*, 118 U.S. 356.

10. Declaration of Marc Van Der Hout, immigration attorney, brief for the appellees, appendix.

11. "President Orders Action to Deport Iranian Students," *New York Times*, November 11, 1979.

12. Kellogg H. Whittick, District Director, Washington, D.C., memorandum to all section heads, November 13, 1979. Brief for the appellees, appendix.

13. Affidavit of Gasem Jaafari, a board member of the National Confederation of Iranian Students. Brief for the appellees, appendix.

14. "50,000 Iranian Students Face Quiz," *New York Post*, November 13, 1979.

15. *Terry* v. *Ohio*.

16. *Washington Post*, November 16, 1979.

17. *Narenji* v. *Civiletti*, 481 F. Supp. 1132 (1979).

18. *Narenji* v. *Civiletti*, 617 F. 2d 754 (1979).

19. "50,000 Iranian Students Face Quiz," *New York Post*, November 13, 1979.

20. *Public Papers of the Presidents of the United States*, November 16, 1979 (Washington, D.C.: Office of the Federal Registrar, 1979), p. 2133.

21. "7,592 Iranians Admitted to U.S.," *Washington Post*, January 16, 1980.

22. "Not Sure Ousted Iranians Have Left Country," *Washington Post*, April 3, 1979.

23. "Iranian Round-up," *Washington Post*, November 7, 1980.

24. Ibid.

25. Telegram from field investigators in Oregon to Washington, D.C., office. Brief for the appellees, p. 54.

26. Brief for the appellees, *Narenji* v. *Civiletti*, on appeal from U.S. District Court for the District of Columbia, p. 31.

27. President's news conference, November 28, 1979.

28. Proclamation 4705, December 6, 1979. *Public Papers of the President*, p. 2198.

29. Cyrus Vance, *Hard Choices* (New York: Simon and Schuster, 1982), p. 380.

30. *U.S. News & World Report*, November 19, 1979.

31. Ibid.

32. None of the major works refer to the student deportation order, including Jimmy Carter, *Keeping Faith* (New York: Bantam Books, 1982); Cyrus Vance, *Hard Choices*; Hamilton Jordan, *Crisis* (New York: Putnam, 1982); Zbigniew Brzezinski, *In Quest of National Security* (Boulder, Colo.L Westview Press, 1985); Mark Rozelle, *The Press and the Carter Presidency* (Boulder, Colo.: Westview Press, 1985); Kenneth Oye, Donald Rothchild, and Robert Lieber, *Eagle Entangled: U.S. Foreign Policy in a Complex World* (New York: Longman, 1980); Thomas Weigele, *Leaders Under Stress* (Durham, N.C.: Duke University Press, 1989).

ADDITIONAL SOURCES

Congressional Quarterly. *President Carter*. Washington, D.C.: Congressional Quarterly, 1977).

Konvitz, Milton. *Civil Rights in Immigration*. Ithaca, N.Y.: Cornell University Press, 1953.

U.S. Department of Justice. *Annual Report of the Attorney General*. Washington, D.C.: U.S. Government Printing Office, 1979, 1980.

---. *Annual Report of the Immigration and Naturalization Service*. Washington, D.C.: U.S. Government Printing Office, 1979, 1980.

12

The Iran Rescue Mission:
A Case Study in Executive Distrust of Congress

FRANK J. SMIST, JR.

INTRODUCTION

When the founding fathers wrote the U.S. Constitution at Philadelphia in the summer of 1787, they deliberately created a national government that had power divided among the executive, legislative, and judicial branches. The founders were very concerned with the danger of the national government becoming a tyranny that could come to rule over the people it was created to serve. To prevent this from happening, the founders first divided power among the branches. Then they created a system of checks and balances through which no one branch could subvert American democracy. In the words of James Madison in *Federalist* no. 51, the key was to give to each branch "the necessary constitutional means and personal motives to resist encroachments of the others."[1]

In the intelligence policy area, power is divided between the executive and legislative branches. The president, as the chief formulator of foreign policy and commander in chief of the military, appoints the heads of the various intelligence agencies, sets intelligence goals and priorities, and uses intelligence in formulating U.S. foreign policy and assessing its implementation. In this area, the Congress also has a key role. Because of its "power of the purse," Congress has the responsibility and the duty to examine executive branch requests for intelligence funding. The Congress has the power to approve what the executive requests and, if it chooses to exercise it, the power to raise or to cut executive funding proposals. Besides its power of the purse, the Congress has claimed the power to oversee covert actions desired by the executive branch.

Following the creation of the Central Intelligence Agency (CIA) in 1947, the Congress chose to defer to executive branch leadership in the intelligence area. Only a few senior members of the Appropriations and Armed Services committees in each chamber were kept informed of intelligence spending and activities. Presidential funding requests in the intelligence area were routinely approved with little questioning or debate. However, this period of benign neglect ended suddenly in late 1974. In the aftermath of Vietnam and Watergate, on December 22, 1974, the *New York Times* printed on its front page an article by Seymour Hersh that charged that the CIA, in direct violation of its charter, had "conducted a massive, illegal domestic intelligence operation during the Nixon administration against the anti-war movement and other dissident groups in the United States."[2]

What resulted in 1975-1976 was a firestorm of intelligence investigations. Vice President Nelson Rockefeller chaired a commission, similar to the Warren Commission that investigated the Kennedy assassination in 1963, that was appointed by President Gerald Ford to examine charges of illegal CIA activity in the United States. In addition, both the Senate and the House formed select investigative committees to examine allegations of past improprieties and to recommend ways to improve intelligence oversight in the future. The investigators unearthed many examples of both illegal and improper activities by U.S. intelligence. Assassination attempts, illegal buggings, and other improprieties were unearthed and revealed to the public.

The Senate select investigative committee, headed by Senator Frank Church (D.-Idaho), issued fourteen volumes of hearings and reports to the public that detailed the abuses of power that had occurred in the intelligence area in the past. Senator Church's committee also made 183 recommendations to the Senate designed to prevent such abuses from occurring in the future. The most important was the creation of a permanent committee that would exercise oversight in the intelligence area. Budget oversight and covert action oversight were the two most important responsibilities assigned to this proposed committee. On May 19, 1976, the U.S. Senate created the permanent Senate Intelligence Committee when it approved S. Res. 400 by a vote of 72 to 22. The Senate thus sent a signal to the executive branch that the deferential respect with which it had treated executive leadership in the intelligence area had ended.

During the presidency of Jimmy Carter, there was a struggle between the executive and legislative branches as the Senate Intelligence Committee sought to establish a partnership with the executive branch. The committee sought for the first time to exercise, on behalf of the Senate, real budget and covert action oversight. In seeking to realize these goals, the Senate Intelligence Committee encountered executive branch hostility and resistance. This paper examines how the relationship between the Senate Intelligence Committee and the Carter administration evolved in the 1977-1980 period. In particular, the failure of the Carter administration to inform the Senate Intelligence Committee in advance of the Iran rescue mission will be examined and the consequences for future congressional intelligence oversight will be discussed.

CHAIRMAN BAYH AND HIS COMMITTEE

When the Senate Intelligence Committee was established in 1976, Majority Leader Mike Mansfield had personally recruited Senator Daniel Inouye (D.-Hawaii) as its first chairman. However, Inouye stepped down as chairman after only two years because he was concerned that if he or any other chairman served longer than two years, the danger of being co-opted by the intelligence community was too great.[3] Senator Birch Bayh (D.-Indiana) succeeded him as chairman, since Bayh was second in seniority among the Democrats. He served as chairman until January 1981, and thus was chairman of the Senate Intelligence Committee for most of the Carter administration.

Bayh came to the chairmanship of the Senate Intelligence Committee with solid liberal credentials. Serving his third Senate term, he had been the floor leader and was largely responsible for Senate passage of the constitutional amendments that strengthened the presidential succession, gave eighteen-year-olds the right to vote, and approved the Equal Rights Amendment. In addition, he had been the floor leader for the successful campaign to defeat the Supreme Court nominations of Clement Haynsworth in 1969 and G. Harrold Carswell in 1970. On the Intelligence Committee, Bayh chaired the Subcommittee on Intelligence and the Rights of Americans, and was a member of the Subcommittee on Charters and Guidelines.

As chairman of the Intelligence Committee, Bayh continued some of the precedents established by Inouye. For example, he worked closely with his vice chairman, Senator Barry Goldwater (R.-Arizona). Unlike Inouye, Bayh met with the president on his own. (Inouye had refused to meet with the president on intelligence matters unless the vice chairman was also present.) Bayh made a practice of keeping Goldwater fully informed of what he had been told. Then the two of them decided if and when other members of the committee would be informed.[4] Like Inouye, Bayh sought to keep the committee together. For example, in October 1979, the committee released a five-page report entitled *Principal Findings on the Capabilities of the United States to Monitor the SALT II Treaty*. The report did not state definitively that the United States was capable of monitoring the treaty. This was because Bayh had made a deliberate choice not to divide the committee. He noted:

I opted in the end that it was better to get a unanimous report through there than to force through a report that would have divided the committee. It would have been strongly along party lines that we would have supported SALT II. I believe the benefit gained by doing that was not compensated for by the damage that would result to the committee's structure.[5]

Finally, Bayh attempted to maintain Inouye's strict standards of security by occasionally calling members in when their public comments endangered secrets entrusted to the committee.[6]

Bayh also did some things his own way. Inouye had chaired while the committee was being established and, not surprisingly, there was little legislative activity. Under Bayh the committee assumed intelligence leadership as the Senate passed the Foreign Intelligence Surveillance Act of 1978 and the Intelligence Oversight Act of 1980. Bayh's leadership was important in the passage of both. In addition, Bayh brought a significant change in tone and emphasis. Inouye had been concerned about becoming "co-opted" by the intelligence community and so stepped down as chairman after only two years. Bayh had no such concern. As he put it, "The concern I had was not being co-opted but rather how you have complete communciation."[7] A key turning point came when President Carter refused to tell the committee in advance about the Iran rescue mission in April 1980 because of security concerns. Under Bayh's leadership, the committee fought for and won the provisions in the Intelligence Act of 1980 that gave it the right to be "fully and currently informed."[8]

In 1980 there were major changes in the U.S. political environment that had a significant impact on the committee and its chairman. The political changes were due largely to the revolution in Iran and the Soviet invasion of Afghanistan. Before mid-1980, the committee was motivated in its actions by the findings of the investigative committee headed by Frank Church and sought to enact reform proposals made by that committee into law. However, in mid-1980, the committee adopted a new mind-set in which it became a supporter of and strong advocate for the intelligence community. The attempt to enact the reforms proposed by the Church committee ended.

Bayh's last year as chairman was a difficult one. The time he could devote to the committee was interrupted by a tough reelection campaign in Indiana, which he lost to Dan Quayle, and by his wife's slow and painful death from cancer. Because he was preoccupied with these matters, the committee's discipline was loosened, especially among the staff. Staff became increasingly involved in other activities for the members, and some even took an active part in the 1980 political campaigns. Inouye had attempted to establish a precedent by having his personal designee be devoted totally to committee work. However, in the last year of the Bayh chairmanship, the members increasingly came to view the designees as patronage employees.[9] Nevertheless, under Bayh the Intelligence Committee remained united and became solidly established in intelligence policy.

CARTER ADMINISTRATION ATTITUDES TO
CONGRESSIONAL INTELLIGENCE OVERSIGHT

Three different views of congressional intelligence oversight emerged within the Carter administration. These views were also found in the Reagan administration. The first, the Brzezinski-Casey view, saw congressional intelligence oversight as an unnecessary activity fraught with danger. This view, adopted by both Carter and Reagan, was best summarized by Brzezinski himself:

There is a very debilitating tendency for Congress to inject itself into details for which it has neither the competence nor the mandate. The intrusion of Congress into these areas is like the liberum veto in the Polish Parliament. In the middle of the sixteenth century any single nobleman could veto the decision of the entire parliament. Today any single member of Congress can veto a covert action by going public.[10]

Adherents of the Brzezinski-Casey view saw congressional oversight as (1) compromising sensitive information, (2) giving power to persons who had no expertise to do oversight, and (3) revealing bits and pieces of a puzzle that might enable an enemy to complete a picture that could do great harm to U.S. national security interests (the mosaic theory).[11] Holders of the Brzezinski-Casey view had great contempt for the members of Congress as individuals and for the Congress itself as an institution. During the Carter administration, this viewpoint led the president to fail to inform Congress in advance about the mission to rescue hostages in Iran. It later led the Reagan administration not to be honest with the Congress about what it was doing in Nicaragua. Since this view of oversight was held by both Carter and Reagan, the Senate Intelligence Committee had to contend with the president when it sought greater access to sensitive information.

A second view emerged that might best be termed the "Turner thesis," since it was developed by Admiral Stansfield Turner, the director of Central Intelligence (DCI) under President Carter. Here, oversight by the Senate and House intelligence committees is seen as a necessary evil with some distinct tactical advantages for the executive branch. Turner observed: "Congressional oversight gives a lot of power to the DCI. With this oversight process, I have a way of getting off the hook. I'd like to do this, but I have these committees to report to."[12] Yet this view is not limited to the executive branch. As a close aide to Turner observed, this view can be elaborated to severely limit congressional options:

Admiral Turner felt it was important to share information and responsibility with the Congress. Then when something was blown or a disaster occurred, this would shut them up entirely and immediately. They can't say anything. If other committees raise questions, you tell the intelligence committee to get the other guys in order. It's a very effective tactic.[13]

This view uses the oversight committees as a shield to fend off requests for information from other parts of Congress. Ironically, it is a great device for co-opting the Congress and its overseers. Had President Carter or President Reagan adopted this approach, either one might have been able to minimize congressional criticism and opposition. But this view required a modicum of trust in the Congress and a willingness to share power and responsibility with it, two prerequisites neither president was willing to concede.

The third viewpoint might be called the "Vance thesis." Here congressional oversight was a positive good in and of itself. As former Secretary of State Cyrus Vance observed:

Congress should be informed of the whole range of intelligence matters. Congress should be able to express its views on the covert side to the president and the senior officials in the executive branch so that the commonsense view of elected representatives can be brought to bear on such matters.[14]

Agreeing with this view, David Newsom, a former ambassador who worked closely with both intelligence committees on covert action during the Carter administration, noted: "The committees performed a very useful role in looking at actions from a . . . different perspective and asking questions that the executive branch, under the pressures of time, did not ask. Congress represents the best repository of domestic attitudes."[15] All too often White House officials are not familiar with intelligence and the intelligence agencies tend to be insulated from political realities. In such a policy environment, congressional oversight offers the executive branch a perspective to identify what might be politically feasible. However, for this viewpoint to operate, the Congress and its intelligence oversight committees must be seen as equal partners with the executive branch, a perspective neither Jimmy Carter nor Ronald Reagan was willing to adopt.

From a historical perspective, the number of contacts between the executive branch and congressional intelligence overseers and the amount of information given to these individuals grew enormously during the Carter administration. From 1947 to 1976 there was limited access. During the investigative period of 1975 to 1976, access to information and witnesses was only grudgingly given. However, the permanent Senate and House intelligence oversight committees have had unprecedented access. Even with this tremendous change, though, there has been some information that presidents and senior officials have simply refused to share with the Congress. For Jimmy Carter, it was information about the Iran rescue mission. For Ronald Reagan in the 1980s, it was information about what the United States was doing in Nicaragua and the selling of arms to the Iranians.

THE BAYH COMMITTEE AND COVERT ACTION OVERSIGHT

With respect to covert action, the Senate Intelligence Committee exercised a crucial oversight role. In 1974, Congress passed the Hughes-Ryan Amendment, which required that eight Senate and House committees be informed in advance about covert action proposals. Critics maintained that Hughes-Ryan let 57 senators, 143 representatives, and untold numbers of staff know the most sensitive secrets the U.S. government possessed.[16] But in reality very few members or staff were informed. For example, from 1976 to 1980 the Senate Foreign Relations Committee had fifteen members and more than fifty staff members. When covert action briefings were given, the information was severely restricted. One staff director of the Foreign Relations Committee described how they followed the process:

The Foreign Relations Committee was one of the committees that had to be informed under the Hughes-Ryan Act. Agency representatives would come and talk to me and my deputy. We write that all up. Me, my deputy, and the secretary who types it up know. [DDCI] Carlucci would come and brief [Chairman Frank] Church and [ranking minority Jacob] Javits. I don't remember any instance where we went further. We were "established eunuchs."[17]

This was typical of the procedures followed by the other committees that had to be informed. Instead of hordes of members and staff having access to information, access was severely restricted.

The Bayh Committee took its responsibilities toward covert action very seriously. S. Res. 400 had required that the committee be kept "fully and currently informed" with respect to "intelligence activities" and "significant anticipated activities." However, the resolution also stated that the committee had no veto power over such activities.[18] The Bayh Committee developed a set procedure it followed in examining proposed covert actions. All the members and four staffers were cleared for covert action briefings.[19] First, the committee was notified after the president signed a "finding" approving a specific covert action before it was implemented. Briefings were provided to explain and justify the details of the operation. The committee then had five options: (1) comment to the executive branch; (2) refer information to other committees; (3) seek public disclosure; (4) restrict funds; or (5) do nothing. For covert actions that were implemented, the committee received semiannual status reports on ongoing operations, briefings at the annual authorization hearings, and termination reports when an operation ended.[20]

As the committee noted in its 1976 report, covert actions undertaken after such a process "will reflect the national will as expressed by both the legislative and executive branches and not by just the executive branch alone."[21]   This process allowed the committee to consider each covert action individually.   After being briefed, each member would vote on the proposed covert action.   The only one of the options the Bayh committee chose to exercise was to comment to the executive branch.   The key problem for this committee and its successors with respect to covert action was gaining access to highly sensitive information.[22]

THE BAYH COMMITTEE AND THE IRAN RESCUE MISSION

On April 25, 1980, a rescue operation ordered by President Carter to free Americans held hostage in the American Embassy in Tehran was aborted, and an accident that occurred while American forces were leaving Iran killed eight U.S. servicemen.   Prior to the operation, President Carter had ordered information about it very closely held.   No one in the Congress was told in advance.   Even within the executive branch, Carter severely restricted information.   As one senior adviser to the president noted: "Carter personally approved the list of people to whom the existence of the plan was disclosed in advance.   Carter refused to allow the attorney general to be informed.   The president felt so secretive he didn't want even his own attorney general to be informed."[23]

Reaction to Carter's decision not to inform the Congress was very sympathetic, even in Congress.   The reaction of a senior Democrat on the House Intelligence Committee at the time was typical: "The Congress should not have been informed in advance. This was not an intelligence-gathering operation.   It was kind of a special military mission."[24]   Similar sentiments were found on the Senate side.   Minority Leader Hugh Scott (R.-Pennsylvania) observed: "Congress can't be trusted.   If Ford had waited on Congress in the Mayaguez case, the ship would have been elsewhere by the time he was able to act."[25]   On the Bayh committee itself, one senior Republican member supported Carter's action, noting: "The more people you tell, the more danger there is of losing life.   I say: 'To hell with the Congress.'"[26]   A Democrat on the committee observed: "The problem is telling too many people.   My sympathies lie with the administration."[27]   Thus President Carter had support in both houses of Congress for not informing the Congress in advance of the mission.

One Senate Democrat, however, was extremely upset about not being informed. Birch Bayh, the chairman of the Senate Intelligence Committee, noted: "It would have been so easy to tell us.   Any leaker of that information would be hung up by his thumbs.   I expressed my anger to Carter about not informing us.   Carter had a thing about not being able to trust the committee."[28]   The Iran mission was not the first instance of the Carter administration failing to keep the committee properly informed. There were other, equally sensitive operations about which the committee and its chairman had not been told.[29]

Bayh had previously cooperated with President Carter. He commented: "There were a couple of other areas where the president wouldn't tell the entire committee. He let me know but not the entire committee. I suggested to Goldwater we keep it to ourselves. Barry concurred. There were a couple of others we decided to tell to the entire committee."[30] Bayh proposed that one remedy might be to formally limit the number of members to be informed. He suggested the creation of a special subcommittee of five or seven "so you'd know somebody in the oversight mechanism knew,"[31] because "if oversight is to function better, you first need it to function."[32] Ironically, this was just what had been done on an informal basis during the 1947-1976 period.

Although not widely recognized at the time, the failure to inform Congress in advance about the Iran mission led Chairman Bayh and the Congress later in 1980 to pass legislation that more clearly delineated executive responsibilities in this area. The Intelligence Oversight Act of 1980 eviscerated the Hughes-Ryan Amendment of 1974 by reducing the number of committees to be notified of covert action from eight to two. The executive branch was directed to keep only the two intelligence committees "fully and currently informed" of all intelligence activities. In addition, this information was to be provided "in a prompt and timely fashion." Moreover, the intelligence agencies were required to provide the two oversight committees advance notice of "significant anticipated activities."

Also, in those circumstances where the president did not want to inform the entire committee membership, special provisions were added that prior notification be given to eight leaders (known as the "Gang of Eight"): the majority and minority leaders of each chamber and the chairmen and ranking minority members of the two intelligence committees. In cases where prior notification was not given, the president was required to inform the select intelligence committees fully in a "timely fashion" and provide a statement why prior notice was not given.[33] In passing the Intelligence Oversight Act of 1980, Chairman Bayh, his committee, and the rest of the Congress had fashioned a compromise with the Carter administration. The president was left with some flexibility in sensitive situations and emergencies while the Congress believed it had secured access to the information necessary to carry out its intelligence oversight function.

THE AFTERMATH AND SOME CONCLUSIONS

Would the Carter administration have lived up to its obligations under the Intelligence Oversight Act of 1980 had Jimmy Carter been reelected in 1980? It is impossible to know, since Carter was swept out of office by the Reagan landslide of November 1980. It is safe to say, though, that in a tough situation, President Carter was willing to go to great lengths to keep sensitive operations secret, and had a future mission as sensitive as the one in Iran been necessary, he still might not have trusted the Congress and gone it alone again despite what the law required.

The new Reagan administration shared with the Carter administration a contempt for Congress as an institution. Reagan's DCI William Casey detested congressional intelligence oversight, a view shared by Reagan. In 1984, the Reagan administration violated the understandings reached in the Intelligence Oversight Act of 1980 when it secretly mined the harbors of Nicaragua. Later, in the fall of 1986, the Iran-Contra disclosures revealed that again the Reagan administration had failed to obey the law and inform the Congress as required. Secretly, a president who regularly denounced "terrorists" in Iran in public had, in private, sold these same "terrorists" sophisticated weapons in an attempt to ransom Americans held hostage. On April 7, 1990, Reagan's national security adviser Robert McFarlane was convicted in U.S. District Court of violating the law by deceiving and lying to the Congress. The spirit of mistrust of Congress and the willingness to do anything to maintain secrecy that had characterized the actions of President Carter with respect to the Iran rescue mission lived on in the two terms of a conservative Republican successor.

What can be learned from all this? Perhaps the real lesson is that the system devised by the founding fathers and characterized by separation of powers and checks and balances really does work if given the chance. The tragedies of the Iran rescue mission, the Nicaragua harbor minings, and Iran-Contra might have been avoided if Presidents Carter and Reagan had been able to trust the Congress and treat it as an equal power, as the Constitution requires. Congress, through its intelligence committees, can be trusted and, if given the chance, can offer helpful criticism and advice to the executive in fashioning a bipartisan foreign policy. In the long run, the failure to do this is a sure path to disaster. As Winston Churchill observed so well:

Many forms of government have been tried, and will be tried in this world of sin and woe. . . . No one pretends that democracy is perfect or all-wise. Indeed, it has been said that democracy is the worst form of government except all those other forms that have been tried from time to time.[34]

For American democracy to work, presidents must cast aside the gowns of the imperial presidency and treat Congress as an equal partner. That is a lesson neither Jimmy Carter nor Ronald Reagan learned. Hopefully, their successors will look, listen, and learn.

NOTES

1. *The Federalist* (Indianapolis: Modern Library, 1937), p. 337.

2. Seymour M. Hersh, "Huge CIA Operation Reported in U.S. Against Anti-War Forces, Other Dissidents in Nixon Years," *New York Times*, December 22, 1974, p. 1.

3. Interview, Daniel Inouye, March 22, 1983.

4. Interview, Birch Bayh, April 26, 1983.

5. Ibid.

6. Ibid.

7. Ibid.

8. Ibid.

9. Confidential interview.

10. Interview, Zbigniew Brzezinski, June 15, 1983.

11. Confidential interview.

12. Interview, Stansfield Turner, January 30, 1983.

13. Confidential interview.

14. Interview, Cyrus Vance, May 17, 1983.

15. Interview, David Newsom, September 30, 1983.

16. Confidential interview.

17. Confidential interview.

18. Senate Select Committee on Ingelligence, *Annual Report*, 95th Cong., 1st sess., May 18, 1977, p. 17.

19. Confidential interview.

20. Senate Select Committee on Intelligence, *Annual Report*, May 18, 1977, pp. 19-20.

21. Ibid.

22. Confidential interview; Senate Select Committee on Intelligence, *Report to the Senate*, 96th Cong., 1st sess., May 14, 1979, p. 48.

23. Confidential interview.

24. Confidential interview.

25. Interview, Hugh Scott, September 15, 1983.

26. Confidential interview.

27. Confidential interview.

28. Interview, Birch Bayh, April 26, 1983.

29. Confidential interview.

30. Interview, Birch Bayh, April 26, 1983.

31. Ibid.

32. Ibid.

33. Senate Select Committee on Intelligence, *Report to the Senate*, 97th Cong., 1st sess., September 23, 1981, pp. 3, 4, 31, 34.

34. *Winston S. Churchill: His Complete Speeches, 1897-1963* (New York: Chelsea House, 1974), vol. 7, p. 7566.

Discussant: Moorhead Kennedy

I'm very pleased to be with this group to commemorate Jimmy Carter. I've noticed that today, questions are being raised about why, when Iraq seized Kuwait, we were so totally unprepared, as if this could never have happened--despite all the warnings, despite newspaper articles. And of course, the same thing happened to us in Tehran on November 4, 1979. I'd like to raise that question and give you some examples of why, when a crisis is pending, and you seem unprepared, in fact you are.

The shah was admitted to the United States on or about October 22; I remember when the charge called me in to give me the news. There wasn't anybody in the U.S. Embassy who didn't instantly see the very deep trouble we were in, and we wondered how much time all of us had left. At the same time, in Washington, Henry Precht, who was the country director for Iran, the officer immediately responsible for Iranian affairs, was about to get on a plane and come out for one of his regular visits to the embassy. He got a call from the department: "Henry, don't go out there; you'll be killed." I've often wished that the concern expressed for Henry had been a little wider.

Henry Precht told me this when I got back. He came out anyway. He said, "I felt that my place was with all of you." He told me that he found us curiously relaxed, curiously, perhaps, stiff-upper-lipped about the danger that was clearly facing us. And I, as head of the economic section, set up for Henry an opportunity in the ambassador's residence to address the American business community, such as it was, left in Tehran. Henry gave a very good speech in which he said, "Who in their right minds would imagine that Americans in Tehran--or in Iran--were in any danger?" This was within a week of the takeover of the embassy.

On the Wednesday before the takeover--which was on a Sunday, November 4, so this was the end of October--I went to see my friend Benny Osidee, the son-in-law of the prime minister. He had arranged for me to travel in south Persia around Shiraz with a group that, I discovered later, was very much affiliated with the group that took over the embassy. Benny said, "Our students are getting out of hand. They're not collaborating with the government." He was very worried about it. He said, "Tomorrow there's going to be a very major demonstration against the embassy." I went back and duly reported this to the chargé, and it went in a telegram.

I talked to an old Tehran hand--the head of the American Chamber of Commerce, who had an Iranian wife and lived all his life out there. We were talking about the seizure of hotels by students, and the government, which was really crumbling, unable to do anything about it. And I remember saying, "If they're taking over hotels now, and the government can do nothing about it, what will they take over next?" Now, if the British Embassy had been in trouble, I think we could have diagnosed that quite accurately, but because it affected us, we were unwilling to draw the necessary conclusions.

On Thursday, the day of the Beid, or religious festival, there was a massive demonstration. Many of us were in our apartments; we'd withdrawn from the compound and were overlooking it. The place was shaking with the decibels of the compound and were overlooking it. The place was shaking with the decibels of the rhythmic cheers. They got to the top of the wall, and then they withdrew. I think some of us thought it was like a wave--the maximum wave of a tide coming up--that was withdrawing. I remember, however, a Marine saying to me, when I went back on the compound, "Man, we're gonna have an Alamo."

But again, the process of denial came in. We had just had a Hallowe'en ball; I taught my secretary how to waltz. That Friday and Saturday was the Muslim weekend, and the chargé insisted that we all go out and play volleyball or softball-- both of which I hated. There was no burning of documents, there was no getting the embassy ready. The denial process was very strong. The trouble with denial is that the danger gets to you in other ways, and one very good symptom for me, which I refused to accept--this apart from the fact that my elimination system wasn't working, and various other things were happening to me--was that Wednesday night, before the Beid, at a dinner party with some Iranians, all my social fine-tuning was off. But one clear indication should have been that I left my safe open--I think it was Monday night--and the Marines gave me a security violation--a pink slip. And on Tuesday night (I think), I left my safe open again. The security officer looked very doleful, and I thought I was in for a reprimand, which is a very serious thing to have in your file. And I remember, when the embassy was under siege, we looked out the great big windows in the ambassador's office. There was the security officer, Al Goliszinsky, who had gone out to negotiate, his hands tied behind his back, being paraded around for us to see. I said to myself, "Well, at least no more pink slips."

Normally I never would have left my safe open; I had a very good security record. So this shows the upset that was taking place, the rigorous denial that we were in any danger, until finally, as has been recorded, the siege happened. We retreated upstairs, behind a steel door. The Iranian militant students lit newspapers, smoke came under the door, and we recognized that had the siege continued, they might have been maddened to the point where none of us would have survived, so we surrendered. Having done that, I remember someone saying, "They're lining us up"; we lined up. I was blindfolded for the first time, my hands were tied behind my back for the first time, and again for the first time, a student said, "Step down, step right," as he guided me down the stairs. My principal concern was, I've got a luncheon today with an important banker. Will I be released in time for the lunch, or how can I get word to him?

So the denial was very strong, and I think strengthening that was a feeling of outrage, a feeling that something so outrageous could never happen. We just didn't want to believe that it ever could. I think that applies to Kuwait as well as to Tehran.

Finally, I'd like to say one word about Jimmy Carter. I had the honor, about a year and a half ago, to introduce him at a breakfast. I said, "Ladies and gentlemen, I have the honor to introduce the president of the United States, who brought his hostages home."

Discussant: Barry M. Rosen

I'd like to be a bit more global than Mike about the Iran crisis, and perhaps say a little less concerning the crisis itself, concentrating on what occurred before. But first, I'd like to thank President Carter and his administration for the valiant efforts that they pursued over that long and tortuous period, and to thank some of the individuals who are sitting here right now--Hal Saunders and Hamilton Jordan--for the attempts, the very difficult and tortuous efforts that they had to go through. It's to the credit of these individuals, and to the sensitivity of President Carter and the real human being that he is, that Mike and I are standing here today.

The first time I met President Carter was in Wiesbaden, several days after we were released--or a day after. He met us in that horrendous room upstairs in the hospital. We were all wearing medical robes, and he came in with Vice President Mondale and several other people. Jimmy Carter--I suspect by many of us--is considered a very stolid individual with less than an affable personality, but he was warm, gracious, sensitive, apologetic--unnecessarily so, in many ways--and a fine and decent human being. Someone mentioned yesterday in the conference on SALT II that it would be interesting if Jimmy Carter had been president while Mikhail Gorbachev was in power in the Soviet Union. I am convinced it would be more than very interesting if he were president today.

Second, I'd like to say that Jimmy Carter might have been portrayed as weak and vacillating, but he was hardly so when it came to the Iran crisis. He was a hard-liner in the administration, if history could read that correctly. In many ways, the advice he was given moderated his more hard-line attitude. I'd like to quote Hamilton Jordan's book--and this relates to Ms. Reilly's paper, to the president's true personality, not to his public personality. Several days after we were taken hostage, Iranian students-- pro-Khomeini students--were marching around the White House, and for very important reasons, the president was agitated, and so was Jordan--they were concerned about our survival and what this might mean. Hamilton came to the president--ran in and disturbed him--and asked him, "What are we going to do about these Iranians?" The president said, "I may have to sit here and bite my lip and show restraint and look impotent, but I'm not going to have those bastards humiliating our country in front of the White House. And let me tell you something else, Ham. If I weren't president, I'd be out there in the streets myself, and I would probably take a swing at any Khomeini demonstrator I could get my hands on."

Let me move along to something a bit more global about the Iran crisis--not specifically the Iran crisis, but what I think more or less needs to be understood about the U.S.-Iran relationship, and that really doesn't deal only with Jimmy Carter and his administration. Jimmy Carter and his administration are only the last and bitter end of a failed U.S. policy vis-à-vis Iran. As an Iranian poet--a very famous Iranian poet, and believe me, Iranians are very poetic, even though they may not seem that way these days--a thirteenth century poet by the name of Sa'di said, "A wolf's offspring will always be a wolf." Sa'di was in some ways referring to the shah of Iran. The United

States fell in within the parameters of the shah's domestic policies, from at least 1941 to the end of his reign. After Iran fell apart and the revolution occurred, Americans were wringing their hands and saying, "How did Carter lose Iran?" It wasn't Jimmy Carter who lost Iran; I believe it was the shah of Iran who lost Iran. Yes, we were involved--very, very closely involved--in that relationship, and for thirty-seven years we were sucked into a policy that was based on the shah's domestic considerations--his own legitimacy. All too often, we think of great powers pushing around, or controlling, patrons or client states. That's usually not the case. The Iranian situation should not be considered an American loss, per se; it was also an Iranian loss, in terms of the shah and his own policy.

Let's look at several issues. Let's look at the shah and how American policy paralleled his. One, the shah's obsession with military prowess, the need to use military might and arms for his own political legitimacy; two, the use of economic modernization aimed primarily at internal and external political gains; and three, superficial political liberalization used as a tactical device, to avoid sharing real power with any opposition. To the extent that American policy in Iran reinforced the main thrust of the shah's policies, it contributed to the fall of the shah and the collapse of any U.S. influence in Iran.

First, the shah's obsession with military power paralleled America's overemphasis on strategic considerations during every administration from 1941 until 1979. The so-called exceptions were President Kennedy and President Carter. These were exaggerations; President Carter specifically talked about political liberalization and human rights in Iran, but unfortunately that policy was unconvincing, and that had a lot to do with the problems of the Carter administration in dealing with issues like Camp David and SALT II, and the notion that the shah was more or less taking care of Iran and the Gulf for the United States.

Unfortunately, President Carter's good intentions in terms of human rights policy in Iran quickly turned. In May 1977, Secretary of State Vance had visited the shah and, after that, the United States seemed to keep the pipeline going with AWACs and other armaments. Throughout 1978, the arms transfers were still going on. If President Carter were able to look at and analyze his policies in Iran today, I believe he would feel very strongly that those were very mistaken.

Let's move on to the last point. While the shah's political liberalization was primarily a tactical device, the record shows that at no time did the American interest in democratization of the political process in Iran override strategic considerations. Again, unfortunately, during the Carter administration a great deal of time was spent on the strategic considerations of the Soviet Union; very little was spent on the political opposition in Iran. There was much distrust of the Iran desk, the ambassador in Iran; there was tremendous dissension between the National Security Council and the State Department, with the National Security Council winning in terms of supporting the shah to the bitter end. That spelled a policy that had absolutely no way to go but backing the United States against the wall, and with that, the Iranians--the opposition, both liberal and very right wing, particularly--saw us as the cause of all of their problems. Khomeini said, "The United States is the cause of all our problems."

I believe, as one scholar said, that our intentions were very good; essentially we walked into Iran with open arms, but by 1979, we were pushed out. That policy was a failed policy, but it does not really reflect only the administration of Jimmy Carter; it reflects every president from 1941 on.

Discussant: Hamilton Jordan

I've got to leave at 10:30, so I'll try to speak quickly and not repeat maybe points that were already made here by Barry and Moorhead, because I suppose I'm the only ones here who are representing President Carter and the administration. We appreciate your kind comments about at least the results of the hostage crisis.

I'm probably going to forgo responding to the numerous papers that were presented here, but as that is one of our charters--to listen to these papers and respond to them--I will respond briefly to Dr. Smist. Did we mistrust the Congress? Yes. To Ms. Reilly, did our administration at some point in time overlook some basic legal or human right of Iranian students in this country? Possibly; if we did, regrettably. But we were more concerned about the life-and-death rights of our hostages in Tehran than we were the residence or deportation rights of Iranian students in this country, and I don't apologize for that. If you would put yourself back into that time frame, our greatest concern--everything that was happening was being flashed around the world--was that angry Americans would do harm to some Iranian demonstrators; that would be flashed to Tehran, and would be the pretext or the reason for the execution or torture of our hostages. That was the overwhelming concern, and with all due respect to Ms. Reilly, the underlying premise of your paper was that Carter's actions were taken out of some political motivation. I think that's harsh and unfair.

Let me make some general comments about the hostage crisis then and the hostage crisis now. The great historical irony is that ten years later, we have people being held with the active cooperation of a foreign government, people whose rights have been denied them. The two crises are similar in some ways and different in others. The similarities are, in both cases, human lives are involved. In both cases, in a way that's outrageous, in terms of international law, as Dr. Gunter presented, their being held hostage is condoned by the government. It is an international news crisis today, as it was then. There has been international condemnation of the Iraqi government, as there was of the Iranian government then. There is an enormous difference between the two cultures and countries, and we don't understand them and they don't understand us; that was, I think, underlying Barry's comments. That was true then, in terms of Iran; it certainly is true today, in terms of Iraq. It is a story that has a tremendous appeal to the media: East versus West, Christianity versus Islam, cultural differences. It's a story of great passions, great feelings. In both cases, sanctions were applied. In both cases, war is possible. In both instances, we have enormous national interest at stake--we did then in the Persian Gulf; we still do, of course, today. Both crises have enormous political consequences for the sitting president, and of course both crises have enormous policy and political consequences for our nation.

There are also some differences that we should not overlook. If you'll remember, subsequent to the hostage crisis, the Soviets invaded Afghanistan. The present crisis, fortunately, doesn't take place in the context of East-West relations; indeed, we have the Soviets actively helping us, trying to resolve the crisis in Iraq. There are thousands of people involved in the situation today in Iraq; there were fifty-three in Iran. The attitude of the American people--and I have to confess, my own personal attitude--has changed. Some may say that the attitude of the American people toward hostages today is more mature; some might say that it's more callous. But I believe that as a nation, while we place an enormous value on human life, we also balance that against the principle involved in the taking and holding of innocent people who happen to be American nationals. We had no way to reach Ayatollah Khomeini; I was involved for three months with Harold Saunders and Henry Precht; the evidence suggests that probably nothing we did actually reached Khomeini. We had emissaries, we had back channels--nothing worked.

At least today, in the Iraqi crisis, we're dealing with a person who is more Westernized than Khomeini was, and he is able to receive emissaries from our country, from the Soviet Union, so there is some direct communication with the people in charge. I'm not sure that we ever had that in our hostage crisis. The press was manipulated, to some extent, in the Iranian hostage crisis; Saddam Hussein, I think, is very effectively manipulating the global press today--appearing to be moderate by dribbling out, every few days, a few more innocent people, responding to a German visit or a Japanese visit with the release of thirty or forty hostages; and in that way, I think, he is creating an atmosphere that makes it more difficult for the forces allied against him to make a difficult decision to use military force. And finally, the striking difference is that the Iranian hostage crisis was highly personalized. The names of our fifty-three hostages were well-known to the American people; President Carter met with their families; we knew something about every one of them. Today, the numbers of hostages being held is so large that it's a faceless group of people, disproportionately Americans; thousands of people being held. So the hostage crisis today is not as personal as the one was ten years ago.

I'll take two more minutes and then close. I hope to be around to hear that and maybe be around to take some questions. If you back way off and look at what happened, we certainly made many mistakes. I would agree with Barry's analysis that our policy was a continuation of a flawed policy; I would argue that we tried to moderate or slow that policy down, but ultimately were not successful. It was just a question of when there was going to be a revolution. It could have happened in Gerald Ford's term; it could have happened in our term; it could have happened in Ronald Reagan's presidency. But the basic elements of discord and unhappiness were present in the Iranian culture, as I think these two gentlemen will attest. We had made the shah the policeman of the Persian Gulf; we had played to his ego by sending him modern military weapons; he obviously had lost touch with the Iranian people; and it was just a question of when certain things would come together and lead to his downfall. I am sure that there are certain policy judgments and decisions that we could have made that might have delayed that for a couple of years, or there were things that we could have done that might have brought his fall sooner.

But I doubt, by the mid-1970s, that it was just a question of when all of these elements in his culture were going to rise up and force a different form of government. There will be people who argue that if the Ford administration had done X, Y, and Z, and if the Carter administration had done X, Y, and Z, maybe there would have been a way to moderate that transition to a different kind of government. I doubt it. The seeds of unhappiness, of distrust, of alienation, of failed expectations in terms of various programs of the shah that had been implemented with great fanfare--all of the elements were there for a revolution, and it happened while Jimmy Carter was president.

You'll remember that at the outset, it was demanded that we extradite the shah; it was demanded that the United States apologize to the Iranians; it was demanded that we unfreeze Iranian assets that had been frozen. If you take a historical view of what happened, the ultimate result had to be what happened to our hostages, how our country responded to those demands. We never extradited the shah; indeed, it was the humanitarian concern for his health that led us to admit him into this country for medical treatment, which, of course, precipitated the crisis. So we did not extradite him. Second, we never apologized for our actions; indeed, we condemned the Iranians constantly and the international community condemned them. Ultimately, by the time our hostages were released, Iran stood condemned in the community of nations as a nation that had done an outrageous thing. And of course, we froze Iranian assets, billions of dollars; President Bush took an action recently to continue to hold those monies.

Ultimately, we paid an enormous political price. I disagree with President Carter; I do not think, if the rescue mission had been successful, we would have been reelected. I believe there would have been an enormous euphoria at that point in time--that was back in the spring. We still had two problems: We had a divided Democratic party, a president who was trying to take that party--a liberal party--in a moderate direction; and second, we had bad economic circumstances. When we came into office, the price of a barrel of oil on the world market was eight dollars; when we left, it was thirty-two. That drove our economy and created an economic set of problems that I think made President Carter's reelection impossible. I recognize and accept that only in retrospect; at that point in time, I did in fact think we might be elected.

Finally--and kind of poignantly--I've found many ironies in the hostage crisis. It was as if anyone who touched the hostage crisis had some misfortune befall them. Of course, Jimmy Carter was defeated, and he and many other people attribute his defeat to the hostage crisis. My friend Omar Torrijos, who had accepted the shah in Panama when no other country would accept him, was killed in a plane crash. There were people then and now who think Manuel Noriega was responsible for that plane crash. Of course, the shah went from Panama to Egypt, and died--some people think due to the medical care he received. President Sadat, who received the shah in Egypt, was assassinated. Sadegh Ghotbzadeh, whom I met with on two occasions, as Harold and Henry Precht and I were trying to release the hostages--he was Khomeini's alter ego and, to some extent, a major player in the revolution--was executed by that revolution while Khomeini stood silently by. I developed cancer of the exact type that the shah of Iran had. The Ayatollah Khomeini lived seven more years and was in power in Tehran. The most important thing is that our people came out alive.

Discussant: Russell Leigh Moses

This is the way you should treat anybody from academe, I've found: give them about forty-five clicks or so to sum up everything. I'm supposed to offer an academic perspective here; unfortunately, what I find is that my views mirror and correspond more closely to those of the participants in the crisis than to those of some of my colleagues on the academic side. I only want to say a couple of things very, very quickly.

One is that I would agree completely that errors were, in fact, made. We misread the situation in many ways throughout the 444 days; we did not quite understand who was in charge in Iran (it was always Ayatollah Khomeini); and at certain points, I think we did talk to the wrong individuals--individuals who had access, but not the sort of deep and sustained access that we required. Second, I think we misread the Soviet view. Very quickly, I'll just say that I think the Soviets, by and large, wanted the crisis solved; wanted it solved as quickly as possible. And from the work that I've done, I would argue that their intervention in Afghanistan was, at least in part, driven by the fact that they were afraid we would move to free the hostages or do something else first--namely, a military invasion or some form of overt military intervention on a large scale.

Another point that I think is important is that not only did we not understand the Iranian viewpoint, or the various elements that fed into it, but we became so obsessed with freeing the hostages that we lost sight of other trends in the area that I think came back to haunt U.S. policy there in the years that followed.

Finally, I think that in many respects, the criticism of the Carter administration regarding the hostage crisis has, by and large, been much too strong. The fact is, not only did Carter get everyone out, but he didn't sell arms to do it. He did not lose a single hostage in the process, and most important, I think, is the fact that we can be, and we have been, critical of how he acted and how the advisers around him acted, because that's what Carter taught us to do. In large part, his was a time when we were forced to confront ourselves, and to look inward and to reexamine our assumptions about our role in the world at large, and how we cope with a very importantly changing world. I wish I could say the same these days, but given the evolving situation in the Persian Gulf and Iraq, I don't see much evidence for it.

Part III

The Carter Administration and the Third World

Relations with the Third World were of necessity one of the foci toward which American foreign policy was directed. Not only did that portion of the world figure in the continuing struggle between the two superpowers, but it was an area not to be neglected for many other reasons. Because the Cold War between the American alliance system and the Soviet bloc coincided with the vast and tumultuous processes of decolonization of the major Western empires, American concern with the Third World is now difficult to disentangle from that overarching struggle. One needs to be reminded that U.S. interests in major portions of the Third World preceded by a long time the coinage of the name by which that world came to be described.

At the Carter Conference two panels attended to a discussion of those problems. One discussion focused on Asia and Africa, and the other on the Panama Canal treaties.

The Asia-Africa panel heard two papers on the Carter human rights effort in India and in Cambodia. They illustrate in lively terms the difficult choices emerging from the commitment to promote such a policy. The paper on Africa departs somewhat from that pattern and considers the opportunities and difficulties encountered in attempting to apply foreign policy management to regional groups of emerging countries on that continent.

The commentators included one former assistant secretary of state and career diplomat, one scholar of Asian affairs, a former staff member of the U.S. Embassy in Beijing, and a former U.N. expert in African matters.

Of very great interest was the panel on the negotiations of the Panama Canal treaties, which were brought to successful conclusion during the Carter years. The single paper discusses in detail the president's struggle in the domestic arena over the formulation and ratification of the agreements.

On this panel the commentators were also on the most intimate terms with the content and the processes of the events delineated. They consisted of one former diplomat assigned to the area, one journalist experienced in that area, and one former diplomat responsible for the treaties' formulation and the negotiations, as well as involved in the battle over ratification.

AFRICA AND ASIA

13

Principled Pragmatism:
Carter, Human Rights, and Indo-American Relations

SRINIVAS M. CHARY

In sharp contrast to the realpolitik of the Kissinger years, President Carter's chief characteristic was his idealism. Unlike his predecessors Nixon and Ford, he did not regard communism as the chief enemy. He said repeatedly that America had become too fearful of the communists while giving little attention to the great danger of the arms race and too much support to repressive right-wing dictatorships around the world. America had forgotten its historical role as protector of democracy and individual liberty, human rights had been neglected for realpolitik, and Third World countries such as India had been ignored in the pursuit of an East-West condominium.[1] Of the various transformations wrought during the Carter years, none was more remarkable than the revolution in American attitudes toward human rights and the Third World, especially in India.

During his presidential campaign, Carter attacked the style and substance of Nixon-Ford-Kissinger policies, stating that America's image had been tarnished by the use of Machiavellian tactics such as secret diplomacy, back channels, "Lone Ranger" diplomacy, excessive concern with power politics, and an accompanying neglect of principles and morality.[2] The Kissinger legacy included a grand design to build a new structure of peace based on an enduring balance of power. This would avert nuclear disaster and pave the way for the solution of global problems through a strategy of interdependence. Détente with the Soviets would be achieved through a mixture of power, persuasion, threat and the creation of a network of vested mutual interests. This diplomacy, however, would require cunning, secrecy and maneuvering.[3]

Carter, on the other hand, decided to make a concern for human rights the cornerstone of his foreign policy. He believed that the United States had been damaged by Watergate, Vietnam, and the CIA revelations, and that the best thing the country could do to change its image as a nation with no moral values or with moral values that it had forgotten would be to deal fairly with the world's downtrodden, persecuted, and abused under the aegis of freedom, democracy, and human rights. Carter said, "It is a new world, but America should not fear it. It is a new world and we should help shape it. It is a new world that calls for a new American foreign policy."[4]

Carter hoped to build a new international system that contained a new worldwide mosaic of global, regional, and bilateral relations.[5]   Interdependence was the new international reality, and neither the United States nor the Soviet Union could control the world's destiny. Mutual cooperation was not just a convenience but a necessity.[6] The old order of the post-World War II era was thought to be over. The focus on East-West issues and the U.S.-Soviet rivalry was considered anachronistic. Human rights and democracy, normalization and improvement of relations with countries such as India, the resolution of conflict in Africa and the Middle East, arms control, the health of the global economy, and Third World development were considered to be significant issues. Clearly the Carter administration thought it could improve the new world[7] by emphasizing the positive aspects of America with a new, different, and better foreign policy. As President Carter put it:

Our national security was defined almost exclusively in terms of military competition with the Soviet Union. This competition is still critical because it does involve issues which could lead to war. But however important this relationship of military balance, it cannot be our sole preoccupation to the exclusion of other world issues which concern us both.[8]

Carter felt that Third World countries such as India had not been given sufficient recognition in America's excessive preoccupation with the superpower struggle and with regional and domestic rivalries such as the Bangladesh crisis of 1971 and the Chilean issue in Latin America. Like President Kennedy, Carter regarded India as a key area in South Asia. The spectacle of a great nation weighed down by legacies of centuries making a brave attempt to achieve economic modernization within a democratic polity captured his imagination. "We can never be indifferent to the fate of freedom elsewhere," Carter declared in his inaugural address. "Our commitment to human rights must be absolute." The concept that every human being has certain inalienable rights is essentially Jeffersonian and American, but it had received worldwide backing in the United Nations Charter of 1945 and in the Helsinki accords of 1975. In Washington, the president's desire to give U.S. relations with India a new cast received ardent support from key foreign policy advisers, such as Zbigniew Brzezinski[9] of the National Security Council, and Secretary of State Cyrus Vance.[10] For an understanding of Carter's contribution, one must examine the assumptions of the often uneasy American diplomatic experience during the early years.[11]

Basic political differences between the United States and India are nothing new. Divisions over foreign policy fundamentals go back to the earliest days of the Cold War. India's leaders engaged in consolidating a new state, strove to protect India's autonomy in foreign relations by establishing an "area of peace" removed from great-power conflicts. As early as 1946, Jawaharlal Nehru, who became independent India's first prime minister, announced that India would keep itself "free from the great power groups,"[12] thus prefiguring nonalignment. Indian leaders questioned the utility of Western-led military alliances to contain communism in the new states of Asia where nationalism reigned supreme. For India, the application of military power outside Europe to counter the expansion of communism was apt to aggravate the very resentments on which communism fed. Indians argued that rapid economic development was the best antidote to communism.[13]

But the American perception of the situation was sharply different. In its opposition to China's communist regime, the United States insisted that the communist success in Asia represented not self-determination but conquest, and posed a threat to neighboring countries. Even American policymakers sympathetic to democratic India considered Nehru's notions naive. Furthermore, Nehru's efforts to establish friendly relations with China in the middle of the Korean War created bitter resentment in Washington. Before long, suspicions in both capitals began to replace efforts at understanding. In Washington there was widespread acceptance of Secretary of State John Foster Dulles's belief that nonalignment was neutrality between right and wrong, and a sign of anti-Americanism.[14] On the Indian side, V. K. Krishna Menon, Nehru's key foreign policy adviser and India's representative to the United Nations, began to denounce containment as a U.S. strategem for replacing Great Britain as the dominant power in Asia.[15]

The Eisenhower administration's decision to anchor its South Asian alliance system on a mutual defense agreement with Pakistan became the most important irritant in Indo-American relations. After the traumatic partition of the subcontinent, Pakistan sought a military alliance with the United States not only for protection but also to permit it to challenge India in disputed Kashmir. Although President Eisenhower assured Nehru that the military equipment Pakistan received would never be used against India, not all senior American policymakers were as sympathetic to India's concerns. Vice President Richard Nixon reportedly favored the treaty with Pakistan as a means of weakening Nehru's "neutralist influence" on the nonaligned bloc. After the 1954 defense agreement between the United States and Pakistan, Nehru concluded that the United States intended to equalize the two states' military power.

The Kennedy years marked the high point in Indo-American relations. Kennedy objected to the Dulles doctrine as both morally self-righteous and politically self-defeating. Prompt U.S. military assistance to India when the Chinese invaded in 1961 won India's immediate affection and gratitude.[16]

The U.S. tilt toward Pakistan during the Bangladesh crisis of 1971 suggested that Nixon never changed his views about the subcontinent.[17] The United States became involved in a crisis that it had not anticipated in a part of the world where it was aligned with an authoritarian regime that was using brutal measures against its own people and against the dominant power in the subcontinent, while its major international adversary, Soviet Russia, was aligned with the stronger and more democratic power. It was a no-win situation for the United States at best, and the policies of the Nixon administration that followed only served to make the position even more difficult--indeed, virtually untenable and indefensible.

The newly elected president was committed to a more forthcoming policy toward the Third World and an approach that downplayed the importance of the Soviet Union. Carter and his national security adviser, Zbigniew Brzezinski, elaborated a policy of cultivating influential countries of the region as a means of devolving some of the excessive U.S. responsibilities that had been assumed during the postwar decades. India held a general election that replaced Indira Gandhi after the emergency and brought Morarji Desai to power. Desai was known to be well disposed toward the United States and committed to a greater balance in Indian foreign policy. The new leaders in the altered political situation were seen as an immense change for the better over their predecessors in terms of improving Indo-American relations. Moreover, Carter was the first president who had any sort of personal tie to India. His mother had served in the Peace Corps in a suburb of Bombay in the late 1960s.[18]

Even more significant than the national political equation was the state of international politics. The Carter and Desai teams came in during the period of détente. Angola was hardly a cloud on the Afro-Asian scene, and the bipolar relationship (between the United States and the Soviet Union) appeared to be conducive to cooperation between the United States and India, quite unlikely to impose demands on either side that would result in straining the relationship.

The Carter period had an auspicious beginning even before Indira Gandhi's exit from office. The president of India, Fakhriddin Ali Ahmed, died only a few days after Carter's inauguration, and Carter seized the opportunity make a gesture of symbolic importance. He sent his mother, Lillian Carter, as his personal representative at the funeral. Mrs. Carter drew vast press coverage and captured the imagination of a large number of Indians who genuinely respected her for her Peace Corps service in suburban Bombay. The symbolism of her visit turned out to be warm and powerful.[19] Meanwhile, the Janata coalition swept Mrs. Gandhi out of power on an agenda of democratic principles that closely paralleled the human rights concerns that played such a significant role in the Carter administration's foreign policy. The termination of the emergency and the restoration of democratic freedoms in India came as a relief to most Americans. While Americans were rather intrigued by Desai's enigmatic personality, they respected him for his experience, ability, and integrity. Furthermore, his views on economic and foreign policies seemed to be much more favorable to the United States than those of his predecessor. In particular, Desai favored economic policies that gave more of a role to the private sectors and more opportunities for foreign investments and operations than those followed by Indira Gandhi's more socialist regime. His emphasis on a more genuinely nonaligned foreign policy was widely interpreted in the United States as more favorable to American interests and less pro-Russian than Mrs. Gandhi's foreign policy had been. The stage was set for a vast step forward in Indo-American relations.

Both sides showed their increased interest by ambassadorial appointments designed to effect closer ties. Nani Palkhivala was a prominent champion of Indian democracy. His appointment as Indian ambassador to the United States elicited a cordial response in America. Robert Goheen was a distinguished American scholar with close personal ties to India. His appointment as U.S. ambassador to India reminded everyone of the appointment of John Kenneth Galbraith during the Kennedy years.

The priority given to the relationship on both sides appeared healthily congruent with the foreign policy priorities of Brzezinski[20] and the human rights concerns of Carter.[21] Out of ten policy goals of the Carter administration, seven were devoted to North-South and world order issues. This reflected the true priorites of the administration, or more specifically of the president and his key policy advisors. The priorities seemed to bode well for India, which played an important role in nonaligned and North-South matters, and was sympathetic to American priorities in world order issues. There were frequent calls for "initiatives' to be taken toward India. The aid program was reinstituted and other initiatives were launched, such as trade matters and scientific and technical cooperation. Emphasis was also placed on personal diplomacy --the announcement of a Carter visit to India and the launching of a voluminous correspondence between Carter and Desai. They exchanged views in July 1977 on a variety of matters of special concern to their two countries, including "such sweeping subjects as the gap between the rich and poor countries, nuclear safeguards and peace through disarmament."[22]

The Carter visit to India went off well and made a considerable impression on public opinion there, especially on a small village that he Carter visited and that was renamed Carterpuri in his honor. Personal understanding with Desai was good. Carter's major speech in New Delhi to the Indian parliament was a strong affirmation of his principles as they related to South Asia.[23] He emphasized the restoration of democracy and praised India's program of development, especially to meet basic human needs and stimulate the growth of the rural sector. President Carter offered assistance in exploring development of the Ganges and Brahmaputra valleys for the benefit of India, Bangladesh, and Nepal. In all these, human rights was the key.[24]

The highlight of the visit was the statement released jointly by Carter and Desai, known as the Delhi Declaration. The two leaders decided to make this a ringing declaration of broad principles and concern for human rights, development, and democracy. Seen from the perspective of the United States, this indicated how the Carter administration viewed India--as a repository of shared values and as a natural ally for an America that sincerely hoped to base its policy on moral values and to see those values extend to the rest of the world. India was, in a sense, once again the model it had been in the eyes of the Kennedy administration; this time, however, it was not simply an alternative to China. To a great extent the Carter administration appeared to seek identification with India as a way of strengthening and even legitimizing Carter's approach to American foreign policy. India was symbolically important for the Carter administration, preeminent among other "regional influentials" of the Third World.

The much-discussed event of the Carter visit to Delhi was not the Delhi Declaration but the "microphone" incident in which Carter was heard to whisper some tough things to Secretary of State Cyrus Vance.[25] The incident did not affect the visit much, but it served to focus attention on an issue where American and Indian interests were directly and sharply in conflict--nuclear nonproliferation, particularly in the continued supply of nuclear fuel to the Tarapur power station near Bombay. New Delhi viewed this issue as a matter of principle as well as of substance, and Washington was not agreeable to compromise because it was a key element of global nonproliferation.[26] For the remainder of the Carter presidency and beyond, Tarapur was an all-consuming factor in Indo-U.S. relations. Whatever either side did in bilateral matters--and the United States made sincere efforts to favor Indian interests-- was overshadowed in the same way media coverage of the Carter visit came to be dominated by the nuclear issue.

The instructive aspect of the Tarapur problem is its relationship to the American global priorities. The American competition with the Soviet Union and China has long been the major problem of American bilateral policies in South Asia, and that competition has consistently won out over regional and bilateral interests.[27] For all of India's importance, it was overshadowed by the issue of nuclear nonproliferation.

Even though Carter had moved the global issue of U.S.-Soviet relations from center stage, there were many in his administration who considered it a matter of central importance. Their expectations had been raised by Prime Minister Desai's pledge to move away from India's excessively close ties with the Soviet Union, and some hoped for a realignment of India alongside the United States based on shared concerns with democracy and human rights. From the Indian perspective the Soviet Union is critical to India's security. While Desai improved the balance of his nonalignment, he ensured that there would be no break with Moscow.

By late 1979, however, the world--including India and the United States--had changed. The Soviet-U.S. relationship was once against strained, primarily as a result of Soviet and Cuban actions in Ethiopia, and the United States assumed a much more direct interest in Southwest Asia after the fall of the shah. In India, the Desai government had fallen, and soon Indian politicians lost interest in foreign policy. India rapidly receded from the consciousness of the Carter administration except in connection with the disasters to come--the Tehran hostage crisis and the Soviet invasion of Afghanistan in December 1979.

Jimmy Carter said that the Soviet invasion of Afghanistan taught him more about the Soviet Union than he had ever learned before. Pakistan, which shared the U.S. perspective of the seriousness of the Soviet occupation of Afghanistan, became a frontline state. The Carter administration reversed its policy toward the Soviet Union, but it did not despair of a constructive Indian role in the new South Asian situation. Clark Clifford was dispatched as a special presidential envoy in January 1980 to explain the American position to Indira Gandhi, who was returned to power in India's seventh general election, and to evoke productive responses. Ultimately, New Delhi did take some steps to distance itself from the Soviet aggression, but by then much greater forces had taken charge of the Indo-U.S. relationship. The Cold War polarization had again overshadowed any bilateral or even regional interests the United States had in South Asia. The rapid coincidence of American interests not only with Pakistan but also with China provoked understandable Indian concern. As American concern skyrocketed over the Southwest Asian situation, India's potential relevance to U.S. interests receded for the time being.

CONCLUSION

The Carter administration evolved from an initial philosophy of foreign policy that embraced liberal idealism to one of political realism in its final years in office. Brzezinski has suggested that Carter's foreign policy embraced power and principle, and that it tried to blend idealism and realism into what Anthony Lake called "principled pragmatism."[28]

The Carter administration was hardly a historical aberration or a failure across the board, as the conventional wisdom tried to characterize it.[29] It accomplished some notable achievments in foreign policy during its four years, such as improving the Indo-American relationship, the Camp David accords in the Middle East, and the Panama Canal treaties in Latin America. "On human rights, the Carter Administration raised the banner of American concern and showed the world that America was not solely occupied with superpower relations."[30] Carter's efforts toward normalization of relations with China continued the process begun under Nixon.   Certainly the establishment of formal diplomatic relations and the extraordinary visit of Vice Chairman Deng Xiao-ping did much to advance U.S. relations with the world's most populous nation.

The Carter Doctrine has not as yet taken on the historic importance of the Truman Doctrine.   However, with the continuing high stakes involved in the Persian Gulf politics and the volatility of the Middle East generally, the day may come when President Carter's pronouncement will take on more than symbolic importance.[31]

Soviet actions (for example, the invasion of Afghanistan) contributed to a great extent to Carter's political failure in the United States.   Suspicion, rigidity, and insensitivity were characteristics of the Brezhnev foreign policy.   Brezhnev, unlike Mikhail Gorbachev, put the worst possible interpretation on every American gesture and thereby undercut those in the Carter administration who wanted accommodation while strengthening those who were eager for confrontation.   Soviet policy could scarcely have been better designed to provide arguments for those who wanted to discredit Carter's initial emphasis on human rights and global issues.   Bad luck and the uncooperative behavior of the Soviet Union are not the full explanation for Carter's failure, however.   The differences between his two principal advisers, Brzezinski and Vance, and Carter's strong inclination to use alarmist and exaggerated rhetoric (for example, his description of the Soviet invasion of Afghanistan as the greatest threat to world peace since World War II) contributed to the failure.   Finally and tragically, Carter failed because he asked the American people to think as citizens of the world with an obligation toward future generations.   He offered a morally responsible and farsighted vision.   "But the clamor of political critics, the behavior of the Soviet Union, the Iran hostage issue, the discordant views of his advisers and the impossibility of seeing clearly what needed to be done--all combined to make Carter's vision appear naive."[32]

In the final analysis, the successes and failures of Jimmy Carter's foreign policies depended upon Jimmy Carter.   John Stoessinger, in his study subtitled *Movers of Modern American Foreign Policy,* perceptively summarizes the strengths and weakness of Carter's approach to foreign affairs:

Jimmy Carter . . . falls somewhere between the crusader and the pragmatist. His religious conviction, while profound, did not have the rigidity of Wilson's or Dulles'. His tenacity and perseverance did not lock him into an obsession. Unlike the crusader's zeal, his faith did not become a dogma. It always remained a quest. . . . On the other hand, his global human rights campaign was often ineffectual and even boomeranged with the realities of power. . . . The President's faith lacked a practical dimension and thus his foreign policy, especially in the human rights arena, had some aspects of the amateur. But then perhaps even the most sophisticated statesman would be bound to fail if he based his foreign policy on the cornerstone of human rights. Such an attempt might always come to grief on the rocks of national interest and power. Perhaps it cannot be done.[33]

Jimmy Carter tried, and if he did not always succeed, he did not always fail. Winston Churchill once said, "The further back you look, the farther forward you can see."

The further back we look at the Carter achievements in the area of foreign policy, and especialy Indo-American relations, the better they may look in the future.

Carter's doctrine of human rights offered a common cause that carried its appeal far beyond the Iron Curtain. Like no one since Roosevelt, he was identifying the United States with popular democracy and with the hopes and aspirations of different people. Carter's India policy represented a considerable break from the Washington view of the 1950s and foreshadowed a fundamental reconstruction of U.S. policy toward South Asia. Indo-American relations during the Carter years emphasized and developed areas of cooperation rather than of conflict.[34] Carter's relationship with India conveys the sense of decency and purpose that represented the main thrust of the Carter presidency in the conduct of U.S. foreign policy.

In seeking to build the world community on the idea not of uniformity but of diversity, Carter expressed his own sense of the dynamic of modern history.

NOTES

I would like to thank Richard Holbroke, Guo-Chung Huan, Murray Silberman, Donald Mrozek, Kenneth Hagan, Gardel Fuertado, Mrs. Nagaratna Mudambai, and others for their helpful comments and suggestions.

1. Jimmy Carter, "A Foreign Policy Based on America's Essential Character," speech at Notre Dame University, South Bend, Indiana, May 22, 1977, *Department of State Bulletin (DSB)*, June 13, 1977. See *Public Papers of the Presidents: Jimmy Carter, 1977* (Washington, D. C.); Jimmy Carter, *Keeping Faith* (New York: Bantam Books, 1982).

2. *DSB*, June 13, 1977. See Raymond A. Moore, "The Carter Presidency and Foreign Policy," in M. Glenn Abernathy, Dilys M. Hill, and Phil Williams, *The Carter Years: The President and Policymaking* (New York: St. Martin's Press, 1984), p. 55.

3. Gerald Ford, *A Time to Heal* (New York: Harper and Row, 1979); Seymour Hersh, *The Price of Power: Kissinger in the Nixon White House* (New York: Summit Books, 1983); Henry A. Kissinger, *White House Years* (Boston: Little, Brown, 1979), and *Years of Upheaval* (Boston: Little, Brown, 1982); Richard M. Nixon, *RN: The Memoirs of Richard Nixon* (New York: Grosset and Dunlap, 1978); Moore, "The Carter Presidency and Foreign Policy." See also Phil Williams, "Carter's Defense Policy," in M. Glenn Abernathy, et al., *The Carter Years* (New York: St. Martin's Press, 1984), p. 86.

4. *DSB*, June 13, 1977, p. 622.

5. Ibid.

6. *DSB*, August 15, 1977, pp. 193-197.

7. Jerel Rosati, "The Carter Administration Image of an International System: The Development and Application of a Belief System Framework" (Ph.D. diss., American University, 1983), ch. VI. See also Jerel Rosati, "The Impact of Belief on Behavior: The Foreign Policy of the Carter Administration," in Donald A. Sylvan and Steve Chan, eds., *Foreign Policy Decision Making: Perception, Cognition, and Artificial Intelligence* (New York: Praeger, 1984).

8. *DSB*, August 15, 1977.

9. Zbigniew Brzezinski, *Power and Principle: Memoirs of the National Security Advisor, 1977-1981* (New York: Farrar, Straus and Giroux, 1983), p. 81.

10. Cyrus Vance, *Hard Choices: Critical Years in America's Foreign Policy* (New York: Simon and Schuster, 1983), p. 27.

11. Writing on U.S.-Indian relations during the Cold War has been limited. There are a few published works, such as Norman D. Palmer, *South Asia and United States Policy* (Boston: Houghton Mifflin, 1966); and William J. Barnds, *India, Pakistan and the Great Powers* (New York: Praeger, 1972). These argue that the balance-of- power premise shaped the diplomacy of the United States toward South Asia. Gary R. Hess, *America Encounters India, 1941-1947* (Baltimore: Johns Hopkins University Press, 1971), is a well-balanced, scholarly work dealing with President Roosevelt's policy toward India. See also Srinivas Chary Mudambai, *United States Foreign Policy Toward India, 1947-1954* (New Delhi: Manohar Publishers, 1980). Based mostly on unpublished manuscript material at the Truman Library, Eisenhower Library, and National Archives, this work provides an interpretive analysis of postwar Asia and the special dilemmas of American policy.

12. Many of Nehru's views are in *India's Foreign Policy: Selected Speeches, September 1946-April 1961* (Delhi: Government of India, Publications Division, 1961).

13. *Jawaharlal Nehru Speeches, 1949-1953* (New Delhi: Government of Indian Information and Publications Division, 1954), p. 139. See also *Constituent Assembly of India Legislative Debates*, pt. 2, March 8, 1949, p. 1968.

14. See Dulles's testimony in *The President's Proposal on the Middle East*, U.S. Senate Committee on Foreign Relations and Armed Services, 85th Cong., 1st sess. (Washington, D.C.: U.S. Government Printing Office, 1957). See also Srinivas M. Chary, "Sources for the Study of Mutual Security Policy Toward South Asia," *Military Affairs*, 29, no. 4 (December 1975):208-210.

15. Michael Breecher, *India and World Politics: Krishna Menon's View of the World* (London: Oxford University Press, 1968). For a comparative view of the perspectives of United States and India, see Srinivas M. Chary, "An Analysis of Indo-American Relations--Chester Bowles' Views," *Indian Journal of American Studies*, 10 (January 1980):3-9.

16. Srinivas M. Chary, "Kennedy and Nonalignment: An Analysis of Indo-American Relations," in Paul Harper and Joanne M. Krieg, *John F. Kennedy: The Promise Revisited* (Westport, Conn: Greenwood Press, 1988), pp. 119-131.

17. Nixon, *RN: The Memoirs of Richard Nixon*; Kissinger, *White House Years*. See also Srinivas M. Chary, "Indian Ocean as a Zone of Peace: The Policy Options of the 1980s," in *Proceedings of the Sixth International Symposium on Asian Studies, 1980*, vol. 14, *South and Southwest Asia* (Hong Kong: Asian Research Service, 1980), pp. 1035-1044.

18. Miss Lillian worked for two years (1966-1968) at Vikhroli, a suburb of Bombay, as a nurse and a medical counselor. *Times of India*, February 16, 1977.

19. Ibid.

20. Brzezinski, *Power and Principle*. See also his *Ideology and Power in Soviet Politics* (New York: Praeger, 1967); and Thomas Thornton, "American Interest in India Under Carter and Reagan," *SAIS Review*, 5, no. 1 (Winter-Spring 1985):179-190.

21. Carter, *Keeping Faith*. See also Department of State, *American Foreign Policies: Basic Documents, 1977-1980* (Washington, D.C.: U.S. Government Printing Office, 1983), and Thornton, "American Interest in India."

22. M. V. Kamath, "Indo-U.S. Accord," *Times of India*, July 6, 1977.

23. *DSB* 78 (February 1978):7-11.

24. Ibid. See also *DSB*, June 13, 1977, p. 622.

25. Carter said to Vance, "I told him [Desai] I would authorize transfer of fuel now . . . it didn't seem to make an impression on him." He then added, "When I get back, I think we ought to write him another letter, just cold and very blunt." See *Wall Street Journal*, January 3, 1978.

26. See Robert Goheen, "Problems of Proliferation: U.S. Policy and the Third World," *World Politics*, 31 (January 1983). See also Thornton, "American Interest in India."

27. See Thornton, "American Interest in India."

28. Brzezinski, *Power and Principle*; see Moore, "The Carter Presidency and Foreign Policy."

29. Donald Spencer, *The Carter Implosion* (New York: Praeger, 1988); Clark R. Mollenhoff, *The President Who Failed* (New York: Macmillan, 1980); M. Glenn Abernathy, Dilys M. Hill, and Phil Williams, *The Carter Years: The President and Policymaking* (New York: St. Martin's Press, 1984).

30. Moore, "The Carter Presidency and Foreign Policy."

31. Ibid.

32. Gaddis Smith, *Morality, Reason and Power* (New York: Hill and Wang, 1985).

33. John Stoessinger, *Crusaders and Pragmatists: Movers of Modern American Foreign Policy* (New York: W. W. Norton, 1979), p. 262.

34. Norman D. Palmer, *The United States and India: The Dimensions of Influence* (New York: Praeger, 1984), p. 82.

14

Managing Foreign Policy:
Carter and the Regionalist Experiment toward Africa,
January 1977-May 1978

R. BENNESON DeJANES

This investigation of Carter foreign policy utilizes Africa as a case study. It explores how and why certain aspects of U.S. policy toward Africa were developed and administered from January 1977 to May 1978, a period labeled Carter 1. Carter 1 was a period that reflected early courageous attempts by the new president to redirect Africa policy along a "regionalist" rather than a "globalist" perspective. The core of our concern is how foreign policy decisions were made and why the decision-making machinery produced less than rational policy.

Over the past several decades attempts to structure theories of decision making in international politics have resulted in a wide variety of suggested models. While one instinctively concludes that situational dynamics generate almost severely unique models for each circumstance, in this paper I attempt to engage a specific arena with a U.S. president over a closed time frame.

I hypothesize that a modification of what has been called the Organizational Process model in conjunction with the Bureaucratic Politics model takes precedence over the theory of the Rational Actor (Allison, 1969). I argue that intense competition and conflicting conceptions of U.S. national interest between bureaucracies in the White House, the National Security Council, and the State Department's African Bureau often led to confused decision making and inadequate policy.

Decision making at the top levels of U.S. international policy is dominated by large, structured organizations only partly coordinated by an elected or appointed elite. This organizational process has been refined by Glenn Snyder and Paul Diesing. They argue that these bureaucracies, whether in Congress, the executive branch, or civil service, often do not pursue logical policies designed to enhance state interests but, on the contrary, seek authority, power, and control to impose their perspectives on competing bodies. Such a Bureaucuractic Politics model "focuses on the internal political imperatives of maintaining and increasing influence and power rather than on the purely intellectual problems of choosing a strategy to deal with an external opportunity or threat" (Snyder and Diesing 1977, p. 355). Rational state action then is subsumed under petty bureaucracy.

Using the Horn of Africa as a case study, I intend to review the personalities, organization, and perspectives that helped to shape Africa policy during the first seventeen months of Carter's tenure.   U.S. policy toward the region may be administratively and geographically separate but, I suggest, is not unique and therefore reflects much of the general atmosphere of the period January 1977 to May 1978.

The term "Africa policy" is used to describe the pluralistic U.S. positions toward the states normally dealt with by the Africa Bureau of the Department of State. Africa policy, as shaped by the Bureaucratic Politics model, includes positions advocated not only by the Department of State but also by other bureaucracies, including the Central Intelligence Agency, the U.S. Mission to the United Nations, both houses of Congress, the National Security Council, and the White House.

At the time former Governor of Georgia Jimmy Carter ran for the presidency in 1976, the necessity for radical departures in American policy toward Africa became critical to a point far greater than our knowledge about it or our ability to cope with it.

The "Portuguese revolution," when Portugal voluntarily but too quickly exited its former colonies of Angola and Mozambique, generated a billowing wind of progressive world opinion.   Dilplomats worldwide, including State Department optimists, were caught up in what was viewed as a major event signaling global change.

Carter himself was not immune to this sense of euphoria. The new Democratic president surged into office on the crest of revolutionary change in Africa when it appeared that the South African dilemma, by means of first Angola and then perhaps of Namibia, would neatly unravel.

On the edge of such phenomenal events, a visionary Carter attempted to ride the wave of the inevitable. Buoyed by his Democratic liberalism and at the head of world events, the new president was caught up in his own ideals, trapped by competing bureaucracies, and unable to capitalize on the times.

Persuaded by Congressman Andrew Young (D.-Georgia) and other close advisers, Carter resolved to establish a new priority and new direction for Africa policy. In sum, this high-profile strategy demanded closer ties with African leaders and a clearer definition of common concerns.

In an effort to foster the perception of mutual interests, for example, Carter became the first American president to go to the continent. There he attempted to clarify and strengthen an approach termed "regionalist" by encouraging "African solutions to African problems." In a speech at Lagos, Nigeria, Carter focused on three commitments that summarized America's policy of regionalism in his first seventeen months.

We share with you [Africans] a commitment to majority rule and individual human rights. . . . We share with you a commitment to economic growth and to human development. We share with you a commitment to an Africa that is at peace, free from racism, free from military interference by outside nations, and free from inevitable conflicts that come when the integrity of national boundaries are [sic] not respected. These three commitments shape our attitude toward your continent. (Legum, 1979, p. 642)

To bolster the new conception, Carter attempted to arrange policy machinery to reflect the new interest in Africa. He became the first chief executive to be attentive to day-to-day policy toward Africa and events on the continent. Andrew Young's appointment as ambassador to the United Nations emerged as the salient symbol of Carter's new direction.

Like ambitious presidents of the past, Carter was not above a desire to burn his presidency into the historical consciousness of the world by providing major agreements in South Africa. Such a settlement would affirm U.S. world leadership as protector of Third World peoples. It could be partial fulfillment of the idealist dream. Like the accords later reached by Anwar Sadat and Menachem Begin at Camp David, South Africa could emerge as a major diplomatic triumph.

Upon arrival at the White House, Jimmy Carter found Africa policy in disarray, with foreign policy-making machinery having a history of organized turmoil rooted in the Kennedy administration. At issue were a series of ongoing arguments between the State Department, other federal bureaucracies, Congress, and the White House. Deeply felt organizational confrontations over power, perceptions, values, and priorities tended to shape the substance of Africa policy. In many cases the substance of policy fell victim.

Instead of transforming or solving these problems, Carter appointments and decisions only seemed to exacerbate them. As a result, international policy machinery as organized by the Carter team ended up as a schizophrenic structure with multiple and competing centers of decision making.

The State Department, at first generally recognized as the purported focus of authority, found itself in competition with a moody and intemperate Congress, a strengthened National Security Council, Andrew Young as an almost independent ambassador to the United Nations, and an ambitious group of White House "amateurs."

In order to grasp a sense of the fundamental tensions toward Africa policy in the Carter administration, we must first consider the major players, their characteristics and assumptions, and their advocates and allies

As early as the late 1960s, a conflict over the means and ends of U.S. foreign policy took shape within the State Department. These perspectives, for lack of a better term, finally surfaced in open confrontation in the Carter administration and created policy tensions at almost every link in the decision-making chain.

This undercurrent of antagonism between "regionalists" and "globalists" was produced by radically different assumptions about American policy in general, and consequently different policy alternatives toward Africa as an area (Bender, Coleman and Sklar 1985, pp. 9-10).

The regionalist point of view was shared by a circle of officials and disgruntled bureaucrats ranging from Foggy Bottom to Democratic liberals on Capitol Hill. According to this perspective, issues in Africa are unique to the region and should be evaluated accordingly.

The regionalist orientation urged special attention to the continent, and had been developed along three major policy thrusts that, its supporters argued, should directly impact American policy: Black nationalism is the dominant historical force; economic development is the major goal to be supported by the United States; and, as far as possible, Cold War competition should be excluded from Africa.

Regionalists thus argued for the United States to press for broader changes in South Africa and for increased funds for purely economic development elsewhere. Equally important, perhaps, Marxism or socialism was seen as less of a threat to U.S. interests. America therefore should attempt to develop policy with substantially less regard for a state's ideological orientation. Of critical importance, moreoover, African issues should not necessarily be judged on the singular fact of a Soviet presence in the region. Regionalist policy, therefore, sought to break free of the stifling and rigid dichotomy inherent in Cold War thinking. The Kissinger conception of linkage, which tied Africa and other "peripheral" regions to the central questions of U.S.-Soviet bipolar relationships, was rejected.

The regionalist perspective dominated policy making in the early months of the Carter presidency, the period we call Carter 1. It found support in State's Bureau of African Affairs, the Bureau of International Organization Affairs, the Mission to the United Nations, and the top-level Policy Planning Staff headed by Anthony Lake. Cyrus Vance, secretary of state, and Andrew Young, ambassador to the United Nations, both sided with the regionalists on African issues. Congressional advocates of the regional argument could be found in the House Foreign Affairs Committee's Subcommittee on African Affairs, chaired by Charles C. Diggs (D.-Michigan), as well as the Congressional Black Caucus.

Also competing for the right to make policy in the new Carter administration were globalists, who recognized the U.S. role as a great power with central security concerns of containing Soviet expansionism. The Soviet Union and NATO demanded primary attention, they argued. Africa, as well as other Third World nations, generally ranked low on the list of important issues confronting a global power with global responsibilities.

Furthermore, globalists argued that Kissinger's notion of "linkage" applied to internal African politics. Not only were U.S. policy goals directed toward the Soviet Union and Europe, but other international issues should, if possible, be linked to such a focus. Cuban troops in Angola, therefore, became tied to questions of a general improvement in U.S.-Soviet relations. Trade and technology transfers, for example, became dependent on the exodus of Cuban troops and the termination of Russian influence in Angola.

Regionalists pointed out that such a position poisoned with longstanding and rigid Cold War hostilities the entire framework of bilateral relationships with potentially friendly African states. Globalism froze progress in U.S. policy toward changing African nations.

A regional focus, globalists said, and a serious interest in specific issues such as apartheid, could well sink the United States into the mire of localized civil conflict. Deeper American involvement in an African domestic imbroglio such as Chad, Angola, or South Africa, for example, would weaken U.S. resolve at some critical future time when the stakes might be much higher.

While they advocated aid to Jonas Savimbi in his challenge of the Marxist Angolan government, globalists shuddered at any possibility of direct U.S. involvement in domestic problems of unstable African states.

Globalist views had directed policy since the Truman Doctrine, and were well entrenched in bureaucratic patterns of power and behavior. In a broader sense, globalism's major supporters included the State Department's Soviet desk, the staff of the National Security Council, and the Central Intelligence Agency. The Department of Defense, from still another point of view, sided with globalists and agreed that Africa was only a part of the "troublesome periphery filled with unpredictable and unreliable states" (Foltz 1980, p. 72).

Another major asset of the globalist perspective was the long years of dominance by Europeanists within the foreign service. This historic bias in the State Department lent increased influence to Europe-oriented officers. Until the mid-1960s, for example, the distribution of personnel reflected the preeminence of the European point of view. Forty percent of foreign service officers abroad in 1962, for example, were stationed in Europe (Harr 1965, p. 22). Arthur Schlesinger, Jr., as adviser to Kennedy on Latin American affairs, had early noted the pro-European orientation of the State Department to the exclusion of other world regions (Schlesinger 1965).

Carter appeared well aware of traditional problems at the Department of State. If he and his close-knit White House team were not hostile to the cluster of buildings in Washington's Foggy Bottom, they were certainly distrustful. Such disagreement between regionalists and globalists, plus confusion and caution at State, only confirmed Carter's suspicions about bureaucracies and underscored his animosity toward petty bureaucrats.

But if Carter's entourage was hostile to State, that department reciprocated with distrust and apprehension. An anti-establishment Southerner president, and one with a record of administrative reorganization, clearly worried well-entrenched and elitist foreign service bureaucrats.

State envisioned Carter's electoral success as less of a foreign policy mandate and more the result of the American voters' frustration with Vietnam and other issues of foreign policy past. But campaign eloquence on the stump should not be accepted at face value. The chief executive should not believe his own PR. The new president, foreign service officers complained, began to believe his own antiestablishment rhetoric and ignored the advice of State's long-standing and well-informed resident experts (Interviews 1987 and 1988).

Not unexpectedly, the internecine conflicts at State that gradually took on characteristics of well-established dogma not only persisted but emerged to plague Carter's ambitious plans for a radical departure in U.S. policy on Africa. Carter responded as presidents had done before him. He organized competing sets of foreign policy machinery over which he had closer and more direct control in the White House.

Carter appointed Zbigniew Brzezinski as assistant to the president for national security affairs; Andrew Young, close friend and former congressman from Georgia's Fifth District, as ambassador to the United Nations; Vice President Walter Mondale as his day-to-day adviser on Southern African affairs; and Cyrus Vance, a Washington insider, as secretary of state.

Carter's deep interest in and his appointments addressing the region only appeared to confirm the fact that the State Department had failed and that future success meant taking foreign policy in general, and African policy in particular, by the presidential hand.

The appointment of Brzezinski placed the new national security adviser in charge of the National Security Council (NSC). It was a position from which, in policy formation, execution, and access, Brzezinski garnered substantial advantage.

NSC, the bureaucracy directly competing with the State Department for influence, normally lacks organizational strength to develop and coordinate policy. But that disadvantage was rapidly overcome by four characteristics that gave NSC a competitive edge. First, NSC was manageably small, as well as narrow in scope and composition. Second, the NSC was composed of individuals who had proven loyal to the Oval Office. Third, NSC's size allowed it to act on short-term policy with a rapidity that disturbed other foreign policy bureaucrats. Last, the narrowness of membership and singular loyalty could exempt the National Security Council from either ability or desire to reconcile domestic constituencies (Cohen 1981, p. 68).

The arrival of Brzezinski seemed to breathe new life into the NSC staff office. Though Brzezinski did not demand equality with Secretary of State Cyrus Vance, Carter appeared to treat the two as equals and used both to balance influence and information. The paper trail reflects the fact that State officially managed international affairs, with the NSC looking over the department's shoulder. It may well have been Jimmy Carter's intent (Inderfurth and Johnson 1988, pp. 119-121).

The reviews of international issues done by NSC show that the longer-range fundamental orientation, as well as the day-to-day drift of policy, had been penetrated by the NSC staff. By the end of the first year of the new administration, a pattern of dominance had been established. While the letter of policy was laid down by State's bureaucracy, clearly the tone of policy gradually took on a Brzezinski cast (Memo 1977).

Even State's official relationships with Congress seem to have been detoured through a screen in the NSC. There the Congressional Relations Office often passed on State's proposed reports to Congress on pending legislation, such as the South African arms embargo (Schecter 1977).

Moreover, self-assured and confident of his cause, Brzezinski wisely used the media to enhance his bureaucratic bargaining strength. While cautious of being labeled an "anonymous gossip," the NSC director clearly wanted his views well publicized. In that way he mobilized administration opinion to support a globalist strategy.

Brzezinski's influence within the White House grew weekly. In the struggle to decide who would direct foreign policy, a major issue evolved as to who would answer the president's personal mail relating to international issues. Communications from important constituents to the Oval Office may well have "detoured" to the NSC director. After some deliberation, the White House staff concluded that the president had to be careful that letters regarding national security issues passed to Brzezinski were not actually answered by the national security adviser. Substantive replies to Carter's mail should be routed to and answered by the secretary of state.

From the perspective of the State Department, this position of Brzezinski and the NSC became even more significant by means of the theory of the president's ear. That notion argues that policy is propounded and established by the individual or groups with the ability or persuasiveness to speak directly to the chief executive without an appointment. In this competition for influence, Brzezinski thus became a major force within the Carter White House. His powerful personality, coupled with strong opinions, brought hostile response from traditionalists. With a weltanschauung well modeled in his own mind, Brzezinski became locked into definite opinions about issues. In the competition to shape policy, the national security adviser's globalist view naturally saw any Soviet action "as part of a wider global offensive" to challenge U.S. power in all world arenas (Newsom 1987, p. 4).

The presence of such a dominant and powerful personality in the White House competing with the Oval Office generated shock waves throughout the government. Brzezinski created internecine conflict even among those who had similar philosophies. The national security adviser's views were apparently so intense that even among those with a globalist perspective there emerged bureaucratic infighting

The Central Intelligence Agency struggled to present a balance to the chief executive. According to Stansfield Turner, director of the CIA, Brzezinski's lack of flexibility so dominated policy that "If the conclusion fitted with the Brzezinski view of the world," the CIA would be urged to reevaluate the data to give Carter two sides of the issue (Newsom 1987, p. vii).

Brzezinski's strong personality created personal animosity within the struggle. Vance and Brzezinski became principals in a tug-of-war. Department of State bureaucats quickly became inflamed over their weak position vis-à-vis the director of NSC. Former Assistant Secretary of State David Newsom points out that within the globalists' argument, Brzezinski's aggressive tactics isolated potential ideological allies. Secretary of State Cyrus Vance, reflecting the views of State's Soviet desk, argued that it was absolutely necessary "to keep channels open to the Soviet Union and to govern rhetoric to minimize differences" (Newsome 1987, p. 3).

CIA Director Turner described the clash of State and NSC over the Soviet combat brigade in Cuba, for example, as a serious deterrent to rational policy development. He accused Brzezinski of "publicly inflaming the issue at the same time the Secretary of State was trying to damp it down" (Newsom 1987, p. xii).

From within the State Department came charges that Carter and his foreign policy amateurs could neither govern nor deal with the "nuts and bolts of everyday administration" (Interviews 1987 and 1988). The perception of the foreign policy establishment was that the Carter organization thought it was "more fun running for president than running the government" (Interviews 1987 and 1988).

Foreign service officers were blunt in their personal criticism of the Carter team. They charged that the Carter "gang" were "loose cannons rolling about the deck" and Hamilton Jordan would "rather drink a beer and get laid than talk with Giscard d'Estaing or the German head of State" (Interviews 1987 and 1988). To foreign service officers under fire from foreign officials, Hamilton Jordan's escapades, alleged and otherwise, became a personal embarrassment.

If foreign policy in general suffered, so did the development and execution of policy toward Africa in particular. A struggle ensued between the Africa Bureau and the National Security Council for operational control of Africa policy. By the late fall of 1977, Brzezinski's everyday access to the president allowed him to persuade Carter that State's unfolding regionalist conception of Africa should be reconsidered for one based on incident, that is, actions taken by Soviet Russia (Interviews 1987 and 1988).

The Africa Bureau's well-thought-out and well-developed program had obtained the backing of major components in the policy chain, but the State Department complained that "Assistant Secretary of State for African Affairs Dick Moose could not get past Brzezinski" to present another point of view to Carter (Interviews 1987 and 1988). State Department Africanists thus tended to blame Brzezinski for the collapse of Carter's early attempts at regionalism. Brzezinski's bureaucratic contentiousness, they declared, tended to allow and even magnify the Soviet Union as primary player to affect even more narrow African issues that could be defined as regional (Interviews 1987 and 1988).

Congressional advocates of the regional perspective besieged the Oval Office with criticism of a renewed globalist tilt. "The most effective policies toward Africa," wrote Senator Paul Tsongas, a leading Democratic liberal from Massachusetts, "are affirmative policies. A negative, reactive American policy that seeks only to oppose Soviet or Cuban involvement would be dangerous and futile" (Tsongas 1978).

Tsongas, William Goodling (D.-Pennsylvania), and the Congressional Black Caucus all attacked Carter for allowing the recurring conflict between Brzezinski and Vance. Goodling urged the president to publicly address American interests in Africa in order to "put to rest the lingering doubts about confusion within your Administration over the proper course of action in Africa, and ease policy implementation." (Goodling 1978). The Congressional Black Caucus threw its weight on the side of the State Department regionalists. They openly backed Vance, who, they wrote, had "done more to outline and clarify the elements of U.S. foreign policy toward Africa than any other spokesman for the Administration" (Diggs 1978). Such a pointed statement could hardly be ignored.

Initially, the Oval Office seemed to be caught between Brzezinski and Vance. When that happened, Carter's administrative answer was to utilize Vice President Mondale or Hamilton Jordan as personal White House envoy.

It was just such a tactic that led Hamilton Jordan, tapped by Carter to bypass the traditional policy network, to be the go-between in a major foreign policy imbroglio in the Ethiopia-Somalia conflict. This confrontation on the Horn of Africa emerged as the event that broke the back of Carter attempts at regionalist policy.

CASE STUDY: HORN OF AFRICA

Although it is unclear where his advice came from on the issue, Carter, on February 25, 1977, utilized human rights violations as the immediate cause to halt U.S. aid to Marxist military dictator Mengistu Haile Mariam, leader of the Derg in Ethiopia (Selassie 1985, p. 173).

The president's action brought the regionalists and globalists into a sharp and highly charged disagreement. Almost immediately, suggested goals for U.S. policy direction diverged. There were two points of view.

White House political advisers, along with Brzezinski, believed that shifting alliances in the Horn had placed the Russians in an untenable position. While attempting to remain friends with the Somalis, the Soviets had seized the opportunity to support Somalia's Marxist neighbor and longtime adversary, Ethiopia. This "opportunism" provided an opening for possible American displacement of a growing Soviet influence in Arab East Africa.

As Vance tells it, it was, the globalists felt, "to damage the Soviets by tying them down in a costly and endless struggle and even forcing them to back down in a confrontation" (Vance 1983, p. 75). In such a Cold War confrontation, the Russians could be ousted from Somalia and replaced with U.S. influence. On the other hand, regionalists at State, backed by the secretary of state, saw a broader opportunity to mediate conflict between the two African parties and "to work with European allies and African nations to bring about a negotiated solution to the broader regional issues" (Vance 1983, pp. 74-75).

This shifting alliance in the Horn of Africa, combined with Saudi interests in and financial support for Arab Somalia, aided in Carter's rejection of an increasingly pro-Soviet Ethiopia. The White House foreign policy team, Brzezinski, the National Security Council, and Hamilton Jordan developed a scheme that would allow the Somalis to "try and snatch" Ogaden, a desert region of questionable importance sandwiched between the two nations (Interviews 1987 and 1988). This major miscalculation resulted in a severe Somali defeat and the rapid escalation of Soviet and Cuban military influence in Marxist Ethiopia.

State Department professionals point the finger at Hamilton Jordan. It was Jordan, in their assessment of events, who, under Carter's authority, sought to gain advantage for U.S. influence in the Horn. As Carter's envoy, Jordan conferred with President Mohammed Siad Barre of Somalia in the early summer of 1977. He apparently promised not only U.S. economic support but also arms to defend Somalia against possible Ethiopian encroachment.

Evidence suggests that Jordan "encouraged" the Somalis to attempt to regain the Ogaden held by Ethiopia but historically claimed by Somalia. Jordan led Siad Barre to believe the United States would back Somalia, concluded an agreement, and flew back to Washington. The State Department was neither consulted nor required. On July 26, 1977, Washington announced an agreement to supply direct military aid to Somalia. The mystery surrounding this accord and the State Department's isolation from it is confirmed by other authorities. Edmond J. Keller notes: "How this accord was reached and under what terms is not clear" (Keller 1985, p. 187).

Sometime in July, the Somali army, strengthened by Soviet arms supplied at an earlier time, invaded the Ogaden region and threw back a surprised Ethiopian army. Donald K. Petterson, who was director of South African affairs at the time and ambassador to Somalia soon after the event, explains what happened. He writes that the sudden Somali attack took Washington by surprise (Petterson 1985, pp. 194-204).

The State Department, angry that African policy had slipped into the hands of "amateurs" on the White House staff, attempted to regain control. A furious Vance told Carter to void the arms agreement. Caught between Vance and Brzezinski, the president agreed. He quickly ordered termination of any U.S. arms transfers until Somalia evacuated the Ogaden.

Jordan and the NSC's ploy was quickly answered. In an extraordinary logistical coup, the Soviet Union airlifted eleven thousand Cuban troops from Angola and ferried in one billion dollars' worth of military equipment to aid the faltering Ethiopian army. One thousand Soviet military personnel were dispatched to the Ogaden. The conflict turned in favor of Ethiopia.

This major foreign policy defeat shocked the Carter administration. Not only did U.S. intelligence not know the Soviets had the capability to carry out such an airlift, they did not know, in fact, that it was being done (Interviews 1987 and 1988).

Ethiopia, which had heretofore been only a modest recipient of Soviet aid, was transformed into a major point of Soviet influence in Africa. In retrospect, it was through some good fortune, plus negotiations between Vance, Ambassador Anatoly Dobrynin, and Foreign Minister Andrei Gromyko, that the Soviets restrained Ethiopia from invading Somalia after the former's reconquest of the Ogaden.

What followed was a major attempt by the State Department to wrest control of Africa policy from Brzezinski. Apparently, there was some success. In March 1978, Carter sent a State Department spokesman, Assistant Secretary Richard Moose, to Mogadishu, Somalia, to salve the wounds and reestablish the ground rules for U.S. aid (Petterson 1985, p. 198). But Jordan's trip and subsequent events had created their own logical result. Carter readily agreed to Brzezinski's request for a review of U.S. policy on the Horn. He ordered a complete reassessment of U.S. policy toward Africa and the Persian Gulf region. The regionalist experiment had survived for seventeen months.

Edmond Keller argues that it was the assertiveness of human rights policy in Ethiopia, that is, the situational dynamics, that backfired. I would argue that the policy itself was not flawed, that, in fact, failure in the Horn could be traced to a contest, more correctly a tug-of-war, between rivals in the White House and Foggy Bottom.

In a misguided effort by a pugnacious Brzezinski and Hamilton Jordan, no doubt surreptitiously backed by Carter himself, the United States sought a Western-oriented Somalia as a Cold War counterweight to Marxist Ethiopia. The globalists seized the policy initiative from their Foggy Bottom rivals on the assumption that U.S. presence and influence on the Horn of Africa was of greater priority than localizing issues and dampening conflict.

As a result of reassessment, militarization of Carter's African policy rapidly followed. Arguing that Moscow's duplicity took on added sinister intent, Brzezinski perceived an "arc of crisis," a concerted Soviet attempt to threaten sea-lanes in the Persian Gulf region (Brzezinski 1983, p. 188).

The long-term consequences could only be categorized as a major defeat for the Carter team. Since the human rights criterion had no apparent effect on conditions in Ethiopia, U.S. charges of violations became more tempered. Of greater concern was the massive escalation of the arms race in the vicinity of the Horn. From 1976 to 1979, military forces in Ethiopia increased from 65,000 to 250,000. By 1982 there were 2,400 Soviet military advisers, 550 East Germans, and 5,900 Cubans in the country. The ripple effect carried over into neighboring Kenya and Sudan. There the sense of crisis escalated and the need for a sense of security grew. In Kenya, for example, military expenditures increased fivefold.

Carter's shift to globalism swung regionalists to an attitude of opposition. In a futile effort, State Department regionalists desperately urged moderation by the White House. Backed by Secretary of State Vance and led by Harold Saunders, Warren

Christopher, and Assistant Secretary of State for African Affairs Richard Moose, the group opposed militarization of the perceived threat (*Africa Contemporary Record* 1979, p. A-73).

Charles C. Diggs, a member of the Congressional Black Caucus, pleaded with Carter not to "erode the trust you have built up in this continent in a remarkably short time" by introducing Cold War politics and supplying weapons. In an open warning to the president, Diggs said that his Subcommittee on Africa would handle military assistance "with caution" and view any requests "very carefully" (Congressional Black Caucus 1978).

Increasing militarization of African regional political complexities further escalated in May 1978, when forces from Marxist Angola invaded, for a second time, Zaire's Shaba (once Katanga) province. Carter provided C-141 air support to assist French and Belgian military airlifts. His advocacy and support for the establishment of an all-African force to prevent other border intrusions, to be backed by the United States and Europe, met with public hostility from African leaders (Vance 1983, pp. 89-90).

Brzezinski's account of the Ethiopia-Somali conflict is brief. He covers the entire episode in a single paragraph, only emphasizing the necessity for a globalist outlook (Brzezinski, 1983 p. 178). Moreover, Brzezinski fails to assess the Soviet airlift and sealift along with the bungled White House efforts as a major turning point in American policy.

The omission leads one to surmise not only that the NSC most likely had a hand in the events, but also that interview testimony from foreign service officers as well as the literature is accurate.

CONCLUSION

Carter's experience with Africa policy substantiates Allison's theories on the Bureaucratic Politics model. Organization or the absence of it impacts policy. Intensity of competition between senior government players over maintaining and increasing power and influence, coupled with a dominating personality and the intrusion of extraordinary events, severed the last bits of Carter's idealist vision for reorienting U.S. policy.

Several points should be made. First, initially hailed as a "management president," it seems odd that Carter ran aground in his attempts, at least in this instance, to adequately direct and supervise his foreign policy team. As might be expected from his appointments, regional Africa policy became crippled early on. A schizophrenic administrative machinery, split by personalities, bureaus, opinion, and the search for power, clearly failed to function.

It was to become, admittedly, a common problem. The overall issue of the role of the NSC director was viewed seriously enough to be the subject of congressional hearings, as well as a special presidential investigative commission in the post-Carter years.

It was a startling beginning, however. Carter's regional approach and emphasis on Africa, combined with Young's appointment, created false hopes among African leaders and people alike for a new departure in American policy. In that it tended to raise expectations that perhaps could never be, and clearly never were, achieved, many African states emerged from the experience severely disillusioned. Hopes for change, increased development aid rather than military aid, and a greater focus on the continent's distinct problems separated from great power clashes never came to fruition (Interviews 1987 and 1988).

Third, it is difficult not to conclude that the appearance of vacillation and irresolution as a result of bureaucratic infighting contributed to the Carter enigma.

Evidence is strong that the Soviet Union viewed the new president as ambivalent and indecisive. While the White House appeared as a vigorous symbol of American vision, enactment of policy itself seemed cautious and weak-willed. Having evaluated the diffident response in Ethiopia, the Soviet Union may have calculated a similar reaction to its military operations in Afghanistan and thus inadvertently increased the odds of an Afghan invasion (Interviews 1987 and 1988).

Finally, the commonly held prescriptive notion to reorganize the executive branch in order to improve the decision-making process seems moot in the face of constitutional strictures. The checks and balances of powers placed in the Constitution never envisioned the massive challenges of global political and economic responsibilities.

It may be that one needs to return to John Locke's assessment of British global influence at the end of the seventeenth century for relief. An independent foreign policy-making team separated from the executive and legislative branches, like that envisioned by the original Brownlow Report, might well hold answers consistent with questions of the twenty-first century.

REFERENCES

Allison, Graham T. "Conceptual Models of the Cuban Missile Crisis." *American Political Science Review*, 63, no. 3 (September 1969):689-718.

Allison, Graham T. and Morton H. Halperin. 1972. "Bureaucratic Politics: A Paradigm and Some Policy Implications." In Raymond Tanter and Richard H. Ullman, ed., *Theory and Policy in International Relations*, pp. 40-79. Princeton: Princeton University Press.

Bender, Gerald J., James S. Coleman, and Richard L. Sklar, eds. 1985. *African Crisis Areas and U.S. Foreign Policy*. Berkeley: University of California Press.

Brzezinski, Zbigniew. 1983. *Power and Principle*. New York: Farrar, Straus and Giroux.

Carter, Jimmy. 1982. *Keeping Faith: Memoirs of a President*. New York: Bantam Books.

Cohen, Stephen D. 1981. *The Making of United States International Economic Policy*. 2nd ed. New York: Praeger.

Congressional Black Caucus. 1978. Letter to President Carter. June 23. "CO-1-1," Box CO-4, WHCF Executive File, Jimmy Carter Library.

Diggs, Charles C. Jr. 1978. Letter to President Carter. March 31. "Diggs," WHCF-Name File, Jimmy Carter Library.

Foltz, William J. 1980. "United States Policy in Southern Africa: What Next?" *Friedrich Ebert Stiftung* (October).

Goodling, Bill. 1978. Letter to President Carter. August 15. "CO-1-1," Box CO-4, WHCF Executive File, Jimmy Carter Library.

Harr, John E. 1965. *The Anatomy of the Foreign Service--A Statistical Profile.* Washington, D.C.:
Carnegie Endownment for International Peace, p. 22.

Inderfurth, Karl F. and Loch K. Johnson. 1988. *Decisions of the Highest Order: Perspectives on
the Natonal Security Council.* Pacific Grove, Calif: Brooks-Cole.

Interviews. 1987, 1988. Atlanta, Georgia. March 1987, November 1987, April 1988.

Keller, Edmond J. 1985. "United States Foreign Policy on the Horn of Africa: Policymaking with
Blinders On." In Gerald J. Bender, James S. Coleman and Richard L. Sklar, eds. *African Crisis
Areas and U.S. Foreign Policy,* pp. 178-193. Berkeley: University of California Press.

Legum, Colin. 1978. "The African Crisis." In William P. Bundy, ed. *America and the World, 1978.*
New York: Pergamon Press.

Legum, Colin, and Marione Doro, eds., *Africa Contemporary Record, Annual Survey and
Documents.* New York: Holmes and Meier, 1979.

Memo. 1977. Notes on proposed toast to French prime minister by Carter. September 15. "CO-51-
Ex," WHCF Executive File, Jimmy Carter Library.

Newsom, David D. 1987. *The Soviet Brigade in Cuba: A Study in Political Diplomacy.*
Bloomington: Indiana University Press.

Nolutshungu, Sam C. 1985. "South African Policy and United States Options in Southern Africa."
In Gerald J. Bender, James S. Coleman and Richard L. Sklar, eds., *African Crisis Areas and U.S.
Foreign Policy,* pp. 49-63. Berkeley: University of California Press.

Petterson, Donald K. 1985. "Somalia and the United States, 1977-1983: The New Relationship." In
Gerald J. Bender, James S. Coleman and Richard L. Sklar, eds., *African Crisis Areas and U.S.
Foreign Policy,* pp. 194-204. Berkeley: University of California Press.

Rothchild, Donald, and John Ravenhill. 1983. "From Carter to Reagan: The Global Perspective on
Africa Becomes Ascendant." In Kenneth Oye, Robert J. Lieber, and Donald Rothchild, eds.,
Eagle Defiant: United States Foreign Policy in the 1980s. Boston: Little, Brown and Co.

Schecter, Jerrold L. 1977. Memo to James Frey, Office of Management and Budget. June 30. "CO-
141-Ex," WHCF Executive File, Jimmy Carter Library.

Selassie, Bereket H. 1985. "The American Dilemma on the Horn." In Gerald J. Bender, James S.
Coleman and Richard L. Sklar, eds., *African Crisis Areas and U.S. Foreign Policy,* pp. 163-177.
Berkeley: University of California Press.

Snyder, Glenn H., and Paul Diesing. 1977. *Conflict Among Nations: Bargaining, Decision-Making
and System Structure in International Crises.* Princeton: Princeton University Press.

Taulbee, James Larry. 1988. "Premises, Promises and Compromises: Human Rights." *Southeastern
Political Review,* 16:231-261.

Tsongas, Paul. 1978. Letter to President Carter. July. "CO-1-1," Box CO-4, WHCF Executive File,
Jimmy Carter Library.

Vance, Cyrus. 1983. *Hard Choices: Critical Years in America's Foreign Policy.* New York:
Simon and Schuster.

15

The Reaction of the Carter Administration to Human Rights Violations in Cambodia

CARL LIEBERMAN

HUMAN RIGHTS POLICY IN THE CARTER YEARS: AN OVERVIEW

While campaigning for the Democratic presidential nomination in 1976, Jimmy Carter made a presentation to the Chicago Council on Foreign Relations in which he enumerated the basic principles that should guide American foreign policy. In that speech he declared, "it must be the responsibility of the President to restore the moral authority of this country in its conduct of foreign policy. . . . Policies that strengthen dictators or create refugees, policies that prolong suffering or postpone racial justice, weaken that authority."[1] Carter's concern for human rights and the moral authority of our foreign policy was reiterated in speeches delivered after he secured the nomination.[2]

Upon assuming the presidency, Carter and key members of the administration asserted the importance of the human rights component of our international relations. On March 7, 1977, speaking to the Subcommittee on Foreign Assistance of the Senate Committee on Foreign Relations, Warren Christopher, the deputy secretary of state, said, "The concern for human rights will be woven into the fabric of our foreign policy."[3] In an address to the General Assembly of the United Nations, the president noted, "All the signatories of the United Nations Charter have pledged themselves to observe and to respect basic human rights. Thus, no member of the United Nations can claim that mistreatment of its citizens is solely its own business."[4]

During his first year in office, Carter appointed Patricia Derian as coordinator and later assistant secretary of state for human rights. Derian, who had taken an active role in the civil rights struggle in Mississippi, was inexperienced in foreign affairs. She faced opposition from some of the professional career officers within the State Department, as well as high-ranking officials such as Richard Holbrooke and Terence Todman, who were more concerned with maintaining good relations in their areas of interest (Southeast Asia and Latin America, respectively) than with applying sanctions against human rights violators.[5]

Secretary of State Cyrus Vance assigned Deputy Secretary of State Warren Christopher the task of making human rights policies compatible with the overall objectives of foreign policy. After exempting most military aid and food aid programs from human rights review, the Christopher group, which included representatives from Defense, Treasury, and Agriculture, focused most of its attention on American voting on multilateral bank loans. Although Treasury officials were concerned that the use of multilateral lending banks as a weapon of American foreign policy would undermine the effectiveness of the banks, the United States abstained or voted against loan proposals to seventeen nations in Africa, Asia, and Latin America.[6] It also suspended economic or military aid to eight Latin American nations--Argentina, Bolivia, El Salvador, Guatemala, Haiti, Nicaragua, Paraguay, and Uruguay.[7]

Trade sanctions were imposed against Uganda, the Ian Smith regime in Rhodesia, and South Africa. Although there was discussion in the State Department about applying sanctions against Iran, no action was taken to do so. Despite human rights violations in the Philippines and South Korea, limits on military aid were not applied against these countries.[8]

Complaints arose in Congress and elsewhere concerning the inconsistent application of human rights policies by the administration. Some critics suggested that we were too quick to condemn or penalize friendly governments.[9] Spokesmen for, and defenders of, the Carter policies suggested that they helped the nation regain credibility in the world, strengthened long-run relations with other countries, and advanced freedom within U.S. borders. Human rights were seen as the appropriate and particular concern of the United States.[10]

During the Carter years, one of the most egregious examples of human rights violations occurred in Cambodia, where the Khmer Rouge government of Pol Pot killed thousands of people. Although the American government condemned these violations, its position was not entirely consistent. After the invasion of Cambodia by Vietnam, for example, we sought to prevent the representatives of the new Heng Samrin regime from taking its place in the United Nations while continuing to recognize the representatives of the previous government.

This paper examines the Carter administration's reaction to the human rights violations in Cambodia. It will consider the steps it took and the significance of this case for understanding the human rights policy of the Carter years.

CAMBODIA BEFORE AND AFTER WORLD WAR II

Cambodia became a French protectorate in 1864. Until that time, it was a collection of vassal states controlled by Thailand and Vietnam. During the period of French colonial domination, while Cambodia was part of the Indochinese Federation, trade was mainly under the control of Vietnamese and Chinese, and the Vietnamese particularly were employed in lower-level positions of the civil service and police. This pattern of economic and governmental domination by persons not of Cambodian origin probably exacerbated ethnic hostilities.[11]

The Japanese occupied Cambodia and declared it independent during World War II. Norodom Sihanouk, chosen as king in 1941, when he was nineteen, renounced agreements between his country and France at the urging of the Japanese. During the wartime occupation, a group known as the Khmer Issarak was founded. It became the nucleus of anti-French guerrilla activities after the war, cooperating with the Vietnamese liberation movement.[12]

When the war ended, the French sought to resume control of Indochina, only to face armed resistance. In 1953, in order to prevent the Left from coming to power, France granted independence to Cambodia.[13] The Geneva Conference of 1954 brought an end to the first Indochina war and confirmed Cambodia's independence. All foreign troops, both French and Vietnamese, were to be withdrawn, and no foreign bases were to be established, thus ensuring the country's neutral status.[14]

In 1955, Prince Sihanouk abdicated in favor of his father but maintained effective control of the government. A movement founded by Sihanouk, the Sangkum, came to dominate Cambodian politics. The left- and right-wing factions within the Sangkum struggled with one another until the military coup of Prime Minister Lon Nol in 1970.[15]

Sinhanouk established diplomatic relations with China and the Soviet Union, and signed trade and economic agreements with both countries. His purpose was not so much to tilt toward the Communist bloc as to maintain balance at a time when pro-Western forces had established the Southeast Asia Treaty Organization, consisting of the United States, Great Britain, France, Thailand, the Philippines, Pakistan, Australia, and New Zealand. Indeed, Cambodia continued to turn to the United States for economic and military aid.[16]

However, the Eisenhower administration, fearing Sihanouk's attempts to improve relations with the communist powers, began to aid the rightist Khmer Serei guerrillas opposed to his government, who had established bases in Thailand and South Vietnam. In 1961, Cambodia broke off relations with Thailand. It later ended a military aid agreement with the United States and ceased to have diplomatic relations in 1965.[17]

The ending of American aid adversely affected the Cambodian economy at a time when the war in Vietnam was becoming increasingly violent and destructive. Politicians with leftist views joined the government. One, Khieu Samphan, became minister of the economy and nationalized private banks and financial institutions.[18]

The American government gave more direct support to right-wing forces within Cambodia. In 1966, elections put the Right under Lon Nol and Sirik Matak in control of the government. Leftists were purged from the government and several individuals, including Khieu Samphan, Hou You, and Hu Nim, fled to the countryside in 1967 to organize armed resistance to the rightist regime. Peasant rebellions in 1967 and 1968 were harshly suppressed, thus enlarging opposition to the government and strengthening the emerging Khmer Rouge guerrilla movement on the Left.[19]

In March 1970, while visiting Moscow, Sihanouk was overthrown by a military coup led by Lon Nol. The Kingdom of Cambodia was abolished and the Khmer Republic was established. The causes of the coup were complex. There were obvious foreign policy differences between the pro-American Lon Nol and Sihanouk, who had permitted the North Vietnamese and the National Liberation Front guerrilla forces opposed to the government in Saigon to establish sanctuaries in the border areas of his country. There were also internal political struggles over the economic direction of the country.[20]

The American role in the coup is not clear. Whether it was engineered by the United States, as some have charged, cannot be ascertained. It is clear, however, that the Lon Nol government was greatly aided by the United States, receiving hundreds of millions of dollars in military and economic assistance.[21]

During the five years of the Khmer Republic's existence, American bombing of rural areas, designed to weaken the forces opposed to the South Vietnamese government and the guerrilla struggle in opposition to the Lon Nol regime, created massive disruption. Hundreds of thousands of persons perished, one-third of the rural population became refugees, rice production fell dramatically, and there was an enormous increase in the prices of basic foodstuffs.[22]

Sihanouk, who fled to China after the coup, called for resistance to the military government of Lon Nol. The National United Front of Kampuchea was founded; it included not only supporters of Sihanouk but also leftists who had fled to Vietnam in the 1950s and the communist-led Khmer Rouge.[23]

By January 1975, the government of Cambodia was faced with a large-scale offensive by the guerrillas and was clearly in danger of falling. President Ford complained that congressional limits on economic and military aid threatened to undermine efforts to negotiate an end to fighting in Cambodia. The Defense Department said it would need $100-150 million in supplemental military aid to fund the Cambodian government thorugh the end of June.[24]

On February 23, 1975, appearing on the ABC news program "Issues and Answers," Secretary of Defense James Schlesinger said that Cambodia would fall into communist hands unless Congress allocated $222 million in military aid requested by the administration.[25] Two days later, President Ford and Secretary of State Kissinger reiterated Schlesinger's appeal for aid. In a letter to Speaker of the House Carl Albert, President Ford said, "If additional military assistance is withheld or delayed, the Government forces will be forced, within weeks, to surrender to the insurgents."[26]

Despite pleas for additional aid, supplemental funds from Congress were not forthcoming. Opponents of aid saw continued military assistance as merely prolonging the suffering of innocent people and lengthening the painful involvement of the United States in Indochina.[27] Thus, on April 17, 1975, only twelve days before the American evacuation from Saigon, the Lon Nol regime surrendered to the guerrilla forces.[28]

When Phnom Penh, the capital of Cambodia, fell, the Khmer Rouge forces compelled the evacuation of virtually its entire population. Indeed, the cities were generally emptied. The peasants who made up most of the guerrilla army were often repulsed by the cities and their inhabitants, whom they saw as exploiters and traitors. Also, the Khmer Rouge feared that a concentrated urban population would serve as a source of potential opposition. Dispersal to rural areas would make it easier to control the people. Finally, movement from the cities may have been part of the new government's attempt to overthrow the existing social order and re-create the society.[29]

The new regime was led by Pol Pot (previously known as Saloth Sar), Nuon Chea, Ieng Sary, and Son Sen. Pol Pot served as Communist Party secretary. His deputy was Nuon Chea. Ieng Sary became foreign minister, and Son Sen the defense minister of the new government. For a year after the takeover, Sihanouk, who had returned to Cambodia, was recognized as head of state. He was replaced in the summer of 1976 by Khieu Samphan, and the old Kingdom of Cambodia was renamed Democratic Kampuchea.[30] The Khmer Rouge tried to destroy the market economy, compelling the people to work in rural communities under highly regimented conditions. The use of money was ended, and a new calendar was introduced. Traditional schooling was largely terminated.[31]

Thousands of people--some have estimated more than a million--died during the four-year period in which the Khmer Rouge were in power. The regime proceeded to murder those who were believed to belong to the intelligentsia. Others targeted for persecution and even death included Chan Muslims, Christians, Buddhist monks, and members of the Vietnamese and Chinese minorities. Often the families of those perceived as enemies of the regime were arrested and eliminated.[32]

A short time after the Khmer Rouge gained power, active fighting between Cambodian and Vietnamese forces broke out along the borders and on certain islands. Border clashes escalated in 1977 and created increased animosity between the two communist governments.[33] It is possible that the border fights were encouraged by the Khmer Rouge because it wanted to unite the people against an external enemy. In fact, the causes of the conflict were probably more complex. There were long-standing tensions between the Cambodian and Vietnamese populations as a result of the history of domination of Cambodia. As early as 1970, the Cambodians killed thousands of Vietnamese residents in their midst who were alleged to have communist sympathies. Vietnam feared Chinese domination and was an ally of the Soviet Union. Democratic Kampuchea's main ally was China, and it looked to that country for support.[34]

By 1978 a state of war existed between Kampuchea and Vietnam. The Vietnamese invasion of Kampuchea began in December 1978, and was completed by January 1979. Its purpose was to replace the Pol Pot government with one led by a Vietnamese-endorsed opponent of the regime, Heng Samrin.[35] During the war, thousands of persons in eastern Kampuchea were killed because the government doubted their loyalty.[36]

In January 1979, as the Vietnamese-backed forces entered Phnom Penh, the remnants of the Khmer Rouge fled to the interior and the border areas near Thailand. The People's Republic of Kampuchea was proclaimed.[37] Vietnamese military forces continued to occupy the country for the next decade.

AMERICAN REACTIONS TO EVENTS IN CAMBODIA

A complete description of U.S. reaction to the events in Cambodia cannot be provided because much of the relevant material is in classified documents, particularly those of the president's national security adviser, Zbigniew Brzezinski. However, available evidence suggests that the response of the Carter administration to the large-scale killing of civilians in Kampuchea and to the overthrow of the Khmer Rouge government was a mixture of moral outrage, humanitarian concern, and political calculation.

From 1977 to 1980, representatives of the administration condemned human rights violations in Cambodia and provided aid to help ease the famine that threatened the population. On July 26, 1977, Richard Holbrooke, assistant secretary of state for East Asian and Pacific affairs, testified before the Subcommittee on International Organizations of the House Committee on International Affairs concerning the human rights record of the Cambodian government:

Based on all the evidence available to us, we have concluded that Cambodian authorities have flagrantly and systematically violated the most basic human rights. They have ordered or permitted extensive killings, forcibly relocated the urban population, brutally treated supporters of the previous government, and suppressed personal and political freedoms.[38]

Holbrooke's statement to the House subcommittee is of interest not only because it condemned human rights violations but also because it suggested one problem of influencing Cambodia--its isolation. "Since 1975," he said, "Cambodia has been almost completely sealed from the outside world."[39]

In January 1978, speaking at the National Foreign Policy Conference for Editors and Broadcasters at the Department of State, Warren Christopher described human rights abuses in Cambodia as "flagrant and massive." Though he pointed out that we had no relations with Democratic Kampuchea, he said:

we condemn what has taken place there and will take every suitable opportunity to speak out, lest by our silence we seem to acquiesce in the unspeakable human rights abuses that are occurring there.[40]

Despite these statements of condemnation, the administration was reluctant to suggest any specific actions to halt the killings in Cambodia. Following a foreign policy speech in Cincinnati in the spring of 1978, Secretary of State Vance was asked, "what we can do as individuals or as a nation to stop the holocaust in Cambodia?"[41] His response was as follows:

I am afraid to say that I don't have a good answer to that. The situation there is, indeed, a tragic one. We have no contact at all with the Cambodians. We have tried to establish some contact so as to find out at least what is going on there. We have been unable to do this.

    What knowledge we have, we have to gain from others. I think that what one can do is to focus world attention on this situation and hope that the effect of world opinion may change the situation there. But in terms of what we actually can do other than working with others in the world bodies, such as the United Nations and other international fora, there is really nothing practically that I can suggest that we can do.[42]

As suggested by Secretary Vance, the administration response to events in Cambodia included appeals to the United Nations. The government had ruled out military action and an economic boycott (American trade had largely ended as a result of implementation of the Trading with the Enemy Act, while aid was terminated through congressional legislation), but it sought measures within the United Nations to apply pressure to the Pol Pot regime. Thus, the State Department prepared a three hundred-page document that contained reports of atrocities committed by the Cambodian government. The report was submitted to the Subcommission on Prevention of Discrimination and Protection of Minorities.[43]

Administration reactions to the situation in Cambodia appear to have been influenced by three major considerations: domestic political pressure, the difficulty in formulating specific actions to reduce human rights abuses, and our perception of the struggle between Kampuchea and Vietnam.

From 1977 to 1980, the White House received a number of inquiries and letters concerning human rights violations from members of Congress and the general public. For example, Representative Les AuCoin of Oregon noted that he had received a letter from a professor at Eastern Oregon State College, expressing his dismay at the failure of the United States delegation at the United Nations and of the president to speak out about the genocide in Cambodia. AuCoin stated that he, too, was concerned "about the bloodbath that has taken place."[44]

The president also was sent letters by private citizens, including Jane Fonda and Tom Hayden, and a news assistant at the journal *Christianity Today*. Edmund F. McWilliams, Jr., country officer for Laos and Cambodia, noted in his response to Jane Fonda that the president had condemned violations of human rights by the government of Cambodia. He pointed out that Zbigniew Brzezinski had raised our concern about human rights in Kampuchea with Chinese officials and other governments that maintained relations with Phnom Penh.[45]

Congressman Edward P. Boland of Massachusetts, chairman of the Permanent Select Committee on Intelligence, forwarded to Secretary of State Vance a letter sent to Representative Morgan Murphy of Illinois by a member of the Peace Corps. The letter, written in September 1978, expressed concern that we had not developed a policy to deal with genocide in Cambodia. The writer called for the CIA to prepare option papers "regarding possible alternatives for ending the genocide in Cambodia or for bringing peace and stability to Southeast Asia."[46]

It is clear that the White House was concerned about criticism from Senator Edward Kennedy, who announced his candidacy for the presidency shortly after making a speech on October 24, 1979, in which he complained of "past indifference" by the administration to the situation in Cambodia.[47] A memo to Press Secretary Jody Powell, one day after the speech, noted that Kennedy had not so far sent any correspondence regarding Cambodia to the president, the secretary of state, or the national security adviser.[48]

The Carter administration did provide aid to refugees who fled Cambodia, and it also contributed to programs to forestall a famine that threatened to engulf the population after the overthrow of the Khmer Rouge government. As early as 1977, the president asked the attorney general to admit fifteen thousand more Indochinese refugees into the United States through the use of his parole authority.[49] The administration also created an inter-agency task force to develop a longer-term solution to the problem of Indochinese refugees. In 1978, the American government reacted favorably to pleas from voluntary agencies to allow additional Cambodian refugees in camps in Thailand to enter the United States.[50]

Despite the early aid to Cambodians who fled from Democratic Kampuchea, Washington became increasingly confused about the desirability of resettling the Indochinese, particulary after the Vietnamese invasion. On the one hand, the president sent his wife to visit refugee camps in Thailand in the fall of 1979. Her trip focused attention on the plight of the Cambodians, though the refugees included members of the Khmer Rouge, a group denounced by her husband.

On the other hand, critics of American policy, including some members of the bureaucracy, agreed with officials of the office of the United Nations high commissioner for refugees, who believed that the existence of large resettlement quotas in the West encouraged the Indochinese to leave their countries. The U.S. government did not protest the decision of Thailand in 1980 to repatriate or relocate Cambodians who fled across the border. However, the American ambassador to Bangkok, Mort Abramowitz, with the help of his principal refugee aide, Lionel Rosenblatt, lobbied forcefully to allow Cambodians the same opportunity for resettlement as other Indochinese refugees. Shortly before the end of the Carter administration in Jauary 1981, they secured a quota of thirty-one thousand places for Cambodians in the United States.[51]

Food aid to Cambodia was not easily supplied in 1979, despite the widely recognized need to alleviate hunger. The forces of Pol Pot and Heng Samrin both wanted complete control of whatever assistance was provided.[52] Whether there was need for massive food shipments to avert large numbers of deaths is not clear, but there was a widely shared impression among Western journalists, voluntary agencies, and U.N. officials that it was necessary.[53]

Help for Cambodia began in earnest in the autumn of 1979. By February 22, 1980, the international community had donated over $113 million for Khmer relief. About $62.9 million was contributed by the United States. Most of the money and the food it purchased was funneled through the International Committee of the Red Cross, the United Nations high commissioner for refugees, and the United Nations Children's Fund (UNICEF).[54]

If the Carter administration was willing to provide assistance to Cambodia to alleviate hunger, it showed much less support for any forceful action to resist the depredations of the Pol Pot regime. In fact, it refused to recognize the Heng Samrin government installed by the invading Vietnamese, and it supported the continued seating of representatives of Democratic Kampuchea at the United Nations.

The reason for American resistance in recognizing the government of the People's Republic of Kampuchea lies in our interpretation of the geopolitical conditions of Southeast Asia. One of the key elemnts of our foreign policy from the onset of the Carter years was the normalization of U.S.-Chinese relations.[55] Vietnam, by contrast, was seen as a client state of the Soviet Union with ambitions to dominate its neighbors.[56]

Although Carter had campaigned to seek normal relations with Hanoi, negotiations with Vietnam in 1977 had not proven fruitful. Neither Leonard Woodcock, U.S. ambassador to the People's Republic of China, nor Richard Holbrooke, assistant secretary for East Asian and Pacific affairs, had been able to bring about improved relations, though the United States agreed to support Vietnam's admission to the United Nations. Vietnam held out for the payment of $3.25 billion in aid promised secretly by President Richard Nixon in 1973. In the years following American disengagement from the war in Vietnam, support for such assistance had evaporated, and no public figure of prominence was likely to endorse such a proposal.[57]

China was deeply suspicious of Vietnam. The Chinese government was fearful of American efforts to improve relations with the Soviet Union, and it saw the possibility of greater Vietnamese power as enlarging Soviet influence in Southeast Asia.[58]

Brzezinski, who deeply distrusted the Soviet Union and viewed it as an expansionist power, increasingly favored the Chinese position. When the border war between Vietnam and Cambodia first broke out, he referred to it as a "proxy war" between the Soviet Union and China. Experts at the State Department vehemently disagreed, believing that the war was rooted mainly in the rivalries of the two countries and fearing that Vietnam and Cambodia might draw China and the Soviet Union into a wider conflict.[59]

When Deng Xiaoping, the vice premier of China, visited the United States in January 1979, he revealed to Carter a tentative Chinese plan to make a punitive strike across the border into Vietnam. In his memoirs, Carter says that he tried to dissuade Deng from taking such action. Vietnam was being isolated as a result of its aggression against Kampuchea, he argued, and a military strike by China might create sympathy for Hanoi.[60]

Brzezinski, while not contradicting Carter's account, describes it somewhat differently. He points out that he had mentioned to the president growing Chinese concern over Cambodia and that it was important not to convey undue alarm over possible Chinese actions. He was relieved when Carter merely pointed out the seriousness of Chinese action against Cambodia in his discussins with Deng, and suggested that it could be highly destabilizing and that restraint was desirable.[61]

Brzezinski later outlined his views on how the United States should react to Chinese incursions into Vietnam. He proposed that the United States should criticize the Chinese but should also condemn Vietnam for invading Cambodia and call for China and Vietnam to pull out their forces. Thus, we could appear publicly critical of the Chinese action while proposing a plan unacceptable to Vietnam and the Soviet Union.[62]

When the Chinese struck against Vietnam, Brzezinski felt that their action might be beneficial to American interests. He reasoned that it would show that a Soviet ally could be attacked "with relative impunity," thus allaying fears of some of those potentially threatened by the Soviet Union.[63]

In the United Nations we condemned Vietnam for the invasion of Cambodia. Speaking before the Security Council on February 27, 1979, Ambassador Andrew Young noted, "The attack on Kampuchean territory heightened the tensions in the region, leading to the Chinese attack on Vietnam."[64] Richard Petree, our alternate representative to the United Nations for special political affairs, spoke of the conflict in Cambodia as part of a broader problem of instability that threatened Southeast Asia and required Security Council attention.[65]

Our position on normalizing relations with Vietnam was made clear in a statement by the State Department on August 9, 1979:

There have been no talks, secret or otherwise, on normalization of relations between the United States and Vietnam since last fall. As we indicated at that time, Vietnam's actions toward its neighbors and its policies toward its own people resulting in a flood of refugees have made it impossible for us to continue with normalization.[66]

At the United Nations our representative said that the U.S. government supported on technical grounds the recommendation of the Credentials Committee to accept the credentials of the representative of Democratic Kampuchea. "In the absence of a superior claim," he noted, "the General Assembly should seat the representatives of the government whose credentials were accepted by the previous General Assembly."[67]

CONCLUSION

Jimmy Carter has been widely regarded as a political leader whose moral and religious beliefs influenced his policy positions, particularly in the area of human rights.[68] How, then, do we explain his administration's tepid response to the killings and human rights violations in Democratic Kampuchea? Why did the United States tend to favor China and the government it supported in Cambodia in the struggle with Vietnam?

One obvious answer to these questions is that human rights was not the only factor considered in making our foreign policy. Improvement in relations with China and curbing Soviet influence in Southeast Asia were of greater importance to key decision makers than ending abuses against the Cambodian people. Perhaps nongovernment organizations (NGOs) with a more single-minded concern about human rights, such as Amnesty International, are in a better position to pursue their objectives than the government of a major world power. Of course, NGOs lack the diplomatic and economic influence of important nation-states.

Among the factors that made it difficult to formulate consistent and effective policies regarding the human rights situation in Cambodia was the moral ambiguity of our involvement in that country. It may have been clear to Henry Kissinger, Gerald Ford, and Richard Nixon that our failure to continue mili tary aid to Lon Nol and the intransigence of the Vietnamese government helped to bring about the bloody excesses of the Pol Pot regime.[69] Other observers, however, believed that American military involvement in Cambodia and the prolongation of the struggle to overthrow Lon Nol were largely responsible for the serious human rights abuses by the Khmer Rouge.[70] Thus, direct intervention in Cambodia may have seemed a questionable policy option for Carter and his advisers. Certainly, the record of the Vietnamese government regarding its own population created serious problems for anyone who might wish to support its attack against Democratic Kampuchea and its attempt to install a regime under its control.[71]

Within Southeast Asia, Vietnam was often perceived as a greater threat to stability and peace than the repressive regime of Democratic Kampuchea. Thus, any support in the United Nations of the Heng Samrin government, which had been put into power by Vietnam, would have run the risk of offending friendly Asian states. It could also be seen as subtly endorsing the invasion of one's country and overthrow of its government by a neighboring state.[72] Of course, one wonders whether we might have opted for the alternative of not seating either the representatives of Pol Pot or of Heng Samrin.

Domestic political pressures also greatly constrained American foreign policy toward Cambodia. After the war in Vietnam, it was unlikely that we could sustain a policy of active intervention in Indochina. There was little public support for significant involvement in Southeast Asia. Nevertheless, while most Americans were indifferent to events transpiring in Cambodia, the concern of some private citizens and members of Congress was probably responsible in part for the vocal criticism expressed by the administration of human rights abuses by the Pol Pot government. Indeed, one writer has suggested that it was only after the prodding of New York Congressman Steven Solarz that the administration became actively concerned with the suffering in Cambodia.[73]

The failure of the United States and other Western nations to stop the killing and torture of hundreds of thousands of Cambodians points to a major weakness of our human rights policy. Despite the existence of a body of international law designed to suppress genocide and protect the political and cultural rights of people throughout the world, there is not an effective means of enforcement against govermental officials who control the means of coercion in their own countries.

When Senator George McGovern spoke of the need to send an international force to end the killings in Cambodia, he elicited little support within either Congress or the executive branch.[74] A spokesman for the administration might write to a private citizen of the president's "revulsion for a U.S. role of international policeman,"[75] but what alternative is there to the use of force if we wish to end massive violations of human rights?

Economic sanctions, moral condemnation, or diplomatic pressure might work to reduce repression in some cases, but how useful would such weapons be against the government of a country that is isolated, economically underdeveloped, and run by persons with extreme, even fanatical views? Those who suggest the need to try former Cambodian government officials for acts of genocide[76] may be unable to put their plans into operation. However, they have focused on a real need of those concerned with human rights: to make legal and moral norms effective positive law throughout the world.

There are, it must be said, reasons why it would be difficult to secure popular support for the use of coercion against serious human rights abusers in distant lands. Many people are still uneasy about intervening in the "internal affairs" of other countries. They believe that it is not the business of our government (and perhaps other governments) to protect the rights of persons who are not under our jurisdiction. Practically speaking, there is no permanent international law enforcement agency with the ability to accomplish this task.

Moreover, the horrors of modern warfare and repressive governments during the twentieth century may have lessened the sensitivity or the attention span of most people. Thus, we move from one tragedy to another, without being able to understand fully the significance of the suffering we have witnessed.[77]

Some critics of the Carter administration's human rights policy have attacked it for naïveté in a world where power considerations are more important than morality in determining the relations between nations. Others have see it as part of a tradition of ineffective moralizing that has characterized American foreign policy for many years.

There are critics who charge that the Carter policy was mostly rhetoric and not very different in substance from the actions taken by the Reagan administration.[78]

However, before we condemn the Carter policy as largely ineffective, we should consider the actions that we took in relation to Cambodia. If we did not end the killings and the massive suffering of the people of that country, at least we condemned human rights abuses, provided sanctuary to some refugees, and helped to alleviate hunger. Given the imperfect nature of the world order, these are actions more worthy of limited praise than of scorn and rebuke.

NOTES

The author wishes to express his gratitude to Joe Orosz for his assistance in gathering bibliographical materials. He is also grateful for the comments of discussants in the panel on Africa and Asia at the Jimmy Carter Presidential Conference at Hofstra University, November 15-17, 1990.

1. "Our Foreign Relations," address to the Chicago Council on Foreign Relations, March 15, 1976, in *The Presidential Campaign 1976: Jimmy Carter*, 1, pt. 1 (Washington, D.C.: U.S. Government Printing Office, 1978), p. 112.

2. Address at Notre Dame University, South Bend, Indiana, October 10, 1976, and address at the Pulaski Day dinner of the Polish-American community, Chicago, October 10, 1976, in *The Presidential Campaign 1976: Jimmy Carter*, 1, pt. 2 (Washington, D.C.: U.S. Government Printing Office, 1978), pp. 993-998, 1001-1006.

3. "Human Rights: An Important Concern of U.S. Foreign Policy," *Department of State Bulletin*, March 28, 1977, p. 289.

4. "Peace, Arms Control, World Economic Progress, Human Rights: Basic Priorities of U.S. Foreign Policy," *Department of State Bulletin*, April 11, 1977, p. 332.

5. Gaddis Smith, *Morality, Reason and Power: American Diplomacy in the Carter Years* (New York: Hill and Wang, 1986), pp. 51-52.

6. Ibid., p. 53.

7. David Carleton and Michael Stohl, "The Foreign Policy of Human Rights: Rhetoric and Reality from Jimmy Carter to Ronald Reagan," *Human Rights Quarterly* 7, no. 2 (May 1985):215.

8. Smith, *Morality, Reason and Power*, p. 54.

9. Ibid., p. 55; *Congress and the Nation, 1977-1980* (Washington, D.C.: Congressional Quarterly, 1981), pp. 37, 57.

10. Patricia M. Derian, "Human Rights and American Foreign Policy," *Universal Human Rights* 1 (January-March 1979):8-9; Jerel A. Rosati, *The Carter Administration's Quest for Global Community: Beliefs and Their Impact on Behavior* (Columbia: University of South Carolina Press, 1987), pp. 45, 67-68.

11. Kimmo Kiljunen, ed., *Kampuchea: Decade of the Genocide* (London: Zed Books, 1984), p. 2.

12. Ibid., p. 3.

13. Ibid., p. 3.

14. Ibid.

15. Ibid.

16. Ibid., p. 4.

17. Ibid. Also see Roger M. Smith, *Cambodia's Foreign Policy* (Ithaca, N.Y.: Cornell University Press, 1965), pp. 128-136.

18. Kiljunen, *Kampuchea*, p. 4.

19. Ibid., p. 5.

20. Ibid.

21. See, for example, Tom Wicker, "Cambodian Disaster," *New York Times*, February 25, 1975, p. 35; "Cambodia: Time Running Out," *U.S. News & World Report*, March 24, 1975, p. 13; and William Shawcross, *Sideshow* (New York: Simon and Schuster, 1979).

22. Kiljunen, *Kampuchea*, pp. 5-7.

23. Ibid., p. 7.

24. "A New Aid Bill, Sharply Limited," *New York Times*, January 5, 1975, IV, p. 3; and John W. Finney, "Pentagon Says Congress Must Widen Cambodia Aid," *New York Times*, January 8, 1975, p. 3.

25. Leslie H. Gelb, "Pentagon Fears Cambodia's Fall," *New York Times*, February 24, 1975, pp. 1, 9.

26. Bernard Gwertzman, "Ford and Kissinger Warn Cambodia Will Fall Soon if Congress Denies Funds," *New York Times*, February 26, 1975, pp. 1, 8.

27. Wicker, "Cambodian Disaster, p. 35; Anthony Lewis, "The Kissinger Doctrine," *New York Times*, February 27, 1975, p. 35; and "Cambodia Aid Rejected," in *Congressional Quarterly Almanac, 1975* (Washington, D.C.: Congressional Quarterly, 1976), p. 313.

28. Kiljunen, *Kampuchea*, p. 10; and "White Flags Over Phnom Penh," *Newsweek*, April 28, 1975, pp. 27-29.

29. Kiljunen, *Kampuchea*, pp. 10-11; and Sheldon W. Simon, "Cambodia: Barbarism in a Small State Under Siege," *Current History* 75 (December 1978):197-201.

30. Kiljunen, *Kampuchea*, p. 14. Kampuchea was renamed Cambodia by its government in 1989.

31. Ibid., pp. 14-18; Simon, "Cambodia," pp. 198-199; and Michael Vickery, *Cambodia: 1975-1982* (Boston: South End Press, 1984), pp. 171-174.

32. Gregory H. Stanton, "Kampuchean Genocide and the World Count," *Connecticut Journal of International Law* 2 (Spring 1987):341-348; Kenneth M. Quinn, "The Pattern and Scope of Violence," and David Hawk, "The Photographic Record," in Karl D. Jackson, ed., *Cambodia 1975-1978: Rendezvous with Death* (Princeton: Princeton University Press, 1989), pp. 179-213; and Hurst Hannum, "International Law and Cambodian Genocide: The Sounds of Silence," *Human Rights Quarterly* 2 (February 1989):82-138. There are widely varied estimates of the number of people killed by the Pol Pot regime. Michael Vickery maintains that all estimates are imprecise but figures that about three hundred thousand persons were executed. Others have said a million or more persons died at the hands of the Khmer Rouge. Vickery, *Cambodia*, pp. 184-185, 187; Morton Kondracke, "Thanks, but No Thanks," *New Republic*, January 20, 1979, pp. 16-17; and David Aikman, "Cambodia: An Experiment in Genocide," *Time*, July 31, 1978, pp. 39-40.

33. Kiljunen, *Kampuchea*, pp. 22-23.

34. "Communist Quagmire," *New Republic*, January 21, 1978, pp. 5-6.

35. Sheldon W. Simon, "Kampuchea: Vietnam's 'Vietnam,'" *Current History* 77 (December 1979):197-198; and Kiljunen, *Kampuchea*, p. 22.

36. Craig Etcheson, *The Rise and Demise of Democratic Kampuchea* (Boulder, Colo.: Westview Press, 1984), p. 192.

37. Kiljunen, *Kampuchea*, p. 22; and "Cambodian Exodus," *Newsweek*, May 7, 1979, p. 50.

38. "Human Rights Situation in Cambodia," *Department of State Bulletin*, September 5, 1977, p. 323.

39. Ibid.

40. Warren Christopher, "Human Rights: Cambodia," *Department of State Bulletin*, February 1978, p. 32.

41. Cyrus Vance, "Question-and-Answer Session Following Cincinnati Address," *Department of State Bulletin,* June 1978, p. 19.

42. Ibid.

43. David Binder, *New York Times,* August 29, 1978, p. 21. Supplementary material from The New York Times News Service and the Associated Press.

44. Letter to President Carter from Rep. Les AuCoin, 1st District, Oregon, July 8, 1977. Jimmy Carter Library, White House Central File (hereinafter referred to as WHCF), Subject File, C081 (Kampuchea or Cambodia).

45. Letter to Jane Fonda from Edmund F. McWilliams, Jr., country officer for Laos and Cambodia, September 20, 1978, Jimmy Carter Library, WHCF. The Chinese, however, refused to raise human rights concerns with Phnom Penh. Binder, *op. cit.*

46. See letter to Cyrus R. Vance from Rep. Edward P. Boland, October 13, 1978; and letter to Rep. Morgan F. Murphy from Ed Strinko, September 13, 1978, Jimmy Carter Library, WHCF.

47. Memorandum to Richard Moe from Ray Jenkins, November 1, 1979, Jimmy Carter Library, Press Office, Jenkins, "Kampuchea (Cambodia), 1979."

48. Memorandum to Jody Powell from Frank Moore, October 25, 1979, Jimmy Carter Library, WHCF.

49. Letter to Sen. James O. Eastland, chairman, Committee on the Judiciary, from President Carter, October 4, 1977, Jimmy Carter Library, WHCF.

50. Telegram to President Carter from John Richardson, Jr., president of Freedom House, April 25, 1978; and letter to Leo Cherne, chairman, International Rescue Committee, from Zbigniew Brzezinski, May 17, 1978, Jimmy Carter Library, WHCF. Altogether, the United States agreed to accept twenty-five thousand additional refugees from Southeast Asia annually. "The Vice President: America's Role in Southeast Asia and the Pacific," *Department of State Bulletin,* July 1978, p. 25.

51. William Shawcross, *The Quality of Mercy: Cambodia, Holocaust and Modern Conscience* (New York: Simon and Schuster, 1984), pp. 188-190, 323-325.

52. Mark Frankland, "The End of Cambodia," *The New Republic,* October 27, 1979, pp. 12-14.

53. Shawcross, *The Quality of Mercy,* pp. 362-379.

54. "Contributions for Khmer Relief," *Department of State Bulletin,* April 1980, p. 33. For a discussion of some of the problems associated with food distribution, see Shawcross, *The Quality of Mercy,* Chapters 17 and 18.

55. Zbigniew Brzezinski, *Power and Principle: Memoirs of the National Security Adviser 1977-1981* (New York: Farrar, Straus and Giroux, 1983), pp. 3, 54. Normalization came about after negotiations in 1978, which led to the issuance of a joint communiqué. The United States would enter into full diplomatic relations with the People's Republic of China. The question of Taiwan would be resolved peacefully, and the United States would continue trade relations with that country. Jimmy Carter, *Keeping Faith: Memoirs of a President* (New York: Bantam Books, 1982), pp. 193-200, 210-211.

56. Frankland, "End of Cambodia," pp. 13-14.

57. Elizabeth Becker, *When the War Was Over: The Voices of Cambodia's Revolution and Its People* (New York: Simon and Schuster, 1986), pp. 385-392.

58. Ibid., p. 395.

59. Ibid., pp. 394-396.

60. Carter, *Keeping Faith,* p. 206.

61. Brzezinski, *Power and Principle,* p. 409.

62. Ibid., p. 411.

63. Ibid., p. 414.

64. "Ambassador Young, February 27, 1979," *Department of State Bulletin*, June 1979, p. 64. See also "Ambassador Young, February 23, 1979," *Department of State Bulletin*, June 1979, pp. 62-63.

65. "Ambassador Petree, March 16, 1979," *Department of State Bulletin*, June 1979, pp. 64-65.

66. "Issue of U.S.-SRV Relations," *Department of State Bulletin*, October 1979, p. 37.

67. "Kampuchean Credentials," *Department of State Bulletin*, December 1979, p. 57.

68. Gaddis Smith, *Morality, Reason and Power*, p. 50; Rosati, *Carter Administration's Quest*, pp. 44-45; and Brzezinski, *Power and Principle*, pp. 49, 124.

69. Henry Kissinger, *Years of Upheaval* (Boston: Little, Brown, 1982), pp. 335-369; Gerald R. Ford, *A Time to Heal* (New York: Harper and Row, 1979), pp. 243, 247; and Richard Nixon, *No More Vietnams* (New York: Avon Books, 1986), pp. 124, 175-176, 179.

70. Shawcross, *Sideshow*; and "Monsters in Our Footsteps," *Nation*, editorial, April 2, 1977, p. 388. Arnold Isaacs, while recognizing the responsibility of the Khmer Rouge for massive human rights abuses, argues that American policy from 1970 to 1975 contributed greatly to the suffering of the Cambodian people and helped to bring the Pol Pot government to power. See *Without Honor: Defeat in Vietnam and Cambodia* (Baltimore: Johns Hopkins University Press, 1983), pp. 194-240, 289.

71. Becker, *When the War Was Over*, pp. 384-385; and *Report of an Amnesty International Mission to the Socialist Republic of Vietnam, 10-21 December 1979* (London: Amnesty International, 1981).

72. For a discussion of views concerning the seating of Cambodian delegates in the United Nations, see the following articles by Bernard Nossiter: "Soviet Loses UN Skirmish over Cambodia's Seat," *New York Times*, September 20, 1974, p. A-7; and "UN Assembly, Rebuffing Soviet, Seats Cambodia Regime of Pol Pot," *New York Times*, September 22, 1979, pp. 1, 2.

73. Becker, *When the War Was Over*, pp. 393-394. For a more general discussion of the influence of domestic politics on human rights policies during the 1970s, see Sandy Vogelgesang, "Domestic Politics Behind Human Rights Diplomacy," in Tom J. Farer, ed., *Toward a Humanitarian Diplomacy: A Primer for Policy* (New York: New York University Press, 1980), pp. 49-92.

74. Lawrence L. Knutson, *New York Times*, August 22, 1978, pp. 76-78. Supplementary material from the New York Times News Service and the Associated Press.

75. Letter to John Maust, assistant, *Christianity Today*, from Jim Purks, special assistant media liaison, October 14, 1978, Jimmy Carter Library, WHCF.

76. Stanton, "Kampuchean Genocide"; and Hannum, "International Law."

77. See William Shawcross's comments about the reporting of recent tragedies in *The Quality of Mercy*, pp. 12-13, 385-386.

78. For some of the criticisms of Carter's human rights policy, see Fouad Ajami, "Human Rights: Sermons or Substance," *Nation*, April 2, 1977, pp. 389-390; and Carleton and Stohl, "Foreign Policy of Human Rights," pp. 205-229. See also Sandy Vogelgesang, *American Dream, Global Nightmare: The Dilemma of U.S. Human Rights Policy* (New York: W. W. Norton, 1980), for a discussion of some of the problems associated with our human rights policy. Vogelgesang briefly discusses the violation of human rights in Cambodia in ch.1.

Discussant: Gardel Feurtado

The discussion here has been very nonacademic, as we might expect when policymakers and their chroniclers gather; but sometimes returning to the ivy-covered walls is helpful in escaping the trap of looking at policy qua policy, as if the narrow issues of the moment that we address--what some of the participants here call "history"--enhance our insight. The assumption is that such policy "analysis"--really justification or defense of a particular administration's decisions--can actually enlighten us about world events and the underlying bases and contexts of the dynamics of the relations between nations. Given, however, that looking at policy within a limited time frame can tell us *some* things of significance. Although Jimmy Carter was roundly criticized for allegedly abandoning his human rights policy, the issue of human rights has become the cornerstone and the catalyst for much fundamental political change in the world (note the Philippines and China, for example).

But what was the framework within which President Carter attempted to restructure America's relations with Asia and Africa? The pure policy framework actually tells us little, and for this reason we need to remember the lessons of academe. I recall a long time ago, Harold Isaacs's *Scratches on Our Minds* addressed the superficial approach of the West to the non-West, particularly Asia. The thrust of this study was that our policies toward Asia suffered from our failure to fully comprehend the totality of the impact of the Western intrusions on the societies we so lightly label "non-West" or "Third World." And it seems to me, after observing the many years of profound economic, political, social, and cultural turmoil in the Third World, the "scratches" Isaacs deciphered on the modern mind remain that, and have not gone much deeper. Lack of historical insight results in policies devoid of compassion or realism. This, after all, was Isaacs's point: How can a country like America move beyond the superficial knowledge of the Third World and develop policies based on comprehension? We still do not know from whence comes this so-called Third World.

As I recall the three papers here, particularly how they perceive the United States, my reaction is that even someone as seemingly empathic and compassionate as Jimmy Carter misperceived the Third World confronting the United States. One of the most important conclusions of these well-researched papers is that Carter was unable to seriously come to terms with the history of the Third World, most especially when it directly contradicted the touchstone of American postwar foreign policy--the Cold War. Indeed, while most people in the Third World admire American democratic ideals and respect for individual rights, the "true" American history that counts, it seems, is the one Jimmy Carter in the end could not change: that America defined and structured its relations with Third World countries in terms of its Cold War struggle with the Soviet bloc. Anti-Americanism as such, then, is also policy-defined and -driven. For instance, America was not one of the principal colonial powers in terms of territory directly controlled, yet we are the current enemy. We need to go back and rethink some of these kinds of problems, because even Jimmy Carter misunderstood the people, the countries, and the regions he was dealing with.

For instance, if we start with the paper on India, it is clear that Carter believed he had a meeting of the minds with Indian Prime Minister Desai. But Desai was probably an anachronistic Third World leader. He was transitional between the policies established by Jawaharlal Nehru and those of Indira Gandhi. Nehru, for example, in his policy of nonalignment and neturalism as represented in the pronouncements of the Bandung Conference in 1954 and the Afro-Asian People's Solidarity Organization calling for Third World solidarity, coupled with institution building at home, contrasts sharply with Indira Gandhi's persistent willingness to undermine democratic institutions at home, coupled with her readiness to ally with one of the superpower blocs. For Gandhi, the issue was consolidating political power, and given the structure of world politics, no Third World nation could achieve that by adhering to a "nonaligned" foreign policy. This is no news; it occurs almost daily in the Third World. We hear rumblings of democracy, yet leaders seem to grasp at political power in ways Machiavelli might have marveled at. But this again is the datum of history that we sometimes ignore, and seemingly are incapable of comprehending even when it rears its head, as if our perception of what is needed is directly, in undistorted form, communicated to those we wish to influence.

This principle of perception--ours, as well as others'--is so critical, yet we walk by, our eyes askance. Jimmy Carter's "problem," I think, was that he believed his understanding of the Third World was universally valid, and that those countries so classified accepted his understanding of their history and their relations with America. Desai and Carter got along well. The former was an enigmatic personality, reminiscent of Mahatma Gandhi. Carter himself tended toward the introspective. At the same time, Desai vouchsafed private-sector development for India, a concern that was only just making inroads into American foreign aid policy. But Desai, for all that, did not have a substantial power base within India. Later, Carter was unable to work with Indira Gandhi, even as she sought to build a strong, independent, autonomous India. For her, this meant distancing India from the West and cementing close ties with the principal enemy of the United States, the Soviet Union, if necessary. Clearly, it did not help U.S. relations with Gandhi that we supported Pakistan. Jimmy Carter may have seen himself as the personification of the "new" United States of America-- the creator, in Dean Acheson's words, of a new world order. But the old world was not yet dead and buried. In fact, it continued to exist, full of vigor and threat, parallel to Carter's vision of the new world where human rights reigned supreme.

When we turn to Africa, as with India, we see most clearly Carter's predicament in this regard. The "globalists" in his administration were in a life-and-death struggle with the "regionalists," who called for American support for the development of strong African states as a way Africans could manage regional disputes, reducing the possibility and opportunity for superpower engagement on the side of client states. Both sides forgot the objective was to ensure the success of the Carter administration, not merely particular views on the shape of world politics. It is to state the obvious to note that regionally dominant African states would not automatically support American interests on the continent (or in other venues, such as international forums); this held true even for African states that received American economic assistance. That it was the person of "Jimmy Carter, nice guy," and a sympathetic American black official (Andrew Young) behind this new American posture toward Africa seemed to make precious little difference in the political gaming on the continent.

U.S. policy foundered despite the best efforts of the Carter administration (for instance, the treaty returning control of the Panama Canal to the Republic of Panama engendered only a few expressions of gratitude from the Third World). The shoals upon which Carter's policies failed in part lay in the history of the Third World and how we perceive that history. The very use of the term "Third World" suggests that the member countries share a common history and that their postcolonial relations with the West--in this case, America--must perforce be similar. Given, they were all affected by the phenomena of imperialism and colonialism. But the time sequences were different: At least for the major geographic-cultural regions, the beginnings of Western intrusion differed, as did the modes of colonial administration, and the time and manner of their eventual independence.

Third World elites, of course, willingly accepted the term and used its implications of solidarity and unity of large parts of the world to gain leverage and advantage against the Western powers. Organizations such as the Group of 77 (G-77) and the nonaligned movement, and the various United Nations efforts, such as UNCTAD conferences in the areas of science and technology, education, and the role of women, with their focus on both economic and political issues in development, grew from the earlier movements, such as the Bandung Conferences and the Afro-Asian People's Solidarity Organization in the 1950s and 1960s, which were highly critical of the West and the attempt to divide the world into two power blocs.

But the truth of the matter is that Third World history regarding the West is variegated, and this affects the response to U.S. policy-making efforts. Briefly, there is a genuine history (not just that manufactured by ruling elites to justify their power) behind the "radical regimes" that it appears Carter did not fully appreciate. For example, Latin American countries experienced independence long before African countries. Moreover, the Latin American elites rarely were unclear about the postindependence path they would follow. Their future lay with the West; to them, Latin America was an extension of white Europe. Incorporating the indigenous populations of Latin Ameri can into the political movements and giving them a role in determining the future of the various countries were therefore never issues for these elites, since the nations were destined to become overseas versions of modern Europe. The Latin Americans' political ideology, which derived from classical liberalism, supported these perceptions.

In Africa, on the other hand, independence movements sought indigenization and a mass base--although the commitment to mass participation was, in many cases, a cover for attaining political power and constructing popular dictatorships. In addition, the African elites in many cases were strongly influenced by the dominant international ideology at the time of the emergence of pressures for independence: revolutionary Marxism.

The above, I think, sketches out some of the unacknowledged hard issues in U.S. policy toward the Third World that the three papers presented to this panel draw on in various degrees. Clearly, the Carter administration was caught between the seeming necessity to play Cold War global power politics--and had, in fact, appointed someone to guide this effort: National Security Adviser Brzezinski. One gets a sense of division within the Carter administration, that there was fundamental disagreement among Carter's top aides on the conduct of policy. In any case, Brzezinski and U.N. Ambassador Andrew Young, the latter the apparent moving force behind the "new" approach to the Third World, sought to satisfy different constituencies even as they needed to persuade the president of the validity of their positions.

In the harsh light of the media and the subsequent public perception of the administration's foreign policies, explanations that underneath the public disarray was a fundamental unity in goals and instruments are weakened. Even at the time, such statements were relegated to the inside pages of newspapers while the disagreements and infighting received front page treatment. When an issue such as Cambodia emerged, it became the litmus test: Can Carter really do it? Will he really adhere to his personal commitment to defend human rights where they are violated, given the seemingly immovable Cold War issues that made Southeast Asia a pawn in superpower policies?

Clearly, we have a very complex issue here, an issue that the three papers on this panel shed light on. The strong reaction to the suggestion that conflict existed in the administration over the viability of Andrew Young's "new" approach to the Third World, in light of Brzezinski's championing of a firm posture toward the Soviet Union, affirms this point. The adoption of the global Cold War position jeopardized the "new" Third World policy because U.S. aid, alliances, and subsidiary efforts in Asia and Africa, as the papers demonstrate, could be delimited and shaped only by considerations of their effect on the larger, more important struggle against the Soviet Union.

Discussant: Guo-Chung Huan

I'm going to talk briefly about the papers. There are a few issues involved here. One is, of course, the principle itself: What kind of principle the was United States, at the time, formulating and implementing in its foreign policy--not only globally but also regionally? I think human rights had become one of the principles. I use the term "principles" because other principles were involved. The second issue involved here is, of course, how do you define national interests? I think human rights was certainly part of it for Carter, but he had other national interests as well--economic, political, strategic. The third issue involved, if he decided what he wanted--whether you have the ability to do it--is, I think, quite important. Some people here, and one of the papers, asked, What can you do, how much can you do, and at what kind of costs? And those kinds of issues, it seems to me, are fundamental when we're talking about human rights, vis-à-vis other foreign policy issues.

More than that, if you look at the situation in South Asia, the relation between Pakistan and India, I think it's much more complicated, particularly during the Carter administration. Not only have you one country publicly announcing that it's committed to human rights and democracy; another country probably still had a military dictatorship. What about India's internal human rights situation? What about Indian relations with the Soviet Union? These kinds of things are not only what we call globalism but also regionalism. How to make sure the two countries do not have war? For me to suggest that because India is a country supporting the U.S. human rights principle, the United States therefore should be on the side of India, not Pakistan, seems to me a little bit too simple. The relation between these two countries is much more complicated than that you have a democratic system in India, and a military dictatorship in Pakistan. You do have a cultural history, and even religious conflicts between these two countries. That's one point I want to make.

The second thing, talking about Cambodia: The United States couldn't do much to stop the killing. What can you do? Nothing much. And that's why the whole issue can be divided in two phases: one is before the invasion and one after the invasion. The second issue involved here is, of course, China. More specifically, what kind of leverage did the United States have to press China to stop its support of the Khmer Rouge? At least at that time, I did not see much.

Second, particularly after the invasion, China and the United States started a diplomatic relationship, and they both tried to get the Vietnamese out. And the key issue here is, if the Vietnamese get out--as they did in 1989--what will happen? If we are going to war, the Khmer Rouge will probably win the war. They will probably kill many people again. So I think the issue involved here is, we see the tragedies and the horrible massacring by the Khmer Rouge; the question is, what can we do? I think that there are limited means available that the United States can use, and that there was limited access to the resources the United States had in the 1970s, during Carter's administration.

And today, of course, the situation is a little bit different, not because the policy has changed that much, but largely because the geopolitics has changed; it's easy today to talk about what's going on there, largely because the Cold War is over. But when the Cold War was still going on, I think the policy issues were very different. And in 1979, you had a Soviet invasion of Afghanistan. If you add those things together, I think the policy issues have to be much more complicated than what we have thought about. For instance, the Soviet-sponsored Vietnamese invasion actually benefited the Cambodian population. But on the other hand, it's not ended yet. What about boat people from Vietnam? You have a lot of other things to be considered.

What I'm saying is that it's not easy to draw a generalization, to categorize Carter's foreign policy, to say it is simply the contradiction or conflicts between moral principles, on the one side, and political calculation, on the other. Sometimes these two have to be put together.

Discussant: Murray Silberman

I would like to make some observations on all three papers, recognizing that I'm a little bit of an expert on each area, perhaps a little bit more on Africa. One point that strikes me in all three papers is that despite promises and pronouncements about the need for a regionalist approach, or a more regional approach, to problem solving, the United States, by the time the Carter administration came to an end, tended to find itself following the globalist approach, which I think is something of a code word for East-West conflict. We saw this in India, notwithstanding Carter's visit to India. By the time his administration was over, he tended again to approach U.S.-Indian relations in terms of the Cold War. Of course, the Afghanistan issue made this almost a certainty, India being a frontline state, offering all sorts of possibilities for helping the United States aid the Afghan insurgents.

We saw this as well in Africa, where Jimmy Carter--who also made a trip to Africa, to Lagos--talked about promoting economic development and human rights. And by the time his administration came to an end, he was just mucking around in the Horn of Africa. Yesterday he said he had never heard of the Ethiopian conflict-- excuse me, the Eritrean civil war. Anyone who takes a course in African history knows about the Eritrean conflict. It was totally incredible to me that here was a civil war that had been going on since 1960, at least, and he had never heard of it. I'm sure that people like Brzezinski did hear of it; this was simply a footnote in his larger scheme of promoting or pursuing a globalist approach to resolving conflict between the United States and the Soviet Union.

I'd like to focus on Asia and Africa, and to point up some of the ambivalences or the tensions in the Carter administration's approach to the Horn of Africa, about which I know a little bit. Carter came to office promising of deal with problems on a regional basis, and part of that was to champion human rights. However, when the conflict broke out between Somalia and Ethiopia, he made a number of fundamental mistakes, some of which were due to a visceral approach by Brzezinski, as well as Carter, toward viewing Africa through an East-West prism. Number one, he did not understand the emerging forces in the Horn of Africa; he did not understand Somali interests in the Ogaden; he did not understand the Somalis' desire--and I'm not justifying it; I'm merely explaining it--to unite the Somalis in Djibouti and the Ogaden and northwest Kenya under one Somali flag. He did not understand that by giving arms to a Somali government, he was virtually giving tacit support to any enterprise it was planning in the Ogaden, despite all disclaimers to the contrary. To give weapons to Siad Barre meant, in effect, to support this enterprise.

Carter also failed to build on the very long relationship that had existed between the United States and Ethiopia. One has to keep in mind that Ethiopia had been an important friend, or ally, or client--what have you--of the United States. There was a long tradition of providing military and economic support to Ethiopia. Some of the leading elites in Ethiopia's military, including members of the Derg who took power, had undergone military training in the United States. Carter quickly assumed that these people were Marxists; instead of attempting to investigate this situation, instead of trying to bring the Derg to a more moderate policy, he simply wrote them off and stopped providing military support, on grounds that the leaders of this military junta were violating human rights.

Of course, the violation of human rights is an integral aspect of conducting politics in Ethiopia, and it's no less true in Somalia. Why Carter would abandon Ethiopia and support Somalia, which had no more of a brilliant record in the field of human rights, can be explained only in terms of the East-West conflict, and a basic lack of understanding of what was going on in this very important part of Africa. And what did Carter do? He was prepared to exchange--if I may use this metaphor--a pearl for a pebble. He was prepared to exchange, as an ally, Ethiopia for Somalia. Consider, for a moment, the differences between these two countries. Ethiopia was one of the few countries in Africa that had never been under colonial domination. Ethiopia was the seat of the Organization of African Unity. Ethiopia had a population of some thirty-four million people, as against a far smaller population for Somalia. Ethiopia was considered, in many respects, a major power in Africa.

Carter jettisoned all this because there were Marxists in Addis Ababa. Whether this was true or not at that stage--it still is hard to know for sure--the result was a flip-flop. His support went to Somalia; the Americans moved into the bases that the Soviets had had in Berbera; the Russians moved into Ethiopia. Of course, they also inherited a mess--the war in Eritrea and the Ogaden. Nonetheless, this behavior reflected a lack of understanding on the part of the Carter administration, and it exploited the human rights issue as one justification to abandon a long-standing ally, charging that Addis Ababa was violating human rights. The United States thus engaged in a policy that led to the introduction, in a very serious way, of the Cold War into the Horn of Africa.

So there was something of a self-fulfilling prophecy. It's still uncertain whether this area would have become a site of East-West tensions; that might have happened in any event. But there's no doubt that the United States contributed, just as the Soviet Union did. My feeling is that had there been a willingness on the part of the Carter administration to persist with its regional approach to problem solving in Africa, this tremendous problem might not have developed in the Horn of Africa. There might have been more of an attempt to bring both sides together--say, in Eritrea--just as President Carter is trying to do now that he's out of office. There might have been an attempt at that stage to deal with the problems between Somalia and Ethiopia. These are not problems that cannot be resolved; if anything, we see indications now that both governments are willing to settle their outstanding differences. This policy also introduced a considerable militarization in the whole region, because the Kenyan government was deeply afraid of the Somali militarization, the armaments that were being poured into Somalia by the United States. So the United States, by pursuing a Cold War position, created a situation of hostility and tension in the region that I believe was not necessary, and could have been avoided had there been a more sensitive approach to dealing with this area.

There was a tendency on the part of the Carter administration to say that they understood the Third World. This was, to my way of thinking, an exaggeration. There was no real understanding. They were willing to understand it in terms of what they believed was the reality of Third World politics and Third World economics, in terms of the larger ethos they still had not disabused themselves of: the ethos of East-West conflict, which Brzezinski represented and Carter, at key moments, supported. And in the final analysis, we saw that in India, the United States supported an East-West approach; we saw this in Africa and in other parts of the world.

Questions and Answers

DeJanes: First of all, Professor Silberman's brilliant comments have negated any need for me to say a great deal, so let me read one quote. The changes in Jimmy Carter, in the Carter administration, came when Carter stopped fighting the Washington establishment on tax reform, energy policy, and a host of other issues. In foreign affairs, this most definitely came when Carter began to rely on the flawed and bitterly jingoistic advice of Brzezinski. As that grand old curmudgeon of the establishment, Averell Harriman, observed to Edmund Muskie in the spring of 1980, "The administration had come off the track, particularly because of Zbig's advice. Brzezinski was with the President all day, and was giving him a lot of distorted judgments."

Q: Could Carter have pursued a policy regionally, given the political climate? He had Reagan breathing down his back shortly. Could he have gone to a regional approach, even if he had wanted to? Was it a realistic possibility?

Feurtado: I have one comment. Mr. Silberman made a comment that now it seems to be working, and Carter is pushing that approach. Even though I was critical of his globalist approach, I still wonder, at that time, whether the Soviet Union would have sat back and allowed us to do it without interfering. But it might have been worth trying, in any case, even with that. That's the point of view I would take on it.

Silberman: I think that where a regional approach was tried--and we saw this with the Camp David agreements--where the Soviets had a far greater interest in the Middle East, Carter did succeed. I think that one has to create, number one, an intellectual and a policy context in which to carry this out. The Camp David process created such a context, which made possible the treaty between Egypt and Israel. I think if there was a similar commitment in Ethiopia, for example, the same might have happened. I'm not so sure the same might have happened in Cambodia. Nonetheless, even if so many people were killed by this regime, the Carter administration still supported the decision to support the Pol Pot claim to the U.N. seat. I was in New York at the time; I was a member of the U.N. Secretariat. I have been in touch with friends of mine who were members of the U.N. Mission at the time, and there was a great deal of unhappiness over the willingness of the Carter administration to support the claim of the Pol Pot regime for the seat. And taking into account the vast numbers of people who were killed, this is still hard for me to explain and justify.

THE PANAMA CANAL TREATIES

16

Foreign Policy Interest Groups and Presidential Power: Jimmy Carter and the Battle over Ratification of the Panama Canal Treaties

DAVID SKIDMORE

Under the strains produced by the Vietnam War, the Cold War consensus of the 1950s and 1960s gave way during the early 1970s to a decade of intense elite conflict over the direction of American foreign policy. Survey analyses reveal the emergence of several separate elite groupings, each committed to a distinct and internally coherent belief system. The most politically significant cleavage divided Cold War conservatives from post-Cold War liberals.[1]

Relatively little research has been done, however, to uncover the political consequences of this division in elite opinion. In particular, we need to know much more about how these competing elites organized themselves politically and what sorts of constraints these forces placed upon presidential power. Only with such knowledge can we understand the significance of elite divisions for the actual making of U.S. foreign policy.

By examining the debate over ratification of the Panama Canal treaties, I hope to shed light upon the political organization of competing liberal and conservative factions of the U.S. foreign policy elite at a particularly crucial point during the 1970s. By the time of the Panama Canal treaties debate, the battlelines between liberals and conservatives had been well established; indeed, a great deal of political mobilization and coalition building had already taken place on both sides. Early skirmishes between liberal and conservative forces over issues such as arms control and détente had, however, brought only inconclusive results. The battle over the Panama Canal treaties emerged as the first major test of the strength of the two coalitions. The outcome of the ratification debate, coming early during the term of liberal President Jimmy Carter, would greatly influence the domestic political viability of Carter's foreign policy agenda.

Both sides therefore saw the treaties debate as a pivotal contest and as an excellent opportunity for mobilizing supporters and consolidating organizational networks in anticipation of future battles. Each side had reason to believe that victory could be theirs. Liberals took comfort from the fact that the power of the presidency fell on their side. Conservatives counted on the high hurdle set by the constitutional requirement that treaty ratification must be by two-thirds of the Senate. Liberals and conservatives alike hoped that a win on the Panama Canal treaties would provide momentum for their future efforts to exert control over U.S. foreign policy.

In the end, the outcome of this important contest proved ambiguous for both sides. Carter and his liberal supporters won the battle with a narrow Senate vote favoring ratification. Yet the Panama debate revealed the frailty of the liberal interest group network. Victory rested not upon the political and organizational strength of the liberal coalition but, rather, upon the surprisingly sophisticated political skills of President Carter. Yet Carter's virtuoso performance was hardly the sort of asset that could be relied upon in the long run to fend off an increasingly well-organized and well-endowed conservative opposition.

Conservatives emerged strengthened from the battle despite their defeat. While no doubt disappointed at the results of the Senate vote, conservative leaders could rejoice at the astonishing successes achieved in mobilizing grass roots opposition to the treaties. The treaties debate provided opportunities for refining the tactics and organizational forms that later proved effective in tapping popular support for a wide-ranging conservative agenda on both foreign and domestic issues.

SETTING THE STAGE FOR A SHOWDOWN

The Panama Canal negotiations resulted in two agreements: one providing for the gradual transfer of management of the canal from the United States to Panama by the end of the century, and the other providing for the canal's neutral status and U.S. defense rights after the year 2000. The Carter administration considered these treaties emblematic of its new approach to U.S.-Latin American, and more generally U.S.-Third World, relations. Carter's foreign policies would show greater sensitivity toward the symbolic sources of North-South tension. Before his appointment as U.S. negotiator on the Panama accords under Carter, Sol Linowitz wrote that the long-standing dispute between the United States and Panama over the status of the canal "significantly affects the relationship between this country and the entire Third World, since the nations of the Third World have made common cause on this issue--looking upon our position in the Canal as the last vestige of a colonial past which evokes bitter memories and deep animosities."[2]

Fearing that a continued impasse between the United States and Panama over the issue could lead to violent attacks upon the canal, Carter pursued a speedy diplomatic solution. As Secretary of State Vance suggested in 1977, the pacts symbolized the administration's emphasis on preventive diplomacy: "These treaties . . . are, above all, a triumph for the principle of peaceful and constructive settlement of disputes between nations. That is a principle we seek to apply in all aspects of American foreign policy."[3]

Another important purpose in seeking a quick settlement of the Panama Canal dispute sprang from the Carter administration's hopes that a victory on Senate ratification would strengthen its domestic position with respect to other foreign policy issues. As the Senate debate over the treaties neared, Richard Strout of the *New Republic* observed that "Carter would like to make a battleground of the new Panama Canal Treaty, in hopes of . . . using the victory as momentum for tougher tests yet to come."[4] The most important of these, of course, was the SALT II Treaty, still under negotiation at the time. Indeed, according to the *New York Times*, Carter told aides that "the fate of the treaties [would] set the tone for the remainder of his first term."[5]

With respect to this last objective, the treaties proved a bitter disappointment to the administration. Though Carter succeeded in negotiating a new agreement with Panama and even managed a narrow victory in the Senate on ratification, the experience did little to advance his overall foreign policy agenda. Instead, Carter found his efforts mired in controversy, and the high price the administration paid for its final triumph provided a measure of its domestic weakness.

MOBILIZING THE OPPOSITION

The Panama Canal treaties proved among the most contentious pieces of legislation in American history. Certainly no treaty or set of treaties had ever brought forth a comparable level of interest group opposition. The list of groups that mounted substantial campaigns against the treaties is a long one. It includes the American Conservative Union, the Conservative Caucus, the Committee for the Survival of a Free Congress, Citizens for the Republic, the American Security Council, the Young Republicans, the National Conservative Political Action Committee, the Council for National Defense, Young Americans for Freedom, the Council for Inter-American Security, and the Campus Republican Action Organization.[6]

The coalition mobilized in opposition to the treaties was notable not only for its unusual size and breadth but also for the novelty, sophistication, and effectiveness of the techniques employed by its member groups. Conservatives mounted a highly organized and well-endowed campaign built around a populist, grass-roots strategy for rallying opposition to the treaties. Treaty opponents focused principally on influencing public opinion and only secondarily on direct congressional lobbying. Conservatives saw the anti-treaties campaign as part of a long-term strategy for building popular strength and reasserting control over the nation's foreign policy agenda. In line with these goals, the rationales that conservatives used in urging opposition to the treaties often focused less on the canal issue itself than on broader themes relating to America's role in the world. Attacks on the treaties became a vehicle through which conservatives sought to challenge the overall worldview epitomized by the Carter administration and its liberal supporters.

One of the striking features of this campaign was the high degree of coordination among the groups involved. Altogether, twenty anti-treaty organizations cooperated through two ad hoc umbrella groups: the Committee to Save the Panama Canal and the Emergency Coalition to Save the Panama Canal. According to Michael Hogan, these groups played a critical role in coordinating the activities of their member organizations. Through them, "The heads of various organizations planned and coordinated strategy and divided tasks. They taught each other lessons learned in earlier campaigns and they pooled their resources to sponsor projects beyond the means of individual groups."[7]

This was not the only occasion during the Carter years when conservative groups mobilized under ad hoc coalitions. Similar umbrella organizations sprang up to manage the campaigns against the confirmation of Paul Warnke as Carter's arms control negotiator, the battle over the fate of the B-1 bomber, and the Senate ratification of SALT II. Indeed, many of the same groups involved themselves in all four efforts. This proved an innovative and effective means of making the most efficient use of the resources collectively available to Carter's opponents.

Anti-treaty groups placed secondary emphasis on direct congressional lobbying and rejected the path of bargaining with the administration over specific treaty terms. These traditional sorts of interest group activities were generally eschewed in favor of a grass-roots, populist strategy designed to generate and mobilize public opposition to treaty passage. In contrast with the Carter administration's strategy for gaining treaty approval, which "emphasize[d] direct appeals to the Senators and to opinion leaders throughout the country," conservatives focused on gaining "public support directly, with the hope that such support [could] influence the Senators' decisions."[8]

As Richard Viguerie, a conservative political activist, explained:

We're doing some direct lobbying but not as much as the White House. Our strength is not in Washington. Our strength is in Peoria and Oshkosh and White River Falls. And that's where we're going. We want to have the Senators and Congressmen hear from the folks back home, and the closer it gets to Election Day, talking to Ham Jordan and Gen. Brown isn't going to be that effective when the Senator has by that time accumulated 80,000 letters, 20,000 phone calls, 10,000 telegrams against the Treaties, or when 80 percent of his home state press is hollering at him.[9]

Treaty opponents devoted impressive sums of money to this strategy. Their principal weapons included a massive direct mail campaign supplemented by paid media advertising. To provide some sense of the dimensions of this crusade, it is worth detailing the activities of some of the more prominent groups involved in efforts to defeat the treaties. The American Conservative Union spent $1.4 million, sent out 2.4 million pieces of mail, broadcast a 30-minute video on 150 stations in 18 states (seen by an estimated 10 million viewers), and took out newspaper ads in 30 cities. The American Security Council and the Council on Inter-American Security each sent out 2 million pieces of mail while the latter group also ran radio spots in 13 states. The Conservative Caucus spent $850,000, shipped 2 million pieces of mail, mounted a national billboard campaign, held rallies in all 50 states, advertised on 500 radio stations, and sent a fact-finding mission to Panama. The National Conservative Political Action Committeee sent out 500,000 pieces of mail, and the Young Americans for Freedom collected 35,000 names on petitions. Many other groups weighed in with smaller efforts.[10]

The most obvious and immediate purpose of all this activity was to place public pressure on the Senate to reject the Panama Canal treaties. To this end, many groups targeted their efforts on undecided senators. The Committee to Save the Panama Canal, for example, dispatched a "truth squad" on a seven-city speaking tour through states represented by uncommitted senators. This "truth squad" consisted of conservative politicians such as Senator Paul Laxalt and Ronald Reagan, as well as retired military officers such as Admiral Thomas Moore, former chairman of the joint chiefs of staff, and General Daniel Graham. As expressed by Graham, the group's principal message was that other nations would consider handing over the canal "an act of weakness" on the part of the United States.[11]   One senator targeted by the group was Colorado's Floyd Haskell. At an event in Denver, Paul Wyrich, a political consultant to the "truth squad," explained, "We feel a definite show of constituent sentiment might help [Senator Haskell] clarify his thinking."[12]

Yet the principal organizers of the anti-treaties campaign saw its goals in broader terms from the outset. Derailing Senate ratification was only a proximate objective. The fight against the treaties was viewed as a vehicle for building a conservative movement and challenging the legitimacy of the foreign policy worldview espoused by the Carter administration.

Gary Jarmin, legislative director of the American Conservative Union, considered the Panama Canal dispute "a good issue for the conservative movement. It's not just the issue itself we're fighting for. This is an excellent opportunity to seize control of the Republican Party."[13]

Jarmin's hopes were not disappointed.   The Republican National Committee officially joined the anti-treaty campaign when it voted "overwhelmingly" to oppose ratification at a meeting in late September 1977. The committee's resolution included language denouncing the "fragmented, reactive, inconsistent and dangerously weak" foreign policies of the Carter administration. Terrence Smith, in his report on the event for the *New York Times*, commented, "The vote seemed to be an expression of . . . the increasing strength of the conservative elements in the party."[14]

Viguerie, who masterminded the use of direct mail as a means of mobilizing support for conservative causes, shared Jarmin's views on the broader purposes of the anti-treaties fight:

It's an issue the conservatives can't lose on. If we lose the vote in the Senate, we will have had the issue for eight or nine months. We will have rallied many new people to our cause. We will have given our supporters an issue, a cause to work for. The Left has had this over the years and the Right hasn't. . . . Now conservatives can get excited about the Panama Canal giveaway and they can go to the polls, look for a person's name on the ballot who favored these Treaties and vote against him.[15]

Consistent with these objectives, the popular message crafted by treaty opponents stressed the broader ideological symbolism of giving up control over the canal far more than any concrete interests that might be damaged by the treaties' passage. While opponents of the treaties often argued that the Panama Canal was still vital to American military and economic interests, and that continued American control was the best way to secure those interests, these aspects of the debate were, as George Moffett suggests, "largely subordinated to popular frustrations over the 'vanished mastery' of the United States."[16]

Conservatives adroitly played upon public uncertainty over America's global role in the wake of Vietnam. Opponents of the new accords treated the "giveaway" of the Panama Canal as symbolic of America's declining power and as proof that this erosion of dominance was due not to long-term trends in world politics but to mismanagement of the nation's foreign policies and a lack of will on the part of America's leaders generally and of Jimmy Carter in particular. Treaty foes also closely linked the canal issue with the East-West conflict and fears of communism by portraying Panama's Omar Torrijos as a "Marxist thug" and raising fears, in retired Admiral Thomas

Moore's words, of a "Torrijos-Castro-Moscow Axis."[17] New Hampshire governor Meldrim Thomson incorporated both these themes in his warning that America must "stand brave and firm for freedom in this real world of spreading Communism" or "crawl into historical obscurity in the face of the hysterical howling of world opinion."[18]

New Right spokesman Phillip Crane presented the case against the treaties in similarly apocalyptic terms in a book distributed widely by anti-treaty forces during the Senate debate. Crane warned that surrendering to Panama on the issue of the canal would be "one more crucial American step in a descent into ignominy--to the end of America's credibility as a world power and deterrent to aggression."[19] According to Howard Phillips, head of the Conservative Caucus, the secret of the opposition's appeal was simple: "It's patriotism, and that's the issue we do the best with."[20]

The anti-treaty campaign struck a chord with significant segments of the public, resulting in great pressure on many senators to vote against the treaties. In response to conservative appeals, unprecedented numbers of constituents hammered the Senate with "a barrage of letters opposing the new Canal Treaties."[21] Cecil Crabb and Pat Holt report that "Hundreds of thousands of letters and postcards poured in, at one point in ratios as great as 300 to one against the Treaties."[22] According to Michael Hogan, "a radio and television blitz promoting the Conservative Caucus' 'pledge card' campaign flooded Senate mailrooms with the prefabricated, yet signed threats to 'never' vote for a Treaty supporter."[23] An ad placed by the American Conservative Union in the *Nashville Banner* asking readers to write their senator to oppose the treaties "generated some thirty-six hundred pieces of mail in Senator Howard Baker's office in only a week."[24] By November 1977, well over a year before the treaties came up for a vote in the Senate, Baker "had already received 22,000 letters on the issue, only 500 in support of the Treaties."[25] At one point, Missouri Republican John Danforth's office had received 12,284 anti-treaty letters, compared with only 241 in praise of the treaties.[26] These cases were not atypical. Hogan notes, "A compilation of Senate mail by the American Conservative Union showed that some Senators received as many as four thousand communications in a single week, with opposition to the Treaties running from 90 to 100 percent."[27]

IN SEARCH OF SUPPORT

The Carter administration's campaign in support of the treaties took a very different tack from that chosen by treaty opponents. The administration held little confidence that the public could grasp the complexities of the pro-treaty argument. More significantly, it lacked an extensive grass-roots network of interest groups upon which it could call for help. As a result, the administration relied principally upon appeals to opinion leaders, direct congressional lobbying, and a late television plea for public support by the president. When these proved inadequate, Carter found himself forced into difficult concessions on treaty language as well as some last-minute arm-twisting and logrolling in order to secure the votes necessary for passage.

As its campaign for ratification began in earnest, the administration found it especially worrying that interest group support for the treaties appeared so weak and disorganized. While liberal, religious, and business groups offered their aid, none seemed capable of or willing to mount especially vigorous efforts.

The assistance provided by liberal and religious groups proved especially disappointing. In contrast with conservative forces, these organizations failed miserably in their efforts to rally public support. Undoubtedly this was due in part to the fact that many such groups suffered from poor organization and scarce resources. Just as important, liberals found it difficult to craft a message that would resonate with the patriotic and ideological values of most Americans. Both liberal and religious groups often chose to stress moral as opposed to pragmatic themes. These sorts of arguments, which emphasized American guilt for past injustices toward Panama, proved both unpopular with the American people and in large degree contradictory to the themes preferred by the White House.

A recently organized foreign policy lobbying group known as New Directions emerged as one of the principal liberal groups to campaign on behalf of the treaties. Calling itself a "citizens lobby" akin to Common Cause, the group hoped not only to ensure passage of the treaties but also, in the manner of many conservative groups, to use the campaign as a vehicle to build a long-term, mass organization that could institutionalize pressure for a generally liberal set of U.S. foreign policies, such as those pursued by the early Carter administration. Funded by liberal groups such as the AFL-CIO, the Democratic National Committee, the United Auto Workers, the Americans for Democratic Action, and the Washington Office on Latin America, New Directions sent out a 1.1 million-piece mailing to liberal supporters asking for backing of the Panama Canal treaties. New Directions also set up a separate Committee for Ratification of the Panama Canal Treaties, which, however, possessed an operating budget of only $19,000.[28] Michael Hogan points out that the ambitious hopes of New Directions were soon dashed: "The group quickly learned . . . that few Americans would rally to liberal causes out of support for the Treaties. Instead of building its support with the Panama campaign, New Directions collapsed under the financial burden of its direct-mail effort."[29]

A variety of religious groups also mounted campaigns in support of the treaties. The National Council of Churches and the United States Catholic Conference publicly backed the treaties and financed the campaigns waged by the Washington Office on Latin America and the Ecumenical Program for Inter-American Communication and Action (EPICA). Organized religious backing, however, proved of dubious value to the administration. Some religious groups based their support for the treaties primarily upon moral grounds and a reading of history that branded U.S. involvement in Panama as "colonial."[30] The Carter Administration, however, feared that most Americans would reject a pro-treaty argument that featured the United States in the role of the villain and appealed to American guilt over past sins. The White House not only supported the treaties primarily on pragmatic groundsbut also believed that these would be most influential with the public and the Senate.

In his televised appeal to the American people, for instance, Carter stressed that "The most important reason--the only reason--to ratify the treaties is that they are in the highest national interest of the United States and will strengthen our position in the world."[31] The Carter administration, while it did raise the issue of "fairness" with respect to the legitimacy of Panamanian claims on the canal, rejected interpretations that charged the United States with "colonialism" and joined opponents in pointing with pride to the difficulties Americans overcame in building the canal.[32]

This led to considerable tension between the administration and a number of the religious groups involved in the pro-treaty campaign. The administration found itself uneasy with the support of those whose arguments struck moderates as "un-American," while many religious groups were disappointed that the administration seemed reluctant to base its appeal on the grounds of morality and American guilt. Indeed, one major group, EPICA, reversed its support of the treaties in protest over the manner in which the adminstration decided to "sell" the treaties as well as concerns that the treaties did not go far enough to right the historical wrongs done Panama.[33]

Business support proved ephemeral as well. Early during the pro-treaties campaign, the State Department helped organize the Business and Professional Committee for a New Panama Canal Treaty, which was backed by two dozen American multinational corporations. The group soon folded, however, after its organizational head had a change of heart about the treaties.[34]

Leaders of the Business Roundtable, the National Association of Manufacturers, and the U.S. Chamber of Commerce all lobbied persuasively for the treaties, but because their memberships were divided, none of those organizations took an official stance on the issue.[35]

The major business group to campaign on behalf of the Panama Canal treaties was the Council of the Americas, a group representing two hundred major corporations accounting for 90 percent of U.S. private investment in Latin American and the Caribbean. The council produced and distributed pro-treaty pamphlets, met with senators and opinion leaders, and courted broader business support. But the group shied away from grass-roots organizing or a visible public profile. This was because both the White House and the council "feared creating the public perception that the Treaties were 'written by Wall Street' for the benefit of big business."[36]

Another semiprivate elite organization involved in the campaign for treaty passage was the Committee of Americans for the Canal Treaties (COACT), which consisted of prominent political leaders. While nominally independent, COACT was, to a large extent, created and directed by the White House. It produced a handbook intended to guide the efforts of local organizers in mounting grass-roots campaigns on behalf of the treaties. This handbook was distributed to opinion leaders from around the country who were invited to the White House for briefings on the treaties. COACT's ambitions for stimulating local campaigns, however, proved wildly unrealistic. The enormously complex, expensive, and time-consuming plans and methods outlined in its handbook called for heavy commitments on the part of organizers. Yet, not surprisingly, very few of the local notables reached by the White House were so moved that they felt compelled to single-handedly rally the support of their communities behind the treaties.

COACT's contribution proved disappointing in other respects as well. It raised and spent only $350,000, compared with initial funding projections of $1 million. It placed some newspaper ad-vertisements and sent out 300,000 pieces of mail, but even its organizers conceded the ineffectiveness of its advocacy efforts on behalf of the treaties.[37]

On top of the weak interest group support, Carter received little help from the Democratic Party establishment. In October 1977, Carter, conceding that ratification of the treaties was "in doubt," appealed to the Democratic National Committee to "help him win over Congressional and public support" for treaty passage. He soon found the response disappointing, however, when the four hundred-member committee passed a resolution supporting the "treaty negotiations" and the "ratification process" but neglecting to endorse the treaties themselves.[38]

PULLING CHESTNUTS FROM THE FIRE

With only weak interest group support for the Panama Canal treaties, the burden of the pro-treaties campaign rested heavily upon the administration. Contrary to the common image of Carter as politically inept, the president performed brilliantly in guiding the treaties toward Senate passage against long odds.

Carter staffers flew hundreds of locally influential opinion leaders from around the country to the White House for elaborate briefings. It was hoped that by influencing public opinion in their communities, these allies could offset some of the political pressure to vote against the treaties that the Right's grass-roots campaign had placed on many senators. Carter also sent cabinet members and aides on extensive speaking tours on behalf of the treaties, carried out intensive lobbying among uncommitted or wavering senators, and made a major network television address on the issue shortly before the vote in the Senate.[39]

The Carter administration's public appeal stressed the pragmatic benefits to the United States from the treaties, as well as the safeguards contained within them to protect American interests. Carter argued that the United States and Panama shared common interests in keeping the canal open, and that the principal threat to the safety and operations of the canal might come from Panamanian resentment and anger were the treaties to be rejected. In his televised address, Carter predicted, "The new treaties will naturally change Panama from a passive and sometimes deeply resentful bystander into an active and interested partner whose vital interest will be served by a well-operated canal. This agreement leads to cooperation and not confrontation between our country and Panama."[40]

Defense Secretary Harold Brown indicated that the U.S. military could not hope to protect the canal from determined saboteurs: "According to the best informed military opinion, we can't defend the canal from a hostile Panama. It is too vulnerable to a sack of dynamite--or to a glove in the gears."[41] Brown, like Carter, argued that the treaties, by giving Panama a greater interest in the canal's continued operation and providing the United States with the right to act to protect the canal even after it was turned over to Panama, offered the best hope for the canal's future security. Brown's appeal was seconded by the joint chiefs of staff, who publicly threw their support behind the treaties.[42]

The administration also contended that passage of the treaties would remove a chronic irritant in U.S. relations with Latin America and rob radical nationalists throughout the region of a potent symbol of alleged U.S. "colonialism." Finally, Carter maintained that the U.S. image around the world would benefit from its perceived act of fairness toward a small country such as Panama. The treaties, he asserted, would "remove a major source of anti-American feeling" and "provid[e] vivid proof to the people of this hemisphere that a new era of friendship and cooperation is beginning and that what they regard as the last remnant of alleged American colonialism is being removed."[43]

Many senators remained concerned, however, over whether the language of the treaties offered sufficient legal protection of U.S. rights to protect the canal and expedite the passage of U.S. ships through it in case of war or emergency. These became critical issues in the Senate debate, and although Carter maintained that the treaties provided sufficient guarantees of these rights, the administration was forced to make a series of compromises that were designed to strengthen the treaties' assurances in these regards. Carter and General Torrijos of Panama first issued a clarifying statement affirming the right of the United States to defend the neutrality of the canal and to move U.S. ships to the head of the line in an emergency.

On the issue of defending the canal's neutrality, the Carter-Torrijos joint statement declared:

The correct interpretation [of the principle of U.S. intervention rights] is that each of the two countries shall, in accordance with their respective constitutional processes, defend the Canal against any threat to the regime of neutrality, and consequently shall have the right to act against any aggression or threat directed against the Canal or against peaceful transit of vessels through the Canal. This does not mean, nor shall it be interpreted as, a right of intervention of the United States in the internal affairs of Panama.[44]

The Senate subsequently insisted that the Neutrality Treaty be amended by the language contained in this statement. With Carter's tacit acquiescence, these "leadership amendments" passed overwhelmingly in the Senate.[45]

The Neutrality Treaty was the first to come to a vote in the Senate. As the vote approached, the White House was still unsure of passage. In this atmosphere of uncertainty, Carter was confronted with an unexpected development that almost led to Panamanian rejection of the treaties.

Senator Dennis DeConcini (D.-Arizona) demanded that a new condition be attached to the Neutrality Treaty that would be designed to strengthen U.S. defense rights of the canal still further. DeConcini "represented a conservative state where . . . opposition to the new pacts ran high."[46] Hoping to minimize the political damage of voting for the treaties through a highly visible effort to extract additional concessions from the president, DeConcini asked that language be inserted into the treaty guaranteeing that should the operations of the canal ever be interfered with, the United States had the independent right "to take such steps as it deems necessary . . . , including the use of military force in Panama, to reopen the Canal."[47] At least one other senator announced that his vote would turn on whether this condition was made a part of the Neutrality Treaty. Believing that the treaty would fall without these votes, Carter reluctantly endorsed DeConcini's condition despite his fears that the new language would cause problems with Panama.

Only after the passage of the Neutrality Treaty by a one-vote margin did it become apparent just how seriously Panama objected to the DeConcini condition.

Panamanians viewed its language as granting the United States the unilateral right to use military force for the purpose of interfering with Panama's internal affairs. Torrijos threatened to denounce the treaties on Panamanian television. The situation was salvaged only when Senate leaders helped Carter persuade DeConcini to accept an additional amendment to the second canal treaty designed to undo the damage caused by the original DeConcini condition. The new amendment stated that any action taken by the United States to defend the canal "shall not have as its purpose or be interpreted as a right of intervention in the internal affairs of Panana or interference with its political independence or sovereign integrity."[48] Inserted in the second Panama Canal treaty, which passed by a vote of 68-32, this language served to soothe Panamanian tempers.[49]

Both the leadership amendments and the DeConcini condition were important not so much for their substantive effects on the treaties--the rights they asserted were already guaranteed within the treaties to a substantial degree--as for the perception they helped to create that the Senate had forced a reluctant administration to toughen up the protection the treaties offered for U.S. interests. Many senators who felt under enormous pressure to oppose the treaties came around to supporting them once they could take credit for strengthening the treaties. Carter understood these concerns and proved flexible enough to accommodate them.[50]

Another factor that worked in Carter's favor was the widespread acceptance of claims that the administration's efforts to educate the public about the treaties, along with the leadership amendments, had produced a turnabout in public opinion on the issue. In fact, the evidence of such a shift in sentiment was very weak and was based primarily on misleading polling results. Nevertheless, the perception, however erroneous, that the public had finally rallied to the side of the administration played a crucial role in allowing Carter to convert a number of wavering senators to his cause in the days and weeks before the Senate vote.

Survey results on the Panama Canal issue were particularly sensitive to question wording. Some questions provided respondents with only negative information. These tended to produce overwhelming percentages against the treaties. The Opinion Research Corporation, for instance, was commissioned by an anti-treaty organization, the American Council for World Freedom, to ask people, "Do you favor the U.S. continuing its ownership and control of the Panama Canal or do you favor turning ownership and control of the Panama Canal over to the Republic of Panama?" This question contained no reference to the treaties being negotiated, to the transition period through the year 2000 before full control over the canal would be given to Panama, nor to the rights the United States would continue to enjoy through the treaties, both during and after the transition period. Moreover, by referring to "ownership," the question implied an answer to the controversial question of whether the United States held sovereignty over the Canal Zone or merely use rights.

Not surprisingly, when asked in May 1977, this question produced a stunning majority of 78 percent opposed to the transfer of the canal, compared with only 8 percent in favor. The early timing of the poll made these figures a misleading benchmark against which later polling results were measured. Later surveys, based upon less negatively biased questions, showed smaller majorities against the treaties and therefore allowed Carter to claim progress.[51]

This was especially the case since, as the treaty vote drew closer, some polling organizations began to provide more information in their questions, typically including implied rationales for favoring the treaties. Some questions, for instance, included reference to U.S. defense rights or to the leadership amendments. Whenever this sort of additional information was provided, the results tilted more in favor of the treaties and in some cases showed supporters outnumbering opponents. As polling organizations emulated one another in altering their questions over time to include more favorable information, the appearance of a trend was created.

In fact, this appearance waas misleading. The most neutrally worded questions simply asked respondents their position on the treaties without positive or negative qualifications. These neutral questions consistently produced 5-3 majorities against the treaties throughout the treaty debate. Indeed, a survey in June 1978, several months after the Senate vote, which simply asked respondents, "Do you think the Senate should have approved the Panama Canal Treaties or should not have approved them?" once again evoked the familiar 5-3 ratio against.[52] Michael Hogan, in his comments on trends in public support for the treaties, concludes that "the turnabout was illusory."[53] Carter nevertheless encouraged and astutely played upon these illusions to reassure nervous supporters that a vote for the treaties need not be politically damaging.

In addition to Carter's concessions on treaty language and perceptions that the public had become more supportive of the treaties, the other essential ingredient in his recipe for victory involved the wooing of individual senators whose votes were considered crucial.

Carter's political courtship of uncommitted senators did not always prove successful. As indicated earlier, passage of the first treaty remained in doubt even during the final days before the vote. Some senators who privately supported the treaties were too intimidated by opinion polls showing large majorities of the citizens in their home states against the treaties to take the risk of siding with the White House.

Senator Edward Zorinsky was a case in point. In his memoirs, Carter recalls that Zorinsky "said he wanted to vote for the Treaties," but he was concerned about "the lack of support back home."[54] As described by Thomas Franck and Edward Weisband, Carter went to comical extremes in his campaign to win over Nebraska's junior senator:

The Catholic Archbishop of Omaha was called to see what he could do about . . . Zorinsky. . . . Zorinsky, alone, got 250 Nebraskans invited to the White House. Every one of them accepted. Carter talked to the Senator on several occasions. Rosalynn Carter called Mrs. Zorinsky to hope she would urge her husband to do the right thing. Ambassador Sol Linowitz, one of the two top negotiators with Panama, played tennis with Zorinsky and, it is said, let him win. On the hill, the Senator was visited by Vice President Mondale, Zbigniew Brzezinski, Cyrus Vance, Defense Secretary Harold Brown, Treasury Secretary Michael Blumenthal, and even Henry Kissinger.[55]

Despite all of this, Carter's ardent pursuit of Zorinsky came to naught when the senator, deferring to home state pressure, cast his vote against the treaties.

Other senators proved more open to Carter's entreaties, but often at a steep price. Carter was able to nail down the final votes necessary to bring victory only by "pull[ing] out all the stops in dispensing favors to key Senators. For example, the administration switched positions on a government copper purchase, an important public works project, and a costly farm bill."[56] In return for his vote in favor of the treaties, Senator S. I. Hayakawa of California demanded and received assurances that Carter would consult with him in setting African policy, where Hayakawa was interested in seeing the United States support the white minority regime in Rhodesia, and respond more vigorously to Soviet and Cuban activities on the continent.[57] One high-ranking Carter official remarked, "I hope the Panamanians will get as much out of these treaties as some United States senators."[58]

THE PRICE OF VICTORY

Carter's carefully orchestrated campaign succeeded in nailing down the final votes necessary for treaty passage. This in itself was a daring political feat, one too often ignored by the many Carter chroniclers who trace his troubles to political naïveté.[59]

Nevertheless, Carter's "victory" on the Panama Canal treaties proved extremely costly. Gaddis Smith observed, "Ordinarily, a President grows stronger by winning a hard political fight. But Carter's narrow triumph, while it prevented possible disaster abroad, gained him no credit at home."[60] George Moffett has called the passage of the treaties "a Pyrrhic victory" for Carter and notes that "the administration was not able to generate any discernible sympathy for its guiding world view" from the treaty campaign.[61]

After the passage of the treaties, Hedrick Smith predicted that "this was not the kind of victory that will provide long term political momentum or produce much spillover for the Administration in Congress on . . . other key issues," such as arms control. Smith also noted that "Mr. Carter's final bargaining with a few individual Senators is not the kind of tactic that builds bloc support" in the Senate.[62]

Conservatives had vowed during and after the treaty fight that senators voting in favor of the treaties would be punished at the polls. This prediction was partially borne out. When the 1978 midterm elections arrived, conservatives targeted for defeat, with considerable success, a number of liberal senators who had helped lead the fight for passage of the treaties. George Moffett notes, "In the elections of 1978 and 1980, 20 of the 68 Senators who voted for ratification were defeated in bids for re-elections."[63] Only one senator who voted against the treaties, by contrast, was defeated for reelection in 1978 and 1980.

Another cost to the administration was that, as one contemporary account put it, "the President gave out many IOU's, using up political capital that might be needed later on."[64] Carter's success on the Panama Canal treaties weakened his ability to succeed in future legislative contests. Moderate senators from conservative states, such as Howard Baker, endured considerable criticism over their pro-treaty votes and came under great pressure to balance their vote on the canal by opposing later Carter foreign policy initiatives targeted for opposition by the Right, such as the SALT II treaty.[65]

All in all, Carter won the legislative battle but lost the political and ideological war. Conservatives outorganized Carter and his liberal supporters and clearly won the fight for public support. The struggle for ratification of the Panama Canal treaties proved a costly affair for Carter and helped encourage a growing cautiousness and conservatism in his approach to foreign affairs.

A LOPSIDED BATTLE: ORGANIZING INTERESTS
AROUND CARTER'S FOREIGN POLICIES

Perhaps the most important, and for Carter the most worrisome, political fact to emerge from the Panama Canal debate was the obvious contrast between the high level of organization among conservatives and the disorganization of Carter's supporters. Conservatives succeeded in using the canal issue as a rallying point for grass-roots support of conservative causes. During the anti-treaties campaign, conservative groups added four hundred thousand new members to their rolls.[66] Conservatives succeeded in working out a division of labor among the various groups in their coalition and pioneered new political techniques, such as direct mail, that allowed them to raise unprecedented amounts of money and mobilize thousands of supporters on relatively short notice. The momentum and experience gained from the treaty ratification debate made it far easier for conservatives to mobilize similar campaigns on other foreign policy issues in the ensuing years, thus placing Carter perpetually on the defensive. Opponents of the SALT II treaty, for instance, managed to outspend supporters by a ratio of 15 to 1.[67]

By contrast with conservatives, the coalition that stood behind Carter's foreign policies was deeply divided. The two distinct groups that supported Carter's policies found it difficult to work together, and each possessed liabilities that limited its popular appeal.

Carter's policies appealed first to the most internationally committed sectors of American business. These firms were generally more sensitive to global trends and pressures than firms less heavily engaged in international business. As a result, many of them appreciated the administration's preference for a cooperative rather than a confrontational foreign policy approach.

These sectors of the business community were heavily represented, for instance, on the Trilateral Commission, which served as Carter's training ground in foreign affairs and as the source for many of his foreign policy reforms. The same sorts of firms lobbied on behalf of the Panama Canal treaties through the Council of the Americas. Moffett remarks that the latter's support of the Panama Canal treaties "underscores the counter-intuitive fact that for four years the most natural constituency Jimmy Carter had for his new policies in the Third World were the banks and corporations. By virtue of long exposure in the developing world they were the first to comprehend the significance of the changing milieu to which the Treaties themselves were a direct response."[68]

The problem with relying heavily upon this set of allies was that such interests were concentrated in specialized elite circles and possessed little grass-roots organization, power, or appeal. They were weak precisely where conservatives were strong. In fact, close connection with such groups could prove damaging, as when conservatives charged that Carter was pushing the Panama Canal treaties in order to bail out big banks to whom Panama owed significant amounts of money.[69] Moreover, many of these groups, reticent about taking the spotlight for fear of just such populist attacks, were happy to let the White House carry the ball alone.

A very different source of support was available to the Carter administration. Many of Carter's policies appealed to ideological liberals, such as those who had protested the war in Vietnam and who could be found among activists on the left wing of the Democratic Party. These individuals were represented by groups such as New Directions and the Coalition for a New Foreign and Military Policy. Liberal church groups could also be included in this category.

Carter, however, generally avoided close ties with such groups. The reasons were several. Liberal groups often possessed too few resources to command much political clout. Moreover, ideological liberals tended to favor more far-reaching reforms than Carter was willing to contemplate.[70] As a result, a significant degree of distrust distanced ideological liberals from the White House. Finally, Carter feared, probably correctly, that explicit association with groups considerably to the left of the general public might hurt more than it would help the administration politically.

Given the asymmetries in the interest group environment Carter faced, it is not surprising that his early victory on the Panama Canal issue did not clear the way for domestic acceptance of other elements of his foreign policy agenda. Although a skilled political performance by Carter succeeded in overcoming concerted conservative opposition in the Panama case, the balance of forces during the late 1970s worked against the long-term success of Carter's efforts to bring about broad and lasting reforms in U.S. foreign policy.

NOTES

1. For findings on elite opinion during the 1970s, see especially James Rosenau and Ole Holsti, *American Leadership in World Affairs: Vietnam and the Breakdown of Consensus* (Boston: Allen and Unwin, 1984).

2. Quoted in George D. Moffett III, *The Limits of Victory: The Ratification of the Panama Canal Treaties* (Ithaca, N.Y.: Cornell University Press, 1985), p. 67. For a review of Carter's general Latin American policy written by a former Carter National Security Council staffer, see Robert Pastor, "The Carter Administration and Latin America: A Test of Principle," in John Martz, ed., *United States Policy in Latin America: A Quarter Century of Crisis and Challenge* (Lincoln: University of Nebraska Press, 1988).

3. Cyrus Vance, "Meaning of the Treaties," statement before the Senate Committee on Foreign Relations, September 26, 1977, reprinted in Elaine Adam, ed., *American Foreign Relations, 1977: A Documentary Record* (New York: New York University Press, 1979), p. 372.

4. Quoted in Moffett, *Limits of Victory*, p. 107.

5. Martin Tolchin, "White House Woos Holdouts on Canal," *New York Times*, March 14, 1978.

6. The larger project from which this paper springs is primarily concerned with tracing the evolution of competing liberal and conservative interest group coalitions over time and across issues during the 1970s. The discussion of the Panama Canal treaties debate, therefore, gives greatest attention to groups that played an enduring role in either of these coalitions while devoting little discussion to groups that were motivated by specific and particular ties to the Panama issue alone. Nevertheless, a number of such groups played significant roles in the treaties debate, including the

American expatriates, or "Zonians," who lived in the Canal Zone and lobbied against the treaties, and various maritime and economic interests, whose positions varied. On the former, see William Jordan, *Panama Odyssey* (Austin: University of Texas Press, 1984), pp. 302-303, 456. On the latter, see Moffett, *Limits of Victory*, pp. 181-202.

7. Michael Hogan, *The Panama Canal in American Politics: Domestic Advocacy and the Evolution of Policy* (Carbondale: Southern Illinois University Press, 1986), p. 120.

8. William Lanouette, "The Panama Canal Treaties--Playing in Peoria and in the Senate," *National Journal*, November 8, 1977, p. 1556.

9. Ibid., p. 1560.

10. The information contained in this paragraph has been drawn from David Maxfield, "Panama Canal: Groups Favoring Treaties Fight to Offset Opponents' Massive Lobbying Effort," *Congressional Quarterly*, January 21, 1978, p. 137; "Panama Canal Treaties Spurred Intense Lobby Effort as Supporters, Opponents Sought Senate Votes," *Congressional Quarterly Almanac* 4 (1978):389; "Panama Canal Fight: Senators Feel the Heat," *U.S. News & World Report*, February 13, 1978, pp. 37-38; Hogan, *Panama Canal*, p. 119; and Moffett, *Limits of Victory*, p. 171.

11. Graham Harvey, "Canal 'Truth Squad' Plans a 5-Day Blitz," *New York Times*, January 10, 1978, p. A-11.

12. Clyde Haberman and Caroline Rand Herron, "Truth Squad Marches On," *New York Times*, January 22, 1978, sec. 4, p. 2. Also see "Panama Canal Treaties Spurred Intense Lobby Effort," p. 389.

13. Lanouette, "Panama Canal Treaties," p. 1560.

14. Terence Smith, "GOP Committee Votes to Oppose Canal Treaties," *New York Times*, October 1, 1977, p. A-9.

15. Lanouette, "Panama Canal Treaties," p. 1560.

16. Moffett, *Limits of Victory*, pp. 172-173.

17. Ibid., p. 173; and Thomas Hollihan, "The Public Controversy Over the Panama Canal Treaties: An Analysis of American Foreign Policy Rhetoric," *Western Journal of Speech Communication,* Fall 1986, p. 371.

18. Quoted in Hollihan, "The Public Controversy of the Panama Canal Treaties." Thomson reportedly warned Senator Thomas J. McIntyre (D.-New Hampshire) that he would run against McIntyre in the 1978 election if McIntyre voted for the treaties. See "Panama Canal Fight: Senators Feel the Heat," *U.S. News & World Report*, February 13, 1978, p. 37.

19. Quoted in Craig Allen Smith, "Leadership, Orientation and Rhetorical Vision: Jimmy Carter, the 'New Right,' and the Panama Canal," *Presidential Studies Quarterly,* Spring 1986, p. 323.

20. Ken Bode, "Carter and the Canal," *New Republic*, January 14, 1978, p. 9.

21. Moffett, *Limits of Victory*, p. 171.

22. Cecil V. Crabb, Jr., and Pat M. Holt, *Invitation to Struggle: Congress, The President, and Foreign Policy* (Washington, D.C.: Congressional Quarterly Press, 1980), p. 73.

23. Hogan, *Panama Canal*, p. 124.

24. Ibid.

25. Thomas Franck and Edward Weisband, *Foreign Policy by Congress* (New York: Oxford University Press, 1979), p. 198.

26. Bode, "Carter and the Canal," p. 8.

27. Hogan, *Panama Canal*, p. 121.

28. "Panama Canal Treaties Spurred Intense Lobby Effort," pp. 388-389.

29. Hogan, *Panama Canal*, p. 110.

30. One EPICA publication referred to the "colonial environment of the Panama Canal Zone," and another condemned the "gringos" for "the slaughter and exploitation of [Panama's] people." Modest pro-treaty campaigns were waged by religious groups taking more moderate positions.

Among these were the Synagogue Council of America, the Church of the Brethren, and the Disciples of Christ Christian Church. See Hogan, *Panama Canal*, p. 107.

31. Jimmy Carter, "The Treaties with Panama," radio and television address on February 1, 1978. Reprinted in Adam, *American Foreign Relations, 1977*, p. 347.

32. Carter himself refused to "condemn my predecessors for having signed" the original Panama Canal Treaty. Michael Hogan says that "pro-Treaty advocates refused to call the situation 'colonialism'" while the Carter administration encouraged "veneration for Theodore Roosevelt and the glorious canal-building project." Indeed, in his televised address, Carter claimed that Roosevelt would have supported the new canal treaties. While rejecting the charge of colonialism against the United States, the Carter administration did argue that existing arrangements harmed America's image in many parts of the world by creating the "perception of colonialism." This, however, was a pragmatic argument and not a moral judgment. It is also consistent with Hogan's observation that the administration preferred to build public support for the treaties around "reasons of expediency." Quotes from Hogan, *Panama Canal*, pp. 149-151.

33. Hogan reports that "Many religious leaders reconsidered their early support for the Treaties precisely because of the administration's refusal to indict the United States on charges of 'colonialism.'" See Ibid., p. 151. For more on the role of pro-treaty religious groups in the campaign, see also Moffett, *Limits of Victory*, pp. 140-144.

34. Hogan, *Panama Canal*, p 102.

35. Ibid., pp. 102-103.

36. Ibid., p. 103.

37. It is perhaps significant that, unlike many conservative groups opposed to the treaties, COACT disbanded following the Senate vote, thus diluting the organizational momentum that liberals might have derived from the treaties victory. The above account of COACT's activities rests upon Ibid., pp. 95-100; Moffett, *Limits of Victory*, pp. 82-85; and "Panama Canal Treaties Spurred Intense Lobby Effort," p. 388.

38. Terence Smith, "Carter Asks Democratic Leaders to Help Him on Panama Treaties," *New York Times*, October 8, 1977, p. A-24.

39. See Hogan, *Panama Canal*, pp. 92-95; and Moffett, *Limits of Victory*, pp. 71-112.

40. Carter, "The Treaties with Panama," p. 348.

41. Harold Brown, "Challenges Confronting the National Security," address before the World Affairs Council of Northern California, San Francisco, July 29, 1977, in U.S. Department of State, *American Foreign Policy: Basic Documents, 1977-1980* (Washington, D.C.: U.S. Government Printing Office, 1983), document 4, p. 12.

42. David C. Jones, the air force chief of staff, called the Panama agreement "a treaty the Joint Chiefs of Staff can fully support," and pledged that "we will do what we can to help its ratification." James Wooten, "Joint Chiefs Pledge to Help Carter," *New York Times*, August 12, 1977, p. A-6.

43. Carter, "The Treaties with Panama," p. 349.

44. Moffett, *Limits of Victory*, p. 90.

45. For a discussion of leadership amendments, see Ibid., pp. 87-92; and Hogan, *Panama Canal*, pp. 192-196.

46. Moffett, *Limits of Victory*, p. 97.

47. Ibid., p. 98.

48. Ibid., p. 103.

49. For a discussion of the DeConcini episode, see Ibid., pp. 96-106.

50. In addition to the sources cited above, information concerning congressional bargaining over the treaties can be found in William Furlong and Margaret Scranton, *The Dynamics of Foreign Policy-Making: The President, The Congress and the Panama Canal Treaties* (Boulder, Colo.: Westview Press, 1984).

51. Moffett, *Limits of Victory*, pp. 115-155, 209.

52. Based upon Roper survey. For results, see Ibid., p. 212.

53. Hogan, *Panama Canal*, pp. 200-207. Moffett echoes Hogan's view that the turnabout in public opinion was more illusion than reality. See Moffett, *Limits of Victory*, pp. 112-137. Also, for a survey of the public polling on the canal issue, see Bernard Roshco, "The Polls: Polling on Panama--Si; Don't Know; Hell, No!" *Public Opinion Quarterly*, Winter 1978.

54. Jimmy Carter, *Keeping Faith: Memoirs of a President* (Toronto: Bantam Books, 1982), p. 166.

55. Franck and Weisband, *Foreign Policy by Congress*, p. 277.

56. "Carter's Panama Triumph--What It Cost," *U.S. News & World Report*, March 27, 1978. On Carter's efforts to win votes through pork barrel politics, see also Franck and Weisband, *Foreign Policy by Congress*, p. 278.

57. For an account, see Carter, *Keeping Faith*, pp. 175-177.

58. Quoted in Tolchin, "White House Woos Holdouts."

59. For examples of interpretations that stress Carter's political ineptitude, see Kenneth Adelman, "The Runner Stumbles: Carter's Foreign Policy in the Year One," *Policy Review*, Winter 1978; Arthur Schlesinger, "The Great Carter Mystery," *New Republic*, April 12, 1980; Walter LeFeber, "From Confusion to Cold War: The Memoirs of the Carter Administration," *Diplomatic History*, Winter 1984; and Donald Spencer, *The Carter Implosion: Jimmy Carter and the Amateur Style of Diplomacy* (New York: Praeger, 1988).

60. Gaddis Smith, *Morality, Reason and Power: American Diplomacy During the Carter Years* (New York: Hill and Wang, 1986), p. 115.

61. Moffett, *Limits of Victory*, p. 107.

62. Hedrick Smith, "After Panama, More Battles," *New York Times*, April 20, 1978, p. 1.

63. Moffett, *Limits of Victory*, p. 176.

64. "Carter's Panama Triumph."

65. John Spanier, *American Foreign Policy-Making and the Democratic Dilemmas*, 4th ed. (New York: Holt, Rinehart and Winston, 1985), p. 211.

66. Moffett, *Limits of Victory*, p. 176.

67. Jerry Sanders, *Peddlers of Crisis: The Committee on the Present Danger and the Politics of Containment* (Boston: South End Press, 1983), p. 265.

68. Moffett, *Limits of Victory*, p. 148.

69. See Ibid., pp. 174-175.

70. While perhaps exaggerated, Jerry Sanders makes an interesting point on this issue: "There were deep and compelling reasons why the President and his Trilateral advisers eschewed the path of popular mobilization even as its alternative pointed toward revival of the Cold War. . . . As the chief steward of managerial elitism, Carter had little interest in a mobilization sure to activate progressives who were as opposed to empire as an end as they were to militarism as a means." Sanders, *Peddlers of Crisis*, p. 267.

Discussant: William J. Jorden

Ladies and gentlemen, it's a pleasure to be with you this morning, to talk about a subject that's close to my heart, and that accounted for a good chunk of my life, because I was involved in the Panama issue long before the final negotiations began. I followed them carefully, and then became, in the final stages, one of the participants in trying to get this job done.

I asked Dr. Rosenbaum, the organizer of this conference, what he expected and what I should be doing. He said, "You can either comment on the papers or make any other comments you wish to make on the general subject." I thought I might do a little of both, but first, let me say that these last few days have been an interesting experience for me. I have visited a number of sessions and read half a dozen papers and heard ten or twelves others summarized in fifteen- or twenty-minute segments. My overall comment and gut reaction to this is that I miss, in the papers I have read and many I have heard, the sense of life and excitement and tension, and occasionally a sense of impending doom, that pervades the history I know. I don't think there's anything carved in granite that says history must be carefully balanced and cool and aloof, that for every pro there must be a con, and that every action must fit into some grand scheme. The history I have lived for the last forty or fifty years has included wars and political battles and so on. Wars are quite simple to cover historically, because they tell their own story. But there is a good deal of blood and sweat and tears in the other parts of history. Certainly, in the Panama treaties, there was a tremendous amount of blood and sweat, and I don't feel that coming out as much as I would like, in at least a few of the papers that I have read.

But in any case, that is a footnote, and I want to make it clear that I'm not talking about Dr. Skidmore's paper, which I found to be excellent and thorough on the ground that was covered--with, perhaps, a couple of caveats, if I may be permitted. I think that when one talks about the foreign policy interest groups and Panama, it's easy to get wrapped up in the American Conservative Union and the Conservative Caucus and the Citizens for the Republic and Young Americans for Freedom and so on. One omission that I see in this paper, in the listing of groups that actively worked against the treaties, was what I regard as one of the most successful, best-organized groups that opposed them. That group was not in Washington or San Francisco or Chicago; it was in Panama. It was organized by Americans who lived in the Canal Zone, who worked on the Panama Canal, and who were fighting vigorously not for some abstract political issue but for a way of life, as they saw it. And it was a way of life that, for many families, had been their way of life for three generations. And they saw this crumbling if the treaties came to life. They saw the end of the Canal Zone, a ten-mile-wide, fifty-mile-long area in the very heart of Panama, extending on both sides of the canal, where, in effect, the United States had had a colony for seventy-five years.

And so they went to work, and they met regularly; they collected a tremendous amount of money; they sent delegations to Washington; they inundated the Congress with letters and telegrams; they sent speakers around the United States pleading their cause. And I must say that they were quite effective. I talked to many senators and congressmen who said that the single most effective group, as far as they were concerned, was not any of the others we have mentioned, but the citizens of the Canal Zone. Most of those letters and telegrams got a more serious reading from the Congress than did the prepackaged, prewritten postcards that were sent out by many of the other organized groups. So if you revise the paper at any point, I think it's worth at least a footnote.

I think that to get away from the paper and to stick with this point of the way of life of the Zonians is worth doing. We had had, as I said, in effect a colony in Panama for seventy-five years, since the original treaty went into effect in 1903. When President Carter praised Teddy Roosevelt, it should be remembered that Teddy Roosevelt and William Howard Taft made it very clear that the last thing in the world we wanted was a colony. We wanted to build a canal, and we wanted to see that canal operated efficiently and effectively; they had no notion of creating, in effect, a colonial enclave in the heart of Panama. But under later administrations, that is exactly what happened. And I think one of the ironies of the Panama Canal debate was to hear Senator Helms and Congressman Murphy talking about defending the American way of life by protecting the Canal Zone. Well, it was not the American way of life; it was a totally different life from the one you and I and all Americans know here. With further irony, it was about as close as one could come to socialism in the Western Hemisphere. Not just socialism, perhaps, but edging over toward communism, in that there were no elections; there was no elected government; people paid no taxes; all of the services of life, from birth in the clinics to burial, were handled by the government. That was supposedly the American way of life that was being protected by the old arrangement. I think most Americans never realized that we had a system there that was like the colonies in Africa, controlled by the European powers. But in any case, I thought it ironic that archconservatives could so vigorously defend the socialist way of life.

The other irony that has always struck me is that the opponents of the treaty argued vigorously and at length about the inroads of communism into Panama, and I think Dr. Skidmore mentioned the description of Omar Torrijos as a Marxist thug, which was about as far from the truth as one could get. But in any case, when the treaties went into effect, it cut the ground from under the most powerful argument that the communists in Panama, and in neighboring countries in Central America, Venezuela and Columbia, had used against the United States for the past thirty years. Suddenly, when the treaties went into effect and the Canal Zone was eliminated, and the cooperative arrangement between the United States and Panama went into effect to operate the canal, all of those long and tiresome attacks by the communists disappeared.

The Communist Party, by the way, has never been very powerful in Panama, and after the treaties, it lost almost all influence and effect. And this, again, is rather ironic, in that the opponents of the treaty were claiming that it was moving into the hands of the communists, and that we were aiding them, and that we were going to have a Cuban Panama, and so on. The exact opposite was true.

The second comment I wanted to make was, moving on from the point that Dr. Skidmore made, that in the Panama Canal treaty fight, the conservatives lost the battle but won the war. I think that the various groups he mentioned moved on to a longer and broader and wider agenda, and proved very effective over the years in promoting their cause. I think, however, that the point should be made that the transition of the conservative lobbying groups to opposing foreign policy was not as long as has been suggested, nor was it divorced from the Panama issue. It took shape and was effective against the SALT treaty, but it was also active and effective on Panama.

A treaty is a bit like a budget: the Congress passes the budget, but it is fairly meaningless until you have appropriations, and until you have authorizations. A treaty is largely ineffective until you have implementing legislation that carries out the intent of the treaty. Once the hurdle of Senate approval was cleared, the next problem became implementation, and the treaties went to the House of Representatives as well as the Senate. In the House, they were turned over to the tender mercies of Congressman John Murphy of New York, who headed the Merchant Marine and Fisheries Committee. John Murphy was an extreme conservative; he was anti-treaty; he was a roommate at West Point and a lifelong friend of Anastasio Somosa--hardly the kind of dispassionate advocate one would like to turn over business to, especially one as sensitive as the Panama Canal treaties. But he was the mastermind of implementing legislation in the House of Representatives.

As a result of his operations, and of those of many like-thinking representatives around him--Bob Baumann of Maryland jumps to mind, and Bob Dornan from California--in many ways, the treaties were gutted; they reduced their effectiveness; they approved measures that undercut the intent and the purpose and the goals of the treaties. I won't go into the long and bloody battle that went on in the House, and later in the Senate, but one significant change was that under the treaties, all of the people who negotiated it and the senators who approved it had visualized a system for operating the canal under a joint U.S.-Panamanian enterprise with equal rights and equal responsibilities, that would set tolls according to financial need, and that would not depend on any money from the U.S. Congress or the U.S. Treasury. In other words, it would pay for itself.

That was the intent; that was the purpose; and that was, in fact, the way the canal had been operating for thirty years. Murphy and company turned back the clock to the late 1940s. They made the new Canal Commission an appropriated agency of the U.S. government, which meant that all of the tolls taken in by the Panama Canal went into the U.S. Treasury, and every dollar that was spent by the Panama Canal Company to operate--whether it was dredging a new channel or buying paper clips--had to be appropriated by Congress. In other words, the Canal Commission would have to go back to the House every year for appropriations; would have to justify every penny; would have to explain what it was doing. And it gave the House Merchant Marine Committee and the Panama Subcommittee a stranglehold on the future operation of the canal, the selection of personnel, and all of the other things that go into the operation of a large enterprise. And that effort was broadly and intensively supported by the groups that Dr. Skidmore has mentioned.

So it wasn't a case of taking the Panama Canal treaty machinery of opposition and later transferring it to other issues; it was immediate, and its effect on the treaties and on their operation was devastating. It was a sore disappointment to the Panamanians that we had turned things around on them, and it has been the source of constant complaints from 1979 to date because it--in Panamanian eyes, at least--violated the spirit of the agreement they thought they had.

Let me close by saying a few words about the treaties overall, and their history. When I think of the Panama Canal treaties, I think of tension and a thousand nights that were sleepless for dozens of people, both in Panama and in Washington. It was a long, tiresome, demanding battle that we thought, in April 1978, had been won. My memory is of a courageous president who led that fight, a fight that many politicians and pundits and editorial writers had told him could not be won. I think of a number of very brave senators--men like Bob Byrd of West Virginia, and Howard Baker of Tennessee, and Frank Church of Idaho, and Paul Sarbanes of Maryland--who led the fight on the Senate floor, knowing every day that they were risking their political lives to do what was right. I also cannot forget a number of other senators who filled the *Congressional Record* and the airwaves and the columns of newspapers with emotional arguments and distortions and, in many cases, outright lies. I hope history will do something about that. And I think, finally, of a lot of wonderful Panamanians who worked with the United States, and who wondered if--and hoped that--this great country would finally treat them fairly and with justice and as partners. And that, of course, was the name of the Panama Treaty game.

Let me close by recalling one thing: We have the treaties; we barely got them through; they have been effective. The Panama Canal is operating beautifully, and there are no problems that we didn't have forty years ago. What if the treaties had not been approved? It was a question that the anti-treaty forces never asked, and most assuredly never answered. What would have happened, I am persuaded--and it is not based on supposition--is that the canal would have been closed, and it would have been kept closed until some form of justice prevailed. In the meantime, we would have been forced to send fifty thousand or a hundred thousand young Americans to Panama to try to reopen the canal, to kill Panamanians, to be killed by Panamanians; and we would have been the subject of opprobrium and opposition and criticism by the entire world. That painful possibility was avoided by the approval of the Panama Canal treaties.

Discussant: George D. Moffett

I would begin by underscoring one point made by Bill Jorden. I would have to say, after twenty years or so of hovering around the edges of the policy process--as a journalist and at the White House and as an academic--that I've never dealt with an issue that has offered such a satisfying marriage of national interest and idealism. I think all of us who had the privilege of being a part of the ratification debate look back on it as one of the most rewarding experiences in government service.

David Skidmore has covered the ground admirably; he leaves us little room to comment. What I would like to do is put a finer point on a couple of aspects of the ratification debate that stand out in retrospect as being particularly important.

The first has to do with the atmosphere of the ratification debate. One of the most important points to be made about the Carter administration--and I think it's too often missed--is that the public mood that elected Ronald Reagan in 1980 was not a product of the campaign of 1980, but in fact was something that pollsters began to see evidence of as early as the first year of the Carter administration--just about the time President Carter was readying the treaties for submission to the Senate. That is a fact of inestimable consequence, not only to the life of the treaty debate but also to future Carter administration initiatives.

What was this public mood? In essence, it was a reaction to a whole series of changes in the international environment that most Americans were having great difficulty understanding, that they didn't like very much, and that, above all, they feared were about to threaten American supremacy in the international arena. As Tom Hughes described this mood in an article in *Foreign Policy* about this time, as Americans contemplated defeat in Vietnam, the loss of energy independence at the hands of OPEC, the achievement of strategic parity by the Soviet Union, they suddenly found themselves gripped by one of the rare crises of confidence in American history. And in response to this crisis--this sense that events were somehow out of control, that America was no longer in charge, that America had become irrelevant--there was a strong reaction. It took the form of support for high defense spending; it was expressed in terms of a heightened sensitivity to the imperatives of national honor; it took the form of more support for a more muscular foreign policy backed by greater defense spending. And this occurred at the very moment Jimmy Carter was about to go to the Senate with treaties that, although they certainly addressed America's national interest, were nevertheless ultimately based on an idealistic notion that it was the right thing for a great nation to do.

In the jargon of political scientists, Jimmy Carter was suddenly forced to operate in a nonpermissive environment. One can easily think of historical analogies. Franklin Roosevelt, at the height of his popularity, for example, was not capable of convincing many of his countrymen to back a policy of all aid short of war to the Allies in the late 1930s, because his feelings and the public mood were so completely out of sync. I guess the most telling example is Woodrow Wilson, whose idealistic appeals for U.S.

membership in the League of Nations at the end of World War I were largely lost on a public that was retreating into unilateralism and isolation.

Ultimately, I think it is the increasingly conservative public mood that explains four or five of what I find to be the most intriguing anomalies surrounding the ratification debate. Let me tick off a few.

First, I think it explains why the Carter administration came so close to losing the debate, even though it began with almost every conceivable advantage. The president inherited treaties drafted by three predecessors, including two Republicans; the treaties had the backing of the bipartisan leadership in both houses of Congress; they had the support of the joint chiefs of staff; they were treaties that had the editorial support of two out of every three American newspapers; they enjoyed, unexpectedly, the support of influential conservatives like George Will and Bill Buckley. Moreover, the treaties faced what everyone thought at the beginning would be nominal opposition, waged mostly by groups that were outside the political mainstream and that had no solid base inside the Republican Party. But in spite of all of these advantages, after thirteen years of negotiations, forty days of congressional hearings, and the longest floor debate in the Senate in over fifty years, the administration came within a hair's breadth of losing.

I think the shifting public mood accounts for a few other anomalies. One is the fact, as David pointed out, that the intensity factor lay almost entirely on the side of those who opposed ratification, and not on the side of those who supported it. As Howard Baker commented once, "Those who were opposed to ratification were really opposed, and those who were in favor were just sort of."

I think it also explains another point that David mentioned in his remarks: that the Panama Canal debate ended up doing for conservatives what the Carter administration had hoped that it would do for itself--it created a constituency and laid the groundwork for future policy intiatives.

I think this public mood also accounts for the fact--and I find this the most enduring paradox of the ratification debate--that, in a nuclear age, the fate of a seventy-five-year-old, largely outmoded canal in Central America should become the object of some of the most heated political passions in American diplomatic history. I think it explains the anomaly that millions of Americans rallied to the symbol of the Panama Canal--American supremacy in world affairs--just as the reality behind that symbol was slipping irretrievably away. Just as Jimmy Carter turned to give away the Panama Canal, millions of Americans suddenly began to project onto the canal all of their fears and concerns and confusion about the vastly changing international environment. In short, the issue became something much greater than the canal itself, which is ultimately why it proved so difficult and costly for Carter to get the treaties ratified.

In the end--and I think this is the most important point to be made about the Canal debate--Jimmy Carter was caught squarely between two fixed and immovable forces. One was the new international circumstances, which made the conclusion of a new treaty arrangement with Panama all but inevitable. The other was the domestic mood in the United States, which made the ratification of these treaties all but impossible. Let me say that again, because I think it's crucial. Jimmy Carter was a victim of timing because the very international conditions that made a new treaty with Panama unavoidable also made the job of winning domestic support almost impossible.

I don't know if the bright young men and women who managed this debate really had any sense of what they were getting into. I don't suppose they could have known. I think, given the circumstances they had to deal with, they did marvelously well. I concur wholly with David's judgment that the administration's ratification strategy was smart, comprehensive, and well thought out. Having said that, there is no escaping the fact that the administration was forced to live for its remaining three years with the dark consequences of the fact that it never had a public mood on its side that was receptive to the kind of worldview of which the Panama Canal treaties were the consummate expression.

Let me make another point about public opinion. It's not clear to me, to this day, whether the managers of the ratification debate in the White House and the State Department actually understood that the apparent trend in the public opinion polls toward support for the treaties was largely illusory. David has talked about this.

What seems clear in retrospect is that the Panama Canal treaties provide a textbook case in the uses and misuses of public polling. Where things went wrong in understanding the polls was in mistaking the fact that what was true in a clinical sense was never true in practice. It was true that if respondents knew about the two Senate leadership amendments (giving the United States the right to intervene to keep the canal open, and to send its ships to the head of the line in case of a national emergency), they were more inclined to support ratification. The problem was that despite the administration's extraordinary public relations campaign--perhaps the largest in history on a foreign policy issue--the only people who did know by the end of the ratification debate were that 5 to 7 percent of Americans who are typically well informed about public affairs, plus that infinitesimally small fraction of people who were actually asked the pollsters' questions. So while it is true that, in theory, the administration *could* have won support, the fact is they *didn't*, despite their best efforts and those of various powerful allies.

Beyond the point that there was no trend is the counterintuitive fact that there was little actual likelihood of creating one. At the start of the ratification debate, administration strategists made the reasonable assumption that there was a large pool of undecided Americans who, when coaxed out of inattentiveness and undecidedness, would create a groundswell of support for ratification. A similar assumption was held by those in the New Right who managed the opposition to ratification. In fact, there never was a large pool of convertible public opinion. What it comes down to, largely-- and this risks oversimplifying a complicated subject--is that there was such a close correlation between certain demographic characteristics and the disposition either to favor or to oppose ratification that efforts to convince largely fell on deaf ears. The administration had on its side only a relatively small number of Americans who, by virtue of education and experience, were able to comprehend why, all of a sudden, after seventy-five years, it was necessary to give away the Panama Canal.

What was worse for the administration--or potentially worse--was the fact that in the process of trying to make the issue more salient to Americans, the administration risked swelling the ranks of the opposition. I can tell you that the Panama Canal treaties are something you should think about, that they're important, and that you should support them for the following six reasons. You may well say, "Ah, yes, I understand now that this is an important issue. But I draw completely different conclusions from the evidence that you've given me." To a large extent, this is what happened. And I think that fact underlies the most important point to be made about the public opinion: that after the longest, most intensive, and most comprehensive effort to shape public opinion, attitudes toward the Panama Canal treaties simply did not change. At the end of the ratification debate, they were exactly where they were before Jimmy Carter was even president of the United States. To look at that static graph--the straight line that shows the 5:3 ratio of opposition to support that David mentioned--is to look at a line that betrays nothing whatsoever of the intensity of the struggle that took place between supporters and opponents of ratification.

I would make one more point before turning the podium over to Bob Pastor. I have lauded the Carter administration's ratification performance. But administration strategies did make two potentially fatal mistakes. One was not paying enough attention to concerns that were persistently raised by a number of interest groups--the owners of American-flag ship, some East Coast and Gulf port authorities, and some Midwestern farmers, whose goods entered the world market through the Panama Canal. They tried, unsuccessfully, through the several months of the ratification debate to get the administration to face up to the economic implications of increasing canal tolls, as required under the terms of the treaty. They never succeeded; the administration never had a very good response to their questions. I mention it because if the political Right had been alert enough to seize the issue, and to publicize the possible loss of jobs and revenues that ratification could have entailed, it might well have found the two additional votes needed to defeat the treaties.

The other strategic mistake the administration made was on the matter of the DeConcini amendment, which nearly brought the treaty to its knees at the eleventh hour. This is a long story; I won't get into it except to say that I think the administration's mistake was in dealing directly with Senator DeConcini, rather than turning that job over to the Senate leaders, who themselves had an enormous stake in the successful outcome of the ratification debate. As it was, in spite of those two mistakes, the administration fared well. Ratification was a success in the near term. But as I've argued in my book, I think, on balance, the Panama Canal victory turned out to be a Pyrrhic victory for the Carter administration.

Discussant: Robert A. Pastor

Sol Linowitz, one of the negotiators of the Panama Canal treaties, liked to tell a story about how it felt to negotiate the treaties and to promote their ratification. He said it felt as if he were a high school football player in the very last game of his senior year. He had sat on the bench for the previous four years. In the last minute, the coach turned to him and said, "Okay, Jim, go in and play." Excited, he jumped up and asked the coach, "What do you want me to do?" And the coach said, "We have one minute left, and no time-outs. I want you to go in and get hurt." And that's the way many of us who worked on the canal treaties felt, throughout the course of the administration.

Professor Skidmore is quite correct that opponents of the treaties were in a no-lose situation: even if they filed to prevent ratification, the general public, and conservative groups in particular, could rally to the opponents. Indeed, Ronald Reagan and others in the conservative movement used the canal treaties as a potent talking point in their broader political agenda. Perhaps the best illustration that his motives were political rather than substantive was that he did not touch the issue for the eight years he was president. If he had believed just 1 percent of all that he had said in opposition to the canal treaties, one would have expected him to use his eight years as president as an opportunity to revise the treaties. He didn't.

One minor disagreement, however, with the paper is that I do not believe the Carter administration came into office seeing the canal treaties as an excellent opportunity to mobilize supporters. I think many of those who were working in the White House, as well as in the State Department, viewed it as a no-win issue from a domestic political standpoint. The administration would get no credit for ratifying the treaties in the United States and, unfortunately, little credit in Latin America. Indeed, the only reason that eighteen Latin American heads of state came to Washington to witness the signing of the canal treaties in September 1977 was not their deep and real support for the treaties--although they did support it. They came because Carter promised a private meeting with each one of them. However, it was clear that the treaties had failed, the United States would have been unable to structure any relationship with Latin America.

On April 17, 1978, the day before the final vote on the second canal treaty, Zbigniew Brzezinski and Hamilton Jordan asked me to write short statements for President Carter to issue the next day if it were approved or if it failed. I went back to my office. It was very easy to write the one Carter would read if it was approved; we'd all been saying the same things over and over again -- that took a few seconds. I sat down, however, to write up the one if it failed, and it finally occurred to me what would happen if, in fact, the treaty was not ratified the next day. And although we look back on the ratification and think that it was a sure thing, it was not a sure thing; I can assure you of that. And as I began thinking that the canal would probably be closed; Ambassador Bill Jorden would be in desperate shape in the embassy. Probably three or four U.S. embassies in Latin America would be firebombed. So I put the speech aside and wrote a memorandum for Brzezinski to call an NSC meeting that morning to look into contingencies. He did that and the NSC agreed to send several planes to the canal area to improve the canal's readiness and security.

So the problem of the canal treaties for the Carter administration was simply that it was a no-win situation at the end. But the canal treaties were also the most urgent and important part of Carter's Latin American policy. Let me use my remaining time to comment on how that fit into the broader policy. In fact, the Carter administration came in with a very clear agenda for Latin America, which it was able to complete, to a great extent, in its first two years.

For the last two years, it had to confront a very different agenda--a more security-oriented agenda--that, to a great extent, was imposed on it by international events. The preferred agenda was, in effect, developed partly as a result of the moral bankruptcy of Watergate and the demoralization of Vietnam, but also because of the many issues in Latin America that had been subject to benign neglect over a decade. The plague of repression that had descended upon Latin America in the previous years; the economic issues that were increasingly viewed by Latin Americans in a North-South context; the arms race within Latin America--those issues had been completely ignored.

Sol Linowitz, who chaired the Commission on U.S.-Latin American Relations--a private group of twenty distinguished individuals--proposed a very coherent strategy for dealing with those issues, a new approach to Latin America based not on the paternalism of the past but on the centrality of human rights and cooperative relations. The principal issues that needed to be addressed, besides Panama and human rights, were arms control, nuclear nonproliferation, and the economic concerns of Latin America in a broader, global, North-South context. In two reports, the commission made twenty-eight very specific recommendations for the new administration to adopt when it came into office. Carter in effect adopted the report, and in the first eighteen months of the administration, all but one of those recommendations were implemented. That reflected the preferred agenda of the Carter administration.

For the second half of Carter's term--although it's not a precise division--a different agenda was imposed, actually beginning with the Cuban-Soviet intervention in Ethiopia and Cuban expansionism in Africa, and continuing with the fall of the Somoza regime in Nicaragua; the problem of the Mariel exodus of 125,000 Cubans to the United States; and the Soviet brigade in Cuba. This was an agenda that the Carter administration dealt with very uncomfortably; indeed, to a great extent, it exacerbated contradictions within the administration. These events were described by Ronald Reagan as part of a broader picture of U.S. weakness that included much more significant events, such as the Soviet intervention in Afghanistan, the fall of the shah of Iran, the Soviet military buildup. All of these larger reasons left Americans uncertain.

What explains the dual agenda? There is a critique from the left that suggests the ascendancy of Zbigniew Brzezinski in the last two years of the administration accounts for the separate agenda. The problem with that argument is that it omits the principal decision maker in the Carter administration, Jimmy Carter. It also omits the simple fact that the basic principles Carter had developed in the first two years of his administration were, to a great extent, continued.

A critique from the right, by Jeane Kirkpatrick and also by Ronald Reagan, suggests that the last two years--the security-oriented years of the Carter administration--were actually brought on by the first two years, by the emphasis on human rights, by withdrawal of support from dictators. Ronald Reagan argued, in an article in 1978, that Carter had strained U.S. relations with friendly governments in Chile, Argentina, Brazil, Guatemala, and El Salvador. He neglected to mention, of course, that each of these at the time was a military regime and that the whole purpose of the human rights policy was to strain relations, to increase the cost of repression by these governments. To a great extent, it accomplished that.

A third explanation for the dual agenda is that the world had changed, and no administration in Washington could ignore security concerns. But here, I think President Carter remained true to the basic principles he had laid down at the beginning. On human rights, for example, in the case of El Salvador in 1980, he conditioned U.S. aid on improved human rights, and that was one of the reasons U.S. aid was not delivered to El Salvador in the last year of the administration. On Nicaragua, for example, though he was under substantial pressure, he never departed from a principle of nonintervention, or from consulting and working with other Latin American governments. The principal objective of the Carter administration in Nicaragua--which I go into in great detail in my book--was to try to find a middle path between Somoza and the Sandinistas; it did not succeed.

In assessing the overall policy, we've heard a lot on the importance of the canal treaties. Human rights policy probably was the most enduring of Carter's legacies. The number of political prisoners in Latin America declined markedly; even Fidel Castro released 3,900 prisoners, and Duvalier released thousands. Disappearances in the Southern Cone declined or ended. The American Convention on Human Rights and the Inter-American Commission on Human Rights were both strengthened. The nuclear nonproliferation regime was strengthened by Carter's signing the Treaty of Malelolco.

In conclusion, let me cite a Caribbean foreign minister in the OAS General Assembly after Carter's defeat in November 1980. In reviewing the various criticisms that had been leveled against Carter and his human rights policy, this foreign minister--Henry Forde of Barbados--said, "It is our view"--and he was speaking as president of the OAS General Assembly--"that the policy has been the single most creative act in the hemisphere in many a long year. It has raised the consciousness and stirred the consciences of many a leader in the region. It has given hope to many an oppressed citizen. It has helped, perhaps more than any other element of policy, to correct the image of the United States as an unfeeling giant casting its shadow over its neighbors." In view of the importance that Carter had given to consulting and working with democratic neighbors in the hemisphere, perhaps that assessment is at least as important as any other.

Questions and Answers

Q: Tom Wicker commented yesterday that perhaps the biggest political blunder that President Carter made was to press for the ratification of these treaties during his first term.

Moffett: I think the short answer was that they did not have that luxury. This process had started thirteen years before Jimmy Carter became president; it had reached the point of near conclusion by the time of the 1976 election campaign. Because it became a highly charged political issue in that campaign--thanks primarily to Ronald Reagan--there was a sort of tacit understanding between the American administration and the Panamanians that little would be said about Panama, but that it would become, early in the next administration--whether it was a Ford administration or a Carter administration--a matter of high priority. The implied threat here, on the part of the Panamanians, was that if the United States did not make it a high priority, there would be a price to pay in Panama. I think no one who knows the subject has any doubt that Omar Torrijos could have turned on violence like a spigot, if he felt the Americans were reneging on that commitment. The concern that is built into your question is certainly a valid one, and I have no doubts that the administration would have loved not to have had to deal with this issue in the early stages of the administration, especially given what we know now about the price of the ratification debate. But I think there was no choice.

Pastor: I agree totally with George. Torrijos had a pungent phrase: "Panama's patience machine had run out of gas" by 1977. I don't think there's any question that if we had failed to address the issue at the very beginning of the administration, we would have had to deal with all of the negative consequences that Bill Jorden alluded to. I don't think there was any question of the political costs of the decision. Anybody who ran in the 1976 campaign understood that there was a resonance throughout the country against the canal treaty. So Tom Wicker is correct that it was very costly politically. Carter understood that, but he didn't see that there was any way to avoid it. I wrote a memorandum in the summer of 1976, during the campaign, that it was urgent to complete negotiations by the summer of 1977, in order to to get ratification by the spring of 1978, which was sufficient time before the midterm elections. So the political cost was known.

Jorden: If I may say, with respect to my friend and colleague Tom Wicker, he was not really on top of the Panama issue, and if he took that position, he owed it to his audience to say what would have happened if the treaty path had not been pursued. I've suggested what the consequences would have been, and it would have made the Iran hostage issue look like a Sunday school picnic.

Q: I'd like to address this to the ambassador, though I welcome commentary from anybody who'd be so inclined. In retrospect, I'm struck by the fact that President Carter was able to get this enacted so soon in his administration. In comparison with the three prior administrations, he was really a neophyte when it came to dealings with the Congress and foreign policy matters. So my question would be, does the success of the enactment of the treaties owe more to President Carter being an outsider, if you will, being unencumbered with the normal political considerations? Is its success owed to the fact that he was, in general, perhaps a little more earnest in seeing it to fruition? Or is it more the fact that he was the right person at the right time to evince change in the New World? And, as a follow-up to that, would you contrast your counsel to President Ford on his approach to the treaty negotiations and to President Carter in his first year in office?

Jorden: Well, it's a long question, and it would take a long answer to try to be comprehensive. But the short, quick, honest answer is that under Nixon, under Ford, there were no treaties to ratify. There was negotiation, there was talk, there was back-and-forth. It had gone on since 1965, and what happened was that the process had not matured.

Part IV

The United States and the Soviet Union

Like all other post-World War II American governments, the Carter administration confronted the relationship with the Soviet bloc. Efforts to build on prior administration's attempts to decrease the level of tensions and to harness and limit the more dangerous and wasteful elements of the long struggle proved far from simple, as they had previously. The barriers consisted not only of the rigidities of a Soviet regime in apparent decline but also of the long-lasting suspicions and distrust among American political leaders, built since the commencement of the Cold War. One gets the distinct impression that leaders on both sides of this deep divide identified their continued political survival with the maintenance of the schism, fearing that accommodation would lead to the defeat of their parties, factions or elites.

In reading the papers of this panel, one ought to keep in mind that we now look at these events and relationships from the newly gained perspective of the post-Cold War era. The content and tone of both papers offered at this panel greatly increase one's objectivity about the events of that time.

The description of the early Carter initiative in the form of the 1977 Vance mission to Moscow underlines the massiveness of the distrust during those years. That paper's author is a noted Soviet scholar whose perspective from the interior of that system contribute greatly to our understanding of the difficulties of that time. The narrative of the U.S. Senate's management of the SALT II treaty forms an apt counterpart to the story of the Vance mission, since it demonstrates that distrust was by not means one-sided.

In this panel, as in so many others, the discussants contributed the distinctiveness of their wide experience and expertise in the thinking about and the mangement of the Cold War and its intricacies. Both American discussants are former governmental leader and scholars; their Soviet counterpart is a well-known academician and diplomat.

17

The Carter Administration, the Senate, and SALT II

DAN CALDWELL

The greatest consultative privilege of the Senate--the greatest in dignity--is its right to a ruling voice in the ratification of treaties with foreign powers.

Woodrow Wilson, 1885

When President Carter signed the SALT II Treaty and submitted it to the Senate for advice and consent, a new set of negotiations concerning SALT II began, negotiations between the executive branch and the Senate. Carter recognized this fact: "my restraints were just as much with the Senate as they were at the bargaining table with the Soviets."[1] Members of the Senate believed that the task before them was very significant. Minority Leader Howard Baker called SALT II "the most important treaty this country has undertaken since World War I."[2] Democrat John Glenn agreed: "Not since Woodrow Wilson's time and the League of Nations debate has a treaty been so important, yet so contentious, as the SALT II Treaty."[3] In this paper, I will describe (1) the political environment in the Senate in 1979; (2) the senators, committees, and staff members who played a prominent role in the SALT II debate; and (3) the Senate's action on the treaty.

THE POLITICAL ENVIRONMENT IN THE SENATE IN 1979

Many observers have noted that for years the U.S. Senate resembled a gentlemen's club rather than a serious legislative body. In the "old Senate," influence and power were centralized and determined by seniority; deference was paid to certain older, "bellweather" members; only rarely would younger members challenge senior, established members; and senators often deferred to the White House. Vietnam and Watergate destroyed this atmosphere, for both of these episodes demonstrated the disastrous consequences of inadequately checked executive power. The "new Senate" was decentralized, democratized, and junior-member oriented.[4] As I. M. Destler noted, "In the Cold War period, three things combined to make Congress a tolerable policy partner: deference to the president on the big things; centralization of power;

and, if not consensus, a functioning internationalist coalition. By the 1970s, all had disappeared."[5]

A number of those elected to the Senate in 1974 had been caught up in the anti-Vietnam War movement; they included Gary Hart (who had been George McGovern's campaign manager in the 1972 presidential race), John Culver, and Dale Bumpers. These three freshman senators requested and received places on the Senate Armed Services Committee, where they were able to exert their influence on defense issues. The presence of these three liberal senators on the Armed Services Committee in itself was a departure from past practice; previously, members of the committee had rarely challenged the positions or budgets of the Department of Defense.

As the 1970s wore on, public opinion about Soviet-American relations and presidential power took a conservative turn, and this change was reflected in the composition of the Senate. In 1978, twenty new senators were elected, eleven Republicans and nine Democrats. This was the biggest single turnover in the Senate since 1946. Included in this group were a number of conservatives, including Gordon Humphrey and Alan Simpson. In many respects, the "gadfly role" that liberal senators such as William Proxmire, George McGovern, Mark Hatfield, and Frank Church had played in the early 1970s was played in the late 1970s by Jake Garn, Malcolm Wallop, Humphrey, and Jesse Helms.[6]

Thus, the Senate that Jimmy Carter faced in the debate over the SALT II Treaty in 1979 was composed of a diverse group of politicans, including some elected in the early 1970s, who reflected the antiwar orientation of that period, and others of a conservative orientation who reflected the more assertive orientation of the 1980s. As a political body, however, the Senate went from being the "most dovish body in the U.S. government" to being the most hawkish by the end of the 1970s, an orientation that had a dramatic impact on the SALT II debate.[7]

JIMMY CARTER AND THE CONGRESS

Jimmy Carter was the first elected president following Watergate, and the residual tension from both Vietnam and Watergate added to the normal amount of conflict that exists between the executive and congressional branches even in the best of times. Added to this, Carter had campaigned as a Washington outsider, trying to make a virtue out of his lack of Washington experience. Once elected, Carter and his advisers did little to dispel the wariness that many members of Congress felt toward the new president. Things did not begin well. When Speaker of the House Tip O'Neill requested tickets for his family to attend a gala at the Kennedy Center the night before Carter was inaugurated, he received tickets in the last row of the second balcony. O'Neill blamed Hamilton Jordan for slighting his family, and although Jordan apologized, O'Neill believed that the slight had been intentional. Subsequently, after Jordan failed to return several of his phone calls, O'Neill referred to Jordan as "Hannibal Jerken."[8] O'Neill concluded that "during the Carter years, congressional Democrats often had the feeling that the White House was actually working against us."[9] There were other petty slights that alienated some members of Congress; for example, the White House sent bills to House and Senate leaders for meals consumed there.

Carter had a kind of disdain for legislators. During the presidential campaign, he was asked whether some cattle on a South Dakota farm reminded him of Georgia's legislators. He replied, "No, they're more intelligent."[10] Carter later recognized his problems; he entitled one chapter of his memoirs "My One-Week Honeymoon with Congress."[11]

Neither Carter nor his staff members and senior cabinet members enjoyed spending time with members of Congress. One Senate staff member saw John Stennis at the White House and asked him if he met often with the president. Stennis, chairman of the Senate Armed Services Committee and one of the most influential members in the Senate at that time, remarked that he had been to the White House only once during the Carter administration.[12] Carter and his principal cabinet members with foreign policy reponsibilities, Cyrus Vance and Harold Brown, enjoyed mastering the technicalities of complex issues and did not enjoy interacting with members of Congress. According to political scientist Charles O. Jones, "Separation was preferred to intimacy in presidential-congressional relations."[13]

Carter's problems with Congress were not simply due to personality conflicts. During the ninety-sixth Congress (1977-1979), Carter sought to deal with a number of complex and controversial issues, including windfall profits, comprehensive energy legislation, Taiwan, the Panama Canal treaties, defense spending, and Iran. Interestingly, despite his problems in dealing with Congress, he accomplished a great deal. The Panama Canal treaties were ratified; sales of aircraft to Saudi Arabia and Egypt were approved; the arms embargo against Turkey was lifted; the sanctions against trading with Rhodesia were retained; the Taiwan Relations Act was passed; and the largest development assistance bill in history was passed.[14] These victories were achieved at some cost, as President Carter later recognized: "The battles with Congress over the Panama Canal treaties and energy legislation had been long, drawn-out, and debilitating to the members [of Congress] and to me."[15]

Carter's problems with Congress were exacerbated by another factor: the White House Office of Congressional Relations was not effective. Jimmy Carter had brought the director of the office, Frank Moore, with him from Georgia, and he had no previous experience in Washington. In the interviews conducted for this paper, both senators and Senate staff members were very critical of Moore. Several went so far as to say that Moore was the worst White House congressional liaison with whom they had dealt.[16]

Early in the administration, Senators Gary Hart and Alan Cranston went to the president and suggested that he appoint a senior official to act as a liaison betwen the White House and the Senate. They suggested Robert Strauss, who, as the special trade representative, had served as the administration's chief lobbyist for the legislation on the multilateral trade negotiations.[17] Senator William Proxmire believed that the president should have appointed the respected former Senate majority leader, Mike Mansfield to such a position rather than naming him as ambassador to Japan.[18] Instead, the president relied on Frank Moore until it became obvious that he needed help. Robert Beckel, who had assisted with the ratification of the Panama Canal treaties, was brought in and did a creditable job, according to almost all accounts. In early 1978, the White House decided that an overall coordinator for the SALT II ratification effort was needed, and Matthew Nimetz, the number-three person at the Department of State, was appointed. Although the members of both the executive branch and the Senate interviewed for this paper believed that Nimetz did a good job, they also felt that he was not at a high enough level within the bureaucracy. Finally, in August 1979, the president appointed the respected Washington attorney Lloyd Cutler to act as the "SALT II tsar," but this appointment came very late in the ratification process.

Despite the problems in dealing with the Congress, the executive branch devoted substantial resources to working with the Congress. Although the White House Office of Congressional Relations had a small staff of several professionals, there were at least 675 staff members from executive branch departments and agencies who were directly involved in congressional liaison work, more than one congressional liaison staff person for each member of Congress.[19] The Department of Defense alone had a congressional liaison staff of 227.[20]

In sum, according to Department of Defense official William Perry, "The Carter administration did not have a good working relationship with the Congress, partly because the president didn't recognize the importance of that and didn't work at it hard enough, and partly for reasons out of his control."[21]

THE SENATE'S INVOLVEMENT IN SALT

During the negotiations that led to the first SALT agreements, the Senate was not actively involved in the oversight of the negotiations.[22] Following the conclusion of the SALT I negotiations, the Anti-Ballistic Missile Treaty was submitted to the Senate for its advice and consent. It was approved by an overwhelming majority of 88-2. According to the 1961 law that established the Arms Control and Disarmament Agency, any agreement related to arms control must be submitted to the House and the Senate for review.[23] Therefore, the Interim Agreement on Offensive Forces was submitted to the two houses of Congress. Senator Henry Jackson was concerned about the disparity in numbers of missiles that the agreement allowed for the United States and the Soviet Union, and sponsored an amendment calling for equal levels in all future agreements. The Jackson Amendment marked the first significant congressional involvement in the SALT process.

Vietnam and Watergate had stimulated the involvement of the Congress in foreign policy, and the Carter administration recognized that increased congressional involvement was a fact of life. In May 1977, Paul Warnke, the director of the Arms Control and Disarmament Agency, wrote to Vice President Walter Mondale and requested that he designate several senators to serve as advisers to the SALT delegation, "in order to facilitate Congressional knowledge and involvement and to increase public understanding of the objectives of these negotiations."[24] Subsequent to this, Secretary of State Vance wrote to the entire membership of the Senate, extending an invitation to visit Geneva to observe the SALT II negotiations firsthand. By the time SALT II was signed, thirty-six senators had visited.[25] In addition, in mid-1977 the administration named twenty-five senators and fourteen representatives as official advisers to the American SALT II delegation. Although this action was clearly designed to assure the members of Congress that their views were being taken into account in the negotiations, not all members of Congress were convinced that their views were seriously considered.

Tension, struggle, and competition have characterized executive-congressional relations throughout most of American history. But during the Carter years, the Congress was more activist than during previous periods. It had not only the will to challenge the executive branch; it also had expanded legal, structural, institutional, and political capabilities to do so.[26]

By the late 1970s, the Congress had significantly increased its staff support. In the mid-1960s, the total staff for House and Senate committees was approximately eleven hundred. By the late 1970s, there were more than three thousand. The personal staffs of individual members of Congress also increased dramatically, from fewer than six thousand in the mid-1960s to more than ten thousand in the late 1970s.[27] In percentage terms, the growth in the personal staffs of senators from 1947 to 1979 was 512 percent, and the growth of the Senate's committee staff was 373 percent.[28] In addition to the growth in the number of staff members, there was a difference in the quality of staff members. In the early 1960s, it was unusual for a senator to have an aide whose specific responsibility was foreign policy; by the late 1970s, this was the rule rather than the exception.

In addition to increasing the number of staff members during the 1970s, Congress increased the number and the analytical capabilities of congressional support agencies. The Office of Technology Assessment was established in 1972, and by 1979 had a staff of 145. The Legislative Reference Service was reorganized as the Congressional Research Service (CRS) and was given greater responsibilities, more staff, and a larger budget that enabled it to focus on a wide variety of topics, including SALT II.[29] Between 1965 and 1979 the CRS staff rose from 231 to 847, an increase of 367 percent. The Congress directed the General Acounting Office to enlarge its staff and to expand its scope to evaluate the implementation of programs. Its staff rose from 4,278 in 1965 to 5,303 in 1979, an increase of almost 25 percent. The Congressional Budget Office (CBO), founded in 1974, was designed to provide the Con gress with an in-house capability to analyze budgets presented to the Congress by the executive branch. During the SALT II debate, for example, CBO staff members prepared analyses concerning the costs of strategic weapons programs with and without SALT II.[30] By 1979, CBO had a staff of 207.[31]

Members of the Congress also had boosted their power by increasing the number of committees and subcommittees. By the ninety-sixth Congress (1979-1980), all but two Democratic senators chaired either a committee or a subcommittee, and nearly half of the Democratic members of the House chaired either a committee or a subcommittee.

The interaction of the White House and the Senate during the debate over the Panama Canal treaties sensitized senators to both their responsibilities and their power in the ratification process. According to William Bader, the staff director of the Senate Foreign Relations Committee at the time SALT II was debated, "It was during the Panama Canal treaties' deliberations that the Senate rewrote the 'marriage manual' on ratification procedures. The Senate developed a taste and a technique for modifying, and not simply reviewing, submitted treaties."[32]

Given the power and the increased inclination of Congress to use that power, President Carter, Hamilton Jordan, and Frank Moore considered the possibility of concluding SALT II as an executive agreement rather than a treaty. One of the SALT II agreements--the Interim Agreement on Offensive Weapons--was an agreement rather than a treaty, so there was a recent precedent. Vice President Mondale was concerned about sending the treaty to the Senate and the possibility that it would become the hostage of a few conservative senators.[33] In addition, many members of the House of Representatives--including Robert Carr, Thomas Downey and Clement Zablocki--had suggested that the administration submit the final agreement to both houses of Congress. In an interview with Prof. James McGregor Burns, President Carter indicated that he might submit SALT II to the Congress as an agreement rather than a treaty.[34] There was a strongly negative reaction to this trial balloon, and the president backed away from this alternative.[35] Once this decision was made and SALT II was signed as a treaty, it was submitted to the Senate for its advice and consent.

SENATORS' POSITIONS ON SALT II

Once the treaty was submitted to the Senate, four groups of senators emerged. First, there was a group who were irreconcilably opposed to the ratification of SALT II in the form that it was submitted to the Senate. This group included Henry Jackson, John Tower, Jake Garn, and Jesse Helms. A second group consisted of senators who were strong supporters of the treaty, including Alan Cranston, John Culver, Gary Hart, and Joseph Biden. A third group that emerged during the debate on the treaty consisted of liberal critics of SALT II who believed that the treaty did not do enough to control the arms race. This group was led by Mark Hatfield, George McGovern, and William Proxmire. The fourth group consisted of the "undecideds," those who had not made up their minds about how to vote on the treaty. The senators in this group were clearly the most significant, for their votes would determine whether the treaty was ratified or rejected. The most important members of this group were Majority Leader Robert Byrd, Minority Leader Howard Baker, and Armed Services Committee Chairman John Stennis and member Sam Nunn.

Senators influenced the debate on SALT II in a number of ways: Some were experts in their own right and issued press releases concerning the treaty; others worked through the committees that they were on. I will first review the positions of a number of prominent individual senators and their staff members, and then I will review the debate within the three Senate committees that held hearings on SALT II.

The Irreconcilable Opponents

A number of senators were irreconcilably opposed to the SALT II treaty. One Senate staff member said, only partly facetiously, "There are twenty members [of the

Senate] who would vote against ratification if the treaty provided for unilateral Russian disarmament."[36]

Henry M. Jackson was the most prominent irreconcilable opponent of the treaty. Jackson first came to Washington, D.C., in January 1941 as a twenty-eight-year-old member of the House of Representatives. He was elected to the Senate in 1952 and served there until his death in 1983, at age seventy-three. During his forty-one years of service in the Congress, Jackson devoted his attention to two principal issues: energy and national security. He closely reviewed any matters concerning arms control, and often influenced the way in which the Senate dealt with these matters. Paradoxically, during his service in the Senate, Jackson voted in favor of every arms-control agreement that was reported to the Senate for a final vote, including the Antarctic Treaty, the establishment of the Arms Control and Disarmament Agency, the Limited Test Ban Treaty, the Outer Space Treaty, the Nonproliferation Treaty, the Seabed Treaty, the Anti-Ballistic Missile Treaty, the Interim Agreement on Offensive Forces, the Biological Weapons Convention, and the Environmental Modification Treaty.[37]

Despite this apparent support for arms control, Jackson had demanded a price from the executive branch for his support of a number of these agreements. When the Limited Test Ban Treaty was considered by the Senate, Jackson demanded and received a promise from the Kennedy administration to continue nuclear tests at the same or higher level following the entry into force of the treaty. Jackson wrote the amendment to the 1972 Interim Agreement demanding that future agreements contain "equal aggregates" for the United States and Soviet Union. After the SALT I agreements were concluded, Jackson demanded that the Nixon administration replace almost all of the high-level officials of the Arms Control and Disarmament Agency. It was during this "purge" of the agency that Gen. Edward Rowny replaced Gen. Royal B. Allison as the representative of the joint chiefs of staff on the U.S. SALT delegation. Given the central role that Jackson had played in the Senate on national security affairs, it was clear that he would continue this role when SALT II was submitted to the Senate.

Columnist Rowland Evans noted: "of all the sources of power in Washington today, the most nearly invisible--yet in some ways the most influential--is the congressional staff . . . a staff of professionals is no less essential to the care, feeding, and orderly operation of Congress than Merlin was to King Arthur or Cardinal Richelieu to Louis XIII."[38] With allowances for journalistic license, the point that Evans makes is a good one; the staff of members of Congress perform vital roles. Like other senators, Henry Jackson had a staff to assist him, and his advisers remained with him for a much longer period than the staff members of most other senators. Jackson's professional assistant and adviser on foreign and defense policy, Dorothy Fosdick, worked for him from 1955 until his death in 1983.[39]

Of all of Jackson's advisers, Richard Perle was undoubtedly the most influential and effective. Perle served Jackson in various professional and staff positions from 1969 to 1979, and he attracted the attention of officials at the highest level of the executive branch throughout that period. Henry Kissinger noted: "I actually considered Jackson a good friend, and I agreed with many of his analyses of Soviet intentions. The difference between Jackson and me was that he wanted all-out confrontation, under the influence of one of his associates, Richard Perle. . . . he liked a policy of constantly 'needling' . . . the Soviet Union."[40] Looking back on his presidency, Jimmy Carter noted, "I never did have much hope that I could convince Richard Perle that we needed the SALT II Treaty or [that we] ought to negotiate any treaty with the Soviet Union."[41]

Part of the reason Perle was so effective is that he had very good ties with Washington journalists. A correspondent for a national magazine recalled that Perle would frequently call him at seven o'clock in the morning, several hours before his weekly deadline, with news items. Often, the correspondent would incorporate these tidbits into his story even though he did not have time to check them.[42] According to a former Senate aide, "Richard Perle understood how to get his point of view across in a timely, appropriate, and convincing way to the national media, and that created a symbiotic relationship with the media and Perle."[43]

Richard Perle was an effective opponent of the SALT II Treaty. Part of his opposition may have been personally motivated. He was a Democrat, and Zbigniew Brzezinski had considered him for a position on the National Security Council; however, he was not offered anything in the executive branch.[44] Nancy Ramsey, the executive director of Americans for SALT, the principal interest group working for ratification of the treaty, when asked who the most effective opponent of the treaty was, replied: "Richard Perle, because everywhere we moved on the Hill, Perle had already been there, or he was right behind us."[45]

Perle was hardly alone; there were a number of conservative staff allies working for other seantors. Sven Kramer had worked for Henry Kissinger before Senator Tower hired him to work for the Republican Policy Committee. Ty McCoy had worked in the CIA and the Department of Defense before going to work for Senator Garn. David Sullivan had worked for the CIA before joining the staff of Senator Gordon Humphrey in 1979. James Lucier and John Carbaugh were Senator Jesse Helms's foreign policy aides.[46] Other aides listed as "available to work on SALT" in Henry Jackson's files included "John Lehman, Sy Weiss, Fred Iklé, Burt Marshall, Charlie Kupperman (Committe on the Present Danger), Bill Schneider (Jack Kemp and Hudson Institute), Colin Gray (Hudson Institute), Bill Van Cleve [sic] (University of Southern California), Dick Pipes (Harvard), Ron Lehman (Senator Tower), Chris Lehman, Mark Schneider (Senator Garn), and Mark Edelman (Senator Danforth)."[47] A number of these aides began meeting regularly at the Madison Hotel, and hence became known as the "Madison group."[48] The members of this group had very good ties to, and obtained sensitive information from, the Department of Defense. They sought to draft amendments that would result in the renegotiation of the treaty, so-called "killer amendments."

Jackson and the other irreconcilable opponents worked against the SALT II Treaty even before it was concluded; a press release by Jackson of May 9, 1979, stated: "From what I know of the SALT II treaty it is substantially unequal and unverifiable. It favors the Soviet Union. In its present form it is not in the security interest of the United States."[49] Despite Jackson's opposition, President Carter had tried to win his support for the treaty, but by the time that the treaty was sent to the Senate, Jackson's opposition was firm.

Henry Jackson was the most prominent opponent of the SALT II Treaty in the Senate, though there were a number of other senators who would have voted against SALT II regardless of the changes that could have been made in the treaty.

The Treaty Supporters

Larry Smith, a former Senate Armed Services Committee staff member, recalled: "A number of the SALT II supporters were intimidated by the presumed expertise of Senator Jackson and his staff on SALT II."[50] In order to defend against Jackson's and other critics' attacks on the treaty, Senators Cranston, Culver, and Hart developed a case for the treaty and a strategy for dealing with the critics' attacks.[51] The case that they developed was based on the premise that the SALT II Treaty would increase the national security of the United States rather than on the idea that arms control was inherently good or that it would contribute to détente. The "national security case for SALT" claimed that the treaty would cap the threat to the United States; that it would help the United States to assess the threat from the Soviet Union; and that the treaty would help us to better evaluate Soviet capabilities. The pro-SALT senators and staff members also developed tactics for dealing with the critics' attacks. They would make sure that an "officer of the day" was on duty at various committee hearings, particularly Senator Jackson's Arms Control Subcommittee, to respond to any questions or attacks by the SALT II critics.

Supporters of the treaty invited twenty senators to form a group, according to the organizer of the group, Alan Cranston, "to consider the strengths and weaknesses of the treaty and to develop supporters within the Senate so that we would be ready to deal with counterarguments."[52] The "Cranston group" met regularly with officials from the administration to discuss treaty issues. In interviews, former Senate staff members gave the Cranston group high marks for stimulating support for the treaty in the Senate. William Bader commented, "The Cranston group was doing what the Foreign Relations Committee should have been doing: holding seminars, inviting people in, and building an internal constituency. The committee was not prepared to do that."[53] Senators Robert Dole and William V. Roth, Jr., organized their own SALT study groups, but these were not as active or effective as the Cranston group.[54]

Just as the staff members who opposed the treaty formed the Madison group, so the staff members who supported the treaty formed several groups of their own. Larry Smith and Charles Stevenson were instrumental in developing the "national security case" for SALT while working for the Senate Armed Services Committee. Senator Edward Kennedy's foreign policy adviser, Jan Kalicki, assembled a group of staff members to meet periodically to discuss various aspects of the treaty. In a memo to Deputy National Security Affairs Adviser David Aaron, the administration's SALT ratification coordinator, Matthew Nimetz, identified a "core of friendly Senate staffers meeting weekly for strategy meeting [sic], including"--(with the Senator or committee for whom or which they worked indicated in parentheses)--"Jan Kalicki (Kennedy), Tom Dine (Budget), Charlie Stevenson (Culver), Lynn Parkinson (Bumpers), Peter Gold (Hart), Larry Smith (Armed Services), Cas Yost (Mathias), John Haynes

(Anderson), Bruce Van Voorst (Clark), Bill Miller (Intelligence), and Bill Ashworth (Foreign Relations).[55]

The Liberal Critics

On March 2, 1979, Senators Hatfield, McGovern, and Proxmire wrote to President Carter: "After considerable thought we have concluded that the proposed SALT II treaty is very difficult, if not impossible, for us to support."[56] The "gang of three" was particularly concerned that "the price of SALT II" would be too high; that to gain the support of conservative senators, the administration would agree to develop and deploy new weapons systems such as the MX missile.[57]

In an interview with the author, Senator Hatfield indicated that he and his two colleagues thought that the Carter administration was trying to buy the support of conservatives. According to Hatfield, "We viewed our strategy as a way to slow down and perhaps stop the constant yielding and placating of the promilitary senators. . . . The more [the Carter administration] placated, then the more they demanded."[58] In fact, the Carter administration was not completely hostile to the criticism of the three senators. After they announced their position, several members of the White House Office of Congressional Relations met with the senators and their staff members on Capitol Hill. They indicated that the "White House would support strong language in the treaty, if the Senate were to put it in, suggesting that the next round [of the SALT negotiations] have very deep reductions." According to one of Proxmire's staff members who was present at this meeting, "We felt that this was a tactical victory of sorts, that we got their attention."[59]

Those in the White House believed that Hatfield, McGovern, and Proxmire were posturing, and that they would vote in favor of the treaty if their votes were needed for it to be ratified.[60] Looking back on the treaty debate, Proxmire believes that he probably would have voted for the treaty if the Senate had voted on the treaty. In an interview, Hatfield noted, "If I had been the deciding vote, I probably would have voted to approve the treaty."[61]

The Undecideds

There were approximately thirty senators who had not decided whether they would vote for or against SALT II by the time it was signed.[62] This clearly was the most important group because it would determine the fate of the treaty.

The two most important formal leaders of the Senate are the majority leader and the minority leader. At the time SALT II was signed, these two positions were held, respectively, by Robert Byrd and Howard Baker. Their support had been crucial during the Panama Canal treaties ratification effort, and the Carter administration wanted their support for the SALT II Treaty.

Majority Leader Byrd did not come out in favor of SALT II at the time it was signed. Instead, he studied the hearings in great detail and considered the testimony before the Foreign Relations, Armed Services, and Intelligence committees. Byrd carefully read not only the treaty but also the transcript of the testimony of various witnesses. According to William Perry, "My single most impressive meeting with any senator was with Senator Byrd. We spent five or six hours one-on-one discussing the treaty, and I found Senator Byrd exceedingly well informed."[63] Byrd may have adopted his noncommittal approach in order to win over the undecided senators. In early July, Byrd led a delegation of senators to Moscow, where they were received by Foreign Minister Andrei Gromyko and General Secretary Leonid Brezhnev. According to reports, Byrd was pleased with his trip to the Soviet Union and the answers that his received to his questions. Nevertheless, Byrd waited until late October to announce his formal support for the treaty.

The Senate minority leader has played an important role in the ratification of past treaties. During the debate on the Limited Nuclear Test Ban Treaty in 1963, President Kennedy was able to obtain the support of the minority leader of the Senate at that time, Everett Dirksen, in order to counter Henry Jackson's criticism of the treaty. Sixteen years later, President Carter sought to convince Senator Dirksen's son-in-law and Senate minority leader, Howard Baker, to support his arms control treaty, SALT II.

Senator Baker had supported several previous arms control agreements, including the SALT I agreements and the Vladivostok Accord. In addition, he had supported President Carter on some important foreign policy issues, including the ratification of the Panama Canal treaties and the lifting of the embargo on arms shipments to Turkey. Perhaps because of this past support, Baker felt vulnerable to conservative attacks within the Republican Party. This was an important consideration at any time, but was even more significant in 1980 because Baker was seeking his party's nomination for president.

At the beginning of 1979, Baker indicated that he was undecided on SALT II and that his vote would depend upon how the Soviets conducted themselves in the world.[64] He also somewhat ominously indicated that the era of bipartisanship in foreign policy was over: "[Arthur] Vandenberg was right in his time, and I think I am right in my time."[65] Within several months, Baker indicated that he was "leaning against" the treaty because of his concerns about the restrictions placed on U.S. strategic programs, the Soviet Backfire bomber, and verification.[66] As late as June 6, Baker was still publicly undecided. He told the National Press Club: "I would like to support SALT II, but, my friends, the issue is not whether I support SALT, the question is whether I support this treaty. And I simply cannot give you the answer to that question at this time."[67] The answer came on June 27 when Senator Baker announced his formal opposition to the treaty: "If the Administration does not signal a willingness to consider amendments, and if the Soviet Government does not desist in trying to threaten the Senate, then I will work diligently and, I trust, effectively to defeat this treaty."[68]

Baker was one of the first members of the Senate Foreign Relations Committee to question the Carter administration's first witness, Harold Brown. According to Paul Warnke, "On the first day of the hearings, Baker came armed for bear, and Brown, who had great experience in the [arms control] field, peeled Baker like an onion, and he did not come back to the hearings."[69] On November 2, Baker formally announced his candidacy for the Republican nomination for president, and one week later, in the

Foreign Relations Committee, he voted against reporting the treaty favorably to the Senate. Baker had gone from the undecided to the opposed column of the vote counters. According to Baker, "SALT II is a disaster for the deterrent effect of our weapons system. It gives us nothing of value in return, it validates Soviet strategic arms superiority, and it thus endangers national security."[70]

Both critics and supporters of SALT II viewed Sam Nunn's role in the debate over the treaty as crucial. Just three weeks after his inauguration, President Carter sent Nunn a hand-written, "personal and confidential" note in which he assured the senator, "As you know, I will be the monitor and actual negotiator in arms limitation talks, and I will stay close to you and others."[71] Eugene Rostow recalled that he believed the treaty was doomed when three senators--Nunn, Baker, and Jackson--requested research help from, and began meeting with the members of, the Committee on the Present Danger.[72] One White House official commented, "I can envision winning SALT without Jackson and possibly even without Baker. . . . But without Nunn, we're dead."[73] In January 1979, Frank Moore and Zbigniew Brzezinski wrote a memo to President Carter concerning the administration's ratification strategy in the Senate. They pointed out, "Nunn is, perhaps, the most crucial Senator in the SALT ratification battle. . . . He may be one of the only Senators who can effectively counter Jackson."[74] During the height of the debate over SALT II in the summer of 1979, Madeleine Albright, Brzezinski's aide for congressional liaison, wrote a memo to him saying, "Sam Nunn is going to be crucial to the passage of SALT. Within 24 hours, he managed to switch the debate from one which was focused on verification, Protocol, and heavy missiles to one about overall defense posture."[75]

Prior to his election to the Senate, Sam Nunn had served as a state senator in Georgia, and before that as president of the Perry, Georgia, Chamber of Commerce, his first elected office. Because Nunn and President Carter came from the same state, they knew and had dealt with one another before either came to Washington. When he was a state legislator, Nunn supported Carter in both of his gubernatorial campaigns. In 1972, Nunn defeated the candidate for the U.S. Senate whom Carter had appointed to fill the vacancy created by the death of Richard Russell. During the early 1976 Democratic presidential primaries, Nunn remained neutral, but he strongly supported Carter in the general election. Following his election to the Senate in 1972 with a respectable 54 percent of the vote, Nunn went to Washington with his great-uncle, Representative Carl Vinson, who served as chairman of the House Armed Services Committee. The two men called on John Stennis, Henry Jackson, Robert Byrd, and Mike Mansfield to request that the new senator be appointed to the Senate Armed Services Committee. The Senate leadership was impressed with Nunn and appointed him to the committee; within several years of his arrival in the Senate, Sam Nunn was a respected expert on military affairs.

During the Carter administration, Nunn criticized the president for unilaterally canceling the B-1 bomber program, and he was influential in convincing the Senate not to cancel the enhanced radiation weapon (the "neutron bomb"). According to one senator, "Nunn has more credibility on SALT than just about anybody in the Senate. When I first came to the Senate, we just naturally looked to Scoop [Henry] Jackson for leadership on arms control, but Jackson has used up a lot of his credibility in recent years."[76] Senator Lawton Chiles noted, "SALT is incredibly complicated. It hurts your head. Most senators are involved in so many things they don't have time to be an expert on everything, so you look around for somebody you can trust. Sam is not an ideologue. He is not going to influence the kneejerks on the right or left, but his credibility will sway some votes among the uncommitted."[77]

Nunn was concerned about a number of aspects of the SALT II Treaty, including the vulnerability of U.S. land-based missiles, the Soviet Backfire bomber, the verification of the agreement, and the effect of the protocol to the agreement.[78] When asked about the strategic impact of the treaty, Nunn replied:

One of the principal questions is whether we are tranquilized into thinking we really do have overall parity and that this treaty will allow us to continue our spending levels with the Soviets continuing theirs, as they are now. If that happens, they will achieve superiority. If the whole debate stimulates the United States to adopt strategic programs and overall military posture is substantially enhanced, then it will have served a good purpose, whether the treaty is ratified or rejected.[79]

To Nunn, the most important question was not the effect of the treaty on arms control but the effect of the treaty on U.S. defense programs. Following the signing of the treaty, Nunn led the battle to force the Carter administration to increase the defense budget in exchange for his support of SALT II. The administration was committed to a 3 percent increase, but Nunn wanted an increase of 5 percent. In early September, Nunn criticized the administration's approach: "Voltaire once said of the Holy Roman Empire that it was neither holy, Roman, nor an empire. As of July 1979, the administration's three percent real growth was neither three percent, nor real, nor growth."[80]

President Carter recognized the key role that Nunn played in the SALT II debate. He recalled:

Sam was one of the senators who took the position that a SALT II Treaty was beneficial to our country, that it was a balanced treaty, and I was able to confide in Sam about the ultrasecret verification capabilities we had in nations around the Soviet Union. These couldn't be revealed to the public and couldn't be revealed to other senators. But Sam used the SALT II Treaty in a legitimate fashion to extract from me promises for a higher level of defense expenditures, and I didn't particularly object to that."[81]

On December 17, Nunn, along with eighteen other senators, sent Carter a letter in which they expressed their concerns about the SALT II Treaty.[82] Three days later, Nunn voted with six other members of the Senate Armed Services Committee who were opposed to the committee's release of its critical report on the treaty. By that time, although he never made a formal commitment on SALT II, Nunn was reportedly leaning toward supporting ratification of the treaty.[83]

THE COMMITTEE HEARINGS

Following President Carter's submission of the SALT II Treaty to the Senate, the treaty was referred to the Senate Foreign Relations Committee (SFRC), which, since its creation in 1816, has had exclusive jurisdiction over treaties. When the SALT II

Treaty was submitted to the Senate, the conservative members of the Armed Services Committee, led by Senator Jackson, pressured chairman Stennis to hold hearings on the treaty. Founded in 1976 and specifically charged with the responsibility for overseeing intelligence activities of the executive branch, the Senate Intelligence Committee was given the task of assessing the verification procedures of the treaty. In this section the actions of the Senate Foreign Relations, Senate Armed Services, and Intelligence committees will be reviewed.

The Senate Foreign Relations Committee

Because of the responsibility and the prestige of the Senate Foreign Relations Committee, positions on the committee have been highly sought after. And the chairmanship of the SFRC has traditionally been one of the most important positions in the Senate. The character and the effectiveness of congressional committees are heavily influenced by the persons who chair them. Previous chairmen of the SFRC have included some of the most influential members of the Senate: Henry Cabot Lodge, William Borah, and J. William Fulbright, who served for fifteen years. Following Fulbright's defeat in 1974, John Sparkman served as chair from 1974 to 1978; most considered his leadership to have been mediocre at best.

Soon after his election to the Senate in 1956, then Senate Majority Leader Lyndon Johnson appointed Frank Church to the SFRC. At the end of 1978, Sparkman retired, and Church, with twenty-two years of experience on the committee, became the chairman. Superficially, one would have thought that Church and Carter would have been complementary; both were moralists concerning foreign policy. However, they had run against one another in several 1976 Democratic presidential primaries, and harbored some resentment as a result of these contests. According to William Bader, "The White House Staff, the 'Georgia mafiosi' . . . hated Frank Church for political reasons. Church had beaten Carter in four out of five primaries."[84] Rosalynn Carter believed that Democratic Party liberals, presumably including Frank Church, had launched a movement known as "ABC (Anybody But Carter)" during the last three weeks of the campaign.[85] Despite whatever ill will existed between Carter and Church, Carter indicated a desire to work closely with the SFRC and its chairman by meeting with the members of the committee before inauguration, an unprecedented action for a president-elect.[86]

Following the 1978 elections, there were two significant changes within the committee. First, three conservative Republicans--Jesse Helms, Richard Lugar, and S. I. Hayakawa--joined the committee. The other three Republican members were moderates, Jacob Javits (the ranking Republican member), Charles Percy, and Howard Baker. The nine Democratic members of the committee (in descending order of seniority) were Frank Church (chair), Claiborne Pell, George McGovern, Joseph Biden, Jr., John Glenn, Richard Stone, Paul Sarbanes, Edmund Muskie, and Edward Zorinsky. Biden and Lugar were also members of the Senate Intelligence Committee, which reviewed the verification procedures of the treaty.

The second important change within the SFRC was the decision to do away with the former bipartisan staff and to create a minority staff. As was the case with congressional staff overall, the staff of the SFRC had grown significantly in the late 1960s and 1970s. In 1965, there were nine professional staff members; by 1979 the number had grown to thirty. Both the addition of the three conservative Republican members and the creation of a minority staff heightened partisan division within the committee.

On the same day that President Carter signed the SALT II Treaty, the staff director of the SFRC sent a memorandum to the members of the committee outlining a proposal for the schedule of the hearings.[87] This proposal called for twenty days of hearings, four days for the committee's markup, and a target date of September 25 to submit the committee's report to the Senate. By way of comparison, the SFRC had held seven days of hearings in 1972 during its consideration of the SALT I agreements, and had held sixteen days of hearings, two days of markup, and three days of executive session briefings during its consideration of the Panama Canal treaties. As it turned out, the schedule outlined by the SFRC staff director could not be kept for reasons related primarily to events that were only indirectly connected to SALT II.

On July 9, the SFRC began hearings on the treaty. They were held for a total of twenty-seven days from July through October. The public hearing record filled 5 volumes of 2,266 pages with the testimony of 88 witnesses.[88] In addition, the committee held thirteen executive sessions, and the transcripts of these sessions totaled more than twelve hundred pages. Six witnesses testified only in executive session, bringing the total number of witnesses who testified before the committee to ninety-four.[89]

The Senate Armed Services Committee

The SFRC and the Senate Armed Services Committee (SASC) have competed for the right to review treaties. Following President Kennedy's submission of the Limited Nuclear Test Ban Treaty to the Senate in 1963, the SASC held hearings on the military implications of the agreement. In 1968, Senator J. William Fulbright, then chairman of the SFRC, called hearings on the need for antiballistic missiles, an area the SASC considered to be its exclusive jurisdiction. In 1972, the SASC held hearings on the "military implications" of the SALT I agreements. During the Carter administration, both the SFRC and the SASC held hearings on the Panama Canal treaties.

Opponents of the SALT II Treaty were anxious to have a formal, public forum in which to review and criticize the treaty. Senator Jackson, a member of the SASC, pressured the chairman of the committee, John Stennis, to hold hearings on the treaty. In addition to Stennis and Jackson, the other Democratic members of the committee (in descending order of seniority) were Howard Cannon, Harry Byrd, Sam Nunn, John Culver, Gary Hart, Robert Morgan, J. James Exon, and Carl Levin. The Republican members of the committee were John Tower (the ranking minority member), Strom Thurmond, Barry Goldwater, John Warner, Gordon Humphrey, William Cohen, and Roger Jepsen. The SASC held hearings on 16 days; the testimony of 29 committee witnesses filled 1,610 pages of 4 volumes.[90]

Henry Jackson and Richard Perle used the SASC as a forum in which to criticize the SALT II Treaty. According to Nancy Ramsey, Perle was "absolutely unstinting in his opposition and his ability to use the [Senate] Armed Services Committee for his purposes."[91] Jackson's and Perle's files contain a number of memoranda concerning their preparations for the SASC hearings. One memo, entitled "An Outline for the SASC Hearings: What We Hope to Establish," notes: "It should be our purpose in the hearings to demonstrate that pivotal administration arguments are not supported by evidence and/or logic, that the treaty is unequal and unverifiable, that it is flawed with loopholes and ambiguities."[92]   Another memo reviews the strengths and weaknesses of various Carter administration witnesses.[93] Harold Brown was viewed as "probably the administration's strongest witness." The newly appointed director of the Arms Control and Disarmament Agency, retired Gen. George Seignious, was portrayed as "a weak witness--if he claims that he is only recently involved we help make the point that it is Warnke's treaty." Clearly, Jackson and Perle wanted to characterize the treaty as Warnke's: "Even though retired, Warnke should be called as the principal architect of the treaty."

The supporters and the opponents of the treaty worked with the witnesses who bolstered their respective cases. Larry Smith, the staff member who was working closely with senators Culver and Hart on the SASC, coordinated the questions that the SASC supporters were going to ask administration witnesses.[94] Senator Jackson's office coordinated the testimony of the witnesses opposed to the treaty. A memo of October 1979 from Jackson's office notes, "Nitze is best speaking from his own experience--in this case as a SALT negotiator during the last administration. There are several issues that he wishes to address, including: (1) a comparison of his force ratios ... with Harold Brown's . . . ; (2) the administration's lack of candor in relating the Soviet position on MX deployment; [and] (3) the irrelevance of the 10 RV [reentry vehicle] (fractionation) limit to the survivability of Minuteman."[95] This memo also noted, "Ed [Rowny] wants a chance at least to paraphrase the assessments he made for the JCS and their views as expressed in the memoranda they refuse to turn over. I will prepare a couple of questions that will give him an opportunity to lay that out."[96] The SASC's hearings on the treaty provided the forum for opponents to publicly express their criticisms.

The Senate Intelligence Committee

The Senate Intelligence Committee was created to oversee executive branch intelligence operations and to consider matters related to the intelligence capabilities of the United States. Consequently, the SFRC requested that the Intelligence Committee review the verification issues related to the SALT II Treaty. There were three specific reasons that the request was made: (1) the issues involved were of a highly sensitive nature; (2) verification was clearly going to be a significant issue in the debate over SALT, and it therefore deserved the most thorough and professional treatment; and (3) the Intelligence Committee was set up to deal with these issues.[97]   Several members of the Intelligence Committee were also members of either the SFRC (Biden and Lugar) or the SASC (Jackson). According to William Miller, the staff director of the Intelligence Committee in 1979, "about one-third of the Senate reviewed the material collected by the Intelligence Committee, and nine or ten of these considered it very closely. . . . Senator [Robert C.] Byrd was one of those who was rigorous in reviewing the material."[98] Verification became an important issue in the debate over SALT II, and the Senate Intelligence Committee played an important role in addressing this issue. On October 5, the committee issued its unclassified five-page report.[99]

THE SENATE'S ACTION ON THE TREATY

After the president submits a treaty to the Senate for its advice and consent, it is referred to the relevant committee or committees, which hold hearings and issue a report. The full Senate may act on the treaty in several different ways. First, the Senate may advise and consent to the ratification of a treaty as it is submitted, without proposing any changes. Second, it may reject a treaty. Third, the Senate may attach specific stipulations in its resolution of ratification. There are several different types of conditions, including amendments, reservations, understandings, and declarations.[100] An amendment changes the actual text of the treaty, and therefore the terms of the contract between or among the signatories. Therefore, a treaty that is amended by the Senate has to be resubmitted to the president and the other parties to the treaty. A reservation is "a limitation, qualification, or contradiction of the obligations in the treaty, especially as they relate to the party making the reservation."[101] A reservation may have such a significant effect on the terms of a treaty that the president has to notify the other signatories of treaty, which, in turn, can file a reservation of their own or refuse to proceed with the treaty. During the hearings on the SALT II Treaty, there was some question as to the legal status of reservations. In his testimony to the SFRC, Eugene V. Rostow argued that "a reservation has the same legal effect as a letter from my mother."[102] To remove any doubts about the legal status of reservations, the SFRC drafted the resolution of ratification to require that the Soviet Union explicitly accept all reservations adopted by the Senate.

Understandings or interpretations may be part of the resolution of ratification in order to explain, elaborate, or clarify certain aspects of the treaty. If an interpretation does not affect the terms of the treaty, it has no legal effect; however, the president informs the other negotiating parties of any such interpretations. Such understandings are commonly used to clarify the meanings of treaties. Similar to "sense of the Senate" resolutions, declarations are "statements of the Senate's position, opinion or intentions on matters relating to issues raised by the treaty in question, but not to its specific provisions."[103]

A number of amendments to the SALT II Treaty were considered by the SFRC. The opponents of the treaty drafted amendments designed to make the treaty unacceptable to the Soviet Union. A number of these "killer amendments" were presented by conservative senators. Other amendments were presented for other reasons. According to Senator Garn, "I didn't expect any of my amendments to be accepted in the Senate. . . . I wanted to use them as an educational process. . . ."[104]

The SFRC concluded its hearings and began its markup sessions on the treaty on October 15. The committee held sixteen public sessions and six executive sessions during markup, and considered thirty-six conditions to the SALT II Treaty. The committee divided these conditions into three categories. "Category I" conditions were those that did not require formal notification to the Soviet Union.[105] "Category II" provisions were those that "would be formally communicated to the Soviet Union as official statements of the position of the United States Government in ratifying the Treaty, but . . . do not require their agremeent."[106] "Category III" provisions were those that would require the explicit agreement of the Soviet government in order for the treaty to enter into force. Twenty of the thirty-six proposed conditions were adopted; of these, thirteen were "Category I" conditions, five were "Category II" conditions, and two were "Category III" conditions. Clearly, the latter were the most important conditions because they required the explicit approval of the Soviet Union. The first of these conditions was a reservation adopted by the SFRC by a vote of 14-0 that stipulated that the agreed statements and common understandings contained in the SALT II Treaty and protocol would be of the same legal status as the treaty. The second "Category III" condition adopted by the committee was a reservation that the letter given by General Secretary Brezhnev to President Carter concerning the capabilities and production of the Backfire bomber would be legally binding on the Soviet Union.

On October 5, 1979, the Senate Intelligence Committee issued a unanimous report that concluded: "Overall, the Committee finds that the SALT II Treaty enhances the ability of the United States to monitor those components of Soviet strategic weapons forces which are subject to the limitations of the Treaty."[107] Considering the fact that the members of the Intelligence Committee included such hard-liners as Henry Jackson, Jake Garn, Richard Lugar (who voted aginst the treaty in the Foreign Relations Committee) and Malcolm Wallop, the unanimous approval of the Intelligence Committee's report significantly strengthened the claim of the Carter administration that the treaty was verifiable.

On November 9, 1979, after four months of hearings and what SFRC members characterized as one of the most exhaustive considerations of any treaty to be submitted to the U.S. Senate, the SFRC, by a vote of 9-6, voted to recommend the ratification of the treaty to the full Senate. Seven Democrats (Edward Zorinsky, Frank Church, George McGovern, Joseph R. Biden, Paul S. Sarbanes, Edmund S. Muskie, and Claiborne Pell) and two Republicans (Percy and Javits) voted in favor of the treaty. Two Democrats (Glenn and Stone) and four Republicans (Helms, Hayakawa, Baker, and Lugar) voted against it.

On December 20, 1979, over the objections of SASC Chairman John Stennis, the committee adopted a report denouncing the treaty as "not in the national security interests of the United States." According to reports, Henry Jackson and his staff aide, Richard Perle, were the principal authors of the report.[108] The report specifically cited the following areas of concern: (1) certain inequalities, such as the Soviet advantage in throw weight, the Soviet possession of modern, large ballistic missiles, the exclusion of the Soviet Backfire bomber, the inclusion of Western theater nuclear forces, and the potential precedents established by the protocol to the treaty; (2) loopholes concerning "new types" of ICBMs; (3) the verification of the treaty; and (4) ambiguities contained in the treaty.[109] Ten senators voted in favor of releasing the report and seven senators voted "present," indicating their opposition to the release of the report.[110] Although the report was released in December 1979, Majority Leader

Byrd did not allow it to be filed until a year later, at the end of the ninety-sixth Congress. One Senate aide noted, "People in the White House were absolutely crushed by the vote in the Senate Armed Services Committe," and in an interview, Anne Wexler confirmed that this vote was viewed as a major setback.[111]

Estimates vary as to what the vote count was on the treaty. Alan Cranston, known as one of the best vote counters in the Senate, estimated that shortly before the treaty was signed, the tally stood at twenty firmly against, ten leaning against, forty leaning heavily toward ratification, ten leaning slightly toward ratification, and twenty undecided.[112] In retrospect, Richard Perle recalled, "The treaty was dead after the hearings."[113] Larry Smith estimated that after the hearings the vote stood at fifty-seven in favor of the treaty, twenty-seven opposed, and sixteen undecided.

CONCLUSION

Jimmy Carter, Hamilton Jordan, Jody Powell, Gerald Rafshoon, and Carter's other advisers from Georgia were very good at running elections, as Carter's nearly miraculous election in 1976 showed. Once in office, the members of the new administration prided themselves on being Washington "outsiders." In the aftermath of Vietnam and Watergate, the American public viewed not being from Washington as a virtue. Viewed from another angle, however, not being from Washington meant that the administration had no experience in the city's arcane ways. Initially, the members of the Carter administration believed that they could operate the way they wanted to, without regard for what they viewed as the stuffiness and pretension of official Washington.

The Carter administration had some early successes in dealing with the Congress, not so much because of the administration's adeptness but because the administration went around Congress and appealed to the American people. In the debate over the Panama Canal treaties, the members of the Carter administration did what they did best: they ran a political campaign in order to get the treaties ratified. Influential citizens from key states were invited to attend briefings and encouraged to urge their senators to vote for the treaties.

Buoyed by the Panama Canal treaties experience and success, the members of the administration decided to adopt the same approach once the SALT II Treaty was signed. But the domestic and the international contexts were quite different in 1979 than earlier in the administration. The adminstration had used a great deal of its political capital by 1979, and this capital had not been replenished. Indeed, the minor slights and personality conflicts between administration officials and members of Congress had exacerbated relations between the White House and Capitol Hill. In addition, Jimmy Carter and his principal foreign policy officers, Cyrus Vance and Harold Brown, were not inclined to meet, nor did they enjoy meeting, informally with members of Congress.

The Carter administration did not begin its campaign to ratify the SALT II Treaty until it was signed in June 1979, but the treaty opponents had been working against the treaty for several years. A political campaign takes time, money, and personnel to run. The members of the Carter administration could devote their attention and the resources of the executive branch to the ratification of the treaty, but there were many other issues that demanded their attention. And there were legal restrictions against the use of federal funds for lobbying for a particular program such as the SALT II Treaty.

At the time President Carter signed the treaty and submitted it to the Senate for its advice and consent, it appeared that public opinion favored the treaty and the Senate opposed it, just the opposite of the case with the Panama Canal treaties. Despite this fact, the administration adopted a ratification strategy based on the Panama Canal treaties model. As three Senate committees conducted hearings on the treaty during the summer of 1979, at the other end of Pennsylvania Avenue the White House sought to win public support for the treaty.

On Capitol Hill, a group of pro-treaty senators led by Alan Cranston, John Culver, Gary Hart, and Joseph Biden and staff members Larry Smith, Charles Stevenson, and Jan Kalicki sought to increase support for the treaty. The anti-treaty senators were led by Henry Jackson, Jake Garn, Jesse Helms, and John Tower and staff members Richard Perle, John Carbaugh, and James Lucier. Each side sought to use the hearings as a forum in which to prove its case. Because this treaty concerned defense issues rather than simply foreign policy issues, the SASC hearings and critical report were significant. In other cases in which the SFRC and SASC had held differing views, the report of the Foreign Relations Committee was often given greater weight because other treaties dealt primarily with foreign policy rather than defense issues. Nevertheless, by the end of the summer of 1979, it apeared that the treaty proponents had won the battle. In its lead editorial of August 20, 1979, the *Los Angeles Times* predicted: "it appears probable that the agreement will be ratified by the Senate."[114] Politically conservative publications such as *Business Week* supported ratification of the treaty.[115] If the Senate had voted on SALT II in mid-to-late August, it would have been ratified. But such a vote was not taken because the SFRC had not completed its hearings and report on the treaty.

At the end of August, the announcement by Senator Frank Church of the "discovery" of a Soviet combat brigade in Cuba caused great concern and a delay in the consideration of the treaty. Although the SFRC's original schedule called for the committeee to submit its report to the full Senate on September 25, the Soviet combat brigade caused the submission of this report to be held up. When it was finally sent to the Senate on November 19, a second external event--the Iranian students' takeover of the American Embassy in Tehran--had taken place just two weeks earlier. The Iranian hostage crisis diverted the attention of President Carter, the Senate, and the American people from SALT II. At the end of December, a third external event, the Soviet invasion of Afghanistan, made it politically impossible to proceed with ratification efforts in the Senate, and President Carter asked the Senate to suspend its consideration of the treaty.

NOTES

1. Jimmy Carter interviewed by Michael Charlton, in *From Deterrence to Defense: The Inside Story of Strategic Policy* (Cambridge, Mass.: Harvard University Press, 1987), p. 72.

2. Howard Baker, "Press Conference on SALT II," unpublished transcript, June 27, 1979.

3. John Glenn, "SALT: A Congressional Perspective," press release, May 17, 1979, p. 1.

4. Michael Foley, *The New Senate: Liberal Influence on a Conservative Institution, 1959-1972* (New Haven: Yale University Press, 1980).

5. I. M. Destler, "Congress," in Joseph S. Nye, Jr., ed., *The Making of America's Soviet Policy* (New Haven: Yale University Press, 1984), p. 54.

6. Joshua Muravchik, "The Senate and National Security: A New Mood," in David M. Abshire and Ralph N. Nurnberger, eds., *The Growing Power of Congress* (Beverly Hills, Calif.: Sage Publications, 1981), pp. 251-252.

7. Ibid., pp. 200-201.

8. Thomas P. O'Neill, Jr., with William Novak, *Man of the House: The Life and Political Memoirs of Speaker Tip O'Neill* (New York: Random House, 1987), pp. 310-311.

9. Ibid., p. 308.

10. Jimmy Carter, quoted in Robert Shogan, *Promises to Keep: Carter's First Hundred Days* (New York: Crowell, 1977), p. 207.

11. Jimmy Carter, *Keeping Faith: Memoirs of a President* (New York: Bantam Books, 1982), p. 65.

12. Author's interview with Larry Smith, Washington, D.C., October 20, 1987.

13. Charles O. Jones, *The Trusteeship Presidency: Jimmy Carter and the United States Congress* (Baton Rouge: Louisiana State University Press, 1988), p. 96.

14. Memo from Madeleine Albright to Zbigniew Brzezinski, "Overview of the 95th Congress," October 20, 1978, "FG 6-1-1/Aaron, David: 1/20/77-12/31/79," Box FG-23, WHCF-Subject File, Federal Government-Organizations, Jimmy Carter Library.

15. Carter, *Keeping Faith*, p. 108.

16. This was also the view of congressional staffers interviewed by Eric L. Davis, "Legislative Liaison in the Carter Administration," *Political Science Quarterly* 94 (Summer 1979):292.

17. Author's interviews with Larry Smith and Alan Platt, Washington, D.C., October 23, 1987.

18. Author's interview with Senator William Proxmire, Washington, D.C., June 4, 1987.

19. Davis, "Legislative Liaison in the Carter Administration," pp. 290-292.

20. William Bader, "Congress and the Making of U.S. Security Policies," *Adelphi Papers* 173 (Spring 1982):18.

21. Author's interview with William Perry, Menlo Park, Calif., January 15, 1988.

22. Alan Platt, *The U.S. Senate and Strategic Arms Policy, 1969-1977* (Boulder: Westview Press, 1978).

23. Public Law 87-297, 75 Stat. 631, sec. 33.

24. Letter from Paul Warnke to Vice President Mondale, May 7, 1977, in Henry M. Jackson Papers, Accession no. 3560-6, Box 61, Folder 12, University of Washington Libraries.

25. Author's interview with Ralph Earle II, Washington, D.C., October 23, 1987.

26. Muravchik, "The Senate and National Security," p. 1.

27. John F. Bibby, Thomas E. Mann, and Norman J. Ornstein, *Vital Statistics on Congress 1980* (Washington, D.C.: American Enterprise Institute, 1980), pp. 71-73; Jones, *The Trusteeship Presidency*, pp. 62-63.

28. Charles O. Jones, *The United States Congress: People, Places and Policy* (Homewood, Ill.: Dorsey Press, 1982), p. 58.

29. See, e.g., Mark M. Lowenthal, *SALT Verification*, Report no. 78-142F (Washington, D.C.: Library of Congress, Congressional Research Service, 1978); and Harry L. Wren, *SALT II: Major Policy Issues*, Issue Brief no. IB79074 (Washington, D.C.: Library of Congress, Congressional Research Service, 1979).

30. U.S. Congress, Congressional Budget Office, *SALT II and the Costs of Modernizing U.S. Strategic Forces* (Washington, D.C.: Government Printing Office, 1979).

31. Bibby, Mann, and Ornstein, *Vital Statistics on Congress*, p. 74.

32. Author's interview with William Bader, Arlington, Va., October 20, 1987.

33. Strobe Talbott, *Endgame: The Inside Story of SALT II* (New York: Harper and Row, 1979), pp. 215-216.

34. James McGregor Burns, "Jimmy Carter's Strategy for 1980," *Atlantic Monthly* 243, no. 3 (March 1979):41.

35. Richard Burt, "Carter Will Submit Treaty on Missiles," *New York Times*, January 15, 1979, p. A-1.

36. Unidentified Senate aide quoted in Rudy Abramson, "GOP Liberals, Moderates Hold Fate of Arms Pact," *Los Angeles Times*, May 11, 1979, pp. 10-11.

37. Richard Perle, "The Senator and American Arms Policy," in Dorothy Fosdick, ed., *Staying the Course: Henry M. Jackson and National Security* (Seattle: University of Washington Press, 1987), pp. 194-195.

38. Rowland Evans, quoted in Harrison W. Fox, Jr., and Susan Webb Hammond, *Congressional Staffs: The Invisible Force in American Lawmaking* (New York: The Free Press, 1977), p. vii.

39. Dorothy Fosdick's father was Harry Emerson Fosdick, one of the most respected Protestant preachers of the twentieth century and a prominent pacifist. Given Senator Jackson's hard-line positions on foreign and defense policy, it was more than a little ironic that Fosdick's daughter was his principal adviser during his Senate career.

40. Henry Kissinger, interviewed in Charlton, *From Deterrence to Defense*, p. 43 (emphasis in original).

41. Author's telephone interview with Jimmy Carter, April 12, 1988, transcript, p. 2.

42. Author's confidential interview.

43. Author's interview with Alan Platt, Washington, D.C., October 23, 1987.

44. Perle denies that he wanted a position in the Carter administration, but other sources indicated that he wanted to go into the executive branch. Author's interviews with Alan Platt; Barry Blechman, Washington, D.C., October 23, 1987; Richard Perle, telephone interview, November 10, 1988.

45. Author's interview with Nancy Ramsey, Washington, D.C., June 5, 1987.

46. Muravchik, "The Senate and National Security," p. 255.

47. "List of Staff Available for Work on SALT," Henry M. Jackson Papers, Accession no. 3560-6, Box 61, Folder 12, University of Washington Libraries.

48. Jody Powell, *The Other Side of the Story* (New York: William Morrow, 1984), pp. 252-262.

49. "Statement by Senator Henry M. Jackson," press release, May 9, 1979, in Henry M. Jackson Papers, Accession no. 3560-6, Box 13, Folder 15, University of Washington Libraries.

50. Author's interview with Larry Smith.

51. Author's interviews with Larry Smith; Alan Cranston, Washington, D.C., June 5, 1987; and John Culver, Washington, D.C., July 12, 1988.

52. Author's interview with Alan Cranston. The members of the group were Senators Cranston (chair), Dale Bumpers, John Chafee, Frank Church, John Culver, John Durkin, John Glenn, Gary Hart, Daniel Inouye, Edward Kennedy, Patrick Leahy, Carl Levin, Charles Mathias, Robert Morgan, Edmund Muskie, Claiborne Pell, William Proxmire, David Pryor, James Sasser, Robert Stafford, and Paul Tsongas.

53. Author's interview with William Bader.

54. The participants in the Dole Group were William Armstrong, Henry Bellmon, Pete Domenici, Gordon Humphrey, Robert Jepson, Harrison Schmitt, Richard Schweiker, Alan Simpson, Strom Thurmon, Malcolm Wallop, and John Warner. The Roth Group included Henry Bellmon,

Rudy Boschwitz, Lawton Chiles, Dennis DeConcini, Walter Huddleston, John Melcher, Larry Pressler, James Sasser, and Alan Simpson.

55. Tab 1 of memo from Matthew Nimetz to David Aaron, January 18, 1978, WHCF-Subject File, FO 6-1, Jimmy Carter Library.

56. Letter from George McGovern, Mark Hatfield, and William Proxmire to President Carter, March 2, 1979, printed in *Congressional Record--Senate*, March 5, 1979, p. S2044.

57. Richard Burt, "Liberal Senators Say Arms Pact Would Not Curb Weapons Race," *New York Times*, March 5, 1979, p. 1.

58. Author's interview with Mark O. Hatfield, Washington, D.C., June 7, 1987.

59. Author's interview with Ronald Tammen, Washington, D.C., June 4, 1987.

60. Author's interview with Anne Wexler, Washington, D.C., October 28, 1988.

61. Author's interviews with Hatfield; and William Proxmire, Washington, D.C., June 4, 1987.

62. Author's interview with Ralph Earle II, Washington, D.C., October 23, 1987. In July, the Friends Committee on National Legislation estimated that twenty-nine were likely to vote for the treaty, thirteen were leaning toward support, twenty-eight were undecided, sixteen were leaning against, and fourteen were definitely against the treaty. *FCNL Washington Newsletter,* July 1979, p. 8.

63. Author's interview with William Perry, Menlo Park, Calif., January 15, 1988.

64. "Baker: Senate Undecided on SALT II," *Washington Post*, January 15, 1979.

65. Comments on "Meet the Press," January 14, 1979, quoted by I. M. Destler, "Trade Consensus, SALT Stalemate," p. 345.

66. Steven V. Roberts, "Baker Is Inclining Against Arms Pact," *New York Times*, April 12, 1979, p. A-1.

67. "Speech by Senator Howard Baker to the National Press Club," June 6, 1979, unpublished transcript, p. 3.

68. "Statement by Senate Republican Leader Howard Baker on the SALT II Treaty," June 27, 1979, unpublished transcript, p. 2.

69. Author's interview with Paul Warnke, Los Angeles, May 20, 1987.

70. Howard Baker, *No Margin for Error: America in the Eighties* (New York: Times Books, 1980), p. 192.

71. Letter from President Carter to Sam Nunn, February 14, 1977, "Executive, FG 264, 1/1/78-12/31/78," Box FG-209, WHCF-Subject File, Federal Government-Organizations, Jimmy Carter Library.

72. Author's interview with Eugene V. Rostow, Washington, D.C., October 1988.

73. Albert R. Hunt, "In the SALT Debate, Senator Sam Nunn's Role Could Prove Decisive," *Wall Street Journal*, March 22, 1979, p. 1.

74. Memo from Frank Moore and Zbigniew Brzezinski to President Carter, January 23, 1979, WHCF, Foreign Affairs, Executive, FO 6-1, 11/21/78-2/10/79, Jimmy Carter Library.

75. Memo from Madeleine Albright to Zbigniew Brzezinski, July 30, 1979, "Executive, FO 6-1 (7/13/79-7/31/79)," Box FO-42, WHCF-Subject File, Foreign Affairs, Jimmy Carter Library.

76. Unidentified senator quoted in Phil Gailey, "Nunn May be Key in Senate's SALT Debate," *Washington Star*, April 27, 1979, p. A-7.

77. Ibid.

78. Sam Nunn, "SALT II," unpublished speech delivered to the Air Force Association, Warner Robins, Ga., July 17, 1978, p. 1.

79. "Three Senate Experts Discuss the Pros and Cons of SALT II," *New York Times*, July 8, 1979, p. 7.

80. Sam Nunn, "SALT II and Defense Spending," *Congressional Record--Senate*, September 7, 1979, p. S12167.

81. Author's telephone interview with President Carter, April 12, 1988, transcript, p. 3.

82. Letter to President Carter from Sam Nunn, Lawton Chiles, John Danforth, Harrison Schmidt, Edward Zorinsky, David Boren, Lloyd Bentsen, J. J. Exon, Dennis DeConcini, Alan Simpson, John Warner, Henry Bellmon, Rudy Boschwitz, Peter Domenici, John Heinz, Richard Stone, S. I. Hayakawa, Larry Pressler, and David Durenberger, December 17, 1979, author's files, p. 4.

83. Congressional Quarterly, *Weekly Report*, December 15, 1979.

84. Author's interview with William Bader.

85. Rosalynn Carter, *First Lady from Plains* (Boston: Houghton Mifflin, 1984), p. 132.

86. U.S. Congress, Senate, Foreign Relations Committee, *Meeting with President-Elect Carter*, 94th Congress, transition period, November 23, 1976.

87. Memo from William Bader to the members of the Senate Committee on Foreign Relations, June 18, 1979, Henry M. Jackson Papers, Accession no. 3560-6, Box 49, Folder 26, University of Washington Libraries.

88. U.S. Congress, Senate, Committee on Foreign Relations, *The SALT II Treaty*, hearings, 5 vols., 96th Congress, 1st sess., 1979.

89. U.S. Congress, Senate, Committee on Foreign Relations, *The SALT II Treaty*, report no. 96-14, November 19, 1979, 96th Congress, 1st sess., 1979.

90. U.S. Congress, Senate, Committee on Armed Services, *Military Implications of the Treaty on the Limitation of Strategic Offensive Arms and Protocol Thereto (SALT II Treaty)*, hearings, 4 vols., 96th Congress, 1st sess., 1979.

91. Author's interview with Nancy Ramsey.

92. Office of Senator Henry M. Jackson, "An Outline for SASC Hearings: What We Hope to Establish," Henry M. Jackson Papers, Accession no. 3560-6, Box 61, Folder 12, University of Washington Libraries.

93. Office of Senator Henry M. Jackson, "SALT Hearings Witness List," Henry M. Jackson Papers, Accession no. 3560-6, Box 61, Folder 12, University of Washington Libraries.

94. Author's interview with Larry Smith.

95. Office of Senator Henry M. Jackson, "Memorandum on Nitze and Rowny Hearings, October, 1979," Henry M. Jackson Papers, Accession no. 3560-6, Box 61, Folder 12, University of Washington Libraries.

96. Ibid.

97. Author's interview with William Miller, Washington, D.C., October 21, 1987.

98. Ibid.

99. U.S. Congress, Senate, Select Committee on Intelligence, *Principal Findings on the Capabilities of the United States to Monitor the SALT II Treaty*, report, 96th Congress, 1st sess., October 5, 1979.

100. Senate Foreign Relations Committee Report, *SALT II Treaty* (report), p. 34.

101. Ibid.

102. Testimony by Eugene Rostow, Senate Foreign Relations Committee, *SALT II Treaty* (hearings), vol. 2, p. 393; also see vol. 4, pp. 13-14.

103. U.S. Congress, Library of Congress, Congressional Research Service, *Treaties and Other International Agreements: The Role of the United States Senate* (Washington, D.C.: Government Printing Office, 1984), pp. 109-111.

104. Author's interview with Senator Jake Garn, Washington, D.C., June 3, 1987.

105. Senate Foreign Relations Committee, *SALT II Treaty* (report), p. 18.

106. Ibid.

107. Senate Select Committee on Intelligence, *Principal Findings*, p. 5.

108. Destler, "Congress," p. 52.

109. Senate Armed Services Committee, *Military Implications*, pp. 16-17.

110. Rudy Abramson, "Divided Senate Panel Attacks Arms Pact," *Los Angeles Times*, December 21, 1979, pt. I, p. 4.

111. Author's interviews with Ronald Tammen, Washington, D.C., June 4, 1987; and Anne Wexler, Washington, D.C., October 28, 1988.

112. Abramson, "GOP Liberals, Moderates Hold Fate of Arms Pact," pp. 1, 10.

113. Author's telephone interview with Richard Perle, November 10, 1988.

114. "The Shadow of Soviet Might," *Los Angeles Times*, August 20, 1979, pt. II, p. 6.

115. *Business Week*, August 13, 1979, p. 100.

18

An Offered Hand Rejected?
The Carter Administration and the Vance Mission
to Moscow in March 1977

VLADISLAV M. ZUBOK

There is no possible means of isolating ourselves from the rest of the world, so we must provide leadership. But this leadership need not depend on our inherent military force, or economic power, or political persuasion. It should derive from the fact that we try to be right and honest and truthful and decent.

Jimmy Carter, *Why Not the Best?*
(1975), p. 146

The resurgence of Ronald Reagan's militant conservatism, followed by the Bush administration, has screened from public memory the short period of the Carter administration, as if it were an unpleasant episode that would better be forgotten. Carter's foreign and domestic policies were painted in black, and the explanation of that boiled down mostly to the president's personal flaws.   Meanwhile, recent fundamental changes in the international situation and in the domestic setting in the Soviet Union have brought forth the familiar dilemma: Can leadership try to be "right, honest, truthful, and decent" in its foreign policy and be regarded a success in terms of domestic policies?   The leadership in question is the now-embattled Mikhail Gorbachev and his two-headed team in the Communist Party and the Supreme Soviet. There are some striking similarities between the situation of Jimmy Carter and that of Gorbachev in 1987-1990: a "crisis of confidence," a syndrome of "never again" using force and repression inside or outside, an acute realization of the "end of Pax Sovietica and/or Americana," and mounting conservative backlash.   Observers also reasonably point out that the "new political thinking" in Gorbachev's Soviet Union has clear antecedents in the liberal and "trilateral" scheme of the Carter people.

To avoid these shallow analogies, a more perceptive and balanced view must be taken of both the original intentions of the Carter administration in the international field and of their initial implementation, especially, in Soviet-American relations.

LIBERALISM, POPULISM, AND A BRAVE NEW CROWD

Carter's victory brought to the executive branch an extremely wide array of individuals with various backgrounds. Among those who had to deal with national security and foreign policy at least five patterns were discernible:

1. The President's inner circle of assistants and advisers, usually called the "Peanut Brigade," who directly helped to run his political campaigns. Among them were Hamilton Jordan, Stuart Eizenstat, Jody Powell, and Gerald Rafshoon.
2. Mainstay experts with mostly liberal backgrounds in law and political science, who in various ways had been affected by the "Vietnam trauma" and by profound changes on the international scale. Among them were Cyrus Vance, Zbigniew Brzezinski, Paul Warnke, Warren Christopher, Samuel Huntington, Marshall Shulman, and Adam Yarmolinksy.
3. Experts with backgrounds in both civilian and military science and engineering, like Harold Brown, James Schlesinger, and W. Perry;
4. The "junior varsity" of foreign policy and military experts, mostly liberals, from Congress and Washington consulting firms, including Anthony Lake, Leslie Gelb, Richard Moose, Richard Holbrooke, David Aaron, Robert Hunter, Karl Inderfurth, James Woolsey, Walter Slocomb, and William. A. Jackson.
5. Populists, civil activists, and former McGovernites like Andrew Young, Patricia Derian, Hodding Carter III, Patrick Caddell, and Midge Costanza.

People with backgrounds in groups 2, 4, and 5 were predominant among the political nominees to the State Department. Individuals from group 3 were heavily represented in the Department of Defense.

Several basic factors influenced the composition and spirit of Carter's foreign policy/national security crowd. The first was the disintegration of the Cold War "liberal establishment" as it existed from Truman to Johnson. Infighting and recrimination, brought about by the traumatizing events of the late 1960s and early 1970s, especially the McGovern presidential campaign of 1972, drove many liberal ideologues to the right. A sense of collapse of old schools of thought and the enviable example of Henry Kissinger prodded new gurus like Brzezinski and Huntington to new geopolitical schemes. But in most cases the mainstream experts sought to return to a "moral and just" foreign policy, if only to heal the nation's wounds inflicted by the Vietnam war. Self-therapy also was a driving force behind the "move to the left" of many former establishmentarians.

They argued for détente with the Soviet Union, but even more they wished to bury the hatchet of the Cold War rivalries and to turn the attention of the nation to new requirements. Their attitudes were strongly reflected in the reports and discussions at the Trilateral Commission, an international public organization that counted among its members the governor of Georgia, James Earl Carter. It was in the Trilateral Commission and related elite seminars that the concepts of multilateralism, interdependence, strategic sufficiency, and negotiations for finding a common ground had been coined and elaborated--ideas that are now propagated as "new challenges" by Soviet reformist experts.

A second factor was the emergence of an immense talent pool of "neoliberal experts," as a result of Watergate and other events, in and around the Democratic

Congress. In the last Nixon-Ford years, it became a haven for dissenters from Kissinger's personal style and substance in foreign policy. They participated in many coalitions struggling for military cuts and reduced involvement abroad.

Many of them were young and strongly affected by the civil rights movement and great reform ideas of the 1960s. They found Kissinger's "realpolitik" cynical, Machiavellian, and repugnant, and proposed that future U.S. foreign policy should tap the best resources of American idealism, as called for by President Kennedy fifteen years before.

The Watergate disclosures and the Church Committee testimony on CIA activities even more strongly convinced them that "Cold War" methods must be relegated to the "dustbin of history." They cherished an idea of transplanting the lessons of the 1960s civil rights reforms and other conflicts onto the international field, primarily the Third World. Anticommunism and the communist threat seemed to them completely anachronistic concepts when compared with such new global challenges as pollution and North-South relations.[1] They voiced their criticism in journals such as *Foreign Affairs, Foreign Policy, Atlantic Monthly*, and *Harper's*, and in influential newspapers such as the *Washington Post* and the *New York Times*.

Generally, people with backgrounds 2 and 4 reinforced each other in the Carter administration. The younger ones, at the working levels, helped to substantiate the opinions of those on the policymaking level, notably Cyrus Vance and Paul Warnke. Initially, they were reinforced also by populism, a strong desire for a "new beginning," widespread among Carter people and the country as a whole. Every administration wants to distinguish itself from its predecessors, but the long social turmoil over Vietnam and Watergate made it almost an obsession. Carter and his "Peanut Brigade" went out of their way to prove that "people," not the "old establishment," now ruled in America. Jordan, in a well-known interview, derogated the candidacies of Vance and Brzezinski in a clear attempt to project the populist image of the future Carter administration.

All rhetoric aside, President Carter had to turn to those who had experience. But he did tap a new source of talent, with backgrounds of group 5. These people were appointed to substantial positions in many departments and agencies, and influenced the atmosphere of the administration. In fact, some of them imagined themselves in antisystemic terms, like guerrillas descending into corrupted Washington and firmly set on doing so "in a right way."

A major factor in the process of recruitment and nominations was the marked absence, with few exceptions, of those who had openly supported Nixon against McGovern in 1972, and advocated rigid confrontational approaches in the foreign policy/national security area. In no small part that sprang from the personal priorities of Carter, who felt himself uncommitted to the conservative flank of the Democratic Party and, furthermore, spoke a language different from the fervent, dedicated "Cold Warriors." Carter, so to speak, preached a different sermon; his favorite model was not Truman but Wilson, not Andrew Jackson but Thomas Jefferson. Illustrative is the case of Paul Nitze, who displeased Carter by his stern lecture on "imminent danger."[2] Despite Carter's admiration for him, Henry ("Scoop") Jackson, along with the militaristic Committee on the Present Danger, could claim only a few true allies in the new administration. From their long list of candidates (Paul Nitze, Elmo Zumwalt,

Michael Rashish, Jeane Kirkpatrick, Eugene Rostow, Michael Novak), only James Schlesinger was nominated, and he became secretary of energy instead of defense.[3]

Finally, Carter's inexperience was a factor in the strange mixture of liberal experts and populists in his administration. He later admitted,

My staff and I were inexperienced in the ways of Washington. . . . We still suffered from some incompatibility with Washington's leaders, particulary in the news media.   . . . Initially, I was convinced that choosing a cabinet that was broad and diverse in its background would compensate for any lack of experience in my personal staff.[4]

With the benefit of hindsight we know how vulnerable the Carter administration was. The period of nominations left it with some scars. The nomination of Paul Warnke to be the chief of the Arms Control and Disarmament Agency and chief SALT negotiator gave "Cold Warriors" in the U.S. Senate a chance to warn Carter about their ability to block any treaty with the Soviets calling for the advice and consent of the legislative body. Another nomination, that of Theodore Sorensen to become the director of the CIA, encountered opposition from the military and intelligence communities, who blamed him for disclosure of classified information in his writings. Many legislators, whose protégés had been ignored during the nomination process, felt acrimony toward Carter.

In fact, the diversity of backgrounds of the appointees did little to save Carter and his "Peanut Brigade" from the severe criticism and scorn of the Washington community; instead, it created additional problems. One arose from the nominations of the "conventional" Cyrus Vance and the "controversial" Zbigniew Brzezinski, creating a soil for rivalry between the State Department and National Security Coucil. Because the appointees did not include many leading advocates of military preparedness and "hard-liners," the Right felt free to attack the administration.

INTENTIONS AND IMPLEMENTATION

According to two authoritative scholarly accounts, Carter came to office without a clear or consistent idea of détente and of arms negotiations.[5] On the operational level that was true, but Carter's Wilsonian vision and political instincts should not be altogether discounted. On the level of general intentions, Carter pursued at least two goals. The first was to restore moral domestic support for foreign policy in general, and for U.S.-Soviet détente in particular. The second was to substitute the power of persuasion and negotiations for the power of nuclear weapons.

At the beginning of 1977, détente was stalled, and the very term was discredited as a result of events in Angola and the uproar about repression of Soviet dissidents. Détente's architects were either utterly discredited (Nixon) or under harsh criticism (Kissinger). But the national consensus was still against increases in military spending; any effort in the military area smacked of global involvement and interventionism abroad. Congress reflected this mood and blocked efforts of the Ford administration to build up a military budget.

Reflecting his second goal, Carter, six days after his inauguration, made a truly Wilsonian gesture: he sent personal letters to Leonid Brezhnev, stating that his goal was "to improve relations with the Soviet Union on the basis of reciprocity, mutual respect and benefit." He expressed the hope that early progress in relations could be reached through a quick SALT accord, early agreement on a comprehensive nuclear test ban, and agreement on MBFR. He also stated his desire for an early summit meeting.[6] He received a response carefully crafted by Brezhnev speechwriters.

To meet a first and major goal, however, Carter had to distance himself even more from the Nixon-Kissinger policy in order to integrate those groups and values that had been antagonized by that policy. The specter of Watergate haunted Carter and his administrative leaders in the White House,[7] making them eager to fulfill their campaign promise of a "moral foreign policy."

One remedy was a vigorous human rights campaign. Post-Vietnam liberals and civil rights populists agreed with Senator Henry Jackson and liberal right-wing Republicans who had castigated Kissinger for ignoring the issue of human rights in the Soviet Union and Eastern Europe. Where the "Cold Warriors" simply discovered an updated formula for the struggle between "democracy and totalitarianism," the "bleeding-heart liberals" found a natural projection of American idealism and moral imperatives beyond national boundaries. But the success of the Jackson-Vanik amendment, basing U.S. trade on free immigration for Soviet Jews, the uproar against the "Sonnenfeldt doctrine," the indignation at President Ford's refusal to invite Alexander Solzhenytsin to the White House, and the importance of the Helsinki "humanitarian" basket indicated that in all these cases, both groups held similar attitudes.

Therefore, Carter's public praise and his February letter of support to Andrei Sakharov, his inviting Vladimir Bukovsky to the White House, and the sympathy offered to other Soviet dissidents were both morally gratifying and politically expedient.[8]

Another crossroad of populist inexperience and political calculus was nuclear disarmament. Carter seemed to be an advocate of minimal deterrence, and at his first meeting with his staff on SALT after taking office, he declared with tight-lipped intensity that he had been serious in his inaugural address about dreaming of the day when the earth would be rid of nuclear weapons, and that his "most cherished hope" was to contribute to progress in that direction.[9]

One may risk suggesting that both this idealism and his background in nuclear engineering contributed to such emotional involvement. In a much more somber way, Secretary of Defense Harold Brown and other "science and technology" people in the administration sponsored the idea of deep cuts of nuclear weapons. Brown, Brzezinski, and his deputy David Aaron subscribed to the doctrine of mutual assured deterrence, which by its inherent logic united the concepts of a wide band of vulnerability, strategic redundancy, and sufficiency. In addition, liberally inclined arms controllers such as Paul Warnke and Leslie Gelb had never been enthusiastic about SALT I and the Vladivostok agreement, because they legitimized the qualitative and even quantitative nuclear arms race instead of stopping it. They were pushed by many other liberals with radical antiwar backgrounds, who were always ready with "new bold proposals."[10]

On the hard-line flank, Senator Henry Jackson, who grew into the leading strategic expert of the Senate, his aide Richard Perle, and Paul Nitze demanded parity in ICBM throw-weight, implying not a freeze but real cuts of strategic systems--albeit for the Soviet 300 "heavy" missiles but not for the other two legs of the triad, where the American side had superiority.[11]

So the general idea of moving from the agreed-upon Vladivostok guidelines to deep cuts enjoyed the support of a wide spectrum: from Jackson to the joint chiefs of staff to those post-Cold War international affairs experts who wished to break the ice of parity, the limits and sublimits in artificial schemes, in favor of bold moves to stop the arms race by unilateral reductions and sacrifices in the national security area.

As happened many times during his term, Carter took the erroneous road of seeking as wide a spectrum of expert opinions as possible, often with fratricidal views and proposals. In fact, the first memorandum that reached his desk--its authors were Jackson and Perle--became a base for consensus, despite the fact that its goals were a far cray from Carter's longing for a nuclear-free world, or from the Warnke-Vance-Gelb ideas of negotiations with the Soviets. With Warnke stuck in the Senate confirmation process and Vance immersed in the trimming of the large diplomatic bureaucracy, liberals could not produce a timely proposal of their own.

In a secret meeting of principals, a new comprehensive SALT proposal was thrashed out. It called for reducing the aggregate of strategic systems from 2,400 (the Vladivostok guidelines) to 1,800-2,000 missiles, with MIRVs going from 1,320 to 1,100 or 1,200, and ICBMs with MIRVs to 550. Soviet "heavy" ICBMs were to be reduced to 150. Most important, this new proposal put a ban on development, testing, and deployment of any new type of ICBM, including mobile ones. At the same time, American forward-based systems were not affected by the proposal, and were even to be reinforced by limitless long-range ALCMs and short-range land- and sea-based missiles.

These substantial reductions were all to be on the Soviet side.[12] Despite certain misgivings, Vance and Warnke joined in supporting the presidential decision. What was really egregious was that no serious effort had been made to consult Soviet experts in and out of the administration regarding possible Soviet reactions. It seems that domestic needs and inspirations mattered more than the perspectives of international understanding.

It was not the first time that American foreign policy/national security mechanisms proved unable to work out an equitable, balanced proposal that took into account the legitimate interests and/or idiosyncrasies of the Soviet side. The array of misplaced unilateral American initiatives started with the Baruch plan and was followed by "open skies."[13] This phenomenon tells us something about the patterns of U.S.-Soviet negotiations during the Cold War and the détente of the 1970s. It is enough to say here that even the largest pool of idealism and goodwill in the Carter administration could not overcome the huge inertia of the Cold War and of secrecy in diplomacy. So the gap between the noble and idealistic intentions of Carter and of his advisers in groups 2, 4, and 5 and the final proposal was quite critical in putting in doubt the seriousness and sincerity of the administration's desire to negotiate a mutually acceptable agreement.

INTENTIONS MISUNDERSTOOD

Carter's victory in November 1976 came as a complete surprise to Soviet leaders. Every transition, especially from one party to another, was an unknown quantity--but so what? After all, the Brezhnev leadership had already seen détente survive a wrenching transition during the Watergate scandal from Nixon to Ford. The Vladivostok summit and agreement considerably firmed up Soviet optimism about the prospects of continuity in U.S.-Soviet relations. Soviet leaders were fully prepared to "save detente" by taking all necessary measures to form good relations with a new administration.

However, there were clear objective and subjective limits. The Soviet system of decision making in the area of U.S.-Soviet relations, especially on military strategic matters, had never been flexible. The most glaring shortcomings were the following:

1. The absence of any central policy-level body to coordinate flows of information, to carry out midterm and even short-term planning in the foreign policy/national security areas
2. An effective ban on all forecasting in foreign policy, including attempts to assess possible action-reaction dynamics in U.S.-Soviet relations
3. The ideologization of policy-making, reflected in systematic intrusions into the domain of U.S.-Soviet relations of high Communist Party officials specializing in propaganda and in relations with the "brother" socialist countries and communists movements
4. The utter impossibility for diplomats, international affairs experts, arms controllers, and other civilian officials to prevail over the military in national security affairs, which were universally considered the prerogative of the Ministry of Defense and the General Staff.

As Carter moved on his comprehensive SALT proposal in complete secrecy, the clumsy and compartmentalized Soviet foreign policy/military mechanism was not ready to shift gears. Signals from Washington were contradictory. On the one hand, in September, Carter authorized W. Averell Harriman to go to Moscow and tell Brezhnev that if Carter was elected, he would move quickly to sign a SALT II agreement based on the Vladivostok accord and incorporating a compromise on the issues left unresolved at Vladivostok.[14] In his first press conference and first personal letter to Brezhnev, the president reiterated his intention to reach a "rapid conclusion" of SALT II before going on to more contentious issues. In all of their responses, the Soviets made it absolutely clear that any agreement had to be based on Vladivostok.[15]

But information leaked to Moscow about an impending radical change in the American position. In fact, Carter himself gave some hints in his "populist" foreign policy press conferences and speeches. Although Secretary Vance, in a break with previous practice, informed Soviet Ambassador Anatoly Dobrynin of the change only shortly before the start of his visit to Moscow, Soviet diplomats had time to inform Moscow that the new administration was going to lay out a new proposal. The reaction from Moscow was one of disbelief. Neither the leadership nor the experts could imagine that Americans were so blatant or naive as to present such a one-sided suggestion.[16]

Even without archival evidence it is clear that both the top leadership and the working levels of Soviet foreign policy-making misinterpreted U.S. intentions. The position of those at the working level was of importance, because many times in the history of U.S.-Soviet relations, the experts standing behind the political leaders had made them reconsider some initial reactions, working laboriously from below in favor of a wiser, more balanced approach to negotiations and agreements. However, this time was different. Working-level experts lacked the time to enlighten leaders on the substance and meaning of the new American proposal. More important, they misjudged several indicators:

- The message of Carter's presidential campaign and the pressures on his foreign policy in the wake of Watergate. While stressing Carter's inexperience, they tended to explain his rhetoric as propaganda. For example, his campaign for human rights was widely characterized as political expediency, and as the anti-Sovietism of Carter's advisers. Brzezinski was a primary target and bête noir in the eyes of most of the Soviet officials and experts.[17]
- The importance of Carter's antinuclear sentiments. His statements on that score were generally ignored or downplayed. On the eve of Carter's inauguration, Brezhnev delivered a high-profile foreign policy speech in Tula. It contained for the first time a rejection of the goal of strategic superiority and explicitly used the word "sufficiency." Designed primarily by Foreign Ministry experts as a sign to Americans that the Soviet side was ready to follow up on military détente, the draft of this speech met with serious opposition from Communist Party ideologues and was approved only on the pretext that it was meant to stake out for the Soviet Union a vanguard role in a struggle for nuclear disarmament. Carter's antinuclear pronouncements in this context were interpreted as attempts to "steal our thunder."[18]
- The specific background of the Carter administration and its potential domestic vulnerability to attacks from the Right. Never did experts attempt to foresee the repercussions in the United States in case of a Soviet rebuff to the Carter proposals.

Many times during the Cold War the intervention of top leadership helped to reorient Moscow's foreign and security policy to achieve a breakthrough in negotiations. But in early 1977, top authority was on the ropes: the ailing Brezhnev, after a heart attack and the death of his mother, could not master the details of talks, and detached himself more and more from day-to-day U.S.-Soviet diplomacy. Practical decision making was already in the hands of a triumvirate: Foreign Minister Andrei A. Gromyko, Minister of Defense Dimitrii Ustinov, and Head of the KGB Yuri V. Andropov.[19]

Still, Brezhnev was far from a puppet in March 1977, and, being emotionally committed to the idea of détente and a summit with the American president, could still make a difference. That would have happened if the Americans had come up with a "Vladivostok plus" variation. But the new proposal was received by Brezhnev and all major experts at the working level as a suggestion to bury Vladivostok and all the years of efforts expended to reach that agreement. A Soviet expert close to Brezhnev and Gromyko recalled:

If the Americans had put it differently--say, let's finish that job and address this proposal in a parallel way, we're not against modifying it, etc. . . . Then our psychological attitude would have been positive. But they bluntly told us: Let's forget about Vladivostok--and that provoked a very sharp negative reaction. At the moment we all were convinced that it was the only right approach. . . . There was a unanimous impression that the Carter Administration was weaseling out of the SALT process.[20]

Incidentally, according to the same source, the human rights issue did not play a critical role in the diplomatic failure of Vance's visit. If the American approach to SALT had appeared more reasonable to the Kremlin, that irritant would not have prevented a cordial welcome in Moscow.[21] More objectionable to both Gromyko and the military was the idea of asymmetry in cuts implied in the new American proposal. At that moment Soviet leaders tended to look at the strategic parity in numerical terms, believing that it must be gauged "on drugstore high-precision scales."[22]

Brezhnev had one more reason to become annoyed at the idea of throwing the old agreement into the garbage. He had invested a lot of personal political capital in the Vladivostok agreement. That was the last time the general secretary directly managed the thorny process of consensus-building, and he had to overcome serious opposition-- especially since the hard-line minister of defense, Andrei Grechko, had been joined by Chairman of the Presidium of the Supreme Soviet Nikolai V. Podgorny.[23] There was simply no one in the Kremlin at this time to spill his political blood for the chance for success. Brezhnev barely let the American delegation present its case before starting to scold them for bringing "a piece of propaganda" to the negotiating table.

This impression was confirmed by the badly coordinated American public presentation of the subsequent events. The administration had not planned a retreat. To Moscow, "Carter seemed to be saying, 'Either you accept our position or we start the arms race and the Cold War again.' His statement was taken as a diktat or ultimatum."[24] Accustomed to negotiate and make concessions in privacy, Soviet leaders were unused to that sort of stampede. Typically in this situation the visceral reaction from Moscow was automatic: teach the Americans a lesson, raise the propaganda ante, and discredit American "imperialism." That reaction indeed followed, and Gromyko publicized the American proposal, thus effectively ending the seven-year period of U.S.-Soviet tacit negotiations and "quiet" diplomacy.

DRAWING SOME CONCLUSIONS

It is tempting now to indulge into counterfactual specu-lations about what would have been achieved or prevented if the March diplomatic debacle had not happened. Ten years afterward, the United States and the Soviet Union returned to the ideas of deep cuts (although until now they have remained hesitant to pursue them). But a direct comparison clearly does not hold with the appearance of such first-rate variables as Gorbachev, *perestroika*, and new thinking in the Soviet Union, and the rapid melting of the Cold War. So, for these reasons, comparative and counterfactual analysis does not pass many tests.[25]

But in two aspects, a "what if" approach might be useful. One deals with such important things as first impressions and levels of confidence in international relations. Here a serious opportunity was squandered for both sides, especially the Soviet side, to tap the reservoir of goodwill and cooperative intentions that existed in abundance in the Carter administration, not only on the highest level but also on the working levels of the foreign policy/national security apparatus.   Now, when watching the supercautious and temporizing approach on both levels of the Bush administration, some people in the Soviet Union cannot help thinking with nostalgia and sympathy about the "moral and compassionate" diplomacy of the Carter administration.

But in 1977 those characteristics were overshadowed by an adverse impression. After the Vance visit, many in the Kremlin and on the working level became convinced that the Carter administration was insincere, unpredictable, contradictory. The Vance-Brzezinski rivalry brought more grist to this mill.   After Vance's visit it became an axiom for many in the Kremlin and on the working level that Carter's Soviet policy was drifting to the right of the president, who was haplessly falling between two stools and unable to choose between the Brzezinski line and the Vance line.[26]   Future research will show how this image of a vacillating administration affected Soviet actions abroad, including the decision to get involved in Ethiopia and Afghanistan.

Another "what if" lesson concerns the ability of the two sides to assess and carefully heed the probable reaction-counteraction dynamics.   The events of March 1977 are an outstanding negative example of how both great powers should not act if they don't want to undermine the fragile base for understanding and cooperation. Carter's proposal was designed and conducted in such a way that it went against the grain of Soviet psychology and negotiating style. But the Soviets' decisive rebuff did even more harm, since it left the Carter administration open to scathing criticism that it was weak on national security and unqualified to deal with the Russians. Vance, and especially Warnke, already hurt by the Senate confirmation hearings, came out of this experience with diminished political capital to mastermind Soviet policy.[27]

Later the Soviet side found the explanation for the weaknesses of the "doves" in the Carter administration exclusively in the internal correlation of forces in the United States, including the rise of economic problems and a plot of "reactionary forces." But the truth is that without the disaster of March 1977 and the continued Soviet buildup of ICBMs, it would have been problematic for hard-liners to understand the "imminent danger."   The spiral of tough reactions worked against parallel Soviet and U.S. interests, and certainly helped to destroy liberal-populist alternatives to the dominant hard-line logic in U.S.-Soviet policy.

This episode bears on the current state of U.S.-Soviet affairs in reminding us that under present international conditions, the superpowers can miss critical opportunities if they do not learn to sympathize with each other and avoid any action (or inaction) that might discredit positive developments on the other side.   It also stresses the importance of some joint coordination and study of unilateral and reciprocal initiatives, so that they lead toward gradual reduction of tensions and an increase of cooperation, and not toward perilous misunderstandings and propaganda contests.

NOTES

1. David Broder, *Changing of the Guard* (New York: Simon and Schuster, 1980).

2. Strobe Talbott, *The Master of the Game: Paul Nitze and the Nuclear Peach* (New York: Knopf, 1988), p. 149; Paul Nitze, *From Hiroshima to Glasnost: A Memoir of Five Perilous Decades* (New York: Weidenfeld and Nicolson, 1989), p. 347.

3. *Washington Post*, January 28, 1977, p. A-15; December 16, p. A-5.

4. Jimmy Carter, *Keeping Faith: Memoirs of a President* (New York: Bantam Books, 1982), p. 47.

5. Strobe Talbott, *Endgame: The Inside Story of SALT II* (New York: Harper and Row, 1980), p. 42; R. L. Garthoff, *Détente and Confrontation: American Relations from Nixon to Reagan* (Washington, D.C.: Brookings Institution, 1985), p. 564.

6. Garthoff, *Détente and Confrontation*, p. 565; Zbigniew Brzezinski, *Power and Principle: Memoirs of a National Security Adviser, 1977-1981* (New York: Farrar, Strauss, Giroux, 1983), pp. 146-150.

7. Carter, *Keeping Faith*, p. 27; Rosalynn Carter, *First Lady from Plains* (Boston: Houghton Mifflin, 1984), pp. 149-150.

8. Garthoff, *Détente and Confrontation*, pp. 569-571.

9. Talbott, *Endgame*, p. 43.

10. Ibid., p. 45.

11. Ibid., pp. 52-54; Garthoff, *Détente and Confrontation*, pp. 803-804.

12. Garthoff, *Détente and Confrontation*, p. 806.

13. Vladislav Zubok, "Open Skies: Dilemmas of U.S. and Soviet Security in 1955," *International Affairs* (Moscow) (1990).

14. Talbott, *Endgame*, p. 39.

15. Garthoff, *Détente and Confrontation*, pp. 802-803.

16. Interviews with former Soviet officials.

17. Interviews with former Soviet officials.

18. Interview with former Deputy Foreign Minister Georgy M. Kornienko, February 22, 1990.

19. Interview with Kornienko, November 23, 1989. This fact is corroborated by observation on the American side by Paul Warnke, interview, May 5, 1989.

20. Ibid.

21. Ibid.

22. Well-known expression of Andrei Gromyko.

23. Personal observation from participant in Vladivostok summit.

24. Talbott, *Endgame*, p. 74.

25. See J. L. Gaddis, *Nuclear Weapons and International Systemtic Stability--Emerging Issues*, Occasional Paper no. 2 (Cambridge, Mass.: AAAS, January 1990) pp. 11-15.

26. Later Soviet publications revealed in detail that prevailing view. See R. S. Ovinnikov, *Zig-zags of U.S. Foreign Policy: From Nixon to Reagan*, Politizdat, Moscow (1986), pp. 147-153 (in Russian).

27. Interview with Paul Warnke, May 5, 1989.

Discussant: David L. Aaron

I will try to be very brief, because I know you would like to get to questions. There's an old proverb--it may even be Russian in origin--that says, "Never appear on the dais with anyone who knows more about a subject than you do." It goes on to say that if you appear with one person who knows more than you do, that's a misfortune; if you appear with two, it's carelessness. And here I am with four gentlemen who may know more about this subject than I do.

Let me make a few general comments about Soviet policy when we first came into office in early 1977, to set a framework. I think the most important point is that, in contrast to the Republican Party and the Republican candidate, who had dropped détente from his vocabulary and then had frozen his relationship with the Soviet Union, and who was responding to conservative concerns that somehow the Soviet Union was not only taking advantage of us but outdistancing us--certainly in the military sphere and perhaps in other areas as well--the Carter administration came in with a sense of optimism about the future. Indeed, the first general survey that we took of world events, of our strengths, of our adversaries' strengths and weaknesses--a thing called "Presidential Review Memorandum #10"--came to the conclusion that, generally speaking, we were not only stronger but we had more advantages, that we had stronger allies, that the problems in the world that needed to be dealt with could be dealt with more on our terms, and that we needn't, as the president later said, have an inordinate fear of either communism or, for that matter, the Soviet Union.

However, as we came into office, the campaign of 1976 did not end, and there was a continuing series of statements, organizations, concerns, movements, stressing the fact that the Soviet Union was moving ahead; the United States, inexplicably and, lacking leadership, was not doing so. Of course, this is all rather ironic when you look back in history, because this is a period that the Soviet officials now refer to as the period of stagnation in the Soviet Union. We were prepared to pursue détente, and we made that very clear in the campaign, and the president made that very clear in his first days in office. We respected and were concerned about Soviet military capability, and the momentum particularly of their strategic defense programs but also their conventional military programs.

But it was not an accident and it was not, in fact, the liberal State Department that wrote the line that said that the United States should not have an inordinate fear of communism; it was Zbigniew Brzezinski who wrote that line. He wrote the line because he felt that there was a consensus in the administration that we did not believe the Soviet system worked, we did not believe it was the wave of the future, and we did not believe every Third World problem was Soviet-inspired. And, insofar as there were problems that the Soviet Union did have a hand in, we did not necessarily believe the problems could be resolved by dealing only with the Soviet Union; in fact, there were problems in a particular region that had to be dealt with by themselves. And we also had concern about issues that really had only a tangential relationship, and sometimes none whatsoever, to the Soviet Union, such as peace in the Middle East, the Arab-Israeli problems, the problems of southern Africa, the problems of energy independence, and so forth.

We tried our best to try to sort out those issues and deal with each one in specific terms. This was a failure. Domestically, this did not work, and I think the example Dan Caldwell gave of the linkage that grew up between Panama and the SALT treaties is a perfect example. Shortly after he voted for the Panama Canal treaties, Howard Baker told the president, "Mr. President, I'm not going to be able to do that for you again." Indeed, when the SALT treaty came around, he couldn't, and he didn't.

Interestingly, I think it's important to recognize that the biggest problem in the Carter administration period--the biggest, most damaging political events in foreign policy--were not Soviet. They were the events that unfolded in Iran. And equally, while I believe that SALT II was an important achievement, and Ronald Reagan kept it despite his professed opposition to it, I believe that President Carter's greatest achievement was the Camp David accords. Without them, we would not have the alliance that we now see in the Middle East arrayed against Saddam Hussein.

Let me make some brief comments about some of the things that the other speakers have said. First of all, on the question of linkage, it was a great debate at the time: What should linkage be? But I don't believe it was ever properly seen in public for what it was. There were really three kinds of linkage. One is the question of how far you can go with the Soviets in one area, such as arms control, without hoping for and seeing and having some modification of Soviet behavior in other areas. In other words, can you deal with strategic arms alone, regardless of what's going on elsewhere in the world, regardless of political relationships, regardless of human rights abuses, and so forth? And the answer to that is, really, you cannot do that. The purpose of strategic arms control agreements is not merely to try to curtail the growth of strategic arms, because if that were the criterion, we haven't done a very good job--in either SALT I or SALT II. The purpose of it is political as well--to improve the climate and the relationship between the two countries--and other things have to happen for one to feel that that has been accomplished.

The second kind of linkage is, in fact, an error, when you see, in events throughout the world, the hidden hand of the Soviet Union, or the communist menace, or what have you. That is a kind of linkage that only becomes self-defeating. Finally, there is the question of domestic linkage, and I'd like to comment on it a little further. It's the question of what this particular agreement, what this set of activities, has to do with the nature of the presidency, with the president's political power, with the political conditions in the country at a given time. Let me give you an example. By the time SALT II came to be ratified, almost every important player was playing politics with this very important treaty.

I'll give you a specific example. George Bush called the White House and said, "I really am very concerned about this treaty. I know it can be a very important thing for U.S.-Soviet relations. I'm troubled by the criticisms. I'd like to have a meeting with some senior people in the White House to talk about it." We'd known George Bush, many of us in the government, for a long time; he'd been director of the Central Intelligence Agency and was considered to be a sensible person. So we invited him into the White House, which he announced to the press; he brought along two aides; and when we sat down in the Roosevelt Room to begin to brief him on SALT II, he said, "Now, there's just one thing that you need to know before we start." I said, "What's that?" He said, "I'm actually against the treaty, and I'm going to be against the treaty, but I'd like to hear what you have to say about it." That kind of took the heart out of the discussion a little bit.

Since we're talking about personalities, I might comment on one of Dan's questions about Paul Nitze: If he had been included, being a friend of Scoop Jackson's, in the team--he'd been on the Nixon SALT team, and I had worked with him in the SALT I negotiations--would it have been helpful? I couldn't help thinking of the day that we signed the ratification instruments in the White House, and all the delegates were in line, going in to see President Nixon sign the SALT I ratification instruments. As Henry Kissinger walked down the line, he stopped at Paul Nitze and said, "Paul, I really want to thank you for what you've done. If it wasn't for you, we would have concluded this agreement two years earlier."

I might just make a passing comment about the rivalry between Vance and Brzezinski, which I think was very painful and destructive and not helpful to the president's conduct of foreign policy. I've often wondered whether it was avoidable. I spent a good deal of time with Tony Lake; we used to meet once or twice a week, he representing Secretary Vance and I representing Dr. Brzezinski, to see if we couldn't sort out the fact that rumors were coming from the State Department, from the White House--backgrounders, criticisms, sniping, and what have you--in an effort to reconcile our positions and try to go back to our bosses and see if we couldn't be good intermediaries. One day--I guess that we were a couple years into this rather worthless exercise--we sat at lunch. As we compared notes on a specific incident, we discovered that the very unpleasant comments made in the State Department about the National Security Council, and the very unpleasant comments allegedly made in the White House about the State Department top leadership, did not come from people in the woodwork; did not come from senior officials--they came from our bosses. That afternoon, we had several glasses of wine and decided that, from then on, when we had lunch, we would have lunch because we were friends, not because our bosses were ever going to be friends.

I think that as the administration unfolded, we were faced with increasing challenges from the Soviet Union, and there was a sense in the Congress that somehow we were not conducting our policy toward the Soviet Union with sufficient strength and consistency. And we felt that, politically, very keenly in the White House. I don't think the State Department felt it quite as keenly. They had much broader and diverse interests, and I think that the general frame of mind of Secretary Vance was that you focus on a few key issues, you push very hard on those, you get them done, and you accomplish something. And that very much fit in with the president's frame of mind, whereas Dr. Brzezinski's concept was "Listen, everything is connected." We have to understand the political context. We're not going to get very far here if we can't get far with other issues. And I think it was a philosophical, it was a personality, it was an outlook difference that reflected the differences that existed in American society and in Washington at the time.

Let me make a passing comment about the Vietnam syndrome, partly because it became a part of subsequent lore and legend that the Carter administration was full of people who were traumatized by the experience of Vietnam and therefore couldn't stand up to the Soviets, couldn't make decisions involving strength of military forces, or what have you. I think there's something to it, but I believe that that syndrome affected the more senior policymakers in the administration, and not the "junior varsity" that Dan Caldwell's paper referred to. I think that the more junior people-- myself, Tony Lake, and Les Gelb, who's now with the *New York Times* and who had written *The Pentagon Papers* as an exercise in self-criticism in the Johnson administration, to try to understand where we went wrong--were determined not so much somehow to pay dues for what had happened in Vietnam as to understand the mistakes we made then, try not to make them again, and try to make the government work better. We all knew each other; we had grown up together in Washington. But unfortunately, that was not enough to overcome the divisions that grew up at an even more senior level in the government.

Finally, let me make a comment about the March meeting and SALT II, and whether we should have just gone ahead and signed an agreement, and what a terrible tragedy all of that was. I really don't see it that way. First of all, the SALT II agreement that had been negotiated by Henry Kissinger was not ready to be signed or agreed to in any way, shape, or form. In particular, there was a very large question about naval nuclear forces, and by the time we arrived in office, Dr. Kissinger, through the back channel, had a number of proposals, ideas--it was difficult to keep track of all of them--that he was discussing. We were going to limit the number of ships that could have nuclear weapons on them; we'd limit the number of weapons that could be on the ships; and the ships could be in only certain areas of the ocean. There were ideas that were wild, that would have been extremely upsetting to the Defense Department if it had known about them--sometime it did--and there were some very important open questions.

Second, if we had gone forward even with the main provisions of the agreement, we wouldn't have done something about the one big issue that the entire American defense establishment had been concerned about, long before the SALT process ever began: the ability of Soviet ICBMs to destroy American ICBMs in a first strike. The issue here wasn't whether the Soviets were going to launch a surprise attack, or conduct a first strike, or any such scenario. The issue was how we would respond, because as defense planners, we would do something. The Reagan answer was to come up with the Star Wars program. So the concern was not trivial, and it could well lead not only to a greater number of offensive strategic forces but also to the deployment of defensive strategic forces, the breakdown of the ABM treaty, and a number of other things. So the purpose of the March proposal was to try to turn the corner on the heavy missiles, the heavily MIRVed missiles, that the Soviets had.

I don't think the meeting was handled very well on our side. We didn't inform the Soviets in advance; we gave them very little indication of what was going to happen. We took a huge delegation over there; we built up expectations that there was going to be some major breakthrough when, in fact, we were presenting a lot of very new ideas. And finally, when the Soviets quite logically said no--which is what you would expect them to say--Secretary Vance and Paul Warnke held a press conference to announce that the meetings had been a failure. This was not exactly designed to move the ball along, and then, Andrei Gromyko of course felt compelled to have his own press conference--something he almost never did--in order to denounce our version of events. Henry Kissinger called me not long after that and said, "You know, I don't understand what you guys are doing. I've been to Moscow a dozen times, and I almost never succeed in my discussions. It's just one more step in the process, but I don't hold a press conference to announce that we had a failure." I think he had a very good point.

Finally, I'm not shocked by the fact that the Soviets rejected us, because six months later, they came back and agreed to reduce their heavy MIRV missiles. That was a real turning point in the negotiations, and for the first time, it introduced serious reduction into that entire process--something that the Reagan administration then tried to carry forward. So I don't think that proposal and the moment it represented should be seen in the way I think it is generally seen.

Discussant: Vladimir O. Pechatnov

It's an interesting coincidence to comment on the paper by Zubok, who happens to be a former student of mine. So maybe I'm not totally impartial when I say I like the paper. I think it throws new light on the perceptions on both sides during that critical episode of Soviet-American relations, and treats the whole episode largely as a case of mutual misunderstanding, which I tend to agree with.

But though the misunderstanding was mutual, I find the Soviet one more understandable, or perhaps even more excusable than the American one. Of course, the Soviet side didn't see all the nuances and contradictions and diverse intentions that went into the March proposal of the Carter administration. Perhaps they should have listened more to the Institute of the United States and Canada in this respect, but after all, there was a new president, almost totally unknown in Moscow, who was rejecting, it seemed, the previous frameworks, agreements, and discussions in a way that was, in Soviet eyes, very one-sided. And it was one-sided.

So the Soviet reaction was not surprising. What I'm surprised with is how the American side, with all its knowledge and expertise on the Soviet leadership, with all its emphasis on playing out different scenarios and forecasting, was unable to foresee the Soviet reaction. I remember talking to Marshall Shulman, who at that time was chief Soviet adviser to Secretary of State Vance, just before their trip to Moscow, and he seemed to be worried about the outcome. He didn't, of course, reveal anything, but obviously he had some apprehensions about the Soviet response. I would be interested in comments that Admiral Turner and Mr. Aaron would have about their view of the possible outcome of Secretary Vance's mission at that time.

Second, about the impact of that trip on subsequent events. Later, both sides essentially got back to the Vladivostok framework and real negotiations resumed. But as a result of that false start, precious time was lost that we needed so badly in 1979. And the atmosphere of the relations was spoiled considerably. America's withdrawal of its initial proposal, the deep cut idea, although it remains to be verified by the archive materials and future research, may have stiffened the Soviet attitudes and self-righteousness in the months to come. But more important, I think, it turned strongly against the administration domestically, because instead of appeasing Henry Jackson and those like him, which was one of the original motivations behind the deep cut proposal, the administration became more vulnerable to the criticism of this reversal and of its subsequent SALT II agreement.

Which brings me to Professor Caldwell's paper, which is, in my view, a very solid piece of work, heavily documented by very interesting material from both primary sources and interviews. It's very strong on the Senate side, and I was glad to learn that this paper is to be a chapter of a forthcoming book on the subject. But that book would not be complete, in my view, without a full story of the administration's side, the administration's effort in that battle. To the extent that Professor Caldwell deals with that, he seems to subscribe to the prevailing view that the administration was doing too little too late, as was its general pattern of operation in congressional relationships.

I wouldn't totally agree with that. I recollect that in the Institute of the United States and Canada we were watching this fighting very closely, and we saw clearly that the administration was very serious and very active about the whole operation. Later on, I had a chance to go through some of the relevant documents in the Jimmy Carter Library, and I was even more impressed with the quality and detail of that effort. I think that along with the Panama Canal treaties, it might be one of the best-organized, most massive operations of this kind in American history. The administration clearly understood the importance of the treaty for both Soviet-American relations and its own political future. Let me very briefly read one quotation from a memo to the president, most probably written by Hamilton Jordan, as early as the fall of 1978:

Politically and substantially, SALT II is the most important issue you will deal with as a President. SALT has come to represent in this country and around the world the ability of the American President to effectively manage the U.S.-Soviet relationship. Politically, it will be the greatest and toughest fight of your presidency. If we ratify the SALT II agreement in 1979, and if the economy is in a reasonably good shape, I believe it will ensure your reelection in 1980. If we are defeated on SALT II, I believe it will destroy your ability to be an effective President and probably cost you re-election.[1]

The administration also had a realistic understanding of the problem and of the obstacles that it faced in that struggle. In my view, it also had a pretty comprehensive strategy for dealing with those obstacles. Long before the ratification campaign, the groundwork for that operation was beginning to be laid at the end of 1977, and the overall plan of the ratification campaign, judging by the documents I saw, was ready by the end of the next year and the beginning of 1979. It was an all-round comprehensive plan, stressing public education, and grass-roots lobbying, working in the Senate, getting consensus within the administration, media support, and so forth.

Of course, some mistakes in that strategy were made; perhaps there should have been more attention to working directly with the Senate and less to public opinion, although I think, as American politics shows, the best way to get to the Senate sometimes is through its constituencies, so that may have also been the point here. But anyway, my overall impression is that while the administration was well prepared for the fight--it didn't start from scratch with the ratification campaign, but too many things were beyond its control--it was an uphill struggle against great odds from the very beginning.

First of all, the mood and correlation of forces in the Senate. From Paul Warnke's nomination vote on, the administration understood that votes in the Senate would be extremely hard to get. Second, the mood of the public. Although in general it supported the arms control agreements, again, as Pat Caddell showed in his constant flow of memos on SALT to the president, the public was ambivalent--although it agreed in principle with the desirability of the measure, it was also very suspicious of the Soviets. And the administration had to fight the growing public perception of the alleged shift in military balance between the United States and the Soviets in favor of the Soviets.   The administration was vulnerable to the usual right-wing and conservative criticism of being "soft on communism," and therefore not credible to strike the right deal with the Soviets.

The Soviets didn't help much.   We did almost all we could to reinforce by our behavior the image of an expansionist power bent upon gaining strategic superiority over the United States.   There were also some mistakes in timing, which were already referred to, and there was simply bad luck, like the issue of the Soviet brigade in Cuba. The hostages, of course, and Afghanistan were the final blow.   But it's interesting to remember at this point that even after Afghanistan, from what I could see in the documents, the president was still thinking about getting back at some point in the future, when the situation permitted, to this unfinished battle in the Senate.   That shows his commitment, I think, to the arms control idea, which he demonstrated from the very beginning.

In conclusion, one might say that although the treaty was never ratified, it served its purpose: it was more or less observed by both sides, and it paved the way for future negotiations.   All this may be true, but the damage was done--to Soviet-American relations, to the arms control process as such, and politically to the administration, contributing to its defeat in 1980, as Hamilton Jordan had warned two years earlier.   So it's with some sadness that we now can look back both at March 1977 and the SALT II as opportunities lost, and the promise only half fulfilled.

NOTE

1. Memo (unsigned) to President Carter, Box 34, Chief of Staff Hamilton Jordan's Files, Jimmy Carter Library.

Discussant: Stansfield Turner

In response to your question, Dr. Pechatnov, as to why we didn't anticipate the Soviet reaction to President Carter's arms control proposal of 1977, I can only say mea culpa. It was my job, and I didn't do it. In part, I think you overestimate how well we understand you and how hard we work at it. It's not as good as it should be. In this instance, it was in part because of the speed with which this came about; the administration was less than two months old when Mr. Vance went to Moscow. In part, it was because there was in the administration a penchant for secrecy and for not including the bureaucracies, but unless you take an issue like this and digest it in the normal bureaucratic process, foreign cultures can get overlooked. I was wrong; unfortunately, I came to my job only six weeks after the administration got started, so my first meeting of the National Security Council involved the description of what Vance was going to propose. I don't try to excuse myself, but I'm saying that at that meeting, nobody asked me if the CIA had evaluated the possible Soviet reaction. I should have looked for that and anticipated it; I did not. But I don't think it was on the policymakers' minds. David was closer to that, and he will probably pick that up and either refute me or confirm it or give a different view. I think that will be helpful.

Let me very quickly try to move to a slightly different sphere of the SALT II issue, and draw some lessons for looking to the new arms control negotiations from our errors in that one. As chief of intelligence I was involved primarily with the question of whether we could verify this treaty. I took a very strong stand that as chief of intelligence, I could tell the president and the Senate only how well we could monitor what the Soviets were doing, not determine whether that was adequate verification. Taking that stand made me very unpopular in the White House and elsewhere, because the media interpreted it as my not being in favor of the treaty, not being willing to come out and say it was adequately verifiable. I was viewed as an unreconstructed military hawk who didn't want the treaty. In point of fact, I really did, and was very enthusiastic about it. I tried to conceal my enthusiasm as much as I did any possibility that I was opposed to it, because the chief of intelligence must be seen as objective on these issues. If I were seen to be for the treaty in saying it was adequately verifiable, or against it in saying that it wasn't, then people might question whether the monitoring evaluations I was giving them were accurate or skewed to support my position.

I could tell the president things like "Mr. President"--and I'm making these numbers up--"if the Soviets build a hundred more ICBMs than they're allowed, at that point, we will be able to detect it with a 90 percent confidence." Is that adequately verifying the treaty? I don't know. That is a political judgment. How badly off would the United States be if the Soviets obtained a hundred additional missiles, and we had a 90 percent chance of finding out? What would the United States be able to do to counter that if it happened? Those are not matters of intelligence; those are matters of political judgment, of what risks the country can and should take in order to have a treaty. The point I'd like to make in looking forward to new treaties is that there will never be total, absolute verification. There's always going to be this element of risk, of maybe they can get a hundred before we find out about it with a 90 percent probability. And you've got to accept that. The opponents of START or whatever treaty comes up next will almost undoubtedly demand absolute verification. That's a canard, don't fall for it. We've got to be able, as a country, to measure what risks we're willing to take.

And as I look back on the SALT II verification procedures, I think one error we made was that we didn't judge what risks we were willing to take. We measured and tried to monitor values that were not very important. I can't tell you how many hours I spent studying, debating, and testifying about the throw weight of Soviet ICBMs. Throw weight determines how many warheads can be put on a missile, and therefore how many weapons there are. But we're dealing with only about three hundred Soviet missiles. What if they put ten more warheads on each one than we thought they had? Three thousand more warheads, added to a total of some twenty-five thousand. Insignificant.

Just a few weeks ago, I was in Moscow. I had the privilege of going into the Kremlin and meeting with a Soviet marshal. I said to him, "I wonder, sir, because of all the time it has taken us to negotiate this START treaty, and we're going to get only a 15 percent cut in warheads--and that's insignificant on twenty-five thousand-- shouldn't one of our presidents just stand up and say, 'I'm going to unilaterally, without any agreement, without any verification of rules, cut my warheads in half'? I don't believe, sir, you could tell your president that if we cut ours in half and you retained all of yours, and you had a two to one advantage, you would be able safely to attack us." And the marshal said, "Da." He instantly agreed; he instantly understood that at these kinds of numbers, a few thousand here or there is insignificant.

We've lost sight, in arms control, of our objectives. We've had schizophrenia between a school of thought that considers numbers and quality of these weapons for purposes of fighting and another school of thought that says mutual assured deterrence is what we need, the ability to survive and retain an invulnerable deterrent force. We want Soviet marshals or generals to say to their president, "We cannot destroy the American deterrent to the point that they can't retaliate against us so devastatingly that it won't be worth it, no matter how much damage we do to them." So we must, as we go forward, look at our verification procedures and realize they will never be absolute and perfect; that we will take some risks; and that the risks we should take are risks that don't affect the vulnerability of our deterrent. Risks as to qualities and numbers are much less significant.

In the SALT II Treaty, for instance, we opposed the Soviets going to mobile ICBMs. We said, "We'll develop no new ICBMs, mobile or otherwise." Yet, here's the Soviet Union, a nation that's not a sea power, a nation that has a large landmass around which you can place mobile ICBMs, and naturally will gravitate in that direction to find invulnerability. And we should want them to have invulnerability, because if they don't, if they feel vulnerable, then we don't know how they will react under stress. We achieve our invulnerability by going to sea, because we're a sea power. In SALT II, we weren't interested as much as we should have been in invulnerability and deterrence. We worried too much about measurements of war fighting.

Part V

Carter Biographers

Assessing the characer and tenure of American presidents has become something of an industry whose existence is justified by the importance of its subject in the political life of the country and the world. Occupancy of the seat of power brings with it exposure to scrutiny of one's deeds, moods, dispositions--one's entire life. Carter's biographers have been, and continue to be, actively at work plying their craft, and the Hofstra Conference was able to attract a number of them to share their views. The focus of each participant was different; their works were published at different periods of Jimmy Carter's emergence and tenure; and they varied considerably in their viewpoints.

Mr. Carter makes a particularly interesting subject because of the uniqueness of his background and political emergence. Few "outsiders" have become president, and, since the end of the Civil War in 1865, fewer still have been from the South. In addition, the 1960s and 1970s were politically and socially turbulent. That Jimmy Carter could emerge as president toward the end of such a period seems in itself a sign of the thoroughness of the alteration of the American political landscape. Thus, political biography has a rich soil in which to do its work, and the biographers' panel testifies to that in ample ways.

Moderator: Erwin C. Hargrove

I want to say a word on my thinking about the presidency before I began to work on Carter and how he affected my thinking about the presidency.

A very important book was published in 1960 by Richard Neustadt, the title of which was *Presidential Power*. He was then at Columbia, subsequently at Harvard. It became the basis for all subsequent writing on the presidency, I think, by both journalists and political scientists. The thesis was that the presidency is a weak office, with weak formal powers. The president can't necessarily get his way with Congress; he doesn't necessarily control the bureaucracy, even his own cabinet; public attention is infrequent, and it's difficult to get it; and therefore, the prescription is that the president has to make up for those gaps betwen authority and power by personal political skill. It's a personal concept of the presidency. Presidents get along with Congress by bargaining, by persuading other people that their goals are consonant with the president's goals. There is no such thing as command of bureaucracy, and presidents can capture the attention of the public only in connection with events. They can teach in connection with events. FDR was the exemplar; Ike was the foil, and in fact, he was portrayed as a somewhat weak, passive president who didn't understand how politics worked in Washington. Subsequent revisionist biographers, particularly Fred Greenstein of Princeton, have shown that was not an accurate reading of Ike; he was very skillful politically, but he just pretended he wasn't, and it worked. But anyway, Neustadt's book was read by John Kennedy; Dick Neustadt was an adviser to Kennedy. I think it became the implicit standard by which both journalists and political scientists evaluated presidents: the FDR norms.

Lyndon Johnson seemed made to order. I remember an interview that Neustadt gave in *U.S. News & World Report* early in the Johnson administration, still in 1964, in which he talked about how Johnson matched his norms. That evaluation, of course, didn't last. The subsequent criticism of Neustadt's model in the political science literature pointed out at least two things. One, he ignored the great executive powers of presidents. I don't think it ever occurred to Neustadt that a president would take us into a war by using his executive authority. Second, Dick wrote that the search for personal power in the office is the key to political influence. Again, I don't think it ever occurred to him that people like Lyndon Johnson and Richard Nixon would show that the search for personal power is necessary but not sufficient, and even damaging, to the search for presidential power. So what developed out of that was the general criticism of the "textbook presidency," in which the president was presented as the first among equals in the three parts of our governments. The president articulates the public interest, Congress is provincial--that view, which was implicit in Neustadt, came under criticism in response to Johnson and Nixon, in response to Vietnam and Watergate.

And a countermodel developed--not fully developed, but it became important--democratic character in the presidency is important. Moral charcter is important, but so is democratic character, openness. Presidential restraint in the use of power is important. And Ford and Carter seemed to embody these norms. Carter conveniently forgot that Ford was in the White House; he campaigned against Nixon. But Ford had done many of the things to restore civility to government that Carter had said he was going to do. But Carter's 1976 campaign explicitly appealed to these themes, I think, and I predicted in an essay published in 1974 that this democratic model would not last; that at some point, events would impel the American people to want a hero in the White House--someone who could dominate events. I think it's an irony that Carter came into office with this implicit democratic character model in the air, but he was actually evaluated in terms of the earlier, Neustadtian model of power and power relationships.

I brought these two models to my study of Carter, which I began in the early 1980s. If you compare him against the Neustadt model, he comes out rather poorly in terms of canons of presidential skill. He lacked bargaining skills with Congress; he disdained bargaining with Congress; he was very naive about executive politics. A number of people have talked about this: his naive notion about cabinet government, and his assumption that he wouldn't have to use White House staff to manage policymaking. He was poor at presentation of himself and issues to the public, although a brilliant campaigner in 1976. A reporter for the *Wall Street Journal*, Allan Otten, told me during the campaign that Carter was the best one-on-one campaigner he had ever seen, and I've had that confirmed by any number of people. But he separated campaigning from governing. He didn't undrestand that governing is politics. And these were the judgments of Washington professionals--Congress, interest groups, certainly journalists, and a good many political scientists--and eventually those filtered down to public opinion. The democratic character model, which he deliberately tried to exemplify, seemed wanting.

I could have stoppped there and I could have written a critical book, a negative portrait. But the theory didn't cover all the facts. How to explain his great achievements if he's so inept? That's one question. And a second one was, What about the context? Was it fair to blame Carter for policy failures--especially for domestic policy failures--when the Congress had changed so in its reform and response to Nixon: the great democratization of Congress; the power of subcommittee chairs; the great number of centers of power within the Congress; the political parties' unraveling--as a consequence of Vietnam, a decline in party identification, a decline in party loyalty, and so on.

My own work on the presidency had, before that time, emphasized the importance of historical context in presidential power. Skill has to be bolstered by political support, and presidents can't create it all. Neustadt had a static view of presidential power: that the president is always going to be weak institutionally, and it's a question of personal skill. I think that's incomplete. It's really a question of the political mood of the times, the kinds of events that concern people, the degree to which people are prepared to get behind presidential leadership. And so I think the Ford and Carter presidencies both faced declines in the instruments of presidential power: the parties, the rise of voracious and selfish interest groups--in many ways filling the vacuum caused by the decline of the parties--the congressional fragmentation. And therefore Carter was caught, I think, between two stools. He entered office with a moralistic, democratic style, and he was judged by the previous model, but under conditions in which it was not possible to act in terms of the Neustadtian model.

He hoped to lead the Democratic Party in a centrist direction, but he had great difficulty with his own coalition, which was breaking apart. He introduced comprehensive legislation--welfare reform, energy, and so on--and had great difficulty with it. Still, despite all the criticism that he took--particularly for the disastrous first year, in which he sent too much up to Capitol Hill--his batting average with Congress, as a number of papers here have attested, was quite good. Compared with Kennedy and Johnson, his congressional staff got their act together after the first year and were very effective and very efficient. I think my colleagues can probably speak to that. In fact, it suggests that personal skill may be less important than we might think. Carter had the Democrats there; in fact, the Democrats who were so angry at him supported his program in Congress more than any other group.

Carter's greatest personal achievements, however, were ones in which he played to his own strengths. Maybe this is the other side of pride: tenacity, homework, vision. He transcended the immobilism of Washington government, I think, in his great foreign policy successes. Camp David was, of course, the principal one. I was very struck with the panel the other night. Each of those very impressive professionals-- foreign service officers, very professional, sophisticated, intelligent men--said Jimmy Carter was a better man than I was and than we were, because he had a clearer vision of what could be achieved in the way of an agreement between Israel and Egypt. He had the tenacity, he had the vision, he had the toughness. These things were not particularly caught by the Neustadtian model. Last night Robert Strauss called the Panama Canal treaties a great second-term issue; Rosalynn Carter repeated that to Jimmy Carter, and he said, "Yes, but I may have only one term. I want to achieve something in that term."

I made a lot of fun of the human rights business when it was going around at first, because I thought it was very naive. But think about it today: think about Marcos; think about South Korea; think about South Africa; think about the Soviet Union. I do think his greatest failure was his inability to strike the right kind of rapport with the public; he was too much of a rationalist. He couldn't put on the kind of performance that he put on for us yesterday afternoon. He was very good in town meetings, terrible on televison, terrible reading speeches, couldn't project himself well.

So what's my estimate? He faced hard questions--very hard questions--and resolved some of them. He was honest with the country. He spoke sense to the Democrats--I don't think, personally, they've learned it yet. It was a presidency of considerable achievement flawed by a president who would not act to protect his political reputation--who, if anything, disdained his political reputation, I think, in Washington and the country. For example, the decision to admit the shah was a terrible mistake. I heard Carter say in a group, "I was the one who was opposed to admitting the shah. It was a mistake. We woudn't admit the shah for political reasons. But once they told me he was ill--so ill that he had to have American doctors--I said okay, let him in." I submit that was a terrible mistake. Carter was quite prone to confuse personal morality with political morality, and they're very different. Political morality would have said, "Don't let him in, you have other responsibilities."

So I think this is a great man who is happiest when he can do good without the constraints of politics. As Louis Koenig said, he's "the last serious president" of the United States that we've had.

Discussant: Haynes Johnson

When I got up this morning in Washington--I just flew in--I picked up my *Washington Post* and found a story by my colleague and friend E. J. Dionne, formerly of the *New York Times*, reporting on what President Carter said here yesterday. It struck me in reading it how ironic and yet how contemporary the Carter presidency is, especially given the kind of comments that he made. This was directly on the Gulf situation. I won't repeat it to those of you who were here. But it struck me again that the conjunction of the moment now makes us look at the Carter presidency in a special way, because he said--in E. J.'s quoting of him, at least--"I don't think the Arab world will ever forgive the massive death that will occur by American weapons against Arab people." He went on to say that he had supported very much--I'm paraphrasing--President Bush's initial handling of the actions in the Gulf: the sanctions, international coalition, and the rest. He was raising the questions that we don't hear raised, either by the White House or in the political system today, on what the long-term consequences of a war there will be. And I thought to myself, that's Carter at his best. That's why Carter looks good in retrospect: a longer view of history, a sense of linkage between past and present, and a rather wise and tempered view of the world we are now entering. In that sense, I won't take long to make some introductory comments.

I have just finished a book; I'm pleased that you laughed at, or enjoyed, the title, *Sleepwalking Through History*. I agree with Erwin's provocative analysis that, in many ways, Jimmy Carter prepared the way for Ronald Reagan; and that for ten years --or at least the eight years of the Reagan presidency--there was always strong political capital to be made by "running" against the "inept, weak, vacillating, wimpish leadership of Jimmy Carter in the White House." What's interesting now--and ironically exquisite--is the latest evidence of one of history's continually fascinating turns. It must give Carter some small pleasure. Carter now has higher public opinion ratings than Ronald Reagan, and only two years since Reagan's presidency. In a much more serious way, the kinds of issues that the Carter presidency was addressing, and that he himself was talking about, are today even more the issues that the United States will be grappling with as we go on into the next century: energy; long-term depletion of resources; the ability of the political system to make long-term choices, not short-term ones; ethical standards, so that the system is believed and not collapsing in cynicism; and all the rest.

When I wrote about the Carter term, I looked at the first two years of his presidency and felt that he would be an extremely important figure if a transitional president: a president who came to power when the New Deal period was ending, and when the Democratic Party was about to experience even more of a decline in terms of its hold on the national political sense of the country. It was also a time when the country was looking for a different approach--a more conservative, if you will, practical, realistic approach--to the problems of governance and long-term issues-- economic, political, social--that are still very much with us, now even more so.

Furthermore, I thought it was extremely important to see what happened to the experience of a Southern president who came to Washington as the true political outsider of the century. It is not by happenstance, to close the circle, that the Democrats have not elected another president since Jimmy Carter--it's already been fourteen years--and I would argue that the next president to be elected from the Democratic Party will probably *have* to be from the South. It's an interesting turn of the wheel. That's a logical conclusion to be drawn from the cracking, or the fraying, of the Republican lock, so called, on the Sunbelt states in the most recent congressional elections, when the Democrats elected governors in Florida and Texas, and almost took California. You can see the beginnings of a possibility there for the Democrats, if they have the right approach, which probably won't occur, since they have booted their political opportunities ever since the Carter presidency.

The Carter presidency today deserves more examination, particularly in the aftermath of the Reagan years. Ronald Reagan used everything in reverse of the Carter presidency, and used it brilliantly. He used the symbols of the presidency to give us a picture of strength and to recapture and rekindle an almost mystical belief in American might. And he used these images of the presidency in quite an effective way in contrast to Carter, whose earnestness he made fun of; even in the last campaign, George Bush deprecated the Carter presidency. But the country is beginning to come to terms with the Carter presidency, especially given the enormous cleanup process coming out of the 1980s. We're being forced to look back on how we got to where we are, and discovering that the issues that were so much at the center of public attention in the Carter period are even more so now.

Discussant: Betty Glad

I'm not going to talk about my biographical techniques unless you have questions during the question-and-answer period. But I do think, in reevaluating the Carter presidency, it's important not to overlook some of the problems in that presidency. In a balanced assessment of Jimmy Carter, one should look at his flaws as well as his virtues.

Certainly Carter had many virtues as president of the United States. In the foreign policy arena in particular, he was a risk taker. In the Camp David negotiations of 1978, he tackled very difficult problems and exceeded all expectations of those in his immediate political environment. In his human rights campaign, something many of us who deem ourselves political realists were somewhat cynical about at the time, he made a very important contribution to the world political community.

But the biographer cannot take lightly or pass over Carter's political shortcomings, treating them as amiable eccentricities of no real importance. Sometimes, he sabotaged his own goals. I'm going to talk today on his handling of the SALT treaty to illustrate this point. My thesis is that Carter's political choices and rhetoric made it more difficult to conclude a treaty in the first instance and contributed to the political environment that made Senate approval of the treaty problematical.

The SALT treaty was one of Carter's most important commitments. As Rosalynn Carter noted, "Of all the goals Jimmy had as president, reducing the threat of nuclear war and preventing an expensive and dangerous nuclear arms race was the most important of all to him."

Yet Carter stumbled at the very beginning of negotiations with the Soviet Union on this issue. The SALT II agreement was near completion before the 1976 campaign. If Carter had been willing to build on what President Ford and Secretary of State Kissinger had done before him, he might well have had a SALT II agreement by the end of his first year in office.

Carter was not content, however, to build on the work of his predecessors. He wanted massive arms reductions, and he thought he could accomplish this without paying attention to the signals the Russians were sending him. Shortly after coming to office, the president wrote to Leonid Brezhnev that he was going to offer some proposals for deep cuts in nuclear weapons. Brezhnev wrote back on February 25, stating that any departure from the Vladivostok formula was "deliberately unacceptable." Jimmy Carter, however, did not proceed more cautiously and explore formulas with the Soviet leader to see what might be acceptable.

Instead, he proceeded with the elaboration of what would be his proposal for massive arms reductions, and invited Henry Kissinger to the White House for dinner in mid-March, to seek out his views. Carter recalled that Kissinger "thought that the deep cut proposal we had put together on SALT had a good chance to be accepted by the Soviets if they are sincere and want to make progress on disarmament." He never considered the possibility that Kissinger, recalling Carter's 1976 campaign critiques that he was a "Lone Ranger" in his foreign policy-making, may not have had his best interests in mind.

In late March, Secretary of State Cyrus Vance traveled to Moscow to present Carter's plan for major arms reduction. Vance had convinced Carter to let him also present a more modest fallback proposal should the first one not fly. When presented with Carter's plan, however, the Soviet leaders cut the talks short. In an angry press conference, the Soviet foreign minister, Andrei Gromyko, publicly rejected the Carter proposal as "a cheap and shoddy maneuver for unilateral advancement."

At this time, the Soviet leaders were already suspicious of Jimmy Carter's intentions toward them. During the 1976 campaign, he had criticized the Kissinger détente policies, running television ads in the South that piggybacked on Ronald Reagan's critique of Ford policies. Once in office, Carter put his human rights campaign at the very top of his agenda. From the Soviet perspective, it seemed to be aimed at them--a form of anti-Soviet posturing. On January 27, at Carter's direction, the State Department warned Moscow against violating the rights of the Soviet dissident Andrei Sakharov. The State Department had been concerned that statements such as this could get in the way of his arms control agreement, but Carter would not be deterred. In February, the president sent Sakharov a letter saying that the United States would use its influence to seek the release of political prisoners. It was the first direct communication between a Western leader and a political prisoner along these lines. On March 22, Carter announced his intention to increase expenditures for Radio Free Europe and Radio Liberty so these organizations could extend their broadcast range into the Soviet Union.

The Soviet leadership had responded to Carter's human rights campaign with editorials in *Izvestia* and *Pravda* complaining that these American activities were undermining relations between the Soviet Union and the United States. When Vance arrived in Moscow to present the American proposals, Brezhnev greeted him with the statement that "constructive development of relations" was "impossible" if the United States did not respect the principle of noninterference in other nations' internal affairs.

Yet when the Soviet leaders rejected Carter's initial arms control program, he was surprised. Their defensive reactions to his human rights campaign, he suggested, might be motivated by "their desire for political reasons to exaggerate the differences between the two countries."

By 1988, the administration was explicitly linking human rights violations to possible U.S. punishments. On April 13, 1978, the U.S. ambassador to the Soviet Union, Malcolm Toon, issued an unusually blunt statement warning that U.S.-Soviet relations would be adversely affected should the Soviet Union proceed with the treason trial of dissidents Anatoly Shcharansky and Alexander Ginzburg. When these two men were sentenced, the White House canceled the sale of advanced computers to TASS, the Soviet news agency, and ordered all sales of U.S. oil technology to be placed under administration review.

The administration at this time was suggested that Soviet activities in the Horn of Africa could undermine support for the SALT treaty within the United States. On March 1, 1978, Brzezinski made the first public suggestion of this nature. Carter, even while denying formal linkage between SALT and Soviet activities in the Horn of Africa, noted that American opinion would turn against SALT and lead to its failure if these activities were continued. At Wake Forest University in March 1978, he warned that a continued Soviet military buildup and adventurism could erode popular support for cooperation in any area. In his speech at the U.S. Naval Academy on June 17, 1978, Carter suggested that the Soviet Union was attempting to export "totalitarian and repressive forms of involvement" through its military programs and use of proxies.

Finally, in January 1979, Carter played the China card. In his speech at Notre Dame on March 22, 1977, he had given the Soviet leaders a glimpse of his intentions when he suggested the Soviet Union's archrival, the People's Republic of China (PRC), was a "key force for global peace." The United States, he said, would work with "creative forces" in that country in the future. Less than two years later, the United States and the PRC worked out diplomatic normalization, and cultural and scientific agreements. Carter and Deputy Premier Deng Hsiao-ping issued a communiqué stating that the United States was going to work with the Chinese to oppose those who were attempting to "establish hegemony or domination over others." "Hegemony" was a frequent Chinese characterization of Soviet activities in the Far East, and the use of the term suggested that anti-Soviet motives were behind the agreements.

After a series of delays and reversals, however, the SALT II treaty was finally signed at Vienna on June 18, 1979. The United States had moved back toward the Vladivostok formula, and the secretary of state had downplayed U.S. human rights concerns at the final negotiating sessions in Geneva. Opponents of the treaty had mobilized, however, and the administration brought in Lloyd Cutler to orchestrate the administration's efforts to win Senate support. By the late summer of 1979, as Brzezinski noted, the campaign on behalf of SALT was making steady progress.

But then some behind-the-scenes politicking orchestrated by Zgibniew Brzezinski got out of hand. In late July, the national security adviser had warned Carter that there was evidence of a Soviet combat brigade in Cuba, and he asked for increased intelligence surveillance. On August 14, Brzezinski told the president that the intelligence reports showed there was a Soviet brigade in Cuba. This was an extremely serious development, he noted, and could jeopardize the SALT II treaty.

Yet Brzezinski was not so alarmed by these reports that he felt obliged to cancel a short vacation he had planned to take over the Labor Day weekend. While Brzezinski was away from Washington, however, the chairman of the Senate Foreign Relations Committee, Frank Church, went public. He charged that the Soviets were testing U.S. resolve by these actions. Running for reelection in a close contest in Idaho, he was evidently trying to correct his earlier image as a foreign policy dove.

The resulting pandemonium caused Brzezinski to rush back to Washington. Secretary of State Vance argued at this time that the United States should demand the withdrawal of the brigade and noted that the status quo was unacceptable. Brzezinski, surprisingly, took the position that the brigade had possibly been in Cuba for some time, and that it was not really an issue. What was needed, he urged, was the development of a comprehensive, worldwide strategy toward the Soviet Union, which would include opening talks on the exchange of military technology with China.

Carter, in a televised statement on the matter on September 7, sent a mixed message on the matter. The Soviet combat unit in Cuba, he noted, may have been in

Cuba for quite a few years, and it was not an assault force. Still, these developments in Cuba were ominous and the status quo was "not acceptable."

Behind the scenes Carter's top advisers continued the fight over policy. Cyrus Vance, Robert Cutler, and Walter Mondale urged that the conflicts with the Soviet Union be confined to the brigade in Cuba. Brzezinski and Harold Brown wanted to use the issue to force a great anti-Soviet front. Thus Brzezinski urged the president to increase defense spending and develop a dialogue with China on the possible sharing of sensitive technology and other military issues.

Carter saw the full implications of the Brzezinski stance for his SALT II treaty only when he met with Senator Robert Byrd at the White House on the evening of September 23. The senator told Carter that the Soviet brigade in Cuba was a phony issue, and urged him to forgo the hot rhetoric and find a more appropriate response. Another week went by before Carter resolved the issue in public. In a televised address on October 1, he said that he had Soviet assurances that the brigade had been in Cuba for some time and had no offensive intentions. Still, he would increase surveillance over the area. He would establish a Caribbean Joint Task Force, and there would be new military and economic assistance to Caribbean nations.

Brzezinski's response to the president's relatively moderate action on the brigade issue suggests that Brzezinski had embraced an agenda quite a different from the president's. On October 4, the national security adviser made what he called "the most disagreeable comment" he had ever made to the president. The United States had told the Russians on several occasions that it took great exception to their actions in Vietnam, Iran, the Middle East, and Africa, and more recently in Cuba, he told the president. "But then we do nothing about it." This could be dangerous for the future, he argued, because the Russians could miscalculate our responses. The president was livid. He told Brzezinski that he "had no intention to go to war over the Soviet brigade in Cuba."

By this time, however, considerable damage had been done to the campaign to ratify SALT II. Senator Church, on September 4, postponed the hearings on the SALT treaty and stated that he saw no likelihood of Senate ratification of the treaty so long as Soviet combat troops were stationed in Cuba. The whole crisis had shaken the public's confidence in the administration and had heightened hostility toward the Soviet Union, as Brzezinski later noted in his memoirs. The SALT ratification process had been slowed, Brzezinski concluded, and would have to be put off until later in the year, or perhaps early 1980.

When the Russians went into Afghanistan in late December, the final nail was driven into the SALT II coffin. When informed of the Soviet action, the president exclaimed, "There goes SALT II." Rosalynn Carter noted in her memoirs that she had never seen "Jimmy more upset than he was the afternoon the Russian invasion was confirmed." Carter stated in his memoirs that this was the most "profound disappointment" of his presidency.

This frustration may well have contributed to his subsequent efforts to isolate the Soviet Union politically, economically, and culturally. Some of these measures--such as the boycott of the Olympic Games in Moscow and the embargo on the export of American grain--were controversial and adopted against considerable resistance at home and abroad. But the president's goal, as he told Rosalynn right after the invasion occurred, was "to make sure that Afghanistan will be their Vietnam."

His rhetoric, moreover, foreshadowed the "evil empire" rhetoric of the Reagan administration. In an exchange with Hamilton Jordan, he suggested that the invasion had "made the prospects for nuclear war more likely." In a speech on January 14, 1980, Carter saw the Soviets' action as a reflection of their lack of central moral values. The invasion, he said, was "a deliberate effort by a powerful atheistic government to subjugate an independent Islamic people." In his January 23 State of the Union address, he said, "The implications of the Soviet invasion of Afghanistan pose the most serious threat to world peace since World War II."

Many of the problems that I have delineated here cannot be understood simply as manifestations of Carter's political inexperience. The biographer who draws from a broader perspective can see patterns in his approach to several different issues, and these patterns suggest that certain personality and stylistic characteristics influenced him.

Carter, as I pointed out in my biography of him, is a proud man, very certain of his moral and intellectual superiority to many others in his political environment. That kind of pride contributed to his willingness to take risks. He aimed high, in part, because he saw himself as destined to accomplish great and difficult goals. Morever, because his ambition was accompanied by extraordinary tenacity and considerable intellectual ability, he sometimes succeeded.

This combination of traits paid off during the Camp David negotiations on the Middle East in 1978. But those same qualities led him to overshoot at times. Carter's original misstep during the SALT II negotiations can be understood in these terms. He hungered for a major arms reduction agreement, as Strobe Talbott has suggested. He wanted something that would distinguish his work from the relatively modest accomplishments worked out within the Vladivostok framework. The result--when Secretary of Defense Harold Brown presented him with the package for deep cuts in the Soviet arsenal, he bit at it, as one participant in the process told Talbott, like a "beautifully tied, juicy fly dropped right in front of a hungry trout's nose."

This adherence to an exalted image of his mission was accompanied by a tendency to downgrade the importance of the interests and concerns of political others, even when their assistance was requisite to the accomplishment of his political ends. Carter undermined his following in the U.S. Congress, as I have shown in my biography, by his insensitivity to the interests and political territories of many of its members. That same kind of insensitivity contributed to his rejection of Brezhnev's objections to plans for a major arms limitation program that clearly ran contrary to Soviet interests. It was almost as if he did not fully realize at the beginning that he could not achieve an arms control agreement without the consent of the Soviet leaders.

The certainty that his goals were morally right contributed to another kind of political innocence. Carter had difficulties, as I have pointed out elsewhere, in seeing that two good ends might compete with each other, and that sometimes people have to prioritize their values so that they can make the trade-offs required in this less than perfect world. Carter's failure to realize the problems his human rights campaign presented for his SALT II objectives can be understood in these terms. He simply could not see that the unencumbered pursuit of one righteous goal could conflict with the accomplishment of another righteous goal.

Carter's response to the Soviet intervention in Afghanistan can also be understood, in part, in terms of his rage at the final demise of his SALT II treaty. He saw the Soviet intervention as *the* cause of the failure of his SALT treaty. He thereby avoided recognition of his own responsibility for the delay in negotiating the treaty, as well as his own contributions to the political climate that made approval of that treaty problematic. His exaggeration of that crisis into "the most serious threat to world peace since World War II" was influenced by his proclivity for inflating the significance of all major events that touched upon his career. There had been more serious Soviet challenges in the postwar period. The Berlin blockade of 1948 and the Cuban missile crisis of 1962 were clear efforts to change the balance of power between the United States and the Soviet Union. The Soviet intervention in Afghanistan, by way of contrast, was an attempt to maintain dominance in a country that had been within the Soviet sphere of influence for some time. For Carter, however, the crisis he had to deal with was the greatest, just as his programs were the best.

The Carter presidency, in short, presents us with the problem of interpreting a president who aimed high, accomplished much, but sometimes undermined his own objectives. Portraits that either overlook his real accomplishments or blame his failures on factors over which he had no control do not do justice to an interesting and complex man.

Discussant: Robert Shogan

First, I'd like to thank Hofstra for the opportunity to participate, and I thank all you folks for coming. I hope we all learn something together. My remarks are going to be focused on Carter as the anti-politician as president, and particularly as exemplified by his so-called malaise speech. Let me talk briefly about being anti-politician.

We're all familiar with the fact that Carter prided himself on not being a politician and disliking politics, separating himself from politics. And a number of people--myself included--at times have ascribed that to his sort of newness to politics, and also to his Southernism. Professor Hargrove has talked about his being in the Southern progressive tradition. But I don't really think this tradition can be regionalized. Let's recall a couple of comments by a Democrat, as it happens, and a candidate for the presidency that were very similar to the things Carter said. One of the things that make Carter a nonpolitician--and I think hurt his effectiveness--was his oratory, or his difficulty with oratory. Milt Gwirtzman once told me that if Carter haddelivered Roosevelt's "We have nothing to fear but fear itself" speech, the Depression would still be going on. And Jim Fallows said that Carter used to admonish him not to put any flourishes in his speeches, that he was really anxious not to be interesting. We can go back--not all that long ago--to a Democratic nominee who said, "I don't want to be a great communicator." That, of course, was Michael Dukakis. I don't think there was any great danger that he ever would be, but he kept emphasizing it.

When I first encountered Jimmy Carter as a candidate before the 1976 campaign, he said there were two principles that he was going to campaign on. One was trust, which was tied to his religion; the other was competence. Again, we don't have to go far back to remember who told his party at their convention in Atlanta that this election is not about ideology; it's about competence. So you have two people who would seem so disparate, yet both of them sort of saw themselves as Governor Goodwrench. Mostly, I think what bothers me as a citizen--maybe as an individual, certainly as a journalist--is that being against politicians is an even easier card to play in this country than racism. People feel guilty about being racist; nobody feels guilty about disliking politicians.

What it does and what bothers me--and I think that this is getting to the root and to what, I think, approaches the problem of the Carter presidency, and what would have been the problem if there had been a Dukakis presidency--is the lack of accountability; you don't feel you have to explain yourself to anyone, because if you're Carter--and, in a way, if you're Dukakis--you already know what's right, and the people, if they have enough sense, given enough time, will appreciate and understand you; and if they don't, well, the hell with them. That creates problems for all of us, for the country, and for the anti-political president.

I think many of those problems were pointed up by the so-called malaise speech. Briefly, to refresh your memory, the energy shock drove up gas prices; there were people lining up for gas they couldn't afford to buy. Carter was in Tokyo; Stuart Eizenstat shot up a flare of alarm, and he came back. He was going to give an energy speech; he talked to Rosalynn and said, "God, I can't give this speech again. I've got to say something to get some people's attention." Well, he certainly accomplished that. What he did was go to Camp David, and he took a bunch of people with him. I think this demonstrates--as a corollary to his anti-political attitude--a kind of self-absorption. If you believe you know what is right, and you don't need to explain it to people, what becomes important is how you feel and how you arrived at those judgments. Probably the most seasoned politician in the Carter administration, Walter Mondale, did not like the idea of Carter delivering such a speech, yet Carter went ahead and did it. This was self-absorption personified. This went on for more than a week, and wise (or not so wise) men went to Camp David to see him. Republican Senator Ted Stevens of Alaska, never one of the more tactful legislators but sometimes perceptive, wondered aloud if the president was approaching some sort of mental problem, and suggested that he ought to go off and take a rest.

Well, Carter finally gave this speech, and he said there were a lot of things wrong with the country. He never, as you know, used the word "malaise"; he said we were suffering from "a crisis of confidence." I think the word came from a Caddell memo, but at any rate it was a reasonable description of the mood that Carter painted. Carter accepted some responsibility for what was going on, but not much. He said, "I've worked hard to put my campaign promises into law, and I have to admit,with just mixed success." The real culprits, he made clear, were Congress and, to some extent, the people. As a matter of fact, because Americans tend to rally around the president in times of crisis, even if he has sort of invented the crisis himself, the speech by itself created a little positive blip, as things were measured, for Carter's image.

However, he not only stepped on his own lines, he trampled all over them, because then he fired a large portion of his government. If you remember, he asked the whole cabinet, and I think all senior political appointees, for their resignations, and went ahead and fired four of them. Carter himself said, in a masterpiece of understatement, "I handled that very poorly." The purge not only cost him some of his most experienced advisers, but also antagonized the many influential friends of these influential people. One quote that deserves repeating at this time is from a Democratic Congressman, Charlie Wilson of Texas, who said about the people who were fired and the people who were left, "They're cutting down the big trees and keeping the monkeys." The result, by the time Carter got through--first with the speech and then with this purge--was that if there hadn't been a malaise, it was about as close to it as you could get.

The malaise speech, I believe, by being an artificial crisis, set the stage for another episode that, while it was a real crisis, was largely inflated by Carter. That was the Iran hostage crisis, in which the whole focus of the country became tuned in on the fate of the fifty or sixty American hostages in Tehran. This may have been humanitarian and compassionate, but there was nothing Carter could do about them. In fact, putting that kind of emphasis on it was counterproductive, because the more attention we paid to them, the more it was profitable for the Iranians to hold on to them. In terms of political consequences, I think some idea of the impact can be gained from Richard Wirthlin, the pollster for Ronald Reagan, who was preparing to run in 1980. He told me later that he was "absolutely ecstatic" when Carter gave his malaise speech. He said, and I tend to agree with him, "He completely misread the perception of what people wanted a leader to be. He set us up with a perfect foil. It made him sound impotent. It was the most important political speech in the last four years."

The problems Carter faced were real enough, but he had real opportunities, too. Briefly, his election as a white Southerner who could attract black votes gave him the potential for at least offsetting what had been a problem that, since the 1948 convention, had divided and convulsed the Democratic Party. He had a way to reduce and erode the terrible toll of racism. Before Carter was president, many people believed that if you could find a way--if you were a Democrat--to alleviate the edge of racism, then you could really deal with what many people think are the serious national problems. Carter had that way, and God knows he had all the good intentions of doing it, but he was unable to fully realize it. I think it was because of his being an anti-politician.

Carter became, as you know, the first elected incumbent president since Herbert Hoover to fail to win reelection, and that's not an insignificant event, if we remember what it took to defeat Hoover. I feel, as I think everyone has said here, that he paved the way for Ronald Reagan. In the malaise speech, Carter said, "Our people have turned to the federal government and found it isolated from the mainstream of our nation's life." In essence, Reagan won the 1980 presidential campaign by reminding people that it was Carter whom they had chosen to head that government.

Discussion among Panelists

Hargrove: Let me address a question to the panel, picking up from Betty's thesis about pride. Were his successes and failures two sides of the coin--his tenacity, his ambition, his vision? It was pride going before a fall. Does that explain his successes and his failures? Does anybody want to speak to that?

Johnson: Let me try. I remember a discussion with Carter at the White House where we got into the question of politics and the familiar "inside Washington" view, about why he wasn't dealing with Congress, why he didn't get rid of Frank Moore, and so forth. Carter was very angry about that. But the conversation turned to Lyndon Johnson, and someone said, "Well, Lyndon used to operate this way," and Carter looked aghast. He said, "Well, I can't imagine operating that way." He went on to say some things he had heard about Johnson trading judgeships and the politics of the court, and so forth. He couldn't imagine dealing that way, which seems to me was the perfect moral position, the proper position, but I also wondered what world he was living in. There was somehow the sense that politics was almost ignoble, whereas, it seems to me, that's not the case if you want to achieve something. I think that was part of the problem.

Shogan: Insofar as the good things he did and the things he didn't do, I think there is a range of things that a president can try to do and can accomplish. I think the first responsibility of a president is to communicate the relevance of what he's doing to the people who've chosen him. Carter talked, as Haynes said, about politics as if it was an indulgence, and that it was noble to rise above it. I think that it was an abdication of responsibility. Politics is like writing or journalism; it's a discipline. You have to explain what you're doing and why you're claiming people's attention. I don't think he saw it or recognized it that way, whether because he was an engineer or because of some psychological emphasis in his personality. Any number of the things he did would have taken on more meaning for the country if he had gone through the exercise of getting across to the country why he was doing them and then how they fit into some overall plan. But he didn't do that, and it's also possible that if he had tried to go through that exercise, maybe he would not have done some of those things and would have done others. What goes hand in hand here is a failure to set priorities; instead, there is comprehensiveness. Also, a self-indulgence of doing things that happened to appeal to him without going to the trouble of explaining to people why they should care about what happens.

Glad: I would like to say something here, too. I think the problems with pride are not simply that you can set extraordinary standards--actually, that's an asset; that's the upside of pride--for yourself and do the impossible, if you're lucky. I think Carter's problems as a politician were not that he was not a politician in terms of his own campaign interests. When I looked at his governorship, he traded with the best of them. Bert Lance was the highway commissioner; he used to stand outside the Georgia Senate and watch how people voted, and he clearly traded jobs for support in the campaign. He certainly did it in the 1980 campaign. Suddenly the federal coffers were opened up for New Hampshire and Florida--I wonder why--in 1979-1980. I think his problem as a politician--and this is the negative side of pride--was a lack of empathy with significant political others. I think it's important not only to explain yourself to the public but also to respect others in the game--other politicians--to realize they have political territories to defend, that they have expertise, that they've been around. Why not bring them into the game at the very beginning? The interesting thing I have found since writing Carter's biography is that I'm not his harshest critic in this area. I've looked at some of the memos his aides were writing him in 1979 and 1980, and I'm sure they knew these things. They were constantly telling him and advising him to get the political considerations into the discussions earlier on. Hamilton Jordan had a diagram showing how the Domestic Policy Council people had to be in touch with the political people earlier, so they were not running ahead with their policy formulations without touching important political bases.

In terms of the 1979 "malaise" speech, if you look at what the aides were writing behind the scenes, Patrick Caddell, the one who was feeding Carter this view, knew him and understood him. I think he was, in a sense, manipulating Carter by appeals to his being a great Wilsonian leader. He said, "If you don't make this statement public, that's what will put you in that category." And he had the polls showing how Carter had gone downhill; he had the polls saying there's a great malaise in the public, and you can address it. On the other hand, practically every one of Carter's staff aides opposed this speech until it was clear that Carter was going to go with it. Then Hamilton Jordan switched and said, "Now I'm convinced it's a good idea. But . . . ." Greg Schneider said, "The people are waiting for action now. They don't want another speech." Carter was getting awfully good advice from his aides, except from Patrick Caddell, and he ignored most of what they told him.

Hargrove: I said here the other morning that Joe Califano once said to Carter, "Why don't you have Russell Long down to the White House for dinner and have a chat with him?" Carter said, "I don't understand him when he talks. Do you understand him?" But the extraordinary thing is how much study he put into trying to understand Begin and Sadat. Now, what's the difference?

Johnson: You raised a very interesting question: whether he was doomed by the times in any event, no matter what he might have done. I think that is very important to look back on and wonder. We're talking today about the problems of divided government, as though that's the reason there's difficulty in Washington. The Democrats had greater margins in Congress than they have today--in both House and Senate--when Carter was elected President. That was the last time a president and a Congress of the same party were together, starting fresh, and yet it fell apart; it didn't work. Why was that? Was it the times? Was it the man? I don't know. Probably all of them.

But I do know that the feeling among the Democrats in Congress--the leaders of the Democratic Party and across the board--toward Jimmy Carter was that they didn't dislike him, but later they didn't feel comfortable with him, and they came to have absolute contempt for him. I remember a conversation with one of the leaders of the Senate Democrats. He said to me--this was in the second year--"You know, he"--

speaking of Carter--"doesn't have a single friend up here." And it was chilling, because it was true. It wasn't that they didn't respect Carter, but something had happened. I also have to add that the Democrats were arrogant, they were so sure they were going to be holding power for a long time, and the world would never turn on them.

Shogan: Two quick thoughts on Carter as a politician. It seems to me there are two routes to political persuasion, and they're not mutually exclusive. One is to work through interest groups and try to build a coalition, and we know what Carter thought of interest groups. They were special interest groups, and it was an epithet. He couldn't stand them. The other is to deal with the public. Haynes mentioned that he was a terrific one-on-one campaigner; it apparently was difficult for him to deal with more than one person. He did not try to communicate--you can ignore interest groups, as Reagan sometimes did, if you are really good at speaking to the mass electorate. He didn't want to do the latter either, so he kind of handcuffed himself. I think he saw politics purely as manipulation, but in a very limited sense and a very private way. I think that led to his early success in the nominating campaign. By May 1976, things turned down for Carter; Gerry Brown and Frank Church took turns beating him, week after week, and he didn't have many more political successes. The early part of the nominating schedule, when he took people by surprise, when one-on-one campaigning could pay off--when you could be manipulative and use the liberal sphere of George Wallace--brought his success. When he went beyond that, he didn't have the political resources or acumen to develop it.

Hargrove: After I'd spent a day with Carter in Plains in 1982, listening to him talk, I was trying to get a fix on him. I didn't quite have the sense of him. I decided that his religious faith was the key to his personality. And then I went and talked to a lot of Southern Baptists--and there are all kinds of Southern Baptists, but he's a certain kind of Southern Baptist: not Calvinist; really an early anti-Baptist who believes that with God, all things are possible. Not much conception of original sin in Carter's worldview, I don't think. You add that to the engineer; engineers seem to believe there are correct answers to questions. And then, I think, a deep psychological need for mastery over problems. He must master; he must master problems. Take all those things and put them together, and you have someone who has no tolerance for the conventional politician who believes that truth is ambiguous and uncertain; that you must have tolerance for human failings. Carter often quoted Reinhold Niebuhr, but I don't think he understood him at all. The editor of the *Christian Century* told me that Mrs. Niebuhr wrote a letter to Carter and said, "You don't understand my husband." I don't know if that's true.

Johnson: It's true. Niebuhr's daughter was the editor of the book I wrote. She thought he didn't understand her father.

Hargrove: The sense of ambiguity, paradox, irony, and tragedy in Niebuhr's work was not in Carter. If Southerners don't have a sense of tragedy, they're not Southerners. Carter was not a very good Southerner in that sense, I think.

Glad: I'd also say, if he wasn't a very good politician, he wasn't a good Southerner, either. When I went to Georgia, I was impressed at how many really good Southern

Baptists are also fine politicians. It may be a matter of being a certain kind of Baptist, but I certainly wouldn't say his religion was the major explanatory factor in his political failings.

Questions and Answers

Q: First, I want to thank you all for a wonderful series of insights in beautiful capsule form. It's been a lot of fun. This is a very broad question that asks you to move out of your reflections on Carter alone, but I think it's a question that comes out of the many sessions in the conference. If I have to put it in one sentence, it would be, What is your personal prognosis for human authenticity in the Oval Office? Professor Hargrove spoke of the tremendous strength that came out of Carter being himself, having studied the personalities of Begin and Sadat, and having presented himself as a straightforward human being in the Camp David process. And Mr. Johnson, if I understood him correctly, presented a contrast between Carter and his belief that you could just tell the truth--the contrast between that and the experience of the 1980s, when politicians seemed to feel that you have to respond to the polls, and we came down to the sound bite and the image makers and the response to the public opinion polls. So you have two contrasts here, and I'm just wondering, in terms of your sense of the presidency and where it's been and where it's going, how you see this difference between the late 1970s--the Ford-Carter approach to authenticity--and the experience in the 1980s and early 1990s. Where do you see that coming out? Is the next president from the Democratic Party, for instance, going to be not just a Southerner but also a woman or a black, because there's more willingness to be authentic among those groups than there is among the image-made male white Protestants?

Shogan: I don't think that just being yourself is really enough. I think maybe that's where you start from. I think the responsibility is to show how whatever it is that defines yourself as a personality and an intellect, should make a difference to the people you ask to elect you president. I think being authentic ought to start when you're seeking office, and that if you can be authentically yourself and convince people that that's something which matters to their lives, then whether you're white or black, tall or short, male or female, that authenticity will serve you well in the office. Otherwise, it gets to be irrelevant. Carter was authentically himself as president, but it didn't always do him a lot of good--or us, either.

Glad: I would like to say something. I think "authentic" means not only not having two faces but also knowing yourself. And I certainly think if you know yourself, you're going to be a better politician: you have your goals clear, and are better able to make your hierarchy of needs clear--the kinds of things that contribute to being a good politician. But when it comes to the public, I think the mass media today make it almost impossible for you to show your entire self. So we ask, in a sense, for somebody to be inauthentic in public in order to succeed. It's a real paradox.

Johnson: I recently finished my book on the Reagan years, and I concluded that everybody's looking for the leader who can take us out of the morass that we're in; that's what we were looking for when we got Reagan, as a matter of fact. I suddenly realized that what the country was looking for--maybe what I'm looking for--is the perfect president: Jimmy Carter to run things, to make the right issues, to plot out the strategy, to deal with the long term; and Ronald Reagan to sell it to the country and to the world. The blend of the two--the public performer and the theoretician, the strategist and the person of honor and dignity--of course doesn't exist.

Hargrove: I think you have to tap chords in people to which they're responsive if you're going to be an effective political leader. You can't be interested in technical issues to the exclusion of the things that actually move people. In that sense, I think Reagan was authentic. I also think Reagan knows who he is. I don't happen to care for him much, but I think he knows who he is.

Johnson: That's right. He had just a few objectives. Carter, over and over in conversations and interviews, would say, "It was not my nature to do this, it was not my nature to do that." He knows himself very, wery well. But it's excluded in these political roles.

Q: Mr. Johnson, you've been reading my mind, to a degree. I'm in the process of stealing one of your terms--that we have been sleepwalking for eight years. And it seems to me that we are now in a process of rude awakening. Yesterday, I had an uplifting experience. I heard Jimmy Carter. Having heard you, I am discouraged from putting him in nomination for the next presidency. What do you think?

Johnson: Well, I'm not going to make a nominating speech here. As I said earlier, the Carter that we see now--the exemplary ex-president, taking on issues, negotiating crises, dealing thoughtfully--is a person the country has come to have great respect for. But I do think that when you're in the office, you have to be able to convey clearly to the country where you're going. That was the test I'm afraid the Carter presidency didn't measure up to, and I suspect Carter would say that himself.

Hargrove: I think probably that's right.

Q: There was certainly an unnerving side to Jimmy Carter: the lack of predictability and stability in the things he did. One of the things that finally unnerved me was PD 59, and nothing's really been said in this conference about that. I realize that when the president abandoned MAD (mutually assured destruction) and seemed to try to tell the people that he really believed nuclear war could be winnable, and that we should be positioning ourselves to do it, he was restating a targeting condition that already existed. But this was the president, and it just didn't seem to fit. Why did he do that? Does anyone have any insights?

Glad: Yes, I have. I think Carter had two sides to his personality--what I call the Brzezinski and the Vance sides--and they were constantly fighting within him. PD 59 was the Brzezinski side. I think the Brzezinski side became more salient the longer he was in office. I think now that he's out of power, we're seeing the Vance, the Woodrow Wilson side. I'm not so sure that if he were back in power, we might not find the same split again, however. I think, in a sense, he had not really integrated these two sides, had not worked out a clear position for himself.

Hargrove: Could I add a thought to that? I think in the fourth year, Carter learned that his style of leading had not worked--either domestically or in foreign policy--and then there were reversals, particularly regarding the Soviets. And therefore, he fell back on conventional politics--conventional Cold War foreign policy, with which he was ill at ease, and conventional domestic politics, using the pork barrel to try to win the election. It's come through in a number of papers here that the fourth year was extraordinarily uninspired; he really let go his effort to be a unique president, and became a kind of conventional Democratic politician. Do you agree with that?

Johnson: Yes, I agree with that.

Q: During this conference, several of the speakers have attempted to pin political labels on Jimmy Carter. I heard "neoconservative," "neoliberal," "moderate-conservative." I even heard somebody say that he seemed to be a liberal to liberals, and then ended up disappointing them; he seemed to be a conservative to conservatives, and ended up disappointing them. How do you see Jimmy Carter fitting into the political spectrum, if it's possible to fit him in?

Johnson: I hate labels; I don't even know what to call myself. That's where I begin in today's world. We talked about Carter's religious background, and I don't want to make too much of that; I think Carter was a good person. I think he tried to be a good president, by his own standards and his own values. And I think maybe he was a moderate, out of the progressive tradition. Carter was a great admirer of John McPhee, who wrote for the *New Yorker*, and he could talk with great eloquence about nature and the environment. I don't know where you put that. He was sort of a humanist, I suppose. But in terms of political labels, I would say he came out of a moderate progressive tradition.

Shogan: He himself said that he was an economic conservative and a something-else liberal, whatever the something else was. In areas like civil rights--if not civil liberties and human rights--he was a liberal. Some said he was the most conservative Democratic president since Grover Cleveland. I think what sets him apart from his immediate predecessors--Kennedy, Johnson, Roosevelt, Truman--is not so much the content as the ideal. It was his approach to process. They were all in the same New Deal tradition, and they all marched with a party that Roosevelt had built, which was based on organized constituencies and using political power. It's been called all sorts of pejorative names--interest group liberalism, for example--but that's what made the Democratic Party go. Carter was very uncomfortable with that concept. He resisted it all the way. He catered to it a little bit when he was a candidate in 1976, but he was very unhappy. And I think his resistance to having to deal with these interest groups defined his policy decisions more than any particular consistent philosophy of Left or Right.

Q: I would make two short comments, and then ask a question. One, I think my recollection is that President Carter's aides, when he first came into office, really ticked off the Democratic leadership. And second, I think if you want a combination of Reagan and Carter, we had it in Franklin Delano Roosevelt. Now, my question is whether the blame is in us, the electorate: that we want programs, but we're not willing to pay for them; that any person running for public office who presents the realities--that if you're going to have these programs, we're going to have to raise taxes--is going to lose.

Glad: I'd say yes.

Johnson: Well, you're right, of course. The test of the political leader is to persuade the public to go where that leader wants to go, to have an idea of what he or she wants to do, and then to get the backing of the public to follow it. And there is no consensus on mobilizing the public on the problems of the future.

Hargrove: I'm less inclined to blame the public because I think people's politics are automatically self-seeking. People have to be led and instructed and inspired by leaders. I think publics are responsive to the kind of leadership they get, and we've had lousy leadership in this country for the last ten years in terms of truth-telling. It's going to take some time to reverse that.

Shogan: I think that blaming the public is a little bit like my blaming readers because they bought more of Teddy White's books than any of mine.

Q: In his book, Professor Hargrove makes a good case for the Democrats' needing what he calls--I think I've got this right--a "politics of public good," and that the problem with the politics of public good is the kind of people who support it--like, to some degree, Jimmy Carter. They tend to believe that their conception of the public good is the only correct one, and that the grubby process--otherwise known as democracy--through which we negotiate it becomes nothing but interest politics. To me, the political and the substantive failures of the Carter administration are essentially one and the same; Carter never understood that one of the purposes of a Democratic president was to deliver to Democratic interest groups, who are otherwise known as the poor working class, and that he could have done what Bob Shogan suggested: unite lower-income whites and blacks who had been at war for so long. Why didn't Carter understand the imperatives of a Democratic president, and why did he view these as somehow an unseemly form of politics, as special interest politics?

Shogan: I'd like to respond, because there's something I think should have been clarified earlier. I talked about Democratic interest groups. I think Caddell made the point in a sometimes brilliant, sometimes murky memo right after Carter took office, in which he talked about the need to build a new coalition. I want to say, before someone else says it, that the coalition that Roosevelt and Truman had created and established was fading and losing relevance. What you needed to do was create another kind of alliance. I asked Carter what he thought his natural constituency was, and he said, "Well, consumers." I said, "Gee, that's kind of broad. Could you go a little beyond that?" He said, "Yeah. Small businessmen." I think he didn't see the political process in terms of bargaining, in terms of giving and taking, in terms of explaining--whether the groups had marched behind Truman and Stevenson, or whether they were new kinds of groups. He didn't do coalitions. He did Jimmy Carter up there, doing the public good, and you can get into trouble that way. The one politician, I think, who's come closest to doing that--I don't know that he recognized it--is a rather tall senator from New Jersey. He operates in the same kind of League of Women Voters style, and that goes along all right if nobody is challenging you very seriously; you don't have any trouble with it. We saw in this last election that there were some problems--not of his own making--and we saw that support was weak. I think Carter had some of that same kind of high-minded view. What's striking about this conference is that no one has impugned his motives or his goals or his direction, but I don't think that's enough. I don't think Carter saw the need to deal with people that way. Whether that was religion or character, I don't know.

Glad: I would like to add something to that. V. O. Key talked about the importance of keeping your base coalition fairly narrow and satisfied. If you tend to go too far, you wind up with nobody really supporting you. So I think it's very important to pay attention to the coalitions in your party. I'm also astounded that there are all of these new interest groups. Are they women? Are they blacks? Are they getting so much? Are they being indulged? I think that the Republicans have stolen the rhetoric of interest groups. It's no longer bankers or Wall Street, but all kinds of people who have traditionally been the dispossessed and who can exercise power only through taking to the streets, combining and acting in ways where they're seen.

Johnson: I'd forgotten about Carter having an opportunity to take blacks and whites in a unified political coalition that hadn't really existed, hadn't formed. That was the real tragedy, as I look back on the Carter years. I think there was an extraordinary opportunity. I'll just tell you one brief story. At the Democratic convention of 1976, in New York, I went up to Harlem to do a story. I spent the day talking to blacks, and when I came back, my editors didn't believe what I was telling them. Those blacks in Harlem were absolutely for Jimmy Carter, the white Southerner with the accent. So there was that opportunity to do something, to meld something, and I think there was a failure of leadership there to seize that moment. Whether it could have worked, I don't know, but it seems to me tragic that it wasn't implemented.

Hargrove: I don't think Carter had any sympathy with the traditional constituencies of the Democratic Party. In that sense, I think his small businessman, Southern background was a handicap. Stu Eizenstat told me once that at the end of every budget cycle, they try to find some extra millions to put into traditional Democratic programs; Carter did a lot for those groups, but he would never take credit for it. He didn't think it was important to try to take credit for helping his own basic constituency. Another member of Stu's staff told me that there was a debate about whether to do welfare reform or national health insurance first, and some of the politically savvy people said, "Welfare reform will get nothing for you; you're going to fail. But there's a constituency out there for national health insurance." But Carter had it fixed in his mind that welfare reform was important, because he'd seen, as a governor, how wasteful welfare was.

Q: I'd like to probe again Carter's religious background and its influence. It's interesting that Professor Glad dismisses that. I'm curious about that. Professor Hargrove regards the religious aspect as an important explanatory factor. I would sharethat latter view, and I wonder if it's given adequate attention, especially in light of Carter's own claim that it's so very important. It seems to me that with his religious background and coming out of a consensual, Democratic tradition that emphasizes the moral base of issues--he's not moralistic, but there's a moral base of issues that's very important to him--when he enters the presidency and has to deal with some of those horse-trading, hauling, tugging aspects of the presidential office that are repugnant to him, it's the politics of governing that he rejects. I think there's plenty of evidence that he resisted such politics in the first year. I think the best test for Carter's coming to terms with the office is not 1980 but 1979, during which, it seems to me, he began to come to terms--his initial responses to the office were stretched, and he began to reconcile some of the things he had to do within the framework of his basic religious impulses. For example, in 1978, on hospital cost containment and gas deregulation, he bargained in a way that brought great criticism, because he had claimed not to be a trader, not to be a bargainer. By 1979, he was working much more cooperatively with the Congress; I think he had come to terms with the political hierarchy. This was his original resistance to the Washington community: he didn't like a hierarchy; he wanted to deal with the people. And he wanted to bring the people into the process. By 1979, that had begun to dim in his mind; he'd grown a bit disappointed with the American people's capacity to process issues and, on the other hand, come to terms with the Washington community. Now, I think there's a religious response thread that runs through those things that needs to be taken very seriously. I would like Professors Glad and Hargrove to respond or to clarify how one sees it as so important and the other regards it as unimportant.

Glad: I wonder in what respect his religion influenced him. You've emphasized the importance of Carter's religion for his political style, and I think it's more important than making a generic statement about what specific aspect of his religion influenced what specific aspect of his political style, or his value system.

Part VI

The Past as Prologue

The concluding part of this volume is graced by the transcripts of three of the most distinctive moments of the Carter Conference, as well as the proceedings of a panel dealing with the Carter post-presidency and the Carter Center. It was our good fortune that President and Mrs. Carter agreed to be present for part of the three-day event, and that Robert S. Strauss, a prominent and many-talented participant in the administration, delivered the banquet address. The president spoke at noon on Friday to a capacity audience of High School students, and, after a respite for luncheon, at three o'clock to conference participants, faculty, students, and community members. For both events, Mrs. Carter was present onstage, and participated in the question-and-answer period following Mr. Carter's talks.

The Friday night banquet, for which Mrs. Carter could be present, featured Robert S. Strauss as main speaker. His reflections and reminiscences of his varied official assignments, and his insights into the inner workings of the Carter government, especially his characterizations of his relations with the president, were warmly received.

The panel on the post-presidency featured two scholarly papers. One dealt with a description and history of the Carter Center at Emory University by the former president's personal aide, and the other discussed the reevaluation of Mr. Carter's tenure currently under way. The three discussants were two of the program directors of the Carter Center and a journalist.

What makes the contents of this part especially significant is the uniqueness of the Carters' post-presidential years. Their energetic and selfless efforts at social, economic, and even political remediation around the world have resulted in the widespread opinion that "Jimmy Carter is the best former president we have ever had."

At Hofstra, President Carter evidenced his commitments and his convictions in ways that can fairly be described as moving. The students' response to his call for their assumption of responsibility for the fate of their communities and their country was heartening and buoying; the conference audience's reaction to the president's description and analysis of the Carter Center seemed equally strong. In both sessions the questions were pointed and sometimes sharp. A notable aspect of the meetings was the authoritativeness of Mrs. Carter's participation. Acquaintances of Jimmy Carter, in dealing with expressions of surprise about the perceived differences between Jimmy Carter the incumbent president and Jimmy Carter the post-president, respond with assurances that these apparently different people are indeed one and the same, with the same values, goals, and expectations. "We don't notice any big difference from the way he's always been; you're just seeing the real Jimmy Carter close up, instead of on the television screen," says one long-time associate. Another close coworker of recent years opines, "The difference is that the burdens are now gone and that, for the first time in his adult life, he has acquired a sense of fulfillment at being able to pursue goals that reflect his innermost aspirations."

Whatever the case may be--whether President Carter was or was not different form the post-president--the choices he and Mrs. Carter have made since they left the White House clearly point to the possibilities for the useful employment of the talents and commitments of other former presidents. Ideas for including them more formally in the actual operations of government have, in fact, been broached from time to time. Whatever the fate of such proposals will be, the Carters' engagement in critical issues of our day is likely to have dual consequences: they will positively affect the outcomes of many difficult problems not attended to by other organizations, and they are already serving as models of conduct for young and old at home and abroad.

THE POST-PRESIDENCY
AND THE CARTER CENTER

19

Jimmy Carter: The Post-Presidential Years

STEVEN H. HOCHMAN

No American child sets a goal in life of becoming a former president of the United States.   The dream is to become president; what happens afterward is little contemplated.   Jimmy Carter, an inveterate goal setter, achieved the dreams of his youth: appointment to the Naval Academy, success in business, election as Georgia state senator, then as governor, and finally as president. Then, in November 1980, he lost an election.   He had to decide, at the age of fifty-six, what he would do with the rest of his life.

No single pattern exists for former presidents.   Some have retired completely, others have continued to be active in public life or private business.   Recent former presidents, from Herbert Hoover to Gerald Ford, departed Washington, wrote their memoirs, and worked to establish their presidential libraries.   Funds for the libraries were raised privately, but Congress had provided in 1955 that the National Archives would operate the institutions once the buildings and the records they housed were deeded to the federal government.   In 1958, former presidents were assured basic financial security when Congress created a presidential pension.   Up to that time, the only financial benefit given them by the federal government was the privilege of franking their mail.   After the Kennedy assassination, Congress provided former presidents and their wives with Secret Service protection.

By the time he left the White House on January 20, 1981, Jimmy Carter had decided that initially he would follow the example of his recent predecessors, but he also set unusual and ambitious longer-term goals for himself. He intended to resume an active involvement in public affairs without returning to political office. The means to this would be the creation of an institute of public policy to be connected to his presidential library and to a university. He would spend his first year and a half out of office writing his memoirs and planning for his future library and institute.

My personal connection with President Carter began in July 1981 when I went to Plains, Georgia, where he had returned, to help him write an account of his presidency. Although every recent predecessor had published such a book, the Carter approach was distinctive. Unlike these predecessors, he organized no large team of researchers and writers. I was the only assistant. He intended to write the book himself, and in a single year, which seemed extraordinarily fast to me.

During the months when we were working intensely on the book, President Carter seemed to the media to have disappeared from public life. It is true that he made relatively few public appearances, the most notable being his joint representation of the United States with Presidents Nixon and Ford at the funeral of Anwar Sadat, but he was moving ahead on the library and institute. Even before he left the White House, he had decided to establish his office and the library in Atlanta. While he wanted his home to be in Plains, he believed that his public life could best be conducted from the Georgia capital.

In February 1981, representatives of Atlanta-area universities formed the Atlanta Area Consortium for the Presidential Library. The consortium recommended that the library be built on a site in the city of Atlanta called the Great Park. This site was convenient to downtown as well as to local institutions of higher learning. In the 1960s, a major highway to the northeast suburbs had been planned through the area. Much of the right-of-way had been purchased and cleared, but opposition from neighborhood groups had convinced then-Governor Jimmy Carter to stop the project in 1972. A commission was later established to determine what use should be made of the cleared land. In 1979, this commission, chaired by architect and developer John Portman, had proposed using the area for a "great park" that would include a future Jimmy Carter Presidential Library. President Carter was convinced by the recommendations of the commission and of the consortium. In July 1981, he requested that the state of Georgia allow him to build on this site. State and local government officials supported the request, and neighborhood groups were cautiously optimistic that a longtime source of contention would be removed. On October 29, the Carter Library, Incorporated, was established to raise the funds necessary to build the institution.

On April 22, 1982, President Carter joined Emory University President James T. Laney in a press conference to announce his decision to accept appointment as University Distinguished Professor at Emory. President Laney further announced that "Mr. Carter's association with Emory will make possible the development here of a remarkable institute for the study of public policy." Although representatives of the Georgia public universities also had wooed him, President Carter had feared that a connection with them might permanently entangle him in the budgeting process of the state legislature. Since he intended to speak out on controversial issues, he believed that his freedom of speech would be better protected at a strong private university. The recommendations of friends and advisers, his compatibility with Emory President Laney, and the knowledge that the university was an institution on the rise with a sound financial base influenced his decision.

The April announcement left unclear the details of President Carter's professorship and the future institute. Even though both President Carter and the university had spent months in planning, they had not yet agreed on many basic issues. In part, this was because there was no clear model for such a relationship. No former president had served on the faculty of a university since William Howard Taft had taught at Yale Law School, and no former president had ever been actively involved in a university-based policy institute. The initial proposals of an Emory committee of administrators and faculty were quite conventional in scope. They advocated an Emory University Center for Public Policy, linked to the Carter Library, in which junior and senior fellows would conduct scholarly research and policy analysis. Senior fellows, one of whom would be Jimmy Carter, would have joint appointments as Emory faculty. The center would also sponsor public speakers, conferences, and publications.

President Carter had a different and far more ambitious view of the future center and his role in it. He and his wife Rosalynn, his partner in all his activities, intended to make the center the focus of their lives. He expected it to reflect and to promote his personal interests in world peace and human rights. He was not interested in joining an institute where scholary reports were the primary product; his model for the center was much closer to the agricultural experiment stations pioneered by land-grant universities. Practical applications were his goal. One of his dreams, which would become increasingly important to him, was that the center play an active role in the mediation of conflicts.

Recognizing that he needed advice on how to proceed, President Carter consulted with key staff members from his administration and other trusted friends. In July, he brought several of these advisers to Sapelo Island, Georgia, to meet with President Laney and several other leaders in the Emory community. Attendees such as Cyrus Vance, Warren Christopher, Sol Linowitz, and Zbigniew Brzezinski had broad experience with policy research and the academic world. They pointed out that while Emory was a fine institution, it did not yet have a distinguished faculty in political science or international affairs who could provide leadership for the institute. The consensus of the meeting was that President Carter brought special assets to the partnership with Emory, that he should be the guiding force in the formation of an institute with an action-oriented policy focus, and that this institute should carry his name.

The participants in the Sapelo retreat recommended that the institute establish a distinctive identity and not duplicate the work of existing policy institutes. They agreed with President Carter that the emphasis should be on global issues, although domestic issues might also be pursued. It was considered very important that the institute establish a nonpartisan character.

In the fall of 1982, an institution called the Carter Center of Emory University came into existence. Jim Waits, dean of the Chandler School of Theology at Emory, became part-time interim director. I was asked to serve as senior research associate, my primary responsibility being to coordinate President Carter's academic relationship with Emory. A secretary was also engaged. The center was temporarily housed on the top floor of the university's Woodruff Library. President Carter would spend several days a month on campus, teaching and continuing to make plans for the center. His main office in Atlanta was downtown in a federal building, although he spent only a few days a month there. President Carter took no formal position in the center (and never has), but as founder and as chairman of the various boards that were created for the center, he plays a central role.

President Carter insisted that the center immediately initiate its first project, an effort to promote peace in the Middle East. He also decided to follow it with a project addressing nuclear arms control. Two Emory faculty members who had attended the Sapelo retreat were asked to direct these projects. Dr. Kenneth Stein, an assistant professor of Middle Eastern history with a demonstrated talent for developing international programs at Emory, took on the first project, and Dean of the Graduate School Ellen Mickiewicz, a specialist in Soviet Studies, took on the second.

In September, Jimmy Carter's first "reemergence" in public life began. He returned in the new roles of teacher, author, and fund-raiser. His inaugural address as Emory professor drew national and international media attention. Speaking on human rights, he decried the "deafening silence in the world" when the United States fails or refuses to speak out on behalf of suffering people. The next month, another large and highly publicized event was the town hall meeting, an open forum for the entire Emory community. This was the first of nine annual town hall meetings, now a great tradition at Emory. In September and in every following month of the academic year, Professor Carter devotes two or three days to lecturing in classes and special forums. He made it clear that his professorship was not a purely honorary or ceremonial position. He visited every division at the university. Although some faculty members advised him to teach a regular class in history or political science, we found that his impact was much greater as a guest lecturer in a variety of courses. He wanted to have broad involvement in the university.

Soon after the launching of his career in academia came the release of *Keeping Faith: Memoirs of a President*. Officially published in November, the book achieved the goals that President Carter had set for it. It was not a full history of the administration but, rather, a "highly personal report" of his own experiences. The diary he had kept in the White House was our most important source. The book was a *New York Times* best-seller for thirteen weeks, and its success led President Carter to write three other books. He actively promoted *Keeping Faith*, appearing on radio and television talk shows, and giving interviews to newspapers and magazines.

About the same time President Carter began another sort of campaign. This was to raise the funds for the Carter Presidential Library and the Carter Center of Emory University. As a defeated Democratic president, he was anxious about his ability to attract the twenty-eight million dollars or more needed for the buildings and projects. Campaigns such as this are not conducted through mass mailing. Personal appeals must be made to corporations, foundations, and individuals. President Carter could count on some people who were loyal to him or to Emory University, and some Georgians who wanted to support a local institution would contribute. But a major portion of the funds would have to come from people who were convinced that the library and center would make a difference for the United States and for the world.

What President Carter learned during his first months of fund-raising reinforced his confidence in the future of the center. He stressed to potential donors that because of his personal involvement, the center would have an impact beyond that of other centers for public policy. He said that as a former president he had access to world leaders and to the media that was not available to scholars and policy analysts. In fact, he had access to potential donors beyond that possessed by virtually any university or policy center. At every foundation and corporation he asked to visit, he was received warmly and listened to carefully. His visits were historic events in the lives of those with whom he met. While not every visit resulted in an immediate contribution, he was very persuasive in getting across his message and leaving a favorable impression. People were genuinely interested in and impressed by what he was trying to do.

There had been some fear at Emory that President Carter's clear identification as a Democrat might hurt the credibility of the Carter Center. However, it quickly became obvious that this was not an important issue. Furthermore, President Carter reached out to prominent Republicans to gain their cooperation. The most important of these was former President Gerald Ford. In February 1983, President Carter joined President Ford at a conference on domestic policy issues at the Ford Library. It became clear at the conference that the impact of both former presidents was increased when they worked together. President Carter invited President Ford to cochair the Carter Center's November 1983 consultation on the Middle East, and President Ford or other prominent Republicans have participated in all the center's major conferences.

"Consultation" is the term the center uses for high-level conferences. The first consultation, and the ones that followed on other subjects in the next few years, demonstrated President Carter's ability to draw together international antagonists in an academic setting. Decision makers and scholars meet together peacefully and constructively. Issues such as Middle East peace and nuclear arms control are unlikely to be resolved during a consultation, but the dialogue is advanced. Furthermore, the consultations advance public knowledge about these issues. After the Middle East consultation and extensive travel in the region, President Carter wrote *The Blood of Abraham: Insights into the Middle East.*

Besides pursuing international political issues, President Carter involved the Carter Center in a wide range of health policy initiatives. The Emory community possessed exceptional strength and depth in this area. From a task force appointed to explore opportunities emerged an idea suggested by Dr. William H. Foege, then director of the United States Centers for Disease Control (CDC), a federal agency that is located on the Emory campus. Dr. Foege proposed a consultation entitled "Closing the Gap"-- the gap between what we know how to do in health care and what we actually achieve. Since he planned to step down as CDC director, Dr. Foege agreed to become director of the Carter Center project.

The Carter Center remained a very small operation, but it did develop some structure during 1984 and 1985. Kenneth Stein was appointed its first fellow and then its first executive director. Added to the staff were a public relations officer and a development officer who would concentrate on programs. Six additional fellows were appointed from outside the university and one, Ellen Mickiewicz, from inside. Two of these fellows, Karl Deutsch and Harold Berman, were world-renowned scholars. The other four brought to the center practical experience beyond their scholarly credentials. Dr. Robert Pastor, for instance, fellow in Latin American and Caribbean studies, had served on the National Security Council staff in the Carter administration. Dayle Powell, who would develop a conflict resolution program, had served as an assistant federal attorney.

Although very pleased with the projects launched by the center, President Carter was growing frustrated with the slow pace at which Emory was incorporating the Carter Center. The academic culture was not as congenial to activism as he had hoped. There was some fear at the university that this new institutional appendage would end up determining departmental and university hiring priorities. Also, many faculty and staff opposed a parkway that the Georgia Department of Transportation wanted built in conjunction with the library and center. While virtually no one opposed the center and the library, some blamed President Carter for not rejecting the proposed road.

President Carter was still committed to the success of the Emory relationship, but he did not want to delay implementing projects of priority for him. He decided to move forward by initiating projects outside of the Emory structure. By the fall of 1986, the center and library buildings would be completed. President Carter decided to name the complex the Carter Presidential Center, and to house within it a conglomerate of organizations connected primarily through their relationship with him.

On May 15, 1986, it was announced that William Foege would leave CDC and succeed Kenneth Stein as executive director of the Carter Center of Emory University. Dr. Stein would devote himself to developing the Middle Eastern studies program at the center. Dr. Foege had already directed two major center projects, "Closing the Gap" and "Risks Old and New: A Global Consultation on Health." He would also become fellow in domestic and international health policy. Soon afterward it was announced that William C. Watson, who had served as associate executive director of CDC, would come to the Carter Center as associate executive director. Accompanying Foege and Watson was a new organization to be housed at the Carter Presidential Center, the Task Force for Child Survival, dedicated to improving the health of children in developing countries.

Meanwhile, President Carter had been approached to assist with a project proposed by Dr. Norman Borlaug, winner of the Nobel Peace Prize for creating the "Green Revolution" in India and Pakistan. This new project would be to bring the "Green Revolution," agricultural self-sufficiency, to sub-Saharan Africa. It would be financed by a Japanese philanthropist, Ryoichi Sasakawa. President Carter was enthusiastic about this project and adopted it under the name Global 2000, the title of a major report on world resources prepared during his administration. With the guidance of Dr. Foege and the financial support of a Pakistani international banker, Agha Hasan Abedi, President Carter planned a health division for Global 2000. Its first project would be to target for eradication the Guinea worm disease, a debilitating disease afflicting some ten million people in Asia and Africa.

Another part of the new conglomerate would be the Carter-Menil Human Rights Foundation. This was created by President Carter and Mrs. Dominique de Menil, a noted philanthropist, to champion human rights in the world. It would work with human rights watch groups to alleviate oppression, and also award an annual prize to organizations or individuals demonstrating courage and effectivness in protecting and promoting human rights.

On October 1, 1986, President Carter's sixty-third birthday, the Carter Presidential Center opened in a grand fashion. The Carters were joined for the dedication by President and Mrs. Ronald Reagan, numerous other dignitaries, and a crowd of five thousand people. They received extensive international and national media coverage. The Carter achievements as president and as former president were lauded, and special attention was paid to President Carter's vision of the future of the center. Physically, the center was very impressive. A series of four interconnected circular buildings adjoining two man-made lakes and a traditional Japanese garden, it sits nestled into a hill overlooking downtown Atlanta. The beautiful complex gave substance and reality to President Carter's dreams.

The dedication had a strong impact on Emory administrators, trustees, and faculty who participated in the ceremonies and academic procession. The potential of the center and its significance for Emory became much more obvious. It also became clear that President Carter was prepared to move on with new projects that might leave the Carter Center of Emory University as a minor player. Within the Carter Presidential Center itself, there were strong differences of opinion on how the institution would operate. Although the buildings had been designed primarily for researchers and administrators, not for large conferences, some staff members tried to book as many special events into the center as possible. This proved disruptive to research programs. Also, coordination was lacking among the organizations in the conglomerate.

After a few months, President Carter, in cooperation with Emory, acted to reform the operation. Although Global 2000, the Carter-Menil Foundation, the Task Force for Child Survival, and the Carter Center of Emory University (CCEU) remained separate organizations, a far closer relationship was created by naming CCEU Executive Director Foege and Associate Executive Director Watson to be, respectively, the executive director and associate executive director for all organizations. They were also empowered to move ahead with building a truly professonal administrative staff for an umbrella institution, The Carter Center, Inc.

Several noteworthy events were taking place as the Carter Center sorted out its administrative problems. At the first consultation held in the new facilities, President Carter, with the assistance of Fellow Robert Pastor, launched the Council of Freely Elected Heads of Government. The council is an informal group that now includes eighteen current and former heads of government, and it uses its influence in the Western Hemisphere to reinforce the trend toward democracy. President Carter was also moving ahead with other new programs. The $100,000 Carter-Menil Prize was awarded for the first time. In Africa and Asia, the Global 2000 programs were getting under way. President Carter went to Bangladesh, Pakistan, Ghana, Sudan, and Zambia to meet with heads of state and negotiate contracts guaranteeing the support of the governments for Global 2000 projects.

In 1987, Jimmy and Rosalynn Carter brought out a book they entitled *Everything to Gain: Making the Most of the Rest of Your Life*. They wrote about how they had dealt with defeat by starting over and finding new goals to enrich their lives. They offered advice for others who faced setbacks or changes. In this book that grew out of the Carter Center consultation "Closing the Gap," they discussed their many activities since leaving the White House. As they traveled around the country promoting the book, they received an especially warm reception. To be sure, even in 1981, a visit from the Carters was always greeted with enthusiasm, but it was clear at the time that the media and the majority of Americans perceived President Carter as a loser. As a rule, Democratic leaders wanted to disassociate themselves from him. In 1984, some political operatives had tried to keep him off the televised program of the Democratic convention. Now the atmosphere had changed.

Articles of two kinds began to appear. Many praised him for his accomplishments since leaving office. Some said it was time to reevaluate his presidency in a more favorable light. One theme of these latter articles was that the revelations of the Iran-Contra affair had demonstrated that President Reagan's inattention to detail was not the great virtue that had been thought, and that such neglect would have been inconceivable in the Carter administration. As Reagan's approval rating fell, Jimmy Carter's rose.

By the summer of 1988, when the Democratic national convention came to Atlanta, the Democratic Party was again comfortable enough with President Carter to feature him prominently in the program. Many events were scheduled at the Carter Center. Fellows of the Carter Center helped organize policy forums for the delegates and for international political leaders. The results of the convention may not have been the best for the party, but the convention was certainly an enormous success for the center. Besides the political visitors, the Carter Center was host to nearly every major media figure in the United States. President Carter's post-presidential achievements became far better known.

The election of George Bush turned out to be a major advance for the Carter Center. President Carter and President Ford had led a bipartisan committee that prepared a report on policy issues, entitled *The American Agenda*, that was intended for the next president of the United States. Soon after George Bush became president, they met with him to present the report. After this, President Bush offered President Carter access that President Reagan had never offered. Although President Carter had always informed the State Department of all his activities in international affairs, he had no personal relationship with President Reagan. President Bush offered cooperation, which permitted President Carter a more effective role in foreign affairs.

President Carter's ultimate dream for the center was that it would aid in the resolution of conflicts around the world. Through the Council of Freely Elected Heads of Government and another Carter Center organization, the International Negotiating Network, President Carter began to play an active role as an election monitor and mediator. He had experimented with election monitoring in Haiti in October 1987. At that time he had been invited by people who opposed the government, and his presence had little impact. He decided that in the future he would have to be invited by all parties in an election, including the government, before he would involve himself. This happened in Panama in 1989, where the opposition desperately wanted him to observe the election, and Manuel Noriega reluctantly invited him. When the Noriega candidate lost the election overwhelmingly, Noriega tried to falsify the election returns. Demonstrating considerable personal courage, President Carter refused to allow this and exposed the attempted fraud. Noriega chose to abort the election. While Noriega lost any vestige of credibility, Jimmy Carter confirmed his. This provided a quantum leap for his reputation.

Later that year, Jimmy Carter was invited to monitor an election in Nicaragua, to be held in February 1990, and to mediate the civil war between the government of Ethiopia and the Eritrean People's Liberation Front. In September, the cover of *Time* announced that "Jimmy Carter is Back." The magazine said that Jimmy Carter "may be the best former President America has ever had."

Since that article, President Carter has supervised a free election and peaceful transition of government in Nicaragua, successfully monitored an election in the Dominican Republic, and is in the process of monitoring elections in Guyana and Haiti. The Ethiopian Civil War remains unresolved, but he moved the antagonists further than anyone had in twenty-eight years.

Jimmy Carter's reputation is certainly boosted by these widely publicized international achievements, but much of the respect that he has gained comes from more mundane efforts. Since 1984, he and Rosalynn have devoted one week a year to Habitat for Humanity, an organization that helps poor people build homes for themselves. The first year the Carters took a bus full of Georgia volunteers to the Lower East Side of New York City, where they worked as carpenters to renovate an old building. Since then they have led "Jimmy Carter Work Camps" in Chicago, Atlanta, Philadelphia, Milwaukee, San Diego, Charlotte, and Tijuana, Mexico. They also have visited projects in many other cities and countries. In the area of human rights, President Carter practices "quiet diplomacy," regularly intervening with leaders of governments that oppress people. Intentionally, these efforts receive little publicity, but they are well known in the human rights community.

President Carter is now in his ninth year of teaching at Emory. He and the Carter Center have helped the university attain a new level of recognition. In 1987, a *U.S. News & World Report* poll of college presidents ranked the institution among the top twenty-five national universities. President Carter's teaching at Emory was highlighted in the magazine. His publication record has been better than that of most professors, although his writings are not aimed at the academic world. His latest book, *An Outdoor Journal: Adventures and Reflections*, is an autobiographical work about his lifelong love of the outdoors. His essays on public affairs appear in national newspapers and magazines. Scholarly books about him are appearing and in preparation, many based on the papers available at the Jimmy Carter Library. In his hometown of Plains, the Jimmy Carter National Historic Site has been established by the National Park Service, and he and Mrs. Carter are assisting with its development.

The continued advancement of the Carter Center remains his most important goal. It has evolved into a new kind of institution, emphasizing academic application and issues involving the developing world. He plays a special role, giving the center programs an impact beyond that of traditional policy centers. Emory University has grown to understand the strengths of the Center and plans a full merger of the Carter Center and Emory within the next five years. Questions still remain regarding the proper balance between research and application that the center should achieve, but the value and importance of both is recognized.

Jimmy Carter is not the first former president to contribute to the public good, but he has taken advantage of the opportunities available in the late twentieth century, and has gone beyond the best achieved by his predecessors.

A NOTE ON SOURCES

The starting point for research on the post-presidential life of Jimmy Carter must be the books and articles that he has written since he left the White House. Many of his writings are autobiographical, and all reflect his current interests. Most of these publications can be found at any research library, although a few articles and speeches have appeared in relatively obscure publications.

A vast amount of information about President Carter and the Carter Center is available in newspapers and magazines. Indexes are published for major periodicals, including the *Atlanta Journal and Constitution*, an especially important source. However, less widely circulated publications, such as the *Americus Times-Recorder*, his county newspaper, and the *Emory Wheel*, the Emory University student newspaper, regularly have carried accounts of his activities that cannot be found elsewhere. Other publications of Emory University, the Carter Center, and Habitat for Humanity are rich sources. To have a complete picture, a researcher must check numerous local publications, not only around the United States but around the world. President Carter travels widely and often receives heavy local coverage that is not picked up by the wire services.

At the Jimmy Carter Library in Atlanta, an extensive clippings file is available. Ultimately, President Carter's post-presidential papers and those of many of his current associates will be available there as well. Virtually no private papers from this period are currently open to researchers. Processing the papers of the presidency remains the first priority, and it is likely that processing of pre-presidential papers will be given the next priority.

My account of the post-presidential years is based on my own papers and recollections, as well as the published materials described above. I have served as assistant to President Carter since July 1981, and have been involved in one way or another with most of his activities during these years. I give a more personal account in "With Jimmy Carter in Georgia: A Memoir of His Post-Presidential Years," in *Farewell to the Chief: Former Presidents in American Public Life*, edited by Richard Norton Smith and Timothy Walch (Worland, Wyoming: High Plains Publishing Company, 1990), pp. 123-134.

Before writing this account, I interviewed President Carter regarding this period of his life, and I also consulted with Carter Center personnel. For their help, I want to thank President Carter; Faye Dill, personal assistant to President Carter; Carrie Harmon, director of public information; Robert A. Pastor, fellow; Kenneth W. Stein, fellow; and Kathryn B. Hochman, a former member of the development staff and my wife. Nessa Rapoport, who served as editor for *Keeping Faith* and *An Outdoor Journal*, also was helpful.

20

Carter Rehabilitated: What Caused the Thirty-Ninth President's Press Transformation?

MARK J. ROZELL

A remarkable phenomenon is occurring on the pages of this country's elite news and opinion publications--the rehabilitation of Jimmy Carter's reputation. Many of the same opinion elites who previously had characterized Carter's presidency as a failure now tell us that, in retrospect, his leadership and commitment to ethical principles are worthy of emulation by future presidents.

This transformation in presidential reputation is all the more remarkable when we contrast exactly what opinion elites said about Jimmy Carter while he was president with what they are saying about him during his post-presidency years. In what follows I demonstrate the dramatic contrast between Jimmy Carter's presidential and recent post-presidential press, and explain why Carter's reputation is undergoing such a change. I shall argue that there are three explanations for the emergence of the new and improved Carter image:

1. With the benefit of hindsight, a number of opinion elites assess that Carter's administration accomplished a great deal more than was acknowledged by presidency observers during the Carter years.
2. Compared with the leadership failings of his successor, Ronald Reagan, Jimmy Carter's leadership--particularly in the public ethics arena--looks increasingly impressive.
3. Jimmy Carter is a great ex-president. He is not selling his former presidency for personal gain; he is using his former presidency as a vehicle to mediate international disputes, assist Third World nations in dealing with health crises, and build houses for homeless Americans, among other causes. Curiously, some journalists are reassessing Carter's presidency because of his admirable post-presidential activities.

The first section of this study is based upon a comprehensive review and analysis of journalistic commentary on Jimmy Carter's administration from January 1977 through January 1981. The sources consulted are the *New York Times*, *Washington Post*, *Wall Street Journal*, *Time*, *Newsweek*, and *U.S. News & World Report*. The major press themes summarized here are documented more completely in my book, *The Press and the Carter Presidency*.[1]

The second section of this study is drawn from a comprehensive review and analysis of journalistic commentary on Jimmy Carter's presidency and ex-presidency covering the 1985-1991 period. The Newspaper Abstracts on Disk program recalls citations of news stories from the *New York Times, Washington Post, Wall Street Journal, Christian Science Monitor,* and *Los Angeles Times.* I also consulted magazine indexes, including *Time, Newsweek, U.S. News & World Report,* and *New Republic.*

The two major sections of this paper present the tale of two very different Jimmy Carters. But clearly, Jimmy Carter did not change, the press did. During any presidential administration, opinion elites struggle with great difficulty in their efforts to define and interpret a president. This struggle does not end after a president leaves office but begins slowly to give way to more refined and reliable assessments than the instantaneous analyses opinion elites make of incumbent presidents. In the case of Jimmy Carter, opinion elites have started relatively early the process of presidential revisionism usually initiated by scholars.

JIMMY CARTER'S PRESIDENTIAL PRESS

The leading print journalists who covered the Carter years characterized Jimmy Carter as an ineffectual leader. According to the prevailing interpretation, he was not up to the job of president for the following reasons:

1. Carter was an "outsider" to the Washington establishment. Therefore, he lacked the political know-how needed to work around the government. His presidency was an "on-the-job training" experience in national leadership. In August 1980, *Time* magazine's Hugh Sidey wrote:

When Jimmy Carter stood before the 1976 Democratic National Convention and pledged new "leadership," he had never met a Democratic President or slept in the White House. The presidency was a legend from books, the Federal Government a classroom exercise, and Washington was a distinct citadel of power that somehow had been corrupted by its residents. . . . In his own inexperience, the President could not define a mission for his Government, a purpose for the country and the means of getting there.[2]

2. Carter adopted a leadership style unsuited to the traditional ways of political Washington. His approach was apolitical, a derivation of his engineering background. In a political process based on the dynamics of political power and compromise, Carter not only eschewed traditional politics, he naively expected that the rest of political Washington could do the same. Tom Wicker assessed him thus in May 1978:

The inheritor of a profoundly political office, whose most successful occupants have all been experienced and skilled politicians, Mr. Carter seems more nearly to have an engineer's approach-- concern with the details of program and policy rather than with the broad appeals and human exchanges of gaining acceptance for them.[3]

3. Carter brought to the White House a number of his Georgian political advisers who also lacked much-needed experience in political Washington. The backgrounds

of these staffers were too narrow and parochial for the harsh political realities of the nation's capital. A July 1978 *Time* news story commented:

The White House staff reflects Carter's lack of success as a Government manager. . . . The tightly knit and provincial Georgia Mafia, which dominates the staff and enjoys the best access to the President, has slowed Carter's integration into the Washington scene and has limited his effectiveness.[4]

4. The Carter White House did not "play the game." That is, the president and his principal aides did not attach much importance to the social rituals of the nation's capital and thereby offended many influential Washingtonians whose help the White House needed. At the end of Carter's first year in office *Time* reported that "The man from Plains is not the kind of bourbon-sipping, backslapping politician who gets along easily with the good ole boys in Congress."[5] At the end of Carter's term, *Newsweek* assessed that Carter did not know how "to do business in an insider's city." Particularly, Carter acted "standoffish" to "the lords and ladies of Washington society."[6]

5. The President's moralism was unsuited to the harsh realities of national and international politics. Although Carter's commitments to ethical conduct in public office at home and to human rights abroad were admirable, such commitments were based on an overly optimistic and moralistic outlook, if not a holier-than-thou attitude. Syndicated columnists Rowland Evans and Robert Novak wrote in September 1977 that Carter "is still inclined to moralize on issues that, far from being moral, are matters of practical politics. . . . Upgrading conventional political questions to the status of good v. evil is still an ingrained habit for Carter."[7]

6. The Carter White House failed to live up to the high standards of ethical conduct established by the president. Whereas Carter demanded that his administration be above reproach, his White House was mired in ethics controversies ranging from Office of Management and Budget Director Bert Lance's financial probity to Billy Carter's efforts on behalf of the Libyan government. During the late summer 1977 Lance controversy, George F. Will commented:

The Lance affair has reminded Americans that Carter is not Moses, entrusted by God with new standards of goodness. It also has made Carter seem a bit like Gantry, not about to live by the rules he preaches.[8]

7. Carter lacked the ability to provide inspirational national leadership. He was a masterful policy analyst, someone capable of commanding the most arcane details of a policy or program but thoroughly incapable of simplifying a proposal into a saleable slogan or catchphrase. His administration lacked a central, guiding phrase such as "Great Society." According to William Safire's April 1978 commentary, Carter lacked a coherent political philosophy that could bring structure to a confusing policy environment:

Unless some philosophy is articulated that gives an Administration its character and flavor--unless the trumpet is certain--the diffusion of power loses its purpose. All that is left is squabbling and backbiting and end runs.[9]

8. The Carter White House lacked clear policy priorities. The president brought to Washington a too-full platter of controversial proposals without a workable political strategy to enact them. Hence, his administration tried to do too much too fast, and consequently accomplished too little. As David Broder wrote in June 1977:

What's missing is the sense of strategy--of choosing those problems that are important for the idealized goals and ignoring the rest; and of tackling the specific problems in a way that illuminates the principles, rather than contradicts them.[10]

9. Carter's rejection of the imperial trappings of the presidency undermined a major asset of his office--its majesty. Americans truly want their president to be an "elective king," someone to look up to and emulate. The lesson of Watergate was not that Americans dislike power; they dislike the misuse of power. Carter demonstrated that Americans also disrespect the failure to exercise power. In July 1978, *Time* magazine assessed that Carter

seems more comfortable wearing his famed cardigan than the mantle of presidential leadership. . . . Carter has been too reluctant to assert himself, to lean on people, to operate, in a sense, with the ruffles and flourishes that this one job of all in the U.S. may demand.[11]

10. Carter lacked a coherent worldview. Therefore, his administration's policies--both domestic and international--often worked toward contradictory ends. In April 1978, David Broder contended: "The goals a president espouses give a hard edge of meaning to his administration and politicize the country into meaningful blocs. Carter has blunted that process by espousing a bewildering variety of contradictory causes in both foreign and domestic policy."[12]

The generally negative press portrait of Jimmy Carter's leadership took hold early in the presidential term and did not change during his tenure. Even after such significant achievements as the Camp David accords and Panama Canal treaties, the underlying negative press perception of Carter remained. And because Carter's leadership style was incompatible with journalists' expectations, the president often did not receive credit for his successes.

What journalists found most difficult to comprehend was that a Democratic president with large party majorities in both houses of Congress did not seek to lead in a Rooseveltian or Johnsonian fashion. Carter's programs, which emphasized such goals as fiscal austerity, did not have an impassioned following within the Democrat-controlled Congress. Political journalists considered Republican presidents such as Richard Nixon and Gerald Ford more likely to have difficult relations with Democratic Congresses. A Democratic president at odds with his own party's leadership in Congress was unexpected. Intraparty conflicts between Carter and Congress, therefore, fueled the negative press assessments of Carter's leadership acumen.

Carter approached presidential leadership differently than his predecessors. Whereas Carter emphasized such presidential duties as problem identification and policy analysis, he paid less attention to politics-as-usual and public relations. Clearly, journalists criticized him harshly for not emphasizing certain tasks, such as congressional relations, at which Carter never sought to excel. To Carter's contemporaries, that meant the president had failed in his leadership duties. With the benefit of hindsight, political journalists today assess Jimmy Carter's presidency in a much more favorable light.

JIMMY CARTER'S POST-PRESIDENTIAL PRESS

A comprehensive review and analysis of recent journalistic writings on Jimmy Carter drawn from those listed in Newspaper Abstracts on Disk and from major magazine indexes reveal the press rehabilitation of the former president. These more recent assessments stand sharply in contrast to the severely negative reviews that Carter received while he was in office. Three themes stand out in the recent post-presidential press assessments of Carter: (1) Carter's presidency was more successful than initially believed; (2) Carter's leadership looks admirable in the post-Reagan era; and (3) Carter is a great ex-president.

Looking Good with Hindsight

The June 5, 1989, issue of *Time* magazine featured a retrospective article on the controversies surrounding former House Speaker Jim Wright (D-Texas). A major point raised in the analysis was that the Wright scandal seemed indicative of a general decline in ethical conduct within Congress. The article was accompanied by a brief commentary recommending that the House of Representatives employ a little-known constitutional provision to choose a new Speaker from outside the ranks of Congress. The new Speaker should be an outsider to political Washington who was untarnished by "the evanescent ethical standards that have become a way of life on Capitol Hill." The commentary concluded:

Perhaps the Democrat who best personifies this republic of virtue is former President Jimmy Carter. His reputation burnished by the elevated tone of his retirement, Carter would actually bring to the task energy, integrity and his legendary distaste for congressional business as usual. He could even boast a made-to-order campaign slogan: "After the Wright stuff, why not the best?"[13]

Suddenly, the qualities that earned Carter the scorn of his contemporaries--emphasis on moral leadership and rejection of politics-as-usual--uniquely qualify him to lead Congress out of its malaise.

More ironic, perhaps, is a July 18, 1988, *Wall Street Journal* editorial entitled "Jimmy, We Hardly Knew Ye." During the Carter years, the *Journal's* editorialists were among the president's most harsh and unyielding critics, particularly on economic and national security issues. This more recent editorial made a most amazing concession: that the greatest achievements of the Reagan years--the economic recovery and the revitalization of the U.S. military--could be attributed in part to the policies of the Carter administration, particularly "the appointment of Paul Volcker as chairman of the Federal Reserve and the start of the military build-up following the Soviet invasion of Afghanistan."[14]

A prominent theme in the post-presidential press commentary on Jimmy Carter is that the former president can properly claim many significant policy achievements that his contemporaries either overlooked or gave insufficient notice. The *New York Times Magazine* on December 10, 1989, featured a cover story by Wayne King entitled "Carter Redux." King listed a number of Carter's insufficiently recognized presidential achievements, including the Camp David negotiations, Panama Canal treaties, SALT II (which was adhered to throughout most of Reagan's tenure), and the successful negotiations to release the American hostages in Iran, "but not in time to save his Presidency." In King's assessment, Carter received blame for a number of matters largely beyond presidential control, such as the oil embargo. Carter's presidency, therefore, deserved better notice:

Thus, Jimmy Carter, whose vision of a better world may have been ahead of his time, fell afoul of the immediacy of empty gas tanks and 20 percent interest rates and the image of blindfolded Americans enduring God-knows-what at the hands of fanatics halfway across the world. Nonetheless, looking at the Carter Presidency in 1989, a historian may well find much to applaud. If nothing else, none of the American hostages in Iran were killed. The combined four-year budget deficit during the Carter Administration was $227 billion (the eight years under Ronald Reagan, $1.3 trillion). Furthermore, the Carter years were free of the conspicuous corruption . . . that plagued the Reagan Presidency.[15]

Similarly, a January 19, 1987, *New Republic* article by Jeffrey L. Pasley and Adam Paul Weisman examined "Carter's major legislative achievements" and commented: "These days Carter looks pretty good even on the leadership issue." Again, presidential qualities portrayed negatively during the Carter years are given credit for the president's successes:

A major test of leadership is the ability to make opponents see the necessity of unpopular policies. Carter passed it on several critical occasions. In an effort that promised no political gain, Carter pushed the Panama Canal treaties through Congress by personally lobbying Congress in exactly the way that Reagan was praised for doing in support of his 1981 tax cuts. . . . Carter also fought successfully to remove controls on oil prices, though his move was extremely unpopular. . . . With Congress deadlocked on the issue in 1979, Carter lambasted the legislators in a speech that exemplified both the integrity and the abrasiveness of his approach: "I'd rather accept the political blame than spend another two years arguing with you about what ought to be done--when you *know* what ought to be done." Subsequent events proved Carter right and his detractors in Congress wrong. . . . [The] increase in production spurred by decontrol eventually broke the power of the cartel and led to the current low prices. Clearly Carter revisionists will have plenty of material.[16]

On July 19, 1988, the *Christian Science Monitor* featured an article entitled "Polls and History Begin to Deal Kindly with Jimmy Carter." This article acknowledged that Carter "governed at an unusually confusing, difficult time" for a Democratic president. He tried to confront budget deficits during a time when Democratic Party constituencies demanded more from the federal government. Also,

Carter took on some knotty and thankless tasks, such as the Panama Canal treaties and Civil Service reform. His Camp David accords between Egypt and Israel, says [presidential scholar] Bruce Buchanan, was one [*sic*] of the two most significant presidential foreign policy achievements since World War II.[17]

Carter now is respected enough among political journalists that many of them call upon the former president to use his expertise in such areas as budgeting and foreign policy to benefit President George Bush.[18] Such status as a knowledgeable elder statesman has been accorded occasionally to Richard Nixon, rarely to Gerald Ford, and never to Ronald Reagan.

Looking Better Than President Reagan

According to a number of political journalists, Carter's presidency looks increasingly successful when compared with the Reagan years. *Christian Science Monitor* senior Washington columnist Godfrey Sperling, Jr.'s, November 14, 1989 article, "Jimmy Carter Rediscovered," articulated the increasingly common view:

Jimmy Carter is on the rise. People are talking about the Carter trait that won him so many supporters back in 1976: his decency. People are also beginning to remember that it was Carter, not Reagan, who not only talked family values but lived them. . . . Compared with the Reagan years the Carter presidency was scandal-free. The worst ethical allegations during the Carter years were the charges of inappropriate banking practices by Bert Lance--actions that had preceded Mr. Lance's joining Carter in the White House (and of which Lance was ultimately acquitted after resigning from the administration). One does not have to put Reagan down in order to elevate Carter. . . . The important thing is that Jimmy Carter, and rightly so, is being rediscovered.[19]

Pasley and Weisman of the *New Republic* argued that whereas Reagan merely projected a leadership image, Carter actually delivered on a number of leadership pledges:

The truth is that in many ways Carter was a better Reagan than Reagan himself. In the case of Iran, Carter practiced the policy of not dealing with terrorists that Reagan only preaches. . . . Carter imposed a grain embargo on the Soviet Union after the invasion of Afghanistan, a move that was condemned by Reagan. . . . Reagan promised in 1980 to "get government off our backs." But it was Carter who oversaw deregulation in the airline, banking, railroad, trucking, and oil industries. . . . Carter cut the deficit from $79 billion in 1976 to $27 billion in 1979, practically a balanced budget by Reagan-era standards.[20]

The Iran-Contra scandal during the Reagan administration contributed importantly to the new and improved Carter press image. Journalists frequently criticized Carter for a hands-on, scrupulous attention to managerial details, leadership approach. True or not, many journalists assessed that presidential obsession with governing details detracted from Carter's ability to lead effectively. He allegedly did not know how to delegate authority.

Early in President Reagan's first term, journalists drew many contrasts between Carter's managerial style and Reagan's so-called chairman of the board style. The comparisons almost always were flattering to Reagan. Often Reagan's policy successes were attributed to an inattention to details that allowed him to pay greater attention to setting broad themes and building public support. After the Iran-Contra story broke, the conventional wisdom changed. As a former *New York Times* political writer, E. J. Dionne, Jr., assessed in an article entitled "Carter Begins to Shed Negative Public Image":

Mr. Carter may have been the prime beneficiary of the Iran-Contra scandal. Until then, Mr. Reagan's style of delegation to subordinates was often contrasted favorably to Mr. Carter's seemingly excessive attention to detail. Afterward, Mr. Carter's hands-on style looked much better.[21]

Pasley and Weisman agreed:

the obsessive attention to detail, the workaholic's need to be in command of everything, the stubbornly logical approach that made him seem cold and difficult, the fierce devotion to principle that bordered on sanctimony. In the wake of Iranamok, Carter can no longer be easily attacked for such qualities. The stylistic differences that used to make Carter look like a handwringing wimp are now the ones that make him look like the scrupulous executive Reagan is not.[22]

The *Washington Post*'s Sidney Blumenthal commented during the 1988 Democratic national convention held in Atlanta: "Jimmy Carter's resurrection began before the Atlanta Convention. His name, public opinion polls began to show, was no longer anathema. And the themes that carried him into office, especially integrity, may have taken on a renewed relevance with a proliferation of scandals. Carter has come to stand for reconciliation."[23]

A Great Ex-President

Jimmy Carter's rehabilitation also is due to his selfless activities as an ex-president. Whether he is helping to build houses for the homeless or assisting with the negotiations of adversary foreign groups, Carter achieves nearly universal praise for using his ex-presidential status to improve the lives of others. As E. J. Dionne, Jr., noted, "Jimmy Carter the man is winning praise as a role model for ex-Presidents from the Washington crowd that labeled him a feckless chief executive."[24] Consider, too, the following:

According to *Time* magazine's article "Hail to the Ex-Chief," Carter "may be the best former President America has ever had."[25] *Washington Post* columnist Richard Cohen wrote, "If scholars get around to evaluating presidential retirements, Carter's will rank at the top."[26] Syndicated columnist Colman McCarthy added, "Jimmy Carter is becoming the best ex-president we have."[27] And *Washington Post* columnist Mary McGrory's article "Exceptional 'Ex'" added that "Jimmy Carter is experiencing a kind of renaissance. He has been reborn as what *Time* magazine called 'our best ex-president.'"[28]

Significantly, McGrory assessed that Carter's ex-presidential activities proved that his presidential commitments to morality and decency were not contrived. In her words:

Carter has come on in the class of exes. He has demonstrated that he really is a Christian, that the piety that so often got on politicians' nerves is   absolutely   genuine.   His activities bespeak a conviction that he truly believes he is his brother's keeper.[29]

Most of the journalistic commentaries assessing Carter's post-presidential activities draw contrasts between these activities and those of former presidents Gerald Ford and Ronald Reagan (little mention is made of Richard Nixon other than that Nixon has devoted his ex-presidency to being his own revisionist). Consider the following commentaries:

1. Indeed, the worse Ronald Reagan has begun to look--with his $2 million fee for a trip to Japan and with Nancy's bitter book--the better Carter is looking. Carter's approach to life--he mediates international disputes, helps build houses for the poor, and, all in all, lives quite modestly--stands in sharp contrast to Mr. Reagan's self-centered lifestyle.[30]

2.   Reagan's mega-yen deal appeared all the more unseemly contrasted with the recent statesmanlike activities of his own precursor, Jimmy Carter. . . .   Carter has devoted his post-presidential days to the pursuit of do-gooder causes, Ford has capitalized on his gregarious nature to make money while having fun.[31]

3. [Carter] has redefined the meaning and purpose of the modern ex-presidency. While Reagan peddles his time and talents to the highest bidder and Gerald Ford perfects his putt and Richard Nixon struggles to gain a toehold in history, Carter, like some jazzed superhero, circles the globe at 30,000 feet, seeking opportunities to Do Good.[32]

4. . . . of all of them [former presidents], Carter stands out. In debt when he left the White House, eschewing a lecture agent, and accepting only an occasional paid speech, he conducts himself as if his presidency was a priceless heirloom: sacred to him because it was sacred to the people. . . . [Carter's presidency] was redeemed by a retirement that, when compared to Ford's or Reagan's, shines for the price he put on it.[33]

5.   At a time when other politicians, except Ronald Reagan, who denied its existence, were talking about homelessness, the sight of Carter actually doing something about it went down well. He certainly looked better than former president Gerald R. Ford, who spends time on the links or collecting fat fees from all the corporate board meetings he can fit into his schedule. . . . Carter, who is neither greedy nor self-serving nor cashing in on his four years in the Oval Office, is at least an example of rectitude and altruism.[34]

The *Christian Science Monitor* made the same point in its editorial "A Tale of Two Ex-Presidents." Written in storybook fashion, this "tale" reminisced about the one ex-president (Jimmy Carter) who built homes for the poor, led conferences on serious topics, oversaw elections in Central America, and performed many other good deeds, and the other ex-president (Ronald Reagan) who retired to his "2.5 million mansion in the sun," accepted two million dollars from a corporate sponsor for participating in some ceremonies during a trip to the Far East, "gave $50,000 speeches, and agreed to write his memoirs for $5 million. The moral of this story: It's possible to rise from humble origins to become President of the United States. Then retire to do good . . . and to do well."[35]

CONCLUSION

At least one person is intrigued by the rehabilitation of Jimmy Carter in the press. The former president contends that the press, not Jimmy Carter, has undergone a transformation. Carter told an interviewer in December 1989:

It's interesting and gratifying to see the media collectively saying there is a new, different Jimmy Carter, managing the affairs of the Carter Center competently, not uptight, not trying to push his religion forward. But I haven't changed. As far as the press is concerned, there is a revision of perspective.[36]

More bluntly, Carter asserted in July 1988, in reaction to a question about his "vindication": "That's a word the press likes to use. I don't think I needed to be vindicated."[37]

The dramatic change in the press assessments of Jimmy Carter is part and parcel of journalists' propensity to offer instantaneous assessments of political personalities and events, often without regard to context. Such assessments are subject to significant change when the context of events is considered with hindsight.

Indeed, with hindsight, Carter's presidency looks much better today than when he served in the White House. Carter adopted an untraditional leadership approach, but one that suited his personality and goals fairly well. Carter's administration can correctly claim a number of significant accomplishments including the Camp David accords, the Panama Canal treaties, a largely successful energy program, and civil service reform. Carter accomplished such goals despite a most difficult political context. The 1970s congressional reforms dramatically changed the nature of executive-legislative relations. Carter could not reasonably be expected to reproduce Johnsonian leadership tactics, given the increasingly decentralized congressional decision-making apparatus. He recognized the need for the federal government to move from an expansionist to a consolidative policy agenda, a recognition resisted by many congressional Democrats. Carter's commitment to consolidation caused great difficulties with Democratic leaders and powerful interest groups. Such difficulties fueled negative press stories of Carter's leadership acumen. Many leading journalists ignored this context in evaluating Carter's presidency.

Also, the journalists who covered the Carter presidency often focused on the chief executive's stylistic shortcomings. Carter did not cover himself in glory. He eschewed advice even from his own communications advisers to improve his public presentation style.[38] The president's priorities included policy analysis and managing the details of government, but not public relations. These presidential priorities, combined with the journalistic emphasis on the public presidency, undoubtedly played a large role in Carter's negative press image. Journalists tend to evaluate most favorably presidents who excel in the arena that journalists know best--public relations and the press. With hindsight journalists can assess the policy achievements of a president without paying so much heed to symbolism and style. Hence, the new-and-improved Carter press reputation combined with the significant downgrading of the Reagan presidency by leading journalists.

In some ways, the shortcomings in the journalistic perspective of Carter today are as serious as the shortcomings in the earlier press evaluations of his presidency. Those earlier evaluations lacked balance and perspective in part because journalists expected Carter to be something he never intended to be--an activist, interventionsist Democratic president in the FDR and LBJ mold. Today journalists are rewriting the history of the Carter presidency more favorably, in part because of their admiration for what Carter is doing as an ex-president. It is interesting to speculate about the possibilities for ranking presidential stature on the basis of what the president does after he leaves office. Suddenly the Herbert Hoover administration has a whole different look.

It is true that in the current context Carter's selfless activities are noteworthy. To many observers of the Carter presidency, the president's emphasis on public morality and private virtue appeared hopelessly naive in a political environment inhospitable to morality and virtue. Unfettered by the demands and realities of public office, Carter's values now seem very compatible with the role of the high-profile, influential private citizen. And as a private citizen, no doubt, Carter has greater control over his agenda than he did as president. While in office, Carter projected the image of being constrained by events beyond his control. As a private citizen, he has the luxury to pick and choose those issues he cares most about, and thereby exercise considerable control over his own agenda. Carter's ability to project a positive public image is enhanced by his current position.

The recent fast-paced rehabilitation of Jimmy Carter also is tied to specific events, such as former president Reagan's acceptance of huge speaking fees, a stark contrast with Carter's refusal to capitalize on the presidency. Whereas news stories about such contrasts with Reagan's activities elevate Carter's reputation today, it is less clear whether such assessments will make any long-term difference to Carter's standing in presidential history.

The early rounds of journalistic analysis of the Carter presidency have not provided either a very accurate or a balanced assessment of Carter's term. When Carter first emerged on the national scene in 1976, journalists played a significant role in building up his stature. When Carter served in the White House, journalists played a leading role in undermining his repute. The most recent round of political journalism has rehabilitated Carter's stature. Undoubtedly, the last words from journalists about Jimmy Carter have not been written.

Even so, recent favorable news stories on Jimmy Carter's presidential years may mark the early stages of more serious Carter revisionism. Recent academic studies of Carter's presidency by Charles O. Jones and Erwin Hargrove are neither adulatory nor hostile toward the former president.[39] That is a significant departure in itself from much of the early scholarship on the Carter years, which tended to follow the journalistic reviews.[40] To be sure, the purpose of the Jones and Hargrove books is not to justify Carter's actions or to rehabilitate the former president's reputation. Rather, these studies provide important insights into how Carter sought to project leadership. As serious attempts to understand--not to judge--what Carter tried to do and why, they inevitably clash with the earlier, relentlessly negative press attacks on the president's leadership acumen. For that reason, these studies have contributed importantly to the recent upgrading of Carter's presidential reputation. And perhaps future studies of the Carter years will pave the way for an increasingly improved historical standing for the thirty-ninth president. If so, Carter's fate in history may resemble those of Dwight Eisenhower and Harry Truman, and not Herbert Hoover: a president who earns respect and stature over time for what he accomplished as president, not for what he did as a former president.

NOTES

1.   Mark J. Rozell, *The Press and the Carter Presidency* (Boulder, CO: Westview Press, 1989).

2.   Hugh Sidey, "Assessing a Presidency," *Time*, August 18, 1980, p. 10.

3.   Tom Wicker, "Another PR Solution," *New York Times*, May 21, 1978, p. E-21.

4.   "A Problem of How to Lead," *Time*, July 31, 1978, p. 11.

5.   "A Bold and Balky Congress," *Time*, January 23, 1978, p. 16.

6.   Peter Goldman, "Hail the Conquering Hero," *Newsweek*, December 1, 1980, pp. 30, 32.

7.   Rowland Evans and Robert Novak, "Carter's Energy Package: A Problem with Tactics," *Washington Post*, September 30, 1977, p. A-27.

8.   George F. Will, "Lance, Carter, Babbitt and Gantry," *Newsweek*, September 19, 1977, p. 122.

9.   William Safire, "The Floating Anchor," *New York Times*, April 20, 1978, p. A-23.

10.   David Broder, "A Lack of Strategy in the Carter Camp," *Washington Post*, June 8, 1977, p. A-23.

11.   "A Problem of How to Lead: Dissatisfaction Is the Washington Mood," *Time*, July 31, 1978, pp. 10-11.

12.   David Broder, "Will Carter Be Tough on Carter?" *Washington Post*, April 23, 1978, p. D-7.

13.   Margaret Carlson, "How Many Will Fall?" *Time*, June 5, 1989, p. 34.

14.   "Jimmy, We Hardly Knew Ye," *Wall Street Journal*, July 18, 1988, p. 18.

15.   Wayne King, "Carter Redux," *New York Times Magazine*, December 10, 1989, p. 108.

16.   Jeffrey L. Pasley and Adam Paul Weisman, "He's Back! No, Not Nixon--Jimmy Carter," *New Republic*, January 19, 1987, pp. 14-15.

17.   Marshall Ingwerson, "Polls and History Begin to Deal Kindly with Jimmy Carter," *Christian Science Monitor*, July 19, 1988, p. 17.

18.   See William Raspberry, "For Bush, Advice from Previous Tenants," *Washington Post*, November 23, 1988, p. A-21; Godfrey Sperling, Jr., "Drawing on Our Former Presidents," *Christian Science Monitor*, January 24, 1989, p. 18; "Other Presidents and Budget Reality," *New York Times*, December 2, 1988, p. A-30.

19.   Godfrey Sperling, Jr., "Jimmy Carter Rediscovered," *Christian Science Monitor*, November 14, 1989, p. 18.

20.   Pasley and Weisman, "He's Back!" p. 14. This point is also made in a *New York Times* editorial, "A Dubious Reagan Achievement," January 4, 1990, p. A-22. The editorial documents growth in the federal bureaucracy during the Carter and Reagan years and concludes that whereas Reagan promised to shrink government, the growth in bureaucracy during his terms was nearly double the rate of growth during Carter's term.

21.   E. J. Dionne, Jr., "Carter Begins to Shed Negative Public Image," *New York Times*, May 18, 1989, p. B-6.

22.   Pasley and Weisman, "He's Back!" p. 14. A March 1990 *Wall Street Journal*/NBC poll demonstrated that the Carter rehabilitation had taken hold not only among leading journalists but also in the public opinion. The poll noted that while Carter and Reagan had similar post-presidency

approval ratings, Carter's "negative" rating was significantly lower than his successor's ("Carter Edges Reagan . . . ," *Wall Street Journal*, March 16, 1990, p. A-1). And a *U.S. News & World Report* survey of federal, state, and local politicians showed that these people designated Carter as "Best Social Advocate: The 1990 Excellence Award in Government" ("Doing Good: Jimmy Carter," *U.S. News & World Report*, July 9, 1990, p. 47).

23. Sidney Blumenthal, "The Carter Constituency," *Washington Post*, July 21, 1988, p. B-3.

24. Dionne, "Carter Begins to Shed . . . Image," p. B-6.

25. Stanley W. Cloud, "Hail to the Ex-Chief," *Time*, September 11, 1989, p. 60.

26. Richard Cohen, "The Carter Distinction," *Washington Post*, May 11, 1989, p. A-21.

27. Colman McCarthy, "The Best Ex-President We Have," *Washington Post*, November 18, 1989, p. A-25.

28. Mary McGrory, "Exceptional 'Ex,'" *Washington Post*, September 28, 1989, p. A-2.

29. Ibid.

30. Sperling, "Jimmy Carter Rediscovered," p. 18. More recently Sperling recommended that the Democratic Party give serious thought to Carter as a 1992 presidential candidate. According to Sperling, Carter is the answer to the former *New York Times* columnist Tom Wicker's call for "a modern version of FDR." See "Someone Democrats Are Overlooking," *Christian Science Monitor*, July 30, 1991, p. 19.

31. "How to Be an Ex-President," *Newsweek*, May 22, 1989, p. 40. Another *Newsweek* article ("A Diminished Ron, a Refurbished Jimmy," April 2, 1990, p. 36) referred to Carter as "the modern model of a successful ex-president of the United States." And:

while Carter had found his niche in international diplomacy and humanitarian causes at home, the three other living alumni of the Oval Office have taken divergent paths. Gerald Ford first chased the dollar, taking lucrative board seats and riding the lecture circuit, before sinking into comfortable retirement. Richard Nixon has pursued his slow rehabilitation, churning out books and dispensing political and diplomatic counsel. But Reagan has stumbled into one misadventure after another since leaving the White House.

32. Cloud, "Hail to the Ex-Chief," p. 60.

33. Cohen, "The Carter Distinction," p. A-21.

34. McGrory, "Exceptional 'Ex,'" p. A-2.

35. "A Tale of Two Ex-Presidents," *Christian Science Monitor*, May 16, 1989, p. 20.

36. King, "Carter Redux," p. 103.

37. Blumenthal, "The Carter Constituency," p. B-3. In a more recent interview for a *Washington Post* profile, Carter commented:

I did have an incompatibility with the Washington press corps that was distressing to me. But I always felt what I did as president was the best I could do. I've been relaxed about historians' assessments. There's an inclination with presidents who were not at all that well respected when they left office to be refurbished over time: Truman, Eisenhower, Hoover. I was hoping that would take place, and it has begun to. And the fact is that what we've been attempting to do in post-White House years *is* unprecedented and *worthy* of commendation. That's not my motivation, but it's gratifying to get good publicity for a change, for what we are doing now. (Art Harris, "Citizen Carter," *Washington Post*, February 22, 1990, p. B-2.)

38. Mark J. Rozell, "President Carter and the Press: Perspectives from White House Communications Advisers," *Political Science Quarterly* 105, no. 3 (Fall 1990):419-434. See also John Anthony Maltese, "'Rafshoonery': The Effort to Control the Communications Agenda of the

Carter Administration." Paper presented at the Eighth Presidential Conference, "Jimmy Carter: Keeping Faith," Hofstra University Cultural Center, November 17, 1990.

39. Charles O. Jones, *The Trusteeship Presidency: Jimmy Carter and the United States Congress* (Baton Rouge; Louisiana State University Press, 1988); Erwin Hargrove, *Jimmy Carter as President: Leadership and the Politics of the Public Good* (Baton Rouge: Louisiana State University Press, 1988).

40. See, for example, Betty Glad, *Jimmy Carter: In Search of the Great White House* (New York: W. W. Norton, 1980). More recently, a good many of the positive journalistic accounts of Carter's presidency draw on assessments from the scholarly community. See Andrew L. Yarrow, "Kindly Reflections on the Carter Era," *New York Times*, November 19, 1990, p. A-14; E. J. Dionne, Jr., "A Decade Afterward, Carter Record Is Defended," *Washington Post*, November 19, 1990, p. A-6.

Discussant: Wayne King

I'm going to respond to a bit of that. We agree as much as we disagree, but we disagree. We're talking about the journalistic and historic perspectives, and I think we definitely ought to keep those separate. There's also the presidency and the post-presidency, and there the twain should meet. I would say that the clocks are different, first of all--the journalistic clock and the historic clock. The journalistic clock starts the day the man's inaugurated--in the case of Jimmy Carter, the Carter presidency--and each day, that clock runs. At five o'clock, we write or we broadcast, and that's the take on Jimmy Carter that day--sometimes that week, sometimes that month, then the yearly summary. But that's the clock.

And the news in the Carter administration often was not all that good. We had the hostage situation, in which, I will confess, there was a journalistic orgy that I thought was embarrassing. But on the nine o'clock news, eight o'clock news, or eleven o'clock news--whichever segment you watched--we had yellow ribbons and crying families. We had an annualized inflation rate, at one point, of 20 percent at the same time the prime rate was 20 percent. We had runaway inflation at the same time that we had a recession.

And we had a president who never said "malaise": it's nowhere in the speech. Ted Kennedy hung that on him. But the speech was about malaise. I talked to him in Plains, and he said, "Wayne, it was a damn good speech," and he gave a copy of it to me, to refresh me. I remembered it as lacking leadership, as being almost whiny, and I remembered him as blaming the people for the malaise or the failures or the economic situation. I read the speech, and I said, "This is a terrible speech." Whatever President Carter intended to do, he failed to do. That speaks to that question of communication. Whatever it was he had in mind--to say "I need your help, you're participants; I'm sorry that you're feeling so bad"--the speech was a failure. The reality, again, is the clock; that clock ran every day for four years. Much of the news was bad; much of the Carter image thus was bad.

At the end of that four years, Carter went right off the scope, and I think one reason was that he was a defeated president and, in some ways, a disgraced president. The feeling was that the United States was disgraced by the hostage situation. Although Jimmy Carter actually negotiated the freedom of the hostages, Reagan got the credit. So Carter went off to Plains, into a black hole, and Ronald Reagan appeared, and we were dazzled by him--the media and everybody else. A friend of mine said, "We were dazzled, and I was watching his [Reagan's] hands, not so much to see which shell the pea was under, but to see if there was a pea there at all." In any case, we watched Reagan, and he dominated the news. There was no question about it. It was very upbeat, a total change. But the important point that I want to make here is that, at the end of the Carter presidency, the new clock started. That is the historic clock. And it's totally different from the journalistic clock.

The historic clock takes the four years, starts here and ends here. You can look at that four years, and you can do two things that are important. One, you can step back from it and not say, "The hostages were abused today, and they stomped on the American flag in Iran," but look at that in perspective from day one to the end of the administration, and reflect on it, analyze it, and see how it fits against the background of historical perspective to that point. The other thing that happens is that in the succeeding eight years, you get what I call the historic foreground, against which to look at the Carter presidency.

The Carter economic failure--and it was; Paul Volker was about three years too late--came after William Miller had made an utter disaster. But in the perspective of eight years of Ronald Reagan, I don't think that we journalists or historians should upgrade Carter's D, or D-minus, or C-minus, to a C. I think he deserves a C-minus on his handling of economic matters. But Ronald Reagan deserves to be flunked, thrown out of school, and eliminated from the alumni association. Carter might have had a disaster, but what followed is utterly catastrophic; the eight years of Reaganomics, and the Kinard charade and lie of supply-side economics that we're going to be paying for, for decades--not for years, as we did for Carter's missed stance and tentativeness with the economy.

So that historic foreground, of looking at what Carter did compared with what Reagan did, gives us a different perspective. I don't think we reevaluated him because he's a great ex-president; I think we reevaluated him because, compared with the history to 1988, or 1990, he doesn't look all that bad--and not simply because of Reagan. One revision that I think is important is the hostage crisis. It was absolutely unprecedented in the history of any country, to have hostages paraded before the country nightly. Carter was blamed for being a total failure in handling it. In retrospect, considering the only other comparable situation, the Reagan handling, it looks pretty damn good. And I think it's going to look a lot better if Saddam Hussein kills about a thousand. How are we going to evaluate Bush at that point? This is what I told you is the perspective of foreground.

There is more, but we'll leave it for questions.

Discussant: Robert A. Pastor

The papers were so good--or, as Jimmy Carter would put it, "They were superb"--that I don't feel the need to comment directly on them. Instead, I will offer a simpler explanation for post-presidential popularity; second, I will explain what has changed in the world that permits Carter to play a much larger role than other former presidents have played; and third, I will describe what he did in Panama and Nicaragua. In Nicaragua, the result was a free election on February 25, 1990--the first free election that Nicaraguans had ever had, the first time that all of the political parties that started an election completed an election and agreed to accept and respect the results.

F. Scott Fitzgerald once wrote that the test of a first-rate intelligence is to hold two opposing ideas in your head while retaining the ability to function. It's a test that Americans have rarely tried, and when they have, they have failed. The print media and television have especially failed us in this regard. We have elected to the presidency people who are immensely complicated, and yet we try to define them with a single dimension. Sure, we put two colors to those dimensions, as Professor Rozell pointed out; there is a positive color and a negative color, but they're superimposed on a single dimension, like one of those billboards that reflects a second image as you move past it. Carter was typed an "outsider." The positive color of that, when he was elected, was that he was not a part of the moral decay and bankruptcy of Washington. Before too long, the negative side of that single dimension became clear, and it's been emphasized by Wayne King. As an "outsider," he did not know the ways of Washington or, as was suggested, in an earlier incarnation he was a "hick" who didn't appreciate the power and the sophistication of this great nation. So you had a person with a single dimension, an "outsider," with a positive and a negative color.

The same occurred with Ronald Reagan. He was typed a "great communicator," a person with a big picture of the nation. The positive dimension was that he is an eloquent speaker; he did not get into the details, as Jimmy Carter, an engineer, did. And the negative side is that his "picture" of the government was so broad he didn't even bother to manage the government. The truth is that both these individuals are immensely complicated, and we ignored their complexity.

To build on the Fitzgerald statement--perhaps to offer a Pastor corollary--the media focused and fixed on a new image in May 1989 as a result of the congruence of two events occurring at the same moment. At that time, Ronald Reagan was in Japan, collecting a fat fee, while Jimmy Carter was risking his backside in Panama. The new image was based on facets of their presidencies that were known but previously downplayed: Reagan as being regal and perhaps greedy; Carter as being selfless and hardworking--a world citizen. So we now have fixed a new image of both, and frankly, I don't mind if that new image holds for the next ten years.

But that does not sufficiently capture what Jimmy Carter is about. It does, however, mean a new set of stories, some of which you've heard. Wayne King comes down to Atlanta, followed by a stream of other newspaper journalists and magazine writers, and all of them ask the same questions in order to write the same story; it's not necessary to hear the answer. And the same story is the rehabilitation of Jimmy Carter: he's a world citizen, he's doing good. It's the same one-dimensional story. I'm not saying that's wrong; I'm just saying that the true story is a bit more complicated, just as it was the first time.

The question that is often asked is "What has he been doing since he left the White House? We haven't heard of him at all." Well, I can attest that he's run me into the ground during the past few years. He's been running as quickly, as determinedly, on as broad an agenda--as many of you know from hearing him yesterday--as ever. But people were not focusing on it the way they are now.

Let me leave that aside and make a second point very quickly. I think the world has changed in ways that now permit transnational statesmen such as Carter to play a much more vital, much more central role--not just in promoting agriculture and health, as Carter explained, but even politically, in working out differences between opposing sides in civil wars in Africa, or in Central America, or in the Caribbean. In his book *Bound to Lead*, Joseph Nye, professor at Harvard University, wrote about "soft power," as opposed to the hard power of conventional weapons. U.S. "soft power" stems from our values, our pluralism, and our diversity; it permits us to help other nations or leaders see their objectives in ways that are compatible with our objectives. In fact, that is the role Carter played very successfully in Central America.

In Nicaragua, he was invited in August 1989 by all of the political parties. He succeeded because he was the only person the Sandinistas and UNO, the opposition, trusted; neither trusted the other. The opposition did not trust the Sandinistas to permit a genuinely free electoral process, but they trusted Carter to be fair, to call it as he saw it, to denounce it as a fraud if it was a fraud, or to certify a Sandinista victory if in fact they won. And so they transferred the usual trust that opposing parties have from the electoral process to Jimmy Carter--together with a larger international observer presence, which included the Organization of American States and the United Nations. Carter mediated the electoral process step by step, giving new confidence that the election could be free or, in the opposition's case, that we would be able to detect any fraud in that election--and if we detected it, we would denounce it. With this knowledge, the opposition was willing to participate in the electoral process.

On February 25, 1990, the night of the Nicaragua election, we had the results because of a quick count, which both sides wanted us to do because each was convinced it would win, and wanted us to certify its victory. So we had the results as quickly as anybody in that country, and President and Mrs. Carter and I visited with Nicaraguan President Daniel Ortega. We knew that he had lost decisively. Carter came into the room; Ortega followed. Ortega was ashen-faced; he was in a state of shock. Carter sat down and said, "I understand. I have won a presidential election, and I have lost an election, so I know how you feel. Losing an election is not the end of the world." To which Mrs. Carter said, "I thought it was." After everyone laughed, Carter then told Ortega, "You're a young man; you'll have another opportunity." I said, "That's what he told me ten years ago." The initial exchanges broke the ice.

Ortega was looking for some room, some space. He said, "Well, the results are not looking good, but we think they will change." Carter was clear: "The results have indicated a landslide for Mrs. Chamorro." Then he went on to explain all of the great achievements that Daniel Ortega could take credit for, in a way that permitted Ortega's ego, which had shrunk like a balloon without air, to recover and fill up again. He could feel some pride in what he had done. In fact, many of the points that Carter made to Ortega were later made by Ortega in his concession speech.

Carter then said to him, "Now we need to focus on the transition. To be a statesman--and you have this unique opportunity to be a statesman--we're going to have to work on a transition that will permit this country to become fully democratic; that will permit the opposition to govern fully and effectively; that will permit national reconciliation for all of the people of your country." Ortega understood that, and we did work on the transition, and the transition has held, although many felt sure that Ortega would never permit a free election and would never give up power. Nicaragua is in difficult shape today, but not if you compare it against what it had undergone in the past decade.

So the role that Carter played in Nicaragua--to mediate differences between groups who distrusted each other--was a vital role. It's a role that he's played in Haiti, that he played in Guyana about one month ago. He tried to play the role in Panama, but we failed, and we learned from that experience. We learned that you need an ongoing presence to monitor the electoral process over an extended period, and we in fact had one in Nicaragua. We learned that we needed a quick count to be able to know the results; and we learned that you have to keep all parties committed to the campaign to give people a fair chance to vote their preferences.

Let me conclude with a story of Winston Churchill, whose party lost the election in 1945. The war was over in Europe; he was the great victor, and the people of Great Britain threw him out of office. He came back home, and his wife said to him, "Don't worry, Winnie. This is really a blessing in disguise." Churchill looked at her and said, "If it's a blessing, it's certainly well disguised." The blessing of the Carter post-presidency, of course, has not been so well disguised, although perhaps it hasn't been as well publicized as it could be. I think this conference serves as a great opportunity to do that.

Discussant: Kenneth W. Stein

The title of Bob Pastor's book is *Condemned to Repetition*. It seems I am condemned always to follow Bob Pastor. Not only is his office next to mine at the Carter Center, which is a great delight, but I'm forced to compete with him in one-liners. I always lose.

The phone rang. It was June 1982. It was Dan Lee, chief of staff of President Carter's office in Atlanta. "The President and Mrs. Carter would like you to join the president and some of his friends, and a couple of Emory people, at Sapelo Island, Georgia, this weekend."

"You mean, this coming weekend? Dan, what are they going to talk about?"

"Well, they're going to talk about the Carter Center."

Okay. I had served on the university faculty committee at Emory; we had talked about the center's administrative structure and its relationship to the university. I got off the phone and turned to my wife, Ellen. "Ellen, they want me to go to Sapelo Island next week. I don't even know where it is."

"It's off the Georgia coast."

"Great."

"You have nothing to wear."

So we went down to the large shopping mall in northeast Atlanta, Lenox Square, and I was introduced to Brooks Brothers; I bought a jacket, a pair of pants, and this suit. Later that week, on Thursday, I picked up the suit and the jacket. Then I received a phone call Friday morning. "Hello, Ken? This is Jimmy. We decided that this is going to be casual. Only dungarees this weekend."

I walked into the former R. J. Reynolds tobacco family home on Sapelo Island in dungarees. Sitting on the sofa were President and Mrs. Carter. He rose to greet me, and next to him was Cy Vance; on the other side was Zbigniew Brzezinski; on the other side of him was Ham Jordan; on the other side of him was Andy Young. Then there were Warren Christopher and four or five others from the Carter administration. I could not for the life of me understand what an assistant professor of Middle Eastern history, born in Rockville Centre, New York, brought up in Hempstead, was doing among these people.

The next day I found out the real reason: I would have a chance to beat Zbig in tennis, 6-1, 6-1. That evening was, for me, probably the most fascinating evening of my professional life. Knowing that I was Jewish and that I kept reasonably kosher, President Carter had asked the cook to prepare some fish for me. Everyone else was eating shrimp. I sat down and looked at Carter. It was six o'clock at the water's edge on a picnic bench. Carter had just finished working with Steve Hochman on the chapters dealing with Camp David. There were a lot of people sitting around after dinner, including the president of Emory University. Four hours passed; it was now ten minutes after ten, and Carter and I had been in conversation for four hours. I asked him every conceivable question about what happened during those fifteen days at Camp David. The next day, on the plane home to Atlanta, President Jim Laney of

Emory University turned to me and said, "You were engrossed in that conversation with him last night. I can't believe you spent four hours talking about fifteen days!"

I said, "Jim, you graduated from Yale Divinity School. Do you know what it would have been like to interview Matthew, Mark, Luke, or John?"

President Laney looked at me and said, "It was *that* good?" It's been that good ever since.

It's rare for a professor of Middle Eastern history to have had the experiences that I've had in the last eight years: traveling to the Middle East three times with President Carter; planning three major meetings; writing a book with him. We've been through some very difficult times philosophically about the area of the world about which he probably feels most compelled to do something.

What I want to talk about in the five minutes left is what I've learned about his method and the sources of power, which I have seen in him only in the post-presidency. I did not know Jimmy Carter when he was president; I didn't have the good fortune, as Bob Pastor did, to have worked for four years in Washington for him.

There are several points I want to make very briefly. What are the sources of power that Jimmy Carter uses in the post-presidency? Where does he obtain that power?

First, his consummate interest in international affairs, in a period of time when the sitting president of the United States was basically unidimensional in his attitude toward foreign policy. Ronald Reagan looked at the world as Us versus Them--the United States versus the Soviet Union. Jimmy Carter showed a deep interest in the rest. He showed an interest in Third World countries that Ronald Reagan never showed. In addition, President Carter showed not only an interest in, but also a capacity to understand, many of the facts and many of the needs in the Third World.

Second, Jimmy Carter is a good listener, and he's willing to embark into areas of conflict where others have not ventured because it's too risky; he's willing to listen to political leaders who aren't really nice people. He's willing to listen to Daniel Ortega, Mengistu Haile Mariam, Yasir Arafat, and Hafez Assad. These people are considered unsavory, and he's able to do it because he has a moral currency that comes from his human rights record: No one can accuse Jimmy Carter of not defending the rights of the individual if he sits with Assad. He may not say publicly to Assad or to the press in Syria--of course, it wouldn't be published in the Syrian press anyway--"You're doing bad things to your people." But he will say to Assad personally, "You cannot do those things. You cannot condone terrorism." He's willing to do that. He's willing to do the unconventional, to talk and try to persuade the political outcast to alter his views. And I find it interesting--at least in the Middle East--that Middle Eastern leaders treasure his evaluation of their world, their region, in part because he shows an interest. Most sitting presidents of the United States don't pay attention to Third World problems, and Carter has shown a consuming interest in them during his post-presidency.

What do we do at the Carter Center? We are doing the things that Jimmy Carter really wanted to do in Washington but couldn't do because of the bureaucratic constraints and political demands that were upon him as president of the United States. We're not looking at the American presidency; we're not dealing with the budget; we're not looking at domestic issues. We're dealing with those very special issues that he likes to get his teeth into, and he gets his teeth into us to get into them. Bob Pastor and I barely have enough time to spend with our families. We're also enthusiastic about what we do; we're optimists about what we do. But the point is that he loves these issues; it's infectious, and mutually self-reinforcing.

Bob Pastor knows more than I do about how President Carter is able to confer authority in the post-presidency, and that is a very important concept, because he's able to walk to Chamorro and to Ortega and have them confer authority upon him, even though he has no legal power or foreign aid to give. These leaders look to him for guidance, for direction, and for a way to get them out of the malaise in which they find themselves. And last, he's caring. He has a compassion, a sincerity, a forthrightness, an appeal to the common man. Why would the citizens of Damascus throng the streets in 1983, and clap and shout when Jimmy Carter brought about the Camp David accords, which effectively put Syria off to the side in the Middle East peace process? Why would they embrace Jimmy Carter? Because he cared to come to Syria. He cared to talk to their president, even if the Syrians didn't like their president. He also personified the rights of the common man, something absent in Syria. He paid attention to Syrians as people, perhaps more than their own president did. And what we forget to understand is that many of these countries just want to have someone acknowledge that they exist; it's that simple.

And last, let me say a bit about Carter's objectives. I'll use one example. This past March, we were in the Middle East for the third time, and we were scheduled to meet with Yasir Arafat on the trip home. I had planned for us to meet in Tunis, but it wouldn't work because of the Namibian independence celebration, which Arafat had to attend. We received a phone call at the American consulate in Jerusalem. I talked to one of Arafat's advisers on the phone at five o'clock the day before we were supposed to leave. "Chairman Arafat can't meet with you," he said.

I replied, "All right. We can't leave Israel earlier."

"Why can't you leave Israel earlier?" Arafat's adviser inquired.

We dickered back and forth, and the visit to Tunis did not take place. Later, President Carter decided to meet with Arafat in April 1990; he went to Paris, met with him, and received an enormous clamor of outrage from the Jewish community in the United States. Collectively they said, "How dare you give legitimacy to this man who heads the PLO? You don't like Israel; you don't like Israel's right to exist." I still receive reverberations; every American Jewish leader knows my phone number.

But what people do not know, or don't pay attention to, is what Carter said to Arafat. Did he tell Arafat that terrorism is good? Did he tell Arafat it's good to kill Israeli children in settlements like Ma'alot? Did he tell him it's good to have Palestinian kids throw Molotov cocktails in Jerusalem? No! President Carter said approximately the following in a recent interview, so I'm not divulging anything that hasn't been said previously. Carter spent forty-five of the sixty minutes trying to persuade Yasir Arafat why it was essential for him to change the PLO charter, which makes repeated reference to the disestablishment of the state of Israel. That is an important request for an international leader to make: If you want peace with Israel, you have to change the charter: merely recognizing Israel is insufficient. Carter went one step beyond what most people think is permissible or doable, and I'm sure Arafat did not like getting this for forty-five minutes from a former president of the United

States--particularly the very same man who talked about the Palestinians' need to have a homeland.

My work with President Carter has been fun, rewarding, and exhausting. If it were to end today, I would have had a very fortunate experience, one that I would not trade. The beauty is that Jimmy Carter is going to outlive us all, and I'll be delightfully at this probably the day after I die.

Questions and Answers

Q: I'd like to ask Mr. King: In retrospect, the hostage crisis is a minor event compared to what's going on right now. I think things are changing, another clock is ticking now. Do you feel the same way?

King: I'm sorry, I'm not quite following the question. A different standard? Is that what you're asking me?

Q: Exactly.

King: I will admit that it's been difficult for me to understand why Reagan was a "Teflon president." Part of it has to do with that incredible style and wit that he has; there's no question about that. I have a suspicion that Jimmy Carter was held to such a high standard because he set a very high standard for himself. And I think--those who know him better could speak better to this--he's developed, in the past four or five years, a better sense of self-denigrating humor, if you will. He's a much funnier man. He's always been very funny, but publicly so. I remember, at the reunion, he said, "People have asked me to criticize President Reagan for taking the two million dollars, and I certainly won't do that. I refuse to do that publicly, but here among friends, I would like to say, if you find a deal like that, let me know." Now, that's a different kind of Jimmy Carter. I think it does have a lot, unfortunately, to do with style. That's not a very meaningful answer.

D'Innocenzo: I might add that some have suggested that, in moving from Reagan, the Teflon president, in Bush we get the Revlon president--that he's using cosmetics instead of substance.

Q: I wanted to ask a question of Mr. King. He rated Jimmy Carter's economic policy and other accomplishments as a D or C-minus. It seems quite obvious that Roosevelt could not solve the problem with the New Deal, and you can pick up any high school history textbook and see that the complexity of the economic problem cannot be solved within a one-, two-, three-, four-year period, and that Reagan has carried a lot of the groundwork that Jimmy Carter laid. It's beyond me why the press could not look back and see the complexities of these things instead of trying to stick a name on Jimmy Carter. Why can't they put this into perspective? The New Deal was not economically successful; it was the war that got us out of the problem, and Roosevelt shifted to that. So how can you expect Jimmy Carter to succeed?

D'Innocenzo: I think Professor Rozell might want to comment on that, too.

King: I could give you two answers. One is the journalistic--our perspective. I'll confess immediately that our historic perspective in daily journalism is very poor; few journalists are weighty thinkers. But the basic thrust of the news is not such that it's placed against a perspective like Roosevelt, in advance of failure. In the Carter situation, though, if somebody would give me the dates quickly here: Miller was appointed initially, and Volker--how much later was Volker?

Pastor: It was 1979.

King: Three years, yeah. So we had three years of Miller, who was a good banker but who understand. At the time, it was known that Carter was failing to cool off a superheated economy; this is not 20-20 hindsight. Carter was reluctant to tamper. It got so bad that he had to appoint Volker, who used Draconian and necessary measures, and threw us into a terrible tailspin. Maybe a C-minus or a D is too low; I'll confess to that. I did want to say he should get an A-plus for making human rights perhaps the foreign policy consideration of the United States of the 1980s and the 1990s, not only for the United States but worldwide. I didn't talk about accomplishments, and I apologize for that.

Q: I wanted to ask--to anyone who wants to answer it--if President Carter had followed other Democratic presidents who weren't as dynamic and aggressive as LBJ and Kennedy were, do you think public opinion would have been more favorable toward him? Or do you think it doesn't make any difference?

Rozell: One thing I pointed out in the presentation and my book is that many people had expectations of Jimmy Carter based upon previous Democratic presidents--certain ideas of what a Democratic president with a large party majority in each house of Congress should do. But I think the political context was so different in 1977 than it was in 1933 or 1965 that the comparison is not a favorable one. Part of what you're getting at, though, and I would agree with this, is a matter of style, as opposed to substance. On the one hand, I don't think Carter should be criticized for not living up to a standard of presidential leadership that he did not presume to meet in the first place, and that the era of a large-scale, expansionist public policy agenda had long passed. Carter was dealing with a more consolidative agenda, and I don't think you could evaluate him on the basis of the LBJ or FDR model, given that context. Nonetheless, I think as a matter of style, he may be more aptly criticized for not projecting a kind of aura that would have helped him. One chapter in my book deals with how some people in the press office and his communications advisers evaluated his use of the news media. Wayne King was pointing this out, too: that part of the problem was a failure of communication; we're in agreement on that. That's a necessary element of presidential leadership. The image of leadership is a necessary part of its reality, and I think that was a problem Carter had to deal with more effectively than he did. And I think it was his loss that he did not spend more time working at those things that would have enabled him to project the kind of image Americans look for from their president. And it's remarkable to me--seeing him yesterday, in this setting--to think of the criticisms of him as not being effective in dealing with the public. But there were certain formats in which he was just not very good. I don't think he worked at it, and he should have.

Q: I want to ask about a subject that invariably comes up, but I heard it brought out by only one person, who took great efforts to bring it out in great detail. I don't think anybody will argue with the fact that the picture of President Carter now is far superior, much more effective, than it was during his presidency. What I want to ask is, Is it not true that the shortcomings within the cabinet itself, and within Jimmy Carter's administration, came from the fact that he came through the Trilateral

Commission and he had a staff with twenty-four people who were members of the Trilateral Commission, and he filled the gaps between a number of Republican governments before and after him, and therefore, was influenced directly by David Rockefeller and Zbigniew Brzezinski?

Pastor: I think actually a better argument has been made that Carter had inadequate education and experience from the perspective of the New York establishment, if you will, than that he was unduly influenced by the Trilateral Commission. I think the Trilateral Commission was a source of important information and ideas on the world; it did not govern his cabinet or his policies in any manner. I think quite the contrary: David Rockefeller was significantly estranged, I think, from the policy and from the cabinet, to a great extent. Let me make some other points that bear on earlier comments as well.

I think it's clear that Carter was--and remains--more of a policymaker than a politician. He would much prefer to spend time thinking through and articulating a policy than trying to secure broader approval for that policy. In that sense, he is, today, liberated from the problem of what he perceives as the Congress, but in fact is the problem of democracy as well, which is to assure that a particular policy goal is implemented. But again, you can look at his accomplishments and weigh them alongside those failures toward the end of his presidency that have been grafted onto our minds: inflation, Iran hostages, Afghanistan. But if you compare that with the Panama Canal treaties and Camp David and the human rights policy; if you compare that with SALT II, China normalization, multilateral trade negotiations--if you look at all the achievements together, which I think is what people can now do with some distance--I think you will perhaps grade the presidency a little bit higher than Wayne King suggested, and understand that what Carter is doing in his post-presidency is quite similar in approach. But in a sense, as Ken Stein pointed out, perhaps he's liberated from the necessity of implementing more than just articulating.

BANQUET ADDRESS

21

The Unchanging Jimmy Carter

ROBERT S. STRAUSS

Thank you, President Shuart, Dr. Rosenbaum, Chairman Dempster, Rosalynn, ladies and gentlemen, my good friends. It seems forever since Hamilton Jordan, who's here tonight, walked into my office in 1973, when I was chairman of the Democratic Party, and said, "Mr. Chairman, what would you think about Jimmy running for president?" And I said, "Of what?" True story. And now I have the very special pleasure of being on this program, for which I express a special thanks.

I hardly know where to begin. I guess I should begin by saying nothing is more pleasant, Rosalynn, than the joy of being with you and not having to put up with your husband. It's just marvelous! I wish I'd been here all day. But I wouldn't say a thing like that; you know I wouldn't. There are so many things I would like to talk about, but the hour is late and I'm well aware of that. But when I was thinking about how much I had to cover in this short time, I was reminded of a marvelous story I haven't told in a long time--a true story--involving Sir Winston Churchill.

The story is told--and it's been confirmed to me by Pamela Harriman, his former daughter-in-law--that when Sir Winston was engaged in one of his bitter political campaigns, he found himself in a debate with his opponent. His opponent was at the microphone, much as I am at this microphone, and Sir Winston was sitting at his right. They were in a large hall, much like the one we're in tonight. The opponent said to the group, "It is beyond my conception that intelligent people such as you would consider voting for a man who has such little discipline in his life. Why, his alcoholic habits are well known to one and all; and I can assure you the stories of his drinking are not exaggerated." He pointed to Churchill and said, "Sir Winston, if all the alcohol you have consumed in your life was poured into this room, it would fill the hall to here." He drew an imaginary line. "Would fill the hall to here, Sir Winston!" When he said that, so the story is told, Churchill looked at the floor and looked at the imaginary line and looked at the ceiling, looked a second time at the floor and the imaginary line and from the line to the ceiling. Then he said into the microphone in front of him, "So much to do, so little time." I have so much to do, and so little time, that I had better begin.

It was difficult to try to put together a few notes on what I wanted to say this evening. Scholars will tell you that ten years is really far too short a period of time to put a historical perspective on a presidency. But even a ten-year, inadequate perspective is fascinating when you start jotting down some of the things the Carter presidency emcompasses. As a matter of fact, it's amazing what substance there is-- almost too much to list on an evening such as this. It doesn't take long, when one begins to work on a Carter record, to realize that so many of the things that were viewed as flawed policies, if you will, or wrong strategies, or inappropriate issues that should never have been tackled, have now been proven to be just the contrary. And while many of them--a great many of them--took their toll on President Carter's political base, I can begin by saying what I'm sure most, if not all, of you realize: that the nation and the world are certainly far better off because of what he stood for and what he accomplished. So let me list a very few simple, clear examples of what I'm talking about.

One can't start without thinking of the Panama Canal. The effort that went into the negotiations leading to the treaty, and the treaty itself, were viewed with contempt by then nonpresident but candidate Ronald Reagan and the Ronald Reagan wing of the Republican Party--not by Democrats and Republicans of vision and political courage, like Howard Baker. But the simple fact of the matter is that every single president from Eisenhower on was in favor of such negotiations and treaty, but each felt it would be political suicide, far too dangerous to undertake. But not Jimmy Carter. I well remember saying, as others did, "Mr. President, this is a second-term issue. It takes too heavy a toll." But even a ten-year historical perspective has left all but the most hard-line critics understanding that we could never have stabilized our relationships with Panama specifically, or Mexico, or Central or South America, without the Panama Canal effort of the Carter administration. Any constructive role in Latin America would have been almost impossible without this accomplishment, and most thinking people now recognize it.

Next, we can move to SALT II, which, again, the Republicans characterized during the 1980 campaign as "America's window of vulnerability." It's fascinating that although the SALT II agreement had to be withdrawn, never ratified, the same Reagan administration that characterized it as "America's window of vulnerability" explicitly abided by it for the next six years. Abided by it, I would remind you, even to the point of decommissioning submarines to stay within its limits. And I think it's fair to say that SALT II is still the framework that guides us and those who would have been its signatories. It's not much of an overstatement, if any at all, to say that SALT II has probably served as well as if it had been ratified. I've never seen a real study of the impact of SALT II on the world since the presidency of Jimmy Carter, but I have no doubt that it would, in retrospect, be viewed in the most positive light by all but the harshest right-wing critics.

Camp David, the cornerstone of the Carter foreign policy in the Middle East, was an incredible accomplishment. We all tend to exaggerate--even a modest fellow like me--from time to time. But I would suggest to you that although Jimmy Carter had first-class help at Camp David, it is no overstatement to say that this was a personal and individual accomplishment. His single-mindedness, his steadfastness, and yes, his stubbornness and refusal to accept failure when it was obvious, brought about the only real progress toward peace in the Middle East that we've seen. And I would remind you that many at the time, even though they applauded it, said that it could not and would not last, that it could not survive.

Well, let's look at the record. It has survived an invasion of Lebanon, the attack by the Israelis on the Iraqi nuclear facility, the destabilization caused by the Intifada activities, the assassination of Anwar Sadat, and now the invasion of Kuwait. And to this day, not one single drop of blood--Egyptian or Israeli--has been spilled on that border. It has survived, but people tend to overlook the fact that Egypt--the Egypt that was ostracized by the Arab world for entering into the Camp David accords--is once again the center of leadership for the Arab world.

And I think it's also fair to say that, even though we have made no progress in dealing with the rights of the Palestinians, the Golan Heights, and other such issues, the autonomy framework and many of the guidelines of the Camp David accords still remain the only credible answer we've found that is even discussed when the peace process, from time to time, does get some modest attention. As a matter of fact, as far as I can tell, even Prime Minister Shamir, who voted against the ratification of the Camp David accords, now supports them, even if he does little or nothing to build on them.

In human rights, President Carter was constantly criticized. He was viewed as being foolish and naive with respect to what goes on in the real world. Well, having been indoctrinated with the negative press around the country, negative comments from members of Congress and the business community, just where are we after only ten years? It's hard to believe, but I daresay Jimmy Carter's human rights program will eventually be recorded by history not just as one of his significant accomplishments, but as one of the major accomplishments of this country during the past twenty years or so. The world, my friends, would be much different today without the Jimmy Carter human rights program, and it has particularly become a beacon of hope to people and nations around the world. And as I was writing this, I thought to myself that it was in the Carter administration that we learned once again that this nation acts best when it acts across the board according to and in keeping with its values.

It may not be in good taste for me to brag about another major Carter accomplishment, because I had a role in it, but one of the meaningful achievements of the Carter presidency was the lead role our country took in successful negotiation of the Tokyo round of multilateral trade negotiations, which led to the Trade Act of 1979. This accomplishment still receives acclaim around the free world, and let me repeat what many of you have heard me say publicly other times: that we would never have had a successful conclusion of the Tokyo round if Jimmy Carter had not understood every single issue and provided more support than I, as his trade minister, could ever have imagined, or anyone else dreamed possible. And when I give someone credit for something I've been involved in, they've earned it. I could go see Jimmy Carter at any time, day or night, and he always had time to call Callahan in London, or Schmidt in Germany, or Giscard d'Estaing. And he clothed me with the appearance of power by seeing that I attended every economic summit, and sat by his side during critical trade discussions. I'm too nice to ask you to compare President Carter's successful Tokyo round, which received worldwide acclaim, with the status of today's Uruguay round, which is foundering, and is so desperately needed. And compare the Carter involvement with what's taking place in the current administration.

In another dimension of the Carter presidency, there simply is no question that when we examine two of the negatives that caused his defeat--inflation and the hostages--we can surely understand better today what happened, with inflation again on the rise because of outside forces over which President Bush has little control, caused primarily by the same commodity--oil. Even the situation that I think was the ultimate downfall of President Carter politically, the hostage crisis, looks altogether different today. President Carter's leadership, his patience, and his toughness of mind did help us, did take the lead, in our being about to bring out hostages without going to war, without transferring military equipment, and without paying a bribe to the Iranians. Not only did President Carter *say* he wasn't going to pay ransom for hostages; he *didn't* pay ransom for hostages.

We all remember what a difficult, painful time that was, but there is some justice in this world, from time to time. A recent *New York Times* poll listed a series of foreign policy crises from the 1980s and asked the American people which one they thought was handled best. Guess which one came in first? President Carter's handling of the Iranian hostage situation! I was more shocked than the president would have been, had he read it.

I want to talk just a minute more about the president. I often recall President Carter saying to people, "I don't care whether it's the political thing to do or not, it's the right thing to do, and I think we ought to do it." He spent far too much of his time worrying about whether Ham Jordan and Jody Powell and I were cooking up some scheme which might possibly help him politically, and thus diluting the substantive things he wanted to accomplish. God knows, the thought of it drove him crazy, and whenever he saw us together, he was sure we were up to it. And I must also confess, as one of his greatest admirers, that I have never been a tremendous admirer of Jimmy Carter the presidential politician. At times the fella would drive you crazy. I would much rather have Rosalynn Carter handling the politics, and Jimmy Carter handling the policies. And Rosalynn, I don't mean to diminish in any way your accomplishments in the policy area.

Sitting here with Rosalynn and thinking about these remarks reminds me of a wonderful story that she may or may not recall. In the Carter campaign for reelection, Jimmy wasn't leaving the White House and Rosalynn was traveling around the country. I and others were traveling hard, too, both with her and separately. Often we spoke late in the evening--ten-thirty or eleven--when she'd come back from a trip and have a question on her mind. She'd been in Pennsylvania when we removed something called a trigger price, a mechanism to see that steel prices stayed supported. We were just going into the Pennsylvania primary, and the one thing we didn't need to do was make every steelworker and everybody else in the state furious, but the trigger price mechanism did have an adverse impact on inflation. People in the Pennsylvania steel areas went crazy. Rosalynn went up there a couple of days later, and she came back and called me about ten o'clock at night. I said, "How was the trip?"

She said, "It was hard. I think I did some good, but those people are so angry. Bob, who would have been foolish enough politically to have removed the trigger price mechanisms five or six days before the primary?"

I said, "Rosalynn, why don't you reach over there and pat the president of the United States on the rear end and ask him that question."

Her response was, "Oh. Well, goodnight, Bob." And that was Jimmy Carter at his worst politically, and at his best as a president.

It seems to me that, over and above anything else one would say about this president and his administration, the most important thing--the thing that has assumed greater and greater value with each passing year--is that Jimmy Carter was a president determined to do what he believed to be in the best interest of this nation and its people, and he was willing to take the heat for it and not cry. Just think about it for a few minutes. Run through your mind all the major accomplishments of the administration. Each of them--even Camp David, in the end--was a political loser for President Carter, and each turned out to be a major accomplishment, a winner for this country. He paid the price, and the country continues to reap the benefits.

Let me put it another way. Jimmy Carter was a president who was willing--more than that, he was president who felt duty-bound--to tell the American people the truth rather than whatever he thought they wanted to hear at a particular moment. There has been a lot of discussion in the past few months about the cynicism, and even the anger and the disgust, of the American people toward the political process and elected officials. Political pundits, consultants, and pollsters all over the country are scrambling around, trying to figure out what's at the bottom of it. I'll tell you what I think it is. My guess is that Americans have gotten tired of being treated like they shouldn't be told the truth, and my guess is, the public is beginning to realize the price they pay for politicians who make decisions based on what's popular instead of what's right.

I'll tell you something else. My guess is that the reasons for the recent surge in approval of Jimmy Carter go well beyond the splendid record of public service he's compiled since he left the White House. My guess is that a lot of that approval has to do with the recognition that he was a president who did speak the truth, and who did try to do what he thought was right for the country. You know the real secret behind all of this hoopla over the reemergence of former President Jimmy Carter? Of course you do. Many of you in this room, particularly, because you worked with Jimmy Carter, as I did. And you know, as I know, Jimmy Carter. The simple secret here is that Jimmy Carter hasn't changed one bit. He's just as hard-headed, just as stubborn, just as impossible to argue with, and just as hardworking and decent and determined to do what's right and committed to public service, as he always was. That was Jimmy Carter before he came to Washington; that was Jimmy Carter when he sat in the Oval Office; and that is Jimmy Carter today.

HIGH SCHOOL COLLOQUIUM
AND TOWN MEETING

JAMES M. SHUART, CHRISTOPHER M. BELLOMY, AND HERMAN A. BERLINER

Dr. James M. Shuart: Ladies and gentlemen, it's my great pleasure to welcome so many students and their teachers from the high schools of Long Island to Hofstra University for this very special event. I'm delighted that you can share this wonderful experience with Hofstra University. We're very pleased and honored to have President Jimmy Carter and former First Lady Rosalynn Carter with us this day. President Carter will make a presentation to our colloquium, and following that, Mrs. Carter will join with him to answer your questions. And now, it's my privilege and pleasure to introduce our honored guest.

Jimmy Carter served in the White House from 1977 to 1981. Early on, he gave evidence of wanting to be a people's president. At his inauguration, Mr. Carter wore a business suit instead of the more formal attire of his precedessors. During his inaugural parade, he set a precedent by leaving the presidential limousine and walking to the White House, shaking hands with crowds along the way. He carried his own suitcase on his travels. He held town meetings in various parts of the country, staying at the homes of private citizens, and he vigorously supported the widening of civil rights for minorities and women, and the extension of basic human rights to the downtrodden in other countries. Only two men--Grover Cleveland and Woodrow Wilson--previously had become president without having held civilian office in the nation's capital, or having been a commanding general. Like President Carter, each had won election because of a reputation for honesty and reform as a state governor.

President Carter won his greatest triumph in international affairs, and at the same time, he had his greatest difficulties in that area. As a peacemaker, he achieved what was then considered to be the impossible feat of ending the long-standing belligerency between Egypt and Israel, bringing together President Anwar Sadat and Prime Minister Menacham Begin at Camp David to shape a treaty of peace. In the last part of his term, however, Iran's revolutionary government seized the American embassy in Tehran, and held some fifty hostages for fourteen months, resisting all of President Carter's efforts to free them. Thankfully, all of the hostages were eventually freed, and all came home alive.

Mr. Carter was born in Plains, Georgia. He graduated from high school at sixteen years of age, then went on to attend Georgia Southwestern College and studied mathematics at Georgia Tech. He's a graduate of the United States Naval Academy; he was an officer on battleships and submarines, and in 1950, he was named the engineering officer of the U.S.S. *Sea Wolf*, one of the first American nuclear submarines.

In the years since he left the White House, Jimmy Carter has not retired to inactivity. Since 1981, he and Mrs. Carter have written no fewer than six books between them. Each year, they take up hammer and saw for a week, helping to build homes for the homeless. But his greatest contribution, in my opinion, is in international affairs. A recent article in *The Nation* notes that he seems to be everywhere, mediating civil wars in Africa, playing umpire in elections in Haiti, Panama, and Nicaragua. He has created for himself an admirable extra-constitutional role as ex-president. In his quiet, methodical way, he has tackled some of the most intractable of human problems, whether it be guinea worm disease in Africa, or the world's longest-running civil war in Ethiopia. In the process, he has set a new standard of behavior for former presidents.

Ladies and gentlemen, I'm very pleased to present President Jimmy Carter to you.

Carter: President Shuart, I am delighted to be back at Hofstra University for my third visit. The first was during the last few days of the 1976 presidential campaign. I came back in 1980--a very successful visit to Hofstra but not a very successful campaign trip--and I am delighted to be back here again. This arrangement, and the exuberance and welcome of the students, remind me of the Democratic conventions when I was nominated to be president. It makes me inclined to get back into politics to hear your good welcome--I had that thought for about ten seconds before I rejected it.

Today I am going to make a few brief comments that might relate to politics, to government, to student roles, to the experiences that my wife and I and our family have had. We now are involved in a wide range of activities. I am a professor at Emory University in Atlanta; this is my ninth year of lecturing there. This is an ambition I had when I was very young. If you had asked me, when I was your age, or even younger, what I wanted to do later in life, I would have said, first of all, "I want to go to the Naval Academy and be an officer on a ship"; my second choice would be to be become a college professor. I finally reached my goal in life, thanks to Ronald Reagan, four years earlier than I had anticipated.

Since leaving the White House, we have devoted some of our efforts to earning a living. Most of our income has been from the sale of our books. We have written five books that have made the best-seller lists. My wife's book was number one on the *New York Times* list; I never quite made that. Rosalynn asked me to announce that our books are still on sale, if you are interested in helping us out.

I grew up, along with my wife, Rosalynn, in the small town of Plains, Georgia, with a total population, since 1900, between about 650 and 680 people. We now have 680; we had 681 before Amy went off to college, the peak of our population so far. We have a very stable life there. After I went off to college and came back home from the Navy, we were deeply involved in a lot of political affairs on the local level, but primarily public service. I was on the hospital authority, I was on the library board, I was on the county school board, I worked with the statewide seed organizations, I was a Boy Scout leader, Rosalynn was a Cub Scout leader, we were involved in our church. Out of that community experience, learning the needs of our people--we were there during the very difficult racial integration years, civil rights days--we became increasingly interested in politics. I finally ran for the Georgia Senate, and served two terms, then decided to run for governor. We had become familiar with our people. We knew their hopes, their dreams, their aspirations, their fears, their concerns, their doubts about the future; and we were able to launch a kind of grass-roots campaign. Rosalynn and I campaigned regularly, and our young sons--Amy was not born when we began--also were involved in the campaigns. I think they learned lessons during the political campaigns that have helped to shape their lives.

Out of that campaign came election as governor of Georgia. When we began our campaign for president in 1975, after leaving the governor's office, we had a family political team--like a basketball or a baseball team, but scattered all over the nation. I would go one place; Rosalynn would go another; our oldest son, Jack, in a different place; his wife, Judy, in a different place; Chip and his wife, Karen; Jeffrey and his wife, Annette; my aunt and my mother. This is one of the reasons we were able to get elected: we had about ten people campaigning, and the other candidates had only one person campaigning. They never knew what hit them until after I was elected president and they were defeated. The point is that I had found a very wonderful role for our sons--at that time, college or just a little past college age--to become involved in the election campaign for the highest political office in the world. At the end of every week, on Saturday and Sunday, we would get together back in Plains, talk about our experiences, and I, the candidate for president, would learn a great deal from my sons and others in the family about what was going on around the country, what was interesting to the people, and what was an advantageous and sometimes a detrimental policy that we were trying to espouse and explain to the American people.

Also, when we were elected and moved into the White House, we had that same relationship with our family. Young members of our family were still very eager to learn about our country and to bring to me as president the basic concerns of students. Amy brought me the view from grammar school. How could I, as president, help improve the conditions in the school's lunchroom, or in the presentation of opportunities for students to learn? I had learned from the challenging concerns of my sons' generation--Earth Day, withdrawing our troops from Vietnam, dealing with civil rights. The point I am trying to make to you high school students is that a president in office, a candidate trying to become a governor or president, can derive a great deal of benefit from students your age; you have a deep insight into the basic considerations of life.

After we left the White House, Amy reached your age. She has been a very active student leader, promoting two or three causes. The most important cause that Amy has espoused is to eliminate apartheid, racial discrimination, in South Africa; she was also very strongly opposed to the illegal activities of the CIA in the so-called Contra War in Nicaragua. Amy has not limited her activities to talking with other students; Rosalynn and I are very proud of the fact that she has been arrested four times. I am not advocating that you all get arrested; the point is that she believes very deeply in a few basic principles that affect not only her own life and ambitions, but also the integrity, the moral and ethical standards, of our country. I think she has, along with other students her age, been very effective, as my sons were almost a generation earlier, in trying to influence American policy.

As a former president, as one who has been successful in politics, I would like to urge you this morning to ascertain in your own lives what you consider to be important--not just finishing your education, not just finding a wife or a husband, not just building a house or raising a family, but what you consider to be important as an issue or an event or a goal or an ambition or a dream that you would like to see brought into effect under or with your influence. Is it environmental quality? Is it control of nuclear arsenals? Is it basic human rights for people who are persecuted? Is it the alleviation of suffering? Is it the sharing of food with starving people? Is it a hope that now-dying infants in Africa and Asia might live? Is it providing shelter for people who have no place to stay? These are the kinds of things that were burning issues in the 1960s, 1970s, 1980s, and are now in the 1990s; and they will be burning issues in the next century. How do you compare what our government is doing with what you think our nation ought to be doing? Is our nation's measurement of greatness the same as your definition of what a great nation is? What laws would you like to see implemented--in Washington, in your own state--to make our government and democratic society a source of pride and not embarrassment? These are not idle questions that affect other people. These are questions that affect you personally.

You will obviously be students, you will get jobs, you will raise families; those are obvious and legitimate ambitions of many people. But there are other things that you can take as responsibilities that will not detract from your quality as a student. It will not detract from your playing a responsible role as a husband or wife or mother or father, because when you try to shape society for the better by courage and ambition and study and hard work and activity, you expand your own life in a beneficial way. It adds adventure, excitement, gratification to your life to take on a task that might be considered hopeless and work hard to bring it into being.

The last point I want to make, before we answer your questions about our lives in the White House and afterward, is that you are now in a phase of life when you have the greatest possible freedom. I think this freedom might be enhanced to some degree when you graduate from high school, if you do, and go to college; before you take on the responsibilities of a family, and before you take on a job where your public expression of opinions might be shaped by your employers. If you get a job teaching school, you are going to be very sensitive about what the principal of the school thinks about what you have to say if you want to be promoted, if you want to be given a better assignment. And if you work for IBM or a bank or a law firm, or in a construction firm or for Coca-Cola or whatever, you are going to be quite restrained in your freedom of expression and your freedom of activity. So in your student days-- juniors and seniors in high school, and throughout your college years--you have the best opportunity to speak freely as Americans and say, "This is what I want my nation to be. These are the issues that I want to change for the better." That is what politics is. That is what government is. You don't have to wait until you're twenty-five or thirty or thirty-five years old before you start shaping political decisions in this country.

Rosalynn and I have a very good time these days--I do not have the responsibilities of running a country. We have the Carter Center of Emory University. We are involved, as President Shuart said, in negotiating peace where war exists; we try to hold elections in this hemisphere to bring democracy to countries like Panama, Nicaragua, the Dominican Republic, Haiti, Guyana; we are trying to eradicate horrible tropical diseases, like guinea worm, in twenty-two countries throughout the world; we are trying to promote the production of food grains in Africa, where every year for the last twenty years, the per capita production of food grains has gone down; we are trying to teach the Chinese people, at their own request, how to alleviate the problems of handicapped people; we are trying to identify serious human rights abuses in countries around the world, and to intercede with the leaders of those nations to bring an end to persecution; we are dealing with relationships between our country and the Soviet Union; and we are trying to help analyze the peace process in the Middle East.

Those are the kinds of things we are doing now as strictly private citizens, with no government role to play, no authority at all, and very limited funding. We use our influence, whatever it might be, in these very challenging, very exciting opportunities. And you have the same opportunities as students to set your goals, not only for your own lives, but also for the society within which you live. That is the essence of politics. I would hope that in the future, if you see an opportunity to get involved in a political campaign--identify someone you like, whom you think would be a good member of congress, or a good U.S. senator, or a good governor, or a good mayor-- then go and say, "I would like to help you." If you find, during a campaign, that your candidate is not measuring up to your standards, then tell that person, "Mrs. Jones or Mr. Smith, I came to support your campaign for Congress or for mayor. I don't like what you're doing about this particular issue. You're not giving enough attention to environmental quality," or whatever. It could have a profound, beneficial impact on that candidate.

In closing, let me tell you: You can have a major role in shaping society in the future--what your county is, your city is, your state, your nation, and the world might be in the future. It does not take many strong, determined, courageous voices to do it, and those voices can come from you. Whether or not you ever become a congressperson or a governor or a senator or a president, you certainly can help to shape our nation's policies and our nation's ideals. Thank you for letting me make these remarks. Now we will answer questions.

Shuart: Before we continue, I would like to reiterate how pleased we are that former First Lady Rosalynn Carter is with us today. During her husband's presidency, Mrs. Carter handled many active roles. She was one of President Carter's most influential advisers. She often sat in on cabinet meetings, and she diligently pursued her independent interests, including mental health programs, the needs of the elderly, and women's rights. Many students of the presidency have said that the political partnership of Jimmy and Rosalynn Carter was unequaled in the White House since the days of Franklin and Eleanor Roosevelt, but partnership in the Carter marriage, as you have heard, existed long before they moved to Washington. Mrs. Carter took an active role in the family business in Plains, Georgia; campaigned vigorously for her husband's election as governor of Georgia; and for two years campaigned alone across the nation for his election to the presidency. And through it all, she chalked up a record of independent accomplishments. Her greatest achievement was the work she did as honorary chairperson of the President's Commission on Mental Health. She led hearings on mental health in cities across the nation, and held roundtable discussions on the subject at the White House; her work resulted in the passage of the Mental Health Systems Act of 1980. I'd like Mrs. Carter to stand up for a round of applause.

Mrs. Carter: Thank you very much. I just want to add a few words to what Jimmy had to say. You do not have to wait for another election to help improve society. There are always issues out there, and if you think, for instance, that our country ought to be a country where everybody has a place to live, where there are no homeless; where everybody has food to eat, you can join Habitat for Humanity and help build houses, or you can go to a soup kitchen and help with that. All of these things are very important. I think the reason Jimmy and I say this so much is because of where we have been. The problems that are really difficult are the ones that a president sees, or the ones that I saw as first lady. Those that are the easiest to solve do not reach the desk of the president--they are solved before they get there. What we saw were the problems that never go away: problems of the schools or the handicapped or the sick. If you are interested in something, and you think you know what you want to do in life--if you want to be a social worker, for instance--volunteer for that kind of work. Everybody needs help; all organizations need help. You might volunteer, and you might decide that is not what you want to do for the rest of your life. A volunteer job could really be helpful to you in determining your future, what you want to do.

Another thing that I wanted to tell you is that when Jimmy and I were in Plains school, we went from the first through the eleventh grade--we had only eleven grades then, in the same school building--and we had--how many students, Jimmy? Two or three hundred? We had an exceptional teacher. She was the principal, the homeroom teacher for the eighth grade, and taught English; later she became superintendent. She would come to our classrooms when we were little children; she made us all recognize and learn the great artists, and she had paintings she would show us; she played classical music, and we had to learn about composers and so forth. She would come to our room and say, "Now, study hard. Take advantage of all your opportunities, because you never know--someday one of you young men might be president of the United States." Whoever thought Jimmy Carter would be president of the United States at that time! But I would like to correct that statement and say, "Any young man *or* woman may grow up to be president of the United States."

Christopher Bellomy: Good afternoon, everyone. As president of the student government, I'd like to welcome everyone, on behalf of all the students, to our campus this afternoon. You have a unique opportunity this afternoon. Mr. and Mrs. Carter have agreed to accept any questions you might have. There are four microphones at four points in the theater, and at each of those microphones, there's a monitor in charge who will assist students who want to ask questions. Only four people in line at each microphone to ask questions of Mr. and Mrs. Carter, please, and keep your questions brief and to the point, so we can get in as many questions as possible.

Q: Mr. President, Mrs. Carter, I'm Steven Gilroy. I'm a teacher from Manhasset schools, and the question is really for the two of you. I think there's been a great change recently. It used to be that when young people were told they could be anybody they wanted to be, including president, there would be great excitement. Now I think it's almost the opposite; they couldn't care less. They don't want to go to college. I was wondering what advice you could give me as a teacher to try to arouse these young kids' desire to go into politics, and an excitement about being in public service.

Carter: I tried to cover the answer somewhat in my opening remarks. If there are changes you would like to see made in the life of your own family or the people you know--particularly those who are not as fortunate as you--if there are changes you would like to see in the priorities or standards or ideals of our nation, the best way to bring about those changes is in the political realm, where you can become a leader of the nation. You can obviously do a lot as a private citizen, but if you can become a member of the U.S. Congress, or a senator, or president, than you can put your ideals into practice in a much more effective fashion. The ultimate concern of citizens of our country should be not to take care of our own immediate, sometimes selfish needs but to ask how we can share our blessings, the benefits we have derived from a free and open and democratic nation, with others--not just in this country but also overseas? Politics can also be a lot of fun. It is a lot of fun to know that your ideas can be put into effect, and that you can share with many other people an exciting, ambitious, and challenging problem, and ultimately the answer to a problem.

Mrs. Carter: Do you want me to answer that question, too? I have a suggestion for you. I think one thing you could do is get your students involved in a local issue, let them learn everything they can about it, and make up their minds which side they are on. Then try to influence your local officials. Actually take your students to see them and tell them how they feel. They should also write letters to them. The students will be amazed at what a difference they can make. I can tell you that politicians read their mail.

Q: I'm Steve Milner, LIE Tonight. A decade later, do you feel the situation with the United States has changed very much, being that we're in Iraq now, versus Iran, the gasoline prices are high--there are so many similarities. What advice would you offer President Bush at this point?

Carter: Although there are many similarities between now and ten years ago, there are some dramatic differences as well. For instance, in the eight years that President Reagan was in office, we had such terrible fiscal deficits that the total national debt tripled in eight years. President Reagan had twice as much federal debt as all the other presidents put together, from George Washington through me. When I left office, we were the greatest creditor nation on earth; people owed us more money than any other nation in the world. When President Reagan left office eight years later, we had become the greatest debtor nation on earth. We owe more money to foreigners than all the developing nations, all the poor nations, in the world combined. So we do not have the flexibility in our federal budgeting to take care of crucial needs like housing or education or health care.

Also, our nation, when I was president--I believe--had the reputation of being firmly committed to peace. When we had a problem anywhere in the world--including, as President Shuart mentioned, in the Middle East--we worked to bring about a peaceful resolution to that problem. I would advise President Bush to do the same thing. In the last couple of weeks, we have seen a dramatic change in the attitude of our government. We had previously been embarking American troops to protect Saudi Arabia from an invasion. A couple of weeks ago, President Bush, the secretary of state, and others, I believe, decided that now we must prepare our troops for an invasion of Iraq. We are going to start a war; we are not going to wait to defend a nation against war. This is very disturbing to me. I think we ought to maintain the role of a strong, determined, peaceful nation, not starting a war but trying every way we can to prevent a war.

Q: President Carter, do you feel your actions against the Soviets for their invasion of Afghanistan were successful and had any effect--specifically, the decision to boycott the Moscow Olympics?

Carter: As you may remember, in Christmas week of 1979, the Soviet Union invaded Afghanistan, a peaceable neighboring country. They sent in about one hundred thousand troops, and began trying to subjugate that free country. We had three basic options at that time. One was to send American troops halfway around the world to fight the Soviet troops, which I thought was a foolish possibility. The other two possibilities involved economic response and political response. In the political realm, to answer your specific question, we did several things. First, we got the members of the United Nations--104 of them--publicly to condemn the Soviet Union for the invasion. The second thing we did was to restrain the Soviets economically. A third thing we did was to make sure that the world realized that the Soviets could not use Afghanistan as a launching pad to invade Pakistan and Iran, and therefore penetrate to the Persian Gulf. In my State of the Union speech in January 1980, I told the Soviet Union that if it did conquer Afghanistan, and attempted to invade nations adjacent to Afghanistan, we would consider this a direct threat to our own security, and we would respond accordingly.

And the last thing is what you brought up, the Olympics. When the Soviets invaded Afghanistan, they were using the 1980 Olympics as a major propaganda statement: The countries are coming to Moscow for the Olympics because we are a strong and peace-loving nation. At the same time, they were trying to subjugate the people of Afghanistan with military power. The Congress of the United States voted overwhelmingly that we did not want to send an Olympic team to Moscow. I made the same statement. The decision, though, had to be made by the American Olympic Committee, which is totally independent of the president and the Congress. The U.S. Olympic Committee voted, by a two to one margin, not to send our athletes to Moscow until the Soviets withdrew from Afghanistan, and fifty-four other nations decided the same thing: We will not support the Soviet invasion of Afghanistan by sending our athletes to Moscow. It was a very difficult decision to be made, but I thought the Olympic Committee made the right decision.

Q: Good afternoon, Mr. President. My name is Peter Troy, from Herricks High School. Ten years after having faced the energy crisis toward the end of your term as president, the nation is once again facing the possibility of an energy crisis as a result of the Middle East crisis. What are your thoughts on how to prevent an energy crisis and to decrease our chief dependence on foreign oil?

Carter: I think the most difficult political challenge I had as president was trying to convince the American people and the Congress that we had an energy crisis and we needed to do something about it. What we tried to do was to put into U.S. law requirements that would make us more committed to conservation of energy. We passed a law, for instance, that automobiles' efficiency had to be increased. When I was elected president, the average automobile in this country got twelve miles per gallon. We passed a law that each year, efficiency had to increase, up to an average of twenty-eight miles per gallon at the end of eight years. We required that homes had to be insulated better to save electricity and other sources of energy, and that electric power rates, for instance, had to be raised to discourage waste.

When I was inaugurated in January 1977, we were importing 48 percent of our oil. Because of the policy that we put into effect by law, that ultimately got down to 30 percent. President Reagan, though, and I am afraid President Bush, have a different idea about energy conservation. They do not put it as a major goal of our country. So instead of importing 30 percent of our oil, we are importing more than 50 percent of the oil that we use, and that percentage is steadily going up. We are not really emphasizing--from the White House and the State Department, from the government, even from the Congress--the necessity to save energy and to develop alternative sources of energy. I think this should be a major factor in our nation's response to the Iraq-Kuwait crisis.

The other day, the secretary of state said the reason we are in Saudi Arabia, and might have to take military action, was twofold: American jobs and oil. I do not believe that those are the kinds of reasons for us to sacrifice human life on the deserts of Saudi Arabia and Iraq. But if our nation would take a strong stand, enforced by the president and the Congress, to save energy, then I think we would be much less susceptible in the future to blackmail by countries that have a lot of oil but do not have a commitment to the kind of principles that make our nation proud. So we do need a comprehensive energy policy, and we need to enforce the laws that were passed while I was president.

Q: President Carter, my name is Pablo Sinclair, and I'm a senior from Floral Park Memorial High School. You said that we should not be an aggressor in the Middle East. Do you think we should have troops there as a peacekeeping force?

Carter: Yes. When Iraq invaded Kuwait, I think we made exactly the right response. First of all, we went to the United Nations and obtained the support of other countries, including the Soviet Union, China, France, Great Britain, and smaller countries. I think President Bush did a superb job in marshaling that kind of support to prevent what then was considered to be a very likely invasion of Saudi Arabia by Iraq. And so we did station our troops in Saudi Arabia, I think, in adequate numbers to prevent an Iraqi invasion. We also got other countries--France, Great Britain, Syria, Morocco, Egypt--to join in that defensive force. This has all been in accord with United Nations resolutions.

Lately, the thing that concerns me is that President Bush, the secretary of defense, and the secretary of state have been making statements that we are shifting from a defensive role to an offensive role. President Bush has announced that we are going to send two hundred thousand more troops to the deserts of Saudi Arabia, not just to defend Saudi Arabia, for which it is not necessary to have that many troops, but in preparation for an attack against Iraq. There are people who advocate a preemptive strike against Iraq, and they say we can win this war easily, by bombing Iraq into submission. This troubles me, even if it is accurate--which I do not think it is--because the people of Iraq are already suffering under the dictatorship of Saddam Hussein. And everyone who is familiar with military tactics--which I happen to be, having studied military science and served in the Navy--knows that bombs are usually not effective in killing military personnel. The effective target for bombing is civilians. If we bomb Baghdad, it is very likely that soldiers and other military, including Saddam Hussein, would be in trenches, would be hiding, would be behind the lines or in tanks. The civilians would be the ones who get killed. I reject that.

People say that Iraqi forces are inadequate to defend themselves, disregarding that Iraq fought a horrible eight-year war against Iran. Others say we can send in American troops, and they are so superb that the Iraqis will yield. The fact is that historically, it takes about three times as strong a force to invade a country as it does to defend one's own land. I would offer my life to defend my country against an invasion--to defend my wife, my children, my home, my nation, against invading forces. But I would not be willing to give my life to invade someone else's land. There is another important reason why we could suffer very large casualties if we do invade Iraq. If you are defending your country, your infantry troops can be placed in deep trenches and foxholes; your machine guns and artillery can be placed on the most advantageous sites; you can measure exactly how far it is to certain places, so you can make sure your guns are accurate; your tanks and artillery can be placed in holes, covered with camouflage and protected from attack. But if you are attacking that embedded force, you are exposed. And that is a very important consideration.

As I said, people will give their lives to defend their own country. In the Muslim world, part of their religion is that their souls will go directly to heaven if they sacrifice their lives in the defense of what they consider to be their Holy Land. So I think we are greatly underestimating the casualties that will be the result of a war initiated by us--not just on American troops, which will be bad enough; the Defense Department is talking about ten or twenty or thirty thousand casualties. But the casualties among Iraqi citizens and Kuwaiti citizens, who are already suffering, will be even greater. So I think we should do everything we can: be patient, keep the pressures on Saddam Hussein, interrupt his sale of oil, not let supplies enter his country, open avenues of negotiation, and let these pressures build up rather than launch a war, which is what we were trying to prevent in the first place.

Q: I'm Daniel Saul, from Paul D. Schrieber High School in Port Washington. President Carter, you were very influential in promoting a new level of peace between Israel and Egypt. Do you feel a similar peaceful solution is possible for the current Israeli-Palestinian conflict, and if so, how do you think the United States can promote such peace?

Carter: I think it's possible for one basic reason, and that is that the people of Israel, the Palestinian people, the Lebanese people, the Syrian people, the Jordanian people, the Egyptian people all want peace. The obstacle is the political leaders who do not have the courage to bring their people to peace through negotiation or mediation. I hope the time will come when that avenue will be opened up by more enlightened and more courageous political leaders. The second point is that this is almost an impossibility without the full and persistent involvement and influence of the U.S. president and the secretary of state. When President Nixon and President Ford and Secretary of State Henry Kissinger were in office, they were constantly probing for ways to bring the Arabs and the Israelis to the negotiating table to end a war, to find a route for peace.

I did the same thing. It was a major commitment of my administration every day-- among many other things, of course. I was trying to find a way to bring the Israelis and Egyptians and others to the table to negotiate peace. That has not been a priority for the last ten years. I think that after this present Gulf crisis is resolved, after Iraq withdraws from Kuwait and we have a peaceful settlement of that issue, there is going to be a much greater focus of the world's attention on the Israeli-Arab issue than there was in the last ten years. I think that even though the Israelis are reluctant to go to an international peace conference, world pressure is going to be much greater than it has been the last few years, and I would say that the likelihood of such a peace conference is better than it was a year or two ago, before Iraq invaded Kuwait. It is certainly not an easy thing to do, but I think if we can predicate a solution based on the Camp David accords, which I helped negotiate, that would guarantee Israel's security and the recognition of Israel's existence in a peaceful way by all of its neighbors, and also would honor the legitimate needs, the human rights, of Palestinians and give them self-determination and a homeland. Those two things must be done; peace will not come without either of them, and they're not incompatible. I think, to answer your question, peace is possible; it is going to take a lot of work and maybe some more patience on our part.

Q: President Carter, based on your experiences in the White House and your interpretation of the Constitution, do you think that President Reagan should have been brought up on charges of treason for his involvement in the Iran-Contra affair?

Carter: If you compare what actually occurred in the Watergate complex with what occurred in the Iran-Contra scandal, the Iran-Contra scandal was much more serious. But I think the nation reacted wisely in the case of President Reagan--having already been through the Watergate crisis, with the president embarrassed, with the office of the president having been brought into disgrace--not to consider charging President Reagan with a crime or impeaching him. So I would certainly not have approved or supported in any way--even as a Democrat--any effort to impeach President Reagan. We still don't know all the facts about the Iran-Contra scandal. My own hope is that the crime is over, we will forget about it, and we will go on to better things.

Q: Good afternoon, Mr. President. My name is Peter Abar, from Herricks High School. I would like to know, looking back on your term, were there any disappointments, any policies you would have liked to have seen implemented, or any issues that would have been resolved had you been reelected?

Carter: There were a lot of them. We passed the energy legislation and put it into law. Some of the major bills actually were passed after the November 1980 election, when I had been defeated. This was a very fine achievement, but the laws were not enforced by my successor in the White House. Had I been in the White House, I would have embedded much more deeply in the consciousness of American people the need for honoring these laws concerning energy conservation.

Another very important issue was the Camp David accords and the peace treaty between Israel and Egypt. Had I been reelected, I would have maintained the pressure, or the influence, on the participants in the Mideast dispute to move toward further peace agreements--between Israel and Jordan, between Israel and the Palestinians, between Israel and Lebanon and Syria.

We established the Department of Education when I was in the White House. I had always thought that education should be elevated to a cabinet-level interest, and I appointed a very fine former federal judge, Shirley Hufstedler, from California, to be the first secretary of education. President Reagan, in his 1980 campaign, promised the people that if he was elected, he would abolish the Department of Education. He tried to do so, but he was not successful because the Congress was convinced that the Department of Education was necessary. President Reagan did not want secretaries of education who were genuinely committed to improving education in this country; he tried to cut off federal funding going to the department, and therefore made it incapable of reaching its potential.

So there were obviously some things I wish had been different, things I would have reversed. One always comes to mind. As you may or may not know, in April 1980, I sent a rescue mission to Tehran--we called it Desert One--to try to rescue the American hostages. We had eight helicopters; we had to have six to bring out all the hostages. We lost three of those helicopters in accidents. One change I would have made, obviously, was to send one more helicopter. If we could have rescued the hostages in April 1980, I have no doubt that I would have been a hero, that our country would have been gratified, that I would have been reelected president, and that I could have done all these things I just described.

Mrs. Carter: I have an answer to that question, too, because I worked for almost four years to get a good mental health program in place in our country. We passed the Mental Health Systems Act in September 1980; two months later, a new president was elected; and by February of the next year, all my work was gone, and the government changed the way it implemented the mental health law. It was a real disappointment to me, but I have been gratified to learn, since we left the White House, that states are using that plan. And I went to New Zealand and Australia to make speeches to mental health groups. They are using my plan as a guide to developing their mental health programs. So all is not lost, but I felt like it was, and it was one of the disappointments of my life.

Q: Good afternoon, Mr. President. My question to you is, who do you think will obtain the Democratic presidential nomination in 1992, and do you think the problems in the Middle East will have an effect on President Bush's reelection?

Carter: The student body president of Hofstra, Chris Bellomy, said he might be the candidate, but he won't be thirty-five years old. Let me answer the last part of your question first. I do think that what happens in the Persian Gulf will greatly affect President Bush and his chances for reelection. If it is the general impression in our country that President Bush has handled that crisis wisely, with a peaceful resolution, I think that will greatly improve his chances of reelection. As far as whom the Democrats might choose, I would say the major question is who really wants it badly enough to make a commitment to run, to stick with it, to learn about the American people, and to campaign as avidly and as strongly as is necessary to get the nomination. I do not know who that might be. There are a lot of people--governors and members of Congress--who are now being considered. A senator from my state, Sam Nunn; a senator from New Jersey, Bill Bradley; Governor Mario Cuomo of New York; Governor Bill Clinton from Arkansas; and five or six others. I think all of these men--and maybe some women, about whom I don't know--are giving the question some serious thought.

I know from experience that once you decide to run for president, it has to be a total commitment. When you first go around the country, as we did early in 1975, meeting with five or ten people sometimes, which is all we could get together, you must convince those five or ten people that "I'm in it to stay. I'm going to be a candidate when the final votes are counted. If you join my team and help me get elected, I'm not going to back out of this effort and leave you stranded." That total commitment to marshal all your mental and physical and moral resources to seek the presidency is something I have not yet seen in any of the candidates. There are some very fine people, but it is really too early. You have to remember that we didn't start our campaign until January 1975, which many people thought was very, very early; the equivalent time will be January 1991. So folks have a month now before they have to make up their minds to run or not. I think, though, that the Democrats have a good chance to win in 1992, and I obviously would like to see this happen, and to have a Democrat in the White House.

Shuart: I hate to be the bearer of bad news, but we're going to be able to accept only one more question.

Q: President Carter, what is the responsibility of former presidents to challenge an action by a current president that undermines a program you established, such as your solar energy tax credit program?

Carter: One of the nice things about being a former president is that you have total freedom to go where you wish, to say what you want to, to meet with whom you choose, and to express your views to the maximum extent of your ability. Obviously, an incumbent president has much greater access to the press, and the president's words are listened to much more carefully than those of a former president. But I feel not only that I have an opportunity to pursue my own goals as a private citizen, as a professor now, but I also have an obligation, or a duty, to do so. But I do not think that my opportunity and my obligation are any different in character from yours. If you see a Congress or a president or a governor doing something contrary to your standards, or your ideals, or your measurements of what a great state or a great nation ought to do, you should do something about it. You can write letters to the news media, you can write letters to that particular political leader, you can marshal others to join with you in public demonstrations, you can let your views be heard. And as Rosalynn said earlier, this is a very powerful factor, because so few people do it that when one small group of, say, Long Island high school students say, "This is what our government has got to do"--maybe stay out of the war in Iraq--that message will get into the *New York Times*, the *Daily News*, the *Long Island Press*, and be heard and listened to and considered by the president. You can count on that. So my obligations and my freedom are basically the same as yours. I feel an obligation, and I enjoy letting the incumbent president know when I don't like his policies.

Thank you all very much for letting us meet with you.

Jimmy Carter Conference—Town Meeting

JAMES M. SHUART AND
HERMAN A. BERLINER

Dr. James M. Shuart: It's my great pleasure to welcome you to this very special town meeting with President Jimmy Carter and First Lady Rosalynn Carter. We're very pleased and honored to have them with us. President Carter will make a presentation to our town meeting, and following that, Mrs. Carter will join with him to answer your questions. And now, it's my privilege and pleasure to reintroduce our honored guest.

Ladies and gentlemen, I am very pleased to present President Jimmy Carter.

Carter: First of all, let me express to George Dempster and to Jim Shuart my gratitude for being given an opportunity to come back to the Hofstra University campus for the third time. As George pointed out, he has introduced me all three times. In 1976, about four days before the election, he brought me good luck; now, in 1990, I hope he has again brought me good luck. I don't know what the results will be of your analysis of our administration; I have a great deal of timidity about seeing the C-SPAN tapes and looking at the sessions that have been held to say what did he do, why in the world did he do that, what have been the consequences of his mistakes? But I think it is a very great tribute to Hofstra University to be holding this eighth assessment of the administrations of our nation's leaders, beginning with Franklin Roosevelt. I am glad to come back here for this purpose.

At noon today, I met with a group of high school students who asked me questions that were far superior to any questions I ever got from the White House press corps. We will see how your questions compare with theirs.

I have been asked this afternoon to make brief remarks about the relationship between the White House and the Carter Center, so I am not going to spend very much time resurrecting the experiences of the White House. I would like to try to leave as much time as possible for questions, to talk about how the things that we are doing now--Rosalynn and I together--relate, I think quite directly, to some of the goals and ideals, the aspirations, the hopes and dreams of the White House, and how some of the disappointments in the White House--particularly not having been reelected-- have helped to shape our lives since that time.

This is my ninth year as a Distinguished Professor at Emory University--this was my week to teach--and I have enjoyed that most of the time. It has been a very exciting and challenging responsibility. When I was a child, as I told the students this morning, if anyone had asked me what I was going to do when I grew up, I would say, "My first preference is to go to the Naval Academy and be a naval officer. If I cannot do that, then my second choice would be college professor." Thanks to Ronald Reagan, I reached that goal four years earlier than I had anticipated. And when we were defeated in November of 1980, we then found out, two or three weeks later, that the blind trust we had created with our life's work before I was elected President had gone from a very profitable operation down to a million-dollar debt. We can announce today, with great pride, that we have paid off that debt, primarily because of the success of the books we have written. All the books we have written have been best-sellers. Rosalynn's autobiography was number one on the *New York Times* list. She asked me to announce that all the books are still on sale.

We left the White House not really knowing what we wanted to do. We were discouraged, we were in despair. We were somewhat embarrassed at the defeat; we had an unfinished agenda that had propelled us and inspired us not only for the four years in the White House but also for the campaign period before that as we shaped our opinions and knowledge of this country during a very difficult but challenging and exciting campaign. We had learned a lot in preparing for debates, in preparing for the job, and had had some accomplishments, but there was still a lot to do. And we went back to the White House basically in political disgrace. The most disgraceful thing that we ever did was not to be elected in November 1980; it is an almost unforgivable sin for an incumbent president not to be reelected. But we absorbed those defeats and began to say, "What can we do with the rest of our lives?"

One of the most difficult things that we have ever done was to write a book together, *Everything to Gain: Making the Most of the Rest of Your Life*. It almost brought an end to forty-three years of marriage. My advice is never a book on an equal basis with your husband or your wife. If you are the writer and your spouse is a good editor, that is fine; you can make the final decision. But do not ever share it on an equal basis; it is absolutely destructive. That book describes in a very humane, sometimes almost tearful, way the ordeal we went through after the White House. I do not mean it was all black and discouraging, but we were in debt, we were in disgrace, we did not know what we were going to do next; our last child left home; we had illnesses in the family, we lost members of our family. But out of that has come an unprecedented experiment in the life or potential life of a person who has been the president of the greatest nation on earth.

We deliberately have orchestrated the character of, the boundaries of, the principles of, the Carter Center--sometimes trying things out, sometimes with a great deal advice and counsel--and we have done this work with a few simple guidelines. First of all, we do not undertake a project at the Carter Center if we feel that anyone else can or will do the same thing. If the United Nations or the government of the United States or USAID or Harvard University or the Brookings Institution or Norway or Sweden can take on a project, we do not take it on. In other words, we try to fill vacuums that exist in the world community. Second, the projects have to be of notable importance to our country or to the rest of the world. Third, we do not do anything on a partisan basis. We are very careful, being part of Emory University, to have a bipartisan or a nonpartisan approach to the projects that we do undertake. We have dealt with sensitive issues like U.S.-Soviet relations, nuclear arms control, peace in the Middle East, democracy in this hemisphere. President Gerald Ford, my predecessor and a distinguished Republican, is my active cochairman. When we have dealt with global health issues or those in this country, or when we have dealt with world problems on burden of debt, or competitiveness with the Europeans and the Japanese, we have usually brought in a distinguished member of President Reagan's or President Bush's cabinet, to make sure that the world knows--particularly the people we invite to participate--that it is not just a Democratic Party study.

Third, we do not undertake an issue just for an academic or scholarly analysis, with the hoped-for result being advice or counsel or new ideas. We must feel that the result of our work will lead to a direct, specific action. And so in the process, we bring people together at the Carter Center when we do analyze a complicated subject: the foremost experts we can identify, and people who can put into effect recommendations or ideas that might be forthcoming.

So that basically describes what we do. We try to maintain an academic environment. For instance, when we want to have a conference--which we will have later this month on the future of Lebanon, its economic and political status, on which we have been working for a year or so--we want to be sure that everyone can come together without embarrassment. In two previous conferences, when we discussed peace in the Middle East between Israel and her neighbors, we were able to bring to the Carter Center for public forums like this and private discussions the ambassador from Israel, two or three prominent members of the PLO, the foreign minister of Syria, the ambassador from Saudi Arabia, the crown prince of Jordan, and the security minister of Lebanon. The participants do not walk out on each other. When the Israeli gets up to say, "This is the way Israel feels about the peace process," none of the Arabs leave, as they do in the United Nations. They sit there, paying close attention to what is said by their adversary. They will not ask each other questions. They address the questions to me or perhaps to President Ford. "President Carter, would you ask the speaker what he thinks about this?" And I turn around and ask the speaker, "What do you think about this?" And he says, "President Carter, I think this about that," and I tell the audience, "The speaker thinks this about that."

But in the private sessions it is very exciting, because quite often scholars in the great universities in Tel Aviv, Jerusalem, Haifa, and in Damascus, Amman, Cairo, and Alexandria, for the first time in their lives get to know their peers. In Tel Aviv, for instance, there are scholars who devote their entire adult lives to study of the economy of Syria. They have never been to Syria; they don't feel that they will ever go to Syria. But they now have a chance to talk to scholars from Damascus about what is going on in that country. It is very exciting. That is the kind of program that we have at the Carter Center.

Finally, let me describe just a few of the most tangible action programs that we have. We are very interested in alleviating suffering that is not being adequately addressed. For instance, my administration normalized diplomatic relations with China, as you may remember. We announced it on December 15, 1978, and it was consummated January 1, 1979. So I have had a relationship with the Chinese leaders, including Deng Xiaoping, the supreme leader then and perhaps even now, though in the background. And Deng asked us to come to China because he wanted to add a new dimension to the Chinese culture. The Chinese had never been involved in the rehabilitation of handicapped people, and he wanted us to help develop this capacity--a strange request, I thought, but one that was a challenge to us.

So we assessed what we could do, and we came up with two projects. One was to teach the Chinese how to mass-produce artificial arms and legs of the highest technological quality--you have seen the DuPont advertisement with the Vietnam veteran with artificial legs who is playing basketball. This is the kind of thing that we have been able to teach the Chinese to produce. Next April, in Beijing, there will be dedicated a six-story factory, completed outfitted at their expense but with our guidance, that will mass-produce prostheses. The other aspect of this particular Chinese project is how to deal with handicapped children. They have never had a special education program in their elementary schools. So in July, we finished teaching ninety-three outstanding educators in China, in special crash courses conducted by three American universities--not including Emory, by the way--how to train children who are autistic or partially memory-retarded, or who have a speech, sight, or hearing difficulty. And now those ninety-three leaders are all over China, in ninety-three different communities, and they are teaching elementary teachers how to deal with handicapped children.

This is the kind of thing we do. Others can do it, but they will not. What gives us the momentum, or the ability, is that I can negotiate directly with Deng Xiaoping, and we actually signed a contract between the People's Republic of China and the Carter Center.

Another project with which we are concerned is preventing the starvation of people in poverty-stricken countries, particularly in Africa. For the last twenty years, every year, the per capita production of food grain has gone down. The average African now has seventy fewer calories daily than twenty years ago, and twenty years ago the diet was already very inadequate. We have tried to address this, beginning in 1985. In 1987, we began a project called Global 2000; I don't put my name on this--I don't even put the Carter Center name on it--because we want local leaders to get credit for these programs. But with the help of Dr. Norman Borlaug, who won the Nobel Peace Prize in 1970 for the Green Revolution in India and Pakistan, we now are teaching small farmers how rapidly to increase their production of basic food grains: millet, sorghum, corn (which they call maize), and wheat. We have these projects in different countries in Africa, and we have potentially been able to triple the production of those food grains, at least the first year. We furnish maybe two people, highly qualified scientists, in a country; they bring several hundred of their people, at their expense, to be extension workers. It has been a very successful program.

The director of the Carter Center is Dr. William Foege, who for ten years was the director of the Centers for Disease Control. He orchestrated the eradication of smallpox throughout the world a little more than fifteen years ago, and he is a wonderful leader in the health field. We have twenty-six different health programs at the Carter Center. One thing we have undertaken recently is a task force on disease eradication. Since smallpox was targeted for eradication more than twenty years ago, no other disease has been targeted; since we organized our task force, two diseases have been marked for eradication. The first is an indescribably horrible disease called guinea worm that exists in twenty-one nations. About ten million people are afflicted with this debilitating disease in India, Pakistan, and all across sub-Saharan Africa. We have set a goal of totally eradicating guinea worm by 1996. It is a very exciting thing for us to go into a nation with Dr. Foege by our side, and Rosalynn and I negotiate with the leaders: "You've got to do this, we will do that, we will marshal other financial and technical support. In your country, you have this many people, we estimate, with guinea worm--quite often, they don't even know it--and this is how we eradicate it." It is a very challenging opportunity for us.

The next-to last thing I will mention is human rights. We tried to pursue human rights as best we could when I was in the White House. It was basically abandoned, for a while at least, under President Reagan. One of the first visits that the new U.N. ambassador, Jeane Kirkpatrick, made was to Argentina, to the military junta, and then to visit with General Pinochet in Chile. And the first two visitors the Reagans invited to the White House were President Marcos and President Chun of Korea. These were leaders of nations where human rights violations were occurring. Later, to give President Reagan credit, his administration did improve its record. At the Carter Center, we continued to work on these issues. We have a small staff, but we work very closely with the watch committees--with Amnesty International, the Lawyers Committee on Human Rights, Physicians for Human Rights, Americas Watch, Africa Watch, Helsinki Watch, and so forth--and they come to us with their most troublesome cases of oppression.

My role is to go directly to the leader of the nation where human rights violations are taking place. I do this in a very confidential fashion, to give them a chance, without losing face, to correct their problem. They may have political opponents who have never committed a crime of violence sentenced to death, or they may be practicing torture in prison, or incarcerating people without accusations and trials. We try to let the leader correct that problem on his or her own initiative. If that is not done, then I reserve the right to expose those human rights violations to the rest of the world. This can be very damaging to a Third World country, in particular one that is struggling to get economic aid and investments. If I condemn the country, it can have a negative effect. We have had very good success with this approach to national leaders.

The last thing I will mention is that we are particularly troubled about conflicts in the world. I have to admit that when I was president, I did not know the full extent of the conflicts that existed in the world. Obviously, I knew about the conflict between Israel and Egypt, I knew about the war between Iraq and Iran, but there were parts of the world that never came to my attention in the White House. I am really embarrassed to say that, but it is true. I will give you a quick example. The first day of August of this year--I choose that day because it is the day before Iraq went into Kuwait--at the Carter Center we were monitoring the conflicts in the world, joined by the Swedish University of Upsala. At that moment, there were 112 conflicts in the world; 30 of those were major conflicts. A major conflict, in our arbitrary definition, is one in which at least a thousand people have been killed on the battlefield. Some of them are horrendous in scope. The war between Eritreans and Ethiopians has been going on for thirty years; more than a million people have died. In Sudan in 1988, 260,000 people died--and practically no attention was given to this war in our country or the rest of the world.

These wars are quite often between black peoples, in remote countries that do not have oil. So we do not pay much attention to their suffering. This has become a great concern of the Carter Center. The tragedy is that every one of these conflicts was internal in nature. Not a single one of the thirty was between two countries. The United Nations is specifically prevented from dealing with these wars, and so is our own country, and so are Great Britain and France and others, because it is totally improper for a United Nations official to communicate with revolutionaries who are trying to change or overthrow a government that is a member of the United Nations. When we have an ambassador accredited in Khartoum to the Muslim government of Sudan, it is totally inappropriate for our ambassador or his staff to communicate with the revolutionaries, the Sudan People's Liberation Movement. So this leaves a need for a way to address these issues, and that is what we do at our center, working with many other people around the world.

This is a very troubling issue, because it causes so much suffering, so many refugees--there are almost thirty million people now who are refugees from these wars. They are starving, they do not have adequate care, they are homeless, and we give very little attention to them. As we deal with these issues at the Carter Center, we try to refine our techniques of negotiation, mediation, and arbitration. We search for new ways to bring warring groups to the peace table.

One of the new techniques that we have been pursuing, at least in this hemisphere, is the holding of elections that are internationally supervised. We did this for the first time in Panama, in May 1979; General Noriega invited us to supervise the scheduled election. He was totally convinced that his candidates were going to win, and he wanted me and our group to legitimize his victory. So we consulted with the State Department and ultimately went down, and the election was beautiful. The people registered to vote without restraint, they voted on the first Sunday in May without restraint. When the votes were counted, however, Noriega's candidates lost by a three to one margin; they only got 22 percent of the vote. The next morning, I negotiated with him, trying to get him to accept the results and become a hero in Panama. He could stay in Panama, he could retain his commanding position in the National Guard until the following September, he could keep his ill-gotten gains--that's not exactly the way I referred to them--and he could be the one who brought democracy to Panama. But about two o'clock Monday afternoon, the day after the election, he decided to steal the election. He tried and he failed, because I pointed out to the world that he was stealing the election, so he declared it null and void. The real winners of the election were installed after we invaded Panama and are the leaders of Panama now.

In order to resolve the Contra war--a war that the United States organized and financed, in which about thirty-five thousand people lost their lives--we were asked by the Sandinistas to supervise the election in Nicaragua; we did not go until the Supreme Electoral Council and the opposing political parties had also invited us. That is a standard requirement we have: that all sides invite us. We spent a lot of time making sure that the registration to vote was honest, that the campaign was fair, that the balloting was without intimidation, that the counting of ballots was accurate. That was not the end of our troubles, because the Sandinistas, amazingly, lost, and they were very reluctant to accept the results. I spent two or three days negotiating intensely with the Sandinista leaders and with Mrs. Chamorro's UNO party leaders, to get them to accept the results.

Since then, we have monitored the election in the Dominican Republic, and we are now involved in one of the most exciting of all, the elections scheduled for December 16 in Haiti. That republic was established in 1804, but it has never had a day of freedom from tyranny. We hope, if everything goes well, that we will have a successful election next month. The other election that we are working on now is in Guyana, a country in the north of South America, where they probably have not had an honest election since 1964.

These are the kinds of things that we are able to do at the Carter Center. Almost all of these efforts are an extrapolation of what Rosalynn and I tried to do in the White House--human rights, the maintenance of peace, the elimination of suffering. They are all ambitions compatible with the dignity and the ideals and the aspirations and the ethical standards of our great country. Thank you very much.

Dr. Herman A. Berliner: Thank you, President Carter. We now come to the question-and-answer part of our program. As was been noted before, both President Carter and Mrs. Carter will be available to answer your questions. If you want to ask a question, please go to the microphone and wait your turn. I see people starting to do that already. Two microphones have been set on the lower level and two upstairs-- you must use a microphone so that everyone can hear the question. We will distribute the questions between microphones; please keep your questions brief and vigorous; one question per person; and please identify yourselves. After your question has been answered, please take your seat. Our microphone monitors today are Leslie Feldman and Lou Kern of the Hofstra University faculty, and Alison Lang and Ross Levy, Hofstra University students. President Carter and Mrs. Carter, will you please join me at the podium?

Q: President Carter, my name is Dan Ostrander. I know as president, you were always conscious of the use of power. As a matter of personal morality, under what circumstances could you justify the use of power against another individual, and against a country such as in Panama or Iraq?

Carter: Obviously the president, as commander in chief in a time of emergency or crisis, has both the authority and the obligation to act with military authority to protect the integrity or security of our country. When I ran for president, one of the reasons that I was elected was the aftermath of the Vietnam War. I made a frequent promise that I would never intercede in the internal affairs of another country unless the security of my country was directly threatened. I think the president of the United States, leading the greatest and strongest and most influential country on earth, should make every possible attempt to resolve crises or difficulties in a peaceful manner, because we should set an example not only for our own people but also for the rest of the world.

I think we ought to be very reticent about starting a war. I did not approve of the invasion of Panama, which included the death of about a thousand people, and caused the destruction of Panama. The primary purpose of that invasion, in my own judgment, was to capture General Noriega. We have now captured him; he is in prison. Whether he will ever be tried, I think is doubtful. There's some evidence that may not be eagerly awaited by the people who will conduct the trial.

Now we are faced with a much more serious crisis. I wrote an op-ed piece for *Time* magazine about three weeks ago that you might want to look up, if you are interested in the subject. There are only two options, I think, in the Iraqi situation. One is for Saddam Hussein to withdraw from Kuwait, and accede to the basic demands of the U.N. Security Council. The other is for us to force that militarily. I think forcing it militarily will have adverse consequences far beyond what we have been led to believe. The casualties would be enormous, in my judgment. The estimates in Washington have ranged between ten thousand and thirty thousand U.S. casualties, which is quite serious. And that does not count the casualties in other military organizations. But as you have heard mentioned, the primary advice is to minimize U.S. casualties by resorting to massive air attacks, bombings. Soldiers and marines don't suffer much from bombing raids. The ones who suffer from bombing raids are civilians--in Kuwait City, perhaps, if that is where our attack is launched, or in Baghdad and other Iraqi cities. The casualties would be the very people we are trying to protect, the ones who are suffering under the domination of Saddam Hussein. So we will basically be killing, in addition to soldiers, a large number of totally innocent civilians.

Another thing, in using force in the Gulf crisis, do we have adequately marshaled forces? I have no doubt that the United States and its allies can eventually prevail in an attack on Iraq. And President Mubarak, who is one of our major allies in Saudi Arabia, has announced that not a single Egyptian soldier is going into Iraq. I think if we do launch this attack, which will primarily be a unilateral attack by the United States, joined with a token additional force, we will reap great and very serious consequences politically. I don't think the Arab world will forgive the massive death that American weapons will inflict on against Arab people, even those who are on our side.

A third reason to avoid war is the economic cost. There is no doubt that Saddam Hussein will destroy the oil wells in Iraq and in Kuwait that are already under his domination, and what effort he will make to destroy the oil wells in Saudi Arabia, which is pretty nearby, we don't know. He has already said he will destroy them, but whether he will, no one knows. But that could very well increase the price of oil from thirty-five dollars to, say, seventy-five or eighty dollars a barrel. The damage to those oil wells might be long-lasting, if not permanent.

So that is the downside of a military attack. The other side is, What can be done? I think we ought to maintain--maybe increase--economic sanctions on Iraq. They are not inconsequential, and the effect already, to me, is evident. I read in the *New York Times* this morning that Saddam Hussein has agreed to bring in the International Agency on Atomic Power to look at his nuclear installations and assure the world that he is not trying to build atomic weapons. I don't know if he is honest or not, but he has invited them to come in; Iraq belongs to this organization. Another thing is that he sent word--I think through some of the Saudi leaders--that he may be willing to withdraw from Kuwait if he can get some compensatory results--perhaps to lease one of the islands that would give him access to the Persian Gulf. I think we ought to maintain increasing pressure, but at the same time, encourage negotiations. And those negotiations, in my judgment, would have to be done within the Arab community, with the approval at least of King Fahd and Saudi Arabia, perhaps with the participation of King Hussein. I think that we could work out a way for Saddam Hussein to withdraw, to comply with the U.N. Security Council resolution, without having a massive and very destructive war.

Q: . . . election about proposals to limit the number of terms that federal legislators may serve. I'd like to get your feelings on any of these proposals, and what you think the effects would be in terms of an ideological shift in the nation and the balance of power between the presidency and the legislature.

Carter: I was Georgia governor under a constitutional requirement that I could serve only a single four-year term. As you know, the president of the United States is restricted to two terms, as a result of Republican pressure after Franklin Roosevelt's election to a fourth term. I know there is a state initiative to limit the terms of state legislators that was passed with great enthusiasm a couple of weeks ago, and that is strictly a constitutional prerogative of the states. The federal government, I think, should not have any role to play in what state legislatures do. I do not personally approve of that very popular proposal. I think that if a member of Congress is elected from my district, if he does a good job--or she does a good job--keeps contact with the district, learns, over a period of time, the different characteristics or needs or hopes or dreams or aspirations or concerns or achievements of the district, that person can become increasingly effective in representing that district. I think this is better than having someone serve, say, four years or whatever it is, and then have to come home and stay. So I do not favor a constitutional provision, which is what it would require, to limit the term of office of a member in the U.S. House of Representatives or the U.S. Senate.

Berliner: I ask that the next question be for Mrs. Carter. Let's go upstairs, please.

Q: This question concerns the public perception of the presidency, or of the president. In your husband's administration, there was a hostage crisis which involved less than fifty people who returned alive. In Reagan's administration, you had several hundred Marines who were killed through what seemed to have been a military error--they didn't provide adequate security for their installation. This was not--I don't think-- perceived as a failure of the Reagan administration, or of President Reagan. I'd like your feelings about the public perception of a presidency--how it's formed, how public events are manipulated, if you feel they've been manipulated.

Mrs. Carter: I have a good answer, I think, for the reason that the Marines' deaths were not considered really bad: a day or two afterward we bombed Grenada, which was very popular with people. I disapproved of it, but our country did that. So the emphasis was taken off the Marines who died and put on our brief victory of blowing up Grenada. I always told Jimmy that if he had bombed Tehran, he would be reelected president. I still believe that, and yet, all of our hostages would have been killed, innocent people would have been killed; it was not the thing to do. But it took an awful lot of strength to be able to withstand the pressure that was put on him to do something dramatic during that hostage crisis, because all of our friends, supporters, people in the administration felt that if we could get the hostages home, Jimmy would win reelection.

I would come home from a campaign trip and say, "Do something." And he would say, "What do you want me to do?" I'd say, "Mine the harbors!" I didn't really think that, after he would convince me that was not the right thing to do, but I think that peace and human rights are looked on as soft, and people do not want our country to be soft; they want it to be tough. What I think we are beginning to understand now is that we are stronger when we stand for peace. We are stronger when we stand for human rights in the world, and I can tell you that from traveling--I am just back from the Soviet Union--there is no way to describe the feeling that people have there for Jimmy's human rights policies.

Q: I have a question for both President and Mrs. Carter about the campaign of 1976. During that campaign, the two of you crisscrossed America. One of the issues was the pardon of Richard Nixon, and I think many people--including President Ford--may believe that one issue might have helped you win the election. I wondered, after fourteen years and a closer friendship with President Ford, do you still both think the pardon was wrong?

Carter: I do not believe that I have ever commented publicly in criticism of President Ford for that pardon. In my mind, there is no doubt that there were two factors that caused President Ford's defeat that he himself brought about. That was one of them. It was a very difficult thing for him to face; many people were disillusioned, at the immediate end of the Watergate scandal, to feel that there was some sort of deal made between President Nixon and then-Vice President Ford: "If you will pardon me, I will resign and make you President." President Ford has obviously denied it, but that was a feeling that existed. The other was his change from Nelson Rockefeller as vice presidential candidate to Bob Dole. I think Bob Dole, at that time, was looked upon as a very irresponsible vice presidential partner for President Ford. Since my victory over Ford was fairly small, I think that had he kept Nelson Rockefeller on the ticket with him, he would have attracted moderate voters he did not get with Dole, and he might have prevailed.

I have met with President Ford many times since then. He and I have become both good partners in interesting projects and genuine personal friends. When we are riding in an automobile from a meeting to a hotel, we hate to get to the hotel. We like to talk to each other, we are genuine friends, and I have a great admiration for him. So I do not have any criticism to make. President Ford, though, is still sensitive about this. In the assembly programs put on at the Ford Library, he always very carefully designs them so that President Nixon does not get invited. They do not want to be in the same place at the same time, because they know that the first question from the news reporters is going to be "Was there a deal when the pardon came through?" So a few times--this is kind of giving away a secret--President Ford has said, "I would like to have you come to the next conference, but we are going to restrict the participants to those leaders who served at the same time I served." That excludes Nixon; it also excludes me, which is okay. I go to enough conferences.

Anyway, I think that President Ford probably did the right thing. There was a very deep hunger in our country, when he came into office, to get Watergate in the past, and I do not think that President Ford is the kind of person who would have done an illicit orchestration of a pardon in exchange for the resignation of Nixon. I never have thought about him in that way.

Mrs. Carter: I do not have anything to add to that. I do think it was an issue in the campaign, though I do not believe I ever answered a question about it. It was an issue because of the times, with the Vietnam War and Watergate and CIA revelations. I think people wanted a change, and Jimmy said he would never tell a lie, which did not go over very well with the press, but the people liked it. So they trusted him at that point, and distrusted government and politicians. And Jimmy was fresh and new on the scene in Washington, and he appeared honest--and he is honest.

Q: A question for President Carter. I understand that you made some effort at one time to inquire into the case of Raoul Wallenberg. I wonder if you would briefly share that effort, and also share with us any information you might have on the current--if there are any--efforts for Mr. Wallenberg.

Carter: I did, at the request of many people, inquire of the Soviet authorities for information about Raoul Wallenberg's location, or whether he was still alive; if not, the circumstances of his death. The Soviets always denied having any information about him. I do not know exactly what has happened since. I think the Soviets have provided some information that he did die earlier, but I'm not sure. I'm sorry I can't answer your question more definitively.

Q: David Braverman, Class of '92. Mr. President, in a speech on July 15, 1979, you told the people of the United States that a fundamental threat to American democracy was the erosion of confidence in the future. How did you feel about it then, and how do you feel about it now?

Carter: I thought that was the best speech I made when I was president. It was laboriously prepared, and it came at a time when I had repeatedly gone to the people to tell them that we had an energy crisis, and had to do something about it. The earlier fireside chats, instead of inspiring the American people and the Congress to do something to conserve energy, seemed to alienate people. So at the last minute I canceled one of the scheduled fireside chats and went into seclusion at Camp David. I then invited many people to come in and give me advice about the status of our country, and ultimately, I made that speech. We had a means at the White House then--it is much more effective now--to get an instant response from viewers on a speech, and the response was overwhelmingly positive.

It was later characterized as a "malaise" speech. I never used that phrase; I did not think of it in that way. But the basic point I made in the speech was that we had been through an ordeal in this country--with Watergate, with Vietnam, with the assassination of John Kennedy, with the assassination of Bob Kennedy, with the assassination of Martin Luther King, Jr., with other things--but that the nation was inherently resilient; that with democracy, with freedom, we could withstand those crises and we could face the future even stronger, having come through them successfully. I also said that we had an equal crisis on our hands in becoming excessively dependent on imported oil and being such a wasteful nation. The response was very good. It was partially the result of that speech and the follow-up efforts that we passed the final stages of a very comprehensive national energy policy. As a matter of fact, the last major bill was not passed until after I lost the election in November 1980, as a lame duck president. But that was done.

You might be interested in knowing that when I was inaugurated, we were importing 48 percent of our oil, which caused me great concern. Because of the impact of the laws that we passed, that was brought down to about 30 percent. But President Reagan, in his own very attractive and inimitable way, convinced the American people there was no problem, everything's okay; we don't have to worry about this. He tried to abolish the Department of Energy, he didn't adequately finance the implementation of some of those laws, and government excused automobile manufacturers, for instance, from making automobiles efficient. So at this point, instead of importing 30 percent of our oil, we are importing a little more than 50 percent, and that percentage is going up every year. I do not mean to say--I do not want to say--that we are in Saudi Arabia because of a lack of an energy policy. But it is one of the contributing factors, and our country should marshal its efforts, impose restraints on the unnecessary consumption or waste of energy, and encourage the burgeoning production of alternative sources of energy in lieu of importing oil. You might be interested to know that the average American now, for a given level of gross national product, uses two and a half times as much oil as a Japanese, twice as much as a European. This is not only something we can afford because gas is so cheap in this country, but it is also something by which we afflict other people on earth-- particularly the poverty-stricken people in Africa and so forth--and I think we ought to do something about it. But it requires presidential leadership; it's got to come from the White House, and that hasn't come.

Q: Your position with regard to the current situation in Kuwait is persuasive. On the other hand, the analogy has been made--perhaps with some justification--with, say, Czechoslovakia in 1938. If that analogy is faulty, why is it faulty?

Carter: It would help me if you would briefly describe the particular situation of Czechoslovakia in 1938.

Q: Well, certainly, there was a considerable mood in this country at that time that we had no serious interest over there, and why should we get involved. It was quite difficult for President Roosevelt to convince the nation that any serious military commitment was needed, on arguments that might well have been similar to the ones you make.

Carter: Well, the reason I see it as different is that this invasion by Iraq of Kuwait was indeed met, I think, with unprecedented response in this country. And I have been filled with personal admiration, and have expressed it many times, that President Bush handled this crisis extremely well--I think almost with perfection--in the first stages. As he said, we have got to defend Saudi Arabia from potential advances by Iraq; we have got to marshal global condemnation of Iraq's invasion; we have to encourage the United Nations to be involved--all those things I think are quite admirable and I approve of them all. I'm a little bit on shaky ground here because I have not received one word of briefing from the White House or the State Department since the Iraqi invasion took place, which I think is not a proper way to treat a former president. I'm not embarrassed, but I think it would be to President Bush's advantage if they would come down from the National Security Council and say, "President Carter, let us explain to you what our policy is and why we are doing this and what we hope to do, and what our information is." I did that habitually--maybe excessively--with Presidents Ford and Nixon when I was in the White House. That's just an aside. So I do not know the secret details of what is going on. But as long as that was President Bush's policy, I think it was overwhelmingly approved--not only in this country but in other nations.

The change that took place about two weeks ago was very carefully orchestrated, in my opinion. President Bush, Secretary Cheney, and Secretary Baker took the position that we are not planning a defensive employment of U.S. forces and others in Saudi Arabia; we are planning an offensive operation. And to add two hundred thousand more U.S. troops, plus the others that might come, to the forces in Saudi Arabia not only sets up a threat to Saddam Hussein--it is a very expensive threat, by the way, to which Saddam may not respond--but also establishes an element of momentum that is extremely difficult to interrupt or to reverse. And when President Bush says that Saddam Hussein is worse than Adolf Hitler, or when he says that there can be no negotiations with Saddam Hussein until after he totally capitulates, that is a very difficult position to reverse in the future without great embarrassment to the president of the United States. And this is exacerbated by one particular factor: that President Bush has been damaged politically lately, because he has gotten the reputation of being very wishy-washy on the budget and on taxation. And so it is going to be more difficult for him in the future to change his position on Iraq than it would have been had he still been riding a wave of 75 percent popularity.

So I think we ought to maintain our position of staying in Saudi Arabia, not backing down on our demands, protecting Saudi Arabia--which I am not sure was ever in danger, by the way, but just assume it was--increasing, perhaps, the economic sanctions but at the same time, at least condoning if not publicly promoting negotiations with Saddam Hussein to encourage him to withdraw from Kuwait. And that is not an impossibility, in my opinion. As I mentioned earlier, one of the indications of his concern is trying to bring in the International Atomic Energy Agency observers to make sure he is not making atomic weapons. And there may be other very important things that he would be willing to do in addition to withdrawing from Kuwait. I would personally not be averse to Saddam Hussein withdrawing from Kuwait with a secret deal worked out with King Fahd and others: Okay, you withdraw from Kuwait, get all your forces out, let an Arab force come in and monitor the withdrawal. Start rebuilding Kuwait, let the people come back home. And in the future, we will guarantee you that you get one of the islands--maybe not title to it, maybe not sovereignty over it, but get a ninety-nine-year lease for it. Let him have access to the Persian Gulf. I would not object to that in lieu of war.

Q: I'm sorry I'm a little bit slow. I'm signing, and my interpreter is interpreting for me. I'm a freshman student here at Hofstra University, at the New College. I'm very concerned about what's happening today with the price of oil, and the recession. Do you feel it's the same situation that you had during your presidency? I'm the next generation, so I'm wondering what's going to happen. Will it get worse or better?

Carter: Let me say, as a bottom line I am going to put on top--I do not know if that is legitimate at Hofstra University or not--that in spite of the present economic concerns, and even the most negative expectations, we remain a rich country. When we travel to the rest of the world--to Latin America, to the Caribbean, to Africa, to Asia--and see the plight of even the most fortunate people there, we need not go into despair or wring our hands or give up or be hopeless or complain about our own plight if the inflation rate does get up to 10 percent, and if we do have the price of oil two dollars and a half instead of a dollar and a quarter. In some countries now, like Sweden, the price of oil is already four dollars and thirty-five cents. We have among the cheapest oil prices in the world. So that is the bottom line; we are not in a desperate plight, and the basic natural and human resources of our country are so enormous that we are able to weather almost any imaginable economic crisis, even those that are going to be worse than we anticipate.

The other point is, I do not know what is going to happen in the future. The most serious change that has taken place in the last twelve years is one concerning the flexibility of the ability of our nation's government to meet expected and unexpected needs. As you probably have heard in this conference, or as some of you may already know, during the eight years of President Reagan's administration, our national debt tripled. His national debt was twice as much as all the accumulated national debt from George Washington through me. And this means that the tension that evolved in the whole country--certainly between the Congress and the White House--recently on the budget hearings is not going to go away. It is going to continue, and this year, if we removed all the sleight-of-hand tricks of accounting, we would probably have a federal deficit of more than three hundred 300 billion. We are now taking sixty-five or seventy billion dollars from the Social Security fund, and applying it to pay off our current deficit, just to make the deficit look small.

Another very troubling thing that could come home to haunt us even quicker is the debt that we owe to foreigners. When I left the White House not too long ago, we were the greatest creditor nation on earth. Other countries owed us more than they did any other nation in the world. Now we have become the greatest debtor nation on earth. We owe foreigners more than any other country in the world. We owe foreigners more than all the accumulated developing nations on earth owe foreign people. This is a very serious problem. It is okay now, but as you see interest rates rising in Japan, as you see interest rates rising in Germany and so forth, those people who have invested so heavily in U.S. government bonds to pay our bills as we spent more than we took in are going to start changing to Japanese bonds and to German bonds, and we are going to find the cost of our deficit rising.

This means that when we have a legitimate problem with environmental quality, or repairing roads, or education, or health, or housing, we do not have the money to pay for it. So we have lost the flexibility as a nation to deal with legitimate needs of our people, to give us an even better life. Those things do concern me very much, and I think partially the blame rests not on the congressmen and senators and President Bush, but on you and me, because you saw, when members of Congress did exhibit a little courage--maybe for a change--and voted for a very moderate increase in taxes, they went home and faced an irate constituency. They were threatened with expulsion from office and were very seriously stigmatized, and their previous margin of victory went down almost to nothing. So the American people reacted adversely when the Congress did try to do something that was right and needed and courageous. So I do not think we are going to face a future that is dismal, but we do have some serious problems that have to be addressed--not only by the White House and Congress but also by all of us.

Q: Good afternoon, Mr. President. I'm sure, as an active participant in the peace processes in the world, you're well aware that this year's recipient of the Nobel Peace Prize was General Secretary Mikhail Gorbachev. What I'd like to know is whether you consider him a worthy recipient of that award.

Carter: Yes, I think the Nobel Peace Prize award to Mikhail Gorbachev is at least three years overdue. In my lifetime, in this century--and I will even go so far as to say, in the presence of many historians, perhaps in world history--I do not know of anyone who has so dramatically changed the world political and social security in such a brief time as has Mikhail Gorbachev. He is unpopular at home; Rosalynn just got back from the Soviet Union, her second trip over there this year. He is very unpopular there because of the economic problems, but I think the world realizes that what he has done has been a transforming, beneficial contribution. I will give you a brief rundown.

He encouraged--almost forced--the Vietnamese to withdraw from Kampuchea; he admitted that the Soviets should not be in Afghanistan and withdrew; he has opened up and encouraged democracy and freedom in Eastern Europe; he has done the same thing with *glasnost* in the Soviet Union. He has encouraged the world to join in a moratorium on the testing of nuclear devices--he had an eighteen-month moratorium, the Soviets didn't run a single nuclear test, and rest of the world would not join. He has called for the meticulous honoring of every single nuclear arms agreement ever negotiated between the Soviet Union and the United States when President Reagan was trying to do away with SALT II, do away with SALT I, and do away with the anti-missile treaty. He has also called for the total prevention of the deployment of destructive weapons in space. These are the kinds of things that he has done that have not necessarily benefited his own nation, except to restore its friendly relations with other countries, but he has transformed the consciousness of the world. So I do think that, above anyone else on earth, he has long deserved the Nobel Peace Prize.

Mrs. Carter: I was asked to say a few words about Gorbachev. Jimmy and I went to see President Gorbachev in the summer of 1987. It was before his first meeting with President Reagan, and we were talking about things that he was going to do, and that we were doing at the Carter Center. I wrote everything down, everything he said. He said, "We have to wait until this president gets out of office"--that was before he met Reagan--"and then we are going to change the way we conduct foreign policy. It is absolutely ridiculous for the Soviet Union and the United States to be vying for the small countries of the world when what we ought to be doing is working together to lift them out of their poverty, and to raise their standards of living." There was real suspicion about whether Gorbachev was sincere, but Jimmy and I thought that he was.

I have been on a human rights committee with the man that he appointed to be his human rights chairman, or commissioner. In January 1988, we gave a list of four hundred religious prisoners to the Soviets. They let all but one out of prison; he had a criminal record. By the end of 1988, there were no prisoners of conscience, or

Gorbachev said there were none; we monitor that still. But I went to the Helsinki international meeting in Moscow in June, and nobody there likes President Gorbachev now. It was because their expectations were so great, and now the country is just disintegrating. I listened for three days to the human rights people talking about the terrible job Gorbachev was doing. They admitted that there could not have been human rights meetings if Gorbachev had not been in power. Yuri Orlov and Lev Timofeyev, who is another dissident that I know, moderated the meeting the first day, and everybody was able to say anything they wanted to say. It was a transformation, but still, they did not like Gorbachev. So the last day, I was talking to a man who is revered among the human rights people; they said that he is the next Sakharov, if there is anybody who could take Sakharov's place. So I said to him, "I've listened to this for three days. Now, tell me what you would do to make life in the USSR better." He said, "We would have a democracy." I said, "All right, tell me how you would do it." He thought for a long time and then he said, "If I was God Almighty, I'd try to do it with Gorbachev."

Everybody is distressed because there are food lines. They have not seen the sun in two months. It rains; it is cold. It is a sad situation. They do not have any hope for things being better in the future. I left on the sixth; the anniversary of the revolution was on the seventh. They were getting Red Square ready for the big parade that they have. I went to see Sergei Stankevich, who is the deputy mayor of Moscow; I had seen him when I was there before. He had been so excited; Moscow was going to be a model of democracy. Now he does not know what is going to happen. It is a very delicate time, and everybody I met with, from the number three man on down, said that the next thirty to sixty days will be crucial in the Soviet Union. And the headlines in the paper the day before I left were that there might be a coup during the celebration of the revolution, and there were tanks and soldiers in the streets. So I came home hoping Gorbachev could hang on, and hoping that the Nobel Prize will make it easier for him to stay there.

Carter: For the last five or six years, beginning when Chernenko was the leader, before Gorbachev, the Carter Center has monitored every single television news broadcast every day, plus the major documentary films that they promulgate to their people. Ninety-three percent of the Soviet citizens have television; it is the center of their life as far as information is concerned, and it is totaly controlled by the government. So we have been able to tell immediately when there was a change in the basic policies of the Soviet government by seeing what they were transmitting to their people. The Carter Center is forming a very good working relationship with President Gorbachev. Yesterday morning, for instance, when Evgenii Primakov arrived in New York, I talked to him almost immediately, and he gave me a report on two or three things I will not go into detail about. One was that the Soviets are going to hold out as long as possible against any U.N. resolution authorizing a military attack against Iraq. The other one was that Primakov, who is Gorbachev's key representative--he is the one who went to Baghdad, went to Amman, and he has been trying to make some progress in a peaceful way in the Gulf crisis--is cochairman with me.

They have asked the Carter Center to orchestrate a commission that would help the Soviets learn how to use television in the most effective way to deal with ethnic crisis, with economic problems, the holding of referendums, the conduct of elections, and so forth. So we will begin that work under the Aspen Institute's auspices this fall, and then next year, we will start a continuing operation, with Primakov and me being the cochairmen, that will involve a very distinguished group of Soviets and Americans. On the American side are the CEOs or the presidents of ABC, NBC, CBS, the Public Broadcasting System, Turner Broadcasting System, and a couple of others. So we have top-level people. We are trying in every way we can at the Carter Center to understand what is going on in the Soviet Union and to help them overcome some of the horrendous problems that Rosalynn has just reported to you.

Q: I would like to ask Mrs. Carter if she has anything more she wishes to say about her trip to the Soviet Union--any thoughts at all. If she's completed as much as she wants to say, I have another question.

Mrs. Carter: It was an interesting trip. This trip, last week, was in relation to a commission that I am on--the Commission on Peace and Food. There was a World Food Prize given--I think for the first time last year, or the year before last. It was not part of the Nobel Prizes, but it was worked out in some way in connection with that. Dr. Swaminathan from India won that first prize, and with the money he received, he formed a commission on peace and food. At a time when we thought maybe military expenditures were going to go down--this was before Iraq--he wanted to see that money used for bread to feed the world, and to teach people how to grow more food grains. It sounds really exciting to me. I was able to talk about our Global 2000 program, teaching the African farmers how to increase their food production on small farms. And the commission is planning to come up with specific programs that can be used in poor countries. We are not just going to write a paper that looks good, that will be put on a shelf. I think this could be very helpful.

What I learned a couple of things about the Soviet Union. One is that the people do not know how to work, because they have not had to work. They get paid, and whether they are ambitious does not matter. They do not advance, they do not get paid any more. We had a woman from Latvia tell us one night that she went to school in Paris, and she ran a little pizza place where she did everything: she cooked the pizza, she served the customers, she cleaned up at night. And my interpreter, whose father was a diplomat in the Soviet Union--I understand he is retired now--started laughing. I said, "What's funny?" She said, "In Moscow, it would take ten people to do that. A customer would come in and one would say, 'I don't want to wait on him; you do it.' The other one would say, 'I don't want to wait on him; you do it.'" There are no incentives; they have not had any incentives to work hard or to be proud of what they can do.

And the man who is Gorbachev's adviser on agriculture (from the same place that Gorbachev came from, and he's known him forever) was with us all week. He said that they would like to have family farms, but that people do not know how to do everything. For instance, one person services the tractors; some use them; some plant; some harvest. So they are going to have to teach the people to work, to live in a democracy with a capitalistic system. It is a very discouraging situation.

Shuart: President Carter must catch a plane for California, so we have time for one more brief question.

Q: President Carter, as a professor of intercultural communication, I'm aware of how much of your success in human rights and international diplomacy has been attributed to your sensitivity to cultural difference. As we're embroiled in this current conflict in the Mideast, could you offer some thoughts on the relationship between cultural sensitivity and the peace process, from your perspective?

Carter: One of the things that you do not learn when you campaign for president--in Iowa and in New Hampshire and in Florida and New York and Maine and so forth--is how to deal with people in other nations who are dramatically different from you. And that is something you also do not learn in the White House; with the most intelligent and aggressive briefings from the CIA and other agencies, you just do not learn it. If a crisis comes up like the one in Lebanon, we learn the different ethnic groups and religious groups and military groups that are fighting in Lebanon--but we do not really learn. And I would say, again with some embarrassment, that we have tried to put ourselves in the position, since leaving the White House, of breaking down the enormous barriers that exist between the average American citizen--like all of us in this room--and poverty-stricken people in our own country and in particular overseas, who never have a decent meal, who don't have a place to sleep tonight, who don't have enough money to buy food for their children. And these people are increasing, even here. In our Habitat for Humanity projects, for instance, Rosalynn and I work only a week a year; we get a lot more credit than we deserve because they take TV pictures of us hammering nails. The point is that we work side by side with perhaps the poorest people in our country, and one of the things that's startling is that we find what worthy people they are. They are not poverty-stricken because they're worthless. Quite often, they have never experienced success in their lives. They have never seen their parents try anything and succeed. So they develop something like the attitude that Rosalynn just described among the Soviet citizens, who have lived so long under communism that they do not know what it means to think, "I have some control over my own destiny; with my own effort, I can change the future of my life."

We had a very extensive conference at the Carter Center called "Closing the Gap." We found, for instance, that in one suburban area of San Diego that was studied meticulously, there was about a 35 percent unaccounted-for level of suffering within families. If you accounted for the level of income, the quality of their food, their access to medical care, the quality of jobs they had, there was still about a 35 percent level of suffering in those families--from drug addiction, alcoholism, crime, pregnancy among young women--that you could not account for. And the psychologists went in there with a large team, a very competent group, and they found that the reason was that these people were convinced they could not do anything or make any decision that would affect the future of their lives. So if a young woman was tempted to have sex, she just had it. She did not think, "If I say no, I won't have a baby." And if people were offered drugs, they wouldn't say, "I'm not going to take drugs." They didn't think, if they rejected it, that they would live a healthy life.

That is the kind of thing that we run across in Africa and Asia as well. We have food programs in Ghana and Zambia and so forth. We go in among those farmers who are looked upon as worthless, and we sign a binding contract with the nation. One of the things it says is that at planting time the nation has to guarantee the farmers that when they harvest their crops, they will get a competitive, profitable price for their grain. This is very difficult for a socialist country, because they have the principle that you have to have grain cheap at harvest time. But no matter what we do with seed, with fertilizer, with advice, with work, farmers won't grow any more than their families eat unless they can sell their surplus at a profit. This is the kind of understanding that we have never had in the past--at least Rosalynn and I have not.

Another thing: We are in Haiti now; I mention that very much in passing. I pray to God that on December 16, we will have a successful, honest, fair, and safe election. The Haitian people have had a republic since 1804; it is the second oldest republic in the world. It is the oldest black republic in the world. They have never had one week of freedom from despair and persecution and tyranny and suffering and hunger. We hope we can bring into their consciousness a belief that they can be successful one time in bringing democracy and freedom to themselves.

So I think the cultural differences are not just because of race, they are not just because of religious faith; they result from the experiences that have prevailed over generations of people who live in that community. And we are now afflicting these poverty-stricken people with additional burdens. We Americans--all of you in this room, including me--are doing this. At the time of the OPEC oil crisis in 1973, the average woman in the Third World spent two hours a day gathering firewood to cook a meal. Now those same women have to spend eight hours a day finding firewood; the price of oil has gone so high, because we waste so much, that they have to burn wood and they can't burn oil anymore. So they go further and further from their homes every day to get firewood, and eventually they go far enough to meet the villagers from another place who are struggling for the same last tree. And when the tree is cut down, the soil erodes, the stream silts up, they cannot catch fish, the land will not be productive. And whatever problems or tensions or burdens or doubts in their lives that existed are worsened by the fact that they no longer can live a decent life, they no longer can feed their children.

So these are the cultural things--some of them very practical, some of them related to philosophy or religion--that we do not understand in this country because we are basically unconcerned. We live charmed lives, and we have a tendency to think, as fortunate Americans, that we are so secure, we are so influential, we are so rich, because we are superior, because God blesses us; and God blesses us because we are chosen people. And in that process, which is part of human nature, we do not take the time or effort or courage to say, "What can I do to improve the quality of life for people who are different from me, or remote from me, or who have dark skin, or have not been economically successful?" We are good people, we are decent people, we are generous people, we are honest people. But we are basically self-centered, and our nation has never yet reached a level of generosity and sharing and compassion and love that we try to reach as human beings. I think we have a long way to go, even in the greatest country in the world.

Index

About the Editors and Contributors

DAVID L. AARON is an author, a former senior government official, and an investment banker. He has contributed articles to the *New York Times Magazine* and *Foreign Policy*, and is a frequent guest commentator on various network television news and public affairs programs.

CHRISTOPHER M. BELLOMY is a law student at Suffolk University and a second lieutenant at the 114th Personnel Service Company.

HERMAN A. BERLINER is Provost and Dean of Faculties at Hofstra University. He is also Associate Editor of *The American Economist*.

DAN CALDWELL is Professor of Political Science and Chairman of the Council for International Studies at Pepperdine University. He is the author of *The Dynamics of Domestic Politics and Arms Control* (1991) and the co-editor of *The Politics of Arms Control Treaty Ratification* (1991), as well as other books and articles.

HENRY F. CAREY is a Visiting Lecturer in Political Science at the Bucharest Polytechnic Institute. He has previously taught at the Central American University in Managua as a Fulbright Lecturer, and at Connecticut, Manhattan, and John Jay colleges.

SRINIVAS M. CHARY has taught at the New School for Social Research since 1983. He has authored numerous articles and reviews on U.S.-Asian relations in American and Indian journals. His research interests include Asian studies, political psychology, and the yoga systems of Eastern philosophy.

LAWRENCE X. CLIFFORD is the Executive Director of a school for disturbed and behaviorally disordered children. His current research interests combine psychological and historical scholarship to examine important diplomatic events and their participants.

R. BENNESON DeJANES is Professor at Clark-Atlanta University. His principal research interests have been concerned with the relationship among Congress, bureaucracy, and the White House. He is the author of several articles for professional journals and other publications.

HERMANN F. EILTS is Distinguished University Professor of International Relations at Boston University. A former U.S. Ambassador to Egypt, he has authored many books and articles on the Middle East.

GARDEL FEURTADO is Assistant Professor of Political Science and Co-Chair of the program in Third World Studies at the Citadel Military College in South Carolina. His service in the Central Intelligence Agency and the American Diplomatic Corps coincided with the Carter administration. His research and work encompass Asia, Africa, the Caribbean, and American foreign policy and international politics. He has authored works on China and Surinam.

SEYMOUR MAXWELL FINGER is Professor Emeritus at City University of New York. He is the author of *Your Man at the U.N.* and *American Ambassadors at the U.N.*, co-author of *Bending with the Winds: Kurt Waldheim and the U.N.*, and editor of *New World Balance* and *Search for Peace in the Middle East*.

BETTY GLAD is a professor at the University of South Carolina. She has written several biographies employing psychoanalytic psychology, including *Charles Evans Hughes and the Illusions of Innocence*; *Jimmy Carter: In Search of the Great White House*; and *Key Pittman: The Tragedy of a Senate Insider*. Her most recent book is a volume she edited and contributed to, *The Psychological Dimensions of War*.

MINTON F. GOLDMAN is Professor of Political Science at Northeastern University. He is the author of *The Commonwealth of Independent States and Central/Eastern Europe*, and has contributed numerous articles to professional journals on Soviet and American policies toward Afghanistan during the Carter, Reagan, and Bush administrations.

MICHAEL M. GUNTER is Professor of Political Science at Tennessee Technological University and a former Senior Fulbright Lecturer in International Relations in Turkey. He is the author of *The Kurds in Iraq* (1992), *The Kurds in Turkey* (1990), and *A Study of Contemporary Armenian Terrorism* (1986).

ERWIN C. HARGROVE is Professor of Political Science and Public Policy at Vanderbilt University. His books on the presidency include *The Power of the Modern Presidency* and *Jimmy Carter as President: Leadership and the Politics of the Public Good*.

JOSEPH F. HARRINGTON is Professor of History at Framingham State College. His principal research area is twentieth-century East-West diplomacy, especially American-Romanian relations. He is the co-author of *Tweaking the Nose of the Russians: Fifty Years of American-Romanian Relations, 1940-1990*. He has published several other books and hundreds of articles and abstracts in the fields of diplomacy and the education of the gifted and talented.

STEVEN H. HOCHMAN is Associate Director of Programs and Senior Research Associate at the Carter Center of Emory University, and an adjunct professor in the Emory Department of History. He served as assistant to President Carter, with special responsibility for academic and scholarly affairs. As a specialist in U.S. history, his writings have focused on Jefferson and Carter.

GUO-CHUNG HUAN is an Assistant Professor at the East Asia Institute at Columbia University. He was the first Chinese Visiting Fellow at the Harry S. Truman Institute for Advancement of Peace, at the Hebrew University of Jerusalem, in 1987. He served as an economist working on the United States fixed income market and the Far East financial market for the Deutsche Bank Capital Corporation.

HAYNES JOHNSON is a Pulitzer Prize-winning columnist for the *Washington Post*, an author, and a television commentator. He has written many books on national affairs including *The Bay of Pigs, Lyndon, The Working White House*, and *Sleepwalking Through History--America in the Reagan Years*. He was a guest scholar at the Brookings Institution (1987-1988).

BARTLETT C. JONES is Associate Professor of History at Central Methodist College. He is a generalist in American culture and has written numerous books and journal articles. His research interests include the Americanization of Abel Muzorewa (Zimbabwe) and Andrew Young's U.N. tenure.

HAMILTON JORDAN served as the gubernatorial Chief of Staff for Carter from 1977-81, campaign manager for Carter's presidential campaign, and is currently the Vice Chairman of Whittle Communications in Knoxville, Tennessee.

WILLIAM J. JORDEN is a retired diplomat and journalist. He was a foreign correspondent in Asia and the Soviet Union and diplomatic correspondent in Washington. He held numerous high-ranking positions in the State Department and had two tours on the National Security Council staff. He was U.S. Ambassador to Panama (1974-1978) and is the author of *Panama Odyssey*.

MOORHEAD KENNEDY is President of Moorhead Kennedy Associates and Executive Director of Moorhead Kennedy Institute of the American Forum. Both specialize in experiential education and training through role play simulations. A retired Foreign Service Officer, he was taken hostage at the U.S. Embassy in Tehran, Iran, and held for 444 days. He is a frequent guest on television; lecturer; and author of *The Ayatollah in the Cathedral: Reflections of a Hostage*, co-author of *Think about Terrorism, the New Warfare*, and numerous articles.

WAYNE KING is a correspondent for the *New York Times* who has served as bureau chief in Philadelphia, Atlanta, and Houston, and as a political correspondent in the Washington bureau. He is the author of numerous newspaper and magazine articles, including "Carter Redux" in *New York Times Magazine*.

DANIEL C. KURTZER is Deputy Assistant Secretary of State for Near Eastern Affairs, responsible for bilateral U.S. relations with Israel, Egypt, and Palestinians, and for the Middle East peace process. He has served in Cairo and Tel Aviv, and as a member of the Secretary of State's Policy Planning Staff.

ERIC LANE has taught at Hofstra Law Shcool since 1976. He teaches government-related law courses such as those dealing with the legislative and administrative law process. Prior to the presidential conference, he wrote numerous articles on the international protection of human rights.

SAMUEL W. LEWIS is President of the U.S. Institute of Peace. A career diplomat from 1954-1985, he served as U.S. Ambassador to Israel for eight years under Presidents Carter and Reagan, and was a prominent actor in Arab-Israeli negotiations, including participation in the 1978 Camp David conference. He is a frequent commentator on Israeli-Arab issues for television, radio, and the print media, as well as academic conferences, and has written extensively for professional publications.

CARL LIEBERMAN is Associate Professor of Political Science at the University of Akron, where he teaches courses in American government and public policy. He has written a number of articles on the presidency and state and local politics. His most recent book is *Making Economic Policy* (1991).

GEORGE D. MOFFETT is diplomatic correspondent and former Middle East bureau chief of the *Christian Science Monitor*. He served as an assistant to the chief of staff in the Carter White House and is author of *The Limits of Victory: The Ratification of the Panama Canal Treaties*.

RUSSELL LEIGH MOSES is Assistant Professor in International Relations at the Hopkins-Nanjing Center for Chinese-American Studies, Paul H. Nitze School of Advanced International Studies, Johns Hopkins University, in Ninajing, China, where he teaches courses in international relations and American foreign policy. He is the author of *Freeing the Hostages: Reexamining U.S.-Iranian Negotiations and the Soviet Union, 1979-1981.*

ROBERT A. PASTOR is Professor of Political Science at Emory University and Fellow at Emory's Carter Center. Director of Latin American and Caribbean Affairs on the Naitonal Security Council from 1977-1981, he is the author of *Whirlpool: U.S. Foreign Policy toward Latin American and the Caribbean* (1992) and six other books on U.S. foreign policy, Mexico, Nicaragua, immigration, economic development, and democratization.

VLADIMIR O. PECHATNOV is a counselor of the Embassy of the Russian Federation in the United States. His principal areas of research include U.S. political history in the twentieth century and, in particular, the history of the Democratic party. He has written extensively for scientific journals and other publications in Russia, and he is the author of *The Democratic Party: Electorate and Policies.*

WILLIAM B. QUANDT is Senior Fellow in the Foreign Policy Studies Program at the Brookings Institution. He is an expert on the Middle East, American policy toward the Arab-Israeli conflict, and energy policy. He is the author of numerous books, including *The United States and Egypt: An Essay on Policy for the 1990s* (1990).

CHRISTINE REILLY is a graduate of Rutgers University and Brooklyn Law School and currently practices law in New York.

JEREL A. ROSATI is Associate Professor in the Department of Government and International Studies at the University of South Carolina. His area of specialization is the theory and practice of foreign policy, with an emphasis on the study of U.S. foreign policy. He is the author of *The Carter Administration's Quest for Global*

Community: Beliefs and Their Impact on Behavior and the Politics of United States Foreign Policy.

BARRY M. ROSEN is Assistant Vice President for Institutional Advancement at Brooklyn College (CUNY). He was formerly the Voice of America's chief of the Uzbek Service and press attaché at the U.S. Embassy in Tehran at the time of the hostage crisis. He is the co-author of *The Destined Hour*, a Christopher book award winner, and the editor of *Iran since the Revolution.*

HERBERT D. ROSENBAUM is Professor Emeritus of Political Science at Hofstra University. A former Chairman of the Political Science Department there, he wrote *A First Book in Politics and Government* (1972), co-edited *Frankin D. Roosevelt: The Man, the Myth, the Era* (1987), and directed Hofstra Presidential Conferences on Franklin D. Roosevelt in 1982 and Jimmy Carter in 1990.

MARK J. ROZELL is Associate Professor of Political Science at Mary Washington College. He is author of *The Press and the Ford Presidency* (1992), *The Press and the Carter Presidency* (1989), and of numerous articles in such journals as *Political Science Quarterly, Polity,* and *Presidential Studies Quarterly.*

HAROLD H. SAUNDERS is Director of International Affairs at the Kettering Foundation. He served as Assistant Secretary for Near Eastern and South Asian Affairs (1975-1978), where he participated in drafting the Camp David accords and the Egyptian-Israeli peace treaty. He is the author of *The Other Walls: The Arab-Israeli Peace Process in a Global Perspective.*

SAMUEL SEGEV is a Visiting Professor at Hofstra University and formerly an editorial writer and a columnist with the Israeli daily *Maariv.* He has written extensively on the Middle East and is the author of ten books, including *The Iranian Triangle*, the untold story of Israel's role in the Iran-Contra affair.

ROBERT SHOGAN is a national political correspondent for the *Los Angeles Times.* He previously worked as a reporter and editor for *Newsweek* and the *Wall Street Journal,* among other publications. He is the author of five books, including *Promises to Keep: Jimmy Carter's First 100 Days* and *The Riddle of Power: Presidential Leadership from Truman to Bush.*

JAMES M. SHUART is an experienced educator, government official, and civic leader. He is the sixth president of Hofstra University.

MURRAY SILBERMAN is a former senior official of the U.N. Department of International, Economic, and Social Affairs and is Adjunct Professor in the Department of Political Science at Hofstra University and Manhattan College. His current principal research activities and writings are on Central and Eastern Europe. He is the author of *Slavery in the Arab World* (written under the name of Murray Gordon) and of numerous articles on the Middle East and Eastern Europe.

DAVID SKIDMORE is Assistant Professor of Political Science at Drake University. His research interests lie in the areas of American foreign policy, international relations theory, and international political economy. He is the co-editor of *The Limits of State Autonomy: Societal Groups and Foreign Policy Formulation* and co-author of

International Political Economy: The Struggle for Power and Wealth. He is also the author of several other published papers on the Carter administration's foreign policies.

FRANK J. SMIST, JR., is Director of Global Studies at Rockhurst College, and he has been active in the International Studies Association as President of the International Education Section. He has been actively involved in internationalizing college campuses and preparing colleagues for the post-Cold War world. He is the author of *Congress Oversees the United States Intelligence Community: 1947-1989.*

GADDIS SMITH is Larned Professor of History and Director of the Center for International and Area Studies at Yale. His specialties are the history of American foreign relations in the twentieth century and maritime history. He is the author of *Morality, Reason, and Power: American Diplomacy in the Carter Years* and other books.

KENNETH W. STEIN is Associate Professor of Near Eastern History and Political Science. He is Fellow and Director of Middle Eastern Programs at the Carter Center of Emory University. His principal research efforts focus on the political history of the modern Arab world, modern Israel, and the origins and development of the Arab-Israeli conflict. He is the author of *The Land Question in Palestine, 1917-1939,* collaborated with Jimmy Carter on *The Blood of Abraham: Insights into the Middle East,* and is co-author of *Making Peace Among Arabs and Israelis: Lessons from Fifty Years of Negotiating Experience.*

ROBERT S. STRAUSS serves as Ambassador to the Russian Federation. He lectures extensively in the United States and abroad, and has authored numerous papers for professional journals, newspapers, and magazines.

KENNETH W. THOMPSON is Director of the White Burkett Miller Center of Public Affairs at the University of Virginia and formerly vice president of the Rockefeller Foundation. He is the author of over twenty books, including *The President and the Public Philosophy, Winston Churchill's World View,* and *Traditions and Values in Politics and Diplomacy,* and co-author or editor of 150 books, including *The Virginia Papers.*

STANSFIELD TURNER is the John M. Olin Professor in the School of Public Affairs at the University of Maryland. He is the author of *Secrecy and Democracy* (1985) and *Terrorism and Democracy* (1991). He is engaged in private business as a lecturer, television commentator, and columnist. He served as the Director of Intelligence under Jimmy Carter.

ALEXEJ UGRINSKY is Adjunct Assistant Professor of German and Director of Documentation, Finance and Planning at the Hofstra University Cultural Center. Dr. Ugrinsky's published works include *Lessing and the Enlightenment* (Greenwood, 1986), *Goethe in the Twentieth Century* (Greenwood, 1987), *Friedrich von Schiller and the Drama of Human Existence* (Greenwood, 1988), and *Gerald R. Ford and the Politics of Post-Watergate America* (Greenwood, 1993).

VERNON J. VAVRINA is Assistant Professor of Political Science at Marist College. He teaches courses in international and comparative politics, and specializes in U.S. human rights policy.

VLADISLAV M. ZUBOK is the co-author of two books and the author of several articles on American history, politics, and culture. Since 1987 he has been engaged in pioneering research, taking oral history interviews, and working in the Soviet archives on the Cold War. He is an international guest scholar at the Keenan Institute in Washington, D.C.